The Post-Presidency from Washington to Clinton

The Post-Presidency from Washington to Clinton

Burton I. Kaufman

University Press of Kansas

Published by the University Press of Kansas (Lawrence, Kansas 66045), which was
organized by the Kansas Board of Regents and is operated and funded by Emporia
State University, Fort Hays State University, Kansas State University, Pittsburg State
University, the University of Kansas, and Wichita State University

Library of Congress Cataloging-in-Publication Data

Kaufman, Burton Ira.
  The post-presidency from Washington to Clinton / Burton I. Kaufman.
      p.   cm.
  Includes bibliographical references and index.
  ISBN 978-0-7006-1861-3 (cloth : alk. paper) 1. Ex-presidents—United States—
History. 2. Presidents—Retirement—United States—History. I. Title.
  E176.1.K38 2012
  973.09'9—dc23
  [B]
                                    2012019510

British Library Cataloguing-in-Publication Data is available.

Printed in the United States of America

10 9 8 7 6 5 4 3 2 1

The paper used in this publication is recycled and contains 30 percent postconsumer
waste. It is acid free and meets the minimum requirements of the American National
Standard for Permanence of Paper for Printed Library Materials Z39.48-1992.

For
Dr. Richard Schmidt
With deep gratitude

Contents

Preface

What to do with ex-presidents? When one newspaper editor suggested at the end of Grover Cleveland's first administration that they be shot, Cleveland indicated that he thought that might not be a bad idea. In 1913, former president William Howard Taft made clear his preference for poison to having to sit hour after hour on an uncomfortable chair in the chamber of the U.S. Senate and listen, as an ex officio member of the Senate, to the inexhaustible mutterings of his senatorial colleagues. Former president Herbert Hoover said very much the same thing seventy years later. Both Taft and Hoover were responding to suggestions that former presidents be made ex officio members of the Senate with the right to be long-winded themselves.

Such proposals had been, and would be, raised sporadically throughout the nineteenth and twentieth centuries. In 1954, Senator William G. Magnuson of Washington even proposed that former presidents be added to the National Security Council. The rationale behind these proposals was, of course, to take advantage of the wisdom that former presidents had accumulated as holders of the nation's highest office. However, when such proposals were raised, they never developed much traction or support. Least of all were they supported by most of the former presidents.

In fact, the activities of the nation's first three ex-presidents (George Washington, John Adams, and Thomas Jefferson) were bounded by the eighteenth-century republican ideal of politically disinterested private citizens engaging in public service for a limited period before returning to private life. It is well known that Washington set a precedent for future presidents by deciding against seeking a third term as president. He did so for personal reasons but also because of journalistic and other attacks accusing him of acting in an imperial manner. Concerned as always about his honor and his place in history, he did not want even the appearance of violating this essential republican principle of public service as the duty of a virtuous citizen rather than as a quest for personal power and ambition.

Republicanism remained the paradigm of political behavior until the end of the 1820s, when the development of political parties and the rapid expansion of popular sovereignty brought an end to the early Republic. Like everything else political, it continued to define what was expected of former presidents.

Yet the transition to a more active post-presidency began with the retirement of James Madison in 1817. By the time John Quincy Adams retired from the White House in 1829, former presidents no longer even maintained the pretense of abstaining from active participation in the nation's political affairs. Soon after being defeated for reelection in 1828, Adams was elected to the House of Representatives and began one of the most illustrious post-presidential careers in the nation's history. A transition had been completed, therefore, from a republican to a more democratic and participatory ideal of the ex-presidency.

From the post-presidency of Adams to the ex-presidency of Bill Clinton, there has continued to be a steady evolution of the role of former presidents. This is a history of that evolution from Washington to Clinton through the lives of the thirty-one former presidents who lived for at least two years after leaving office. Its major theme is the transition of the ex-presidency from one defined by the eighteenth-century republican ideal of the post-presidency to one in which former presidents became increasingly active publicly. By the end of the twentieth century, former president Jimmy Carter, who may have established a new paradigm for ex-presidents, was even identifying himself as a "citizen of the world," while in the twenty-first century, former president Clinton was referred to in a television documentary as "president of the world." By this time, too, the ex-presidency had evolved to the point that it had assumed some of the characteristics of a formal office, including provisions for office space, a small staff, franking privileges, pensions, and Secret Security protection.

Yet these were the perquisites rather than the powers of office. For the most part, ex-presidents have not had much power or influence on national policy. Although they are regularly given national security briefings, informed before the public of major policy decisions, often consulted by incumbent presidents, and even asked occasionally to carry out an assignment for the White House, such requests are infrequent and usually done as matters of courtesy or when the stakes in terms of the national interest are low. When Jimmy Carter took it upon himself to engage in diplomacy in North Korea, for example, he acted on his own and came under much criticism for behaving improperly.[1]

The fact that the ex-presidency has not carried with it much political power should not diminish the importance of the story that follows. In the first place, the post-presidency has evolved since World War II into a big business, in which ex-presidents have mass merchandised themselves and made untoward millions of dollars through the sale of their memoirs and other books (most of which have been partially or completely ghostwritten), through their appearances on the lecture circuit, and by being featured in different media formats. Increasingly, they have also been employed in various paid capacities by mid- and large-size corporations both at home and abroad. These activities have included being paid huge sums for speaking to corporate executives, serving on boards of directors, and acting as paid consultants. In 2008, just to take one example, former president Clinton became eligible for a $20 million payout for his relationship with a private equity firm, Yucaipa Funds, after he decided to end his connection to Yucaipa in order to avoid any conflict of interests for his wife, Hillary, who was running for president.[2]

Former presidents have also been able to wield considerable influence outside the corridors of the West Wing or the halls of Congress in terms of raising enormous sums of money for their presidential libraries, which have just as often served as monuments to themselves and their presidencies as places for scholarship, and for various philanthropic and humanitarian pursuits both at home and in some of the poorest and most desperate parts of the world.

In these and other ways, the evolution of the ex-presidency has corresponded with the political, economic, and social transformation of the United States over two centuries, including the development of the modern presidency. Following the parallel evolution of the ex-presidency with these other changes throws additional light on the nation's history and on the presidency itself.

Because the evolution of the ex-presidency is indistinguishable from the lives of most of the former presidents, I have chosen a biographical approach to my topic. Another reason for this approach is that, contrary to much of the literature on former presidents, most of them have had fascinating post-presidential careers filled with both accomplishment and failure, humor and pathos. In some cases, their lives after leaving the presidency were as important historically as their careers as president. In other cases, their post-presidential careers offer new or additional insights into their personalities and character.

While there have been excellent histories on the post-presidencies of several of the former presidents, while many presidential biographies have excellent chapters on their subjects' post-presidential years, and while there have been a few slim books on the ex-presidencies of all the nation's former presidents, this is the first book based on primary and secondary sources and covering all the ex-presidents chronologically but within a thematic framework.

Acknowledgments

First I would like to join the chorus of authors who have had their books published by the University Press of Kansas in acknowledging my indebtedness to Fred M. Woodward, director of the press, whom I have known and with whom I have worked for over thirty years. In addition to being director of the press, Fred is an exceptional editor, who combines real concern for his authors with sometimes blistering candor and a scorching pen. His only purposes, however, are to turn good ideas into better ones and to publish quality manuscripts. He is the best in his profession. Like all authors, however, I alone take responsibility for all mistakes of fact and analysis in the pages that follow.

I would also be remiss if I did not acknowledge the help of the wonderful staff at the University Press of Kansas, most notably Susan Schott, the assistant director and marketing editor with whom I have also worked for a number of years, and Kelly Chrisman Jacques, the production editor who went out of her way to make the life of a Luddite a lot easier in an age when technology has overtaken pasted notes in the production stage of book publishing.

I developed the idea for this book on former presidents when I was nearing retirement and about to become a "former" myself. Initial research indicated that there was a need for a book on ex-presidents. I submitted the idea to Fred, who helped me refine it into a formal proposal, which led to a contract from the University Press of Kansas. When I began this project, I had only a vague idea what it would entail in the way of reading and research, especially on the nation's early history. At times I felt like a graduate student preparing again for my qualifying exams. Perhaps that is why I have so enjoyed this project. The quality of scholarship on the new nation and early Republic is simply astonishing.

Helping guide me through this period have been a number of people, but especially my dear friend from the time we were both undergraduate history majors and roommates, Marty Quitt, and his wife, Debbie. As undergraduates, Marty and

I had two experiences few others can brag about. We both skipped class in 1960 to be—along with John Updike and perhaps six thousand others—at Fenway Park to see Ted Williams hit his last home run. A few week later, we were at the Old Boston Garden to see and hear a dashing and handsome young senator from Massachusetts give his final campaign speech for president. Marty and I have since followed remarkably similar academic careers. Marty was dean of the graduate school at the University of Massachusetts, Boston, when he retired. About the same time, I retired as a dean at Miami University of Ohio. We continue to talk on a regular basis, and when we get together with our wives, about once or twice a year, we begin our conversation exactly where we left off. I am deeply grateful for the help that both Marty and Debbie (another trained historian) have given me while preparing this book, including reading large portions of the manuscript.

Rather than list the number of other friends and former colleagues who have assisted me in this project and others over the years, I would like to end on another personal note by thanking my daughter, Dr. Heather Kaufman Moore, and her spouse, Steve; my son, Dr. Scott Kaufman, and his spouse, Julie; and especially my wife of forty-six years, Diane. Heather has a growing medical practice in Grand Junction, Colorado, and Scott is professor of history and Board of Trustees Research Scholar at Francis Marion University in Florence, South Carolina. Heather and Scott (and now their spouses) have always given Diane and me nothing but joy. As for Diane, even after being diagnosed with a serious neurological disease over a decade ago and then surviving an unrelated ruptured brain aneurism and many months of recovery in 2009–2010, she has remained upbeat and supportive. Since her aneurism, she has completed two books, one already published. Her greatest pleasure, however, has always been to make other people happy, none more so than me.

Because he saved Diane's life after her aneurism and has taken an abiding interest in her health ever since, I am dedicating this book to Richard Schmidt, M.D., Ph.D., a gifted neurosurgeon at the University of Utah (UU) Hospital and a faculty member in its School of Medicine. I am also grateful to the hospital's superb staff of doctors, nurses, and therapists who made her recovery possible and to the equally fine doctors at one of the hospital's satellite clinics in Park City. In particular, I would like to acknowledge Diane's neurologist, Dr. John Steffens, the director of stroke rehabilitation at the UU Hospital, Dr. Steven Edgley, and our family doctor in Park City, Dr. Mary Parsons. To each of them, I will be always grateful.

Burton I. Kaufman
Deer Mountain, Utah
April 2012

The Post-Presidency
from Washington
to Clinton

1

The Republican Ideal of the Post-Presidency

Washington, Adams, and Jefferson

Never would an incumbent president look forward more to his retirement than George Washington did in March 1797. Since first announcing his intention to retire in his famous Farewell Address of 19 September 1796, he had grown increasingly anxious to leave the nation's capital, then at Philadelphia, and return to his estate at Mount Vernon, on the Potomac River about eight miles south of the small but flourishing town of Alexandria, Virginia. Across the Potomac from Alexandria was the site of the nation's new capital, still little more than a shabby and muddy piece of land, but one where Washington carried on his lifelong interest in real estate speculation by buying a few parcels of land.

On 4 March, Washington attended the inauguration of his successor, former vice president John Adams, at a large ceremony held on the first floor of Congress Hall, one block from the official residence, simply known as the President's House. Although fewer eyes were on Adams than on the soon-to-be former president, Washington remained attentive and silent throughout the ceremony. Afterward, however, he made clear to his successor just how happy he was to be giving up the reins of power. Adams later described his inauguration: "A solemn scene it was indeed. Washington's face remained as serene and unclouded as the day. Me thought I heard him think, 'Aye! I am fairly out and you are fairly in! See which of us will be the happiest.'"[1]

Washington was not able to leave Philadelphia for Mount Vernon until 9 March. Before departing for home, he hired a sloop to carry by water well over a hundred boxes, packages, hampers, and caskets of personal belongings and other miscellaneous items ranging from carpets to window blinds, fire buckets, a bidet, and a tin shower bath. Accompanied by his family, including the young son of the marquis de Lafayette, whom he had taken under his wing, and Lafayette's tutor, he set out in a coach for the journey of about 150 miles to Mount Vernon. He spent the first evening at Wilmington, Delaware. He reached Baltimore on 12 March and Alexandria the next day.

Fully aware that his presence would be an opportunity in every community along his route to honor him, Washington urged local officials not to make a celebration of his presence. For the most part, his wishes were respected. A plan by one of Washington's friends in Alexandria to provide him with an escort to Mount Vernon went awry. As Washington later wrote, he "avoided in every instance where [he] had previous knowledge of the intention, and could by earnest entreaties prevail, all parades and escorts."[2]

Washington's determination to return quietly to private life at a time when he was already widely acknowledged as the singular embodiment of the American Revolution and the father of the nation and could have had any honor he wanted, including reelection to a third term as president, was a reflection of his deep sense of duty and his abiding commitment to public virtue. To comprehend fully Washington's decision to retire at the end of his second term as president, one has to understand these terms in their late eighteenth-century context, which in the United States was republicanism. Washington defined duty in republican terms and exercised public virtue in a republican idiom.

Although republicanism was the core principal of early American political thought, it defies easy description or definition. At its most basic level, however, it represented a flipping of the divine right of the monarchy to the divine right of the governed. A product of many sources, it was predicated most importantly on neutralizing the depravity the former colonists associated with the unfettered authority of the British monarchy. For the founding fathers, civic virtue was the antidote for political corruption. Fascinated by the literature of ancient Rome— Cicero, Virgil, Sallust, and Tacitus, among others—they took their cues on civic virtue from the golden age of the Roman Republic. The virtuous citizen, in their minds, was the private citizen who put aside his personal career to serve a larger public purpose, fully expecting that public service would be momentary and a return to private life imminent.[3]

This republican ideal of an immediate and unencumbered return from public to private life was decisive in Washington's decision to retire and in the way he conducted himself as a private citizen. The same was true of his two successors, John Adams and Thomas Jefferson. But as these first three presidents prepared for their retirements, they also had other things on their minds, not the least of which was making a living. Part of the republican ideal of former citizen-statesmen was the "vine and fig tree motif" drawn from a biblical phrase, often cited by Virginians, and intended to acknowledge the pursuit of virtue in a pastoral setting. However, the bucolic life of agriculture was more often myth than reality. Each of the nation's early presidents had to deal with the problem of tight finances and ongoing debt resulting from combinations of high standards of living, diminished returns from their lands, and familial obligations. Even Washington, who was the wealthiest of the nation's early presidents and practiced advanced agricultural techniques on his several farms, was land rich and cash poor, and he had difficulty meeting his obligations. Jefferson went bankrupt trying to maintain his high standard of living.

The nation's first presidents were also concerned about their own mortality. Birth and burial records indicate that a newborn in the United States could anticipate living to be about fifty-six years old. Although this figure is skewed by the high infant mortality rate common at the time and by social class, as late as 1790, when the first census was taken, less than 20 percent of Americans could expect to survive from birth to the age of seventy. Less than 2 percent of the population was over sixty-five. Scarcely anyone retired in the modern sense of the word.

When living past sixty-five was still an achievement for a healthy adult and each of the nation's presidents was witness to life expunged unexpectedly either because of the death of a wife in childbirth (in the case of Jefferson) or the loss of a child or close relative because of the scourge of yellow fever, smallpox, or tuberculosis, a constant concern of the nation's early leaders was their own longevity and that of their families. It was natural for them to want to spend the last years of their lives away from the brouhaha of public service.

This was especially true given the intense partisanship associated with the birth pangs of the new nation and the transition from what one writer has called the "Age of Federalism" to what another has defined as "the rise of American Democracy." Notwithstanding the republican disdain of political partisanship, it was more severe in the 1790s than in most decades in the nation's history. Even Washington was not left unscathed by the intense political infighting of the 1790s. The major theme of his Farewell Address was a plea to the nation to avoid the partisanship he feared might tear it asunder. One reason he was so glad to give up the reins of power in 1797 was his fervent desire to escape the nation's political warfare. Unfortunately, he was not entirely successful. Political partisanship remained a reality of American political life, and although Washington and his successors, Adams and Jefferson, continued to espouse the republican ideal of retirement from public to private life, they were swept into its vortex.[4]

Yet the republican concept of the post-presidency, as practiced by the nation's first three presidents, represented something more than an unrealized ideal. In the first place, while all the ex-presidents dabbled in politics, they always did so discreetly and never contemplated reentering the political arena in any significant way. Second, as part of the revolutionary generation that had led the struggle against England, they had on a number of occasions before becoming president given careful thought to the transition from former public statesman to private citizen. Among these former civil servants, the republican image of a bucolic life and abstinence from state affairs resonated with remarkable regularity. Third, the republican ideal of citizen-statesman and abhorrence of political partisanship remained strong enough that even in the intensely partisan campaign between John Adams and Thomas Jefferson to succeed George Washington as president in 1797, both Adams and Jefferson forswore any kind of public role.

Republicanism remained the paradigm of political behavior until the end of the 1820s, when the development of political parties and the rapid expansion of popular sovereignty brought an end to the early Republic. Like everything else political, it continued to define what was expected of former presidents. Not until the retirement of John Quincy Adams in 1829 did former presidents cease maintaining even the pretense of abstaining from active participation in the nation's political affairs.

Yet the transition to a more active post-presidency began with the retirement of James Madison in 1817. For that reason, Washington, Adams, and Jefferson form a separate cohort from the other former presidents of the early Republic.

I

In his Farewell Address of 1796, George Washington expressed the republican ideal of politically disinterested private citizens engaging in public service for a limited period before returning to private life. In his message Washington spoke of his impending retirement, "satisfied that if any circumstances have given peculiar value to my service they were temporary."[5] His words were more than a platitude. Throughout his adult life, Washington had been guided by certain essential qualities and principles. Two of these, ambition and a belief that self-interest guided all human behavior, might seem incongruent with the republican model of civic virtue even though they accounted for a good part of his success both as a land speculator in the West and a Revolutionary hero. However, as John Adams later made clear, ambition (*gloria*) was not incompatible with being a virtuous citizen, and self-interest was not necessarily inconsistent with a concern for honor and reputation—two other matters of fundamental importance to Washington. Even a private citizen pursuing his own interests, Washington believed, could still be working for a greater good.

As a member of Virginia's gentry and House of Burgesses, Washington predicated his honor and reputation on a strong sense of civic obligation and commitment to civic virtue. By the eve of the Revolution, he was also convinced that the English government was lost in corruption. No less than the other founding fathers, therefore, he embraced republican ideals and became a dutiful citizen in the republican cause, believing a noble new experiment in government awaited the colonies. He held to these republican principles for the rest of his life.

Washington's announcement of his intention to retire at the end of his second term as president in 1797 was the fourth time that he had contemplated retirement after providing service to the nation. After successfully leading American forces during the Revolution, he retired to Mount Vernon. In 1787, he served for four months in Philadelphia as chairman of the Constitutional Convention. After the delegates adopted a new constitution to replace the Articles of Confederation, he again returned briefly to Mount Vernon and helped tip the balance in Virginia in support of the new document before being elected unanimously as the nation's first president. In 1792, he once more contemplated his retirement and had James Madison, then serving in Congress, prepare a draft of a farewell message to the nation. However, Madison and others persuaded him to seek a second term, to which he was again unanimously elected.

In these three previous occasions in which he contemplated retirement, Washington expressed all the themes consistent with the republican ideal of a virtuous citizen returning to private life after public service. In this sense, he forecast the message of his Farewell Address of 1796 and the statements he would continue to make over the next three years before his death in 1799. "Having happily assisted in bringing the ship into port & having been fairly discharged; it is not my business to embark again on a sea of troubles," he remarked in 1786 when pressure was exerted on him to participate in a convention to reform the Articles of Confederation.[6]

Yet Washington was not simply being a virtuous citizen in expressing his desire to remain a private citizen living out the remainder of his life in the pastoral surroundings of his Mount Vernon estate. Throughout much of his adult life, he was concerned with his own mortality and with trying to make his estates at Mount Vernon and his landholdings along the nation's Western frontier profitable. As he grew older, these became even more pressing matters for him.

An imposing figure by any standard, measuring about six feet tall, muscular, graceful like an athlete, and weighing 175 pounds as a young man and between 210 and 220 pounds during the war years, Washington owed part of his legendary status to his physical presence. Even when he entered his senior years after the Revolution and his body began to soften and to lose some of its muscularity and grace, he continued to physically overshadow most of those around him. Although he almost died from pneumonia in 1790, he was also, for the most part, healthy until the time of his death. His most serious health problems were faltering hearing, a case of rheumatism, and his teeth, most of which had rotted out by his midfifties and had been replaced by ill-fitting dentures resulting in the tightly compressed lips and sunken cheeks seen in most of his likenesses.

Washington came from a family, however, of short-lived men. His half-brother, Lawrence, died of tuberculosis in 1752 at the age of thirty-four. Just a year earlier, George had contracted smallpox, leaving his face permanently scarred. When he was a surveyor at the age of seventeen, he suffered for the first of many attacks of malaria, called "ague" at the time. In 1757, he nearly died from another recurring problem, severe dysentery. As he entered his senior years, he expressed increased concern about his mortality. In a letter to the marquis de Lafayette, who had visited Mount Vernon in 1784, he wrote nostalgically about his vanishing youth, remarking, "Tho' I was blessed with a good constitution, I was of a short lived family—and might soon expect to be entombed in the dreary mansions of my father's."[7]

Washington claimed not to fear death. "I know it is very doubtful whether I ever shall ever rise from this bed, and God knows it is perfectly indifferent to me whether I do or not," he remarked after the surgical removal of a growth on his thigh in June 1789.[8] At the same time, he remained concerned about his impending mortality throughout his prepresidential years and during his two terms as president. In 1791, he even expressed anxiety to his secretary of state, Thomas Jefferson, about his declining mental acuity. Although there is little to suggest that he was becoming senile, there is much to suggest that during his second term, he became increasingly melancholy, perhaps a result, for the first time in his public career, of political attacks being directed against him personally.

When Washington left office in 1797, the nation was deeply divided between Republicans associated with Thomas Jefferson and James Madison and Federalists associated with John Adams and Alexander Hamilton. At the risk of oversimplification, they divided over three fundamental questions. One was whether the country's future lay with industry and banking, or with agriculture and commerce. A second was whether the role of the federal government should be enhanced or limited. The third was whether the nation should align itself more closely with England or with France in their off-and-on war, which would last nearly another two decades. For the most part, Federalists aligned behind the first of each of these alternatives while Republicans opted for the second. Complicating matters even more, the nation was rife with geographical tensions between the hinterlands and eastern cities, between slave and nonslave states, and between large and small states. In his Farewell Address, Washington sought to address the partisanship threatening to tear the nation apart. The "spirit of party," he wrote, "serves always to distract the public councils and enfeeble the public administration. It agitates the community with ill-founded jealousies and false alarms; kindles the animosity of one part against another; foments occasional riot and insurrection."[9]

Washington's appeal, however, failed to quell the partisanship. Even the president came under attack, especially after his support of the unpopular Jay Treaty, which the Republicans thought aligned the United States too closely with Great Britain. Although Washington remained an icon for most Americans, his administration and policies became the topic of the nation's newspapers, which at the time had a total circulation of about 40,000 but a readership probably two or three times that, and which were known for their malice, partisanship, and even vulgarity. The Republican press, convinced that the president was either himself a Federalist or was being manipulated by the Federalist leader, Hamilton, charged him with being "treacherous," "mischievous," "incompetent," and a "spoiled child." More seriously, they claimed his manner was imperious and that he displayed monarchical tendencies with "all the insolence of the Emperor of Rome." Even as Washington prepared to leave Philadelphia for Mount Vernon on the eve of his retirement, the notorious proprietor of the Philadelphia *Aurora,* Benjamin

Franklin Bache, grandson of Benjamin Franklin and a strident Republican, took a parting shot at him, remarking: "If ever there was a period for rejoicing, this is the moment."[10]

Passionate about his honor and reputation, keen about his place in history, and therefore inclined to bristle at criticisms of his policies, Washington, who had learned to distrust the press during the Revolution, became the first of a long line of presidents to disdain journalists and the press, which he accused of "dissiminating . . . poison." More to the point, the partisan attacks took a toll on him mentally. This, together with concerns about his physical health, led him to decide in 1796 not to seek a third term. "Added to the weight of years which have passed over me," he remarked in the spring of 1796, the troubles and the journalistic attacks of the last two years "have worn away my mind more than my body, and renders ease and retirement indispensably necessary to both."[11]

Of even more concern than the first president's health in his decision to leave the public stage was his wish to oversee his plantation at Mount Vernon, where he was always happiest, and to attend to his vast landholdings in the Ohio and the Great Kanawha river valleys that extended from Ohio through Virginia and western Pennsylvania. There was never a time throughout his adult life when Mount Vernon did not weigh heavily on Washington's mind. "I shall begrudge no reasonable expense that will contribute to the improvement and neatness of my farms," he wrote of Mount Vernon in 1793 while still in office, "for nothing pleases me better than to see them in good order . . . nor nothing hurts me more than to find them otherwise."[12]

Mount Vernon, the estate he had inherited from his brother, Lawrence, was his home for forty-five years. Over this period, he enlarged and twice improved the residence, which was beautifully situated to overlook the Potomac River. He began the first improvements in 1759 and started the second just before the Revolution. He also added other features at different times. He raised the structure from one and a half to two and a half stories, added north and south wings, and incorporated various architectural embellishments, including a two-story piazza on the riverfront, double-height pillars, open and arched colonnades linking the mansion with two main outbuildings, a cupola, and, later, a weather vane in the form of a bird with an olive branch in its mouth.

The residence reflected Washington's attention to detail and his sense of proportion, skills he acquired as a young surveyor. It also mirrored different periods in his life. The first building effort was his attempt to assume a place among Virginia's privileged gentry. The second remodeling and later changes included a large dining room, the most public space in the residence, with agricultural motifs inspired by Washington's belief in the virtuous nature of neoclassical republicanism and meant to recall the legend of Cincinnatus, the victorious Roman warrior and leader who gave up power to return to farming. Even the weather vane was intended as a symbol of his hope for the new nation.[13]

Mount Vernon was a working estate as well as a residence. Washington was also a farmer and landowner—indeed, he was one of the most scientific agricul-turalists in Virginia and one of the nation's largest landowners. Over the years, Washington increased the size of Mount Vernon from 2,000 to 5,000 acres, which he divided into five farms. Although he was originally a tobacco farmer, he ex-perimented with different crops, and he promoted practices to eliminate soil ex-haustion, increase crop yields, and improve the quality of his livestock. He used various types of plows and ways of plowing, and he experimented with other types of farm machinery and fertilizers.

Washington also turned Mount Vernon into a primitive mechanized village. At different times, he established a fishery, a flour mill, and even Virginia's larg-est distillery of grain alcohol. Throughout his public career, he sent his longest letters to his overseers at Mount Vernon, providing management instructions. He kept meticulous records of the costs and profits from his farms. However, he never intended his estate to be solely a commercial operation. Both before and after his public service, he enjoyed showing off to visitors both the mansion itself and its stately grounds and botanical gardens, with its rows of fruit trees, magno-lias, boxwoods, exotic plants, and lilacs, all of which he carefully nurtured and cultivated. The landscape combined beauty and purpose in a serenely harmonious setting.

At the same time, Washington depended heavily on the lease and sale of his vast Western landholdings to supplement his income and to help subsidize his heavy financial responsibilities, including providing for his extended family and a regular stream of visitors to Mount Vernon. At age sixty, the first president owned 58,000 acres of land, including the acreage of Mount Vernon. He bought his first parcel of land, 1,459 acres on Bullskin Creek in the lower Shenandoah Valley, sometime around 1750 from his earnings as a surveyor. As a colonial volunteer during the French and Indian War, he received a grant of land from the British, and after the war, he bought the grants of other veterans and purchased another 20,000 acres of land in the Ohio River Valley. When he married Martha Custis in 1759, he came into an estate of another 8,000 acres and eighty-five slaves, dou-bling his slave force.[14] His properties, however, proved a constant source of worry to him when leaseholders and purchasers of the land, who had bought on credit, failed to make their payments.

Although wealthy in land, Washington found himself frequently short on cash, even in the last years of his retirement. "My Estate (though it might sell on credit for a tolerable sum)," he told Thomas Law, the husband of his step-grand-daughter, Betcy, in May 1798, "has been and probably will continue to be, far from a productive one." The next month, he said much the same thing to Tobias Lear, who oversaw the family finances. Without the sale of some of his landhold-ings in western Pennsylvania, he told Lear, "my business must have stopped, or my embarrassments at this moment would have been great."[15]

Washington's interests and concerns and much of his daily schedule af-ter leaving the presidency, then, were the same as they had been in his earlier

Mount Vernon was a working farm as well as Washington's beloved estate. This undated illustration shows Washington talking to his white overseer while slaves are harvesting his crop of wheat, which had replaced tobacco as the primary crop. Washington was always happiest enjoying the life of a plantation owner. The boy and girl in the illustration might be the children of the overseer. (Courtesy of Library of Congress, Prints and Photographs Division.)

retirements and had mostly to do with the practical and mundane matters of his own economy, family, and health. After rising early and taking breakfast around seven in the morning, he would spend a good part of the rest of the day on his mount, riding for hours, meticulously observing his farms and giving orders to his overseers. He also spent considerable time fixing up the residence, which he found in a miserable state of disrepair when he returned home, and busying himself with his lifelong project, already under way but never completed, to channel the Potomac River and connect it eventually with the Ohio River. At three in the afternoon he would eat dinner, often attend to a stream of visitors anxious to consort with a legendary figure who had become world renowned, write letters, read, have tea, and then retire around eight or nine in the evening. The American Cincinnatus, it seemed, was fully content to assume once again the role of private citizen.

Yet this was never entirely the case. After briefly canceling all his newspaper subscriptions after his retirement, he began reading a dozen newspapers daily and found himself drawn into the political warfare that only intensified after he left office. His own political leanings grew increasing high Federalist as he became estranged from his former secretary of state, Thomas Jefferson, and bitter toward France because of its violation of American neutrality on the high seas. When President John Adams asked him in 1798 to come out of retirement to lead a new army in the United States' quasi war with France, the president even pressured Adams to name Alexander Hamilton as his second in command, even though Adams considered Hamilton his archenemy. Not only did Washington's behavior show a private citizen closely following the affairs of state, but in the case of his confrontation with Adams over Hamilton, it also makes clear Washington's determination to use his special place in the American pantheon to have his way politically.

Washington was therefore not only the United States' first president, but also its first post-president to seek to use his influence to advance his own personal and political agendas. Indeed, as a former president, Washington also employed his vast network of connections throughout the country to obtain information useful to his land speculations in the West.

Yet he decided against seeking a third term as president not only for personal reasons, but also because of the journalistic and other attacks accusing him of acting in an imperial manner. Concerned as always about his honor and place in history, he did not want even the appearance of violating the essential republican principle of public service as the duty of a virtuous citizen rather than as a quest for personal power and ambition. In deciding to deliver his Farewell Address to the American people, he insisted to Alexander Hamilton, who wrote the penultimate draft of the message—which was first published on 19 September 1796 and has since become one of the most celebrated documents in the nation's history— that he include language from the message James Madison had helped write four years earlier. In this way, he wanted to make clear to the nation that he had remained in office a second term not because of personal ambition but out of a sense of civic duty in the wake of the growing partisanship already evident in 1792. As he explained to Hamilton, language from the earlier address showing "that it was much against my inclination that I continued in Office, will cause it to be believed that I could have *no* view in extending the Powers of the Executive." [16]

In his letter to Hamilton, moreover, Washington also included his own first draft of a new message in which he referred specifically to his desire to establish the republican principle of limited terms of office. "May I be allowed further to add as a consideration far more important than even good laws under a free government," he stated in the draft, "that an early example of rotation in an office of so high and delicate a nature, may equally accord with the republican spirit of our Constitution, and the ideas of liberty and safety entertained by the people." [17] Washington did not himself favor setting a limit on public service, remarking to the marquis de Lafayette that he thought it unwise to "preclude ourselves from the services of any man who on some emergency shall be deemed universally most capable of serving the public." [18] Aware of growing concerns not only on the part of his political enemies but also among many who supported him that should he seek and win a third term he would establish a precedent for a monarchical government, he wanted to put these concerns to rest. He understood that his greatest attribute was his reputation, which he considered indispensable to the maintenance of political stability and building of public institutions. Here a sense of his place in history mixed with his republican ideals and goals for the nation.

Although it is also true that in the three years after he left office, Washington became increasingly involved in the partisan politics, he disliked discussing politics with casual acquaintances or with visitors to Mount Vernon, much less speaking publicly against his political opponents. After being been out of office just a few months, for example, he wrote to Oliver Wolcott Jr. in May 1797 about "various conjectures" that Wolcott, a Connecticut Federalist who had been comptroller of the treasury under Alexander Hamilton, had raised as to why President John Adams had recently decided to call Congress into session. In his letter to Wolcott, Washington made clear his wish not to become involved in such political speculation. Agricultural pursuits kept him busy enough, he said. "To make, & sell a little flour annually, to repair houses (going fast to ruin) . . . and to amuse myself in Agriculture and rural pursuits will constitute employment for the few years I have to remain on this terrestrial Globe."[19]

Washington was not being entirely candid in his comments to Wolcott; he often commented privately about political matters and became publicly more partisan in the two years that followed. Yet neither was he being disingenuous. On the contrary, given his abiding concern about his place in history and the nation's commitment to republican principles and abhorrence of unfettered political ambition, abstention from, rather than public engagement in, partisan politics was always his preference. Concern about his historical persona, in other words, dictated as much as possible the lack of a public persona while in retirement.

Even Washington's blatant use of his influence to secure Hamilton as his second in command after he agreed to lead a new army in 1798, which reflected most poorly on his reputation as the virtuous citizen responding without artifice to public duty, must be placed in a proper context. In the first place, Washington hesitated to come out of retirement. He stated that he would accept such an appointment only if the nation was invaded or in imminent danger of being invaded by France, and he made clear his intention to serve a nominal rather than an active role as head of the force. Second, he did not want to be saddled with commanders from the Revolution chosen because of their seniority. As he explained to Secretary of War James McHenry, who had apprised him of Adams's intention to have him lead a new army, he doubted a competent general staff "could be formed from the old generals, some on account of their age or infirmities; some from never having displayed any talents for enterprise; and others from their general opposition to the government or their predilection to French measures."[20]

Third, Washington insisted on having Hamilton as his second in command mainly because he thought Hamilton was the most qualified for the position. In fact, his relationship with his former treasury secretary had not been all that close since returning to Mount Vernon. He had corresponded with him only twice. He rejected his recommendation that he (Washington) make a southern tour to rally the country against France. In contrast to Hamilton, he did not want war with France; nor at the time did he think it imminent.

Having won his way with respect to the appointment of Hamilton as his second in command, Washington's role as commander of the nation's new army was nominal, as he always intended. After spending six weeks in Philadelphia in November and December helping to organize the new force, he returned to Mount Vernon, where he lived out the last year of his life. Apparently in good health, he resumed his normal routine, spending most of his time each day overseeing his farms. He maintained close contact with Secretary of War McHenry and Hamilton about the organization and outfitting of the new army and carefully watched the construction of the new capital city. He also quietly supported a number of Federalist candidates for Congress and the Virginia legislature. Although some Republicans even feared he might become more active politically, that possibility never seemed to have entered his mind.

On 12 December 1799, the former president spent five hours outside during a cold and wet day. The next day he complained of a worsening sore throat affecting his swallowing, breathing, and ability to speak. Doctors summoned to Mount Vernon employed the traditional medical practice of bleeding and purgatives, which only worsened his condition and caused him considerable agony. He died on 14 December 1799. Contemporary studies have concluded that he probably died from a rapidly worsening throat infection, which obstructed his airways and is easily treatable today with antibiotics.

Ironically, although Washington predicated his retirement on the republican ideal of abstention from public affairs, and although he largely stayed true to that principle during the three years he lived after leaving office, his post-presidency—like most of his life—had a more lasting impact on the course of American politics than that of any other former president. The sociologist Barry Schwartz has correctly observed that what Washington did not do throughout his career was often as important as what he did do. As the military leader of the Revolution, he deferred to Congress. As president, he abnegated dictatorial power. As a private citizen, he deferred to and legitimated the political process even when he disagreed with his successor.[21]

As a result, Washington became the symbol of what Americans stood for and the embodiment of what they held virtuous and even sacred. He also became the incarnation of a new civil or public religion in which homage to him was not so much hero worship as homage to the nation's most cherished beliefs and in which the division between the secular and the divine became obscured. His birthday, even when he was alive, became a cause of national celebration, and Mount Vernon a shrine visited by pilgrims. His image was seen on scores of coins, engravings, statues, and other icons. His very name became that of the nation's capital and of numerous towns, counties, and streets throughout the country. No other

American president, with the exceptions of Abraham Lincoln and Thomas Jefferson, would be perceived in the same manner as Washington. However, even lesser American presidents would receive homage. Presidential commemoration would not only survive Washington; it would become an enduring quality of American public religion.[22]

II

As James Madison once observed, "There never was perhaps a greater contrast between two characters than between those of Washington and John Adams."[23] The nation's first president was cool, confident, and reticent, and his successor emotional, insecure, and passionate. Washington was courtly and reserved. Adams was demonstrative, even insulting. Washington sought to avoid conflict. Adams often seemed to welcome it. Washington embodied charisma. Adams seemed to defy it. Washington was the object of envy but rarely exhibited it himself. Adams was driven by envy. Even physically, the differences between the two men could not have been greater. In contrast to the tall, athletic, and striking first president, Adams was short, bald, rotund, and awkward.

It is perhaps not surprising, therefore, that Adams always felt he would be shortchanged by history. His insecurities plagued him throughout much of his career. They flawed his presidency and helped lead to his defeat for reelection in 1800. They also made him an unattractive personality historically. During his life, he complained that his contributions to every major event of the new nation's history—the coming of the Revolution, his diplomatic role in Europe during and after the Revolution, and his own presidency—had gone unheeded or were overshadowed by the other founding fathers. In particular, he cited Benjamin Franklin, Alexander Hamilton, George Washington, and Thomas Jefferson. Most of them he resented (Franklin), detested (Hamilton), envied (Washington and Jefferson), or thought were his intellectual inferiors (all of them except Jefferson). Making matters worse for Adams was the fact that his own administration fell between presidencies headed by two of the nation's most iconoclastic leaders.[24]

Yet the unattractive side of Adams's personality, especially the self-doubt and envy that bedeviled and tormented him throughout most of his life, has made him much more human than the seemingly impenetrable Washington who preceded him and the detached Jefferson who followed him. His well-known irascibility and stubbornness, which often got him into trouble as president, seem at other times to have been nothing more than his understanding of the frailties of human nature and his desire to do right.[25]

The negative side of Adams's character was also offset by his sense of personal loyalty, his devotion to family, his piety, and even his joviality playing with his grandchildren at his Braintree farm (often referred to as Peacefield, about twelve miles south of Boston). Without dismissing his problems as president, particularly his exacerbation of partisanship both among Federalists and between Federalists and Republicans, he was also a generally successful chief executive, avoiding a harmful war with France and maintaining the integrity of his office against strong opposition.

Above all, Adams stands out as a person of gallant public virtue deeply committed to republican principles and a leader passionate in his patriotism and sense of honor. An intellectual, he read many times over the ancient classics, studied the British and Scottish theorists, and had an unrivaled understanding of the British constitution. Ever consumed with his place in history, he confessed his envy of "any man who was in possession of more wealth, more honours, or more knowledge [than himself]."[26] Yet paradoxically, he remained always a person of great humility and self-sacrifice who was bothered throughout his life more by a lack of recognition than by a lack of personal fame or affluence.

Adams's post-presidency reflected his quixotic personality. On the one hand, much of the quarter century that passed between the time he left the new capital city of Washington, where he became the first sitting president—without even attending the inauguration of his successor, his former friend and for the past half-dozen years at least his political enemy, Thomas Jefferson—until the time he died in 1826, was a quest by him to seek historical vindication of his political career. On the other hand, it was part of his ongoing effort to overcome his personal failings and find peace with himself. If he was not entirely successful in the first of these endeavors, he appeared more successful in the second of them.

Playing a major part in both undertakings was a fourteen-year-long correspondence that Adams had with Jefferson, with whom he mended fences after Jefferson left office. Begun in 1812, the Adams–Jefferson correspondence was more than a private set of letters between two retired presidents who were former colleagues and political rivals. They were far-reaching ruminations on political theory and commentary on national affairs, especially by Adams, that have since become widely appreciated as one of the great written legacies of the founding generation.

Even more than Washington's retirement from the presidency, Adams's post-presidency was characterized by its adherence to republican principles. Adams's commitment to republicanism is beyond dispute. He always advocated a mixed and balanced government as the institutional framework of republicanism. At one time, he was even willing to give a wide swath to popular sovereignty. However, he was never a democrat. Throughout his career, he had identified himself closely with the great statesman, theorist, and orator of the late Roman Republic, Marcus Tullius Cicero. Like Cicero, who shared many of Adams's personal characteristics, including being defiant in the name of principle, Adams believed in a nobility of talent, wealth, and accomplishment.

As a result of his encounter in the 1780s with the views of French democratic theorists, which shocked him, Adams moved further away from acceptance of democratic principles. Still advocating a mixed and balanced government, he called now for one that accepted permanent social inequalities and provided for a standing body of the elite, a more representative elected body, and a strong executive able to prevent domination of one body over the other and to encourage civic virtue, which, he believed, had increasingly given way to selfishness. In other words, he favored a government of the one, the few, and the many.[27]

Although as Washington's vice president Adams had expected to succeed him in 1797, he had followed the republican principle of not publicly seeking the office. After being defeated for reelection in 1800, he contemplated a retirement of personal and philosophical reflection in agrarian serenity and simplicity in accord with Cicero's own account of a well-spent life. After he retired to his Braintree farm, to which he had always yearned to return, he maintained that he was never so happy "since some sin to me unknown involved me in politics."[28]

This time, though, Adams went back to Braintree bitter at his failure to win reelection, which he attributed to the machinations of Alexander Hamilton. He also shared Washington's disdain of the press. The Republican *Aurora* had attacked his presidency viciously, and even in retirement, he blamed the press for his relative historical obscurity compared to the other founding fathers. "If I am to judge by the newspapers and pamphlets that have been printed in America for twenty years past, I should think that both parties believed me the meanest villain in the world," he wrote to his friend, Dr. Benjamin Rush, a few years after retiring. "Washington and Franklin could never do any thing but what was imputed to be pure, disinterested patriotism. I never could do any thing but what was ascribed to sinister motives."[29] He was sure that he had been reduced to a political and historical nonentity, a conviction that only ripened in subsequent years. In contrast to Washington, his home did not swarm with visitors hoping to meet, talk with, or merely catch a glimpse of the abiding figure of the American Revolution. "I am not, never was, & never shall be a great man," he wrote in despair in 1807.[30]

Much of Adams's withdrawal into relative obscurity, however, was his own doing. At first, he cut off all public ties, remaining at home and even refusing to travel to nearby Boston. After two years of virtual exile, he mellowed. He began to attend local public functions, such as Fourth of July celebrations, visited Boston occasionally, and enjoyed dinners at the American Academy of Arts and Sciences and the Massachusetts Society for Promoting Agriculture, organizations in which he served as honorary president. He also began an extensive and rich correspondence with a number of old friends, in particular the Philadelphia surgeon, Dr. Benjamin Rush. His life, he remarked after a decade into retirement, had become filled with "serenity and Tranquility."[31]

Adams, however, remained largely apart from the public. Becoming increasingly disenchanted with the Federalist Party, which he believed had become an aristocracy of the moneyed classes and posed the greatest threat to his concept of mixed republican government, he even resigned from both associations. He felt increasingly out of place among its Federalist members and remarked that his presence put "a restraint upon conversation."[32] He also refused to comment publicly on political issues, and he adopted the policy, which he mostly followed throughout his retirement, of not writing to any sitting president.

Like Washington, Adams found a good part of his time engaged in the mundane affairs of daily life. He did not have Washington's extensive estate or vast landholdings. Indeed, he liked to mock Washington, Jefferson, and other members of the Virginia dynasty as well as to engage in self-ridicule by referring to himself as "the Monarch of Peace Field," or later calling his farm "Montezello" to make the point about how humble his landholdings and lifestyle were. "Mr. Jefferson lives at Monticello the lofty Mountain. I live at Montezello, a little hill."[33]

Adams exaggerated. Peacefield was, in fact, a comfortable, spacious, and warm two-story New England colonial house with an attractive front porch, windows and shutters running the length of the second floor, and dormers adorning a third-floor attic that provided additional living space. It had a beautiful garden and verdant fields for Adams to pursue his love of farming. Located about seventy-five feet from the saltbox house where Adams had been born in 1735, the residence had been purchased by Adams and his wife, Abigail, sometime in the 1780s while John was serving as ambassador to Great Britain. It became the home of the Adams family for four generations.[34]

The contrast between Peacefield and Monticello or Mount Vernon was nevertheless striking. One French visitor, perhaps comparing Peacefield to the great palaces of the French aristocracy, by which even the residencies of Washington and Jefferson might not have passed muster, described it as a "small house which a sixth-rate Paris lawyer would disdain to choose for his summer home."[35] Still, it was not incorrect to describe Peacefield as a dwelling more fit for a successful lawyer like Adams than a member of the Virginia landed gentry. The residence also reflected Adams's more modest financial means. Unlike Washington, Adams could not engage in land speculation or sell properties to raise needed cash. Although he did not lead the Virginian's lavish lifestyle, his financial needs were even more pressing.

Having retired with few financial resources and no longer enjoying the lucrative $25,000 salary the nation's first presidents received (the equivalent of about $311,000 in 2009), Adams needed to provide for a large extended family, including children, grandchildren, a niece, and a widowed daughter-in-law who lived with him and his wife, Abigail. Several of the grandchildren married and had their own children, making John Adams a great-grandfather. Adams relished his time with his offspring. The grandchildren were his great joy and brought out the best of him—his humor, spontaneity, and love of life. Josiah Quincy, a cousin who was often invited to Sunday lunch, recalled in later years that "the President," as the family always called him, was always lively, informal, and full of little jokes and bits of information when with his children and grandchildren. However, the costs of maintaining the household put an enormous strain on him. It was only partially relieved when his son, John Quincy Adams, came to his aid financially. Sickness, death, and thoughts of death were also Adams's frequent companions.

His daughter, Nabby, died of breast cancer in 1813. His wife, Abigail, suffered from a severe case of rheumatism and was often seriously ill. The family also had a problem with alcoholism. The former president's oldest son, Charles, died from alcoholism in 1799. His youngest son, Thomas, a lawyer unhappy with his profession, was also an alcoholic, who resigned from the Massachusetts legislature under mysterious circumstances a year after being elected to that body and who was a constant burden to his father.

Adams, who followed a strict regimen of exercise during much of his retirement, including long walks, horseback rides, and supervision of the work in his fields, remained relatively healthy well into his eighties. His most serious ailments were tremors in his hands, which worsened as he grew older, and gradually declining eyesight. However, having already reached the age of sixty-five even before he left Washington in 1801, he wrote to Thomas saying he hoped he would never become "grief and distress to his family, a weeping, helpless object of compassion."[36] His daughter Nabby's death, occurring shortly after the passing of his good friend and brother-in-law, Richard Cranch, and his wife, Mary, and several longtime colleagues, made him ponder the mysteries of life and death, including his own death. Presuming it could not be far off, he commented that he preferred to die in a fatal accident than suffer through a long and painful illness, such as Nabby had endured, or become a dotard and a burden to others.

Yet it was not thoughts of death or family concerns that consumed most of the first twelve years of Adams's retirement. Rather it was vindication of his entire political career. Worried that his father had no plan for his retirement and concerned that he would become bored with his inactive life, John Quincy Adams suggested to him in 1804 that he write his autobiography. The former president expressed reservations. He had started to write an autobiography two years earlier but had stopped after only the first twelve paragraphs. He told his son that continuing with it now would inflame his passions. However, he quickly warmed to the idea.

Reflecting his lifelong vanity, insecurities, and pent-up anger, Adams remarked that he intended the autobiography to be only for his children. "As the Lives of Phylosophers, Statesmen, or Historians written by themselves have generally been suspected of Vanity," he commented in the very first paragraph of the autobiography, "my Excuse is, that . . . some of my Posterity may probably wish to see in my own hand Writing a proof of the falsehood of the Mass of odious Abuse of my Character."[37] In truth, he had decided to write the work in response to the bitterness he still felt because of his defeat in 1800, and he clearly intended that it be published one day by one of his children

Although Adams worked sporadically on the autobiography over a period of five years (1802–1807), compiling a work of several hundred manuscript pages, most authorities who have studied it have concluded that as a literary or historical work, it was a disaster. As a reflection of Adams's own character, it was jumbled and self-indulgent. Adams could be a fine stylist when writing letters, but his autobiography was more a legal treatise than a piece of prose. It even included long sections extracted from printed documents. Lacking any clear chronological or other organizational framework, it wandered from the factually interesting to tedious description of the trivial. Strangely, Adams said little about any of the founding fathers who tormented his soul. Although he intended originally to carry the chronicle through his presidential years, he never got beyond 1780, failing to touch precisely on the diplomatic and presidential years he felt most in need of vindication. He also skipped over such matters as his law practice, the protest movement in Massachusetts leading to the Revolution, and one of the years he served in the Continental Congress. Instead of vindicating his career, his autobiography served only to underscore his own impulsive, insecure, and anguished character.

Even worse in this regard were his emotional outbursts in response to the publication by his onetime friend, Mercy Otis Warren, of her multivolume *History of the Rise, Progress and Termination of the American Revolution*. The sister of the well-known revolutionary patriot, James Otis, who had been a role model for Adams as a young man, and the wife of James Warren, another leading patriot and one of Adams's closest associates during the Revolution, Warren was also one of the foremost female intellectuals of her time. In her writings, she shared Adams's republican views, interpreting history in terms of a conflict between virtue in defense of liberty and avaricious and corrupted power. However, she also emphasized a related conflict between reason and passion, believing the former, together with liberty and virtue, was necessary to avoid licentiousness and sustain a republic.[38]

Although Warren did not publish her history of the Revolution until 1805, she had completed it several years earlier, by which time she had become increasingly cynical of the Federalists. Adams was irate when he read Warren's *History*. He believed she had maligned him by, among other things, belittling the role he had played in the coming of the Revolution, in the Continental Congress, and in the peace negotiations with England. Just as seriously, she also accused him of having become a monarchist while in Europe in the 1780s.

In a series of letters to Warren, Adams vented all the resentment he had built up over the years for what he regarded as a malign neglect of his crucial role in the establishment of the new nation. He also took deep offense at Warren's accusation that he had lost his republicanism in the 1780s because he supported a standing body of the elite. He correctly pointed out to her that "the word republican is so loose and indefinite that successive predominant factions will put glosses on it as different as light and darkness." Warren got the best of the exchange by pointing to the inherent danger of what Adams considered the virtue of passion. Although recognizing that passion in defense of a noble cause might at times be "the heavenly gales that waft us safely to port," she commented that at other times, it constitutes "the ungovernable gusts that blow us down the stream of absurdity."[39]

In the years that followed his exchange with Warren, Adams never lost his passion or his desire to vindicate his career. Beginning in 1809, Adams went public for the first and only time. Over the next three years, he published a series of essays of more than 1,000 pages in the *Boston Patriot,* in which he defended his presidency and his career as a diplomat in the 1780s. He also made clear his differences with Franklin and especially Hamilton. As an effort to recuperate his reputation, it failed miserably. Once more, he allowed his passion, his sense of hurt, and his vindictiveness toward his enemies to undermine the rationale of his argument. In his one important break from the republican ideal of the former citizen-statesman retiring from the public political stage, he became the first and only former president before James Buchanan to seek vindication of his public career using his own heretofore private correspondence.

Beginning in 1812 and lasting for nearly the rest of his long life, Adams's quest for self-justification took a different direction. The vehicle was his famous correspondence with Thomas Jefferson. The ties between Adams and Jefferson stretched back to the days of the Continental Congress; it was Adams who asked Jefferson, a gifted writer, to draft the Declaration of Independence. The two men remained comrades in arms for most of the next twenty years, but their relationship unraveled in the 1790s after Adams defeated Jefferson for president in 1796.

On one level, Adams and Jefferson differed over specific foreign and domestic policy issues—the same ones that divided Federalists from Republicans and were responsible for the intense partisanship of the 1790s. Their differences, however, were as much philosophical and theoretical as political. Although Adams was a Federalist, he was never really a party man, and he broke with the Federalist Party after he retired from the presidency and eventually became a Republican. While Jefferson helped found the Republican Party, he held partisanship at this time almost as in much disdain as Adams.

What separated the two statesmen was a fundamental difference over republicanism and what that implied for the future direction of the country. Whereas Jefferson and his followers believed that the American experiment was predicated on popular sovereignty replacing the traditional balance of separate social orders, Adams believed in a balance among elite and nonelite social groups. Unlike Jefferson, who was essentially optimistic about mankind's ability to control its passions through reason, Adams also doubted the deliberative rationale of the sovereign public and hearkened back to the need of a permanent elite and strong and independent executive to ensure a republican order protective of liberty. In contrast to Jefferson's optimism about the destiny of the new nation's republican experiment, in other words, Adams remained fixated on the past and dubious about the country's future.[40]

These differences manifested themselves most clearly in the Adams–Jefferson correspondence of 1812–1826. Largely as a result of the intercession of Dr. Benjamin Rush, both men's longtime friend, they agreed to resume their former friendship. In their great gift to posterity, each man sought to explain himself to the other. In doing so, they underscored the paradigmatic significance of republicanism for the founding fathers. At the same time, they made clear the major philosophical and theoretical matters not addressed by republicanism, which accounted in significant measure for the intense divisions and partisanship that constituted the birth pangs of the new nation.

Although both Adams and Jefferson went out of their way most of the time to avoid offending each other, Adams could not resist, especially in the first years of the correspondence, defending his views of republicanism and his record as president even at the expense of Jefferson's views and presidential record. The more prolific and aggressive of the two correspondents, whose letters outnumbered the Virginian's by about four to one, Adams also could not keep from bringing up what he considered old slights and prevarications made against him by Jefferson and his allies. In 1798, during the quasi war with France, Adams had signed the Alien and Sedition Acts, the most notorious feature of which allowed for the fining and jailing of those persons convicted of making seditious remarks about federal officials. Jefferson and James Madison responded with the Kentucky and Virginia Resolutions, which claimed the right of states to nullify acts by the federal government not expressly granted to it by the Constitution.

In July 1813, at a time when talk was ripe in New England about seceding from the Union over opposition to the War of 1812, Adams, who vigorously opposed such talk, reminded Jefferson of the danger inherent in the two resolutions. "The Northern States," he wrote, "are now retaliating, upon the Southern States, their conduct from 1797 to 1800. . . . Their Newspapers, Pamphlets, hand Bills, and their Legislative Proceedings are copied from Examples sett them, especially by Virginia and Kentucky. I know not which Party has the most unblushing Front, the most Lying Tongue, or the most impudent and insolent, not to say the most seditious and rebellious Pen." Less than two weeks later, he took another swipe at Jefferson by reminding him of his support for France in the 1790s and the dangers of unrestrained popular sovereignty. "You was persuaded in your own mind that the Nation would succeed in establishing a free Republican Government. I was as well persuaded, in mine, that a project of such a Government, over five and twenty millions and five hundred thousands of them could neither write nor read: was as unnatural irrational and impracticable; as it would be over the Elephants Lions Tigers Panthers Wolves and Bears in the Royal Menagerie at Versailles."[41]

Jefferson remained nonplussed by Adams's jibes. His policy was to strike back occasionally but mostly to deflect onto other subjects reflecting his more scientific and enlightenment orientation. On 28 October, however, he spelled out his views on aristocracy and popular sovereignty and his optimism about American posterity. His differences with Adams could not have been clearer. Perhaps aristocracy was inevitable in the "old world," given its lack of land, he said. However, conditions in the United States were different. America's abundance of land allowed everyone the opportunity to own property and earn his own living. "Every one, by his property, or by his satisfactory situation," he added, "is interested in the support of law and order. And such men may safely and advantageously reserve to themselves a wholesome controul over their public affairs, and a degree of freedom, which in the hands of the Canaille of the cities of Europe, would be instantly perverted to the demolition and destruction of every thing public and private." One may merely contrast Jefferson's remark with Adams's response on 15 November to understand how two republicans could have such dissimilar views about human nature and the future: "Mankind have not yet discovered any remedy against irresistible Corruption in Elections to Offices of great Power and Profit, but making them hereditary," Adams replied to Jefferson.[42]

Throughout the years that followed, Adams and Jefferson touched on a wide variety of issues. As time passed, matters between them became increasingly more philosophical and theoretical. They paid more attention, for example, to the intrinsic value of human existence, to the proper character of a gentleman, and to religious matters. Here Jefferson and Adams arrived at remarkably similar views. Jefferson expressed his belief in the philosophy of Christianity as set forth by the Apostles, while Adams made clear his belief in a Christian God but without identifying himself with any particular Christian religion. One issue on which they rarely spoke until near the end of their own lives was death.

Adams's correspondence with Jefferson had a profound impact on him. He never entirely eliminated the demons haunting his personality. Even his grandson, Charles Francis Adams, later commented on his frequent irascibility and emotional outbursts. In 1818, he lost his wife and soul mate of fifty-four years, Abigail, which for a time left him devastated. His eyesight deteriorated to the point where he had to have others read to him, and the palsy in his hands made it impossible for him to write his own correspondence; instead, he had to dictate to others. This was not an easy task, for he had long ago lost his teeth and refused to wear dentures, making it difficult for him to speak clearly. By the time he reached the age of ninety, he had also become so frail that he was confined to a few rooms at Peacefield and was unable to move without considerable assistance.[43]

Overall, however, Adams appeared more at peace with himself than he had been when he wrote his first letter to Jefferson in 1812. In much of his correspondence with Jefferson, there crept in a playful literary game in which both men assumed the roles of raconteurs, epigrammatists, semanticists, and etymologists. Adams was also delighted at the attention he received from three generations of his family. He loved to pause and reflect when playing with his grandchildren. One evening, while watching his granddaughters, Susanna and Abigail, blowing soap bubbles with one of his clay pipes, he wondered about the "allegorical" meaning of newly formed bubbles, their beauty illuminated by the light of candles and fire, suddenly gone like a wisp of air. "There can be no more perfect emblem of the physical and political and theological scenes of human life," he wrote. "Morality only is eternal. All the rest is balloon and bubble from the cradle to the grave."[44]

In 1820, his fellow citizens honored Adams by choosing him as a presidential

Portrait of John Adams at age eighty-eight in 1824 by the foremost portrait artist of the Federalist period, Gilbert Stuart, who painted the portraits of the nation's first six presidents. The portrait was completed in 1824, the year Adams's son, John Quincy Adams, was elected the nation's sixth president. By this time Adams was in declining health. Although his mind was still sharp, he suffered from palsy in his hands and had to dictate his correspondence. The portrait is on exhibit in the Long Room of the Adams house in Quincy, MA, operated by the U.S. National Park Service. (Courtesy of Library of Congress, Prints and Photographs Division.)

elector for Massachusetts. He cast his ballot for James Monroe. That same year, they honored him again by selecting him to represent them in a convention to rewrite the state constitution, a document that he had largely written in the first place. No longer did he think he would be a forgotten historical figure, but he still regretted that he would not be remembered as a great figure.

Adams was proud but apprehensive about the rising political fortunes of his son, John Quincy Adams. When Quincy Adams was appointed secretary of state by President James Monroe in 1817, putting him in line to succeed Monroe, his political enemies charged that he had been advanced in the diplomatic service because of nepotism. In response, the elder Adams strongly denied that he had ever tried to use his influence to promote his son's career.[45] When Quincy Adams was elected president in 1824, his father worried that he would be slandered, just as he had been, as president. "Our American Chivalry is the worst in the world," he complained to Jefferson in one of his last letters to his old friend before he died. "It has no Laws, no bounds, no definitions; it seems to be all a Caprice."[46]

Despite Adams's growing infirmities, he did not seem to fear death, and when he died on 4 July 1826, probably of congestive heart failure, he appeared far happier than he had been during much of his life. His last words after briefly coming out of a coma were, "Thomas Jefferson still lives."[47]

III

In fact, Jefferson had died a few hours earlier on that same day, the fiftieth anniversary of the Declaration of Independence. However, he lived out his retirement quite differently from Adams. Less interested than Adams in vindicating his political career, he remained far more active politically than Adams—or, for that matter, Washington. He maintained a regular correspondence with his successor, James Madison, in which he sometimes acted as Madison's unofficial adviser, and he engaged in other political activities.

Jefferson remained committed, nevertheless, to the republican ideal of former presidents. Even his correspondence with Madison during the War of 1812 was largely informative and almost always in response to inquiries from the president. After the end of the war, he gave himself over more and more to the collection of books, to correspondence, including his correspondence with Adams, and to inquiries into a vast range of subjects from architecture, to archeology, to paleontology, to horticulture, and to language and literature. He remained concerned about the nation's future growth and place in the world. He also devoted an enormous amount of his time to the establishment of the University of Virginia, and he supported the Missouri Compromise of 1820.

The political world itself, however, had only passing interest for Jefferson.[48] Indeed, as the years went by, a growing number of visitors to Monticello commented on how ill-informed he had become on current affairs. Like his predecessors, he had been the object of a venomous oppositional press as president. In retirement, however, he hardly ever read the newspapers; he remarked in 1816 to James Monroe, "I rarely think them worth reading, and almost never worth notice." Another time, he commented to his friend, Walter Jones, "[Journalists] have rendered themselves useless, by forfeiting all title to belief." He still took the *Richmond Enquirer,* but, he said, only for the advertisements, "the only truths to be relied on in a newspaper."[49]

Jefferson's support of the Missouri Compromise, which provided for the expansion of slavery into the Missouri territory, his refusal to free his own slaves despite his well-known advocacy of democratic principles, and DNA documentation that he fathered a number of children with one of his slaves, Sally Hemings, have fostered robust debate about his attitude toward slavery and his treatment of his slaves that have tarnished his reputation among some historians.[50] Nevertheless, Jefferson remains one of the great icons of American democracy. More than any other American president with perhaps the exception of Abraham Lincoln, he has come to symbolize democratic principles in ways relevant to most Americans, even to those of different political persuasions. The Jefferson–Jackson dinner remains one of the major annual events of the Democratic Party. At the same time, no less a Republican figure than former president Ronald Reagan has claimed the Jeffersonian ideals of limited government and individual freedom as the bedrock of his own political philosophy. Although this identification of Jefferson with a democratic version of republicanism traces back to his authorship of the Declaration of Independence, it was embedded in most of his political career and helped define his post-presidential years.[51]

Six feet, two and a half inches tall (about the same height as Washington), lean, with reddish hair, a ruddy complexion, thin lips, an angular nose, and hazel eyes, Jefferson was perhaps the most inscrutable of the nation's founding fathers, even more impenetrable in terms of his personality than Washington. While being distant and aloof was as much a tactic for Washington as it was a reflection of his personality, the same was not true for Jefferson. Notwithstanding the fact that he was also one of the most sophisticated, worldly, and erudite members of his generation, he relished his privacy and solitude.[52]

That is why Monticello, located in Albermarle County near the Blue Ridge Mountains, was so important to Jefferson: he always preferred the inner peace he found at Monticello to public service. He also took great satisfaction in applying some of his vast knowledge in practical ways to his estate. For most of his adult life, he was planning, building, or remodeling Monticello. Construction of the first design of the residence began in 1769 and was not completed until 1784, when Jefferson left for Europe. In 1796, Jefferson began work on a new design for remodeling and enlarging Monticello involving virtually tearing down the old structure and building it anew; the residence was not completed until 1809, after Jefferson had retired as president. Best known for its portico and the stately columns that embellished the front of the house, its large entrance hall, its north octagonal bedroom and tearoom connected to the dining room, and its domed upper room, Monticello was a brilliant example of Roman neoclassicism modified by Jefferson's own genius as an architect. The structure's uniqueness was complemented by elaborate furnishings and such unusual interior features as parquet floors, windows pivoting on a center pin, rolling double doors, and alcove beds.

Jefferson also nurtured the gardens and fields of Monticello just as Washington did the lands of his Mount Vernon estate. Regarding trees as among the most virtuous of nature's plants because of their practicality as well as beauty, he planted groves of native and exotic trees, 160 species in all, including mulberry and honey locusts, along the roundabouts or roads that girded the mountain leading to the residence, ornamentals adjacent to the house, and living peach trees to fence the borders of his fields. He also planted separate gardens containing more than 170 varieties of fruit and 330 varieties of vegetables, and he built a winding walk bordered by flower beds and verdant lawns. "I find that the limited number of our flower beds will be too much to restrain the variety of flowers which we might wish to indulge," he wrote to his granddaughter, Anne Cary Randolph, soon after returning to Monticello in 1809.[53]

Jefferson's satisfaction came from the horticulture and landscape planning of Monticello rather than from the business side of agriculture, in which he was never Washington's equal. "Too old to learn I must be contented with the occupation and amusement of the art [of farming]," he complained to his friend, Benjamin Rush. "Already it keeps me so much without doors that I have little time to read, and still less to write."[54]

Yet being a planter and landowner was foundational to Jefferson's entire concept of a republican democracy. Throughout the nation's history, there has developed the so-called agrarian myth, the belief of an inherent relationship between the small, landowning, hard-toiling, independent, and virtuous farmers and democratic principles. The association of the yeoman farmer and democracy has historically been one of strongest in the American imagination. No one believed more in this image or was more responsible for its incorporation into the American culture than Jefferson.[55]

Jefferson's views about the interrelationship between opportunities for land ownership in America and the viability of popular sovereignty that he expressed to John Adams in 1813 can be traced back to his imaginative and fictionalized views of Saxon landownership before the Norman conquest of England in 1066.[56] However, they were also based on his true assessment of the changing nature of American agriculture, which by the end of the eighteenth century had become increasingly geared to the production of grain (mainly wheat) for export to Europe in response to the growth of Europe's population. Washington, Jefferson, and other Virginia planters shifted from tobacco to wheat production to meet Europe's growing demand for American foodstuffs. Improvements in husbandry, crop rotation, and agricultural implements also made agriculture more productive. The push of higher agricultural productivity and the pull of export demand opened new opportunities for even small farmers.

An equation followed in Jefferson's mind on one side of which was democracy and on the other landownership and profitable small farmers gearing their crops to the export market. The agrarian myth was therefore not a myth for him but a realistic assessment of the actual and potential political economy of the United States, one predicated on agriculture and commerce over industry and banking; on rural over urban life; on economic security and democracy; and on an expanding nation of unlimited opportunity.[57]

The inclusiveness and optimism of Jefferson's democratic republicanism accounted for the enormous success of the Republican Party in the new nation. It was also responsible for his own victory as president in 1800, which he labeled a revolution because it secured the advancement of democracy. His vision of a growing republic of small farmers engaged in foreign commerce whose future extended westward beyond the horizon also explains much of his foreign policy after he became president, including the Louisiana Purchase (despite his doubts about its constitutionality) and the institution of the embargo of 1807 as a way of forcing the warring powers of England and France to stop their seizure of goods on American ships.

By the time his second term neared its end in 1809, Jefferson was anxious to retire. Although his supporters urged him to seek a third term, he refused even to entertain the idea. The dying Federalist Party accused him and his secretary of state and presumptive heir, James Madison, of squandering the nation's prosperity by the hated embargo, which Congress replaced with the much milder Non-Intercourse Act just before Jefferson left office. Even antiadministration Republicans launched fusillades at the White House. Reacting with hurt and indignation, Jefferson responded two days before the inauguration of James Madison, whom he had battled hard to get elected, "never did [a] prisoner, released from his chains, feel such relief as I shall on shaking off the shackles of power."[58]

After the end of his presidency, Jefferson maintained a regular correspondence with Madison. His relationship with the new president was almost as long as his ties with Adams, going back to their first meeting in Williamsburg, Virginia, in 1776. It flourished after 1779 when Jefferson began serving as governor of Virginia and Madison was a member of Virginia's executive council. There were differences between the two men that surfaced at different times in their long friendship. Jefferson tended to be more theoretical and philosophical than Madison, who was more strategic and pragmatic. Jefferson also had greater faith in human reason than his friend, who focused more on the role of passion and self-interest on human behavior. For that reason, Jefferson regarded even republican forms of government more unfavorably than his colleague, who considered government necessary to combat the dangers inherent in the human frailties that

Jefferson tended to ignore or dismiss. In contrast to Madison, who has often been referred to as the father of the Constitution, a reluctant Jefferson had to be persuaded by Madison to support the Constitution; even then, Jefferson based his support on the addition to the document of what has since become known as the Bill of Rights (the first ten amendments to the Constitution guaranteeing specific individual rights).[59]

The differences between Jefferson and Madison, however, were far less basic, and their relationship more predictable, than those between Jefferson and Adams. In contrast to the volatile Adams, Madison shared Jefferson's sanguine temperament, his confidence, and his optimism about the nation's future. Although Jefferson remained the senior partner in their relationship, Madison's political pragmatism often prevailed over Jefferson's impulsiveness, and despite their occasional differences, their friendship continued to blossom during Jefferson's presidency.[60]

Because of their close relationship and the fact that Jefferson had fought for Madison's election, the popular former president feared that a skeptical public would perceive Madison as merely his puppet. This was an idea that continued to be promoted by the Federalists and even some Republican foes of the former president. In response, Jefferson took the extraordinary step of issuing a circular letter making clear that he had no intention of abusing his relationship with the new president even in the matter of appointments to the new administration.[61] The former president did not always keep his pledge. For example, he successfully secured an appointment to the federal judiciary for Virginia governor John Tyler. "I think there is scarcely a person in the state so solidly popular, or who would be so much approved for that place," he wrote Madison on behalf of Tyler. In contrast, he objected to the appointment of Joseph Story to the U.S. Supreme Court.[62]

Jefferson's most noteworthy intrusion into the appointment process, however, was his successful effort to heal a breach between Madison and his other longtime friend, James Monroe, going back to the rejection in 1807—when Jefferson was still president—of a treaty that Monroe and William Pinkney had negotiated with England. Although the Monroe–Pinkney Treaty resolved many of the differences between the two countries, it omitted any reference to the hateful British practice of impressing American seamen whom the British claimed were still British citizens. Jefferson refused even to consider the treaty, and Monroe blamed both Jefferson and Madison for its rejection. The following year, Monroe ran unsuccessfully against Madison for the presidency. Although Monroe's relationship with Jefferson improved afterward, his relations with Madison did not. They became even worse after Madison offered to appoint Monroe as governor of Louisiana. Monroe, who wanted a cabinet position, considered the appointment beneath him. However, with Jefferson's strong approval, Madison, in 1811, replaced his disloyal secretary of state, Robert Smith, with Monroe.[63]

Jefferson also involved himself in partisan political matters in the first years after he left office. In letters to Madison and other political friends, he took strong exceptions to a number of the rulings of his old nemesis, Chief Justice John Marshall, and to what he perceived as the expanded role of the federal judiciary.

Of the first three former presidents, therefore, Jefferson was the most partisan and politically active after leaving office. However, Jefferson seldom ventured beyond seeking presidential appointments in his private correspondence with Madison.[64] In fact, Jefferson rarely left Monticello or his farms in Bedford County, about ninety miles away, where he designed and built another architectural gem, Poplar Forest. During his retirement, he never even returned to the nation's capital, about a hundred miles away, and only once, in his first year of retirement, did he visit the state capital in Richmond. He also never engaged in the type of public discourse that Adams did in the *Boston Patriot*. As for his influence with Madison, it was limited. Sometimes Madison listened to him, as in the case of the appointments of Tyler and Monroe. Other times, he did not, as in the case of Story.

Jefferson and Madison followed the same pattern with respect to the War of 1812. During this entire period, Madison kept Jefferson fully informed of all important developments. The letters they exchanged were, as they had always been, simple and to the point. Occasionally Madison solicited Jefferson's advice, but usually this was on matters left over from the previous administration. When Madison asked for Jefferson's opinion, the former president was willing to offer it. His distrust of the British was especially palpable. When Madison informed Jefferson in 1809 that the British minister to the United States, David Erskine, had pledged in 1809 that his government would revoke the orders in council establishing a virtual blockade on all countries at war with Great Britain (later repudiated by British foreign minister George Canning) and promised to send a minister to the United States to negotiate a new commercial treaty with Washington, Jefferson made it clear just how he felt about the British: "They never made an equal commercial treaty with any nation," he said, "and we have no right to expect to be the first."[65]

Jefferson came to view the War of 1812 as almost a blessing in disguise. It would both free the United States from the enduring malignancy of British influence and from what he regarded as the larger tyranny of Europe. The war would also foster a spirit of nationalism, make possible the conquest of Canada and the Floridas, and result in an "empire of liberty" such as the world had never seen. "What in short is the whole system of Europe towards America but an atrocious and insulting system," he remarked during the war. "One hemisphere of the earth, separated from the other by wide seas on both sides, having a different system of interests . . . is made subservient to all the petty interests of the other, to *their laws, their* regulations, their passions and wars."[66]

The former president followed the war closely. He was afraid its cost would end his hope of eliminating the national debt and deprive him of a great deal of his agricultural income, based as it was on exports to Europe. He was also obviously disappointed by the conduct and outcome of the conflict. Yet he hardly ever took the initiative in writing Madison about war-related matters. Usually he merely expressed his support of his successor's policy or his views on the situation in Europe, and he rarely objected when the president ignored his recommendations.[67]

Jefferson's correspondence with Madison after he left office was not confined solely to state affairs. When Jefferson returned to Monticello, he realized how greatly in debt he was. Interestingly, he insisted that his debts were an inevitable part of republican virtue. To retire from office in better financial circumstances than when he assumed office would suggest that he had put his own interests above those of the public. To the contrary, he noted, he retired from office with the satisfaction "of having added nothing to my private fortunes during my public service and of retiring with hands as clean as they are empty."[68]

In reality, much of his debt was due to his lavish style of living, which included the purchase of expensive wines, foods, and carriages, and first editions of books for what was the largest and finest private library in the nation. As a result, he had to ask Madison to be the cosigner of a loan for him, which Madison was later able to transfer to the American Revolutionary hero and Polish patriot, Thaddeus Kosciusko.

The problem of debt continued to plague Jefferson to his death. Despite his hope for solitude at Monticello, he faced the same problem that Washington had after he left the presidency. Having been an extremely popular president, he was overwhelmed with guests and curiosity seekers, whom he was reluctant to turn away, and whom he often fed and housed for the night, at great expense to him. He also had to provide for a large expanded family, including his daughter, Martha, his heavily in debt son-in-law, Thomas Mann Randolph, and nine grandchildren. In part to deal with his debt and in part to replace the collection of the Library of Congress, which was burned to the ground by the British during the War of 1812, Jefferson sold the Library of Congress his collection of approximately 6,500 volumes and rare colonial newspapers and manuscripts for $24,000 (the equivalent of about $325,000 in 2009).

Although Jefferson used the funds to pay down his debt, he continued to buy books and live a lavish lifestyle even though he was unable to eke out a satisfactory living from Monticello and the approximately 10,000 acres of land he owned. He tried various new agricultural methods and machinery, experimented with different crops and rotations, manufactured and sold nails, operated a flour mill, and made his own cloth. But he was simply not a good manager or as skilled a farmer as Washington. Indeed, as a planter, household manufacturer, and landowner, he was a failure, and he died impoverished. [69]

Because Madison was a fellow planter and landowner, Jefferson wrote him a number of letters on such agricultural matters as breeding of merino sheep, which were briefly in great demand in Virginia because of their alleged superior wool. A pair of merino sheep had been given to each of them, and Jefferson wanted to breed and make them available at low cost to other Virginian farmers because of what he considered "the scandalous extortions lately practised in the sale of these animals." However, when the wool from merino sheep proved to be inferior to other wool, the widespread craze for merino sheep fizzled, and Jefferson's speculative scheme collapsed.[70]

Over the years, however, Jefferson spent less time managing his lands, which even he acknowledged he did not do very well, and more time on his correspondence and on his other interests such as his library, meteorology (he kept exact records of climate and conditions), and especially his gardens, to which he devoted an enormous amount of attention. Botany he ranked "with the most valuable sciences" both because it furnished the "principal subsistence of life" and because flowers, trees, and other plant life provided everything from shade "to materials for our buildings [and] medicaments for our bodies."[71]

An interest that predated his presidency, and to which Jefferson also devoted an enormous amount of his attention after the War of 1812, was the establishment of the University of Virginia as an institution without religious affiliation and with a full slate of elective courses. He hoped it would rival the major church-related universities located in New England and the middle states, such as Harvard, Yale, and Princeton. He also intended the university to be the capstone of a public education system that extended throughout the entire state. An outpost of the Enlightenment, the institution would be "so broad, so liberal, and so modern as to be worth patronizing with the public support."[72] He considered the establishment of the University of Virginia, despite strong objections from the Virginia legislature over its rising costs, one of the great triumphs of his life, along with his authorship of the Declaration of Independence and the Virginia Statute for Religious Freedom; these are the three achievements he insisted be inscribed on his graveside marker.

Jefferson involved himself in every aspect of the university's establishment, from its location to its construction and curriculum. Appointed rector of the university, he was the architect of its famous portico and colonnades, around which the institution was centered. He sought to draw to the university the finest faculty from Europe. He designed its initial curriculum, and he set its first policies.

Jefferson's plan for the university and his larger educational scheme for the state were unrealistic. He underestimated construction costs and the commitment of lawmakers to a statewide system of public education from the elementary to the university levels. He overestimated the willingness of European faculty to migrate from the world's educational capitals to Virginia's wilderness. The curriculum he designed also included a list of prescribed texts in government reflecting only democratic ideals.

What was so important about Jefferson's plans for the University of Virginia and his larger concept of education, however, was his belief that a republican form of government and education went together. "I have two great measures at heart, without which no republic can maintain itself in strength," he wrote soon after his retirement.[73] These were his plans for a system of general education and for the University of Virginia. The university would not only be free of religious sectarianism, but there would also be no required courses or programs. Faculty and students would live together in an academic village run by the faculty in close collaboration with students. There would be no separate administration, not even a president.

Even though Jefferson's prescribed list of texts in government at the university amounted to the type of political orthodoxy on which he normally frowned, he was willing to make this one exception to free inquiry because he thought that the very foundation of the American government was at stake. In all other academic areas, he was willing to leave it to the faculty to assign texts. As he explained in 1825 to Madison, whom he had drawn into his scheme for the university after Madison had retired from the presidency eight years earlier, "There is one branch in which I think we are the best judges, and the branch itself . . . is that of government."[74]

Madison was able to disabuse Jefferson of the idea of preselected texts. He did so, however, by pointing out that at issue was not so much the texts that students read but the individuals who taught them. "After all, the most effectual safeguard against heretical intrusions into the School of Politics," Madison responded to Jefferson, "will be an Able and Orthodox Professor, whose course of instruction will be an example to his successor."[75] At a time when the republic itself seemed at stake, even democratic republicans like Jefferson and Madison were not prepared to sacrifice it on the altar of what would be regarded today as academic freedom.

Jefferson raised the issue of the relationship between republicanism and education in his correspondence with John Adams. Although Jefferson spelled out his views on republicanism most clearly in his early letters to Adams, he returned to the subject at various times throughout his lengthy correspondence with the former president. After the defeat of Napoleon Bonaparte in the spring of 1814 and the signing of the Treaty of Ghent ending the War of 1812 at the end of the year, Jefferson even expressed his hope that democracy would soon spread throughout Europe.[76]

In 1819, after the Virginia legislature confirmed the establishment of the University of Virginia but before it appropriated adequate funds for its construction, Jefferson linked education to the fall of the Roman Republic. He blamed the end of the republic on the corruption of its government, which he attributed to Julius Caesar. However, then he asked: "What could even Cicero, Cato, Brutus have done had it been referred to them to establish a good government for their country? They had no ideas of government themselves but of their degenerate Senate, nor the people of liberty, but of the factious opposition of their tribunes." This problem might have been avoided had the government been controlled by an educated populace and leadership. "No government," he continued in his letter to Adams, "can continue good but under the controul of the people. . . . Their minds were to be informed, by education, what is right and what wrong, to be encouraged in habits of virtue, and deterred from those of vice by the dread of punishments, proportioned indeed, but irremissible. . . . These are the inculcations necessary to render the people a sure basis for the structure of order and good government."[77]

The battle for the establishment and funding of the University of Virginia, which opened to its first class of 123 students in 1825, consumed much of Jefferson's final years of retirement. In many ways, these were Jefferson's bleakest years. Not only did he lose a granddaughter (Martha's eldest daughter), but he felt overwhelmed by the massive correspondence he received, which he estimated in 1822 at more than 1,260 letters, and to which he felt duty bound to respond at the expense of engaging in the reading he so craved. "Is this the life?" he asked Adams in 1822. "At best it is but the life of a mill-horse, who sees no end to his circle but in death. To such a life that of a cabbage is paradise."[78]

Weighing most heavily on Jefferson's mind was his deteriorating economic situation. Poor harvests, generally declining agriculture prices, the assumption of the debts of his son-in-law, Thomas Randolph, and the Panic of 1819 burst the bubble of credit on which the former president had become increasingly dependent to sustain his way of life. He was left with a debt estimated as high as $60,000 (the equivalent of about $830,000 in 2009). He tried to sell land, but there were no buyers. In the end, Jefferson was forced to ask the state legislature for permission to sell much of his property by way of a lottery.

Interestingly, the legislature approved the lottery, but only after a difficult fight, and only after Jefferson made a special plea, warning that failure to permit the lottery would leave him overwhelmed with fear about the future of his daughter and her children; this suggested how limited the influence of a former president was, even one who had done so much for his own state, who was nearing the end of his life, and who was in obvious need of financial relief. Although Jefferson thought the lottery would provide sufficient funds for his offspring, his friends, shocked by news that the former president was obliged to sell his home, replaced the lottery with a less embarrassing private subscription. However, it failed to generate enough income, and after Jefferson died, all his possessions, including Monticello, were sold in auction.[79]

Still another matter that caused Jefferson considerable consternation in his final years was the Missouri Compromise of 1820, which allowed Missouri to enter the Union as a slave state but prohibited the extension of slavery to any new state carved out of the Louisiana Purchase north of the 36°30' parallel, or the border of the Arkansas Territory (excluding Missouri). His objection to the Missouri Compromise had more to do with what he regarded as a violation of the Constitution, with his concern about a resurgent Federalism, and with his fear for the future of the Union than with slavery. In a well-known letter he wrote to a Republican congressman from Maine, John Holmes, on 22 April 1820, he remarked that the dividing line devised by Congress for the extension of slavery "like a fire bell in the night, awakened and filled me with terror. I considered it at once as the knell of the Union." He even expressed regret that he would "die in the belief that the sacrifices of themselves by the generation of 1776, to acquire self-government and happiness to their country, is to be thrown away by the unwise and unworthy passions of their sons."[80]

Even though Jefferson had assumed a states' rights position on the Missouri Compromise, the former president was never a firebrand in his opposition to the legislation. The University of Virginia remained the main business of his life, and most of his comments about the crisis were made in private. He refused even Congressman Holmes's request to publish his letter to him.[81] Although he supported the revival of states' rights politics in Virginia, he was not a leader of the movement. He never became a sectionalist, and he distanced himself from those who wanted to use his name for their own political purposes. In December 1825, he considered sending to the Virginia legislature for its consideration a statement condemning as unconstitutional a new system of internal improvements being proposed by President John Quincy Adams. While he couched his objections on the basis of states' rights, he was careful to avoid taking the extreme position of nullification as he had done in the Kentucky Resolution of 1798. When Madison advised that even the statement he prepared might be interpreted in a way harmful to the republic, he decided against issuing his remarks.[82]

Indeed, Jefferson's solution to the problem exposed by the Missouri Compromise was the same one he had sketched out forty years earlier: gradual emancipation of the slaves and colonization outside the United States. Although he had heard the fire bell of disunion, he remained hopeful of a solution to the crisis until the time of his death in 1826. "Persuasion, perseverance, and patience," he commented, "are the best advocates on questions depending on the will of the others. The revolution in public opinion which the cause requires, is not to be expected in a day or perhaps in an age; but time, which outlives all things, will outlive this evil also."[83]

After worrying about the future of the Union as a result of the Missouri crisis, Jefferson reached the same conclusion that he had throughout most of his life: democracy would save the republic. In a final letter to Madison written a few months before he died, he asked his longtime compatriot to carry on the cause of democratic republicanism after his death. "It has also been a great solace to me," he wrote him, "to believe that you are engaged in vindicating to posterity the course we have pursued for preserving to them, *in all their purity,* the blessings of self-government, which we have assisted too in acquiring for them."[84]

Although recognizing that he did not have long to live, Jefferson had been in generally good health until the last year or so of his life. He had had his share of medical problems. From the age of nineteen, he had suffered from severe, even debilitating, headaches. In 1785, he broke his wrist while in Paris. Poorly treated by the French doctors, the wrist remained deformed and caused him trouble for the rest of his life. He also suffered, at different times, from severe dysentery, a bad back, and bouts of rheumatism, one of which nearly killed him in 1818. As he became older, he also found it increasingly difficult to walk long distances.

This is an 1856 replica of a portrait that the American artist Thomas Sully, a student of Gilbert Stuart, first painted at Monticello in 1821 for the U.S. Military Academy at West Point, which Jefferson had established as president. While Sully was painting the portrait, Jefferson commented that his talents were being "illy bestowed" on such an elderly person. Because of Sully's own advanced age in 1856, his replica was noticeably harsher and harder than the original. Still, the replica retains Jefferson's unusual dignity and repose and magisterial head with its prominent brow and deep set eyes. (Courtesy of Library of Congress, Prints and Photographs Division [Repro No. LC-USZ-61-537].)

Almost every day, however, he was on his horse, usually riding eight miles a day even at the age of seventy-five. Unlike Washington and Adams, he kept all his teeth. His hearing and eyesight were both good, although he began to wear spectacles to read after reaching middle age. His mind also remained sharp and his curiosity alive. Interestingly, he put little faith in eighteenth-century medicine, rejecting both bleeding and purgatives as curatives. Instead, he was a strong believer in exercise. The fact that he ate a diet of mainly vegetables and fruits may also have contributed to his good health.

Still, old age took its toll on Jefferson, weakening his body and making him more susceptible to his chronic problems with rheumatism and dysentery. At the end of June 1826, after suffering for months from a urinary disease, he became troubled with diarrhea. His doctor was summoned to the house. After examining his elderly patient, he reported little hope that the former president would survive his latest illness. On 2 July, Jefferson lapsed into a coma. Two days later, on 4 July, he died, only a few hours before death also took John Adams. Although more publicly active than Adams after he left office, Jefferson had nevertheless largely abided by republican expectations of former presidents once in retirement.

In the 200 years since his death, Jefferson has achieved iconoclastic status in American history. This saga has been retold in a number of places, most notably in Merrill Peterson's classic, *The Jeffersonian Image in the American Mind*. Although there were many Americans at the time of the Virginian's death who believed that he already deserved a special place in the nation's history, he did not receive the same instant immortality after his death that Washington enjoyed even while he was still alive. Partisan politics, Jefferson's own partisanship, and sectional cleavages that remained even after the Civil War kept that from happening. Not until the establishment of the Jeffersonian Memorial along the Potomac basin in the 1940s was he granted finally the status of America's apostle of democracy, putting him alongside Washington and Abraham Lincoln as one of the great figures of America's public religion—and, even more, of American history.[85]

2

From the Republican to the Democratic Ideal of the Post-Presidency

Madison, Monroe, and Quincy Adams

The coincidence of the deaths of former presidents Thomas Jefferson and John Adams on the Fourth of July 1826, the fiftieth anniversary of the Declaration of Independence, did not go unnoticed. Jefferson and Adams resided more than 500 miles apart when they died. Because news traveled slowly along a still primitive road system, especially in the interior, most Americans did not find out about their deaths for weeks. Even President John Quincy Adams did not learn of Jefferson's passing until 6 July and of his father's death until 9 July.

President Adams expressed what most Americans came to feel when they heard that two of the nation's former presidents and signers of the Declaration of Independence had died within hours of each other on the fiftieth anniversary of the nation's birth. Their paired deaths could not be a mere coincidence, the president stated in his diary after receiving the news his father had died. It was a "visible and palpable" manifestation of divine favor. Attorney General Richard Rush, son of Dr. Benjamin Rush, added, "We should pronounce it romantic did we not believe it providential." This was the common theme at the memorial services held throughout the country in the weeks and months that followed.[1]

Almost as remarkable as the simultaneous deaths of Jefferson and Adams on the United States' fiftieth anniversary was the fact that on Fourth of July 1831, on the fifty-fifth anniversary of the Declaration of Independence, a third former president, James Monroe, passed away. The next ex-president to die, James Madison, did so on 28 June 1836, exactly one week short of the nation's sixtieth birthday. Near death and weakening rapidly, Madison was reportedly even offered stimulants, which he refused, to keep him alive until the Fourth of July. Whether or not the story of the stimulants is true, the fact that three of the first five ex-presidents died on that day, that the two who were signers of the Declaration of Independence died simultaneously on the nation's fiftieth birthday, that a third died exactly five years later, and that the fourth nearly made it to the sixtieth celebration of the nation's independence gave many Americans reason to believe God's work was at hand in the establishment of the new nation.[2]

There was more than this coincidence of death among the nation's early ex-presidents to inspire awe among Americans. As the historian Gordon S. Wood has pointed out, at the time Adams and Jefferson died, "an aura of divinity had [already] come to surround the founding generation. The succeeding generations of Americans were unable to look back at the revolutionary leaders and constitution makers without being overawed by the brilliance of their thought, the creativity of their politics, and the sheer magnitude of their achievement."[3]

Like the three former presidents before him, Madison surely fits this description of the founding fathers. Like them also, he was a republican who rejected personal ambition for public duty and responsibility and looked forward to retiring to private life at his estate of Montpelier. During the nineteen years in which Madison spent in retirement, however, he found himself confronted with two of the greatest events in the nation's short history: the Missouri controversy leading to the Missouri Compromise of 1820 and the nullification crisis of the late 1820s and early 1830s. Because both questions involved fundamental constitutional issues having to do with the relative powers of the state and federal governments, they threatened the nation's very foundation. Because of Madison's reputation as the father of the Constitution, both sides in the two disputes sought his advice and support. As a result, he was drawn increasingly into the public discourse over republican constitutionalism.

However, it was not simply a matter of Madison being pushed into the public arena against his will. For forty years, his every interest and emotion had been subordinated to politics and public affairs—much more so certainly than his closest friend, Jefferson, and in his retirement, he went from being a reluctant draftee during the Missouri controversy to a leading opponent of nullification less than a decade later. He also participated actively as a delegate in the 1829 Virginia Constitutional Convention. The degree of his involvement in the political arena separated his post-presidency from that of his predecessors.

That said, Madison stayed committed to the republican ideal of a virtuous citizen. His abiding concerns as a former president always remained upholding republican constitutionalism and preserving the Union rather than taking a political side or seeking a political advantage. Madison's successor as president, James Monroe, also tried to abide by the republican ideal of a former president after his retirement in 1825. However, he too was forced to assume a more public posture because of financial claims he made against the government growing out of his diplomatic service in Europe in the 1790s and early 1800s.

By the time Monroe left office in 1825, the era of the early Republic was coming to an end as a result of the development of political parties and the rapid expansion of popular sovereignty. Beginning with the retirement of John Quincy Adams in 1829, former presidents no longer even maintained the pretense of abstaining from active participation in the nation's political affairs. Soon after being defeated for reelection in 1828, John Quincy Adams won election to the House of Representatives and began one of the most illustrious post-presidential careers in the nation's history. A transition had been completed, therefore, from a republican to a more democratic and participatory ideal of the post-presidency.

I

Frail and slight of frame, scarcely reaching five feet, four inches in height, and never weighing much more than a hundred pounds, Madison was as physically opposite from Jefferson as Adams was from Washington.[4] As Jefferson's successor in the White House, his major concern was the War of 1812. During the war, he seemed incapable of exerting strong leadership because of his strict views on the constitutional limitations of executive authority. Seeking to show that a president could lead a republic into war without becoming a dictator, he failed to assert the authority of his office or to govern with a steady hand.

Yet the president was coolest in the darkest hours of the conflict and did not take advantage of the war to suppress domestic opposition, as John Adams had done in 1798 with the Alien and Sedition Acts. As a result of concessions gained at the Treaty of Ghent and of General Andrew Jackson's victory at the Battle of New Orleans after the war had already ended, the United States was able to come away from the conflict with a new sense of confidence and national pride. Madison even emerged a hero able to usher in the era of good feelings.[5]

Despite Madison's mixed wartime record, he remains one of the nation's great historical figures. Not only was he instrumental in the drafting and ratification of the Constitution, he was also one of the country's most profound political theorists. He is best known for his argument in the *Federalist Papers* correlating democracy with an extended republic. In contrast to the classical view that democracy could exist only in city-states, he argued that groups of like-minded interests or factions allowed democracy to flourish in a large republic. Extending national geographical boundaries increased the number of competing interest groups. The constant realignment of these groups guarded democracy by preventing a single group from gaining permanent political control. It also allowed the most talented to come to the political forefront.

Although Madison remained a democrat, he worried about the dangers of unfettered majoritarian rule. He never adopted his friend Jefferson's steadfast belief in human reason or his simple equation of democracy with republicanism. Influenced by the Scottish philosophers of the Enlightenment, he shared their concern about the role of passion and self-interest in human conduct and mankind's inherent tendency to engage in destructive conflict. His own theory of democracy was predicated on changing coalitions of competing interest groups, and one of his purposes in drafting the new Constitution was to restrain and guide democracy.[6]

Foremost in Madison's mind was the institutional structure necessary to preserve a democratic republic from the willfulness of human nature. The formative period in his thinking was the 1780s, when he witnessed the constitutional transformation that saved the Republic. As a result of legislative irresponsibility and sheer democratic depravity, the states, in his view, failed to meet their obligations under the Confederation. However, because of a series of developments at home and abroad that exposed the fundamental weakness of the Confederacy and threatened the Republic, they agreed in 1787 to relinquish important powers to a central authority under a strong Constitution.

Had Madison had his way, the Constitutional Convention in Philadelphia would have provided for an even stronger central government than the one it finally ratified. Seeking at the time to limit the role of states in national politics, the future president would have given the national government the power to veto state legislation and base representation in both houses of Congress on proportional representation. Theorizing that democracy in an extended republic would result in the best people assuming leadership roles, he nevertheless worried about the unwashed in power, and he acted in the 1780s not so much out of a concern about democracy as out of the need he felt for order, stability, and a responsible government.[7]

Even in supporting the Constitution, Madison assumed a strict interpretation of the document, believing that those powers not enumerated in the Constitution remained with the states. Outraged by the Hamiltonian program for economic development, which he thought trampled on the powers still reserved to the states, and worried by the administration's policy of accommodation with Great Britain, Madison, a confirmed Anglophobe, joined with Jefferson to form the Republican Party.

In 1798, Madison also collaborated with Jefferson in authoring the Kentucky and Virginia Resolutions, which claimed the right of the states to nullify acts of Congress not specifically delegated to the federal government. In 1800, in a report to the Virginia legislature on the Alien and Sedition Acts, he used language that later came back to haunt him. Referring to the Constitution, he remarked, "The states, then being parties to the constitutional compact, and in their sovereign capacity, it follows of necessity that there can be no tribunal above their authority, to decide, in the last resort, whether the compact made by them be violated; and consequently, that as the parties to it, they must themselves decide, in the last resort, such questions as may be of sufficient magnitude to require their interposition."[8]

As president, Madison took a more accommodating view with respect to national legislation. Goaded by Treasury Secretary Albert Gallatin, he supported a charter for a new bank of the United States, endorsed a protective tariff, made a national university a pet project, recommended a standing army and a strong navy, and called for a system of internal improvements.[9]

The issue of internal improvements raised the still largely unresolved question about the authority empowered to the federal government and the powers remaining to the states. While Madison believed the country needed to build bridges, highways, and canals to promote prosperity and tie the nation closer together, he was convinced that the Constitution did not provide the federal government with the authority to engage in a program of internal improvements. Accordingly, in his last day in office in 1817, he vetoed a $1.5 million bill designated for roads and canals. At the same time, he hinted at his endorsement of a constitutional amendment giving Washington the requisite authority.[10]

Once Madison left Washington, he hoped to put such issues largely behind him and to enjoy instead the quiet retirement of his Montpelier estate. Located about eighty-five miles southwest of Washington, Montpelier never had the same attraction for Madison before his retirement as Mount Vernon had for Washington or Monticello for Jefferson. Madison preferred the public arena to the routine of plantation life, and he sought neither bucolic solace nor rural solitude. Yet the presidency took its toll on Madison, and like his predecessors, he was glad to get away from the nation's capital city whenever possible. In 1815, he took the longest vacation of any sitting president, four months, which he spent at Montpelier with his wife—the former Dolley Payne Todd, a vivacious and attractive widow, seventeen years his junior, whom he had married in 1794 when he was forty-three years old.

Once his term as president ended, he looked forward to returning to Montpelier and actually taking up the life of a farmer. In contrast to his friend Jefferson, he still intended to remain fully abreast of current affairs. However, like the other former presidents, he anticipated being a political observer, not a political participant. He sought to remain aloof from partisan politics and to shun involvement in political campaigns. "I am in the midst of preparations to get to my farm, where I shall make myself a fixture, and where I anticipate many enjoyments, which . . . will be a welcome exchange for the labors and anxieties of public life," he wrote to his former treasury secretary, Albert Gallatin, shortly after his term ended.[11] Over the next twelve years, he never traveled far from the Piedmont area where he lived. Visitors to Montpelier described Madison as content to the point of being euphoric. Although often described as colorless and shy and known for always dressing in black and being out of fashion, he was, in fact, one of the most determined and stubborn men of his time. At Montpelier, however, he was relaxed, jovial, and even sparkling with his guests.[12]

Madison's most immediate concern was the same as the other members of the Virginia dynasty, paying off debts and trying to turn a profit from the 5,000 acres of his Virginia estate and another 1,000 acres he owned in Kentucky. Montpelier, in fact, was as much a working farm as an impressive estate in the manner of Mount Vernon or Monticello. The residency was large and well furnished, with a sixty-foot-long piazza supported by six pillars, a handsome vestibule with a semicircular window divided into thirteen parts symbolizing the thirteen original states, a hall of notables including portraits of all the major Revolutionary figures, and two large wings. The home also had a commanding view of the Blue Ridge, and the surrounding grounds, although well tended, were hardly imposing. A number of Madison's frequent guests even commented on the surprisingly unkempt nature of the countryside and referred to the dirt, smell, and bustle of agriculture that seemed best to characterize Montpelier.[13]

Madison was also confronted with the same problems that Jefferson and other Virginia planters faced: bad harvests, drought, and declining grain and land prices, which did not hit their lows in his lifetime until the 1820s and 1830s, respectively. Over time, the situation caused Madison serious financial problems, which were compounded by his assumption of the gambling and other debts of his scoundrel stepson, Payne Todd, Dolley's son by her first marriage. Between 1813 and 1816, Madison paid out $40,000 to cover Payne's gambling and other debts. There were also other expenses. Although the Madisons had no children together, Madison's mother lived with them. They had large extended families. Relatives frequently visited them, sometimes for weeks at a time. The former president also hosted a regular stream of guests to his home. The declining income he received from his estate simply did not cover his expenses, and he was forced to sell part of his Virginia acreage as well as land in Kentucky and other holdings. Yet Madison's lifestyle was more modest than either of his two Virginia predecessors. Like Washington, he also proved to be an adept and savvy farmer. He read books on the latest farming techniques and tried to put them into practice on his own land. Much of his postretirement correspondence with Jefferson was on such matters as crop and weather conditions and on innovations in planting and plowing. Although he was from Orange County, he was named in 1818 to serve as president of the Albermarle Agricultural Society. In 1818, he delivered a lengthy speech warning Southern farmers of the need for better farming practices, including ending soil erosion and engaging in deep furrow plowing. The thirty-one-page speech was later distributed to other agricultural societies.[14]

Because Madison lived a more modest lifestyle and was a more adept farmer and businessman than Jefferson, Madison never faced the imminent prospect of bankruptcy that his friend did. Like all the Virginia dynasty, Madison had serious financial concerns. He also worried about an adequate income for Dolley after he died. He planned to provide for her by compiling and selling after the death of all the members of the Constitutional Convention, including himself, the notes he carefully kept and later compiled on the historic meeting. After his death, Dolley sold the domestic publication rights for $30,000 (the equivalent of about $578,000 in 2009), less than the $100,000 Madison had hoped at one time she would get. Madison's notes on the Convention have since proven a treasure trove for historians, the best-preserved record of the 1787 debates. In a sense, they marked the first commercial venture of a former president, albeit one completed after his death. Even so, in 1844, five years before Dolley died, she had to sell Montpelier.[15]

In addition to concerning himself with making a suitable living, Madison was drafted soon after his retirement by Jefferson into the latter's campaign to establish and fund the University of Virginia. In 1818, he was chosen a commissioner to find a site for the new university. Over the next decade, he was often at Jefferson's side planning the university, devising the curriculum, reviewing possible candidates for positions, and seeking adequate funding for its establishment. He shared Jefferson's views on the importance of education for a democracy. "Learned Institutions ought to be favorite objects with every free people," he wrote to a group of Kentuckians in 1822 seeking his advice on establishing a plan of education for the new state of Kentucky. "They throw that light over the public mind which is the best security against crafty & dangerous encroachments on the public liberty."[16] When Jefferson died in 1826, Madison replaced him as rector of the university. Over the next eight years, he never missed a meeting of the Board of Visitors, made most of the major decisions, and was frequently seen on campus, strolling the grounds with his wife. He increasingly depended on his young aides to run the administrative side of the still-fledgling institution.

Overshadowing Madison's retirement, especially in the last half-dozen years or so of his life, was the fact that the nation came face-to-face with the very issue left unresolved when the new Constitution was adopted in 1787: the balance of authority between the federal government and the states. As the last of the founding fathers, the father of the Constitution, the nation's elder statesman, and its greatest proponent of republican constitutionalism, Madison was drawn into this argument. Madison was not always successful in trying to show consistency between the arguments he made in the 1780s and 1790s and the ones he adopted in the 1830s, when the earlier claim of the right of the states to nullify an act of Congress reemerged more stridently. The former president always hearkened back, however, to his experience in the 1780s and 1790s to take a strong position in favor of states' rights but against nullification.

Madison began to lay out his postretirement position on the nature of the Union during the Missouri crisis of 1819–1820, when the country debated the extension of slavery into the new states to be formed from the Louisiana Purchase. Even though he was a slave owner himself, he was, by all accounts, the most humane of the Virginia dynasty of presidents in his treatment of his slaves and the one most dedicated to the abolition of slavery. He shared, however, the biases and prejudices of the other Virginia presidents regarding the inferior nature of slaves and their incapacity to mix as freemen with whites. His solution to this conundrum was colonization—preferably in some West African territory—of emancipated slaves, whose freedom would be purchased through the sale of about a third of the federal lands in the West.[17] In 1833, he became president of the American Colonization Society, which was then colonizing former slaves in Liberia.

What concerned Madison, even at this early stage of his retirement, was his belief that Congress was returning to the type of Federalism that he had lashed out against in the 1790s. Although he approved as president the establishment of the Second Bank of the United States, he objected strongly when the Supreme Court, in the case of *McCulloch v. Maryland* (1819), rejected Maryland's attempt to tax the bank. He took issue with the fact that the Court seemed to give Congress sweeping powers by sanctioning the concept of implied powers in the Constitution. He believed the judiciary should act as a restraint on Congress and define the Constitution narrowly. Instead, the Court under John Marshall appeared to be doing the opposite.

Efforts in Congress to limit slavery during the Missouri crisis caused Madison additional concern. Because the Constitution did not prohibit the extension of slavery into newly formed states, he believed that Congress could not bar slavery in these states. He also feared that attempts to do so might tear the Union asunder by dividing the country into permanent parties along geographical lines. "Should a state of parties arise, founded on geographical boundaries and other Physical and permanent distinctions which happen to coincide with them," Madison remarked in 1819, "what is to controul those great repulsive Masses from awful shocks against each other?"[18] Although still dubious about the constitutionality of the final compromise resolving the Missouri crisis, he was able to justify it in his own mind under a clause authorizing Congress "to make all needful rules and regulations respecting the territory or other property belonging to the U.S."

As much as Madison believed that the states retained the authority not delegated specifically to the federal government, he feared the danger to the Union of majority abuse of the states' rights position. When that possibility became even more real at the end of the 1820s, Madison, who had commented on the Missouri crisis mostly in private correspondence, took a more public stance. Although he still preferred the role of concerned private citizen to one of public advocate, he devoted much of his final years to refuting the arguments in support of nullification and even secession.[19]

The nullification crisis began in 1828, when Congress approved the so-called tariff of abominations. Coming on top of a series of protective tariffs beginning in 1816 as well as mounting criticism of slavery and low cotton prices, passage of the 1828 tariff provoked a bitter reaction in the South, especially in South Carolina. In response, Vice President John Calhoun of South Carolina secretly authored the *South Carolina Exposition and Protest,* which stated the right of even a single state to reject or nullify federal legislation. He predicated his argument on the very language that Madison had used in his report to the Virginia legislature in 1800, remarking that Madison's report upheld the doctrine of state sovereignty so convincingly that no additional comment was needed.

The *South Carolina Exposition* touched off a four-year debate over nullification, including even the right of states to secede from the Union. In 1832, the South Carolina legislature passed an Ordinance of Nullification in response to another tariff bill Congress approved, which, although milder than the legislation four years earlier, still kept import duties high. Because nullifiers attempted to rest their defense on the Kentucky and Virginia Resolutions of 1798 and Calhoun had grounded the *South Carolina Exposition* on Madison's 1800 report to the Virginia legislature, the former president felt he had to join the war of words against nullification.[20]

Like all his commentaries on constitutional issues, Madison's case against nullification was carefully crafted, finely textured, lucid, and solid. It was also multifaceted, elaborate, and intricate. At its core was the distinction Madison made between bad, even constitutionally questionable, legislation and a state's right unilaterally to abrogate or nullify a federal law simply because it deemed it unconstitutional. As he had written to Jefferson in 1825, three years before Calhoun even prepared the *South Carolina Exposition*, "the will of the nation being omnipotent for right, is so for wrong also; and the will of the nation being in the majority, the minority must submit to that danger of oppression as an evil infinitely less than the danger to the whole nation from a will independent of it."[21]

Similarly, Madison rejected Calhoun's contention that because the federal government was a compact of sovereign states, each of which retained its sovereignty within its own borders, any state had the right to nullify a federal law it deemed in violation of the original compact. Reviewing the history of the Constitution, including the ratification debates on both the state and national levels, Madison argued otherwise. The document, he maintained, had not been formed by sovereign state governments but "by the people in each of the States, acting in their highest capacity." The Constitution represented, therefore, not a compact of the states, as in the case of the Articles of Confederation, but a union of the people of all the states. Accordingly, it "and the laws formed under its authority could not be altered or annulled at the will of the States individually, as the Constitution of a State may be at its individual will."[22] As for tariff legislation, the former president pointed out that one reason for replacing the Articles with the federal Constitution was to transfer the regulation of foreign trade "from the States to the Govt of the US." There could be no question, therefore, that Congress had the power to pass protective tariff legislation, however pernicious it might be.[23]

In cases where the delineation between the authority of the states and federal government was not so clear-cut, the recourse of the states was the judiciary. Although concerned that the Supreme Court was acting contrary to its intended purpose of restraining congressional authority, Madison stayed committed to the proposition that the final mediator of disputes between the states and the federal government had to remain the Court. By making the judicial branch the ultimate arbiter in such cases, he was convinced that the Constitutional Convention of 1787 had adopted the only means to assure "the object and end of a real Government being the substitution of law and order for uncertainty, confusion, and violence."[24]

In taking up the fight against nullifiers and even more radical secessionists, Madison had to confront the fact that Calhoun and other prominent advocates of nullification had based their position squarely on the writings and comments that he and Jefferson had made in the 1790s. He attempted to do this repeatedly throughout the last years of his life, but he made his strongest defense in a letter at the beginning of August 1830 to Senator Robert Y. Haynes of South Carolina, who had cited Madison's 1800 report in several speeches defending the nullification doctrine. Quoting from the report, Madison challenged Haynes's claim that it declared the right of an individual state to nullify an act of Congress. Rather, it invited other states "to *concur* in declaring the acts to be unconstitutional, and to *co-operate* by the necessary and proper measures in maintaining unimpaired the authorities rights and liberties reserved to the States respectively or the people." He then added, "That by the necessary & proper measures to be concurrently & cooperatively taken were meant measures known to the Constitution, particularly the control of the Legislature and people of the States over the Cong. of the U.S. cannot well be doubted."[25]

Even though Madison succeeded in turning Haynes's defense of nullification, based on his 1800 report, into a strong case against that position, he could never establish complete consistency between what he said at the turn of the century and what he said thirty years later. Even more strained was what he claimed to have been Jefferson's position on nullification. Eventually, he had to concede that, when reading Jefferson's writings, one needed to make "allowances [for] a habit in Mr. Jefferson, as in others of great genius of expressing in strong and round terms impressions of the moment."[26]

Still, Madison's interpretation of republican constitutionalism remained pivotal to the whole debate over nullification. During the historic Haynes–Webster debate of 1830, not only Haynes but also Senator Daniel Webster of Massachusetts, who famously remarked, "Liberty and Union, now and for ever, one and inseparable," commented that the former president's letters on the constitutionality of protective tariffs had led Webster to change his mind on tariffs. Ignoring the real reason why he came out in support of protective tariffs (the expansion of New England manufacturing), he then pointed to the absurdity of the nullifiers' position with respect to the tariff: "Mr. Madison himself deems the same tariff law quite constitutional. Instead of a clear and palpable violation, it is in his judgment, no violation at all."[27]

The nullification crisis did not come to an end until March 1833. After South Carolina issued its Ordinance of Nullification, President Andrew Jackson signed two measures on the same day, the first authorizing him to use military means if necessary to enforce the revenue laws, and the second reducing the tariff over time to a rate of no more than 20 percent. Able to claim victory in its fight over the tariff and facing the threat of military force, South Carolina responded by rescinding its nullification ordinance. Also helping to bring the crisis to an end was the fact that South Carolina found itself standing alone. Several Southern states even dismissed nullification as being rash, revolutionary, and dangerous in practice.

Although one could easily overstate Madison's role in persuading these other states from following South Carolina's lead in ending the nullification crisis, the wide dissemination of his views on nullification was clearly important to the final outcome. Lawmakers in South Carolina, knowing their position on nullification would be discredited without the support of Virginia, tried to dishonor Madison's name in the Virginia Assembly. One of their supporters in the Assembly even noted the "weakness and decrepitude of old age" in referring to Madison. Another called a letter that he had allowed the widely circulated and respected *North American Review* to publish, in which he outlined his position on nullification, "trash." If anything, their attacks on the esteemed former president backfired.[28]

Given the fact that both the nullifiers and antinullifiers posed as Madisonian and Jeffersonian constitutionalists, Madison had little choice except to take an active and public stance in the nullification crisis. He also did so for the most republican of reasons: to save the Union he had helped create. For most of the nineteen years he spent at Montpelier after leaving the White House, he also adhered to the resolution he had made after leaving the presidency—to have nothing to do with party politics. In the elections of 1824, 1828, and 1832, he refused to disclose even to his closest friends his preference for the office he once held. When he wrote on constitutional issues, he did so as a constitutional scholar rather than as a partisan, and he tried to remain anonymous as much as possible. Even during the nullification crisis, he sought to express his views through third persons.

By playing such an active role in the nullification crisis, even furtively, however, Madison broke new ground insofar as the public role of a former president was concerned. Furthermore, his consuming interest in public affairs, which continued throughout his retirement, acted as a centrifugal force pushing him into the political arena in a way similar to the centripetal pull of the voices he heard invoking his name in support of their position on nullification. Before his successor, James Monroe, issued his famous Monroe Doctrine of 1823, for example, he asked both Madison and Thomas Jefferson for their advice on whether to collaborate in a joint statement with England. Although both former Anglophobes now supported cooperation with London, Jefferson remarked diffidently that he had "been so long away from political subjects, and have so long ceased to take any interest in them, that I am sensible I am not qualified to offer opinions on them worthy of any attention." Madison was less qualified in his response. Although he was certain Great Britain's motives for a joint statement were "different from ours," he said, "our cooperation is due to ourselves & to the world."[29]

A readiness to supply information, to defend and justify his own actions, and to correct questionable history led Madison in the last years of his retirement to preempt even more of his time and energy to political matters. Even while involved in the struggle over nullification, the former president accepted election in 1829 as a delegate from Orange County to a convention in Richmond to draft a new constitution for Virginia. The call for the convention came mostly from settlers of western Virginia who, by extending suffrage to those who did not own land and excluding slaves in apportioning representation, wanted to end the stranglehold that eastern Virginia landowners maintained over the Commonwealth.

At the gathering, Madison was sympathetic to the demands of the western settlers on universal suffrage and apportionment of the state legislature. He also made clear that a republic could not rest on control by a minority. His main concern, however, was to find a compromise between the contending factions in the same manner that he worked for compromise during the 1787 Constitutional Convention. While affirming the dangers of minority control of a republic, he also warned of the need for the majority to respect the rights of the minority. Without advocating universal suffrage, he came out for expanding the suffrage and for giving the western part of the state greater representation in the lower house. At the same time, he allowed slaves to be counted in determining representation in the upper chamber. In the end, eastern slave owners maintained control of both house of the legislature, although the requirements for suffrage were loosened. Even Madison was disappointed by his performance at the convention, remarking that he had vitiated his own influence by not standing more resolutely on the side of the western settlers.[30]

Madison returned home from Richmond disappointed by the results of the Convention and in poor health. Frail of body, Madison had been sickly on and off since infancy. Throughout his life, he never even expected to survive into old age. During periods of intense activity, he was subject to sudden cessation of conscious activity, similar to what is referred to today as petit mal seizures or absence seizures, caused by abnormal electrical activity in the brain. His malady may also have been due to emotional and nervous problems. During the Constitutional Convention in 1787, he was forced to cut back in his note taking and participation in the debates because of fatigue and exhaustion. In addition, as president, he suffered from an attack of malaria that lasted for five weeks and almost took his life.

After leaving the presidency and returning to Monticello, Madison had several relapses of malaria, but for the first ten years of his retirement, he remained in surprisingly good health. Beginning in 1827, when he suffered a bout of influenza, however, his health began to decline steadily. His most serious problem was painful bouts of rheumatism, which began in his hands and eventually crippled his arms and legs. He also became little more than skin and bones. By 1834, his eyesight began to fail, and he became deaf in one ear, forcing him to resign as rector of the University of Virginia. During the last year of his life, he spent most of his time in bed or in his chair, barely able to talk. On 28 June 1836, he was moved from his bed to his writing table, where he was served breakfast. While eating, he collapsed and died, becoming the last of the founding fathers to die, just a week short of the nation's sixtieth birthday.[31]

II

James Monroe, who had been dead for almost five years when Madison died, enjoyed a much less notable retirement than his predecessor. The last of the Virginia dynasty of presidents during the early Republic, Monroe was also its least distinguished member. He lacked the heroic stature of Washington, the intellectual

While attending a convention in 1829 to revise the Virginia Constitution, Madison posed for this portrait by the Massachusetts painter, Chester Harding, a former chair maker, peddler, and innkeeper before becoming an itinerant portrait painter in 1823. After studying in England, he developed a reputation painting royalty and nobility. Returning to the United States, he painted the portrait of several presidents, including Madison, Monroe, and John Quincy Adams. According to one observer at the Virginia Convention, Madison's "stock of racy anecdotes was the delight of every social board." (Courtesy of National Portrait Gallery, Smithsonian Institution.)

depth of Jefferson, or the theoretical mind of Madison. He had no talent for abstract thinking, artful speaking, or luminous writing. His own future attorney general, William Wirt, described him as having "a mind neither rapid nor rich."[32]

Monroe was, however, a dedicated public servant who managed to catch the notice of those around him. At an early stage in his career, he caught the attention of Thomas Jefferson, with whom he studied law. Although never as close to Jefferson as Madison, he befriended both men. Despite their occasional differences, Monroe doggedly followed Jefferson's and Madison's ascent into public prominence. Besides serving as America's representative to France during Washington's administration and to England during Jefferson's presidency, he was also special envoy to France in 1803 and helped negotiate the Louisiana Purchase. In addition, he held virtually every high elected position, including congressman and senator from Virginia and twice governor of Virginia. When he was elected to the White House in 1816, he was serving as Madison's secretary of state. By this time, the Federalist Party had ceased to be a serious threat to the Republican Party, and Madison carried sixteen of the country's nineteen states against his Federalist opponent, Rufus King.[33]

Six feet tall with a large and sturdy frame, broad shoulders, wide-set blue-gray eyes, large nose, deeply lined face, high forehead, and gray wavy hair recessed on both sides of his hairline, Monroe was robust and vigorous. He was also intensely partisan and more of an ideological purist than either Jefferson or Madison. At the same time, he was known for being kind, good-natured, and courteous. "Turn his soul wrong side outwards and there is not a speck on it," Jefferson once commented about him. By the time he was elected president, he had also gained a reputation for sound and deliberative judgment and solid administrative skills. Together with his record of long service and the tacit support of Madison, these qualities were enough to win him the Republican nomination for president.[34]

Monroe's presidency ushered in the so-called era of good feelings (a term coined by a New England Federalist newspaper in 1817) and the seeming end of political parties and political partisanship. Monroe actually hoped to end once and for all political factionalism by incorporating the remnants of Federalism into one grand national party. His good intention marked the high-water mark of the republican concept of leadership. Although refusing to name any Federalists to his cabinet, he reached out successfully to the remaining Federalists in Congress and adopted a seemingly Federalist domestic program that included encouragement to industry, trade, commerce, and national defense. By the end of his first administration, he had become an extremely popular president who faced no organized opposition to his reelection. Without opposition, he won every single state and the entire electoral college save one elector. Despite Monroe's good intentions, however, partisanship never disappeared entirely, even during his first administration. During his second administration, it reemerged with a vengeance as four major candidates vied to succeed him in the White House in 1825. One of these candidates, Treasury Secretary William H. Crawford, encouraged his supporters to attack the president's programs because of Monroe's failure to support his candidacy. A second, House Speaker Henry Clay, who had wanted to be appointed Monroe's secretary of state, was openly contemptuous of him. Furthermore, the Missouri controversy had opened sectional wounds. An economic downturn led to the Panic of 1819. Overarching everything else, the United States had changed from a largely homogenous and agrarian nation, tied together by conflict with Great Britain, to a more diverse nation no longer faced with an external threat.

Following the broad policy outlines Monroe set forth, his secretary of state, John Quincy Adams, managed during both terms to achieve a number of major triumphs. These included the Adams–Onis Treaty (1819) extending the boundaries of the United States to the Pacific Ocean, and the Monroe Doctrine (1823) previously noted.

Monroe achieved little domestically, however, instead deferring too much to Congress and being unable to control his cabinet. By the end of his presidency, the era of good feelings had turned sour. Always easily hurt, Monroe was stung by the slings against him—not only by those seeking to replace him, but by others who denounced his policies and even accused him of using public money for private purposes. The latter had to do with $20,000 appropriated by Congress for refurbishing the executive mansion (the so-called Furniture Fund) after the residence had been rebuilt after the War of 1812. Fraud committed by one of the officials appointed to administer the fund, a lack of adequate oversight, and the mixing of personal and public funds provided the basis for these charges. Although there is little evidence that Monroe actually committed fraud, he had acted peculiarly and with less than due diligence in overseeing the expenditures of the fund.[35]

Monroe was relieved when on 4 March 1825, he was able to turn over the reins of power to his successor, John Quincy Adams. Because of the illness of his wife, Elizabeth, he had to remain in the White House for another three weeks before she was well enough for him to return to his new home at Oak Hill in Loudon County in northern Virginia, about twenty-five miles from the nation's capital. He looked forward to a quiet retirement in which his frail wife might regain her health, and he might turn a profit from his lands.[36]

Oak Hill was one of two large estates that Monroe owned; the other was the Highland in Albermarle County near Charlottesville and adjacent to Monticello. Rather than underscoring Monroe's great wealth, the two properties made clear his considerable indebtedness, which plagued him for much of his life. Consisting of approximately 4,400 acres, Oak Hill had been purchased by Monroe with his uncle, Judge Joseph Jones, in 1794. After the death of Jones in 1805, he inherited full title to the land. Monroe had acquired the 3,500-acre Albermarle property a year earlier, just before leaving on his first diplomatic mission to France.[37]

When Monroe bought the Albermarle property, he intended to make it his primary residence and eventually to build on it a home worthy of the Virginia gentry. This never happened. Although Highland remained his home for the next twenty years, he was never able to afford the grand structure he planned. Instead, he built a temporary one-story home of six rooms, to which he later made some modest additions. He and his wife also spent considerable time at Oak Hill. Payments on the Loudon property, on which he had also built a modest six-room, dormer-windowed cottage, proved an ongoing drain on his income. Nor was he able to turn an adequate profit from the extensive acreage he owned, in part because his public duties took him away from his properties so much of the time. To pay off some of his growing debts, he tried unsuccessfully to sell his Loudon property in 1810 at a price he found acceptable.[38]

As late as 1825, Monroe was still trying to sell his Loudon property in order to keep his Albermarle lands. Owning more land than he could afford, yet needing a suitable place to live after he left the presidency, he also put his Albermarle property on the market while building a new, spacious six-room residence at Oak Hill. Set in a grove of locusts, poplars, and oaks, it was constructed of bricks burned on the place, with a wide portico, massive thirty-foot Doric columns, and deep-set windows that looked across rolling farmland. The residence, which Thomas Jefferson had helped design, became his retirement home. With considerable relief, he was able to find a buyer the next year for most of his Albermarle holdings, including his Highland home. He used the proceeds to help pay off debts he owed to the Bank of the United States.[39]

The sad saga of Monroe's two properties does not offer a full explanation for the massive debt, estimated at $75,000 (the equivalent of approximately $1.4 million in 2009), that Monroe had accumulated by the time he left the presidency in 1825. Besides owning more property than he could afford or properly maintain were the lavish lifestyle he led, his personal generosity, including the assumption of the debts of his impecunious brother, Joseph, and the extraordinary expenses associated with his several diplomatic missions, including sumptuous entertainments and lavish residencies, which were the norm for foreign embassies in European capitals.[40]

Besides his financial problems, other matters weighed heavily on Monroe in the six years that he lived in retirement. These included the poor state of his lands, the ill health and death in September 1830 of his wife, the loss of his favorite son-in-law, George Hay, and the friction that developed between his two married daughters, Eliza Hay and Maria Hester Gouverneur.

On the more positive side, the former president found pleasure in farming and worked steadily to increase the value of his estate. Striving to build a large flock of sheep on his lands to supplement the wheat, rye, and other grains he grew, he built a mill, a distillery, and a large barn at Oak Hill. He also enjoyed the years he spent as a member of the board of regents of the University of Virginia, delighted in the visits to Oak Hills of President John Quincy Adams and the marquis de Lafayette, and felt honored to preside over the Virginia Constitutional Convention of 1829. During his retirement, his friendship with Madison grew especially close as the two men rehashed old times during their twice-a-year board of regents meetings in Charlottesville. Although they undoubtedly discussed politics, even more than other members of the Virginia dynasty, the former president avoided all political involvement of a partisan character. In 1828, when he was named with Madison as an elector on the Adams presidential ticket in Virginia, he joined Madison in resigning, remarking that former presidents should abstain from political activity except in major national emergencies.[41]

Overshadowing Monroe's entire retirement, however, was the time he devoted to claims he brought against the federal government for extra salary and expenses and accrued interest that he insisted were owed him from his diplomatic missions to Europe in the 1790s and 1800s. Amounting at one time to over $70,000, or about the amount of his total indebtedness, the claims included ones for salary and living expenses in France in the 1790s even after he had been relieved of his duties, for a residence he bought in France that he assumed the United States would use for a permanent embassy, then sold for a loss when the government decided against purchasing it, and for contingent and out-of-pocket expenses.

Although Monroe had first raised his claims with the government as president, he did not press them until just before he left office. In January 1825, he delivered a message to Congress inviting it to examine all his official financial transactions since 1794. He renewed his request the next year with a memoir in the *National Intelligencer* in which he reviewed his record of public service. In 1827, he began to write his autobiography, which he never completed, in part to impress upon Congress the importance and cost of his two European missions. More importantly, he and his son-in-law, Samuel Gouverneur, lobbied extensively in Congress on his behalf. He also had friends, like the famous Philadelphia lawyer John Seargeant and the wealthy New York banker Silas Burrows, contact influential leaders on Capitol Hill to press his case. He even wrote to General Andrew Jackson seeking his support. "Had I been disposed to take advantage of my country," he remarked to Jackson somewhat curiously, "a thousand opportunities had before presented themselves, in which I might have made an immense profit, & escaped detection." However, Jackson showed no interest in intervening on behalf of Monroe, whom he believed had supported Adams for president in 1824.[42]

After several investigations, Congress agreed in 1826 to pay Monroe $36,000 in fulfillment of his claims for extra salary and expenses. Still not satisfied, the former president continued to press his case with Congress. In 1830, the House and Senate agreed to another $30,000, not so much because of the virtue of his claims but because of public pressure in support of a former president who was old, in dire financial straits, grief-stricken as a result of the death of his wife, and in increasingly feeble health. Former president Madison wrote Monroe to congratulate him on his victory in Congress. Rather than being satisfied, however, Monroe wrote Madison, "I would make no account adapted to the act [of Congress], which fell far short of making me a just reparation. . . . I had rather lose the whole sum than give to it any sanction." Although he still took the money, Monroe continued to believe until the day he died that he had been cheated.[43]

The vigor with which Monroe pursued his case against the government highlighted issues in a far more public way than Jefferson's dire financial situation about the economic problems that faced the nation's former presidents and their families. In fact, Monroe used Jefferson's plight to further his own cause by urging his son-in-law in New York, Samuel Gouverneur, to promote the sale of lottery tickets (then under discussion as a way of disposing of Monticello and settling Jefferson's debt) if the Virginia legislature approved a lottery. Informing Jefferson of his instructions to Gouverneur, Monroe remarked, "If in any way, I may be useful to you, it will be very gratifying to me, to be apprized of it."[44]

Almost certainly the stress and strain of the battle that Monroe fought with the government affected his health. It had begun to deteriorate even while he was in the White House. When he left in 1825, he already looked exhausted and much older than his sixty-seven years. By 1830, his health had deteriorated to the point that he had to resign from the Virginia Constitutional Convention, over which he had been presiding. He developed a chronic pulmonary disease that left him bedridden. In April 1831, he wrote to Madison, "My state of health continues, consisting of a cough which annoys me by night and by day into considerable expectoration [and] renders the restoration of my health very uncertain, or indeed any favorable change in it."[45]

When John Quincy Adams visited Monroe later that spring, he was shocked at how emaciated he had become. Unable to care for himself, and still grieving over the death of his wife, Monroe decided to sell Oak Hill and to move to New York with his daughter, Eliza. There he lived out his last days with his other daughter, Maria, and his son-in-law, Samuel. On the Fourth of July 1831, Monroe became the third successive former president to die on the nation's birthday. Although the precise cause of his death is uncertain, most likely he died of pulmonary tuberculosis. Learning of his death, thousands of mourners followed his casket up Broadway. Buried in a temporary vault in New York, his remains were removed in 1853 to a cemetery in Richmond, where he was buried in a tomb alongside his wife.[46]

Although considerable sympathy had been expressed on Monroe's behalf during his struggle with the government over his claims, this did not suggest any widespread belief that provision should be made for former presidents or their families. Nor did Monroe even suggest that, as a former president, his claims were entitled to special considerations. He did argue that Congress should take into account the sacrifices he had made because of his long career of public service, but lawmakers contested even this view. According to Lewis Williams of North Carolina, the most experienced member of Congress on matters of claims and accounts, all men in the United States were born equal and should be treated as such regardless of former position or other circumstance. When an individual became a public servant, he knew his salary and should live within his circumstances.

Both the artist and the date that this portrait of James Monroe was painted are unknown. But Monroe's full head of white hair and tired look suggest that it was painted after he left the White House in 1825. Yet in contrast to the descriptions of Monroe as looking sickly and older than his sixty-seven years when he left the White House, he appears in this portrait healthy and even youthful for his age. Perhaps the artist purposely portrayed him in this way. (Courtesy of Library of Congress, Prints and Photographs Division.)

If in old age he became indigent because of prior improvidence, it was not the government's responsibility to rescue that person because doing so would only encourage waste and extravagance.[47]

Even though the nation's politics were undergoing substantial change by the end of the 1820s, the republican concept of public service as a civic virtue rather than as a permanent career still remained dominant. However, just as the nation's politics were changing, Monroe's campaign on behalf of his claims, along with Madison's almost simultaneous efforts against nullification, indicated that the role of former presidents was also beginning to change. Increasingly they were becoming more public figures.

III

In contrast to Madison and Monroe, John Quincy Adams became the first former president to reject the concept that former presidents should not be involved in politics. Not only that, he became the first former president to accept the concept of partisan politics, something that he had tried unsuccessfully to avoid during his presidency. He also became the first former president to run for office. Elected to the House of Representatives in 1830, he had an illustrious seventeen-year career in Congress that capped off one of the most distinguished public lives in the nation's history.[48]

About five feet, seven inches, tall, nearly bald, a little paunchy, with dark eyes, a square and chiseled face becoming more rounded with age, sideburns, and a crown of white hair, Adams was one of the most enigmatic figures ever to occupy the White House. Along with Jefferson, he also stands as one of its most brilliant minds—perhaps not the equal of Jefferson in terms of sheer interests, but more learned in language, literature, and most of the fine arts than the Virginian, and his equal in terms of pure intellect.

In many ways, including his love of books and literature, especially the great classics, Adams was the mirror image of his father. He was, however, more of a nonconformist and iconoclast and even more disagreeable. He was the first American president, for example, to wear long trousers rather than knee-length pantaloons and white-topped boots of an earlier day. When living in Washington, his daily exercise was to swim naked for ninety minutes against the tide in the Potomac River. On one swimming excursion, he lost nearly all his clothes and had to hide behind a rock for over five hours before a horse and carriage finally came to his rescue.[49]

Stern, cantankerous, vain, admiring perfection but never expecting to achieve it, Adams also lived an anxiety-filled life and suffered from recurring clinical depression and an obsessive need to succeed that sometimes bordered on paranoia. Even he recognized his shortcomings. "I am a man of reserved, cold, austere and forbidding manners," he wrote in his diary. "My political adversaries say, a gloomy misanthropist, and my personal enemies, an unsocial savage. With a knowledge of the actual defect in my character, I have not the pliability to reform it."[50]

Schooled by both his parents in the virtues of civic duty, Adams shared with all his presidential predecessors a belief in the republican principles of public service. "In a Republican Government the country has a *right* to the services of every Citizen," he wrote to his son, Charles Francis Adams, in 1828. "And each Citizen is bound in duty to perform the service to which he may be called."[51] Since childhood, Quincy Adams was destined by his parents for a public career even though his personal preference was to be a person of letters. Accompanying his father as a young boy to France, where the senior Adams helped negotiate the Treaty of Paris ending the American Revolution, he later journeyed with Francis Dana to St. Petersburg to act as his translator at the Court of Catherine II. Elected as a Federalist candidate to the U.S. Senate in 1803, he became an apostate to both his party and section by supporting Jefferson's purchase of Louisiana and his embargo against Great Britain, and by then attending the Republican caucus to nominate candidates for president and vice president. Denounced as a traitor by Federalist journalists, he was virtually forced by the Massachusetts legislature to resign his seat before his term was up.

Adams is best known, however, for his role as a diplomat, including helping to negotiate the Treaty of Ghent (1814) ending the War of 1812 and then serving as minister to Great Britain during 1815–1817 before being appointed by James Monroe to be his secretary of state. Because of his skill as a diplomat and his achievements during the eight years he served in Monroe's administration, he is widely regarded as one of the nation's greatest secretaries of state.

In the hotly contested election of 1824, Adams was chosen by the House of Representatives as the nation's sixth president even though former general Andrew Jackson of Tennessee won a plurality of both the popular and electoral college votes. His much-disputed victory, which was sealed when House Speaker Henry Clay of Tennessee threw his support behind Adams, marked the end of the early Republic and the beginning of a new era in American politics.[52]

Adams's presidency was the least distinguished part of his political career. One of his problems may have been the fact that he was placed in the nearly impossible position of trying to be a nonpartisan president with an active agenda during a time of political transition resulting in the emergence of the nation's first modern party system.[53]

Adams had always emphasized his distaste for partisan politics. Although he may not always have adhered to his own principles,[54] there also seems little question that as president, he hungered to be a statesman above party. Obviously influenced by his father, he viewed his administration as a patrician return to the rule of "talents and virtue alone."[55] Seeking to promote national development and enhance the nation's cultural, scientific, and general well-being, he advocated high tariffs to encourage manufacturing and pay off the national debt, a broad program of internal improvements, support for geographical exploration, and even the establishment of an astronomical observatory and a national university. Instead of achieving its intended purpose, however, his agenda only antagonized partisan and sectional interests being brought into the political process for the first time through a rearticulation of republican principles along more democratic, organizational, and sectarian lines. By 1828, for example, property qualifications for voting had been eliminated in most states, and voters, not the state legislatures, were selecting the members of the electoral college.[56]

Just the cost alone of Adams's economic programs antagonized most Americans, who were still recovering from the economic and political crises of the Monroe years. Long before his first term was over, he knew he would be defeated for reelection. In an especially dirty election, Jackson gained 56 percent of the popular vote and won in the electoral college by more than a two-to-one margin. Significantly, the size of Jackson's victory was largely the result of his huge margins in the South. Without the Southern vote, the election would have been much closer.

Adams pretended to be genuinely relieved now that the campaign was over. His wife, Louisa, reported that everyone was in good spirits and that the president, who had been sick and depressed throughout the last several years and had lost weight, was getting fat. Adams was, however, bitter at being defeated by someone he felt was unfit to serve as president. He had not expected to win, but he also had not anticipated being trounced. Following his father's example, he refused even to attend his successor's inauguration.

At the same time, Adams was uncertain what he was going to do as a former president. Because he accepted the republican concept of public virtue, he might have been expected to welcome a return to private life and the opportunity to pursue his lifelong love of literature. Instead, he found little attraction in what he considered the tedium of retirement as a private citizen. Although he remarked that he had decided "to go into the deepest retirement and withdraw from all connections with public affairs," he also stated to an acquaintance that he had not deserted his lifelong belief that if people called for his services, he would not decline "any station" he was offered. Although he and his wife avoided official Washington, they remained in the federal capital for several months after leaving the White House.[57]

In May, Adams and Louisa were crushed by the news that their eldest son, George Washington Adams, had likely committed suicide at the age of twenty-eight by jumping from a steamboat on Long Island Sound while returning to Washington. A highly intelligent but sensitive child who was predisposed like his father to melancholy and who seemed never able to live up to his father's high expectations, George had grown up to be an irresponsible alcoholic and a womanizer who had fathered an illegitimate child and who was constantly in debt. A stern disciplinarian with all his children, as his father had been with him, Quincy Adams blamed himself for his son's death. Having to remain strong for his wife, who became seriously ill after learning of George's probable suicide, the former president described himself as being overwhelmed with a grief such as "I never knew before."[58]

There seemed no relief in sight. Back in his home in Quincy (Braintree had become part of Quincy), the former president was faced with the immediate task of fixing up the paternal home, which had become run-down since the death of Abigail Adams in 1818. His father had not been able to keep the home in good repair, and his brother, Thomas, had continued to neglect the dwelling even though he lived there from 1826 to 1829. The grounds had become overridden with weeds, pathways were obstructed, and the dwelling had been stripped of most of its furnishings during the liquidation of the estate after his father's death.

Adams tried to avoid the throes of depression by making extensive repairs on the home, tending to the grounds and gardens, and trying to plant trees from seed, a hobby he had cultivated while at the White House. In addition, he had bookcases built and busied himself unpacking his extensive library of 5,000 or 6,000 volumes, which were still packed in trunks and boxes. His son, Charles, encouraged him to write a biography of his father. Although he made some fits and starts on this project, ennui, a telltale sign of a worsening melancholy, set in. "I can yet scarcely realize my situation," he wrote in his diary. "I cannot yet settle my mind to a regular course of future employment."[59]

Although Monroe's comment in 1828 that former presidents should not become involved in political activities except in national emergencies was still the prevailing sentiment in most political circles, when the opportunity arose in 1830 for Adams to reenter politics, he seized it. Sensing how attractive political office might still be for Adams if called upon to serve, a number of local politicians, anxious to hold on to Adams's congressional district, which was about to be vacated by its incumbent, Joseph Richardson, encouraged him to run for Richardson's seat. Louisa, who did want to return to Washington, was furious at the thought of his running again. So was his son Charles, who considered it beneath the dignity of a former president to serve in a lesser office and would set an unfortunate precedent. Despite their objections, Adams allowed himself to be drafted. In November 1830, the voters elected him overwhelmingly to the House.

Adams was overjoyed. "No election or appointment conferred upon me ever gave me so much pleasure," he noted in his diary.[60] Undoubtedly vanity and a sense of vindication explained much of his glee at the size of his victory. The recent loss of his son, the strain that had existed for many years between him and Louisa, now exacerbated by Charles's death, and his deepening depression, which was even leading him to speculate about his own early death, also factored into what he could only regard as a new lease on life.

At the time of his election, Adams was also under great financial stress. His nominal worth of about $100,000 was mostly invested in real estate. His real debt was about $40,000. In 1823, he had made an ill-advised investment in a flour mill. He had also incurred debt in executing his father's will, and he had made the mistake of allowing his wayward son, George, to mishandle some of his financial affairs. The salary of a congressman of $8 a day (the equivalent of about $159 in 2009) while in session and a traveling allowance would do little to help relieve his debt. Adams hoped it would help pay day-to-day expenses and keep him from becoming another impoverished former president.

Although Adams was elected in 1830, the new Congress did not start until December 1831. During the interim, Adams switched party allegiance from National Republican to Antimasonic. The party nomenclature of the 1820s and 1830s indicated the fundamental change taking place in American politics during this time. Resistance still remained strong nationwide to the idea of competing political parties. The absence of parties was still considered a sign of civic health. With the establishment by the 1826 congressional elections of the Democratic–Republican Party (or Democrats), led by Andrew Jackson, and the much smaller and politically less attractive National Republicans, associated with John Adams and Henry Clay, the concept of permanently organized parties took on new legitimacy. Another political organization, the Antimasonic Party, was also organized in New York in 1826. It had its roots in the murder of William Morgan, a Freemason, for allegedly revealing the rituals of that secret organization. For a short while, it became a significant political movement in the North, tapping into the same dynamics of political change that were spurring on the Jacksonian movement.[61]

Recognizing the growing popularity of the Antimasonic movement, even in his own congressional district, Adams joined the bandwagon, forging a coalition in his district between his old and new parties. The former president acted for more than political self-interest. He was also attracted by the Antimasonic appeal to Yankee moral virtues, its encompassing Protestant pietism, its emphasis on good citizenship, and the opportunity it offered to hoist Jackson, who was a Mason, on his own petard of Democratic Republicanism. As he remarked after attending an Antimasonic meeting in Boston in July 1831, "The application of a blister upon the bosom of the public is wanting. A melodrama, a transparency, a popular ballad well composed, would run like wild-fire."[62]

Between the time of his election and the opening of the new Congress, Adams also read the letters and memoirs of Thomas Jefferson. In contrast to his father, who more than anything else envied Jefferson's fame, Quincy Adams had come to dislike and distrust the friend of his days in Paris when he was a youth and Jefferson was minister to France. Shortly before he died, Jefferson wrote a letter to a fellow Virginian, William Giles, a former friend of Adams but now a bitter political rival, critical of the president's nationalist program. The letter only confirmed what Adams already believed about Jefferson. So did his review of the former president's larger body of writings. "He tells nothing but what redounds to his own credit," he remarked about Jefferson. Throughout his entire career, he had shown perfidy "worthy of Tiberius Caesar."[63]

What made Adams's comments on Jefferson so significant were that they reflected his view of most Southern politicians and that this perception shaped much of his congressional career. Adams thought of the South in terms of a slave power conspiracy—a slavocracy that might eventually destroy the Union. As early as 1820, he even ruminated in his diary that as unwanted as that would be, if it could lead to the establishment of a reconstituted nation without slavery, the breakup could actually be beneficial. "A dissolution of the Union for the cause of slavery would be followed by a servile war in the slave-holding states, combined with a war between the two severed portions of the Union," he explained. "It seems to me that its results must be the extirpation of slavery from this whole continent; and calamitous and desolating as this course of events in its progress must be, so glorious would be its final issue, that, as God shall judge me, I dare not say that it is not be desired."[64] For a unionist and nationalist like Adams to have thought in these terms is nothing less than astonishing.

When he first came to Congress in 1833, though, the South's peculiar institution was not his concern. He regarded slaves as inferior beings and was not particularly interested in challenging the South on the slave issue. Certainly he was not an early abolitionist, and he did not call publicly for the freeing of slaves. Before becoming president, he had supported the Missouri Compromise. After leaving the White House, he said little about slavery publicly. Even as a new congressman, he criticized petitioners seeking the end of slavery. He argued that they had no right to call for changes that affected citizens living in other states and territories, especially when the results were likely to be the stirring of bad blood and harsher slave codes. He also pointed out that there was little interest in his district in exciting emotions over slavery.[65]

Adams was, however, fearful of Southern power, believing that Southern congressmen had done the most to obstruct his presidency. As a nationalist, he also had little tolerance for the Southern argument about the limited role of the federal government and the residual constitutional rights of the states. The nullification controversy especially infuriated him. Appointed chairman of the Committee on Manufacturing (rather than Foreign Affairs, to which he understandably thought he was entitled), he tried to fashion, for the sake of the Union, a tariff acceptable to the South. When he was unable to do so, he became a fierce congressional combatant in the House debates against nullification.[66]

In the mid-1830s, Adams risked the wrath of the South as few other lawmakers would do. By this time, the nullification crisis was over, but slavery was emerging as the singular issue of American politics and the basis of the nation's sectional divide. What continued to concern Adams, however, was not so much the institution of slavery as the rising power of the South. As much as he despised slavery, he still viewed the issue more in political than in institutional terms. For the former president, slavery represented the South, and the South controlled the Democratic Party. Slavery also served as a metaphor for the fundamental issue of state versus national power. This resulted in one of the great ironies of Adams's career. More concerned with wreaking vengeance on a section and party

he detested and with preserving the Union than with ending slavery, he nevertheless became the moral voice and embodiment of the antislavery movement in
Congress.

Adams's view of the Democratic Party had only dimmed after he came to
Congress. Some of this had to do with his contempt for Andrew Jackson. Although he was surprised that the president had taken a strong stand against South
Carolina during the nullification crisis and supported his plan for paying off the
national debt, he considered Jackson, a slave owner, as a tool of the South and dis-
paraged him as uncouth and barely literate, a common depiction of Jackson in the
opposition press. Even when the Tennessean extended overtures of reconciliation
to Adams, the congressman rejected them. He refused, in fact, to be present when
Harvard University awarded the president an honorary doctor of laws degree at
its 1833 commencement. As an "an affectionate child of our Alma Mater," he told
Harvard president Josiah Quincy on 18 June, "I would not be present to witness
her disgrace in conferring her highest literary honors upon a barbarian who could
not write a sentence of grammar and hardly could spell his own name."[67]

Besides Adams's personal disdain for Jackson, he took strong exception to
the president's emphasis on states' rights, and he became a bitter foe of his determination not to renew the charter of the Second Bank of the United States
(BUS). In his mind, the two issues were inseparable. He considered the BUS an
indispensable agency of union, essential to the development of a sound national
banking system and to the integration of a national economy.[68] Once in the House,
the former president became a leading defender of the bank and its president,
Nicholas Biddle, a friend who shared his literary tastes, in their fight with Jackson
over the bank's charter. He was thunderstruck when, in a brilliant strategic move
intended to strengthen his democratic credentials, the president vetoed legislation
in 1832 to recharter the BUS and then transferred the government's deposits to
state banks, which, said Adams, would lead to national bankruptcy.

Jackson's presidency, therefore, confirmed the ex-president's worst fears
about the Democratic Party being in the firm control of Southern interests whose
purpose was to protect slavery under the banner of states' rights. What was at issue was more than the question of slavery. At stake was the very preservation of
the Union.[69]

Adams's fear of the Democratic Party and his concern about preserving the
Union propelled Adams to join the fledging Whig Party. The historian Daniel
Walker Howe has made a compelling case that the Whigs, who emerged in the
1830s and were dead as a party by the 1850s, were as much a cultural as a political movement. In this respect, they had much in common with the Antimasons,
whom they never entirely subsumed but who had become mostly an influential
wing of the party. Unlike the Antimasons, however, the Whig Party represented
a real political challenge to the Democratic Party during its short life. It won decisively in two presidential elections, 1840 and 1848, and lost by less than two
percentage points in 1844.[70]

Like the Democratic Party, the Whig Party was divided along various sectional, ethnic, economic, and other lines. The Whigs were more culturally unified than the Democrats. Foremost, they were opposed to a strong executive like Jackson. At the same time, they placed great faith in the ability of industrialization and modern technology to better mankind, and they looked to the federal government to promote the national welfare through such programs as internal improvements and tariff protection for domestic industry. Reflecting the evangelical spirit of the period, they also regarded the improvement of mankind in moral as well as in material terms; they sought to redeem society of its sins even as they sought to make it more prosperous. This moral imperative shaped the Whig view toward slavery. Although there were Southern Whigs who defended the institution of slavery and Northern Whigs who regarded slavery as less than heinous, most Whigs were drawn from the North and regarded slavery as an odious institution in need of redemption because it robbed its victims of their human potential.[71]

The political and cultural views of the Whig Party matched closely those of John Quincy Adams. Once it had become apparent to him—as it had by 1833, after he allowed himself to run and lose as the Antimasonic candidate for governor of Massachusetts—that the movement served no further political purpose, he gravitated toward the Whig Party. The same year he lost the governorship, he accepted the nominations of both the Antimasonic and Whig Parties for a third term in Congress. Winning the election, he commented that he never considered himself a party man and that he intended to vote his conscience. He also made clear, however, that he would align himself with the Whig Party against the Democrats.[72]

At the time, Adams was in a deep state of despair. Throughout the summer, the health of his second son, John, a longtime alcoholic, had been steadily declining. The former president sank into a deep depression, perhaps the worst of his life. In the few hours he could sleep each night, he dreamed mostly of death. He even talked about death's approach and hoped for an "easy passage." On 23 October, John died at the age of thirty-one. Two years earlier, the former president's brother, Thomas, had died of alcoholism, leaving behind a widow and large family, who became his responsibility. Now he was faced with caring for John's two daughters and widow. He also had to pay off $15,000 in debts that his son had incurred.[73]

Adams felt the afflictions of Job. Alcoholism had killed two of his brothers, contributed to the suicide of one of his three sons, and killed a second. With the deaths of Thomas and John, the former president's financial responsibilities had also mounted. His most immediate problem was simply getting through the winter financially. To do so, he borrowed money and turned for financial advice to his one remaining son, Charles, who had married into one of Boston's wealthiest families. Although Charles proved to be a wise financial counselor and loaned his father money when asked, Adams was not able to resolve his financial worries and pay off all his creditors until the 1840s, near the end of his life.[74]

Plunged into desolation, Adams sought solace in public service. In what can only be described as a remarkable recovery, by November he was discussing local politics and the next presidential election. A few days later, he was taking his seat in the new Congress. The congressman, who had already established a reputation for being self-righteous and cantankerous, returned to his seat more sanctimonious than ever. In a memorable speech in March 1835, which earned him the soubriquet "Old Man Eloquent," he tore into his fellow Whig, Daniel Webster, who had also become his political rival in the arcana of Massachusetts politics, over a fortification bill Webster opposed. "I bested them all," he bragged to his son after he had won his fight over the bill. "I obtained in the House of Representatives of the United States, a triumph unparalleled in the History of the Country," he added shamelessly.[75]

Now in his own element, Adams's congressional career became inextricably linked to his strategically brilliant and unrelenting response to attempts by Southern lawmakers to limit the right of public petition in cases involving the issue of slavery through what became known as the gag rule. The rule represented the Southern response to growing Northern agitation against slavery spearheaded by the American Antislavery Society (AASS). By 1835, the AASS boasted 1,000 chapters and 150,000 members; within three years, those figures had doubled. Because Southern lawmakers had cut off most congressional discussion on slavery and because local postal officials in the South succeeded in banning the delivery of most antislavery literature, the AASS adopted the strategy of submitting antislavery petitions to Congress.[76]

By 1835, the House was receiving hundreds of thousands of petitions demanding an end to slavery in the District of Columbia and the territories. In the past, similar petitions had been routinely referred to committee without disruption in the House's ordinary business. As Southern apprehension mounted over the growing antislavery movement in the North, Southern lawmakers sought to ban all future slave petitions. In 1837, the House approved the first of a series of gag rules barring referral to committee or debate on petitions relating to slavery.

It was the right to petition as provided under the First Amendment to the Constitution, not the issue of slavery, that made the gag rule so offensive to Adams. Because the Constitution was at stake, he was determined to be defiant—to test the bounds of House rules without violating them, and to disregard normal legislative comity without being insubordinate. Beginning in 1836, when the first gag rule was proposed on the House floor, and then in each subsequent year, as the rule was renewed and tightened, Adams kept up an unrelenting attack on the measure. At the beginning of each session, he made sure to present petitions before the rule was renewed. Once it was imposed, he used his mastery of parliamentary procedure to gain the floor, where he excoriated the South. His attacks became increasingly more shrill as he attempted to bait and hold up to public ridicule Southern lawmakers and the Northern Democrats who voted with them. In one exchange, he even had the temerity to suggest that slave owners commonly had intercourse with their female slaves. "I have heard it said . . . and I am inclined to believe it is the case," he remarked, "that in the South there existed great resemblances between the progeny of the colored people and the white men who claim possession of them." As he had intended, his remark caused an uproar among Southern lawmakers.[77]

As Adams continued his battle against the gag rule year after year, and as his attacks on the South and the slavocracy became more intemperate, he was accused by former president Jackson of being insane. Jackson even suggested he belonged in a mental hospital. Southern lawmakers began to refer to him as "the Madman from Massachusetts." His life was threatened. Louisa worried about the personal cost Adams was paying. "Could he only bring his mind to the calm of retirement," she lamented. But Adams could not. His son, Charles, understood his father well: "My own opinion is and has been for many years that his whole system of life is very wrong—that he sleeps by far too little, that he eats and drinks too irregularly, and that he has habituated his mind to a state of morbid activity which makes life in its common forms very tedious."[78]

The climax of Adams's fight against the gag rule came in 1842 when he presented a petition from a group of Massachusetts citizens calling for the dissolution of the Union. Rather than denounce the petitioners, Adams said that it was "not yet time." His remarks threw the House into a frenzy and led one Southern firebrand to make the tactical error of introducing a resolution asking the House to censure Adams and accusing the former president of being complicit in high treason. This gave Adams the opportunity to turn the censure proposal on its head. Taking control of the floor in his defense, he delivered a philippic, charging Southerners with being the ones who had threatened disunion for years and accusing them of various violations of the Constitution, including the right of habeas corpus, trial by jury, and freedom of speech. He also dared them and Northern Democrats to expel him. Adams had so effectively thrown his opponents on the defensive that when, after two weeks of debate, he allowed the House the chance to table the motion of censure "forever," the lawmakers seized the opportunity to pass a tabling resolution by a vote of 106 to 93.[79]

By this time, opinion against the gag rule had begun to turn even among Northern Democrats. Part of the reason was constitutional. In 1840 the House had adopted Rule XXI, tightening and making the gag rule permanent. For some Northern Democrats who had been willing to go along with the subterfuge of yearly tabling petitions, Rule XXI went too far. Believing it represented a clear violation of the First Amendment's right of petition, they refused to vote for it. Even more troubling for a number of them was the growing agitation in the South to annex Texas. Ever since the United States had turned down Texas's request to be annexed to the United States after its independence from Mexico in 1836, the issue of Texas had remained largely dormant. From Washington's perspective, the reason was simple. National leaders from both major parties sought to avoid the implications for the Union of annexing a slave-owning region large enough to

The artist, George Caleb Bingham, known mostly for his paintings of Missouri and the American frontier, painted this portrait of John Quincy Adams in 1844, two years after Adams had won his fight in the House of Representatives over the gag rule and forced his opponents in the House to table a resolution to expel him. When Adams sat for the portrait he doubted that Bingham could produce "a strong likeness" of him. But Bingham succeeded in illustrating the sharp-edged vitality that Adams continued to maintain despite his seventy-six years. (Courtesy of the National Portrait Gallery, Smithsonian Institution.)

be divided into five or six slave states. For various reasons, however, beginning in the 1840s, a movement grew again, especially in the South, to annex Texas. Upset over this possibility, enough Northern Democrats turned against their Southern colleagues and joined with the Northern Whigs to get the gag rule rescinded in December 1844. Repeal of the rule represented Adams's most significant personal achievement since being secretary of state. "Blessed, forever blessed, be the name of God!" he recorded in his diary after the gag rule had been repealed.[80]

By now the former president had become a hero among antislave groups throughout the North. Accepting invitations to lecture throughout the country, he was overwhelmed by the reception he received wherever he went. Although he thrived on the adulation, he still avoided identifying himself with the growing abolitionist movement. His fight continued to be one more in defense of the Constitution and the Union and against the South and the Democratic Party than against slavery. Although increasingly sympathetic to the abolitionist goal of emancipation, he still wanted to delay abolishing slavery until he thought the North was strong and united enough to preserve the Union while emancipating the slaves by martial law if necessary.[81]

Despite Adams's victory over the gag rule, the annexation of Texas in 1845 posed an even greater challenge, in his view, to the future of the Union. The former president's relationship with the Texas question was long, complex, and inconsistent. At one time a continental expansionist, Adams had sought to acquire Texas under the Adams–Onis Treaty of 1819. As president, he tried to purchase as much of Texas as possible, but Mexico was unwilling to forfeit any of its claims to Texas, which included modern New Mexico, Arizona, and most of the Rocky Mountain states. By the 1830s, however, Adams's views had fundamentally changed. Fearful of the consequences of the annexation of Texas in terms of the power of the Democratic South, he became an outspoken opponent of annexation, warning that the Jackson administration was trying to get Texas in order to carve out of the area as many as nine new slave states.[82]

When the issue was first raised in the House in 1836, Adams even warned that the annexation of Texas, along with attempts by the Jackson administration to deprive the Indians of their lands, could lead to a slave insurrection as well as war with Mexico, antislavery Great Britain or France, and the Indians. He even raised the possibility of a civil war. These conflicts might lead Congress to impose its war powers, which could lead to the abolition of slavery. "Mr. Chairman," he remarked on the House floor in May 1836, "are you ready for all these wars? A Mexican war? A war with Great Britain, if not with France? A general Indian war? A servile war? And, as an inevitable consequence of them all, a civil war?"[83]

Even after the movement for annexation was put aside momentarily, the former president continued to worry that the slavocracy had its eyes on Texas; indeed, he purposely tried to keep the issue alive in the hope of rallying public opinion against it. His worst fears were confirmed in 1845, when President John

Tyler of Virginia decided, just before leaving office, to annex Texas by joint reso-lution of Congress. Tyler had succeeded William Henry Harrison, the first Whig to be elected president, after Harrison's death just one month after he took office in 1841. Although the Senate had earlier decisively defeated an annexation treaty, Tyler was able to defy the antiannexationists. After the election as president in 1844 of James K. Polk, a Democrat and an expansionist, Tyler won a joint resolu-tion of annexation, which, unlike a treaty, required only a majority for passage. Even though the House approved the joint resolution by a small margin and the Senate by only a single vote, Adams was beside himself, arguing that the an-nexation of Texas had involved "the perfidious robbery and dismemberment of Mexico" and that "the Union was sinking into a military monarchy, to be rent asunder like the empire of Alexander or the kingdoms of Ephraim and Judah."[84]

The annexation of Texas led to war with Mexico. Adams, a leading opponent of the war, was only one of fourteen House members to vote against it. Just two months before he died, he told his friend Albert Gallatin that he could not be certain what the consequences of the conflict would be beyond strengthening the Southern slave owners. Undoubtedly Mexico would lose California, New Mex-ico, and whatever else the administration might want, including the dismember-ment of Mexico. He doubted that the United States could absorb all this territory. Instead, it would inflame sectional tensions and ignite a civil war. For this reason, he decided "to turn [his] eyes away" from the war.[85]

Although Adams opposed the annexation of Texas and the war with Mexico, he pressed the Polk administration to end the joint occupation of the Oregon Ter-ritory in existence since 1818 and to claim the entire territory to the 54°40' paral-lel (the boundary of Alaska), as Polk had promised in his campaign. The former president claimed to see no inconsistency between his opposition to the annexa-tion of Texas and his urging Polk to press the American claim to the Oregon Ter-ritory. The United States, he stated, had a better claim to Oregon than it had to Texas, and there were no slaves in Oregon. In contrast to Mexico's response to the annexation of Texas, he maintained that Great Britain would not go to war over Oregon. More importantly, the free states carved out of Oregon would help coun-terbalance the new power of the South as a result of the annexation of Texas.[86]

In insisting that Polk claim the full Oregon territory, Adams was almost cer-tainly engaged in saber rattling. In the first place, it is hard to believe that such an experienced diplomat as Adams could truly think that Great Britain would sit idly by if the United States actually tried to enforce its claim to British Columbia. Although Adams was old, he was not senile. Second, he was aware that negotia-tions were already under way to settle the area that had always been in dispute between London and Washington over Oregon: the region between the mouth of the Columbia River and the forty-ninth parallel, or the present state of Washing-ton. In 1846, England agreed to cede to the United States this small part of the much larger Oregon Territory. Once the agreement was signed, Adams seemed to welcome it. What guided his views on foreign affairs in the 1840s was not so much a personal interest either way in the debate over expansionism as his reflexive concern about the Southern slavocracy.[87]

This also helps explains his earlier position with regard to the famous *Amistad* case (*United States v. The Amistad*), in which he successfully argued before the Supreme Court for the freeing of a group of thirty-nine Africans who had been seized illegally and made into slaves. As the slaves were being shipped from one region of Spanish Cuba to another, they seized the ship and killed its captain. Instead of returning them to Africa, as the slaves demanded, their purported owners, whom the slaves had not killed, surreptitiously took the ship to Long Island, where the Africans were arrested and then jailed in New London. Spanish officials demanded that the ship, cargoes, and slaves be restored to Spain.

The *Amistad* case became a cause célèbre for the abolitionist movement in the United States, which argued that the Africans should be freed because they had been illegally forced into slavery. Although President Martin Van Buren was anxious to comply with the Spanish request, lower courts took the side of the Africans. Eventually the case made its way to the Supreme Court. As it went through the court system, Adams became more interested in the plight of the jailed Africans, writing letters in defense of their position. When the case was appealed to the Supreme Court, the former president, now seventy-three years old, in the midst of his battle over the gag rule, and preoccupied with the power of the South, gave an impassioned seven-and-a-half-hour-long closing argument that, by most accounts, convinced the Court to free the Africans.[88]

Adams's long and bitter fight against the Southern slave interests and in defense of the Union had taken a toll on him physically. Not helping his health was another long, frustrating, but ultimately successful crusade to have a sizable donation in 1835 by James Smithson, son of the duke of Northumberland, used "to found at Washington, under the name of the Smithsonian Institution, an Establishment for the increase and diffusion of knowledge among men." It might seem today that Smithson's generosity would have been immediately welcomed in Washington. Instead, Adams devoted eight years, as chairman of a special Smithsonian committee, battling to get the funds appropriated as intended. Holding up action were such issues as the authority of the federal government to accept the gift and to use the funds as Smithson wanted. Not until 10 August 1846 was the enabling legislation signed into law by President Polk.[89]

The next year, while on his way to tour the new Harvard Medical School, Adams collapsed. His face went pale and his legs were limp. His family physician determined that he had suffered a cerebral hemorrhage. "From that day," the ex-president remarked in a posthumously published memoir, "I date my decrease and consider myself for being for every useful purpose to myself and to my fellow creatures as dead."[90] After several months of recuperation, however, the former president was able to return to his congressional duties in Washington. Out of respect for the former president and longtime member of Congress who was nearing eighty years old, who was in feeble condition, and who could barely speak, Congress greeted him with a standing ovation. Even so, Adams was forced to watch sadly as Congress defeated a measure, the Wilmot Proviso, which would have prohibited slavery in any territory acquired from Mexico. His poor health kept him from mounting a defense of the measure.

Despite his declining health, Adams returned to Washington the following December for the next session of Congress. Some of his old feistiness even seemed to return. On 21 February 1848, however, while he was rising to address the House in opposition to a resolution honoring the generals in the recently concluded war with Mexico, he suddenly collapsed and was carried off to the Speaker's room. After lingering in a coma for two days, he died on 23 February at the age of eighty. [91]

Such were the passions toward Adams that continued to linger in the South even after his death that the Virginia legislature defeated a resolution honoring the former president and congressman. Throughout the rest of the nation, however, Americans responded differently to the news that this child of the Revolution, who had devoted his entire life to his country, had passed away. Senator Thomas Harton Benton of Missouri captured the country's mood perfectly when in eulogizing him, he remarked, "Death found him at the post of duty; and where else could it have found him?"[92]

Dying off the floor of the chamber where the former president had spent his last seventeen years was indeed a fitting end to one of the most esteemed careers in the nation's history. As president, Adams had had the misfortune of lacking the skills necessary to navigate a major transition in the nation's political history, but as a member of Congress, he left a legacy that transcended whatever deficiencies he might have displayed as president.

One aspect of that legacy, however, was the end of a transition in the post-presidency that had begun with James Madison. No longer would former presidents be expected to remove themselves after leaving office from the public scene to private retirement. In this respect, as in others, the republican ideals of politics and public virtue had undergone remarkable changes since the days of George Washington, John Adams, and Thomas Jefferson.

3

Former Presidents as Partisan Politicians
Jackson, Van Buren, and Tyler

When George Washington retired from the presidency in 1797 and began his 150-mile journey south from Philadelphia to Mount Vernon, he avoided as many public receptions as possible. When, forty years later, Andrew Jackson retired from the presidency, he followed a route of about 850 miles that took him through Wheeling, Cincinnati, and Louisville before he embarked on a steamboat, sailing the Ohio River to the Cumberland River and then on to his plantation, the Hermitage, in Nashville. Along the way, he welcomed celebrations despite being seventy years old and in poor health.

That Washington chose to avoid a celebratory journey into retirement while Jackson welcomed one reflected in part the differences in personalities between the austere first president and the fiery and passionate seventh president. However, the different ways they entered into retirement also said much about how politics and political expectations of former presidents had changed. Jackson's election as a president had ushered in a new era of participatory politics, so that even former presidents no longer believed they had to maintain the appearance of disengagement from political activity. The seventeen-year congressional career of John Quincy Adams had shattered that pretense forever.

Jackson's presidency not only altered the conduct of American politics in fundamental ways, but it also began a process of change in American political thought that legitimated political parties and partisan politics. Members of both major political parties, Democrats and Whigs, continued to espouse traditional republican values. Both of Jackson's campaigns for the presidency in 1828 and 1832 were predicated on two of the core concepts of republican thought: first, the depravity of unfettered authority, and second, the divine right of the governed. More than any other theme, Democrats used the alleged "corrupt bargain" between John Quincy Adams and Henry Clay, in which Jackson's Kentucky rival supposedly threw his support behind Adams in return for Clay's appointment as secretary of state, to defeat Adams in 1828. Four years later, Jackson made his war against the Bank of the United States (BUS)—the "Monster Bank" as he called it—his primary campaign issue, attributing to the BUS such unfortunate consequences as social inequalities, financial improprieties, and constitutional impieties. As for the Whigs, nothing did more to bind the disparate groups that came together to form the party than their reaction to what they regarded as Jackson's imperial demagoguery, which, they maintained, threatened the integrity of the republic.[1]

With its emphasis on economic progress and the promotion of the national welfare, the Whig Party's message was more positive than that of the Jacksonians, who tended to speak to the fears and resentments of the American people. As a result, the Jacksonians failed to address the dilemma of harmonizing the Jeffersonian image of a stable and virtuous yeoman republic with the emergence of a dynamic new industrial state. By furthering the democratization of American politics already under way even before Jackson took office and then by changing the entire calculus of executive authority, they caused a transformation in the conduct of American politics even more profound than the so-called Jeffersonian Revolution of 1800.[2]

One result of this transformation of American politics was a change in American political discourse. By 1840, common usage blurred the distinction found in dictionaries between a *republic,* in which sovereignty was lodged in representatives of the people, and a *democracy,* in which the people exercised their sovereignty in person. Another change was attitudinal and had more to do with modifications in points of view and opinions than with fundamental alterations in ideology or beliefs. This led to what historian Marvin Meyers has called the "Jacksonian paradox: the fact that the movement which helped clear the path for laissez-faire capitalism and its culture in America, and the public which in its daily life eagerly entered on that path, held nevertheless in their political conscience an ideal of a chaste republican order."[3]

Regardless of the paradox, by its idealization of the people, the Jacksonian movement had a liberating impact on American political thought just as it had on the economy. Rather than being viewed as an inherent threat to republicanism, political parties became the means of sanctifying the popular will and preserving the republic. Partisan politics reflected the competing interests of a permanent party system. It was no wonder, then, that while John Quincy Adams always made a point, even in his congressional career, of his political independence and disdain of partisanship, his successors as former presidents, from Andrew Jackson through John Tyler, made no such disclaimers. On the contrary, they even identified partisan politics with the hallowed ideal of selfless service in the public interest.[4]

|

Few presidents were as popular or as hated as Andrew Jackson. Even today, historians argue over whether Jackson was a heroic figure or a villain, a warrior or a perpetrator of genocide, a tyrant or dispenser of justice, a democrat or a power monger. Because of the changes that Jackson brought to American politics and to the executive branch of government, however, almost all agree that the second quarter of the nineteenth century can rightfully be referred to as the Age of Jackson.[5]

Whether described in heroic or villainous terms, certain elements of Jackson's upbringing and character stand out. Fatherless before he was born, orphaned by age fourteen, and very much a product of the frontier, he was rough-hewn and unruly even as a young adult. He also had a fierce temper and a deep sense of honor that he was prepared to protect to the death. Yet he was intensely ambitious, sought social acceptance, and had an uncanny ability to turn his anger on and off at will. Although a lawyer by training, he was poorly educated and could hardly spell. He made up for this by his charismatic personality and entrepreneurial spirit. He speculated in land, engaged in various business enterprises, and ran a large plantation. One of Tennessee's largest slave owners, he was active in the slave trade. He also liked to gamble, owned a racetrack, and had a passion for breeding and racing horses. Deeply loyal to his friends and those who served under him, he demanded loyalty in return; most of the time, he commanded it by the sheer force of his personality. Yet he was thin-skinned and frequently felt surrounded by enemies. At other times, he felt abandoned by those he had considered his friends. As a result, he could be both compassionate and merciless. Above all, he had a deep commitment to the preservation of the Union, perhaps the one characteristic he shared with John Quincy Adams.

Although Jackson weighed only about 140 pounds, he was an imposing figure. Standing slightly over six feet tall, his body was rawboned, sinewy, and agile. His face was long and angular, with sharp features, and he had a shock of red hair that had turned completely gray by the time he became president. His complexion was sallow and pockmarked from a bout with smallpox. He also bore a scar over one eye from a sword gash he had suffered as a young boy during the Revolutionary War when he refused the order of a British officer to shine his boots. His deep-set blue eyes were often described as steely.

Soon to be sixty-two years old, the Tennessean was at the time the oldest elected president, and the poorest in health. Having one bullet lodged in his chest from a duel he had fought in 1806 and another (until it was removed twenty years later) from a second duel he fought in 1813 that destroyed much of the mobility of his left arm, Jackson was constantly in pain and may have suffered from lead poisoning. The bullet in his chest caused frequent lung hemorrhages, severe attacks of fever, paroxysms of coughing, and discharges of phlegm and sputum. Eventually he also developed chronic bronchitis. The fact that he constantly smoked a pipe undoubtedly worsened his pulmonary condition. During a war with the Creek Indians in 1814, in which he established his reputation as a general, he also became debilitated with chronic diarrhea and dysentery, which further damaged his health. He rarely had an appetite and often substituted diluted gin for food to help relieve his pain. In the years before he became president, he lost most of his teeth, his vision began to fail, and he suffered from increasing headaches. He also used a cane to walk.[6]

The popular image of Jackson when he took office in 1829, however, was not that of an old and sick man but of a heroic leader who had freed much of the South and Southwest from the threat of savage Indians and given the United States its greatest military victory since the Revolution by defeating the British at the Battle of New Orleans in 1815. Most Americans also believed that Jackson had been cheated out of office four years earlier. His overwhelming victory in 1828 over John Quincy Adams was widely regarded as a vindication of the popular will. Indeed, both the size of the vote and the percentage of Americans casting ballots in 1828 compared to four years earlier indicated the spread of democracy taking place in the country. In 1824, just 356,000 Americans, or 26.7 percent of the electorate, voted for president; four years later, the corresponding numbers were 1.56 million and 57.1 percent. For the first time, moreover, Americans had elected a president who was not a member of the patrician classes of Massachusetts or Virginia.[7]

Jackson's election was historic in other ways as well. His administration will always be remembered for his successful battle against the BUS and the Specie Circular requiring payment for federal lands in gold and silver; for his defense of the Union during the nullification crisis despite his support of states' rights; for his veto of the Maysville Road internal improvements bill; and for his defiance of the Marshall Court's ruling against Georgia's efforts to force the Cherokee Indians to cede their lands. Just as important were the changes he brought to the executive branch of government, making it the first among equals and turning the cabinet into a body serving at his pleasure and subordinate to his interests. Previous presidents had been generally unwilling either to challenge the other branches of government or to engage in the wholesale dismissal of their cabinets that Jackson carried out during his first administration. Similarly, he was the first president to engage in what is often referred to as the spoils system and what he called "rotation in office": the replacement of one party's appointees by another, in some cases because of corruption, in other cases because they were not beholden to the party in power.[8]

Significantly, even while helping to change the complexion of American politics and strengthening the executive branch of government, Jackson appealed to traditional republican values. Before he ran for president, he displayed the customary contempt for party spirit. As a candidate, he followed the tradition since Washington's time of not publicly campaigning for office. Throughout his presidency, he stated repeatedly that his underlying purpose was to restore public virtue to a corrupt government by empowering ordinary citizens. He even defended rotation in office in Jeffersonian terms. The duties of government, he said, were so plain and simple that most any citizen was competent to perform them, so that the only effect of the rotation system was the beneficial one of making administrative offices as subject to the popular will as elective offices.[9]

Regardless of Jackson's personal identification with time-honored American values, the changes wrought by his administration carried over into new attitudes toward political parties and partisanship. Much of the credit for this development belonged to U.S. senator Martin Van Buren of New York and his friends, known as the Albany Regency. Even before Jackson ran for the White House, they had begun to develop an elaborate rationalization for political parties. Fundamental to their argument was that nonpartisanship actually encouraged a virulent form of factionalism, resulting in elitist and opportunistic leadership, and that vigorous competition among parties was the lifeblood of a democratic nation. Although Van Buren had reservations about backing Jackson precisely because of his adherence to traditional views on political parties, he decided that the Tennessean could play a powerful tool in creating a new, popularly based political party still largely predicated on Jeffersonian principles.[10]

There is no evidence that Jackson ever came out in favor of permanent political parties. In fact, he may never have fully reconciled himself to their establishment. However, the president and Van Buren shared the same goals of protecting Jeffersonian principles and maintaining the Union. For both men, these goals were to be achieved through the establishment of sectional coalitions predicated on respect for the compromise worked out during the Missouri controversy. This amounted to the construction of a North–South coalition protective of the rights of slave owners. Such a coalition later presented a serious problem for Van Buren when the slavery issue became tied to the question of annexing Texas. Regardless, the outcome of the collaboration between Jackson and Van Buren was a new competitiveness that carried over from the economic arena of laissez-faire capitalism to the political arena of partisan politics.

Because Van Buren and Jackson shared similar goals and Van Buren proved deeply loyal to the president, he became increasingly influential within the new administration at the expense of Vice President John C. Calhoun. Even before Jackson forced Calhoun's resignation during the nullification crisis, he had decided on Van Buren as his running mate in 1832. This assured that Van Buren would be the Democratic nominee in 1836. In the election that followed, Van Buren defeated a coalition of four Whig candidates, winning 170 electoral votes to their combined 124 votes, but gaining only 50.9 percent of the popular vote to their combined 49.1 percent.

By the time Jackson finished his term in 1837, he was looking forward to returning to the Hermitage. One of the most famous and often visited homes of any former president, the residence had not been an especially impressive one during most of Jackson's life, especially for an owner of a large plantation. Jackson had acquired the 425-acre property in 1804. At the time, he and his wife, Rachel, had been living at Hunters Hill, a more valuable property closer to the Cumberland River. To pay off his debts, Jackson sold Hunters Hill and purchased the other acreage two miles away, where they lived in a modest log house until 1819, when they constructed the original Hermitage mansion. By then, Jackson had expanded his farm into a prosperous 1,000-acre cotton plantation employing the labor of forty-four slaves; eventually he claimed to own 150 slaves. The plantation had a number of outbuildings, including a distillery, dairy, cotton gin and press, and slave cabins. The mansion itself was a nondescript, federal-style, two-story, eight-room brick residence on the side of a gently sloping hill whose only striking feature was a formal garden for Rachel.

In 1831, while serving in the White House, Jackson undertook a major addition to the mansion, doubling its size, with flanking one-story wings, a two-story entrance portico with ten Doric columns, a small rear portico, and copper gutters. The inside of the mansion included a library and the overseer's office in the east wing and a large dining room and pantry in the west wing. Outside, Jackson also constructed a Grecian-style temple and monument for Rachel. When a chimney fire nearly destroyed the mansion in 1834, Jackson had it restored in the Greek Revival style familiar to those who visit the Hermitage today.

Like the plantations of other former presidents, the Hermitage remained a working farm as well as a residence and caused Jackson major financial burdens. Because of scarce labor and inflation, reconstruction of the mansion took more time to complete than originally planned and cost the president about double the original estimate. To add to his troubles, the cotton crop for 1836 (the year the restoration was completed) was a calamitous failure.

Also like other former presidents who owned large estates, Jackson was often short of cash. Throughout his life, he had adhered strictly to paying off his debts. His years at the White House, however, had hurt him financially. He received $25,000 a year, but he entertained lavishly and maintained an expensive wine cellar. Although he left for Washington in 1833 with $5,000, he returned to the Hermitage with less than $100. Furthermore, the peak years of the Hermitage as a profit-making enterprise had passed. Jackson's acreage was less productive, and he was facing increased competition from the newly settled frontier areas of the South with richer lands and longer growing seasons. Although he understood the need to diversify, he still had to rely on cotton as his primary crop. Because of the Panic of 1837 and new competition from Brazil and India, cotton prices plummeted. By 1845, the year Jackson died, cotton sold for as little as four to nine cents a pound, prices the former president described as "ruinous."[11]

Making Jackson's financial situation even worse was his determination to pay off the financial obligations of his adopted son, Andrew Jr., who had been raised by the Jacksons as if he had been their natural child. Charming socially, he was reckless, irresponsible, and negligent. In addition to managing the Hermitage poorly during his father's absence, he speculated foolishly and unwisely endorsed his friends' notes. As a result, he incurred a sizable debt. To pay off his son's arrears even as he tried to turn the fortunes of the Hermitage around, the former president sold land he owned in western Tennessee and Alabama. He also looked for buyers for part of his bloodline horses. "I find my blooded stock in bad order and too numerous for empty corn cribs and hay lofts," he wrote to one potential buyer soon after returning to the Hermitage, "but the blood is good. . . . I will give a bargain."[12]

Yet Jackson remained short of cash. The former president lacked money even for a new saddle for his horse. The younger Andrew continued to be a financial burden. Married with two children, he was increasingly incapable of taking care of his family. In 1838, Andrew Jr. bought Halcyon Plantation, a 1,185-acre estate on the Mississippi River for $20 an acre—a high price for a property exposed to the capricious waters of the Mississippi. He secured the property with notes payable over four years. The former president had reservations about the purchase. He knew that if his son got into further financial trouble, he would have to bail him out. However, he did not want to discourage him from starting out on his own. He also hoped a profit might be made by selling timber on the plantation for fuel for the steamboats plying the river as well as from cotton production from its rich fields.

Unfortunately, a combination of poor oversight by Andrew Jr. and constant floods, which washed away crops, timber, and animals, resulted in mounting debts rather than profits. Jackson tried to pay off these obligations by selling the property, but he could not find a buyer. His financial situation became so dire that when he was invited in 1840 to attend the twenty-fifth anniversary of the Battle of New Orleans, he seriously considered not going. His health was not good, and he was reluctant to travel in the winter. He also still resented the fact that after the battle, he had been fined $1,000 by a local judge for imposing martial law on the city. His primary concern was that he could not afford the cost of the trip. As he remarked to his nephew, Andrew J. Donelson, "I cannot bear to borrow or travel as a pauper." He finally decided to go to New Orleans after convincing himself that he could conduct business on the way that would help pay some of his son's bills. To finance his trip, however, he had to borrow against his cotton crop.[13]

Much to Jackson's embarrassment, his financial straits became generally known, a development he attributed to the "calumnies" of the Whig press, which, he claimed, was trying to ruin his credit. "I owe no one a dollar," he said. Nevertheless, he was relieved when Francis P. Blair, the editor and part owner of the Jacksonian organ, the *Washington Globe,* and a member of his former "kitchen cabinet" of unofficial advisers, agreed to lend him $10,000.[14]

In Congress, the former president's supporters also introduced legislation to refund to him, with interest, the $1,000 fine that he had paid New Orleans. His Whig opponents amended the bill from a refund to a gratuity. Although he desperately needed the money, he refused to accept it on these terms. "I would starve before I would accept one cent of the money under that odious and insulting

This is a likeness of a portrait of Andrew Jackson originally painted in 1840 by Edward
Dalton Marchant for which Jackson agreed to sit while he was in New Orleans
celebrating the twenty-fifth anniversary of the Battle of New Orleans. The portrait was
reproduced shortly thereafter by James Tooley Jr., a miniaturist and landscape painter.
It's one of the few portraits to show Jackson wearing spectacles. Tooley died in 1844,
a year before Jackson's death. (Courtesy of the National Portrait Gallery, Smithsonian
Institution; gift of Mr. William H. Lively, Mrs. Mary Lively Hoffman, and
Dr. Charles J. Lively.)

amended legislation," Jackson raged.[15] Only after lawmakers changed the legislation into a measure vindicating him by erasing the New Orleans fine did he agree to accept the funds. The $2,732 he received in 1842 was enough to keep him afloat that year. The next year, his crop was drowned by floods. He was saved only by the generosity of Blair and his partner, John C. Rives, who agreed to loan him $8,000 to consolidate his debts.

Unlike Jefferson and Monroe, Jackson did not die in poverty. His will showed debts of about $26,000, most of it owed to Blair and Rives. He owned more than 100 slaves and the Hermitage. Also, he still had the plantation in Mississippi with another fifty-one slaves, which he had taken ownership of from his son. One estimate placed the value of his holdings, including his land, at $150,000 (the equivalent of about $3.5 million in 2009). Unfortunately, after his death, Andrew Jr., to whom he had left most of his estate against the advice of friends, was still unable to manage his finances. In order to pay off his debts, he was forced to sell off the Halcyon estate piece by piece. Tennessee also agreed to buy the Hermitage, where it allowed him and his family to remain as long as they lived.[16]

Besides attending to his properties and dealing with the financial irresponsibility of his adopted son, in the eight years he lived after leaving the White House, Jackson was also plagued with generally declining health. For weeks and even months at a time, he found himself bedridden with recurring hemorrhages, fever, and a series of other ailments that continued to plague him. "My own health is not good," he wrote in 1839 to Andrew J. Hutchings, the son of a deceased business partner whom he had raised since the age of seven. "I have returns of great pain in my head and ears, and although my cough is nearly cured a hawking up of fleme remains as disagreeable and debilitating as my cough." Throughout his retirement years he lived with, and accepted the fact that, he might die at any time.[17]

Jackson managed, however, to follow the affairs of state and to hurry off letters to President Van Buren, to Francis Blair, and to a host of other prominent Democrats urging them to uphold the policies he had set in place as president and to counteract the mounting Whig attacks on the new administration following the Panic of 1837. If the former president ever saw any inconsistency between his belief in traditional republican values and in his active partisanship in his postpresidential years, it was never apparent either in what he said or did.

Jackson was concerned particularly that the new administration maintain the Specie Circular of 1836, which the Whigs blamed for the depression that followed the panic. They also claimed it was responsible for a downward deflationary spiral, for declining land values, and, more importantly, for the spread of fear and distrust across the nation. Removal of the Specie Circular, they maintained, would restore confidence, stimulate land sales, and increase government revenue. In contrast, the Jacksonians blamed the depression on overbanking and overtrading and argued that the Specie Circular was necessary to check the orgy of speculation that had led to the country's current economic woes.[18]

As the Whigs seized every opportunity to blame the depression on Jackson's economic policies and placed great pressure on Van Buren to repeal the Specie Circular, the former president placed his own considerable pressure on his protégé to hold fast. His relationship with Van Buren was substantially different from that of any former president before him with an incumbent. It ranged from virtually issuing orders to Van Buren to giving him strong advice on how to conduct the business of the presidency. "Persue the energetic course you have adopted," he wrote his successor in June while exhorting him to support the Specie Circular. "Continue to coerce the payment of all public dues in specie, and the moment *a subordinate officer* hesitates to execute the law, remove him, *be whom he may.*" In the same letter, Jackson also instructed Van Buren on how he should run his office. "Permit me here one remark for your consideration, that is, have your plans all matured, your message prepared in due time, to impart to our friends as they arrive, that they may take lead, and carry your views in one solid phalanx."[19]

Throughout his retirement, the former president was also determined to be proven right with regard to his broader view that the nation's future rested in the hands of the nation's largely yeoman and democratic citizenry rather than with its privileged few. Because he identified these elements with the Whig Party, he readily engaged in partisan politics, referring often to the Whigs as "Federalists," "vile calumnators" and "conspirators" who sought various forms of government assistance for their personal profit.[20]

Jackson had made many of these same charges during his presidency, but several developments after he left office made his continued participation in politics all the more significant. In the first place, partisan politics took on even more resonance beginning with the 1838 congressional and state elections. These elections were especially significant in terms of the transition already under way to a modern two-party system. The two parties were better organized, and the Whigs' national political respectability surged after the 1838 election. In New York, they even won the governorship for the first time.[21]

Because the former president continued to command great influence within the Democratic Party, he remained an important voice within Democratic ranks against the growing abolitionist movement, which he identified closely with the Whig Party and believed posed the greatest threat to the Union. Not only did he lash out against the abolitionist movement, he also weighed in heavily in the battle to annex Texas. His interest in annexing Texas had more to do with freeing the United States from potential enemies on its borders than with the expansion of slavery. Both before and after he left office, he worried that if the United States did not annex Texas, it would be faced with an independent Texas Republic aligned closely with Britain and having expansionist ambitions of its own. These conflicted with another of his aims: the acquisition of California.

Although Harrison's election over Van Buren in 1840 seemed to end any immediate chance of annexing Texas, the sudden death of the Whig president exactly one month into his administration opened new possibilities. Harrison's successor, John Tyler of Virginia, had been a Democrat before joining the Whig

Party. After becoming the nation's first nonelected president, he quickly broke with the Whigs by endorsing Democratic policies.

Not surprisingly, Jackson's opinion of Tyler as an apostate to the Democratic Party abruptly changed. He now had full confidence in the president's democratic and states' rights principles, he commented at the end of 1841. By this time, Sam Houston, Jackson's onetime friend from Tennessee, had begun his second term as president of Texas. Reopening the question of the annexation of Texas in 1842, Houston also kept open the possibility of an independent Texas republic aligning itself closely to London if not annexed by the United States.

Prodded by his secretary of state, Abel Upshur of Virginia, Tyler opened up preliminary negotiations with Texas. Although Upshur was killed in a freak accident in February 1844, his successor, John C. Calhoun, completed a treaty of annexation. By coupling approval of the treaty to the security of the South and the defense of slavery, however, he assured its defeat by the Senate in June 1844.

Although plagued by deteriorating health and in constant pain, Jackson followed these developments closely. Not only did he push for annexation, but in March 1844, after Mexico seized some prisoners from Texas, he wrote a letter to Mexico's president, Antonio-Lopez de Santa Anna, urging their release. "It is not my province to inquire into the existing relations between Mexico and Texas," he told Santa Anna. "It is enough for me to know that Texas has been acknowledged by several of the European nations and by the United States."[22]

Jackson's pleasure at the news that Texas had agreed to be annexed by the United States was cut short when he learned that the two most likely candidates for president in 1844, Martin Van Buren and Henry Clay, had issued separate letters opposing annexation. Their purpose was to eliminate Texas as a campaign issue. Making the former president even angrier was a letter he received in May from Francis Blair about Calhoun's comments linking the annexation of Texas to the slavery issue. Blair was convinced the purpose of his remarks was "to unite the whole South upon himself . . . into his scheme of dissolution of the Union." Blair also accused Tyler of being involved in Calhoun's plot as a way of securing for himself the Democratic nomination.[23]

Jackson responded by lashing out at Calhoun and Tyler while breaking with Van Buren. "I say to you emfatically," he responded to Blair, "if Mr. V. Buren had come out in favour of annexation he would have been elected almost by acclamation, and Tyler nor no one else would have been thought of by the democracy, and two thirds of the whiggs. . . . The safety of the great interests of the south and west, and safety of the union are involved."[24] In making these remarks, the former president was being disingenuous because he had already come to doubt whether Van Buren could beat Clay and was now looking for another candidate to replace him.

No longer even nominally supporting his former vice president, Jackson threw his backing behind former Speaker of the House and governor of Tennessee James K. Polk, whom he had already pushed for the vice presidential nomination.

On 16 May he published a letter in the Nashville *Union* calling for the immediate annexation of Texas even by joint resolution of Congress.[25] As the former president understood, a joint resolution of Congress required only a majority of both Houses of Congress instead of the two-thirds vote of the Senate needed for approval of a treaty.

As a way of preventing Van Buren's nomination, the former president lobbied successfully to get the Democratic Party's rules changed to require approval of two-thirds, instead of one-half, of the delegates in order to gain the party's nod. After failing to get the nomination on the first ballot, Van Buren's vote began to erode. With none of the other leading candidates able to get the necessary ballots for nomination, the convention became deadlocked. On the ninth ballot, a stampede started toward Polk sufficient to give him the nomination. Until the previous ballot, he had not even received a single delegate vote.

Polk ran on a platform calling not only for the annexation of Texas but also the entire Oregon Territory. Fully supporting that view, Jackson worked tirelessly throughout the campaign on Polk's behalf. When Southerners threatened to turn a gathering planned for Nashville in August into a rally in support of secession unless Texas was immediately annexed, he used his influence to make the mass meeting into one simply in support of the Democratic Party. He also wrote letters extolling Polk's virtues that were published throughout the country. When Polk was narrowly elected in November, Jackson was overjoyed. "I have the pleasure to tell you that Polk and [his running mate, George] Dallas are elected and the Republic is safe," he wrote his nephew, Andrew Donelson, soon after receiving the election results.[26]

By the time Tyler annexed Texas by joint resolution of Congress just before Polk took office, Jackson was in the throes of death. He could hardly walk because his feet were swollen, and when he walked, he was "at once suffocated for the want of breath," as he wrote to Polk at the end of February. He spent most of his time in bed. He coughed day and night. His entire body began to swell, and he was always in considerable pain. "I have been quite sick for several days," he wrote Blair on 9 April, "and it may be that my life ends in dropsy. . . . Be it so. I am fully prepared to say the Lord's will be done."[27]

Jackson amazed even his doctors by surviving as long as he did. He even continued in his waning days to maintain an active interest in the operation of the Hermitage, where dozens of visitors came to pay their last respects, many of them so that they could claim later that they had seen a national hero before he died. Still attuned to national affairs, he wrote a short final letter to President Polk on 6 June urging him to denounce Tyler's last treasury secretary, George H. Bibb, who had been accused of defrauding the government of $90,000, and to do the same with the incumbent, Robert J. Walker, should he be implicated in the scheme. Two days later, Jackson died, most likely from a chronic infection that led to heart failure.[28]

News of Jackson's death caused more than the usual outpouring of national grief. A commemorative funeral procession in New York City on 24 June may have drawn the largest crowds in the city's history up to that time. Despite an oppressive heat, the procession, which began in the early afternoon, did not conclude until well into the evening. Marching in the parade were groups representing the various interests that had been organized so successfully into the Democratic Party and were part of the new era of partisan politics. For these Americans, and for others across the land who had come to regard Jackson as the embodiment of American democracy, his death was a staggering loss.

II

Martin Van Buren was the third president to be defeated in his bid for reelection. Only John Adams and his son, John Quincy Adams, had suffered a similar fate. Van Buren was the first former president to make a concerted effort to regain the White House. The younger Adams considered running again for president in 1832, but he settled instead for his long career in the House of Representatives. There he joined other Whigs in making life miserable for Van Buren. He was not unmindful that, as a U.S. senator from New York, Van Buren had helped undermine his administration and engineer his defeat in 1828. He also objected to Van Buren's efforts as president to appease Southern slave owners. While arguing before the U.S. Supreme Court in the *Amistad* case, less than a month before the end of Van Buren's presidency, he denounced the administration's efforts to return the former African captives back into slavery. More generally, he found Van Buren to be of mediocre mind and unscrupulous. "His principles," he once remarked, "are all subordinate to his ambitions."[29]

Adams's view of Van Buren was a common but not entirely accurate one. Van Buren, who shared Andrew Jackson's belief in Jeffersonian republicanism and his commitment to preserving the Union, thought this could best be achieved by seeking compromise between the North and slave-owning South. At the same time, his statement of opposition to the annexation of Texas in 1844, while done to avoid a divisive issue in a campaign in which he fully expected to head the Democratic ticket, was also issued because he was genuinely concerned about the spread of slavery into Texas and doubted the legitimacy of the United States annexing a territory Mexico still considered its own.[30]

Unlike most of his predecessors as president, Van Buren was not an engaging figure. Because of his dainty manner of dress and muttonchop whiskers, which he seemed rarely to have trimmed, Van Buren looked almost clownish. At five feet, six inches tall, he was about half a foot shorter than his predecessor. Rather than being rail thin like Jackson, he was trim and solidly built until past middle age, when his love of fine foods and good wines caused him to become overweight. Although as a young boy he had blond curly locks, they had receded with age. By the time he became president, he was nearly bald, with a crown of unruly white hair. He had a fair complexion, deep-set blue eyes, a classic Roman nose, and a high forehead. What stood out about Van Buren's physical appearance were his bushy side whiskers and dapper dress. Even though he toned down his attire over the years from raffish orange cravats and white duck trousers to more appropriate dress, the press remained critical of his wardrobe.

During his administration, the nation suffered through its most serious depression before the Great Depression of 1929. Except for the depression and Van Buren's efforts to establish an independent treasury, little else stood out about his presidency. In terms of foreign policy, it was best known for the *Caroline* affair of 1837, in which the British seized and burned the steamship *Caroline* because it had been carrying supplies across the Niagara River to Canadian rebels leading an insurgency against British rule, and for settling the so-called Aroostook War, involving a disputed border between Maine and Canada. Although these incidents raised briefly the possibility of conflict with Great Britain, they were more in the nature of a tempest in a teapot.

Van Buren also waged a seemingly intractable war against the Seminole Indians in Florida and narrowly gained approval of a treaty providing for the forced removal of the Cherokees from Georgia and Alabama to the far West under shameful conditions. These were reprehensible acts, but they pale in comparison to the genocide committed against the Indians both before and after Van Buren's administration. He also committed no major blunder other than perhaps not responding more forcefully to the economic depression that caused such havoc and despair during his last two years in office.

Before becoming president, however, Van Buren played a pivotal role in the development of the nation's modern two-party system. Raised in the small town of Kinderhook in the Hudson Valley between Albany and New York City, Van Buren was elected in 1812 to the New York state senate. It was in the byzantine world of New York politics that he mastered the techniques of organizational politics and learned how to cope with conflicting interests. In 1821, he was elected to the U.S. Senate. Rather than renounce partisan politics and the concept of permanent political parties, which were so antithetical to classical republican thought, he embraced them. Although he left it mainly to his cohorts to provide the intellectual justification for political parties, he made clear his own belief in the equation between two competing parties and a functioning democracy. More important, he became one of the most brilliant political operatives of his time, first on the state level and then on the national level. He organized and managed coalitions, providing them with a common cause, imposing on them order and discipline, and establishing the machinery of a permanent political party. For most of his political career, he was also able to avoid the thickets that entangled politicians of lesser political acumen.[31]

As a result of his skill as a broker-politician, he developed a reputation as a sly and even duplicitous political figure. Opponents referred to him as the Little Magician (a reference to his size) or the Red Fox of Kinderhook. Because Van

Buren was a sociable man and had a genuinely genial disposition, he never was fully able to fathom the sobriquets attached to his name. He also never gained the same kind of political following that the hero of the Battle of New Orleans enjoyed. Not only did he lack Jackson's charismatic personality, but he also faced a more formidable competition in the emerging Whig Party. With considerable success, the Whigs were able to label Van Buren with the charges of executive usurpation that they had tried unsuccessfully to associate with Jackson.

For the vice president, it must have seemed the height of irony that the very groups he associated with antidemocratic Federalism should accuse the party of Jefferson as being antidemocratic. Although Van Buren was still able to win the presidency in 1836 against a coalition of Whig candidates, he could not stave off defeat in 1840 against a more organized party running a single popular candidate, William Henry Harrison, and mobilizing the mass of voters through such tactics as sloganeering ("Tippecanoe and Tyler Too"), vitriolic antiadministration editorials in Whig newspapers, parades, and mass rallies—techniques that Van Buren had been instrumental in engineering. The master, in short, had been outmastered by the opposition. For the first time in the nation's history, a presidential candidate—Harrison—actively campaigned on the political stump. In an election in which 80 percent of eligible Americans voted, Van Buren gained a respectable 47 percent of the vote to Harrison's 53 percent, but he was trounced in the electoral college 234 to 60.[32]

Unable at first to understand the reasons for his defeat, Van Buren blamed it in on Whig fraud and a "mistake in the public mind."[33] He quickly recovered and wrote to his friend and former attorney general, Benjamin Butler, that he had no regrets and that he looked to a "house to furnish, farm to stock, etc. etc." "Will you believe," he added, "that I begin to hanker after the Hours of Separation between myself and my official honors." With considerable graciousness, he invited Harrison to the White House, hosted a dinner in his honor, and even offered to vacate the White House if the president-elect wanted to move in early. Harrison declined the offer.[34]

After Harrison's inauguration in March, Van Buren spent two months staying with Butler in New York City, by now a major business and cultural center with a population that exceeded 300,000. He then returned to Kinderhook, where he began the remodeling of his recently purchased fifty-acre estate, Lindenwald, a rustically beautiful Dutch colonial estate, with pines, elms, and fruit trees that looked out over gently sloping meadows toward the Catskill Mountains and through which a creek meandered down to the Hudson River five miles away. Unfortunately, the former president was later persuaded by one of his sons, Smith Thompson, whose family lived with him, to expand the residence and turn it into a garish Venetian villa with a four-story loggia tower, a large piazza, and an enormous main hall with twelve-foot-high ceilings and walls covered with cheery Dutch wallpaper.[35]

Soon after buying his new home, the former president added 150 acres of farmland and orchards to the estate's fifty acres and turned it into a profitable working farm by selling his surplus of hay, oats, potatoes, and fruits. Van Buren seemed to enjoy the life of a gentleman farmer. Not only did he prove to be an adept and meticulous farmer, applying the same skills and entrepreneurial spirit to farming that he had applied to his political career, but he enjoyed his growing family as three of his four sons married and had children. Either they lived at Lindenwald, nearby, or visited him often. Moreover, he entertained lavishly and frequently. As his bill for wine, champagne, liqueurs, game, fish, oysters, and other delicacies grew, so did his waistline. Although he worked his farm and commonly rode his horse fifteen miles a day, his small frame was soon carrying 170 pounds.

Despite seeming to enjoy his retirement, politics were never far from Van Buren's mind. Exactly when he decided to run again for president is not entirely clear. Almost as soon as he returned to Kinderhook, he began to receive pledges of support from his followers. In 1842, he began a long tour of the South and West in order to heal wounds and to attempt to reestablish the North–South alliance he considered essential to the unity of the Democratic Party and to his renomination for president. He spent time with friends and former enemies alike, including even a visit to Henry Clay, the likely Whig nominee in 1844 after Harrison's death. While touring the West, he spent a night in Rochester, Illinois, where he met a thirty-three-year-old fledging Whig politician named Abraham Lincoln, who, he later reported, made him laugh so hard with his folksy stories that he went to sleep with aching ribs. Most important during his trip was his visit to the Hermitage. There he renewed his ties with Jackson, who made clear his intention to support Van Buren in 1844. Everywhere he went, he received pledges of support from prominent Democrats. By the end of 1842, he had clearly decided to run again for president. He purposely refrained from becoming a candidate, believing that too early an announcement would be counterproductive.

Van Buren's nomination was not unopposed. Calhoun, who had resigned from the Senate in 1843, launched a vigorous campaign that gained traction even in New York. Senator Lewis Cass of Michigan also vied for the nomination. More generally, Southerners were never fully comfortable with Van Buren's position on slavery, no matter how reassuring he tried to be. Others thought his hard-line money and other policies were out of step with the nation's changing economy and growing expansionist sentiment. Still others simply distrusted him. As Van Buren had anticipated, however, Calhoun's campaign came apart. Party leaders lined up behind Van Buren, and state conventions gave him their endorsement. In December 1843, Calhoun announced he was withdrawing his candidacy. Van Buren's nomination seemed assured.[36]

That did not happen, of course. The fact that the date of the convention was moved from 1843 to 1844 indicated the residual opposition that remained against Van Buren: the later the convention met, the more time there was to rally the opposition against him. His letter of 20 April 1844 to Congressman William Hammet of Mississippi, in which he came out against the immediate annexation of

Texas, sealed his fate. The fact that the letter was published on the same day that the Whig candidate for president, Henry Clay, issued a similar letter suggested to many Democrats that Van Buren had made a deal with Clay to keep the issue out of the 1844 campaign. The coincidence of the two letters published on the same day was enough to deny him the nomination in Baltimore a few months later.

Once again, Van Buren had to endure the embarrassment of defeat, this time by his own party. Again, he displayed one of the most enduring features of his personality: a high degree of self-control even during periods of great distress and disappointment. Although many of his supporters remained furious that he had been denied the nomination, he accepted his defeat with the same grace he had shown after losing the presidency in 1840. During the campaign that followed, he lent his full support to the Democratic nominee, Polk. By persuading his close ally, Silas Wright, the popular U.S. senator for New York, to give up his seat in order to run for governor of New York, he helped carry the key state for the Tennesseean.[37]

What followed was the saddest chapter in Van Buren's long political career. Van Buren expected to play a prominent role in the selection of Polk's cabinet. He believed he had sacrificed his nomination on the hard rock of principle. He had opposed the annexation of Texas not because he was against the expansion of slavery or the eventual annexation of Texas, but because too much of the North was opposed and because the matter of Texas had not been resolved with Mexico. He had made this clear in his letter to Hammet. That was one reason why he was so distressed at Andrew Jackson's response to his letter. He could not believe that anyone "who desires the annexation only when it can be made consistently with what is due to the peace and honor of the country can find anything to object to in my letter," he told his friend Benjamin Butler. In an unusual fit of peevishness, he harped on the fact that he was being accused of being the "enemy" of the South notwithstanding "the opposition and persecution" to which he had been subjected for defending the South in the past.[38]

With the annexation of Texas a fait accompli, it was all the more important, in Van Buren's view, that those Northern interests opposed to annexation be represented in the new administration. Who was better able to represent those Northern interests than the former president? Who had been more instrumental in carrying New York for the new president? Besides, Polk had already told him that he would rely heavily on his recommendations and indicated that he was prepared to give one of his two top cabinet positions, state or treasury, to a New Yorker. In response, Van Buren spent months after the election preparing a list of his recommendations for the cabinet.[39]

Instead of looking to Van Buren to help decide the makeup of his cabinet, however, Polk rejected most of his advice. In fairness to the president-elect, he did consider Van Buren's recommendations seriously and offered the governor-elect, Silas Wright, the position of treasury secretary. He was even willing to consider Wright for secretary of state should he decline his first offer. He later offered Van Buren the position of minister to Britain.

Even so, Polk acted duplicitously. His offer to Wright was made more in deference to the dying Andrew Jackson than to Van Buren and in the knowledge that Wright had no interest in a cabinet position. When Wright declined to serve in the cabinet, Polk looked outside New York to fill the two top positions in his cabinet. His only high-level appointment from the Empire State was Van Buren's rival, William Marcy, whom the new president appointed as secretary of war.[40]

For his treasury secretary, Polk named Robert Walker of Mississippi, who had helped lead the anti–Van Buren forces at the Baltimore convention. For his secretary of state, he appointed Senator James Buchanan of Pennsylvania. Although Buchanan campaigned for Van Buren in 1840, he announced before the 1844 convention that he did not think the former president should run again. He also favored the annexation of Texas and catered to Southern interests. The generally implacable former president was furious at the way Polk treated him. Believing the expansionist and pro-Southern makeup of his cabinet was fraught with danger for the future of the Democratic Party and for the Republic, he rejected the offer of minister to London and planned to withdraw from politics completely.[41]

This proved easier said than done. Although he remained at Lindenwald, he was unable to turn away from politics. He was greatly concerned with a schism between two Democratic factions in his state, one more radical than the other. The more radical group, known as the Barnburners, was opposed to the extension of slavery, expanding the public debt, and the power of large corporations. Among its leaders was Van Buren's own son, John. The second of his sons and the most politically active and astute of them, he had been a free-spending playboy before establishing a law practice in Albany, marrying, and raising a family. Following in his father's footsteps, he became an important force in New York politics. More charismatic than the former president, he was a dynamic speaker, although he was more extreme in his views than his father, as well as less pragmatic.[42]

Opposing the Barnburners were the Hunkers, who were less concerned with the issue of slavery and more concerned with promoting market enterprise through such measures as state banks and internal improvements. They were also more pro-Southern than the Barnburners. Before the election, Van Buren had worked successfully to get the two factions to unite behind Polk. The Barnburners remained incensed at Polk's treatment of Van Buren. They were also angry that the outgoing governor appointed a Hunker, Henry Foster, to replace Wright in the U.S. Senate. As a result, they resumed their struggle against the Hunkers. Already in deep mourning at the recent loss of his wife, John Van Buren was especially unforgiving toward them.

For the former president, developments could not have been worse. He feared the disintegration of everything he had worked for both nationally and at home. He also grieved with John over the loss of his daughter-in-law, and he worried about his son's emotional state. He found some solace in the fact that the Democratic caucus in New York in February reelected John as state attorney general over his Hunker opponent. The state legislature also elected a Barnburner, John Dix, over Foster for the Senate. Still, John won by just one vote, and Dix only narrowly defeated Foster. The Democratic Party remained badly divided.

Over the next few years, matters went from bad to worse. For reasons not entirely of Polk's doing, much of the federal patronage for New York, which Polk had promised to Van Buren, went instead to the Hunkers, who were able to undermine Wright's bid for reelection in 1846 and to deny John Van Buren's renomination as state attorney general. In 1847, the party split in two when John helped lead the Barnburners out of a state party convention dominated by the Hunkers. The annexation of Texas led to war with Mexico and the acquisition of the entire Southwest. In 1846, Congressman David Wilmot of Pennsylvania introduced the Wilmot Proviso. In response, several Southern states passed resolutions that would deny Congress the authority to prohibit the extension of slavery into any of the territories acquired as a result of the Mexican–American War.

Van Buren watched these developments with a heavy heart. Although he opposed his son's plan to call a mass meeting to endorse the Wilmot Proviso, he sided increasingly with his son and the Barnburners. He also took a harder stand against Southern demands to expand slavery into the territories. In 1848, he wrote a long defense of Congress's authority over the territories in which he asserted that free labor and slave labor could not coexist in the same territory. In essence, he enunciated what became known as the doctrine of "free soil, free labor, free men." In April Van Buren's document was published in the *New York Atlas* and came to be known as the Barnburner Manifesto.[43]

Van Buren's intent was not to break up the Democratic Party but to remind the president and the Southern wing of the party that their interests were not in concert with Northern interests. They also conflicted with the Constitution and legislative precedent insofar as the expansion of slavery into the territories was concerned. There was no evidence that the founding fathers ever meant to expand or to protect slavery beyond its current limits. Whether he liked it or not, the former president was entering into an ideological canyon that would echo with the call of "free soil, free labor" for the years remaining before the American Civil War.

Besides the possible disintegration of the Democratic Party, personal matters also persuaded Van Buren to reenter the political arena. Eight months after being defeated for governor, Silas Wright suddenly died. The death of his close friend hit Van Buren hard. Accustomed to having his children near him, he also watched as they scattered in different directions. His second youngest son, and the only one not to marry, Martin Jr., suffered from chronic tuberculosis. All his children depended on him for money. He became lonely at Lindenwald and decided to spend the winter in New York City. It was there that he wrote the Barnburner Manifesto.

In 1848, John asked his father to allow the Barnburners to offer his name for president at the Democratic Convention in Baltimore later that year. "Nothing could be more cruel to me or more destructive of the stand you and your friends have acquired in the state," Van Buren replied.[44] He did not close the door entirely to his son's proposal; he made it clear that the Barnburners should insist on being recognized at the convention as New York's regular Democratic Party.

When the Democrats met again, they refused to give the Barnburners the acknowledgment they demanded. They also adopted an anti–Wilmot Proviso platform and nominated an expansionist, Lewis Cass of Michigan, as their presidential nominee. John and other Barnburners responded by bolting the meeting and attending their own convention in Utica, where they laid the groundwork for a new party. The former president decided to join them. New York Democrats, he told Francis Blair, had been so "grossly humiliated" by the regular Democratic Party that they might never participate again at a national convention.[45]

After the Utica meeting, a much larger gathering of antislavery forces met at Buffalo, where they formed the Free Soil Party on a platform of "Free Soil, Free Speech, Free Labor, and Free Men." In a document prepared for the Buffalo meeting, Van Buren chastised the Democrats for including in their platform the provision against the Wilmot Proviso and called for keeping "the evils of slavery" out of the territories.[46] The new party responded by nominating Van Buren as its presidential candidate. Ironically, it chose as his running mate Charles Francis Adams, the son of Van Buren's inveterate foe for so many years, John Quincy Adams.

The former president doubted he could win the election. He also had qualms about leading a third-party movement against the party he once helped form. He believed that the time was ripe for a new party opposed to the expansion of slavery into the territories. Although he remained a Jacksonian on most other issues, his views on slavery had matured considerably even within the past few months. Not only did he now believe that Congress had the authority to limit slavery, but that it must do so. Reluctantly he accepted the Free Soil Party nomination, the first time that a former president had been nominated by another party. His acceptance sent shock waves through the Democratic Party, which feared the harm Van Buren's candidacy could do to its own nominee. President Polk called Van Buren "the most fallen man I have ever known."[47]

In the November elections, Van Buren failed to carry any state. He received 300,000 votes, or about 10 percent of the ballots cast. Although that was less than what he had hoped for, it was nevertheless impressive for a new party. It allowed the Whig candidate, Zachary Taylor, to carry several states he might otherwise have lost, including New York. Although there had been strong suspicion about Van Buren's candidacy among antislavery forces, the former president worked hard to mobilize them behind him. Continuing his practice of not campaigning publicly, he used all the tricks of modern politics he had introduced into campaigning, including mass rallies and sharply worded newspaper editorials.

The 1848 campaign, however, was Van Buren's last hoorah. Although he lived another fourteen years, he engaged in no more political campaigns. For a time, it seemed that his son, John, might follow in his father's footsteps, seeking state and national office. By 1850, John had become tired of political life, in part because New York politics seemed like quicksand to an aspiring politician. Under his leadership, Barnburners and Hunkers resolved many of their differences, but new cracks reemerged between the so-called Hards and Softs (pro- and anti-Southern factions, respectively). Disgusted with politics, John resumed the dissipated lifestyle he had followed as a youth. Without John's career to support and without influence in the Democratic Party, Van Buren became just a political spectator. In 1852, he returned to the Democratic fold and voted for Democratic candidates for the remainder of his life.

Without political ambition either for himself or his son, Van Buren made the most of this last chapter of his life. In 1849, he lost another daughter-in-law, the wife of Smith Thompson, Van Buren's youngest son, who had been married only a few years and was left with three children. The family lived with the former president at Lindenwald. It was Smith Thompson who persuaded his reluctant father to undertake a major expansion and remodeling of Lindenwald, at great expense to the former president. Hating the gaudy new residence at first, Van Buren came to appreciate some of its modern conveniences, including central heat. Smith ran Lindenwald efficiently. Although he later remarried and moved away, Van Buren willed the estate to him.[48]

During his retirement years, Van Buren watched as many of his longtime friends, allies, and even enemies passed away, including perhaps the greatest cohort of U.S. senators in the nation's history, Calhoun, Clay, and Webster. Increasingly concerned with the deteriorating health of his second youngest son, Martin Jr., who had entered the last stages of his long bout with tuberculosis, the former president sent him to the finest doctors in London and Paris. In 1854, he had him join him at a villa he had rented in Sorrento, Italy, near Naples. On 19 March 1855, Martin Jr. died at the age of forty.

Van Buren had rented the villa in Sorrento as part of an extended trip to Europe, during which he traveled to Ireland, France, Holland, Switzerland, and Italy. Wherever he went, he was received with all the ceremony normally given to a high state official. His schedule of sightseeing, parties, dinners, the theater, and operas exhausted even his friends, who had accompanied him during his travels but found it necessary to go their separate ways.[49]

While in Sorrento, Van Buren began in earnest a project he had started earlier: his autobiography. He continued writing the memoir after returning to the United States in 1855. Although he never completed it, he wrote more than 1,200 pages.[50] Unfortunately, the autobiography was discursive and turgid stylistically and ended in 1835, a year before he was elected president. It contained interesting insights into such historical figures as Jefferson, Jackson, Calhoun, Clay, and Webster. Van Buren also wrote an informative history of American political parties.

During the last years of his life, the now elderly former president had to watch over the dissolution of the Union. Although he always voted Democratic, he lamented the pro-Southern policies of both the Franklin Pierce and James Buchanan administrations. He regretted especially the Kansas–Nebraska Act of 1854, which made the Missouri Compromise inoperative by allowing the two states to organize as territories on the basis of popular sovereignty. Although he did not vote for Abraham Lincoln, he supported the president's efforts to suppress the Confederacy.

Van Buren did not live to see the end of the Civil War. For most of his life, he had been in remarkably good health. Perhaps because of his love of fine foods and wines, he developed gout in his fifties. For most of the remainder of his life, he visited various spas in an effort to find relief from the painful disease. He also suffered from chronic asthma. Although these were relatively minor problems, beginning around 1861, his health deteriorated rapidly. He came down with pneumonia, his asthma worsened, and his circulatory system began to fail. By the spring of 1862, he was spending most of his days in bed. In mid-July, his condition became terminal. On 21 July, he went into a coma, and he died three days later at the age of seventy-nine. He was buried at the Kinderhook Reformed Cemetery.[51]

After Van Buren's death, there was the normal national grief for a dead former president. President Abraham Lincoln prepared a short statement in which he remarked that even while dying, Van Buren's "prayers were for the restoration of the authority of the government of which he had been head." Undoubtedly this was Van Buren's wish, but there is no evidence that was his final prayer before slipping into a coma and dying. Although the Union mourned the passing of a president, there was not the outpouring of grief that had accompanied the death of other former presidents. As president and former president, he never enjoyed the elevated heights of most of those presidents who had preceded him. Lindenwald never became the same tourist attraction that Mount Vernon, Monticello, or the Hermitage did.[52]

Van Buren's activities as a former president, however, were almost as important as his activities in helping to establish the nation's modern party system. He was the first defeated president to seek to reclaim his office, using the techniques of partisan politics he had developed and mastered. He was also the first former president to be the presidential candidate of a third-party movement. Just as in the case of John Quincy Adams, Martin Van Buren's greatest contributions to the nation's history, therefore, were made before and after he served as president. In both cases, they erased whatever vestiges remained of the republican ideal of the role of former presidents.

A daguerreotype (a primitive photographic process) of Martin Van Buren in the 1850s by Matthew Brady, one of the nation's early photographers, who once said that his "greatest aim was to advance the aim of photography" and was most celebrated for his pictorial record of the Civil War. By the time Van Buren sat for this daguerreotype, he was long retired but was deeply disturbed by the South's push to extend slavery westward. (Courtesy of the National Portrait Gallery, Smithsonian Institution.)

III

James K. Polk lived only three months after his term ended. Frail throughout his life, he had a long history of illness due to a chronic kidney condition and surgery to remove a kidney stone while he was still a youth. The surgery, performed under primitive conditions without the benefit of anesthesia, probably left him impotent and explains why he and his wife, Sarah, never had children. As president, Polk fought repeated bouts of illness. A workaholic, he looked forward to his retirement. "I am sure I shall be a happier man in my retirement than I have been during the four years I have filled the highest office in the gift of my countrymen," he wrote in his diary at the very end of his term.[53]

Completely exhausted by the time he left the White House, Polk nevertheless decided to follow a long and circuitous route home to Nashville, Tennessee. Traveling by steamboat and rail down the Atlantic Coast and along the Gulf of Mexico, he visited such cities as Charleston, South Carolina; Montgomery, Alabama; and New Orleans before taking a steamboat up the Mississippi River to Memphis and then into Nashville. During the four-week trip, he was frequently ill with a high fever. After being at home for less than three months, sorting through his papers and books and enjoying retirement, he suffered severe diarrhea. Doctors assumed he had cholera. His condition worsened rapidly. Not a practicing Christian, he sought a deathbed baptism into the Methodist Church. On 15 June 1849, he died at the age of fifty-three, the first president to serve out his term and then be denied any meaningful period as a former president.[54]

Polk had been preceded into the White House by a hero of the War of 1812, William Henry Harrison, whom the Whigs had chosen as their candidate over Henry Clay. Unfortunately, Harrison lived only one month after taking office. He died on 4 April 1841 of pneumonia complicated by poor medical treatment. For the first time, a vice president, John Tyler of Virginia, a recent convert from the Democratic Party to the Whig Party, became president upon the death of the incumbent.

Tyler seemed destined to be president almost from the time he was born on 29 March 1790 into the plantation gentry of Virginia. A graduate of William and Mary College and a lawyer, he was elected to the Virginia House of Representatives in 1816 at the age of twenty-one. This was the beginning of a career in state and national politics that included election to both Houses of Congress and twice to the governorship of Virginia.

Standing just over six feet tall, slender, with an angular face, a high forehead, blue eyes, and an aquiline nose, the future president was a staunch supporter of the South and states' rights, who opposed the Missouri Compromise and the Tariff of Abominations. He also spoke with vitriol against the growing abolitionist movement, which he accused of being part of a British plot to destroy the Southern economy and way of life.

Yet Tyler became known throughout his career for his political independence and for making republican principles foundational to his views on states' rights and strict construction of the Constitution. Although loyal to the South, he had qualms about the evils of slavery and supported the colonization of slaves to Africa. He even served in 1838 as president of the Virginia Colonization Society. He also opposed the nullification movement of the 1830s and the gag rule prohibiting Congress from receiving antislavery petitions because he believed it was unconstitutional and strategically unwise. Because of his opposition to what he considered Jackson's unconstitutional exercise of executive power in removing government deposits from the BUS, he left the Democratic Party to become a Whig.

It was this same streak of independence and adherence to strict constructionalism that got him into so much trouble as president with Henry Clay and other Whig leaders, who had a more expansive view of the role of government, including a protective tariff and the establishment of a new national bank. His opposition to these measures helped undermine his presidency. Disliked by both Whigs and Democrats in Congress, Tyler was often referred to by his contemporaries as the "accidental president." After his veto of several banking and tariff measures supported by the Whig leadership in Congress, there was even the first presidential impeachment investigation in the nation's history. When Tyler left the White House in 1849, the overwhelming consensus in political circles was "good riddance."[55]

Often forgotten about Tyler was that he was responsible for establishing the principle that on the death of a president, the vice president became the president in fact, rather than staying vice president while serving merely as acting president. The Constitution was vague on the issue of succession, including the title and role of a vice president when a serving president died. As the first vice president to be placed in this position, Tyler established the precedent that was followed by other vice presidents after the death of the incumbent until it was formally incorporated into the Constitution by the Twenty-Fifth Amendment in 1967.[56]

Having been read out of the Whig Party as president, Tyler had hopes for a time of winning the Democratic presidential nomination in 1844. Later, he even had himself nominated at his own splinter party convention. When it became clear that he had little chance of being a major political force either within or outside the Democratic Party, he gave up his political aspirations for the moment and retired to a 1,150-acre plantation he had recently purchased along the James River, about thirty-five miles south of Richmond and not far from where he had been born.

Tyler named the plantation Sherwood Forest. Some writers have speculated that he gave it that name to reflect his belief that he had been ostracized by the Whig Party much as the mythical figure Robin Hood had been outlawed to Sherwood Forest. The estate's two-and-a-half-story frame residence, which was surrounded by a beautiful twenty-five-acre grove of large oaks, was over 300 feet long and included a sixty-eight-foot ballroom that Tyler added to cater to the popular dance of the time, the Virginia reel. The dwelling had a large front porch with four columns, two wings on either side of the main house, windows the length of each floor, and dormers along the attic roof. Still being remodeled when the Tylers occupied the mansion, it was elegantly decked out with expensive furniture, mirrors, rugs, and a chandelier, all of which the Tylers had purchased at the time they were married. Between sixty and seventy slaves lived on the plantation. At first unwelcome by the locals, who were mostly Whigs, Tyler and his wife, Julia, whom he had married after his first wife, Leticia Christian, died in 1842, gradually gained acceptance by reaching out to their neighbors, visiting them, and being congenial hosts.[57]

As a former president, Tyler devoted most of his time to overseeing his plantation and raising the fifteen children he fathered with Leticia and Julia—more than any other president. He quickly encountered serious financial problems that remained with him until he died. Because of the illness and death of Leticia, Tyler did not entertain as much at the White House as other presidents. As a result, Tyler managed to save a fair amount from his $25,000 salary (the equivalent of about $613,000 in 2009). Julia also brought a considerable inheritance to the marriage, and the president was able to sell land in Kentucky he had purchased in the 1830s.

The elaborate lifestyle the Tylers enjoyed and the costs of raising a large family still took their toll on the former president's finances. As a farmer, Tyler proved himself able, knowledgeable, and willing to engage in scientific experimentation with different types of seed and fertilizer. As a result, his crops of wheat and corn were generally profitable. In years of poor harvests or low prices, he found it necessary to borrow heavily to make ends meet. Julia was forced to cut back on the social activities she loved. Throughout his retirement years, Tyler found himself having to borrow from one bank in order to pay off the notes due another. To get out of debt, he even dreamed of moving to California or grubstaking a family member to take advantage of the gold rush there. By the time he died in 1862, Julia was already faced with various claims against her husband's estate that only grew worse in later years.[58]

In addition to the cares of his plantation, Tyler had to deal with tensions between the children of his first marriage and their new stepmother and the problems of his wayward married son, John Tyler Jr., who drank, was frequently separated from his wife, and often got into brawls. Not until the mid-1850s did John settle down in Philadelphia, where he practiced law with his brother, Robert. Although all was not bliss at Sherwood Forest, Tyler generally enjoyed the life of a country squire, entertaining visitors, showing off his beautiful and vivacious wife, playing his violin, amusing his grandchildren, hunting for deer in the nearby woods, and serving as rector of the board of visitors of his alma mater, William and Mary College.

Besides tending to his plantation and to family matters, the former president was concerned with establishing his place in history and avoiding becoming an historical nonentity. "All that I should ask of any man," he wrote to his son, Robert, after leaving office, "would be, that as far as in him lies he would represent me to the public as, I feel, justice . . . would require."[59] Encouraged by his brother-in-law, Alexander Gardiner, he even entertained the possibility of a political comeback should the Democratic Party, which he rejoined in 1844, become deadlocked in 1848. He wrote letters to newspaper editors about issues of the moment in order to keep his name before the public. In 1846, he made a highly publicized return to Washington to defend Daniel Webster against charges that, as his secretary of state, Webster had made personal use of a presidential secret service fund. Webster was later acquitted of these charges.[60]

Mainly, however, the former president was concerned about being given proper credit for his role in annexing Texas. He was touched by various tributes he received from Texans thanking him for the annexation. At the same time, he was deeply annoyed when former secretary of state Calhoun announced on the Senate floor that he was responsible for bringing Texas into the Union and that the expansion of slavery was the core reason for annexation. National, not sectional, interest dictated his actions, the former president insisted. "If ever there was an American question . . . Texas was that very question," he explained.[61]

Similarly, he took umbrage when various critics claimed, without accusing Tyler himself of corruption, that speculators in Texas land and bonds had been instrumental in his decision to annex Texas. In two letters to the *Richmond Enquirer,* which were subsequently published in the Northern press, the ex-president rejected these charges emphatically. He did not deny, however, that several friends and members of his administration had engaged in land and bond deals before Texas was annexed. When these shady deals were exposed in the press, Tyler was mortified. He was further embarrassed by a bitter exchange with the former president of the Lone Star Republic, Sam Houston, who raised probing questions about how Tyler would have reacted constitutionally if Texas had been invaded by Mexico immediately after annexation. Instead of resonating to his credit, therefore, the former president's decision to annex Texas was a burden he had to bear for the remainder of his life.[62]

Increasingly, Tyler turned his attention to the mounting sectional crisis that led to the Civil War in 1861. Although always hoping for a peaceful resolution of the growing divide between the North and South and never a firebrand himself, he became more and more outspoken on the issue of slavery and the abolitionist movement. Whatever doubts he might have entertained about the evils of slavery were consumed by his determination to maintain the Southern way of life and by his hatred of the abolitionists.

In the past, as Tyler insisted in his colloquy with Calhoun, his strong emphasis on territorial expansion had been motivated primarily by a Jeffersonian concept of an expanding agrarian republic rather than by thoughts of slavery expansion. Although he always opposed efforts at keeping slavery out of the

This portrait of John Tyler was painted by George Healy in 1859 at his plantation in Virginia. By this time Tyler was nearing his seventies, but still deeply concerned with trying to avert the Civil War. The artist, George Healy, had studied in Europe and had painted the portraits of a number of prominent Americans, including Daniel Webster, Henry Clay, and John Calhoun. (Courtesy of National Portrait Gallery, Smithsonian Institution; gift of Friends of the National Institute.)

territories, he argued as a young congressman during the Missouri crisis that diffusion of the slave population through expansion increased the prospects for the abolition of slavery in states like Virginia. A quarter of a century later, he even expressed serious misgivings about a war between Mexico and the United States over Texas because it would exacerbate the entire debate over the expansion of slavery.

Like other Southerners, however, the former president came more and more to regard the denial of slavery expansion into the territories as immoral. Once the war with Mexico began in 1846, he lent his full support to the conflict, referring to it as "the most just war ever fought by the American people." Later, he blasted the Wilmot Proviso as a "gratuitous insult on the slave States." He also grew more defensive about the slavery system itself. In this he was joined by his wife, Julia. In 1853, she attracted national attention by writing a lengthy article, first published in the New York *Herald* and Richmond *Enquirer,* in which she attacked the British abolitionists' interference in American internal affairs. She then portrayed the Southern treatment of slaves as benign. Tyler boasted proudly of the "universal approval and admiration" his wife's article received. He even claimed it was unmatched "in the annals of our history."[63]

At the same time, the former president reluctantly supported the Compromise of 1850 because it was purposely vague on the issue of slavery in the new territories of Utah and New Mexico, incorporated a strong fugitive slave measure, and offered an alternative to tearing the Democratic Party apart and chancing a civil war. He also endorsed the Kansas–Nebraska Act of 1854 because it nullified the Missouri Compromise and incorporated the concept of popular sovereignty, which he hoped against hope might be a way of resolving the question of slavery expansion in the territories. As he feared, the bloody conflict in Kansas between pro- and antislavery forces only brought the nation closer to the sectional conflict he sought to avoid.[64]

As Tyler's own views on slavery hardened, his worries about a possible slave insurrection also mounted, especially following the raid on Harpers Ferry in 1859 by the abolitionist John Brown. Emotions ran high as residents debated the relative merits of union or secession. For Tyler, the raid amounted to proof of the abolitionists' determination to lead a slave rebellion against the South. Although still firmly on the side of remaining within the Union, the former president, who was approaching the age of seventy and not in good health, became a captain, in a mounted security force of elderly men, to guard against a slave revolt.[65]

Having come to regard himself as an elder statesman, who in the mid-1850s even offered to negotiate a peaceful solution to the Crimean War between England, France, and Russia, Tyler entertained notions again in 1860 of gaining the Democratic nomination for president in an anticipated deadlocked convention in Charleston. He was buoyed by the enthusiastic reception to recent speeches he had given at several commemorative events. He convinced himself that if his name was placed before the convention, the whole South would rally behind his nomination.

That proved wishful thinking, based on an exaggerated sense of his popularity among the party faithful. Instead, when dissident Southern Democrats walked out of the Charleston meeting, they held their own gathering and nominated John C. Breckinridge of Kentucky for president rather than accepting the nominee of the regular Democratic Party, Stephen Douglas of Illinois. Tyler reluctantly threw his support behind Breckinridge. He might have supported and voted for the moderate, John Bell, of his native state, running as a Constitutional Unionist, except he thought Bell had no possibility of winning. Instead, he pinned his hopes on the chance that Breckinridge would get enough electoral votes to throw the election into the House of Representatives, where his own choice for president, Joseph Lane of Oregon, a South-leaning Northerner, might emerge as a compromise candidate.

When instead Lincoln was elected in November, the former president thought the outcome would likely lead to the breakup of the Union because of Lincoln's outspoken opposition to the extension of slavery into the territories. Even after South Carolina seceded from the Union and six other deep cotton states followed by the end of January, Tyler sought a way to prevent a civil war by supporting a compromise proposed by Senator John Crittenden of Kentucky that would extend the Missouri Compromise line of 36°30' across the territories and guarantee to maintain slavery where it already existed. When Lincoln rejected the compromise, the former president headed a peace convention in Washington of twelve border states, half slave and half free. Virginia had called the convention in a last-ditch effort to prevent a war. He held two meetings with outgoing president James Buchanan in which he won Buchanan's assurances that he would take no military action against the seceded states.

The Northern press, however, ridiculed Tyler. Reporters even raised questions about the former president's loyalty to the Union. The *Paterson Daily Guardian* referred to him as a "powerless, brainless, old, office-seeking curmudgeon whom all parties and all peoples abhor," while the *New York Times* simply called him a "traitor." The fact that his granddaughter, Leticia Tyler, who had been born in the White House while he was president, raised the new flag of the Confederacy above the capital in Montgomery, Alabama, seemed to substantiate what was being reported in the Northern press.[66]

There was probably never any doubt in Tyler's mind that should his efforts to keep the Union together fail, his loyalty would be to the new Confederacy. His view on states' rights and the importance of permitting the extension of slavery dictated that course. He did not announce his decision until after the Washington Peace Conference amended the Crittenden Compromise to remove the guarantee on slavery expansion south of the Missouri Compromise line. As a result, Tyler found himself in the embarrassing position of voting against the recommendations of the very gathering he had helped assemble.

On the day after the failed convention, the former president delivered an impassioned speech in Virginia urging his fellow Virginians to join the secessionist movement. He then sat as an elected member of the Virginia State Convention, where he spoke fervently in support of secession. "Where is that Union now which we once so loved?" he asked. "Wrong, abuse, contumely, unconstitutional acts, looking to a higher law than the Constitution," he declared.[67]

After Virginia approved its ordnance of secession in April, Tyler headed the commission that negotiated the terms of the state's admission into the Confederacy, including moving the Confederate capital to Richmond. Not surprisingly, he blamed Lincoln for the breakup of the Union, even suggesting that he acted not for patriotic reasons but as a way of consolidating behind him the "Black Republican" faction of his Republican Party.[68]

In the months that followed, Tyler took great satisfaction at the early Confederate victories, but he protested vigorously to the Confederate government when the harvesting of his crop was delayed because half his slaves had been requisitioned for digging duty around Williamsburg. The war also struck home when Union soldiers, bent on punishing the former president, who had been elected to the Confederate House of Representatives, commandeered, and later ravaged, a summer home he owned near Hampton.

Tyler never took his seat in the Confederate House. For some time, he had been suffering from various gastric problems and was susceptible to heavy colds and influenza. Even more serious, he had recurring bouts of dizziness, probably due to a series of small strokes. On 12 January, while awaiting in Richmond for the Confederate legislature's opening session, he became nauseated and dizzy and later had what was probably another stroke. Believing he was suffering from bronchitis and liver dysfunction, doctors prescribed morphine and ordered him to bed. Although still able to receive callers for several days, he suddenly took a turn for the worse and died just after midnight, 18 January 1862, at the age of seventy-one.[69]

Tyler was buried with the all the honors the Confederacy could bestow on one of its most illustrious citizens. His open, flag-draped coffin lay in state for two days at the Confederate Congress. His funeral service at Richmond's St. Paul's Episcopal Church was attended by Confederate president Jefferson Davis and most other high Confederate officials. A train of 150 carriages followed his casket to the Hollywood Cemetery, where he was buried not far from where James Monroe's body lay. Not unexpectedly, the North reacted to news of Tyler's death by virtually ignoring it. An unpopular president and a traitor to his country had died. During the war, Union forces vandalized his plantation just as they had earlier ransacked his Hampton home. Congress did not even place an official marker at his grave site until fifty years later.[70]

In assessing Tyler's post-presidential career, it seems too harsh to conclude that the former president was a traitor to the Union unless one is prepared to make that same judgment of everyone who had held high civil or military office before the Civil War but then decided to join the Confederacy. Labeling the former president a traitor seems particularly harsh because the thrust of his political efforts in the 1850s was to stave off the firebrands of the secessionist movement by working for an accommodation between North and South.

Like the nation's second president, John Adams, Tyler had been obsessed in his retirement years with redeeming his place in history, especially with being given proper credit for the annexation of Texas, which he regarded as his greatest achievement. The harder he sought to achieve what he believed was his proper place in history, however, the more he and his administration came under unfavorable scrutiny.

Throughout his retirement, Tyler also maintained an unrealistic hope that if he somehow managed to keep his name in the limelight through public comment, letters to the editors, and personal contacts, lightning might strike, and he would be called on to lead the Democratic Party to victory in a presidential election. Notwithstanding entreaties from mostly a small group of Virginians, who did embrace him, most politicians, even in the South, just preferred to forget him. Even his efforts at peacemaking in 1861 were misbegotten, given how late they came and how insoluble the slavery issue had become. As a result, he found himself not only ridiculed in the Northern press but in the untenable position of providing fodder for the very secessionist movement his peace gathering was intended to short-circuit.

The fact remains that like Jackson and Van Buren before him, a former president whose whole political outlook had been premised on republican virtues and values remained a partisan politician. Not only did he fail to see any inconsistency between republican values and partisan politics, but he believed, as a partisan Southern Democrat and slave owner, that he was working selflessly to preserve the Republic.

4

Doughface Former Presidents
Fillmore, Pierce, and Buchanan

In 1850, the great American poet and antislavery advocate Walt Whitman wrote a poem, "Dough-face Song," which was published by the New York *Evening Post*. It read in part:

> We are all docile dough-faces,
> They knead us with the fist
> They, the dashing southern lords,
> We labor as they list
> For them we speak—or hold our tongue
> From them we turn and twist.

In writing these verses, Whitman was directing his anger at pliant Northern congressmen who, he believed, compromised with the South over the expansion of slavery into the territories. The doughfaces were, of course, these Northern congressmen who allowed themselves to be "kneaded," "turned," and "twisted" by the "southern lords."[1]

Whitman did not coin the term *doughface*. Its origin can be traced back to the debate over the Missouri Compromise in 1819, when Congressman John Randolph of Virginia expressed his contempt of Northerners who voted with the South. About these Northerners, Randolph commented, "They were scared of their own dough faces—yes, they were scared at their own dough faces!—We had them, and if we wanted three more, we could have had them." By the time Whitman wrote his poem, *doughface* had become a synonym for Northerners who supported Southern policies, especially as they concerned territorial expansion. Antislavery forces regarded these Northerners as weak and unsubstantial, lacking either character or depth.[2]

Included among those commonly accused of being doughfaces were the United States' three presidents between 1849 and 1861: Millard Fillmore (1849–

1853), Franklin Pierce (1853–1857), and James Buchanan (1857–1861). Fillmore lived twenty-one years after being president (1853–1874), Pierce twelve years (1857–1869), and Buchanan just seven years (1861–1868). Although they led very different lives, they shared two characteristics. They failed to realize that they had been doughface presidents or that they had provided ample reason to be tagged with that label. They also died convinced they had led exemplary administrations. Of the three, only Fillmore's post-presidency was distinctive. The others were undistinguished and even tragic.

I

Perhaps no president has been as much ridiculed as the nation's most forgettable president as Millard Fillmore; there is even a Millard Fillmore Society that meets each year on his birthday to celebrate his obscurity. It is hard, however, not to be sympathetic to Fillmore, not only because he has been the butt of so much banter about his obscurity but also because his was truly a remarkable story of someone who picked himself up by his bootstraps to achieve the nation's highest political office. With the exception of Andrew Jackson, no other earlier president had to overcome so much economic adversity as Fillmore. Born into poverty in 1800 in upstate New York, he received little formal education beyond reading, writing, and basic arithmetic. However, he was ambitious and had a passion for learning. At age nineteen, he enrolled in a nearby academy. With the help of a teacher, Abigail Powers, who was only two years his senior and whom he later married, he furthered his education. Moving to nearby Buffalo, already a booming village of about 8,000 people and the terminal of the Erie Canal, he studied the law with a local attorney. In 1823, he was admitted to the bar.

Fillmore's humble background affected him throughout his life. It left him with a drive to succeed, even if that sometimes meant having to compromise on principles in which he deeply believed. He also remained aware of his limited education and legal training, for which he tried to compensate by constant reading, by careful attention to detail, and by maintaining a deferential attitude toward those he considered of superior education and intellect. He quickly developed a reputation for temperate habits and professional ethics. Lacking oratorical skills, he preferred small groups to large audiences; he spoke slowly and deliberately, and he substituted practical argument and the use of common household words for rhetorical flourishes.

Fillmore's good looks added to his appeal. About six feet tall, well built, with light complexion, blue eyes, thick eyebrows, a high forehead, and a full head of wavy hair, he was strikingly handsome. He was also immaculately groomed and a meticulous dresser. His polished and dignified bearing often made him seem more confident and self-assured than he actually was. Fundamentally, he was a modest man of modest abilities.[3]

First elected to the New York state assembly in 1828, Fillmore ran successfully for Congress in 1832 and rose to become chairman of the powerful Ways and Means Committee. By 1840, he was one of the leading figures in the Whig Party and in control of the party machinery in western New York. In Congress, he supported internal improvements, a national banking system, and a protective tariff. Never an abolitionist or even a leader of the growing antislavery movement in the North, he nevertheless developed an abhorrence for slavery and opposed the annexation of Texas as a slave territory. Elected in 1848 as vice president on the ticket headed by Zachary Taylor, Fillmore assumed the presidency after Taylor's sudden death in 1850 after serving only sixteen months as president.

As president, Fillmore's greatest achievement was his role in winning approval of the Compromise of 1850, which provided for admitting California as a free state but allowed the issue of slavery in the rest of the territory ceded by Mexico following the Mexican–American War to be decided by popular sovereignty. The compromise also incorporated a much-toughened Fugitive Slave Law that required the forced return without the right of trial of any blacks accused of being runaway slaves. Throughout the whole legislative process, Fillmore was guided by the same principles of moderation and conciliation that had become the bellwether of his entire political career.[4]

The president's rigid enforcement of the Fugitive Slave Law, including the use of military force, made him appear, however, as a doughface to antislavery forces in the North. Although he hated the measure and knew that the law "would draw down upon his head vials of wrath," he thought that the Constitution required giving up of fugitive slaves.[5] He also thought that rigid enforcement of the measure was necessary to maintain the Union, especially in the light of growing secessionist agitation in the South. First and foremost, he was a nationalist who believed the best way to maintain the Union was by holding the Northern and Southern wings of the Whig Party together, even if that meant compromising on such matters as runaway slaves.[6]

Fillmore's enforcement of the Fugitive Slave Law cost him dearly. The opposition against him was strong enough to deny him the Whig nomination for president in 1852. He took his defeat remarkably well. For most of his administration, he had resolved not to seek reelection. Although he changed his mind, he had never been driven by intense ambition, and he may have sensed the limits of his own abilities to keep the Whig Party together and to lead the country through a critical moment in its history. At one point, he even encouraged the candidacy of his seventy-year-old secretary of state, Daniel Webster, who was already in ill health.[7]

Yet Fillmore had spent most of his life in politics. He had just turned fifty-three when he turned the reins of power over to Pierce; he was thus still a relatively young man who had given up his law practice for a life in politics. Even as he mouthed platitudes about how much he looked forward to his retirement, he also made it clear that he was still interested in returning to the White House.

"While I shall retire from this exalted station without a single regret," he told well-wishers at a farewell dinner in Washington, "I cannot leave your delightful city . . . without feeling a pang of regret." Even before leaving office, he made plans for a tour of the South, allegedly for sightseeing, but in fact to test the waters for another possible bid for president four years hence.[8]

Within a month after leaving office, Fillmore's wife, Abigail, died. A sickly woman, she had contracted pneumonia shortly after attending Pierce's inauguration ceremonies. Abigail's death was a shattering blow to Fillmore.[9] His plans for a Southern tour were put off, as were those to look for a new home in Buffalo. "I feel that I have no strength—no resolution—no energy—the prospect is gloomy," he wrote to his sister shortly after returning to Buffalo to bury his wife of twenty-seven years.[10]

For a few weeks, the former president tried to busy himself by fixing up his old residence. He also visited his son's law practice almost every day to offer him advice and keep his mind busy. Increasingly, however, Fillmore became bored and restless. After about a year of mourning, he decided to come out of retirement and undertake the Southern tour he had planned earlier. What was significant about his decision was not its purpose—another run at the presidency—but the rationale behind it. He believed that former presidents could not, and should not, be ordinary citizens again.

One reason why Fillmore had been looking for a new residence in Buffalo before Abigail died was because he thought his modest frame house, while a proper residence for a New York assemblyman, was not stately enough for a former president. He also believed that former presidents should be paid a pension. Unlike his predecessors, he had no estate, manor, or farm to which he could retire. His $75,000 in resources (the equivalent of about $1.7 million in 2009) still did not provide enough income for him to live in the fashion to which he thought those in his position were entitled. At the same time, he did not believe ex-presidents should be expected to retire from public life simply because of their former status. Indeed, he had been told repeatedly by friends and acquaintances that he was too young to retire. He agreed. Yet it would not be appropriate for former presidents to seek employment in the private sector. Not only would that be demeaning to the office they had served, but it might be resented by their colleagues in their chosen profession. This meant that they should seek some form of public service.

Fillmore never stated his views on the post-presidency in Jeffersonian or Madisonian terms. Mostly they have to be gleaned from speeches and interviews he gave after he left the presidency. They were developed most fully in a wide-ranging interview he gave to the New York *Herald* in 1873, almost twenty years after he left the White House. "It is a national disgrace," he remarked, "that our Presidents, after having occupied the highest position in the country, should be cast adrift and perhaps, be compelled to keep a corner grocery for subsistence. . . . We elect a man to the Presidency, expect him to be honest, to give up a lucrative profession, perhaps, and after we have done with him we let him go into seclusion and perhaps poverty," he added.[11]

As for choosing a profession after leaving office, Fillmore made clear in the same interview that a former president simply could not take any position. He would "have been glad to continue" to practice law, he said, but it would have been resented by his peers. "My colleagues at the bar would say, and quite naturally, 'Here, you have been to the pinnacle and ought to be content.'"[12] In fact, after leaving the White House, the former president had made arrangements to be a law partner with a firm in New York City, but his friends in Buffalo advised strongly against it. "The honor of Buffalo is concerned in the matter," his former law partner and attorney general during his administration, Nathan K. Hall, wrote him, "the most to secure [the] president from falling back to the ambition of ordinary mortals—laboring daily in the ordinary pursuits of life for his daily bread." Fillmore agreed with Hall. Not only did he not resume his law practice, but he also refused a lucrative offer to be a bank president.[13]

Resolved to resume his political career and to seek the presidency, Fillmore began his tour of the South on 1 March 1854. Its ostensible purpose remained sightseeing. He was accompanied on the trip by Nathan Hall and his former secretary of the navy, Joseph P. Kennedy. He also hoped to include in his retinue the noted novelist Washington Irving, with whom he had struck up a friendship a year earlier. However, Irving, who understood the real purpose behind the trip, declined Fillmore's invitation. "I have no inclination to travel with political notorieties, to be smothered by the clouds of party dust whirled up by their chariot-wheels and beset by speechmakers and little great men and bores of every community who might consider Mr. Fillmore a candidate for another presidential term," Irving remarked.[14]

Leaving Buffalo, Fillmore traveled through Ohio and then down the Ohio River from Cincinnati, to Lexington, Louisville, and eventually to New Orleans, where he embarked for Mobile to begin his northern swing. Traveling northward, he visited virtually every important Southern city he had missed on the first leg of his trip, from interior Atlanta, Chattanooga, and Nashville to the ports of Savannah and Charleston before skirting Washington in favor of Baltimore and then to New York City before returning to Buffalo. He arrived home on 25 May.

It had been an exhausting tour with countless speeches and receptions. Throughout the trip, he dwelled on the Compromise of 1850 without mentioning specifically the Fugitive Slaw Law. However, because of his well-known support of that measure, he was greeted with enormous crowds and warm words. The *Richmond Daily Whig* summed up the feeling of most Southerners when it editorialized, "His magnanimous recognition of our constitutional rights in every act of his administration, and his earnest and brave endeavors to enforce the execution of the Fugitive Slave Law, in spite of Abolitionist denunciation and obloquy should not soon be forgotten."[15]

Any doubts about the real purpose of Fillmore's Southern circuit were dispelled when he followed it with a tour of the West, where he visited Chicago, St. Paul, and Dubuque. Once more, he played the role of a private citizen on a sightseeing trip while testing the waters for another presidential candidacy. He considered himself still a Whig at heart. However, he understood that the party was in the midst of disintegration as its Northern and Southern wings split over the issue of slavery. Fillmore's own enforcement of the Fugitive Slave Law had contributed to the Whigs' ongoing dissolution. Even more harmful was the Kansas–Nebraska Act of 1854, which led to the migration into Kansas of pro- and antislavery forces, each of which established separate governments and engaged in a protracted war. The territory became known as Bleeding Kansas. The Kansas–Nebraska Act also contributed to the formation of the Republican Party, which opposed any further expansion of slavery into the territories. Republicans quickly became a powerful political force, especially in the Northwest.

Another political party that emerged out of obscurity was the American Party, more commonly known as the Know-Nothing Party because its members were instructed to reply, when asked about its origins and purpose, "I know nothing." In contrast to the Republican Party, its origins lay not in the sectional agitation over slavery but in a growing nativist movement directed against the recent arrival of large numbers of Catholic Irish immigrants and fear of Roman Catholic influence. For a short while in the 1850s, it became a powerful political force.[16]

The collapse of the Whig Party gave the Know-Nothing Party a much larger pool of potential converts than any other earlier nativist movement. One of those converts was Fillmore, even though he joined the party for reasons of expediency rather than because he agreed with its antiforeign and anti-Catholic views. Before the 1850s, he had never publicly stated any nativist sentiment. As a congressman in the 1840s, he had even expressed alarm over the growing influence of nativism in politics.[17]

At a time, however, when the Whig Party was in the throes of death and the nation's politics were in a state of turmoil, Fillmore saw in the Know-Nothing Party a convenient vehicle from which to launch his bid for the presidency. The flip side of nativist sentiment, after all, was a strong sense of nationalism. This resonated with the urgency the former president attached to maintaining national unity just as the nation seemed to be heading in the opposite direction.

Of all the political alternatives apparent to the former president, the Know-Nothing Party seemed the only viable one. The Whig Party was terminally ill, as was the Free Soil Party, recently renamed the Free Democratic Party to reflect both its antislavery and Jacksonian principles. Like the Free Democratic or Free Soil Party, the newly formed Republican Party was opposed to the expansion of slavery and therefore bound to be equally anathemic to the South. The former president could never join the Democratic Party, whose opposition to tariffs, banks, and internal improvements he had always opposed. The party was also increasingly unacceptable to Northern antislavery forces, which were leaving it to join the new Republican Party, or in some cases what was left of the Whig

Party or the Know-Nothing Party before becoming Republicans. There seemed no other alternative for Fillmore, therefore, than to join the Know-Nothing Party, which had already shown itself to have a significant political base. The trick was to separate himself from its nativist message and build it into a party that crossed sectional lines and stressed the preservation of the Union.

That was what the former president attempted to do before he formally launched his bid for the presidency. When Fillmore decided to make himself available to the Know-Nothings as their presidential candidate is unclear. The unexpected death from cholera in July 1854 of his twenty-two-year-old daughter, Mary Abigail, left him distraught. As he wrote his close friend Dorothea Dix, the famous reformer and philanthropist, "I feel life has little left for me. My good son only of all my little family remains."[18] Just as Fillmore found solace after Abigail's death by returning to politics, so his daughter's death may have had the same effect. By January 1855, he had clearly made up his mind. In the coming months, he urged his friends and supporters to unite behind him in the new party, give it proper direction, and make it into a truly national party.

Toward the end of May, Fillmore left for Europe. His strategy was to leave it to his managers to build the party into a national one of unity with him as its inevitable candidate for president. By staying away from the United States, he would remove himself from the line of fire about his political ambitions or association with the Know-Nothings. His one reservation was how a former president should be treated by foreign dignitaries. Even though this question seemed to have been answered by Martin Van Buren, who was already being received in Europe with all the entitlements of a former head of state, Fillmore expressed concern about knowingly placing himself "in any position where my country would be degraded or insulted through me."[19] Satisfied that this would not happen, he sailed for Europe in May.

Unfortunately for the former president, his plan for the presidency fell short by one half. His European tour, which lasted more than a year, was a great success. He visited every major capital and numerous other European cities as well as Cairo, Jerusalem, and Constantinople. He was entertained by kings and emperors, prime ministers, and distinguished men of all kind. Wherever he went, he impressed his hosts by his courtliness, modesty, and overall bearing. Despite being associated with an anti-Catholic organization, he had an audience with the pope. While he was in London, he met a number of times with Van Buren, and the two former presidents appeared together at the London Opera and in the gallery of the House of Commons, where they were greeted warmly.

Fillmore's managers in the United States, meanwhile, did their job well. In Philadelphia, in June 1855, the national council of the American Party adopted a resolution calling the existing laws on slavery "final and conclusive." Eight months later, Fillmore locked up the party's nomination despite opposition from those who doubted his nativist credentials and from antislavery forces who had gravitated to the party and believed the former president was a doughface. While in Venice, he received official notification of the party's nomination. He accepted the nomination while in Paris, noting that since the end of his administration he had considered his "political life as a public man at an end." He then made clear that the theme of his campaign would be to "quiet the alarming sectional agitation" dividing the country.[20]

Unfortunately for Fillmore, by the time he received the American Party nomination, it was practically worthless. After returning to New York at the end of June, he began what seemed would be a robust campaign. Instead of leaving it to others to stump for him, as was still the precedent for most candidates, he gave more than two dozen speeches as he made his way home from New York City to Buffalo. In his remarks he emphasized the need to preserve the Union, warning, in particular, that if the Republicans won the election, civil war would follow. "We see a political party presenting candidates . . . selected for the first time from the free states alone," he stated in Albany on 26 June. "Can they have the madness or the folly to believe that our southern brethren would submit to be governed by such a chief magistrate?"[21]

After launching the campaign with great enthusiasm, however, Fillmore remained in Buffalo, believing there was no value in repeating what he had already said by barnstorming the country. As a result, the campaign lost much of its initial enthusiasm. Former Whigs who were antislavery diehards also gravitated mostly to the Republican Party. Southern and Northern Democrats who were not antislavery zealots remained Democrats. Other Northern opponents of slavery who had joined the American Party either left it when it became apparent that Fillmore was going to be its nominee, or refused to be muzzled on their most pressing issue. Former Southern Whigs, whom Fillmore had hoped to attract to his candidacy, put off by this antislavery agitation and believing the former president could not win, joined their Southern brethren in the Democratic Party. The slavery issue and his own reputation as a doughface, in other words, kept the former president from fashioning a new unionist party built on a coalition of former Northern and Southern Whigs. "In the North," he lamented, "I am charged with being Proslavery . . . and in the South, I am accused of being an abolitionist."[22]

When the election results were counted in November, Fillmore received about 872,000 votes to 1.34 million votes for the Republican nominee, John Frémont, and 1.83 million for the Democratic candidate and newly elected president, James Buchanan. His nearly 22 percent of the total vote was highly respectable for a new third-party candidate—more than twice the percentage that Van Buren had received running as the candidate of the Free Soil Party in 1848. A change of about 8,000 votes from Buchanan to Fillmore in Kentucky, Tennessee, and Louisiana would have given him those states and thrown the election into the House. As it was, the former president won only the eight electoral votes of Maryland. Buchanan captured the fourteen other slave states, while Fremont won eleven of the sixteen free states. The Whigs, who had not run a candidate, were dead as a party, as was the American Party.

MILLARD FILLMORE,

AMERICAN CANDIDATE FOR PRESIDENT OF THE UNITED STATES.

Millard Fillmore's 1856 campaign poster, on the Native American Party (Know-Nothing) ticket. A bust portrait of Fillmore is flanked by allegorical figures of Justice (left) and Liberty (right). Both figures wear classical gowns and tiaras. Justice holds a large sword and scales, Liberty a staff and Phrygian cap and Constitution. Atop the Fillmore portrait is an eagle, with American flags on either side. A poster for Abraham Lincoln for president in 1860 is strikingly similar to the Fillmore poster with a portrait of a young Lincoln in place of Fillmore's portrait. (Courtesy of Library of Congress, Prints and Photographs Division.)

After the election, Fillmore retired from politics. His immediate concern was supporting himself. That problem was resolved in 1858 when he married Caroline Carmichael McIntosh, the fifty-two-year-old childless widow of a wealthy Troy businessman. Despite speculation after the marriage that Fillmore had married the widow for her money, by all indications, he loved his new wife, and he even had Caroline keep her wealth in her own name.

At the same time, the marriage relieved Fillmore of any further financial concerns. By a prenuptial agreement, he received a fee of $10,000 a year for administering her estate. Carrying out his belief that former presidents should be involved in public affairs and having the means to engage in charitable endeavors, he and wife became active in philanthropic and civic causes in Buffalo. The Fillmores also purchased a large gabled mansion in Gothic style with parapets, balustrades, and simulated towers in a fashionable part of town.[23]

The former president appeared to be generally content with his new life. He was deeply involved with his wife in the affairs of the city he loved, and he was recognized as its first citizen. Yet he despaired at the fact that his reputation was already being sullied by those who cast aspersions at the fact that he had associated himself with the Know-Nothing movement, and by antislavery forces and others who held that his coddling of the South was at least partially responsible for the mounting sectional crisis leading to the Civil War. In response, he shied away from publicity and from public gatherings. He also refused a commission by New York City merchants to go to South Carolina with former president Van Buren to try to keep it from seceding from the Union after Lincoln's election. It could not do any good, he remarked in explaining his decision. "No conciliation would succeed without the cooperation of Republicans." Before he would go, he wanted assurances that they would "treat our Southern brethren as friends," but he distrusted the Republicans too much to believe that would happen.[24] Despairing of both Democrats and Republicans, he became all the more convinced that his efforts to maintain the Union both as president and as a candidate of the American Party had been the correct one.

The former president's great hero was George Washington. As vice president, he had been present at the laying by President Taylor of the ceremonial stone for the construction of the Washington Monument, which was the first erected presidential shrine. Although Fillmore never had the temerity to compare himself to the nation's secular saint, he commented several times on the similarity between Washington's efforts as president to keep the nation together and his own attempts to maintain national unity during a period of mounting sectional crisis.

In 1860, rumors circulated that Fillmore intended to support the Republican nominee for president, Abraham Lincoln. He denied the speculation, making clear that he deprecated all sectional parties. Although it is not entirely clear for whom he voted, the *Buffalo Commercial Advertiser* speculated that he supported the Constitutional Union candidate, John Bell. Although he remained critical of the Republican Party and in 1864 voted for the Democratic candidate for president, George B. McClellan, he hosted President-elect Lincoln when Lincoln visited Buffalo in February 1861 on his way to Washington. He also strongly supported the Union cause during the Civil War. "Our Government calls for aid, and we must give it. Our Constitution is in danger, and we must defend it," he commented at the beginning of hostilities.[25]

Fillmore adhered to these principles throughout the conflict. During the war, he sponsored a rally to help recruit enlistees into the Union army and gave money to help the families of volunteers. He also organized and led a home guard, the Union Continentals, made up of men too old for active duty who paraded in colorful uniforms, to defend Buffalo from an attack. The possibility of an attack from Canada seemed real after the *Trent* affair of 1861. This incident, which involved the Union seizure of the British mail steamer *Trent* and the removal of two Confederate emissaries on their way to Europe, threatened war between the United

States and Britain. In response, Fillmore demanded troops and ammunition to protect Buffalo. "The safety of this city is absolutely essential to the security of the Great Northwestern lakes," he wrote the War Department.[26] Fortunately, the *Trent* affair was settled peacefully after Lincoln agreed to release the two Southerners and allowed them to go to Europe.

After Lincoln's assassination on 15 April 1865, just as the war was drawing to a close, Fillmore's house was smeared with ink because he had failed to drape his house in black as a sign of mourning. The incident hurt the former president deeply because he had been away caring for his wife when Lincoln died. As soon as he returned home, he draped his doorway as mourners all over the city had done. A few days later, he eulogized the murdered president, remarking, "It is well known that I have not approved of all acts which have been done in his name during his Administration, but I am happy to say that his recent course met my approbation, and I had looked forward with confident expectation that he would soon be able to end the war." At the same time, he expressed his hope that the new president, Andrew Johnson, would emphasize reconciliation with the former Confederacy rather than its punishment.[27] After the war, Fillmore criticized what he believed was the Republicans' harsh treatment of the South. He referred to President Ulysses Grant as "a greater general than statesman." In his remaining years, he also condemned the diplomatic and consular service for their lack of training, especially in foreign languages, and called for the professional schooling of future American diplomats similar to that received by those in the British Foreign Office. In addition, he advocated a single six-year term for presidents, "which would enable the successful candidate to entirely master the duties of the office, and would extend by one-half the periods between which these interruptions occur to the country." Finally, he reiterated his call for pensions equal to half a president's salary for former presidents; he also reiterated his view that former presidents could not and should not be expected to be ordinary citizens again. Whatever one might think of any of Fillmore's specific proposals, they were thoughtful, even prescient: almost every one of them would be adopted in some form after he died. His proposal for a single six-year term for president is still the subject of occasional public comment.[28]

Throughout his life, Fillmore had been in excellent health. His only problem was that he had put on considerable weight in recent years, although he still remained a striking figure who was always well dressed and groomed. On 13 February 1874, however, he suffered a stroke that paralyzed the entire left side of his body and left him permanently bedridden. Although he regained partial use of his left side, on 8 March, he suffered a second stroke, became unconscious, and shortly thereafter died at age seventy-four. After a private service, he was buried in the Forest Lawn Cemetery in Buffalo.[29]

In reviewing Fillmore's post-presidential career, it seems unfair to relegate him to the dustbin of American history. However his presidency may be evaluated, his post-presidential career was long and impressive. Although former presidents John Quincy Adams, Martin Van Buren, and John Tyler had pursued active political careers after leaving the White House and Van Buren had actually run for president as a third-party candidate, Fillmore was the first ex-president to turn on its head the traditional republican concept of the presidency as the temporary duty of a virtuous citizen. Not only did he reject the view that former presidents should be expected to retire from public service, but he was also convinced that they should continue to be involved in public activity of some sort, including even seeking the highest office in the land. "We have received from our fathers a Union and a Constitution above all price and value," he remarked during a campaign speech in 1856, "and that man who cannot sacrifice anything for the support of both is unworthy of his country."[30] Fillmore adhered to that creed throughout his post-presidency. The former president was also ahead of his time in calling for numerous reforms in government, including pensions for former presidents. Notwithstanding his unfortunate but explicable relationship with the Know-Nothing Party, his post-presidency deserves to be remembered as one of the more significant ones.

II

The same cannot be said of the post-presidential career of Franklin Pierce, who succeeded Fillmore into office in 1853. One of the most obscure political figures ever to win a presidential election, he tried as president to hold together the old Jacksonian coalition that was crumbling over the issue of slavery. Uncritically accepting the Southern viewpoint on most matters, however, he regarded those who opposed the expansion of slavery as disloyal. Rejected by the Democrats for a second term as president, he was still widely blamed for the nation's mounting political crisis. Although he remained loyal to the Union after the Civil War began, he was highly critical of the war policies of President Abraham Lincoln. He was even charged with being a Confederate sympathizer. After his wife, Jane, died in 1863, he was left a broken man, whose only solace turned out to be the bottle, a problem that had plagued him at different times throughout his career.

Five feet, ten inches tall, Pierce was slightly shorter than his predecessor. He was also less muscular and thinner, probably never weighing more than 170 to 180 pounds. His eyes were gray rather than blue, and in contrast to Fillmore, his hair was dark and disheveled, with a lock hanging over his forehead. Both his face and nose were also longer and narrower and his lips thinner. But like Fillmore, he was a striking figure.[31]

Although Pierce was the second dark horse candidate to be elected president (the first being James K. Polk) and was not as well known nationally as earlier presidents, his nomination was not all that remarkable. Nor did he come to the White House unprepared to serve as president. A good part of his life had been spent in politics. The son of the leader of the Democratic-Republican Party and

Photo of Franklin Pierce on the eve of retirement (circa 1857) by the most well-known photographer of the time, Matthew Brady. The photo captures Pierce's rugged good looks, with his youthful appearance and locks of his dark and disheveled hair hanging down over his brow. (Courtesy of Library of Congress, Prints and Photographs Division.)

governor of New Hampshire (1827–1829), Pierce won a seat in the state legislature in 1829, just two years after being admitted to the bar. After serving four years as a member of the New Hampshire state legislature (1829–1833), he was elected twice to the U.S. House of Representatives (1833–1837), then to the U.S. Senate, where he served from 1837 to 1842. By this time he had solidified a reputation as a politician's politician who had never lost an election. He was also a committed Jacksonian Democrat and a leader of the so-called Concord Clique or Regency that controlled New Hampshire's Democratic Party.[32]

Unfortunately, Pierce had serious personality problems that continued to plague him throughout much of his life. Born in 1804, he came from what would be described today as a dysfunctional family. Both his father and mother were alcoholics. They were also religious nonpractitioners in a region of southwest New Hampshire where religion played an important role in shaping behavior. As a result, young Pierce grew to maturity feeling insecure and conflicted. His marriage in 1834 to Jane Means Appleton added to his lack of self-confidence. A deeply religious woman from a wealthy New England family, Jane resented Pierce's political career and hated living in Washington. Pierce also evidently inherited his parents' drinking problem. He developed a reputation as a heavy drinker, which may have been a reason why he decided after 1842 to leave Washington for his home in Concord.

Back in Concord, Pierce remained a leader of the state's Democratic Party. Although not well known nationally, he nevertheless developed a reputation as a loyal party activist committed to the ideological principles of Jacksonian democracy. A strong supporter of states' rights, he also defended the South's views on slavery.[33]

When the Democrats met in Baltimore in 1852 to nominate their candidate for president, Pierce was not even among those being considered. Because of the two-thirds rule required for nomination, the convention became deadlocked among the four leading contenders. Not until the thirty-ninth ballot did the Virginia delegation bring forth his name as a compromise candidate. Finally, on the forty-ninth ballot, the delegates broke for him. In November, he easily defeated his Whig opponent, General Winfield Scott.[34]

The new administration seemed doomed even before it took office. A train on which the president-elect and his family were traveling between Boston and Concord went off the tracks. The debris from the wreckage tore the back off his eleven-year-old son Bennie's head. Both Pierce and his wife witnessed the grisly sight. Bennie had been the only one of their three children to live past the age of four. As Pierce entered office, a pall hung over the White House. Pierce's mentally fragile wife suffered a nervous breakdown. Throughout his presidency, he had to contend with his wife's health.

His most serious problem as president, however, was that he came to office sitting on a political volcano while staying committed to maintaining the status quo. He tried to lead, but he lacked the self-confidence often traceable to a rooted upbringing and usually characteristic of inspirational leadership. He also made questionable choices, including selecting an unruly cabinet and deferring to Congress. As a result, he boxed himself in in what proved to be the most divisive issue of his administration, the Kansas–Nebraska Bill. Although he understood the ire the measure would create among antislavery forces in the North, he was sympathetic to the Southern arguments about the South's unfettered right to expand slavery on the basis of popular sovereignty.[35]

Pierce held to this principle throughout his term in office. He also developed a particular hatred for the abolitionist movement and the emerging Republican Party, whose animus toward the South, he believed, inflamed the emotion of the voters and threatened the destruction of the Union. After a bitter debate in Congress, in which Pierce made support for the Kansas–Nebraska legislation a test of party loyalty, the measure passed and Pierce signed it into law. Not only did it undermine the fragile sectional truce established by the Compromise of 1850, it also destroyed the administration, which the nation held responsible for the political chaos that followed.

The nation's major newspapers pilloried the White House. Making matters even worse was the nativist sentiment against foreigners and Catholics that led to major Democratic defeats at the hands of the Know-Nothing Party in 1854. Furthermore, the president vetoed internal improvement projects on orthodox Jacksonian principles just when the full thrust of the industrial revolution was impacting the economy. By 1856, he had alienated almost every faction of his party. Even Southerners viewed him as ineffective. Although he still hoped for a second term, the Democrats turned instead to James Buchanan of Pennsylvania as their nominee.

Few presidents on their way out of office had to endure as much calumny as Pierce. Because the Democratic convention was held in Cincinnati in the first week of June 1856 and he did not leave office until the first week of March 1857, he suffered through ten months of humiliation and vitriol against him and his administration. The Republicans made Bleeding Kansas one of their most effective political issues and brutally attacked the president for favoring what they referred to as "lawless ruffians." Even his home state seemed to turn its back on the president. A reception for him in Concord in September was canceled after a meeting to plan the reception determined that it "would be inexpedient . . . to give President Pierce a reception at this time."[36]

Although Buchanan's election diverted much of the nation's attention away from the outgoing president onto the incoming administration, many of the nation's most respected newspapers continued to rail against Pierce, accusing him of being a doughface and blaming him for the renewal of fighting in Kansas after a period in which the turbulence had seemed to die down. Northern Democrats held him responsible for the fact that Buchanan received only 45 percent of the vote. In Congress, Republican stalwarts repeatedly attacked him. A number of his closest political allies and friends deserted him. Buchanan purged the executive branch of any holdovers from his administration.

After the end of his term, the now former president spent six weeks in Philadelphia, where his wife received treatment for tuberculosis. The couple then returned to New England to spend the rest of the spring and summer. However, because it was obvious that Jane Pierce would not be able to endure the bitter New England winter, they decided to spend the season on the island of Madeira. This was followed by extensive travel to Europe, which included stays in all its principal capitals. Significantly, the Pierces chose to travel as private tourists and to avoid the ceremonial events and meetings that took up so much of Van Buren's and Fillmore's European visits. While in Rome in the winter of 1858, Pierce had a reunion with his old friend, Nathaniel Hawthorne, whom he had first met while both were students at Bowdoin College. Hawthorne commented later on how the former president had aged and on how sad he seemed. "Poor fellow! He has neither son nor daughter to keep his heart warm," the writer said.[37]

Comprehending just how maligned a figure he had become at home, Pierce was in no hurry to return to the United States. Certainly he had no further interest in pursuing a political career. Because he was able to save and invest half his salary as president, much of it in western lands, he left office with approximately $78,000 in resources—about the same as Fillmore had saved, and enough for the moment for him and his wife to live comfortably. Only in the summer of 1859 did the Pierces finally return to the United States.

A few of the former president's allies, including Jefferson Davis, one of his closest friends since his days in Congress who had also served as his secretary of war, urged him to seek the Democratic nomination. Davis argued that only the former president could hold the nation together. Pierce recognized, however, that he had no chance of gaining the nomination even if he had been tempted to do so. Telling his backers that he had suffered enough as president and that he needed to care for his wife, he declined their overtures.

During the 1860 election in which the Democratic Party split, Pierce preferred the Southern choice, John Breckinridge, over the official party nominee, Stephen Douglas. But he decided that he could not abandon his party. Except for offering some advice to the Democrats that went largely unheeded, he did not participate actively in the campaign. Like Fillmore, he was upset by Lincoln's election, which, he commented, "was a distinct and unequivocal denial of the coequal rights" of the states and made secession inevitable. "The declaration's 'no danger' 'no secession' [being espoused in the Republican press]," he remarked, "reminds me of the story of the man who thought there would not be much of a shower when he stood by the ark with the waters of the flood at his hips."[38] Pierce was also critical of President James Buchanan, whom he regarded as incompetent for not acting more decisively once the lower South seceded from the Union.

Even before hostilities began, he blamed the impending war squarely on the

Northern abolitionists. He even seemed to justify the right of the Confederacy to defend itself, should Lincoln employ force to maintain the Union.[39] Once South Carolina seceded from the Union, but before the other Southern states acted, he sent a letter to Judge John A. Campbell of Alabama, whom he had appointed to the Supreme Court, urging the South to give their Northern friends more time to respond to Southern grievances. If after six months the South's wrongs had not been addressed, he told Campbell that the South would be entitled to withdraw from the Union. The letter was published widely throughout the South.[40]

After hostilities broke out in April 1861, Pierce remained loyal to the Union, but rather than make the type of public displays of support for the Union that his predecessor undertook, he showed little sympathy for the Northern cause. In his private correspondence, he became increasingly bitter in his opposition to the war, making it clear that in his view, the South was the victim of antislavery forces. Publicly, he seemed to give up hope that the Union would win on the battlefield or that the nation would be reunited. His own personal problems in the summer of 1861 added to his despair. His wife remained both physically and mentally frail. For the first time since retirement, he also began to experience financial difficulties and even contemplated returning to his law practice.

Instead, the former president decided to tour the West, allegedly to obtain a better idea of its vast resources. During the three-week trip, which took him as far west as Saginaw City, Michigan, and as far south as Louisville, Pierce made clear his bitterness toward the war, even suggesting that it might lead to insurrection in the North. He also remarked that he preferred President Buchanan's former postmaster general and secretary of war, Joseph Holt, as president to anyone else. Why he said this is not entirely clear. During Buchanan's administration, Holt had been sympathetic to the South, but he was always a strong unionist and vigorous opponent of secession. In 1862, he would be appointed by Lincoln as judge advocate of the army.[41]

Pierce's brief trip to the West haunted him for the rest of his life. In December, while visiting family in Andover, the former president received a letter from Secretary of State William Seward enclosing a copy of an anonymous letter in which Pierce was accused of making his Western trip to support an antiwar organization of Democrats based in the northwest known as the Knights of the Golden Circle. In a curt, accusatory fashion, the secretary asked Pierce to respond to the charge. Furious that his patriotism had been challenged, Pierce angrily denied the charges. "It is not easy to conceive how any person could give credence to, or entertain for a moment, the idea that I am now, or have ever been connected with a 'secret league,' or with *any* league, the object of which was, or is, the overthrow the government of my country," the former president responded.[42] Realizing that he had gone too far in accusing a former president of being unpatriotic on the flimsiest of evidence, Seward immediately apologized to Pierce.

The former president made the wise decision not to go public with the exchange of letters. In March, however, the Detroit *Tribune* published Seward's letter to Pierce. It was then circulated widely in Republican newspapers. Although the ex-president got Congress to publish Seward's apology to him, the damage had been done. The secretary's letter only confirmed what many already believed about the unpopular former president: that he was indeed a Confederate sympathizer.

As the Civil War continued, Pierce became unrestrained in attacking the Lincoln administration for its "usurpation against the constitution, against freedom of speech and of the press, [and] against personal liberty." Nothing infuriated the former president more than Lincoln's promulgation in 1862 of the Emancipation Proclamation, which, he stated, proved that the true purpose of the war was to wipe out states' rights and destroy private property. He also could not understand how the American people could tolerate this attempt to "butcher" their own race for the sake of emancipating four million Negroes incapable of profiting from freedom.[43] In a speech on the Fourth of July 1863, the day after the Battle of Gettysburg, he deplored what he referred to as a "fearful, fruitless, fatal civil war" fought "upon the theory of emancipation, devastation, subjugation."[44]

Personal losses added to Pierce's growing despondency. On 2 December, he lost his wife of twenty-nine years to tuberculosis. A few months later, his close friend, Nathaniel Hawthorne, died in his sleep while the two men were touring the White Mountains. The former president's marriage to Jane, a melancholy woman who never forgave Pierce for his political career and who, while in the White House, spent days writing letters to her dead son, Bennie, was never a happy one. The former president, however, was deeply protective of her. His friendship with Hawthorne remained exceptionally strong. In 1852, Hawthorne wrote Pierce's campaign biography and was rewarded the next year by being appointed consul to Liverpool. Unlike most of Pierce's friends, who deserted him during the Civil War, the writer—who believed slavery was evil and remained devoted to the Union—stayed loyal to him. He even dedicated his last book, *Our Old Home,* to him. Although the former president remained a close friend of the writer's family, they thought it best not to have him be a pallbearer at his funeral.[45]

Insults continued to follow Pierce throughout the remainder of his life. One that attracted considerable notoriety was the wide circulation of a pamphlet that accused the former president of breaking his pledge to keep slavery out of politics and of using soldiers in Kansas to make the territory a slave state. What made the pamphlet so damning was that it included a copy of a letter the former president had sent to Jefferson Davis in 1860, later discovered by Union soldiers marching through the South, in which Pierce urged Davis to be the Democratic Party's presidential standard-bearer that year. That Pierce could have even entertained the notion that the soon-to-be-president of the Confederacy would have been the best candidate for president in 1860 added further confirmation for those who already believed that Pierce was another Benedict Arnold.

Even the former president's neighbors distrusted him. When they learned that President Abraham Lincoln had been assassinated and that Pierce had not draped his house with a flag, they descended on his home. When he heard that a mob was on its way, he appeared in front of the crowd and made a speech in which he denounced the assassination. But almost in defiance of the crowd, he added, "If the period which I have served our state and country in various situations, commencing more than thirty-five years ago, has left the question of my devotion to the flag, the constitution and the Union in doubt, it is too late now to resume it by any such exhibition as the enquiry suggests."[46]

Slandered, embittered, and grieving over the loss of his wife and one of his closest friends, Pierce became an alcoholic.[47] Two years after her death, he bought eighty-four acres of land and built a two-story cottage at Little Boar's Head on New Hampshire's narrow coastline. There he did not even try to hide his affliction, often getting drunk in public. His drinking contributed to chronic gastritis and poor nutrition and most likely caused liver damage. He became so severely ill at the end of 1865 that there were fears for his life.

Affected by his near brush with death, the former president, who had never been religious, had himself baptized in the Episcopalian Church. For a time, he abstained completely from the bottle. Sober once more, he resumed his interest in politics. He supported President Andrew Johnson in his battle against the Radical Republicans in Congress and tried to win the president back to the Democratic Party. In 1867, he traveled to Virginia to visit with his old friend, Jefferson Davis, still a prisoner at Fort Monroe in Old Point Comfort. He even invited the Davis family to stay at his cottage at Little Boar's Head.

By this time, however, the former president had started to drink again. He was also in the terminal stage of cirrhosis of the liver. In declining health for several years, he suffered from severe abdominal pains, loss of appetite, nausea, and a chronic cough. "I do not spring up readily from my serious illness [and] have not much strength now," he wrote his friend Horatio Bridges in February 1869.[48] By the summer, fluid began to accumulate in his abdominal cavity. His body became distended, and his weight dropped to less than 100 pounds. On 7 October, he went in and out of consciousness. The next day he died, six weeks short of his sixty-fifth birthday.[49] President Ulysses S. Grant proclaimed a day of national mourning. On 11 October, he was buried at the Old North Cemetery in Concord.

In many ways Pierce was the most tragic of the three presidents who served in the crucial decade before the Civil War. Striking in appearance, honest above approach, seeking to preserve both his party and the Union, he failed to surround himself with a loyal cabinet whose commitment to the preservation of the Union was as strong as his own. He was also deferential to an increasingly fractured and warring Congress. Most important, his Jacksonian belief in states' rights and a limited central government seemed anachronistic during a period of the most profound national change and challenge. His own personal insecurities and hardships made his administration even more unfortunate.

Many of his problems as president, especially his resolute belief in states' rights and a strict construction of the Constitution, followed him after he left the

White House. Once the Civil War began, they made him incapable of being as vociferous a defender of the Union cause as his predecessor, Millard Fillmore, even though their views about the causes of the war and Lincoln's handling of the conflict were not that far apart. While Fillmore was also able to enjoy a long and productive retirement, Pierce became a pathetic figure, an alcoholic whose disease undoubtedly cut short his life and a former president so loathed that after his death, his name was seldom recalled even in his home state.

III

Riding with President-elect Abraham Lincoln to his inauguration in 1861, outgoing President James Buchanan remarked to the incoming president: "If you are as happy . . . on entering [the White House] as I am in leaving it and returning home, you are the happiest man in this country."[50] Buchanan meant what he said. By the time he left office, he was as much reviled as his predecessor had been four years earlier. At his inaugural, Buchanan had vowed to serve only one term. But even if he had decided to seek a second term, there was little chance that he could have been renominated, much less reelected. With seven states of the lower South having already seceded from the Union, a Confederate government established in Montgomery, Alabama, and the other Southern states contemplating secession, Buchanan also understood that the nation was on the brink of a civil war whose epic proportions he could only imagine. He was glad to be able to leave Washington before the ensuing disaster began.

By the time Buchanan became president in 1857, the issue of slavery had become so inflamed on both sides of the Mason–Dixon Line that it would have taken a president of unusual acumen and skills to weather the crisis. Buchanan was clearly not that person. Through his pro-Southern policies, he sustained the South along the road to secession. Furthermore, he foundered catastrophically in the critical months between Lincoln's election in November 1860 and the time he left office on 4 March 1861. Although he did not believe that the South had the constitutional right to secede from the Union, neither did he do anything to prevent it.[51]

Born near Mercersberg, Pennsylvania, on 23 April 1791 (the last president to be born in the eighteenth century), his life spanned nearly the nation's entire history, a point on which he took great pride. Despite an earlier youthful streak of rebellion, he came into his maturity as a serious, meticulous, self-assured, and ambitious young man who worked hard and read widely. He was better known, however for his competence and pleasing personality than for any originality of thought or flashes of charisma.

After being admitted to the bar in 1812, Buchanan opened a law practice in Lancaster, then the state's capital. He was also elected twice to the state legislature. Although still interested in politics, he decided in 1816 to return to Lancaster in order to build up his law practice. Eventually, he became one of the state's most successful and wealthiest lawyers.

A little over six feet tall, with broad shoulders, large blue eyes, blond hair, a large forehead, and fine features, Buchanan was an imposing and distinguished-looking figure, but he had an eye disorder that resulted in his most peculiar feature: the habit of writhing or cocking his head and closing one eye when listening and talking. This made it appear to those with whom he was conversing that they had his full attention and that he agreed with them.

In 1820, Buchanan renewed his interest in elective politics. Over the next thirty-five years, he became a major national political figure. In 1820, he was elected as a Federalist to the House of Representatives, where he served five terms. Reflecting the changing nature of American politics in the 1820s, he changed party affiliations in 1828 and became an increasingly influential Jacksonian Democrat. In 1831, he was named minister to Russia, but he resigned after less than two years. In 1834, he was elected to the U.S. Senate, where he remained until 1845, when he was named by President James Polk as his secretary of state. After the Democrats were defeated by the Whigs in 1848, he returned to private life. But in 1853 he was appointed by Millard Fillmore as minister to Great Britain. He served in London until 1856, when he returned to the United States to run successfully for president.

Having amassed a fortune of about $300,000 (the equivalent of about $6.2 million in 2009), Buchanan purchased a large estate, Wheatland, in 1848. Located about a mile west of Lancaster, his residence at Wheatland was a comfortable three-story brick home that he had recently renovated. Built in a simple Federal style with twenty-two spacious rooms, a formal dining room, a parlor, and a large library, it sat on twenty-two acres of broad and well-groomed lawns and gardens with numerous groves of oak trees. Although a bachelor, Buchanan had a large extended family, including twenty-two nephews and nieces and thirteen grand-nephews and -nieces. Seven of these children were orphans whom he raised. The library was the center of Buchanan's political operations. When he was at Wheatland, he found great pleasure in attending to his gardens in the spring and summer, sleighing in the winter, caring for his family, and entertaining guests.[52]

One reason why Buchanan assumed such a pro-Southern view in the growing sectional crisis between North and South was because he had developed great empathy for the similar gentry life of the Southern planter and plantation owner. Geographically, he was a borderline Northerner, living and working about twenty-five miles from the slave state of Maryland. He viewed slaves more as property than as human beings, and he hated the abolitionists. As a Jacksonian Democrat, he also believed in states' rights and limits on the power of the federal government. As a lawmaker in Washington, he boarded with and developed his closest friendships with fellow lawmakers from the South.

None of this meant Buchanan thought the South had the right to secede from the Union. It did mean he believed that only his party could keep the Union together and that on the issue of slavery expansion into the territories he favored the South. That is why even before he won the Democratic nomination in 1856, he was widely regarded in the North as a doughface.

The new president understood the developing storm facing him when he took office. "The Compromise of 1850 ought never to have been disturbed by Congress," Buchanan wrote in his defense after the Civil War. "After long years of agitation and alarm, the country, under its influence, had enjoyed a season of comparative repose." But with the repeal of the Missouri Compromise, "the struggle immediately commenced in Kansas between the anti-slavery and pro-slavery parties. On this theatre the extreme men of both sections were brought into mortal conflict."[53]

What Buchanan never realized, however, was his own responsibility in turning this brewing tempest into a major crisis by the time he departed the White House in 1861. Rather than including in his cabinet men representing all factions of the Democratic Party, for example, he surrounded himself with persons with whom he felt most comfortable. This meant almost exclusively Southerners or those who shared his pro-Southern views. Partly because he insulated himself from competing views, the president also failed to grasp the depth of the antislavery movement in the North. Instead, he equated the views of antislavery Northerners with abolitionism. He failed to realize that although most Northerners opposed to slavery, including most Republicans, were against the expansion of slavery into the territories, they were prepared to allow it to remain in the existing slave states.

Even more serious was Buchanan's own duplicity in the events that tarnished his administration. This included manipulating the Supreme Court decision in the infamous Dred Scott case, which declared the Missouri Compromise unconstitutional, and supporting the fraudulent proslavery Lecompton Constitution in Kansas even though he knew that the majority of settlers in Kansas were antislavery and refused to be bound by the Lecompton document.[54]

In contrast to Andrew Jackson's handling of the nullification crisis of the 1830s, moreover, Buchanan remained unwilling even to threaten the use of military force against South Carolina when it seceded from the Union in December 1860. Having effectively given other states carte blanche to leave the Union, he then did little, other than to declare secession illegal and to try unsuccessfully to reinforce Fort Sumter in Charleston Harbor, while the other states from the lower South seceded and established a separate Confederate government in Montgomery.[55]

As a result of his pro-Southern biases and his indecisiveness in response to the secessionist movement, by the time he left the White House in March 1861, Buchanan was being pilloried in the North in much the same manner as his predecessor had been vilified four years earlier. The opposition press was especially cruel. Horace Greeley of the New York *Tribune* called him "insane," while other Northern journalists regularly referred to him as a "secessionist." The fact that the press played such an important role in the 1850s—every major city had at least three papers, and each party had its own organ—and that most of the major metropolitan papers in the North were aligning themselves with the Republicans made their attacks on the administration especially baneful. But even Northern Democratic papers found it difficult to defend Buchanan's Kansas policy, and by the end of his administration, many of them had turned against him. Once known for his masterful use of the press, Buchanan became its victim.[56]

Congress also got into the act. After their victory in the 1858 congressional elections, House Republicans took the unprecedented step of forming a special investigatory committee, which concluded in a thirty-page report that the president had used bribes, lucrative printing contracts, and various other fraudulent practices to win approval in Kansas of the Lecompton Constitution. It also found that the former postmaster of New York had absconded to Europe with $160,000.[57]

Always claiming to be the paragon of virtue, Buchanan responded to the committee's report by daring it to recommend his impeachment. When this did not happen, the president declared himself vindicated. But the 800 pages of testimony the committee took and its majority report sullied the administration. Poor management of the War Department, leading to the illegal payment of war contracts with bonds held in a trust for the Indians, further damaged the administration's reputation.

Not surprisingly, therefore, Buchanan was happy to leave Washington when his term ended. He also left office fully convinced that his administration had been an "eminently successful" one.[58] Most of his other Northern contemporaries strongly disagreed. Although he received a warm welcome from his fellow citizens when he returned to his Wheatland estate, he continued to be a target of attack, which became even worse after the Civil War began. Threats against Buchanan's person and home became so serious that members of the local Masonic Lodge to which he belonged took on the responsibility of guarding Wheatland.

In July, President Lincoln suggested in a special message to Congress that Buchanan's administration was responsible for allowing large amounts of money and weaponry to fall into Confederate hands. Picking up on this comment, some newspapers even charged that Buchanan had been in league with the South. In 1862, Garrett Davis of Kentucky introduced a resolution in the Senate accusing the former president of "sympathy" with insurrection in the Southern states for which "he should receive the censure and condemnation of the Senate and the American people." Although the resolution did not pass, Buchanan was infuriated by it. "If two years after a Presidential term has expired the Senate can go back & try, condemn, & execute the former incumbent," he commented, "who would accept the office?"[59]

Buchanan had other cause to be irate. Regardless of his actions as president, the former president always remained loyal to the Union. During the first month of the Lincoln administration, before the firing on Fort Sumter in Charleston Harbor on 12 April, he continued to hope that conflict between the North and South

Portrait of James Buchanan painted by George P. A. Healy in 1859. By this time Buchanan was being vilified even in Congress. When Healy presented the bill for the portrait, which had been painted for the White House, Congress refused to pay for it, and it was many years before the White House acquired a portrait of Buchanan. (Courtesy of National Portrait Gallery, Smithsonian Institution; gift of the A. W. Mellon Educational and Charitable Trust.)

might be avoided and the Union restored. If Lincoln would evacuate Fort Sumter, as South Carolina demanded, then no military action would be taken, the Upper South would remain loyal to the Union, and conflict would be prevented. Reports that Buchanan received at Wheatland in March indicated that Lincoln was intending to evacuate Fort Sumter. If he pursued such a path, then Buchanan's own pacific course in his last months in office would be vindicated.[60]

The former president was bitterly disappointed, therefore, when Lincoln decided to reinforce Fort Sumter, and South Carolina responded by firing what became the first shots of the Civil War. Privately, he condemned Lincoln's decision. In the four years of war that followed, however, he never wavered in his belief that the action taken by the South in seceding from the Union was unconstitutional. He also conducted himself more in the manner of Fillmore than of Pierce. Missing from his many letters during the war was the petulance, the bitterness, and the despair directed at the administration that characterized Pierce's correspondence during the war. He agreed with Pierce and Fillmore that abolitionists and their Black Republican allies had been primarily responsible for bringing the Union to the precipice of civil war, but the sense of Southern victimization that ran through his predecessor's letters was missing in his own correspondence. Although he always retained the naive hope, even late into the war, that a way might be found by which the South could be brought back into the Union assured that slavery would be protected and all would be forgiven, he remained firm in his conviction that Lincoln's war policies deserved his support.[61]

Indeed, Buchanan never uttered a cross word about Lincoln as a person, and after his assassination, he remarked that the dead president had been perhaps the best hope for reconciliation between the sections. In the manner of Fillmore, he urged his fellow citizens in Lancaster and nearby Chester counties to "join the many thousands of brave & patriotic volunteers who are already in the field." It was their duty, he added, to "support the president with all the men & means at the command of the country."[62]

Although Buchanan supported the Union cause and urged his countrymen to join the war effort, the ex-president shunned public attention and almost always expressed his views privately. One reason he remained silent was simply the still lingering tradition that the role of former presidents was to return to private life and not assume a public persona. Here he differed most sharply from Fillmore but also from the succession of presidents going as far back as James Madison. While these ex-presidents had incrementally undermined the republican notion of the role of former presidents, the republican ideal remained alive, especially in the mind of latter-day Jacksonians, like Pierce and Buchanan, who romanticized the nation's agrarian past. In Buchanan's view, the main business of ex-presidents was to refrain from public discourse.[63]

Well aware of his unpopularity as a former president, Buchanan also compared his situation at Wheatland to Napoleon's exile on the island of St. Helena after the Battle of Waterloo. In a melancholy letter, he wrote of living on the "rock of St. Helena." Like Napoleon on St. Helena, he felt deserted even by some of his closest political allies. He was particularly hurt when four former members of his cabinet failed to come to his public defense after Thurlow Weed, one of the leaders of the Republican Party, wrote an account in February 1862 of a cabinet meeting the previous December involving the garrisoning of Fort Sumter and the firing of Buchanan's secretary of war, John B. Floyd. According to Weed, the former president was forced to fire Floyd, who opposed the garrisoning of Sumter, under threat of mass resignation by his cabinet. Weed's account of the meeting was garbled: Buchanan had been planning to force Floyd out because of his mismanagement of the War Department's finances, and Floyd resigned without actually being discharged. Also, evidence that the cabinet threatened to resign en masse still remains circumstantial.[64]

The thrust of Weed's accusations was on the mark, however, insofar as the displeasure of its key members with Buchanan was concerned. Despite the former president's request of them, they refused outright to publicly denounce Weed's article. "Well be it so," Buchanan concluded wistfully after receiving their responses. "They will not contradict Weed, who is powerful & stands high with Mr. Lincoln." Although the former president termed the article "a tissue of falsehoods," he decided against doing anything more about it, persuaded that it would be unseemly for him to become involved in public controversies and that anything he said would be misconstrued by the Northern press as an effort on his part to apologize for his past errors. He also did not want any remarks he made to be misinterpreted in a way that might, as he later wrote, "embarrass Mr. Lincoln's administration in the vigorous persecution of pending hostilities."[65]

In comparing his life at Wheatland during his retirement to Napoleon's exile on St. Helena, the former president had in mind the ostracism he believed he shared with the former French leader. Just as accurate a comparison would have been the leisurely life of a country gentleman he was able to enjoy at Wheatland, notwithstanding his precipitous fall from grace. Despite the war—which at the time of the Battle of Antietam came within ten miles of his estate and led some friends to try in vain to get Buchanan to flee Wheatland—the former president spent much of his time reading, writing, and attending to his private fortune and to the financial affairs of nearly his whole family. He was generous with his money, helping to recruit volunteers for the Union army, and giving small amounts of money to former acquaintances who were not shy to write to him about their needs.

While the winters tended to be lonely, during the remainder of the year, the former president's house was full of family members, neighbors, and former political associates. He always enjoyed entertaining, and he kept a large stock of the best wines, which were constantly being restocked. He also attended frequent public dinners, enjoyed a New Jersey sea resort and the springs of Bedford, where he frequently went to ease his gout, and traveled occasionally to Philadelphia, Harrisburg, York, and Baltimore.

Still, Buchanan remained persuaded that he was being unfairly maligned for a war that he had done everything in his power to avoid. As president, his whole purpose had been to preserve the Union. That he should be held responsible for its dissolution was beyond the pale. Accordingly, he attempted to set the record straight by writing his own account of the coming of the Civil War. The result was *The Administration on the Eve of the Rebellion: History of Four Years before the War,* the first successfully completed memoir by a former president about his administration. Although impressive in many ways, the memoir was a wretched failure in terms of its primary purpose of vindicating Buchanan of his responsibility for the war.

In preparing the volume, Buchanan ran into difficulty almost immediately because he planned to rely heavily on solicited accounts from his former cabinet members most familiar with the events after the secession of South Carolina in December 1860. Obviously unable to depend on the assistance of those Southern members who were now Confederates, he looked to the remainder of his cabinet, including those who had replaced the Southerners. Just as they refused to come to Buchanan's defense against the charges levied by Weed, they declined once more to help the former president. The fact that three of his former cabinet member had become Republicans and joined the Lincoln administration also made them unreceptive to Buchanan's solicitation. Even his former attorney general, Judge Jeremiah S. Black, decided against participating in the project even though he had been the first to broach the idea of a history of the administration. Although Black had offered to write the volume himself for $7,000, he decided against it after Buchanan made clear his agreement with Lincoln's war policies, which Black thought were unconstitutional. "Your endorsement of Lincoln's policy will be a very serious drawback upon the defense of your own," Black wrote Buchanan.[66]

Buchanan remained surprisingly nonplussed by the negative responses of his former political associates. On the contrary, he seemed energized after Black made clear that he would have to rely completely on his own efforts. "I am happy to say you are entirely mistaken in supposing that I suffer from low spirits," Buchanan responded in March 1862 to another letter he received from Black. "I am astonished at my own health & spirits & the zest with which I enjoy the calm pleasures with which Providence has blessed me."[67]

Working alone, Buchanan spent most of his time at Wheatland collecting documents and preparing his defense. The lengthy manuscript, when published, ran almost 300 pages. If the defense was spirited, the writing was legalistic and often turgid, based as it was on lengthy excerpts from his speeches and other documents while he was president. Tracing the origins of the war to the 1830s, the former president made antislavery forces and their allies, including even the British, culpable for the war. "After the formation of the New England [Anti-Slavery Society in Boston in 1832]," he wrote, "the agitation against Southern slavery proceeded with redoubled vigor, and this under the auspices of British emissaries.

One of the first and most pernicious effects of these proceedings was to arrest the natural progress of emancipation under legitimate state authority."[68]

In this single paragraph, Buchanan set the tone of what was to follow. The antislavery movement was responsible for the events leading to the Civil War. The British played a defining role in the antislavery movement in the United States, as later did the Black Republicans. The North was the fomenter, the South the victim in the sectional conflict that followed; indeed, the unprofitable institution of slavery might have disappeared entirely in the 1830s absent Northern agitation against the South. Finally, slavery in all its ramifications, including its expansion into the territories, was an issue beyond the purview of the federal government.

Fast-forwarding to the 1850s, the former president acknowledged that with the passage of the Kansas–Nebraska Act and the repeal of the Missouri Compromise, Southern lawmakers and proslavery forces had to bear some of the responsibility for the war. In Kansas, "the extreme men of both sections were brought into mortal conflict," he conceded. Never, however, did he acknowledge his own complicity in the Dred Scott case. Furthermore, he continued to place most of the blame for Bleeding Kansas on the antislavery forces. He also continued to defend the legitimacy of the Lecompton Constitution and even accused the antislavery opposition of having committed a treasonable act by establishing its own government in Topeka. Quoting at length from one of his presidential messages to Congress, he remarked, "The Topeka government, adhered to with such treasonable pertinacity, is a government of direct opposition to the existing government prescribed and recognized by Congress."[69]

Mostly, though, the former president sought to vindicate his actions in the four months preceding the shelling of Fort Sumter. Indeed, he devoted the bulk of his narrative to a detailed explanation of his efforts to reach an accommodation with the secessionist states, especially with South Carolina over the forts in Charleston Harbor. He made four major points: (1) he sought to avoid war in hopes of restoring the Union, although he acknowledged that would have meant significant Northern concessions on the issue of slavery, including its expansion into the territories; (2) congressional Republicans opposed all efforts at compromise, including the so-called Crittenden Compromise, which would have extended the Missouri Compromise line to the Pacific Coast; (3) he lacked the constitutional authority to take military action against the secessionist states even had he been so inclined; and (4) Congress was, in any case, unwilling to give him the authority to use military force. "We have already seen that Congress . . . refused to adopt any measures of compromise to prevent civil war," he thus wrote. "Failing to do this . . . it was the imperative duty of Congress to furnish the President, or his successor the means of repelling force by force, should this become necessary to preserve the Union. They, nevertheless, refused to perform this duty with as much pertinacity as they had manifested in repudiating all measures of compromise."[70]

Although Buchanan mounted his defense with all the craft of a highly skilled lawyer, and it was for the most part factually correct, his volume fell far short of vindication. Its plausibility was undermined by his one-sided defense of the South; his almost singular attribution of the sectional crisis to the North; his refusal to assess accurately the political consequences of his own actions, such as the choice of his cabinet or to developments in Kansas; and, more generally, his total refusal to accept any blame for the disintegration of the Union during the last months of his administration. Instead, he chose to make Congress the scapegoat. Although the former president produced an important account of the period before the Civil War, for historians, it proved too lopsided in its explanation of the causes of the Civil War and contained too many omissions of fact to influence their judgment of Buchanan's presidency.

Nor did Buchanan's memoirs do much to change contemporary judgment of his administration. To his credit, even though he had finished his memoir four years earlier, he refrained from publishing it until 1866, after Lincoln had been assassinated and the Confederacy had surrendered to the Union. "The publication was delayed," the former president explained in the preface to his memoir, "to avoid the possible imputation, unjust as this would have been, that any portion of it was intended to embarrass Mr. Lincoln's administration in the vigorous prosecution of pending hostilities."[71] Once it was published, it sold several thousand copies. This was enough for Buchanan to commission an autobiography, which was unfortunately never completed.

By the time Buchanan published his memoirs, his defense of his presidency had been undermined by the fact that Lincoln had already achieved the status of martyred savior of the Union. In the flush of the Union victory over the Confederacy, a memoir that was as much a defense of the South as it was of the former president was hardly likely to be well received in the North. Instead, it merely confirmed what those in the North already thought about Buchanan: he was a doughface.

Nevertheless, Buchanan went to his death convinced that he had conducted his presidency in laudable fashion and that history would redeem his reputation. Except for a nervous tic in his leg and some painful polyps that were removed from his nose in a series of operations between 1849 and 1850, Buchanan had been generally fit before his retirement. After leaving the White House, however, his health declined rapidly. He endured recurrent attacks of gout, which caused agonizing joint inflammation. He may also have suffered from a chronic inflammation of the connective tissue supporting the muscle fibers, and he began to have recurring bouts of indigestion and diarrhea. Between 1863 and 1867, he found himself having increasingly to stay in bed because of his joint and gastrointestinal problems. "I fear that I shall not be able to pay you a visit for months to come," he wrote in November 1867 to Henry E. Johnston, the husband of his favorite niece, Harriet Lane, who had served as his first lady (the first time the term was used) in the White House while he was president. "Although relieved from acute pain in my left hand and arm, yet my hand is still so weak and swollen that I cannot carve, and it is but a few days since I ceased to have the meat on my own plate cut up for me."[72]

Sometime in 1867, his health turned for the worse. He suffered from shortness of breath, probably indicating a weakening of the heart. Feeling old and ill, he spoke often of death and seemed to welcome it. By April 1868, he was in the last throes of congestive heart failure manifested by pulmonary congestion and a disabling cough. At the end of May, he developed terminal pneumonia.

Even on his deathbed, he continued to defend his record as president. "I have always felt and still feel that I discharged every public duty imposed on me conscientiously," he told his friend and executor of his estate, Hiram Swarr, on 30 May. "I have no regret for any public act of my life, and history will vindicate my memory."[73] The next day, 1 June 1868, he died at the age of seventy-eight.[74]

Although Buchanan had asked to be buried at the Woodward Hill Cemetery in Lancaster without pomp or public ceremony, he probably would have been gratified after having endured so much calumny that over 20,000 persons attended his funeral. Interestingly, though, in recalling Buchanan's political career, the minister delivering the funeral sermon, the Reverend John W. Nevin, president of nearby Franklin and Marshall College, chose not to dwell on his presidency. "We stand too near the vast and mighty struggle through which we have just passed," he remarked, "to understand [Buchanan's presidency] properly, or to estimate fairly its moral and political merits." Rather, he sought to identify Buchanan with the statesmen that preceded the 1850s. "And in parting with Mr. Buchanan, it is as though we were called to part again with Clay, and Webster, and [Thomas] Benton, and Calhoun, and Jackson, and [Lewis] Cass, and the whole political world to which they belonged."[75]

Unfortunately for Buchanan, his legacy was to be one of a threesome of the nation's most forgettable presidents and whose doughface policies helped cause a civil war, rather than one of a group of some of the greatest legislators and statesmen the nation has ever produced.

5

Former Presidents in an Age of Transition

Johnson and Grant

Historians commonly refer to the presidencies of Andrew Johnson (1865–1869) and Ulysses S. Grant, (1869–1877) as part of the era of reconstruction that ended with the presidency of Rutherford B. Hayes (1877–1881). President Johnson had a radical reconstruction policy forced on him by a Congress controlled by Republicans. President Grant allowed radical reconstruction to fall victim to white supremacy. President Hayes owed his election to a promise to bring the final curtain down on reconstruction. As an interpretative segue into the years 1865–1881, analyzing this time in American history within the framework of reconstruction is compelling. It does not, however, foreclose other ways to view the age or the very different personalities and political perspectives of its presidents.

Indeed, the post–Civil War era marked one of the great divides in American history, not only in terms of bringing a resolution to the issues that threatened the dissolution of the Union and establishing the bedrock of race relations in the South that would last for another century, but also in ushering in an era of unprecedented economic growth characterized by the rise of big cities, big business, big labor, big wealth, and big charity. The era of reconstruction, in fact, overlapped with the so-called Gilded Age, a term coined by Mark Twain (Samuel Clemens) and Charles Dudley Warner to reflect the self-indulgence, corruption, and vulgarity that accompanied this economic change.[1]

The Civil War settled once and for all the issue of secession. Reconstruction invested the central government with new powers not only in determining the provisions according to which the former secessionist states would be allowed to return to the Union, but also in establishing voting rights, defining and affording basic rights of national citizenship, and applying to the states the principle of due process of law found in the Fifth Amendment. Subsequently, the Supreme Court extended due process protections to corporations from unreasonable state regulation even as it limited the rights of citizens.[2]

One can legitimately argue, therefore, that the reconstruction era was both transitory and transitional. Without diminishing the importance of the gains achieved by the freedmen in obtaining the elemental rights of citizenship, most of these gains, especially in the Deep South, were nullified by the return of white supremacy. The reconstruction period was also transitional because the United States went from a fundamentally agrarian nation to a modern industrial state.[3]

The transitional nature of the reconstruction era was mirrored in the post-presidential careers of the first two of the reconstruction presidents, Johnson and Grant. The last of the Jacksonian Democrats to serve as president, Johnson remained a Jacksonian Democrat after he left office. The only president between Andrew Jackson and Woodrow Wilson to serve two complete and consecutive terms, Grant's disastrous speculative financial ventures and his best-selling *Memoirs* were emblematic of new corporate America and were the first conscious attempt to profit financially from being a former president. More important, after leaving the presidency, Grant embarked on a two-and-a-half-year world tour in which he promoted the United States as a developing industrial power.

I

Throughout his political career, Andrew Johnson remained a Jacksonian Democrat.[4] Like Jackson, he appealed to traditional republican principles, believed in limited government, economy in government, and states' rights, and espoused the virtues of a yeoman republic. The two Tennesseans also shared a common heritage. Both men were born into poverty. Both grew up without a father. Both were ambitious, largely self-educated, and self-made. (In Johnson's case, he had no formal education, being apprenticed at the age of ten to a tailor.) Both resented that they were born at the bottom of the social scale, and both sought social acceptance. Both were rough-hewn and had fiery tempers.

The differences between the two former presidents, however, were at least as striking as their similarities. Physically, they were dissimilar. In contrast to the tall, thin, and light-complexioned Jackson, Johnson stood about five feet, nine inches tall; he was well proportioned and swarthy, with a broad forehead, dark, piercing eyes, dark hair, bushy eyebrows, a prominent nose, and a wide mouth with a downward tip at the ends, making it appear that he wore a constant frown. Johnson also lacked Jackson's canny political skills. Although the latter's frequent outbursts often reflected a deliberate political tactic, Johnson's intemperance was profound and uncontrollable. Perhaps that is why words like *vituperative* and *rigid* seem to have been used more regularly against Johnson than they were against Jackson. Conversely, Johnson lacked Jackson's charismatic personality and heroic figure. While both men championed the cause of the common man, Jackson did not engage in the same kind of class politics as Johnson, who always regarded himself as a defender of the poor against the landed aristocracy. Above all, Jackson grew in office. Johnson did not.[5]

Before being named Abraham Lincoln's running mate on the National Union ticket in 1864, Johnson had risen steadily through the political ranks. First elected alderman and then mayor of Greeneville (1828–1833), he served successively before the Civil War in the Tennessee House of Representatives (1835–1837 and 1839–1841), in the state senate (1841–1843), in the U.S. House of Representatives (1843–1853), as state governor (1853–1857), and finally in the U.S. Senate (1857–1862). Deciding to stay with the Union after the outbreak of the Civil War in 1861, he was appointed by President Lincoln as military governor of Tennessee in 1862. Two years later, Lincoln asked him to be his running mate. After Lincoln's assassination a month into his second term, Johnson became the third vice president in twenty-five years to become president on the death of the incumbent.

Throughout his political career, Johnson envisioned a Jacksonian democracy. He also displayed many of the characteristics that would later cost him dearly as president. Enjoying the prominence that went with political office and ambitious for higher office, he developed into a brilliant debater, especially on the stump, where he appealed to the "plebians," as he called the small farmers and tradesman of eastern Tennessee who supported him. At the same time, he launched vituperative attacks against the state's slavocracy, which, he said, controlled the state and were bloated and corrupt, and he steadfastly opposed corporate interests.

In his quest for office, Johnson took no prisoners and frequently made ad hominem remarks against those running against him. Obsessive, self-absorbed, lacking any charm of manner, easily taking offense, he was described later by his secretary of the navy, Gideon Welles, as having no confidants nor seeking any. Although he built a powerful political machine in eastern Tennessee, he usually acted without consulting anyone. Even members of his own party did not much care for him, viewing him as dour, extreme, a maverick on important legislative issues, and untrustworthy. President Polk could not stand him and said as much in the diary he kept.[6]

Throughout his political career, Johnson had always sought higher political office. As early as 1852, he began to eye the presidency, and in 1856, while governor of Tennessee, he entertained the vague hope of being the Democratic nominee as president. Even as military governor of Tennessee, he maintained his interest in running someday for president. He could not, of course, have predicted the dramatic course of events that led him to becoming the nation's seventeenth president in a period of about ten months. But once he learned that Lincoln wanted a war Democrat to be his running mate in 1864, he jockeyed successfully to be that candidate. Having won the second spot on Lincoln's Unionist ticket, he delivered a number of speeches in which he made clear what had been his view about secession throughout the Civil War and would remain his position as president: the Confederate states had never left the Union because they had no legal right to secede. Essentially, he reaffirmed Andrew Jackson's stance during the nullification controversy about the illegality of secession.

As a Jacksonian, Johnson also believed that the states should determine their own course of reconstruction once they had taken loyalty oaths and abolished slavery. However, he made clear his belief in white man's government while failing to spell out, even in the early weeks after he became president, what guarantees and protections the former slaves should be granted. Instead, he finessed the issue of reconstruction in such a way as to satisfy most radical Republicans even as he left hints that he favored a form of reconstruction quite different from the harsher and more extended form, including the right of freedmen to vote, that they had in mind.

The result was the most intense battle between two branches of government in the nation's history, leading ultimately to Johnson's impeachment and trial. This epic struggle over reconstruction has, however, overshadowed other aspects of his presidency, including the national economic transformation that had actually begun before the Civil War and was resumed with renewed vigor after the war ended.[7] The president remained so committed to his Jacksonian vision of an agrarian republic that he failed to understand the dynamic changes taking place in the United States. As a result, he and the Republican-controlled Congress fought not only over reconstruction policy but also over economic and financial policy. Arguing, for example, that the national debt, which he placed in 1868 at more than $3.3 billion (the equivalent of about $52.5 billion in 2009), was the result not only of the Civil War but also of "the perversion of the Constitution and the subjugation of the States to negro domination," the president proposed to repudiate part of the national debt by applying interest payments on bonds funding the debt to the principal on the bonds.[8]

Fearing large aggregations of capital and eschewing fundamental changes in his model of a yeoman republic, Johnson argued in Jacksonian terms that bondholders had already received sufficient interest to compensate them and that if the debt were permitted to become permanent, it "must eventually be gathered into the hands of a few, and enable them to exert a dangerous and controlling power in the affairs of the Government. The borrowers would become servants of the lenders, the lenders the masters of the people."[9] Similarly, he advocated Jacksonian hard money policies. Newspapers and Republicans in Congress excoriated him for the harm they believed his proposals would cause in the nation's financial markets and for his lack of understanding of the way in which modern business was conducted.[10]

Although the Republican Party failed to bring about any major transfer of power in the South, its battle with Johnson solidified its position in the North. It also left Republicans as the party most closely associated with the nation's changing industrial and urban landscape.

Considering how close Johnson came to being forced out of office, one might have expected the former president to seek to escape forever the nightmare of Washington and to retire to the mountains of eastern Tennessee, where he was still regarded as something of a folk hero for having stood up to the demands of the Radical Republicans. Such was not the case. In the first place, despite his identification with the yeoman class of eastern Tennessee, the small-town life of Greeneville bored him. He owned a farm, but he was not a farmer and hated being called an agrarian. He had proven to be a savvy businessman, but the life of a successful entrepreneur was not sufficiently fulfilling for him.[11]

Family life also caused him considerable grief. His wife, Eliza, was ill with consumption and rarely left her bedroom. His oldest daughter, Martha, who had served as official White House hostess in place of her invalid mother, was married to Tennessee's first U.S. senator after the Civil War, David T. Patterson. His other daughter and third child, Mary, was a war widow who had remarried a local resident of Greeneville. Martha and Mary resided in Greeneville, near their father's home and had five children between them. But Mary's marriage was not a happy one and would eventually end in divorce.

Worse for Johnson, his oldest son, Charles, a pharmacist and surgeon in the Union army during the Civil War, had been thrown from a horse and killed in April 1863. Charles's death was an especially hard blow for Johnson, for although Charles had a serious drinking problem, had never married, and had never held a job very long, he had edited his father's newspaper at one time and bought and sold stock for him. His second eldest son, Robert, a lawyer, who had served as his private secretary in the White House, had an even more serious drinking problem than his brother. He became such an embarrassment to the administration that he had to be sent to Asia and Africa, allegedly to investigate abuses of the coolie and slave trades.[12]

What drove Johnson to seek to return to Washington after returning home to Tennessee in 1869, however, was his quest for vindication. Even before leaving the White House, he made clear his interest in a second term as president. The whole South and Northern Democrats anxious to restore the Union as quickly as possible, he hoped, would rally to his support. This did not happen. Notwithstanding the many letters he received urging him to run for president, Democratic leaders did not forgive him for leaving the party in 1864. Although Johnson managed to receive sixty-five votes on the first ballot at the Democratic nominating convention, his support quickly slipped away as the Democrats turned to the wartime governor of New York, Horatio Seymour.[13]

Disappointed and angered by being rejected for another term as president, Johnson even hesitated to endorse Seymour. He also gave up any immediate hope of again holding the nation's highest political office. After the 1868 elections, in which the Republican candidate for president, Ulysses S. Grant, soundly defeated Seymour, a number of his followers encouraged him to run for office in Tennessee. A boomlet even developed for a Johnson campaign for the governorship. An old acquaintance and political collaborator, A. A. Kyle, went to Washington in

January to urge him to run for governor of Tennessee. "The whole Conservative sentiment at Knoxville, & I think I can safely say, throughout East Ten: is in favor of your running for Govr. in Augt next," Kyle later wrote Johnson. "Think of these things and shape your course accordingly." But Johnson discouraged the effort on his behalf. In February, he wrote to newspaper publisher Natus J. Haynes, who had written a long lead article promoting Johnson for the office, that the time was not appropriate for him "to form or publish an opinion" on a possible gubernatorial run.[14]

Not for the last time, Johnson was being coy. What he was already thinking about was a seat in the U.S. Senate. At the end of February, while still in office, he granted an interview to a correspondent from the *New York World* in which he denied any "plan personal to myself for the future." At the same time, he remarked that "[his] temperament, physical strength, and habits, almost forbid [him] to sink into idleness" when his term ended. After denying that he had any interest in seeking retaliation against his enemies, he proceeded to expand on how much a person of high moral character could contribute to the country by serving in the Senate. Obviously having himself in mind, he remarked with respect to the Senate, "I . . . think there is great need there and large opportunity there for any man governed solely by principle." As far as he was concerned, being a senator offered him more opportunities than any other office because a senator represented not only a state but "the country as a whole."[15]

On 4 March, his final day in office, Johnson broke convention by becoming only the third, and last, president (the others being John Adams and John Quincy Adams) not to attend the inauguration of his successor because of the bitter animosity that had developed between him and incoming president Grant over congressional reconstruction. Instead, Johnson remained in Washington for a week before traveling to Baltimore, where he was guest of honor at a large dinner of well-wishers. Toward the end of March, he returned with his family to Greeneville and a hero's welcome. On his way home, he made a number of speeches in which he compared his emancipation from the office of president to the emancipation of the slaves. "For the last four years I have been the completest slave throughout the length and breadth of the United States," he remarked in one speech. "And standing here as a free man I thank God that I am a free man, and have the privilege of speaking as a free man and a private citizen."[16]

By the time he returned home, however, the former president was eager to redeem his political reputation. Still vigorous at age sixty, he had been described a year earlier by the British novelist Charles Dickens as having "one of the most remarkable faces" he had ever seen, "not imaginative, but very powerful in its firmness (or perhaps obstinacy), strength of will, and steadiness of purpose."[17] In making this observation, Dickens was displaying the keen observations characteristic of a great writer. Firmness of purpose and strength of will remained just as much part of Johnson's personality after leaving the White House as they had been throughout his entire political career—except now he was bent on vindicating his presidency and gaining retribution from the enemies who had almost brought him down.

Not surprisingly, given his earlier remarks to the *New York World* correspondent, the former president had his eye on a seat in the U.S. Senate that was about to be vacated by the incumbent, Joseph Fowler, one of seven Republicans who had voted to acquit him during his impeachment trial. Johnson banked his candidacy on the support of both Democrats and Republicans grateful for his efforts to restore the Union as quickly as possible. He also sought to take advantage of internal divisions within Tennessee politics. To bolster his chances with the legislature, which would choose Fowler's replacement, Johnson took to the hustings. In Knoxville, an estimated crowd of 50,000 turned out to hear him defend his record as president, attack bondholders, and promise to seek his vindication. Crossing the state in a special train, he drew large crowds wherever he went. He delivered essentially the same message he had given at Knoxville. He felt rejuvenated by the outpouring of support he received. He dared to deny, however, that he was seeking elected office, remarking in Nashville, for example, that "I am no aspirant for office" and then concluding, "If I can do nothing more, I can retire to my own home . . . and pray for my country."[18]

Tragedy struck in the midst of his campaign when, in April, Johnson's son, Robert, who had never been able to overcome his problem with alcohol, committed suicide. News of Robert's death was almost more than the former president and his wife, Eliza, could bear. Their two oldest sons had died in an untimely manner in less than six years. Only their youngest boy, Andrew Jr. (always referred to as Frank), who was an undergraduate at Georgetown College, remained alive. Abandoning his tour of the state, Johnson went to Washington to see Frank graduate from college.

What was surprising was not Johnson's deep sense of loss but his refusal to give up his quest for vindication. Even while in Washington, he gave an interview to a reporter in which he assailed his successor as "a mere accident of the war." "He hasn't a single idea," he added about Grant. "He has no ideas, no policy . . . nothing. . . . He is mendacious, cunning, and treacherous." Returning to Tennessee, the former president remained just as vitriolic, attacking Grant and Jefferson Davis (to please Republicans), and continuing his tirades against Congress and bondholders, whom he referred to as "credit aristocrat[s] . . . striving to rule the government."[19]

Through his efforts, Johnson helped elect at the beginning of August a governor and a legislature that was solidly conservative and friendly toward him. As a result, he was able in October to come within four votes of getting the seat he so desperately wanted. There were, however, still too many radicals (Republicans) and old Confederates (secessionists) returning to Nashville that refused to forgive the former president. After caucusing, they threw their support behind Judge Henry Cooper, the brother of Johnson's former private secretary and aide, Edmund Cooper. Family ties trumped political loyalty when Edmund abandoned

Johnson in favor of his brother, thereby throwing the election to Cooper by a vote of 54 to 51.

His defeat may have marked the lowest point of Johnson's life, even more so than his impeachment and trial as president. Even during that trying time, he had always believed he was defending constitutional principles and that his presidency would be vindicated. He also felt victimized by a small, but vocal and powerful, group of Radical Republicans. Having campaigned vigorously—and with apparent success—to enthusiastic crowds throughout the state, he felt almost a sense of inevitability about his selection as Tennessee's newest U.S. senator. Although the state elections were not a referendum on his presidency, it must have seemed that way to Johnson. In the weeks before the legislature made its choice for the Senate, the former president received dozens of letters predicting his return to Washington. Once more, however, he seemed victimized, this time by one of his closest political associates.[20]

It is not surprising, therefore, that for the next two years, the former president, whose entire adult life had been consumed by politics, removed himself from the political scene. As a young congressman, he had engaged in a program of self-study, reading numerous works by British playwrights and political theorists. Like many of the nation's early founders, he had been taken particularly by Joseph Addison's play on Cato the Younger, the great Roman statesman, who, in Addison's play, defended the last vestiges of the Roman Republic against Julius Caesar. Regarding himself as a modern version of Cato, Johnson often quoted the Roman throughout his political career and during the recent campaign. "If I can do no more I can follow the advice of Cato to his son in the last extremity in pent up Syracuse," Johnson remarked to a crowd in Memphis. "'Go my son to the Sabine fields, and there praise the gods!' I can retire to my humble home, and pray for my country and the preservation of its liberties."[21]

Johnson may have thought of himself as a contemporary version of Cato, but clearly the Roman identity of civic virtue with retirement after dutiful public service, which motivated the nation's earliest former presidents, had little to do with Johnson's return home to Greeneville. There is nothing to indicate that he was any less bent on his political vindication after his defeat for the Senate than he had been before it. It would have been out of character for him to have accepted defeat and to retire, as he said, to his "humble home" in a small town, which he described to his son, Frank, as "a dull place [that] seems likely to continue so" and from which he had been away the majority of his adult life.[22]

The former president, it is true, did not engage in politics the way he had earlier. Rather, he tended to his wife, his children, and his grandchildren, and he became almost a guardian to a young lawyer and former Confederate who opened a law office in Greeneville, E. C. Reeves. Worth about $150,000 (the equivalent about $2.65 million in 2009), Johnson helped Reeves financially. Soon the young lawyer was in control of the editorial policy of the local newspaper, the *Greeneville National Union*. He also became Johnson's personal secretary. Because of an accident that Johnson had suffered years back, he found it difficult to write, and Reeves usually visited him several times a week at home to take dictation. For the most part, though, he led a lonely existence, remaining at home, sometimes taking a stroll through the town or the nearby woodlands, but rarely visiting even with neighbors. "I feel as though I was among strangers, not to say enemies," he even remarked about his life in Greeneville, which he continued to describe as "lifeless as a grave-yard."[23]

Determined to run for office again, Johnson merely bided his time for the right opportunity. He continued, for example, to make an occasional speech attacking the onerous nature of the public debt and the villainy of congressional Republicans and President Grant. Reaffirming a position he had advocated throughout his political career, he also called for the direct election of presidents and senators and staggered terms for Supreme Court judges.[24]

In May 1871, Johnson delivered a particularly long and often repetitive speech to a group of laborers and mechanics in Knoxville. Identifying himself as a mechanic because of his early career as a tailor, and recounting his life as an example of how even the lowliest citizen could rise to the highest office in the land through the sweat of his brow, he pleaded the case for self-reliance and warned against the "lucre" of capital and the enticements of urban life. "Go to New York; go to Wall street, amongst the bulls and the bears, the bondholders, and the jobbers, and the speculators," he remarked, "and you will find that New York, to some extent is becoming . . . what Sodom and Tyre were to the ancient world." Reminding his listeners of Jefferson's warnings against urban life, he added that "it would be God's blessing if New York should be cut up into four or five cities and spread about throughout the country." Also devoting a large portion of his speech to penitentiaries, which he referred to as "state monopolies of labor" competing against honest mechanics, he proposed a way to eliminate prisons. Preaching a type of eugenics through elimination of a bad human strain, he remarked: "I would divide all offenders into two classes; the first class I would hang, and the second class I would deprive of the power of propagating their species. There you would stop the breed."

As the former president rambled on, he called once more for eliminating the national debt by applying the interest due to bondholders to the debt principal; he referred to the Civil War as a "rich man's war and the poor man's fight"; he compared capital and labor to different sexes, each antagonistic to the other but each "always seeking the other"; and he accused Great Britain of taking sides with the South during the recent conflict because "she believed that the division of the United States would weaken and break down her great rival, and then capital would unite and make war against labor." In sum, Johnson's address in Knoxville was one of the most remarkable and revealing he ever delivered, full of sentimentality and histrionics, sometimes bordering on the irrational and the demagogic, but always held together by his Jacksonian contempt of the monopolies and moneyed interests (bondholders), which, he vowed, would destroy the republic unless constitutional principles and traditional values were restored.[25]

In 1872, the former president surprised a number of his supporters when he decided to run as an independent for Congress. When the results were tallied, the Republican won, and Johnson came in a distant third. Why he decided to enter a race in which he had little chance of winning and which would not give him the type of national vindication he wanted is still unclear. By running and conducting a vigorous statewide campaign in which he was able to take enough votes away from the Democratic candidate to assure a Republican victory, however, he helped cleanse the Democratic Party of its Confederate elements and prepared the way for him to run for the Senate seat in 1874 held by an old political nemesis, Republican William G. Brownlow.[26]

Before being able to kick off his campaign, Johnson was forced to spend much of 1873 recovering from a bout with cholera that nearly killed him. He also became involved in a newspaper debate having to do with allegations made by Joseph Holt, his judge advocate general while he was president, involving one of the alleged plotters in Lincoln's assassination, Mary Surratt. According to Holt, Johnson had seen, and turned down, a petition for clemency, which had been based on Surrat's age and sex, by five of the nine military commissioners who had tried her along with the other conspirators. Surrat was then hanged. Accusing Holt of being a liar, Johnson denied that he had ever seen the petition, and the evidence seemed to back him.[27]

By January 1874, Johnson was ready to launch his second campaign for the U.S. Senate. By now his tactics and message were familiar. He would run an exhaustive speaking campaign throughout the state on behalf of local candidates for the legislature. He would also use another tactic that had become one of his standard operating procedures since being president: holding interviews with reporters from selected newspapers, such as the one he had given to a correspondent of the *New York Herald* in 1869 and two others he had had given to reporters from the *Memphis Appeal* in August 1871 and again in August 1872. More than any of his predecessors, Johnson reached out to the people through reporters and press interviews. He also barraged the press with messages and speeches he had delivered.[28]

Johnson decided once more to make the restoration of constitutional principles and an attack on monopolists and bondholders the focus of his campaign. He anticipated that his message would resonate with conservative Democrats, moderate Republicans, and the first significant agrarian movement after the Civil War, the Patrons of Husbandry or Grangers, who sought protection against the monopolistic abuses of railroad and grain elevator operators and supported some manner of inflation. Despite his own hard money views, he proposed replacing national banknotes with unsecured paper currency, known as greenbacks. "Here are these greenbacks, the government issue," he remarked. "They bear no interest; but those bank notes, they bear 18 percent. How would it do to issue $400,000,000 in greenbacks, and take up those bank notes in the country."[29]

In the months before the statewide elections in November, Johnson crisscrossed the state. Promising to remain independent if elected to the Senate, he sought to heal wounds with Democrats, remind Republicans of the role he had played in helping get a Republican elected to the House, and rally his Jacksonian base of yeoman farmers and mechanics. He even courted former Whigs by eulogizing former president Millard Fillmore shortly after his death on 8 March.[30]

Although the results of the November elections were favorable to Johnson, his election was by no means a certainty. Democrats had swept the state, winning both houses of the legislature by overwhelming margins. Johnson still had to deal with old Confederates ("extreme Democrats" and "radical rebels," he had called them earlier) who had opposed him in past elections.[31] In addition to the former president, they could choose from three former Confederate generals and one colonel. On the first ballot, Johnson led with thirty votes, but he still needed twenty-one more. By the thirty-fifth ballot, the former president had managed to increase his number to forty-three. Realizing that he was close but that the only way he could win was with Republican support, Johnson promised the Republicans that if elected he would not advocate "radical measures" and that he would not oppose Grant's policies "except in very extreme cases." "If elected by Republican votes," he vowed, "I will not forget what I owe that party."[32] The former president, who took pride in his commitment to principle, was willing to subordinate principle to gain the Republican support necessary to return to Washington.

His ploy worked. Although his opponents tried to unite behind a single candidate, they failed. On 26 January, he secured fifty-two votes, one more than needed for victory. When he learned that he had been elected, Johnson responded simply, "I'd rather have this information than to learn that I had been elected President of the United States. Thank God for the vindication."[33]

To deal with several matters, including a reciprocity treaty with Hawaii, President Grant called a special session of the Senate in March. This afforded the former president the opportunity to face many of those still in the Senate who had led the effort to oust him from office seven years earlier and to make a speech on the Senate floor that he had longed to make. Despite a little awkwardness on the part of a few senators, he was generally received well when he arrived in the Senate chambers in March. Although he was given a seat on the Democratic side, he redeemed his campaign pledge not to join the Democratic caucus but to remain an independent.

On 20 March, however, the newly elected senator took to the Senate floor and, ignoring his campaign promise not to oppose the president except in extreme cases, he delivered a blistering attack on Grant. He accused him of violating the Constitution by allowing the army to interfere in elections in Louisiana. He also claimed that Grant was guilty of even broader violations of the Constitution, and he suggested that his aim was a third term as president. "How far off is military despotism?" he asked. Having finished his speech, which added nothing new to what he had been saying almost since the day he returned to Tennessee, he took his seat.[34]

Unfortunately for Johnson, his single address to the Senate proved to be his last. After the special session ended a few days later, he returned to Greeneville, fully expecting to return to Washington in December. Although Johnson appeared to be in good health, he had not been well for many years. In 1864, he came down with either typhoid or malaria, which left him bedridden for weeks.[35] As vice president and president, he had recurring incidents of chronic dysentery, kidney stones, and renal colic. He also suffered from emotional stress and excessive strain, which also often left him bedridden. His failure to see the clemency recommendation for Mrs. Surratt was most likely because at the time the recommendation should have come to his attention, he was sick in bed and allowed no visitors. After returning to Tennessee, he nearly died from an epidemic of cholera and never completely recovered from it. He also continued to suffer emotional stress as a result of the suicide of his son, Robert, and of the strain of seeking office once again.[36]

When Johnson died, however, it came suddenly and unexpectedly. After spending the spring and early summer relaxing and attending to private business matters, the former president and his wife boarded a train at the end of July to visit their daughter, Mary, who lived about forty miles away, before leaving for Ohio, where he planned to make a number of speeches. As some of his contemporaries theorized, he may have been thinking of seeking the Democratic presidential nomination in 1876. While visiting his daughter, however, the former president suffered a stroke. When he was put to bed, he was well enough the next day to reminisce about his entire life, going back to his days as a tailor. However, the next day, he suffered a second stroke that left him totally paralyzed and unconscious. After lingering for a few hours, he died on 31 July.[37]

At Johnson's request, his body, which had been returned to Greeneville for burial, was wrapped in the American flag while his head rested on a copy of the Constitution. Five thousand persons turned out for his funeral on 3 August. Official business in Washington was suspended, and the White House and government departments were draped in black. The former president was buried on Signal Hill just outside of Greeneville, a site that Johnson had picked out years before. His wife, Eliza, was buried beside him when she died just six months later.

In editorializing on Johnson's death, Northern newspapers generally commented on his loyalty to the Union during the Civil War, while Southern newspapers emphasized his efforts on behalf of Southern redemption after the conflict. That newspapers reflected on Johnson's life from the perspective of the Civil War and Southern reconstruction was not surprising. Just as the Civil War and the decade that followed marked the end of one era and the beginning of another, so did Johnson's life. After learning of his passing, President Grant issued a proclamation in which he noted that it was his "painful duty" to announce the death of the "last survivor of his honored predecessors." In making this comment, Grant had in mind the deaths not only of Johnson but also of Franklin Pierce and Millard Fillmore, both of whom had also died while he was president.

DEATH OF THE HON. ANDREW JOHNSON.
U. S. SENATOR FROM TENNESSEE AND EX-PRESIDENT OF THE UNITED STATES.
Died at Greenville, Tenn. July 31ˢᵗ 1875.   Aged 66 years, 7 months and 2 days.

A lithograph of the death of Andrew Johnson in 1875 by the printmaking firm of Currier and Ives, the most successful firm of its kind of the mid- and late-nineteenth century, producing more than a million prints every week for sixty-four years (1834–1895). (Courtesy of Library of Congress, Prints and Photographs Division.)

Although Fillmore was not a Jacksonian, Pierce and Johnson were. As an ex-president, Fillmore had been forward looking in his thinking, making proposals about presidential pensions and reform of the consular service that would not be enacted until the twentieth century and engaging in the type of charitable endeavors that would be characteristic of the Gilded Age. In the political sphere, Johnson also embraced ideas that looked to the future, such as his call for the direct election of senators and even presidents. However, his ideal for the United States was not that of the emerging modern industrial and urban state, which he disdained. Rather, it was of an increasingly bygone era—a yeoman republic of self-sufficient farmers and hardworking mechanics. As president and former president, Andrew Johnson was the last of the Jacksonians.

II

What made Ulysses S. Grant so different from Johnson as a former president was that while the Tennessee politician remained committed to the ideals of a bygone era, the hero of the Civil War held no strong views about the past and readily accommodated himself to the corporate world of modern America. As a former president, he associated with some of the nation's best-known industrial and financial barons. He also took advantage of modern means of transportation and communication to become the nation's most traveled former president. He lent his good name to the speculative ventures in high finance of his son, Ulysses Jr., going bankrupt in the process. And he became the first former president to make a small fortune by publishing his memoirs. Instead of being a slave to the past, he married the past to the corporate world of book publishing to ensure the financial security of his family.

Grant was always more a man of action than of words. The future president, who could not stand music, was once asked which music he liked. He allegedly responded, "I only know two tunes. One of them is 'Yankee Doodle Dandy' and the other one isn't." Whether he actually made that comment, it would have been totally in character if he did.[38] Despite the many scandals that led his administration to be widely branded as one of most corrupt in the nation's history, the former president has hardly ever been accused of being dishonest himself. In contrast to Johnson, he has also seldom been charged with being doctrinaire, vindictive, or willful. In fact, he lacked almost completely Johnson's guile and untrustworthiness. Irrespective of his failure to secure the full rights of citizenship for the freedmen of the South, he has also rarely been labeled a white supremacist in the mode of Johnson. His racial views toward blacks, and for that matter the Plains Indians, were actually more advanced than those of most of his contemporaries.[39]

Not only was Grant's character a study in contrast with Johnson's, but so was his biography. If his predecessor was a self-made man, born into poverty and apprenticed as a tailor without a formal education, who by his own efforts became a successful entrepreneur and politician, Grant's early life was one of privilege and comfort, followed by a checkered military career and virtual bankruptcy in private life before being saved financially by his father. An apt description of his career as a cadet at West Point, where he finished in the bottom half of his class, would be "undistinguished." Although he proved to be an able officer during the Mexican–American War, he began to drink heavily and resigned from the army in 1854, reportedly under pressure. He had difficulty adjusting to civilian life, and after various failures, he was finally forced take a position in his father's tannery business.

At the outbreak of the Civil War on 12 April 1861, Grant hardly seemed destined for historical greatness. Born on 27 April 1822, he was two weeks shy of his thirty-ninth birthday. Five feet, eight inches tall, weighing about 130 pounds, with blue eyes, wavy brown hair, a scruffy beard and mustache, ordinary features, and unkempt dress, he scarcely stood out in a crowd. Married and the father of four children, he centered his life almost entirely on his family.

While some individuals seem fated for greatness, fate uncovers greatness in others. No less than Abraham Lincoln as president, the Civil War revealed Grant's greatness as a military commander. Although he came to be called Butcher Grant during the conflict for the heavy casualties he was willing to sustain in order to defeat the Confederacy, the war brought out his best qualities. His quiet self-confidence but lack of any apparent ego, his ordinary appearance but extraordinary empathy for his forces, his brilliant sense of strategy, his ability to cut to the essence of complex problems, his ability to subsist on existing resources and to pursue victory relentlessly—all made him a superior military leader.

By making Grant into a national hero, the Civil War smoothed his way to the White House in 1868, all but assuring his election as president on the Republican ticket. In 1872, he was reelected to a second term in a landslide, defeating his opponent, Horace Greeley, who ran as a Liberal Republican and Democrat, by a margin of 12 percent (56 percent to 44 percent) and carrying all but six Southern and border states.

What was striking about Grant's presidency is that it was the first to accept and even welcome corporate America. The contrast between Johnson and Grant in this respect could hardly be greater. Although Grant shared Johnson's empathy for the poor and the unfortunate, he did not blame their hardships on monopolists, bondholders, or the bulls and bears of Wall Street. His vision of America was not of a yeoman republic but of an emerging industrial power. As president, his friends and acquaintances included the financier Jay Cooke, the railroad magnate William H. Vanderbilt, and the notorious speculators Jay Gould and Jim Fiske.

Even Grant's monetary and fiscal views were notably different from those of Johnson. Both men held hard money views, but, in contrast to Johnson, Grant was unwilling, even for political expediency, to inflate the currency through the redeployment of greenbacks. Notwithstanding the Panic of 1873 and the depression that followed, he opposed postponement of the resumption of specie payment. Also in contrast to Johnson, he believed the nation's credit hinged on honoring its obligation to make regular interest payments in gold to holders of the debt. Throughout his term in office, Grant's purpose was to guide the nation into a new period after the travails of war and reconstruction.[40]

Grant's second administration was riddled with scandal that led to accusations of criminality on the part of the president's private secretary and longtime aide, Orville Babcock, in the famous Whiskey Ring conspiracy to defraud the government of tax money. In response, Congress overwhelmingly approved a resolution in 1875 stating that it would be "unwise, unpatriotic, and fraught with peril" to depart from the two-term tradition for presidents established by Washington. The press began a drumbeat of attacks on the administration. Yet Grant could have easily been nominated, and probably reelected, for a third term if he pursued it. Certainly his wife, Julia Dent Grant, who had completely refurbished the White House and became its most prominent hostess since Dolley Madison, wanted to remain as White House hostess for another four years.[41]

The president, however, had had enough. After the Pennsylvania Republican Party, meeting in convention, endorsed Grant for a third term, the president issued a statement effectively taking him out of the presidential race. Grant decided against a third term mainly because he had become bored with his office.

Reflecting a lifelong interest in travel, he was instead anxious to see as much of the world as possible. A small investment in the mining company that owned the Comstock lode had grown to be worth $25,000 (the equivalent of almost $500,000 in 2009), sufficient, he thought, for lengthy travel overseas. He also had an additional $60,000 from investments his son, Ulysses "Buck" Jr., had made for him.[42] Relieved of the burdens of office, Grant and Julia remained in Washington while their daughter, Nellie, gave birth to a son. Afterward, they returned to Galena, Illinois, for a short stay before embarking on a world tour that would last two and a half years and have them circumnavigate the globe. On 17 May, the Grants departed down the Delaware River toward the Atlantic on the government steamer *Indiana,* which had been put at his disposal. Other ships on the river blew their horns with long blasts in bids of farewell as the *Indiana* passed by them.[43]

When Grant arrived in Liverpool on 28 May, ships in the Mersey River displayed American flags as a sign of respect. A pattern then began that was repeated in countless places Grant visited, from world capitals to lesser cities and towns throughout the globe. Official greetings by local dignitaries were followed by sightseeing, receptions, and official banquets. Thousands of locals turned out whenever possible to see and greet him. Special treatment was accorded to him by Queen Victoria of England, who had his family as guests at Windsor Castle; by Chancellor Otto Von Bismarck of Germany; by Tsar Alexander of Russia; by the sultan of Turkey; by the viceroy and prince regent of China; and by the emperor of Japan. Part of the reason for the reception Grant received had less to do with his status as a former president of the United States and more with his stature as a commanding general of Union forces during the Civil War. Europeans regarded him as the greatest soldier of his day in the greatest war since the Napoleonic wars, a leader who had broken all conventions of traditional warfare in a conflict characterized by new technologies and means of communication, improved weaponry, and ghastly losses.[44]

Yet Grant's welcome also reflected new respect for the United States as an industrial power. During his travels, he spent much of his time in conversation with John Russell Young, a reporter from the New York *Herald,* who accompanied him on his grand tour. Young not only sent reports back to the United States on the former president's journey, but he also kept a record of it, which he later published. Although most of what Young talked about with Grant had to do with his recollections of the Civil War, the former president talked about the United States' standing in the world, a subject on which he also commented in his correspondence and in some of the hundreds of short remarks and speeches he made during his tour. Together, they made clear his pride in what he believed to be the United States' future as a global power.[45]

As Young reported, the former president was both surprised and heartened by the reception he received from the moment he arrived in England. Writing to his friend George W. Childs, he remarked of his reception in England, "I appreciate the fact, and am proud of it, that the attentions I am receiving are intended more for our country than for me personally. I love to see our country honored & respected abroad. . . . It has always been my desire to see all jealousy between England and the United States abated. . . . Together, they are more powerful for the spread of Commerce and civilization than all others combined."[46]

After a brief tour of the continent, during which he discussed with King Leopold of Belgium the establishment of shipping lines between Antwerp and American ports, he went to Scotland and then proceeded southward through the industrial heartland of England. Young was thunderstruck by the throngs that came out to greet Grant as he visited such places as Newcastle, Sheffield, and Birmingham. "It was here that the General met the working classes of England, and the enthusiasm which his visit inspired makes it impossible to bring it within the limits of a sober narrative," the *Herald* reporter wrote.[47]

Moved by the reception he received, Grant responded by talking about a "common destiny" between the two countries that he believed would "result in the spread of our language, our civilization, and our industry, and be for the benefit of mankind generally." In a related fashion, he remarked that although he was famed for his military career, he hated warfare and wanted the two English-speaking countries to work together to end war. In another speech, he added his hope that the millions of soldiers "who are now supported by the industry of the nations [might] return to industrial pursuits." He even advocated an international congress of nations to discuss "international questions of difficulty . . . whose decisions will be as binding as the decisions of our Supreme Court."[48]

Leaving England for a second time, Grant spent the next six months traveling to Paris, southern France, Italy, the eastern and western Mediterranean, Egypt, the Holy Land, and a return visit to Italy. Remarkably, this turned out for Grant to be the most disquieting and least interesting part of his tour. In Paris, he was the guest of President Marshall Patrice de MacMahon of the Third Republic amid talk that MacMahon was about to launch a coup d'etat. Although Grant toured the famous sights of Paris, including the Louvre, whose paintings drew him back for several visits, he felt limited by the fact that he did not speak French and wound up spending much of his time either with the considerable American colony in Paris or at the New York *Herald*'s office, reading newspapers.[49]

During the remainder of this part of Grant's world tour, the former president wondered at the great pyramids of Egypt, was moved as a Christian by his visit to Jerusalem, was awed by the spectacular architecture of the Parthenon (which was illuminated in his honor), and marveled at Michaelangelo's fresco of the Last Judgment in the Sistine Chapel. What is striking, however, was not how determined Grant was to see every sight, but how unimpressed he seems to have been by what he saw.

He was left cold, for example, by the beauty of Naples, uninterested in such Homeric landmarks he saw as the rock of Scylla and the Charybdis, and depressed by Constantinople's cold March weather. He went through the motions of visiting most of Greece's ancient sights rather than being impressed by them. The same was true of his visits to view the great architecture and art of Renaissance Florence. According to Adam Badeau, his former secretary during the Civil War and now consul general in London, who accompanied him on this part of his world tour, the former president quickly became bored by all the statuary and paintings he saw while in Italy and elsewhere. Unfairly or not, he was best remembered for the remark he made while visiting Venice — that the city would have been more beautiful if its canals had been drained — which seems to have had more to do with his concern about sanitation than with anything else. He also found the government and civilization of the countries he visited repressive and unproductive. "The people would be industrious if they had encouragement but they are treated as slaves." he wrote from Italy.[50]

After Italy, Grant continued back and forth across Europe with visits to Paris, Holland, and Madrid. In contrast to his increasing boredom with Europe's antiquities, he was taken by the evidence of Europe's modern progress. He admired the bridges, roads, railroads, and mines of Europe, which, he thought, might serve as models for the United States. He was also impressed by the cleanliness, industry, and thrift of the Dutch people. At the same time, he was unimpressed by the massive Paris Exposition (World's Fair), which he compared unfavorably to the United States' Centennial Exhibition two years earlier in Philadelphia. Although the Paris fair was the largest of its kind up to that time and included a Gallery of Machines and two avenues illuminated with electric lights, he commented that it was "no improvement on our Centennial show. The buildings and grounds are far inferior to ours."[51]

The most memorable part of Grant's second trip to the continent came when he met German chancellor Von Bismarck in Berlin. The contrast between the two men was striking. Grant had not changed much in appearance since his days as a Union general, except that during the war he had begun to wear a short-cropped beard and mustache, both of which were now neatly trimmed and flecked with gray, as was his hair. Still only fifty-six years old, he had a jaunt to his walk and a youthful appearance. Bismarck, dressed in uniform when he met Grant, and with an ashen face, bald head, and bushy mustache, seemed considerably older than the seven years that separated him from his guest.[52]

Yet the German leader and former president admired each other — Bismarck for Grant's military skill in defeating the Confederacy, and Grant for the German chancellor's ability to forge a powerful nation out of a group of principalities. Although their conversation was interesting in making clear Grant's conviction that total defeat of the Confederacy was necessary in order to end slavery, the two men did not talk much about substantive matters of state. Grant voiced his approval of the Congress of Berlin called by Bismarck to resolve the issue of the Balkan countries that had led to the Russo-Turkish war. He also expressed outrage at the recent assassination attempt of Emperor William. Recalling his fear of social disorder in the United States when Lincoln was assassinated, Grant advocated the "severest punishment" for William's unsuccessful assassin. However, the American Civil War remained the main topic of conversation between Grant and Bismarck.[53]

After his first meeting with Grant, Bismarck visited the former president and his wife, Julia, at their hotel and then hosted a dinner in their honor at his palace. In his account of their conversations, Young later wrote that the former president and German leader "talked mainly upon the resources of the two countries . . . a theme upon which [Grant] never tires." Although the *Herald* reporter did not elaborate, most likely Grant was interested in forging closer economic ties with Germany. While he was put off by the authoritarian and militaristic nature of Germany, he and his party were impressed by the state of German industry and commerce.[54]

Grant's trip through Scandinavia and Russia and then to Vienna was uneventful. Although he marveled at the sights, including St. Petersburg's Hermitage, the "Orient feeling" of Moscow's Kremlin, and Vienna's famed opera house, what continued to impress him the most was the evidence (or lack thereof) of modern progress in the places he visited. He was clearly taken, for example, by the industry of Sweden. In contrast, he and his party were struck by the emptiness of Russia as they traveled the 400 miles between its two great cities.[55]

Since the spring, Grant had become increasingly homesick. In May he had even made plans to return to the United States. "I find that I enjoy european [*sic*] travel just in proportion as I find Americans to associate with," he wrote one of his comrades from the Civil War, William Smith, in September. However, indefatigable in his determination to see as much of the world as possible, he changed his mind and decided instead to continue across Europe before heading south again to the Mediterranean in order to travel by train from Alexandria to the Red Sea and then on to India, Southeast Asia, China, and Japan.[56]

India and the Orient fascinated the former president. He seemed to have been as much impressed, however, by the gas street lamps and the school of arts and industry in the Indian city of Jeypore as he was by India's great marble-domed Taj Mahal.[57] Much the same was true as he continued on to Burma, Singapore, Siam, Cochinchina, and finally China and Japan. As he traveled on this last, vast leg of his journey abroad, he was critical that the peoples of Southeast Asia had governments "forced upon them." At first, he thought British rule was "hard, reactionary, and selfish." He disapproved especially of the high-handed attitude of Westerners in China. "The course of the average minister, consul, and merchant in this country towards the native," he wrote in August, "is much like the course of the former slave owners toward the freedmen when the latter attempts to think for himself in matters of choice of candidates."[58]

Even before Grant arrived in China, he changed his mind about British colonial rule. "I will not say that I was all wrong," he acknowledged from Singapore, "but I do say that English men are wise enough to know that the more prosperous they can make the subject the greater consumer he will become, and the greater will be the commerce and trade between the home government and the colony and the greater the contentment of the government. Should the English leave," he concluded, "the work of rapine and murder and wars between native chiefs would begin."[59] Despite the wonderment of China that had enchanted and enticed Westerners for centuries, Grant was unimpressed by the sights he saw. But he observed that China was "on the eve of a great revolution that will land her among the nations of progress." The country, he added, had "the elements of great wealth and great power too and not more than a generation will pass before she will make these elements felt."[60]

From the moment that Grant arrived in the Japanese port of Nagasaki and went down the landing from his ship on steps covered with red fabric, his trip through Japan was spectacular in every sense. Never before had any Westerner received such a warm, cordial, and opulent welcome. Not only did the emperor, whom the Japanese regarded as a deity, pay him the tribute of an audience at his summer palace, purposely holding his meeting with him on the Fourth of July to honor the birth of the United States, but he shook hands with the former president, a gesture that was unprecedented in the history of the Japanese monarchy. "This is a most beautiful country, and a most interesting people," Grant wrote Badeau in August. "The progress they have made in their changed civilization within twelve years is almost incredible. They have now Military and Naval Academies, Colleges, Academies, Engineering schools, schools of science and free schools, for male & female . . . on as high a basis of instruction, as any country in the world. These people are becoming strong and China is sure to do so also. When they do a different policy will have to prevail from that enforced now."[61]

Grant's worldwide tour had been remarkable. Martin Van Buren and Millard Fillmore had both gone abroad after leaving the White House and had been warmly and appropriately received as former heads of state. Their visits had also been covered in the press. However, the scope of Grant's travels, the coverage of it, and the reception the former president received wherever he went was unprecedented.

During his travels overseas, the former president had read Mark Twain's *The Innocents Abroad: The New Pilgrim's Progress.* In *The Innocents Abroad,* Twain, who had briefly met Grant in 1869 and later played a crucial role in saving him from financial ruin, described his own odyssey to Europe and the Holy Land after the Civil War. In it, Twain seemed to display an indifference about the sights he visited comparable to Grant's often blinkered views by ridiculing those who puffed up the importance of past events and places. At the same time, Twain's conclusion suggested an appreciation of the world that the former president simply lacked. Of Paris, Twain remarked, for example, "We shall remember something of pleasant France; and something also of Paris, though it flashed upon us as a splendid meteor, and was gone again, we hardly know how or where." Of the same city, Grant wrote, "I do not believe there would be a duller place on earth for Americans than Paris if they did not have a large colony of their own countrymen to go with."[62]

Grant had been the quintessential American traveler abroad in the nation's new industrial age. Parochial in certain respects but not in others, he broke down the barriers of distance, time, and communication as a result of his world tour. Unapologetically proud of his nation's industrial prowess, he sought a world community of nations led by the English-speaking peoples but bound closely to other industrial nations. Willing to concede the uplifting value of British colonial rule, he was nevertheless instinctively opposed to colonialism and imperialism, and he was repelled by the arrogance of Westerners toward those they regarded as their inferiors. Impressed, finally, by what he regarded as the march of progress in places like China and Japan, he saw their potential as great powers that might someday come back to haunt the West.

Grant's return to the United States was similar to his trek across Europe and Asia. Instead of heading directly to the East Coast after arriving in San Francisco from Japan in September, he traveled first to northern California and Oregon before heading east again and making numerous detours along the way. Wherever he went, he was greeted by huge crowds and tumultuous receptions. In Chicago, he was welcomed home with a parade of 80,000 people. One of those in the reviewing stand was Mark Twain, whom the former president had remembered from their brief meeting in his White House office in 1869 and with whom he sealed a lasting friendship. The next day, Twain gave a rousing speech to a reunion banquet of the army of Tennessee. Not until December did Grant finally arrive back in Philadelphia, where he had begun his world tour two and a half years earlier. To welcome him back, the mayor of the city declared a holiday, closing all schools, factories and businesses, so that Philadelphians could turn out for a parade in Grant's honor. The parade lasted more than four hours.[63]

By the time the former president arrived back in Philadelphia, he had become the leading candidate for the Republican nomination for a third term as president. By this time, Grant was clearly planning to run for office again.[64] The possibility of serving a third term had become increasingly attractive to the former president as his travels neared an end. For one thing, he did not know what to do with himself once he returned home. Short of resources because of his world tour, he needed to do something major with his life. Meanwhile, a division had developed within the Republican Party between the so-called Stalwarts and Half-Breeds, and the Stalwarts, led by Senator Roscoe Conkling of New York, had been drumming up support for a Grant candidacy. The mass outpouring that greeted the former president as he traveled triumphantly across the continent removed any lingering doubts he still might have had about seeking a third term as president.[65]

Anticipating the reception Grant would receive as he crossed the country, Conkling and other Stalwarts had hoped he would delay his return by six months so that his candidacy would peak just about the time the Republicans were planning to hold their convention. Julia nixed that idea. She was anxious to see her children again. As Grant's handlers feared, however, his candidacy peaked too early. Although the former president continued to keep his name in the front pages by spending the winter traveling to Cuba and Mexico and went into the Chicago convention as the front-runner, his presence back home became a reminder of the scandal associated with his presidency. The New York *Tribune* published stories asserting that Grant could not win if nominated, given the corruption of his previous administrations. In a tactical mistake, which alienated many delegates against Grant, Conkling tried to impose the unit rule on the convention, whereby all the votes of a state would go to one candidate. Even worse, he tried to expel three West Virginia delegates who refused to promise to support the party's nominee. Had the unit rule been adopted, Grant would have had enough support to win the nomination on the first ballot. Unfortunately for him, his opponents, who included Senator James Blaine of Maine, the leader of the Half-Breeds and Conkling's arch foe, and Treasury Secretary John Sherman of Ohio, were able to prevent adoption of the unit rule.

To win the nomination, Grant needed 370 votes; he could count on a loyal 306 delegates, more than any other candidate. But through thirty-five ballots, he could only pick up an additional seven votes. Julia urged the former president to go before the convention in a personal effort to put himself over the top, but Grant said he would rather have his right arm cut off. As Blaine's candidacy lost steam, the anti-Grant delegates turned to Senator James Garfield of Ohio. On the thirty-sixth ballot, Garfield gained 399 votes to Grant's 306 votes, giving the Ohio senator the nomination.[66]

Grant later claimed that he had "grown weary of constant abuse" and was relieved that he had not gotten the nomination.[67] In reality, he was deeply hurt by his defeat. From his home in Galena, he had kept careful tabs on the convention's proceedings, fully expecting to be the nominee. As a result of his extended tour abroad and the reception he received, he had grown more confident in his political skills and his ability as a statesman. He had learned to wow crowds with his extemporaneous remarks. He had managed successful meetings with most of the world's leaders. At the request of the Chinese, he had even engaged in diplomacy between China and Japan over ownership of the Ryukus Islands. He had reason to believe, therefore, that if elected to a third term, he would make a more seasoned and effective world leader than during his first two administrations. But it was not to be.[68]

During the campaign that followed, Grant campaigned actively for Garfield, making a number of speeches on his behalf in New Jersey, New York, Ohio, and Connecticut. After the election, however, relations between the former president and the president-elect soured. Grant anticipated playing a key role in advising Garfield. Although the incoming president was grateful to Grant for the help he had given to him during the campaign, he intended to follow his own course. After Garfield turned down Grant's request that Badeau be left as consul general in London and seemed to side with the Half-Breeds against Conkling over the appointment of a collector of the port of New York, Grant broke with Garfield. "I will never again lend my active aid to the support of a Presidential candidate who has not the strength enough to appear before a convention as a candidate," he wrote Badeau in May 1881.[69] After Garfield's assassination a few months later, Grant tried to offer political advice to his successor, Chester Arthur, but he was again largely ignored. Time had simply eclipsed his role on the political stage.

Even as the restless Grant tried to stay active politically after losing his bid for a third term as president, he was faced with the immediate task of finding employment. Although he had led a relatively frugal life on his world tour—avoiding, for example, expensive accommodations—he had used up most of his resources. From savings, two small pensions his friends had established in his name, and income from small properties Julia owned, he had an annual income of about $6,000 a year. This was scarcely enough to provide for the lavish lifestyle to which the Grants had grown accustomed before traveling abroad. His only recourse was to live in Galena for awhile, then move into a hotel in New York City "at very liberal terms." Wealthy friends came to his rescue, establishing a trust fund for him of more than $250,000 (the equivalent of nearly $5.5 million in 2009) and buying him a brownstone on New York's fashionable Upper East Side. Until then, the former president needed regular employment to supplement his income and keep him occupied.

Grant was soon lending his name to foreign ventures, including the construction of an isthmian canal through Nicaragua and railroad investments in Mexico. During his presidency, he had given considerable thought to building a canal across Central America. On his world tour, he stressed to Young the importance to American and world commerce of an isthmian canal. Because a waterway through Nicaragua posed less of a health hazard and fewer engineering problems, he preferred a Nicaraguan over a Panamanian route, which was then being proposed by the famed French builder of the Suez Canal, Ferdinand de Lesseps. "The Lesseps plan cannot succeed," he told the New York *Herald* reporter while sailing from India to Burma. "As a young officer I crossed the continent on the Nicaragua route, and I have no doubt that it is the true one. I may not live to see it done, but it must be some day."[70] Although he allowed his name to be used in a venture to build a waterway through Nicaragua, the scheme never got off the ground.[71]

Of far more consequence was Grant's involvement in a plan to build the American-financed Mexican Southern Railroad in Mexico and Central America. The proposal for the railroad was one of many schemes by American speculators and promoters to build rails and mines in Mexico. However, it had particular meaning for the former president. Ever since he had fought in the Mexican–American War, he had become fond of Mexico and its people. As president, he followed a policy toward the country that even its own historians have described as the best and most friendly since it gained its independence from Spain in 1821.[72]

In Grant's buildup for the Republican nomination in 1880, he had visited Mexico and met an old friend he had known since 1865, Matias Romero, a former minister to the United States and an entrepreneur. Romero hoped to build the Mexican Southern Railroad as part of an ambitious scheme to connect southern Mexico with Guatemala to the south and Mexico City and the Rio Grande Valley to the north, with branches to the Pacific and the Gulf of Mexico. After obtaining a railroad concession from the governor of the southern Mexican state of Oaxaca, Romero came to New York. At a lavish dinner at Delmonico's, he won over to his scheme two of the greatest railroad magnates of the time, J. Gould and Collis P. Huntington, both of whom had competing interests in the Southwest.

Not by accident, Grant was the guest of honor at the dinner. After the lavish event, Grant and Gould were able to persuade the New York state legislature to incorporate the Mexican Southern Railroad under New York law and to transfer the Oaxaca concession to the new corporation, even though New York had no provision for incorporating companies operating abroad. Grant was then named the railroad's president, with offices on Wall Street. Gould and the other backers of the railroad intended that the former president's primary function would be to go to Mexico and use his reputation to gain the national government's approval for the new railroad's ambitious plans, including higher maximum freight rates and passenger fares than allowed under the original Oaxaca concessions. Three days after being named the corporation's president, Grant traveled with Romero to Mexico City.

The Mexican Southern Railroad proved to be another of Grant's business misadventures—misadventures going back to his life as a civilian before the Civil War. After two months, he was able to persuade dubious Mexican businessmen that his purpose was commerce, not the annexation of Mexican territory. He also gained the approvals he sought from the Mexican government. Over the next several years, he worked assiduously from his Wall Street office, negotiating for additional concessions. He even won the right to build 250 miles of railroad in Guatemala. Although some surveying and laying of track took place, Gould, who had provided most of the initial capital for the project, failed to provide the funds promised to build the northern branch of the railroad. It is possible that he never intended to do so and got involved in the scheme merely to undercut it because it might have competed with his other interests in the Southwest. Without the essential northern branch, the whole scheme was on the brink of collapse. What finally undercut the plan were reports of Grant's own bankruptcy, the result of another failed financial venture. All chances ended of raising additional capital for the railroad. The partnership of Grant and Romero was dissolved, and the next year, the Mexican government revoked the concessions it had made. By this time, Grant was near death.[73]

In becoming involved in the Mexican Southern Railroad scheme, Grant hoped to profit handsomely from the venture. At the same time, his participation in the railroad project reflected the interest he displayed throughout his world tour in the development of railroads and other industrial enterprises and in the expansion of world commerce. For the same reason, at the request of Secretary of State Frederick T. Frelinghuysen, he helped negotiate a reciprocal trade agreement with Mexico. "I never would have undertaken the work I am now engaged in for any possible gain that could accrue to myself," he told Badeau after the treaty had been negotiated. "But I have been much impressed with the resources of [Mexico]. . . . I felt that the development [of these resources] must come soon, and the country furnishing the means would receive the greatest benefit from the increased commerce. I wanted it to be ours." The Senate approved the treaty, but for political reasons having to with the election of Grover Cleveland in 1884, it was never carried into effect.[74]

Even before the Mexican Southern Railroad scheme failed, Grant had been wiped out financially in a banking business founded by his son, Ulysses Jr., and a partner, Ferdinand Ward. In today's terms, the venture amounted to a Ponzi scheme manipulated by Ward, who stole millions of dollars from the business without either of the Grants' knowledge and hid his criminality by milking borrowed money to pay out high dividends. Like all Ponzi schemes, this one eventually failed, but not before ruining Grant financially. Although he had not been actively involved in the business, he had lent his prestige to the firm and invested all of his liquid capital, about $100,000, into it. Even worse, as the business was about to collapse, Ward duped the gullible former president, who had dismissed earlier warnings by friends that the company's assets were being inflated, into turning over to him another $150,000, allegedly to secure a loan to save the business. The former president had to borrow the funds from his friend William Vanderbilt. After Ward absconded with the money, Grant's son informed him on 6 May 1884 that the bank had failed. "I have made it the rule of my life to trust a man long after other people gave him up," Grant told his son. "But I don't see how I can ever trust any human being again."[75] Making matters worse, the $250,000 trust fund established for him in 1881 was invested in bonds of the Wabash Railroad, which defaulted, depriving the former president of even that income.

Left virtually penniless, Grant and Julia began to sell off their property. Learning of the former president's plight, ordinary citizens sent small amounts of money to him. Romero, who was visiting New York, left a check at his home for $1,000. Vanderbilt offered to forgive his loan, and bridge builder James Eads said he would make his bank account available to the Grants; however, the former president refused both offers. To protect Grant's assets, Vanderbilt took ownership of their New York town house, furniture, and Civil War memorabilia (which he then deeded to the government) with provisions that allowed them to live in the furnished home and retain the memorabilia as long as they lived. With this generosity from friends and the public, as well as the sale of two properties Julia owned, the former president was able to survive his immediate financial crisis. The Grants even retained a seaside cottage, which they had bought in Long Branch, New Jersey, while Grant was president and which they had used for summer vacations.

Still, Grant was faced with the problem of earning an income and providing for his family. With no income, he reconsidered an earlier offer *Century* magazine had made to him to write articles on the Shiloh and Vicksburg battles at $500 apiece. The first article on Shiloh seemed like a rehash of his official report of the battle. When, on the advice of his editors, he rewrote it to reflect his personal experiences, he proved his skill as a writer of clear prose. He then applied that skill to his second article on Vicksburg. The articles made so much money for Century Company that the editors encouraged Grant to write his memoirs, offering him a contract with a standard royalty of 10 percent and no advance.

When Mark Twain, who had started his own publishing house, heard about the terms, he was flabbergasted that Century should treat the former president like an unknown author who might sell a few thousand books. "I didn't know whether to laugh or cry," Twain later wrote.[76] He persuaded Grant to turn Century down. Instead, he proposed to publish the memoir himself and gave the former president the choice of a 20 percent royalty or 75 percent of the profits from the book. Because the former president did not want to make any money unless the publisher made a profit, he chose to take 75 percent of the profits.[77]

By the time Grant agreed to sign with Twain at the end of February 1885, he was already dying of throat cancer, a result of a lifelong habit of smoking twenty cigars a day. The first indication of the cancer had happened the previous summer when, at his Long Beach cottage, he suffered severe pain after biting into a peach. However, he delayed seeking medical advice until October. Had he received immediate medical treatment, the cancer might have been surgically removed. By January, however, his condition had become terminal, and newspapers throughout the country reported that he was sinking rapidly. In response, Congress approved legislation to restore Grant to the rank of general of the army with full pay. On 4 March, President Chester Arthur signed the measure just twenty minutes before his term expired. Twain, who was with Grant when he heard the news, wrote his wife, "The effect upon him was like raising the dead." His fondest wish was to die a general.[78]

A race had begun, in the meanwhile, between Grant's worsening cancer and his effort to finish his memoirs. Dictating while he was still able, writing in longhand the rest of the time, and relying mainly on his memory, the former president was determined to complete his memoirs in order to leave Julia with some financial security. At the same time, he made sure each of his facts was checked, using Badeau and his son Fred as his main research assistants. As the weather warmed in the spring, he accepted the offer of Joseph Drexel, president of Drexel, Morgan, and Company, to live on his estate in the Adirondacks about eleven miles north of Saratoga. By the time he moved into the rambling Drexel cottage, the pain from his cancer had become so excruciating that his doctors had to coat his throat with a cocaine solution and administer shots of morphine. He lost his voice completely, and his neck became so swollen that he wore a muffler to hide his disfigurement. Because he had difficulty swallowing food, his weight, which had shot up to 186 pounds a year earlier, dropped to around 130 pounds. Often he could be seen working on his manuscript while sitting in a chair on the porch of the cottage, obviously thin and shrunken, wearing a coat and a woolen cap over his head, a blanket covering his legs, the muffler around his neck, with a pillow supporting his head and a writing pad propped up on his lap.

Grant won his grim race against time, often writing between twenty-five and fifty pages a day when he was not too sick to write or was not being visited by family and friends, including former Confederate foes who came to pay their respects. Toward the end of July, he indicated that his 275,000-word, two-volume work was finished. A few days later, on 23 July 1885, he died. "One day he put his pencil aside and said that he was done—there was nothing more to do," Twain later recounted. "If I had been there I could have foretold the shock that struck the world three days later."[79]

By almost every account, Grant's *Memoirs* was a remarkable piece of prose, the first and best personal memoir ever completed by a former president.[80] Grant wrote almost exclusively on his experiences during the Mexican–American War and the Civil War. He devoted only one chapter to his childhood and years at West Point, and he wrote nothing about his post–Civil War career. He had a gift for capturing the action of war, for concisely and clearly stating his views on strategy and tactics, for describing landscapes and battlefields, and for analyzing the strengths and weaknesses of the commanders under whom he served and who served under him. He showed himself to be a person for whom victory had to be the sine qua non of any commander, even if that meant sending his forces into near-certain death. At the same time, he made clear that he despised the high costs of war, justifying them only in terms of the results they accomplished. On that basis alone, he felt able to justify the Civil War and, by inference, his own action in leading Union troops to victory. He concluded with the proverbial wish: "Let us have peace."[81]

So much was said about the *Memoirs,* even before they were completed, that Grant had to defend himself against charges that Twain or Badeau was ghostwriting them. "The composition is entirely my own," the former president replied publicly on 6 May. Twain, who had been ready to sue for libel, later compared the *Memoirs* to Julius Caesar's *Commentaries,* remarking that "the same high merits distinguished both books—clarity of statement, directness, simplicity, manifest truthfulness, fairness and justice toward friend and foe alike and avoidance of flowery language." After reading the *Memoirs,* Twain's contemporary and long-time friend, William D. Howells, referred to Grant as "one of the most natural—that is *best*—writers I ever read." Over the years, other authors and literary critics made similar comments. Edmund Wilson compared the *Memoirs* to Henry David Thoreau's *Walden* and Walt Whitman's *Leaves of Grass.* Gertrude Stein called them one of the finest books ever written by an American.[82]

Not only were the *Memoirs* a major literary achievement, but they were also hugely successful financially, as Twain suspected they would be when he

Photo of Ulysses S. Grant on 27 June 1885 racing to complete his memoirs while fighting terminal throat cancer at the cottage made available to him by Joseph Drexel, north of Saratoga, NY. As he so often did, he wrote on the porch of the cottage wearing a coat and a woolen cap over his head, his head supported by a pillow and relied heavily on his memory to recount events. He died a month later. (Courtesy of Library of Congress, Prints and Photographs Division [Repro No. LC-USZ62-7607].)

convinced Grant to publish them with his firm. Taking no chances, however, Twain organized a legion of agents to scour the country, persuading veterans of the Civil War to purchase the two-volume set even before it was finished. Three hundred thousand sets were eventually sold at an average cost of $5 apiece. In 1886, Twain presented Julia with the largest royalty check, $200,000, ever written up to that time. Eventually Grant's heirs earned $450,000 from his *Memoirs*. In soldiery fashion, the former president had, in the waning days of his life, carried out his final duty to his family, assuring their financial security.[83]

For months, newspapers had carried the story, almost on a daily basis, of Grant's losing struggle with cancer. In an eerie, almost wakelike, manner, thousands of spectators made their way to Saratoga and then to the Drexel cottage to catch a glimpse of the dying figure. Every day, long lines of tourists walked past the cottage, kept from going onto the porch by a group of volunteers from the Grand Army of the Republic. There were even inexplicable moments when the entire Grant family, including the former president, appeared on the porch, dressed in their finest clothes and jewels, to be photographed. Throughout much of the summer, Grant continued to receive a flock of visitors. His death did not come as a surprise, therefore, to anyone who had been reading the press.[84]

News of Grant's death nevertheless shocked the nation. A period of deep mourning followed. After the former president had become ill, he and his family had considered several possible places for internment. Grant would have preferred to be buried at West Point, but that was eliminated because the academy would not allow his wife to be buried alongside him. Ultimately, the family decided upon a site on the Upper West Side of Manhattan overlooking the Hudson River, now part of Riverside Park, where a temporary tomb was constructed. Here he was laid to rest on 8 August 1885 after the largest funeral in the nation's history. Sixty thousand people, including a large portion of New York's African American population, participated in the funeral procession, which stretched seven miles. President Grover Cleveland and his cabinet, the entire Supreme Court, virtually the entire Congress, and almost every living figure who had played a prominent role in the Civil War were in attendance. Over one million people witnessed the procession.[85]

Almost immediately, plans were made to build a monument to honor the Civil War hero and the nation's eighteenth president. Richard Greener, the first black graduate of Harvard, was appointed secretary of the Grant Monument Association. A competition was held to come up with best design for the monument. The winning architect, John Duncan, broke with the then-current fashion of constructing obelisks by proposing an elaborate granite and white tomb. After considerable delays, the tomb, paid entirely by public donations, was completed in 1897 and dedicated by President William McKinley. The dedication-day parade matched the size of the funeral procession twelve years earlier, with 60,000 marchers led by the West Point corps of cadets and about one million onlookers.[86]

Grant's tomb remains the largest mausoleum in North America. Buried alongside Grant is his wife, Julia, who died in 1902. The monument was the first one of its kind constructed completely with private funds. Together with the Washington Monument, begun nearly fifty years earlier but not dedicated until 1885, it was an early effort at presidential commemoration through the construction of monuments and memorials that was to become such an important part of America's public religion.

Grant's post-presidency had been an important one. If 1877 (the year Grant left the White House) marked a watershed year in the nation's history, both in terms of bringing an end to the era of reconstruction and in ushering in a new era of industrialization and urbanization, the former president's numerous activities after leaving office reflected the transition taking place. He was both a child of the age and one of its senior statesmen, a corporate adventurer and a failed capitalist saved financially only by his coterie of industrial acquaintances and the corporate world of book publishing.

Despite his business misadventures, the emphasis of his post-presidency should be on his accomplishments in the nation's new industrial age, not on his failures. His two-and-a-half-year world tour was a tour de force. He projected the United States onto the world stage by his travels abroad. He took advantage of his legendary status to promote the cause of Anglo-American unity and the gospel of world industrial growth. He became a skilled speaker and experienced diplomat. He mixed comfortably with world leaders, who went out of their way to show their respect for Grant both as the victorious general of the Civil War and as the former leader of an emerging world power.

6

Former Presidents and the Emergent Modern Presidency

Hayes, Cleveland I, and Harrison

Beginning with the administration of Rutherford B. Hayes (1877–1881), important developments took place that strengthened the presidential office and led by the turn of the century to the emergence of the modern presidency.[1] As the stature of the presidency grew, so did the public presence and political prominence of ex-presidents. Hayes had a remarkable post-presidency. Not only did he and his wife, Lucy, engage in a host of philanthropic and humanitarian activities, but he also became an important voice in defense of the working class and a leading advocate for greater federal action in support of universal public education, and against what he referred to as the tyranny of corporate wealth. Grover Cleveland spent a good part of his four years of forced retirement preparing his successful campaign to regain the office he had lost to Benjamin Harrison. After losing to Cleveland in his own bid for reelection, Harrison resumed the practice of law, enjoying a lucrative practice and defending Venezuela in a lengthy arbitration case over the disputed boundary between Venezuela and British Guiana.

There is another significant feature of the Hayes, Cleveland, and Harrison post-presidencies. The historian Morton Keller has written about the last third of the nineteenth century in terms of "tensions as old as America itself—between equality and liberty, between the desire for freedom and the need for social order, between dependence on government and hostility to the state, between localism and nationalism."[2] The tensions that Keller describes so well manifested themselves in each of the post-presidencies of these former leaders as well as in their differences on matters of social order and public and private responsibility.

I

Hayes was well prepared to be president. Born in October 1822 in Delaware, Ohio, just north of Columbus, he was raised in comfortable circumstance. Although his father died ten weeks before he was born, his uncle, Sardis Birchard, a successful businessman and lifelong bachelor who lived in nearby Lower Sandusky, became his guardian and made sure the family had whatever it needed. A graduate of Harvard Law School, Hayes began his political career in 1859 when he ran successfully for city solicitor of Cincinnati. With the outbreak of the Civil War, he helped organize the 23rd Ohio Volunteers and was commissioned a major. During the war, he was elected to Congress even though he refused to take leave in order to campaign at home. At one time a Whig, he had helped organize the Republican Party in Cincinnati and entered Congress as a Republican.[3]

After serving two terms in Congress, Hayes was elected in 1868 to the first of two, two-year terms as governor of Ohio. Although he decided not to seek another term because of the "worry and anxiety" of political office, Republicans drafted him to run again in 1875, and he became the first person in the state's history to win a third term.[4] Although he was not considered a serious contender for the Republican nomination for president in 1876, he emerged the party's standard-bearer after none of the leading candidates were able to secure enough votes for the nomination. In November, he was elected president in the most controversial presidential election up to that time.[5]

Perhaps more than any president who preceded him, Hayes owed his election to the fact that he was the least objectionable and most available candidate for the office. As a candidate, he was not even physically striking or charismatic. At age fifty-four, he stood five feet, eight and a half inches tall and weighed about 170 pounds. He had broad shoulders and a long oval face with a high forehead, deeply set blue eyes, florid complexion, well-formed mouth, and thinning brown hair that was turning gray. He also wore a full moustache and beard and dressed in plain clothes that were often ill-fitting. He was a good communicator and debater with a deep, rich voice who spoke in an enthusiastic and easy manner—but he was no barn burner.

As president, Hayes accomplished little legislatively. Many of the programs he advocated were the same as those he had called for as governor of Ohio. In his inaugural address, he emphasized education, civil service reform, and a sound monetary policy. He placed a high premium on education as a first and fundamental step toward economic and political progress, especially for the freedmen of the South. He called for state-supported schools for all school-age children. Because education was a state matter and the South refused to provide public schools for African Americans, the issue was moot insofar as Washington was concerned. As for civil service reform and a sound monetary system, a merit-based civil service would have to await the Pendleton Act of 1883, while the issue of a sound monetary system would remain one of the most contentious issues into the twentieth century.[6]

Although Hayes failed to accomplish much legislatively, he revitalized the executive branch of government by challenging such congressional customs as senatorial courtesy, repelling congressional assaults on the integrity of his office, and even taking on the powerful Republican machine in New York over reform of the New York City customhouse.[7]

Having enjoyed travel throughout his life, he also often journeyed for weeks away from Washington; he was the first president to travel to California and the Pacific Northwest. He used these travels to promote his programs, turning his presence into a form of bully pulpit years before Theodore Roosevelt transformed that technique into an art form. Although he and his wife, Lucy Ware, also became known for not serving alcohol at the White House (Lucy was ridiculed as "Lemonade Lucy"), they made the executive mansion once more the center of the social season. Lucy, the first wife of a president to graduate from college, even began the practice of allowing children to roll Easter eggs on the White House lawn.[8]

Hayes was also a social reformer, although not in the sense of moving away from his abiding belief in the classical liberal principles of limited government, individual freedoms, and the rights of property; in these and other respects, he remained a creature of his times. He continued, too, to associate himself with a better class of citizens, whom he identified as highly educated, prominent in their communities, and financially well-off. However, he recognized social, racial, and class inequalities, and although he was not an advocate of the type of economic reform or government regulation that characterized the early twentieth century, he believed in change through a process of education and merit. He was also convinced that universal suffrage and an educated citizenry went hand in hand. He even called for the federal government to supplement state-supported schools if necessary.[9]

After he left the White House, Hayes continued to hold to an orthodox political view. He remained persuaded that most of the nation's problems could be resolved through education. At the same time, he became an advocate of even greater change than while he was in office. He talked about "a politics of inequality" and "the rottenness of the present system." He also spoke out against the nation's captains of industry and advocated greater equity across all social, racial, and class lines.[10]

The former president was glad to leave the White House. A political figure who seemed able to avoid internecine politics before he became president, he created so much divisiveness within his own party that it is doubtful he could have won his party's nomination even if he sought it. "I am not liked as a President, by the politicians in office, in the press, or in Congress," he remarked in his diary as early as 1878. Although relations with party leaders improved in his last two years in office, he still remained too independent for them to support his renomination, had he wanted it.[11]

Hayes harbored no such ambition. Even though a number of his supporters urged him to violate a pledge he had made after he was nominated in 1876 not to seek a second term, he turned them down. Not only did he believe he had to honor that pledge, but he was tired of all the infighting and sparring that had taken place during his administration.

In 1874, Hayes had also inherited from his recently deceased uncle, Sardis Birchard, Sardis's estate, known as Spiegel Grove, a heavily wooded twenty-five-acre property with large trees and thick underbrush. It was called Spiegel (the German word for "mirror") because of the nature-made reflecting pools of rain that collected on the property. Hayes loved Spiegel Grove. Even before his uncle died, he moved his family into the two-story, eight-room brick home in order to care for his uncle. He also began the project of enlarging and improving the residence, which lasted for the next twenty years. On the west side of the house, he added a one-story frame addition that included an office–library, drawing room, kitchen, wood house, privy, and wraparound veranda. As he contemplated retirement from the presidency, he built a second major brick addition on the north side, extending the gabled front of the original home and more than doubling its size.[12]

Hayes's ambition for a second term as president was also tempered by his robust family life. He and Lucy had five children, the three oldest of whom lived nearby; the two youngest still lived at home. The family was close-knit, outgoing, and fun-loving. Hayes enjoyed playing sports with his children, especially the emerging national pastime of baseball. He also liked to labor in the yard near the house, working with his middle child, Rud, and two handymen to clear two and half acres for fruit and nut trees, evergreens, berries, and a vegetable garden.

Compared to most of his predecessors, Hayes left the White House financially well-off. Besides Spiegel Grove, his uncle had left him a considerable financial estate. He also invested heavily in real estate. He owned land in Toledo, Columbus, and Duluth, Minnesota.[13] Before the Panic of 1873, he estimated its value at $250,000, which he expected to double in price over the next decade. Because of the depression that followed, this did not happen. The inheritance from his uncle, however, allowed him to weather the depression. After he returned to Ohio in 1881, he valued his property at between $200,000 and $300,000 (the equivalent of between $4.4 and $6.6 million in 2009).[14]

Yet Hayes still had serious financial concerns. The ongoing costs of improving Spiegel Grove and protecting his land investments forced him to borrow from banks and to ask personal friends for money. By selling some of his land, he was able to prune his debt and to provide for his living expenses. Even so, he still owed between $20,000 and $30,000, so that when his friend, William Henry Smith, suggested to him at the end of 1881 that he travel to Europe, he responded that he simply had "no means for the trip." Money matters continued to plague him well into his second year of retirement. "I find it hard to raise enough money for current expenses," he wrote in October 1882 to another longtime friend, Guy M. Bryan. "To sell [land] at fair rates is my wish. When the mania for railroad enterprises and securities, which here prevails has run its course, I hope there will be more capitalists inquiring for real estate."[15]

Despite being land rich and cash poor, Hayes was determined to establish a new life of public service outside of elective office. Never having had the same fiery political ambition as most politicians and yet having won the highest office in the land, he had no desire for any further elective position. Instead, he anticipated a return to private citizenship in the republican tradition—modified, however, by what he still considered the public duty of a better class of citizen. Without perhaps realizing it, he accepted former president Millard Fillmore's important departure from that tradition in maintaining that ex-presidents had a responsibility not to be ordinary citizens again. "If I speak on leaving here to friends," he recorded in his diary the day after his last Christmas in the White House, "I may speak of returning to private life as Washington and Jefferson did; not to shirk the duties of a citizen . . . but ready to do what I may in private life or in humble stations, or if generally called to higher duties."[16]

Even as a private citizen Hayes followed political affairs carefully. Like most Republicans, he was surprised when the dark-horse candidate from Ohio, James Garfield, received the party's nomination in 1880. He was unhappy that Garfield chose as his running mate Chester Arthur, a member of the party's antireform, or Stalwart, wing. As president, Hayes had fired Arthur as collector of the port of New York.

The former president was still pleased by the convention's outcome, including the fact that the Republicans had rejected a third term for former president Ulysses Grant. He had become disenchanted with Grant because of the corruption associated with his administration. During the campaign and before he assumed office, Hayes differed with him on some important matters, which he was not reticent to express to the candidate. He regretted that in his letter accepting the nomination, the Republican nominee did not take a stronger stand in support of civil service reform, and he was upset at the overtures Garfield made to the Stalwarts.[17]

The outgoing president also took umbrage at Garfield's intention to reinstate the practice of serving wine at White House functions. For Hayes, this was not a minor issue. As a young man, he had not been a teetotaler, but he had come to share his wife's views on alcohol. He believed temperance was a societal and moral issue because alcoholism often resulted in crime and disorder. Just as important, he feared that serving wine at the White House would have harmful political consequences for the Republican Party. "Your duty to the Republican party," he wrote Garfield on 17 January 1881, "is to let well enough alone on this subject. The moment you reject the reform it becomes a political question which in the hands of the Temperance leaders will take from us States and congressional districts which we can't spare."[18]

Collaboration still best characterized the relationship between the two men. Hayes especially appreciated that Garfield renominated his college friend and the new president's 1877 rival for the Senate, Stanley Matthews, to the Supreme Court after the Senate earlier rejected him. At Garfield's request, Hayes made a number of difficult late-term appointments that would have caused the new president considerable problems had they awaited his decision.[19]

As inauguration day approached on 4 March, Hayes prepared to leave office not only pleased that his term in office was about to end, but also fully persuaded that he had served his country well. The national press felt the same way. The New York *Graphic* spoke for most of the press when it editorialized, "Take him for all in all, Hayes will step out of office . . . with more peace and blessing than any President in fifty-six years. Who since Monroe has gone out so *willingly* and regretted?"[20]

On the day after the inauguration, the now former president and his family boarded a train for Fremont (the new name for Lower Sandusky). Tragedy struck when the train collided head-on with the locomotive of an unoccupied passenger train outside of Baltimore, seriously injuring twenty persons and killing two others. Narrowly escaping injury themselves, Hayes and his family provided first aid to the wounded. Although the crash delayed their journey by a day, they arrived in Fremont on 8 March. Speaking to a large crowd that welcomed him home, Hayes made clear the role he thought an ex-president should pursue: "Let him, like every good American citizen, be willing and prompt to bear his part in every useful work that will promote the welfare and the happiness of his family, his town, his state, and his country."[21]

Hayes spent the next few weeks putting his house in order. A prolific reader, he had amassed a collection of thousands of books, mostly on exploration, history, biography, literature, and genealogy (a hobby of his). The books lined his narrow library from floor to ceiling and spilled over into other rooms and floors of the residence. Besides being a bibliophile, Hayes was also a hoarder who kept virtually every letter, manuscript, magazine, newspaper, and document that crossed his desk, as well as artifacts ranging from Civil War relics to Indian ornaments, trophies, and souvenirs. These were placed in cases and other receptacles scattered in rooms throughout the house. Much of this material was later transferred to the Rutherford B. Hayes Presidential Library established by the Hayes family and opened in 1916.[22]

Over the next months and years, the former president continued to make improvements to the grounds and residence of Spiegel Grove. He cleared areas around some of the oldest and largest oaks and elms to permit beautiful vistas of fall foliage. He planted avenues of spruces and pines and rearranged the driveways to provide more quiet for those sitting on the porches. In 1889, he made another large addition to the rear of the house that included a new kitchen, a larger dining room, and eleven additional bedrooms on the upper level. He also installed the most modern conveniences, including a telephone in 1881 and hydrant water in 1885 to replace the spring water previously relied upon on the property. By the time Hayes completed his work, he had turned Spiegel Grove into a magnificent estate with handsome grounds and a large, comfortable, thirty-one-room mansion.[23]

Once settled at Spiegel Grove, the former president engaged in real estate ventures and became a director of the First National Bank of Fremont. He also took part in the civic life of the community and was appointed to the boards of trustees of a number of organizations and universities, including Western Reserve, Ohio Wesleyan, and Ohio State. As a proud Civil War veteran, he was a member of the Grand Army of the Republic (GAR) and helped establish the Loyal Legion of Ohio, becoming its first commander. At a time when he had to borrow to protect his land investments, he made generous contributions to many of these organizations and to the local Methodist church even though he was not a church member.

Hayes did not limit his activities to his local community or state. He became a leader in the effort to promote free education for the freedmen of the South. In 1867, the financier and philanthropist George Peabody established a fund of $2.1 million (later augmented by another $1 million) to be used for education in the South regardless of race. As president, Hayes gladly accepted the invitation to become a board member of the Peabody Education Fund. In 1882, he took on similar responsibilities when he became president of the Slater Fund, a $1 million endowment established by John F. Slater, a wealthy Connecticut cotton manufacturer, specifically to provide education in the industrial trades to the freedmen.[24]

When Hayes had promoted universal education as governor and as president, he never singled out industrial education for the freedmen. It would be easy but inaccurate, therefore, to dismiss his new stress on such training to the belief, later expressed most famously by Booker T. Washington, that blacks needed to concentrate on learning a vocation. Hayes remained committed to a general education for blacks as well for whites. He even helped get a fellowship from the Slater Fund to pursue his education abroad for W. E. B. Du Bois, the first African American to receive a Ph.D. from Harvard and a fiery opponent of Washington's philosophy.

Hayes believed, however, that in a modern industrial state competing with industrial powers, traditional education was not giving enough emphasis to the practical aspects of life. He even questioned the stress placed in colleges on Latin and Greek. "The trustees of the Slater Fund have reached one conclusion which I deem of much importance," he commented in 1883, "viz.: That the schools . . . should be prepared to instruct their pupils in mechanical employments—should teach not only what is found in books, but the arts by which to make a living. The failure to do this is a capital defect in our public school system."[25] For that reason, he trained his children to use their hands as well as their minds. He even sent his youngest son, Scott, to a manual training school in Toledo before he matriculated at Cornell University.[26]

Reform of the nation's prison systems was another cause to which Hayes devoted his retirement years. Ever since he was a young lawyer defending what was commonly regarded as the criminal element, he had been concerned with the equitable administration of justice even for the worst offenders. His approach to the legal system and his humanitarian instincts spilled over to his concern about what he considered the appalling operation of Ohio's prisons. As governor, he called for more humane treatment of prisoners and separate facilities for juvenile offenders.

As a former president, Hayes became a leader in a small but burgeoning effort to change the nation's penal system, serving from 1883 to 1892 as president of the National Prison Association, a group of social reformers that met each year. He even linked his interest in industrial and vocational education to prison reform and reduced crime rates, maintaining that with proper training, criminals might become productive members of society.[27]

Another way to reduce the crime rate was by getting rid of alcoholic beverages. Because Hayes continued to believe that the use of alcohol was both a societal and moral issue, he remained a strong proponent of temperance during his retirement years. Until consumers of alcoholic changed their drinking habits and citizens stopped regarding the sale of liquor as a legitimate business, he was convinced that temperance as a political movement would be counterproductive.[28]

Although Hayes accepted the redemptive value of religion and attended church regularly (largely in deference to Lucy), he was never a confirmed Christian or a church member. As a young man, he was moved by a sermon that described Christ as a moderate social reformer, but he did not believe in salvation through baptism or conversion, and he had no answer for what he referred to as the mystery of existence. He was skeptical, in fact, of any form of dogma or organized religion and was a devout believer in the separation of church and state. For these reasons, he was uncommonly harsh in his views on the Mormon Church.

As organized and practiced in the Utah territory in the 1870s and 1880s, Mormonism offended Hayes on several levels. Most importantly, he regarded the Mormon Church as a theocracy whose leaders had absolute control over its members. Mormon leaders also ignored civil authority in the person of the territory's governor. Furthermore, Hayes strongly opposed the Church's polygamous practices, which the Supreme Court had held to be unconstitutional. Not only did polygamy challenge federal law, he considered it an immoral degradation of women.

As president, therefore, Hayes fired the incumbent governor because he was too close to the Mormon hierarchy. He also urged Congress to pass new measures that would keep Mormons from participating in their local government. The legislation he proposed would set up a new territorial government similar to that of the Ordinance of 1787 with the right to vote, hold office, or sit on juries limited to those who could prove that they did not practice or uphold polygamy. Congress rejected Hayes's recommendations as being too extreme.

After leaving the White House, Hayes became even more outspoken in his pronouncements against the Mormon Church. Launching an all-out assault against the church, he took issue with a proposal by President Chester Arthur that the laws against polygamy be more strongly enforced. Even that was not enough,

Hayes recorded in his diary in December: "Utah is governed by the church—and such a church! Take from it political power, and it falls and polygamy with it within five years. How to do this? The measure should be radical. Half-way measures have been tried for twenty-five years. They have failed." His proposals were the same as the ones he had recommended as president:

> Let the territorial government of Utah be reorganized. Let all power . . . be vested in the registered voters of the Territories. . . . Allow no one to be registered who does not prove affirmatively to the satisfaction of United States courts, or other United States officials, that he neither practices the crime of polygamy, nor belongs to or supports any church or other organization which upholds it.[29]

Hayes was disappointed when Congress followed Arthur's recommendation by passing the Edmunds Act of 1882 that significantly increased the number of arrests for polygamy, but went no further. Not until 1890 did the Mormon Church officially renounce polygamy. In the interim, the former president continued to blast the church.[30]

Hayes's attacks on the Mormon Church were unusually visceral for an individual who always prided himself on tolerance, reason, and civility even on matters of dogma. More may have been involved, however, than his disdain for how the church was structured or what it practiced and preached. What was most striking about Hayes's years as former president was that he became more radicalized and outspoken in his political thought. Having always called for a more egalitarian society even as he identified with a "better class" of citizen and advocated classical liberal principles, he became a stronger defender of the working class and spoke out more stridently against the rich and large corporations. "Mayor [Abram] Hewitt of New York is complimented by the newspapers for brave words spoken on the labor question," Hayes recorded in his diary in March 1888. "They are all in criticism of the Labor men. . . . The real difficulty is with the vast wealth and power in the hands of the few and the unscrupulous who represent or control capital. Hundreds of laws of Congress and the state legislatures are in the interests of these men and against the interests of the workingmen."[31]

It would not be stretching matters too much, in fact, to maintain that Hayes came to believe in a form of democratic socialism later shared by no less a figure than the renowned scientist Albert Einstein. Predicated on an ethical desire to eliminate the frightful divide between classes, this form of socialism had liberal antiauthoritarian underpinnings. Its advocates sought to promote equality, social justice, and the reigning in of the emerging corporate economy without simultaneously imposing any highly centralized control. While still emphasizing the dignity of the individual and the protection of individual and political freedoms, they sought nevertheless to use the legislative process to tame the excesses of what Hayes came to regard as class tyranny and corporate greed.[32]

Hayes standing on the porch of Spiegel Grove during the winter of 1888–1889, with William Henry Smith, a newspaper editor and former Ohio secretary of state, whom Hayes appointed as collector of Port of Chicago, and Mrs. Hayes. By this time, Hayes had become more radical in his political views, attacking the concentration of wealth in the United States and speaking out on behalf of the working class. (Courtesy of Library of Congress, Prints and Photographs Division [Repro. No. LC-USZ62-54744].)

Hayes even considered the single tax ideas of Henry George, which called for applying a single a tax on unimproved land. Although he did not think the nation was ready to impose such a radical concept, he was impressed by George's portrayal in his classic work, *Progress and Poverty* (1879), of the power and danger of accumulated wealth. "Money is power," he commented. "Excessive wealth in the hands of the few means extreme poverty, ignorance, vice, and wretchedness as the lot of the many." Although he went on to say that "it was not yet time to debate about the remedy," he concluded, "We may reach and remove the difficulty by changes in the law regulating corporations, descent of property, wills, trusts, taxation, and a host of other important interests, not omitting lands and other property." Two years earlier, Hayes had been even more specific. "Let no man get by inheritance, or by will, more than will produce at four per cent interest an income equal to the salary paid to the Chief Justice, the General of the Army, or to the highest officer of the Navy — say an income of fifteen thousand per year, or an estate of five hundred thousand dollars." If Hayes saw any inconsistency between his willingness to cap the amount an individual could earn or maintain in an estate and his belief in individual freedoms and laissez-faire economics, he never made it clear. A pragmatic man as well as an intellectual, he believed the alternative to what he was proposing would be class warfare that could threaten the very principles he held so dear.[33]

Still a loyal Republican, Hayes was stunned by news in July that Garfield had been shot by a crazed Stalwart Republican office seeker, Charles Guiteau. He feared that if Chester Arthur succeeded to the presidency, his enemy and the leader of the Stalwarts, Roscoe Conkling, would be in charge of the White House. "The death of the President at this time would be a calamity," he recorded in his diary. "Arthur for President! Conkling the power behind the throne, superior to the throne! The Republican party divided and defeated."[34]

Hayes was devastated, therefore, when Garfield died on 9 September. The fact that the assassinated president had been a victim of the intense partisanship among Republicans indicated the need to end the political division he believed was gripping the nation. Because it appeared in August that Garfield might die, he moderated his own views toward Arthur, urging that he be given "a fair trial — a fair hearing" if he became president. Upon learning that the president had died, he urged an end to partisanship and called once more for civil service reform.[35]

Although Arthur's greatest achievement as president was passage in 1883 of the Pendleton Act establishing the modern civil service system, Hayes never warmed to the new president. Arthur remained, in his view, a partisan Stalwart who accepted the reform legislation only because the public demanded it in the wake of Garfield's assassination. Indeed, he believed that by standing up to political bosses and putting the New York customhouse on "a business basis" as president, he had prepared the "corner-stone" of civil service reform. Without saying as much, he viewed passage of the Pendleton Act as one of his proudest legacies as president.[36]

Hayes was no more enamored with the Republican nominee for president in 1884, James Blaine, than he was with Arthur. He regarded Blaine as another hack politician, a "scheming demagogue, selfish and reckless" who would "gladly be wrong to be President." Neither did he care much for the Democratic candidate, Governor Grover Cleveland of New York, whose recently revealed fathering of an illegitimate child ten years earlier he deplored. However, once Cleveland assumed office, Hayes became one of his strongest supporters. "He is sound on the currency, the tariff, and the reform of the civil service," he commented in the spring of 1885. He differed with Cleveland on some matters, especially the new president's stand against expanding the scope of pensions for Civil War veterans to include any disability, not just ones incurred during service, as provided by the Civil War pension legislation of 1878. As president, Hayes had signed the Pension Arrears Act of 1879 by which pensions began on the day of an honorable discharge for disability rather than on the date of the application, but as a former president and a member of the GAR, he continued to advocate for increased pension benefits for war veterans. "I wish there [were] half as much desire to do our full duty by the soldier as there is to take care of the surplus money in the treasury," he remarked in April 1888, the last year of Cleveland's term, when the administration was trying to decide what to do with a sizable budget surplus and was supporting a reduction in tariff rates. Hayes opposed lowering tariffs, arguing that it would do harm to the nation's manufacturing.[37]

Hayes's steadfast loyalty to the Republican Party, rather than his differences with Cleveland, led him to support the Republican candidate for president in 1888, Senator Benjamin Harrison of Indiana, against Cleveland in the 1888 election. Although he would have preferred his former treasury secretary and longtime friend, John Sherman, over Harrison as the Republican nominee, he was satisfied with the nomination of the former Indiana governor, whom he had even considered for a cabinet post when he was president. Hayes referred to Harrison as "a firm, sound man" whose "personal character [was] clear and high."[38]

In 1891, Hayes also successfully supported for governor of Ohio his political protégé, William McKinley, who had fought under his command during the Civil War. In 1892, he hoped that McKinley would receive the Republican presidential nomination over Harrison, whom he had found to be cold and distant and not especially effective as president, but McKinley decided against being an active candidate. When Harrison was renominated on the first ballot, Hayes was relieved at least that the nomination had not gone to Blaine. While publicly supporting Harrison, the former president was not overly disappointed when the Democratic nominee, Cleveland, who was seeking to return to the White House, won the election comfortably. He attributed Harrison's defeat to the protest vote of the nation's underpaid working class.[39]

Although Hayes remained more than just a political observer as former president, he rejected repeated efforts by friends and associates to get him to seek another term as president or some other elective office. His life was too full and he was too content, he told them, to reenter the political arena. The former president also kept an active schedule, tending to his many fraternal organizations and philanthropic causes. He often visited friends and family throughout the country and frequented New York City. "Withdrawn entirely from political life, I was never more actively at work," he told one of his many correspondents at the end of 1886. "Few men, I suspect are more cheerful and contented in their occupations than I am."[40]

Yet all was not bliss in Hayes's retirement. An investigation during Garfield's administration uncovered widespread fraud in the awarding of the so-called star routes—special rural delivery routes in newly established states awarded by the post office to individual mail contractors. Although Hayes knew nothing of the scam, which had been perpetrated by his second assistant postmaster general, Thomas J. Brady, it provided fodder for his political enemies, who accused his administration of skulduggery.[41]

The former president also continued to suffer a number of financial setbacks. None was dire enough to force him to change his comfortable lifestyle, but they were serious enough to cause him considerable concern. In 1885, he lost between $12,000 and $15,000 on his investment in the Fremont Harvester company, a local company gone bankrupt that he and Sardis had thought would be a boon to their community. Similarly, he stood to lose a considerable amount because of the poor management of the Fremont Savings Bank, in which he had invested over $40,000 (the equivalent of about $912,000 in 2009 terms).[42] In March 1892, less than a year before his death, he was complaining again about the "unproductive real estate" that he and his sons owned and their need to borrow $40,000 against their land in order to "warrant going on as we are."[43]

The biggest blow to Hayes, however, was the death from a stroke of his wife, Lucy, on 25 June 1889. Although she was only fifty-seven years old, the stroke did not come as a complete surprise to the former president. While at church not long before her death, Lucy had lost her balance while standing to sing, and she later complained of numbness on her side. Believing that this was a sign that she was going to die soon, she told her husband that she feared paralysis more than death. She appeared well enough, however, that when she was fatally stricken, the former president was at Columbus attending an Ohio State University trustees' meeting. Hurrying back to Spiegel Forest, Hayes found Lucy sitting up but paralyzed and crying. Soon she lapsed into unconsciousness, then lingered for three days before she died.

Lucy and the former president had led a resplendent life together. During the last fifteen years, after they had made Spiegel Grove their permanent residence, they had rarely been apart for long. She had been the shining hostess of the White House during Hayes's presidency, and both during his administration and after, she traveled with him as often as she could. Their last trip together was to New York in April 1889 for the centennial observation of George Washington's inauguration as the nation's first president. She was also in near unison with her husband in thought and deed, and she joined him in engaging in charitable and other good works.

Lucy's death was therefore the most retching moment of Hayes's life. "This is Lucy's birthday," he recorded in his diary on 28 August. "All my thoughts are of her."[44] For the remainder of his life, he continued to pine for his dead wife. Yet almost as part of his healing process, the former president soon began resuming a normal routine. Generally accompanied by one of his children, he traveled extensively. On behalf of the Peabody and Slater funds, he took a tour of the South in order to examine Southern schools and to evaluate the use being made of the two funds' money. He also attended regular board meetings of the various organizations on which he served.

As the former president observed economic conditions in the country, he became more convinced than ever of the need for government to break up the accumulations of wealth he held responsible for so many of the nation's economic and social ills. "The burning question of our time in all civilized countries is the question of wealth and poverty, of capital and labor," he commented in February 1891. "All fair-minded men admit that labor does not now get its fair share of the wealth it creates. All see that wealth is not justly distributed." He found "state action, state regulation, state control" perfectly compatible with his liberal political views. He continued to believe, as he had throughout his political career, that publicly supported education remained the key to resolving the nation's most fundamental problems.[45]

By this time, Hayes's health was failing him. As a young child, he had been so frail that his mother would not permit him to play with other children or even to attend the local school. As he grew older, he toughened himself through rigorous exercise. He worked as a farmhand, took up outdoor sports, and became a first-class runner in college. Throughout his life, he exercised regularly, including playing sports with his children and taking long walks. He was also careful about what he ate and drank, limiting himself to one cup of coffee and a cup of tea a day and no alcohol. At the time of his retirement, he was a model of good exercise, good diet, and good health.[46]

Sometime in his mid- to late sixties, however, his health began to deteriorate. He had difficulty hearing and carrying on a conversation. He suffered from occasional dizziness. Notwithstanding his exhaustive travel and schedule of events, he lost some of his vigor. He may have suffered from some arteriosclerotic changes. After Lucy's death, he began to contemplate his own death, commenting at one point: "Well, let the end come. The charm of life left me when Lucy died."[47]

On 9 January 1893, after attending a board meeting at Ohio State University and going to Western Reserve University in Cleveland, Hayes suffered severe chest pains while at the Cleveland train station. He insisted, nevertheless, on continuing home. "I would rather die at Spiegel Grove than live anywhere else," he commented.[48] Arriving at Spiegel Grove, he was immediately put to bed and given an injection of morphine for his pain. Although the former president seemed to improve as a result of being in bed, on 17 January, his heart gave out. The former president was seventy years old.[49]

After lying in state at Spiegel Grove for three days, Hayes was buried in the Oakwood Cemetery next to Lucy.[50] Veterans of Hayes's 23rd Regiment served as pallbearers. Dozens of other members of the military were also present at the funeral. Although President Harrison chose not to make the long journey to Fremont, President-elect Cleveland did, thereby healing some of the political wounds still remaining between Democrats and Republicans from the disputed 1876 election.

Like the post-presidency of several former presidents whose lives survive in obscurity, the post-presidency of Rutherford B. Hayes deserves to be remembered as one of the more noteworthy of the nineteenth century. Despite the private pleasures he enjoyed in retirement and his sincere lack of interest in elective office after he left the White House, he remained politically active, conferring with and offering advice to four different presidents during his lengthy retirement. He also remained a public figure. No former president lent his name and support to more causes and participated in more public events of a nonpolitical kind than Hayes.

Even more important, while in many ways Hayes fits the common portrayal of the liberal reformer of his time, in other significant respects he does not. Contrary to the traditional narrative that emphasizes an expansive democratic vision during the era of reconstruction giving way to ongoing racism, greater partisanship, intraparty factionalism, class warfare, localism, and laissez-fairism, Hayes became more of a democrat after he left the White House then he was as president. Instead of being part of a retreat away from the national euphoria of reform after the Civil War, he became more of a social reformer. He also became an outspoken foe of corporate power and an advocate of anticorporate state regulation.[51]

Yet Hayes was never able to reconcile the conflict that existed in his own mind between his commitment to laissez-faire principles and his belief in the need for increased state power, between his growing sympathy for the rights of the working class and his antipathy toward social disorder, between his abiding faith in civic virtue and his understanding of the corruption of wealth and power, and between his own democratic and humanitarian instincts and his self-identification with a "better class" of citizens. Although as Morton Keller has reminded us, these types of tension have existed throughout the nation's history, they remain of particular importance for understanding the unique political and social dynamics of late nineteenth-century America.

II

After Grover Cleveland left the White House in 1889 after his defeat for reelection by his Republican opponent, Benjamin Harrison, he wrote a letter to his former law partner and best friend, Wilson S. Bissell, commenting on how relieved he was to no longer be president. "I feel that I am fast seeking the place I desire to reach," he told Bissell, "the place of a respectable private citizen." A week later, Cleveland wrote another letter to his former postmaster general, William Villas, in which he remarked that a suggestion by the editor of the Louisville *Courier-Journal,* Henry Watterson, that former presidents should be "take[n] out and sho[t]" was "worthy of attention."[52]

The truth was that the former president was uncertain about his future. He had not yet decided to make a second bid for reelection. In contrast to Hayes, he had no estimable record of commitment to benevolent causes that he might pursue. He did not feel Hayes's deep sense of civic obligation or have any of his intellectual bent. He loved to fish and hunt, but beyond that, he had few interests or passions. Except for his close friends and family, those who knew Cleveland did not even find him very interesting. Aware that he was not learned or quick of mind, he tended to be silent and uncomfortable among those he considered of superior intellect. His appearance also did not help. One of the nation's most corpulent presidents, he stood about five feet, eleven inches tall and weighed approximately 280 pounds, with a double chin, strong jaw, pale complexion, bull neck, walrus moustache, Roman nose, watery blue eyes, and thinning brown hair. His dress was unflattering. Concerned with making a dignified impression, he tried to keep up with fashion, which by the late nineteenth century was transitioning away from highly tailored frock coats and pinned striped pants to the three-piece sack suit (the modest beginnings of the modern suit). Although Cleveland attempted to follow style, his knee-length, double-breasted coats lacked the tailoring of the still-popular Prince Albert frock coat, and he often wore them fully buttoned, which made him look even heavier than he was. His appearance seemed more crumpled than smart, his countenance more solid than imposing.

Cleveland won the presidency in 1884 as a result of good character and good fortune. Good character was ingrained in him from childhood. The fifth of nine children, the future president was born on 18 March 1837 in Caldwell, New Jersey, but he grew up in upstate New York. His father, a minister, taught and practiced humility, hard work, and sense of duty. His large family had to make do on his father's meager minister's salary and a small annuity that his mother received from her family. This translated into a lot of chores, odd jobs, and few luxuries for Grover and his siblings.

As a student attending the local schools, Grover was a hardworking but never outstanding student. Although he intended to go to nearby Hamilton College, he was forced to help out his family by going to work instead. His lack of a college education was something he always regretted. Unhappy with his circumstances, Cleveland decided to move to the booming western city of Cleveland, Ohio, on the shores of Lake Erie to live with an uncle and study law. On the way, he visited another uncle, Lewis W. Allen, who lived just outside of Buffalo and persuaded his nephew to remain with him.

Within a year, Allen was able to get his nephew a position as a clerk in Millard Fillmore's old law firm of Rogers, Bowen, and Rogers, where he was also able to study law. After four years, he was admitted to the bar and was offered a position with the high-powered firm. What made Cleveland's decision to stay in Buffalo so fortunate for him was that the city was rapidly growing, with a population that had doubled from about 40,000 in 1850 to more than 80,000 ten years later.

Cleveland prospered as Buffalo prospered. In 1865, he formed his own law firm and began to build a reputation as one of Buffalo's most able attorneys. What struck other lawyers was not his superior legal mind or his talent as a trial lawyer. He preferred trying civil to criminal cases and working at his desk to appearing in court. Rather than an imaginative legal mind and a flamboyant presence in court, he became noted for the quality of his briefs. His list of clients grew rapidly, and he became increasingly more comfortable financially.

For nine years, Cleveland lived the life of one of the most respected and successful lawyers in Buffalo, handling mostly local clients and building up considerable savings. Although he was admired as an able litigator and person of sterling character, there were few other qualities that made him stand out from other successful, hardworking professional people—certainly none that would have marked him for high political office. In an astonishing series of events, however, he went in a four-year period (1881–1884) from being a private citizen to mayor of Buffalo, governor of New York, and president-elect of the United States.

The common denominator in Cleveland's meteoric rise to the nation's highest office was his reputation for honesty, decency, and hard work, and the voters' yearning, at all levels of government, for precisely these qualities in their elected officials. His reputation preceded him among Democratic leaders in Buffalo with whom he had already established strong ties at a time when they were looking for a reform candidate to run for mayor in a city that was notoriously corrupt. Although stating his reluctance to run for office, he was attracted by the challenge of office seeking.[53] Campaigning hard from Buffalo's waterfront to the city's more affluent neighborhoods, he beat his Republican opponent by a comfortable margin. Carrying out his promises of municipal reform, he became known as the veto mayor for his repeated refusal to approve bloated contracts for public works that involved payoffs and kickbacks to alderman and other city officials.

Cleveland served less than a year as Buffalo's mayor before he was elected governor of New York. The circumstances leading to his election mirrored those that had elevated him to the mayor's office in Buffalo. At a time when New York politics was dominated by political bosses and machines in both parties, when the capital of Albany was mired in corruption, and when voices of reform were echoing louder and louder, Cleveland's reputation as the veto mayor of Buffalo quickly gained resonance, especially in the western part of the state. Operating behind the scenes, Cleveland was able to unite enough groups within the divided party to gain the Democratic nomination. Running against a fractured Republican Party, he eased to victory in November against a weak Republican opponent.

By virtue of his election as governor of the nation's most populous state,

Cleveland immediately became a potential candidate for the Democratic presidential nomination in 1884. What propelled him toward the nation's highest office was again his distinction of being incorruptible at a time when the nation clamored for reform. As governor, he followed the same practices he had pursued as mayor. He called for the elimination of all "unnecessary offices." He appointed persons to state positions mainly on their merit. He made clear that he viewed his role as governor to be that of the people's trustee. Attacking the inequalities of wealth and power in the state and the unfairness of the existing tax system, he even called for an income tax and an attack on the spoils system. At the same time, he wielded his pen to veto legislation he regarded as unconstitutional or not serving the public interest.

By 1884, Cleveland had emerged as the strongest candidate for the Democratic presidential nomination. The Republicans were in disarray. Liberal reformers, known as mugwumps, were in revolt against the Republican candidate, James Blaine of Maine, who had a reputation for corruption. With Cleveland already having gained the reputation as the veto governor, he was able to win the Democratic nomination on the second ballot.[54]

After one of the dirtiest campaigns in the nation's history, in which Cleveland admitted to having fathered an illegitimate child and placing it in an orphanage and Democrats used the so-called Mulligan letters to show that Blaine had received handsome commissions from the railroads, Cleveland won the popular vote by 29,000 votes out of 10 million cast and the electoral college by narrowly carrying his home state.

Character had elevated Cleveland to the presidency, and character defined his presidency. He delivered on his promise of businesslike reform of government. Following time-honored tradition, he replaced hundreds of Republican officeholders with Democrats. He retained in office Republicans whom he thought merited retention. At the same time, he followed Hayes's earlier assertion of constitutional authority to remove and temporarily replace executive branch officials without congressional interference. His duel with Congress over executive appointments led to the repeal in 1887 of the notorious Tenure of Office Act.

Cleveland also vetoed more than 200 of almost 2,100 private pension bills of Civil War veterans. He argued that the claims were flimsy or fraudulent and that Congress was attempting to establish itself as an alternative to the Pensions Bureau. Over the powerful opposition of the GAR and Republicans, he then vetoed as a boondoggle a measure that would have given a pension to every Union army veteran who had served in the Civil War for at least ninety days and who could claim some disability, including even old age. By defying Congress in these ways, he strengthened the institution of the presidency and reinforced the concept of separation of powers.

While of critical importance to the history of the presidency, however, Cleveland's achievements as president remained largely negative ones. They reinforced his reputation as a person of the highest integrity who spent hours at his desk personally scrutinizing patronage requests and congressional pension measures. He used his veto pen like a sledgehammer. He was tactless and self-righteous. He failed to take into his confidence members of his own party or the public. His relations with reporters did not help. The stew during the campaign over his fathering of a child left him openly contemptuous of the press, a feeling that hardened after he took office. He became known as "His Obstinacy." Because he regarded his role as an administrator rather than as a policy maker, he often failed to provide adequate leadership in pushing through such measures as tariff and civil service reform.[55]

As a result, by the time he ran for reelection in 1888, he had made many enemies even within his own party. Although he was able to win the Democratic nomination on the first ballot, the governor of New York, David Hill, and his supporters were unwilling to campaign actively for Cleveland in New York, which political observers understood would be a key state in the election. The president also ran a lackluster campaign against a formidable candidate, former senator Benjamin Harrison of Indiana, the other swing state in the election. The Republicans were also better organized, and they were able to campaign effectively against the Democrats' support for a reduction in tariffs, which, they argued, would cost jobs at home. Cleveland managed to win the popular vote by less than 1 percent, but he lost the electoral college by a margin of 219 to 182 votes. Had he carried New York, he would have won the election.

After leaving the White House, the former president moved to New York City, where he took a position as general counsel with a prestigious law firm. Because he was not a partner in the firm, he did not share in its profits. Otherwise, he enjoyed all the accoutrements of a senior partner. He also had the luxury of doing mostly what he wanted. He purposely avoided arguing cases in court because he thought that would put opposing counsel at a disadvantage, given his celebrity status. Instead, he devoted most of his legal work to serving as a referee in important cases assigned to him by the courts. He worked hard on the cases he handled, but he intentionally avoided taking on a heavy caseload.

Instead, Cleveland spent a good part of his time at home enjoying his young marriage of three years to his wife, Frances "Frank" Folsom. It was an odd marriage. The beautiful daughter of his deceased law partner, Oscar Folsom, Frances was only twenty-two years old when she wed the forty-nine-year-old bachelor president in June 1886 in the first wedding to take place at the White House. Cleveland had known Frances all her life; she had been his ward after her father's death. He had started secretly courting her while she was a student at Wells College in Aurora, New York. Their marriage proved to be the most popular event of Cleveland's first presidency. Despite their age difference, by all indications, their marriage was a happy one. Outgoing and charming, Frances proved a perfect counterpoint to her husband as well as an excellent White House hostess.

Besides still enjoying the life of a newlywed, Cleveland spent many days after leaving the White House at his favorite pastime, fishing, around lower Cape

Portrait of President Grover Cleveland's marriage in a White House ceremony on 2 June 1886 to Frances "Frank" Folsom. Daughter of Cleveland's former law partner, the bride was twenty-seven years younger than her husband. This was the first wedding ceremony performed in the White House. Despite their age difference, they appeared to have an idyllic marriage, most of which was spent during his retirement years. The portrait was drawn by Thure de Thulstrup, a well-known Swedish-born illustrator, mostly known, however, for illustrating historical military themes. (Courtesy of Library of Congress, Prints and Photographs Division.)

Cod and Buzzards Bay, then largely inaccessible except by water or a six-mile carriage drive. With its pristine beauty and untouched woods, the area became the summer home for many of the nation's successful businessmen and intellectuals, including the former president's friend, Richard Watson Gilder, editor of *Century* magazine, who in 1891 helped persuade the Clevelands to buy a cottage on Monument Point overlooking the tranquil waters of Buzzards Bay. The two-story clapboard house, which the Clevelands named Gray Gables, surrounded on three sides by woods, became the former president's favorite retreat. For the next ten years, he spent every summer vacationing at Gray Gables.[56]

Cleveland's years of forced retirement may have been the happiest of his life. A few years earlier, he had purchased a twenty-seven-acre country estate for $21,500 in the salubrious heights two miles north of Georgetown. After losing his bid for reelection, he sold the estate, which he and Frances had named Oak View, making a profit of nearly $100,000 and allowing him leisure he had never had before. In 1891, Frances gave birth to a baby girl, whom they named Ruth and whom the public affectionately referred to as Baby Ruth, a nickname that smart marketers in 1921 copyrighted for a new candy bar. A middle-aged bachelor when he entered the White House, Cleveland found himself six years later in an Indian summer of life, with a handsome young wife and a baby girl. Not known for being reflective, the former president ruminated on the new joy that had come to him so relatively late in life. "I . . . have just entered the real world, and see in a small child more of value that I have ever called my own before. . . . fame, honor, place, everything," he wrote to a friend on 21 October.[57]

Despite the pleasures of this new chapter in his life, politics was never far removed from Cleveland's thoughts. He watched the new Republican administration carefully. What he saw, he did not like. The tariff was uppermost in his mind. Although he was never a free trader, he believed current tariff rates were immoral because they promoted corporate greed and concentration. Contrary to Republican arguments—that by encouraging domestic manufacturing, high tariff rates led to higher wages—he maintained that they disadvantaged workers (and farmers) by keeping prices disproportionately high in relation to wages and income.

More than that, a protectionist tariff also created a treasury surplus, effectively reducing the circulating money supply, promoting deflation, and leading to calls for unsound monetary policies. In particular, the former president was concerned about the growing movement, especially in the West and South, for the unlimited coinage of silver at a ratio of 16 to 1 to gold. Because the real value of silver relative to gold was lower than 16 to 1, this would have the effect, according to Gresham's famous law of economics, of having bad money (silver dollars) drive good money (gold dollars) out of circulation, something that Cleveland regarded as irresponsible and abhorrent.

In 1890, the Republican-controlled Congress approved, and President Harrison signed into law, a raft of legislation, almost all of which infuriated Cleveland. Among these measures were the Dependent Pension Act, essentially the same legislation he had vetoed as president; the McKinley tariff, the highest tariff in the nation's history; the Sherman Antitrust Act; and the Sherman Silver Purchase Act, which doubled the amount of silver purchased by the Treasury Department each month and required the government to pay for it in paper currency redeemable in gold or silver.

Although Cleveland kept to the tradition of not publicly commenting on the incumbent administration, privately he expressed his disapproval of the so-called Billion Dollar Congress because it was the first peacetime Congress to appropriate $1 billion. "I have thought as I have seen the Republicans getting deeper and deeper into the mire that our policy should be to let them flounder," he commented in April 1890 in response to a proposal for a Democratic tariff bill to challenge the McKinley tariff. Increasingly, he linked the tariff to the social discontent he felt growing in both urban and rural America, and he coupled both to the free silver movement. As he did so, he began to weigh more heavily the possibility of running a third time for president. "I want my discharge from public and political life," he commented in August. "Words of dismissal would be very sweet to me, and I find myself asking, 'Why should I not export them.' [But] I am unable to lose sight of the possibility, or to forget that a contingency may arise, in which duty to my country and my party may require in me the elements of a popular candidacy."[58]

After elections in November in which the Republicans suffered a major defeat and lost control of the House, Cleveland decided to seek the presidency again. Besides his displeasure with the Republicans, he considered Harrison a weak leader whose administration was dominated by his secretary of state, James Blaine. He also feared that unless he sought a second term, his political rival, Governor Hill of New York, would gain the Democratic nomination. Personal drive and ambition, encouraged by his wife—who had told a White House servant just before leaving the executive mansion in 1889 that she and her husband would be back—undoubtedly also motivated Cleveland to run again.

Although the former president remained coy about his plans and continued to deny any further political ambitions, he wrote a telling letter to his friend, Wilson S. Bissell, shortly after the November elections. "Of one thing you may be entirely certain," he commented.

> Hill and his friends are bent on his nomination for the Presidency, and failing in that they are determined that it shall not come towards me. You know how I feel about this matter as a personal question; but if I have pulled out any chestnuts out of the fire I want those who take them to keep a civil tongue in their heads; and further than this, I don't want to see my hard work wasted and the old party fall back to shiftiness and expediency.[59]

Besides Hill's candidacy, another potential obstacle to Cleveland's renomination for president was the power of the silverite movement, which was rapidly growing within Democratic ranks. Democrats from the South and West had provided the margin of difference in gaining approval of the Sherman Silver Purchase Act. They were also in the forefront of the movement for the unlimited coinage of silver at 16 to 1 to gold. Although it might have been politically prudent for the former president to try to finesse the silver issue or remain silent about it for as long as possible, he found the issue so detrimental to a sound currency and economy that he felt obliged to take a public stand. "If we have developed an unexpected capacity for the assimilation of a largely increased volume of [silver] currency, and even if we have demonstrated the usefulness of such an increase," he wrote in a letter that he later published, "these conditions fall far short of insuring us against disaster."[60]

Despite the problems posed by the candidacy of Hill, now a U.S. senator, and the growing free silver movement, Cleveland was easily able on the first ballot to gain the two-thirds vote needed for the Democratic nomination at its Chicago convention in June. Hill's forces had overreached themselves, even in the South and West, by the duplicitous manner in which they gained control of the New York state delegation and imposed the unit rule on it. A month later, the former president broke precedent by traveling to New York from his vacation home at

Buzzards Bay in order to deliver an acceptance speech before a crowd of 20,000 at Madison Square Garden.

Notwithstanding the growing power of the free silver movement, the former president had several factors in his favor in the election that followed. In the first place, his sound money position was orthodoxy among the business and corporate elites, who may not have liked his condemnations of corporate greed and power but appreciated even less the threat posed by the muscle flexing of farmers and workers. The protective tariff, which he made his major campaign issue, the spending programs of the Billion Dollar Congress, the restiveness in the land, and the unpopularity of the cool and aloof incumbent, even among Republicans, also benefited the Democratic nominee. The recently formed Populist Party, which ran its own candidate, General James Weaver of Iowa, on a free silver platform, hurt the Republicans in the West, where the Populists were so strong that the Democrats did not even enter a slate in a number of states.

Although the election was among the least rancorous in memory (in part because of the introduction of the Australian, or secret, ballot), Cleveland worked harder to win than he had in previous campaigns. Reluctant to travel or make speeches, he wrote scores of letters to party leaders throughout the country outlining his views on the tariff, free silver, and other issues. In November, he received over 5.5 million popular votes and 277 electoral votes to Harrison's 5.2 million popular votes and 145 electoral votes. It was the most decisive victory since Lincoln's reelection in 1864. Among the states he won were his home state of New York and Indiana, both of which he had lost to Harrison four years earlier. For the first time since the Civil War, the Democrats also captured both houses of Congress. Weaver received over one million popular votes and twenty-two electoral votes, becoming the only third-party candidate between 1860 and 1912 to win a single state. For the first—and only—time in the nation's history, a former president who had been defeated in his first bid for reelection had been returned to serve a second term.[61]

III

The last of the full-bearded presidents, Benjamin Harrison was characterized by even members of his own party as being colorless, abrupt, and offensive. In terms of the emergence of the modern presidency, however, Harrison's presidency was an important one. Clearly one of the distinguishing characteristics of the modern presidency—perhaps its most distinguishing characteristic—has been the role of the president in foreign policy. As commander in chief during time of war and the dominant world leader for much of the twentieth century, the president's power greatly expanded during this time. Harrison was one of the first presidents to prepare the United States for its expanded role in the world, especially in increasing its commercial interests abroad. In contrast, neither Hayes nor Cleveland had been much interested in spreading American interests overseas. To the extent that Hayes concerned himself with foreign matters, it had mostly to do with preventing the French from building an isthmian canal through Panama.[62] Much the same can be said for Cleveland's first administration.

In contrast, Harrison had a personal interest in commercial expansion abroad. With Blaine as his secretary of state, Harrison pursued a vigorous foreign policy. The administration pushed American claims to distant Samoa, almost causing a naval war with Germany but achieving America's claims to the harbor of Pago Pago. In 1889, Harrison warned Canadians against their overkilling of seals in the Bering Sea between Alaska and Russia, furthering an already existing rift in Anglo-American relations and causing the British to send four warships to the disputed region. In 1891, the president threatened war with Chile after two seamen from the heavily armed *Baltimore* were killed in a saloon fight while on shore in the Chilean port of Valparaiso. At the same time, Secretary of State Blaine pushed for reciprocal trade agreements to promote trade with Latin America. Less than three weeks before leaving office, the president sent to the Senate a treaty annexing Hawaii after a trumped-up revolution was led by American plantation interests against the existing government.[63]

As important as any incident during the Harrison administration, however, were the pathbreaking efforts of the president's secretary of the navy, Benjamin Tracy, to construct a modern United States battleship fleet. Under his leadership, the navy began the construction of three heavily armored steel vessels able to cruise long distances and to engage in major naval battles. In addition, Tracy established the naval reserve, eliminated much of the red tape preventing the design and building of new ships, and issued a contract for the first American submarine. Fully backing Tracy's efforts, President Harrison incorporated the secretary's arguments linking commercial expansion with the need for a big navy into his own presidential messages. As a result of their efforts, the United States changed from having a second-rate navy of mostly wooden ships to becoming a rising naval power.[64]

How and why Harrison became a commercial expansionist, in contrast to some other presidents of the Gilded Age, is not entirely clear. Certainly it had to do with his devout Christianity and his belief that commercial expansion eased the way for the spread of Christian beliefs. The most noteworthy aspect of Harrison's upbringing was less the fact that he was the grandson of former president William Henry Harrison than his Christian background. Born in 20 August 1833 in North Bend, Ohio, near Cincinnati, on the 600-acre farm of his grandfather, a site known as the Point because it stood on the sharp bend of the Ohio River, Benjamin had a strict Presbyterian upbringing. He attended a private preparatory school in Cincinnati, where he received a liberal education under the tutelage of Robert Hamilton Bishop, a Presbyterian minister and highly respected educator who taught history and instilled in his students the redeeming qualities of stewardship and social responsibility.

Already in love with his future wife, Caroline "Carrie" Lavina Scott, Harrison continued his education as a junior at Miami University in nearby Oxford, Ohio, where she lived. His Presbyterian upbringing was reinforced by Miami's small but mostly Presbyterian faculty and by the revival meetings the school frequently held. At Miami, he seriously considered the ministry as a career until he decided to marry Carrie.

In 1852, Harrison graduated near the top of his class. The next year, he married Carrie. Having decided on a legal career, Harrison read law for two years before taking and passing the Ohio bar in 1854. Instead of staying in Ohio, however, Benjamin and Carrie decided to move to Indianapolis, about 130 miles away. His first few years were so lean financially that friends even suggested he move elsewhere. Then William Wallace, the son of a former governor, invited him to become his law partner. Through hard work and Wallace's connections, he was able to build a comfortable practice. With another rising young attorney, William Pinkney Fishback, he later established his own law firm.

By this time, Harrison had become involved in politics. Because of the Republican Party's opposition to the expansion of slavery into the western territories, he joined the new party. In 1858, he successfully ran for city attorney. In 1860, he won election as reporter of the Indiana supreme court. His big break did not come, however, until ten years after the Civil War, when, after losing a bid for the governorship in which he gained considerable national exposure, he was sent on a speaking tour by the Republican National Committee on behalf of Hayes. In 1880, he helped swing the Indiana delegation to James Garfield at the Republican national convention. After Garfield's victory in November, he was rewarded by being elected to the U.S. Senate. Although Democrats in the state legislature denied Harrison a second term in 1887, he emerged as a serious candidate for the Republican presidential nomination after Cleveland's defeat of Blaine in 1884. When Blaine suggested in 1888 that Harrison would be the party's best candidate for president, he was virtually assured the nomination. In November, he defeated Cleveland in the general election by winning the electoral college.

Although Harrison had his greatest impact as president in the arena of foreign policy, he became one of the most involved legislative presidents of the late nineteenth century.[65] A meticulous administrator who organized the executive office in new ways and kept fully abreast of matters on Capitol Hill, he traveled the country in support of his programs and tried hard in other ways to get his priorities through Congress. He played an important role, for example, in determining the outcome of the currency issue during his presidency, and he was also instrumental in getting an amendment included as part of the McKinley tariff of 1890 that gave the president new powers to impose duties on imports.

Yet Harrison was never a popular president, even among Republicans. Nor was he an especially effective leader. Even though the Billion Dollar Congress of his administration passed some of the most notable legislation before the Progressive era, including the Sherman Antitrust Act, the Sherman Silver Purchase Act,

Photo by George Price of Benjamin Harrison in 1888 seated at a table. The last of the full-bearded presidents, Harrison had just defeated Grover Cleveland in his bid for reelection. A well-known photographer of his time, Price also photographed such other notables as President William McKinley making his inaugural address and Mrs. Edith Kermit Carrow Roosevelt. (Courtesy of Congress, Prints and Photographs Division [Repro. No. LC-USZ62-7611].)

and the McKinley tariff, congressional leaders rather than the president were still largely responsible for these measures.[66]

One of the nation's shortest presidents, Little Ben, as he was often called, barely stood five feet, seven inches tall, making him the second shortest president next to James Monroe. Rotund and wearing a full beard, he had a light complexion, blue eyes, and short brown hair that had once been blond. Always fastidiously dressed in a Prince Albert coat and turned-down collar, and speaking with clarity and common sense in a soft tenor voice that still could be heard a distance away, he was a persuasive orator and commanding figure despite his unprepossessing physical stature—commanding, but also icy, distant, and unforgiving, with an overbearing sense of piety and self-righteousness. Even when he did the right thing, he often did it in the wrong way. Stories were legion of patronage seekers and others who came to his White House office and were left standing while he looked at his watch and brusquely asked them to leave after a few minutes. He was cold even to party leaders. As a result, he made many enemies, including much of the press, which, like most presidents, he despised.

In 1892, a dump-Harrison campaign began on Capitol Hill. The campaign backfired, however, when Harrison, who had planned to retire, decided it would be cowardly of him, in the face of opposition to his nomination, not to be a candidate for a second term. His most likely opponent, Blaine, also refused to give the dump-Harrison movement his blessing. His refusal assured that the president would win the nomination. In November, he lost the election to Cleveland by the largest margin for an incumbent in twenty years.

His defeat represented a nadir in Harrison's life, not so much because he had been so resoundingly rejected by the American people but because, two weeks earlier, Carrie, who had been bedridden since May and then diagnosed with pulmonary tuberculosis, died. Carrie's gradual deterioration and death took away whatever interest Harrison might have had in pursuing an active campaign. Instead, he spent much of his time at Carrie's bedside in the White House. After her death on 25 October, he remarked that he felt like "a leader in prison." After taking her body back to Indianapolis for burial and then returning to Washington, he did not even make a return trip home to vote. Although he still wanted to win the election, his rationale was as much one of pride as of desiring four more years in the White House.[67]

Perhaps for that reason, Harrison received the news of his defeat with considerable equanimity. "I was so removed from the campaign that I can scarcely realize that I was a candidate," he wrote one of his backers after the election. To another he remarked, "I have never enjoyed public life [and] do not seem to have the mental adaptation which would enable me to get satisfaction out of it. I always carry care and responsibility heavily."[68]

Harrison described his final day in Washington as "fearfully bad . . . in that it was colder than my Inauguration day. For rain they had snow." Returning home to Indianapolis, he was overwhelmed by the reception he received. Still grieving over the loss of his wife, however, he found it difficult to occupy himself. His house was in disrepair, and he hired workers to renovate the interior and add a new porch and stable. He also spent considerable time unpacking his papers, books, and china. Psychologically, however, he remained depressed as he adjusted to life without his wife of forty years. "I find myself exceedingly lazy, unable yet to do much of any work," he admitted.[69]

Harrison resolved his despondency and lethargy by secretly courting Mary "Mame" Dimmick, a thirty-seven-year-old widow who was also the niece of his dead wife, Carrie. Mame had moved into the White House in 1889 to serve as the first lady's assistant. After Carrie's health began to deteriorate, she became her principal caretaker. Harrison developed a fondness for her that extended beyond niece and uncle. The first letter he wrote after returning to Indianapolis was to Mame expressing to her his "gratitude and love" for nursing Carrie during her last months of life. Within a few weeks, he wrote Mame again, asking her to come to Indianapolis.[70]

Harrison's daughter, Mary, who had come to Indianapolis with her two children, was greatly distressed by the former president's invitation to Mame. Mary had also lived in the White House with her children. Although relations between the two women were civil, she had never cared much for Mame, whose outgoing personality conflicted with her own less gregarious nature. She also probably resented the affection that Harrison displayed toward his niece.

Harrison seems to have had no inkling about his daughter's dislike for Mame, or if he did, he did not let it interfere with his courtship of his niece. "We have all enjoyed her presence," the former president wrote to Mame's sister, Lizzie, in May 1893. At his invitation, both Lizzie and Mame spent the summer at Harrison's vacation cottage in Cape May. Later Harrison wrote Mame from Indianapolis, opening his house to her.[71]

After waiting an appropriate time, the former president asked Mame to marry him. The engagement was announced in December 1895, and they were married the following April. Mary and her brother, Russell, who were horrified at the thought that their father would ever marry after the death of their mother, refused to attend the wedding. Their displeasure did not keep the former president from enjoying the bliss of a newlywed, his life made even happier by the birth in February 1897 of a daughter named Elizabeth. How ironic it was that Harrison and his political rival, Cleveland, one a sixty-two-year-old widower and the other a forty-nine-year-old bachelor, who were known as cold and even forbidding, should break with convention by marrying women both young enough to have been their daughters, both of whom had some filial relationship with them, and both of whom gave them a new family that made their last years among their happiest!

By even Harrison's own account, the former president was still comfortable financially when he returned to Indianapolis. Yet he did not yet feel he was "rich enough to be financially idle."[72] Throughout his life, he had enjoyed traveling and had taken numerous vacations to the New Jersey shore and to the Adirondacks to hunt and fish. As a staunch patriot and veteran of the Civil War who, as president, supported a Flag Day holiday and liked being referred to by his friends and associates as "General," he attended the annual meetings of the GAR and various other reunions of Civil War veterans. Unlike many earlier presidents, he did not spend on a lavish table and expensive wines; in fact, he and Carrie were teetotalers. They gave generously to their church and various charities. He felt, therefore, that he still needed to earn an income in order to continue with his various philanthropies and to carry on his customary lifestyle, especially since Mary, her two children, and then Mame were living with him.

The question was how. For the nation's earliest presidents, who believed public service should be followed by a return to private life, there were few options other than pursuits on their plantations and farms. Over time, former presidents became more active publicly. Yet except for Grant, and to a more limited extent Cleveland, even the most active ex-presidents, like Millard Fillmore and Rutherford B. Hayes, considered it inappropriate to use their former prominence for personal profit.

Not so Harrison, who decided to return to his law practice and was soon demanding and receiving some of the highest fees in his profession. Before holding elective office, he had been one of Indiana's most widely respected and successful lawyers. He owed his success, moreover, to his abilities as an attorney rather than to his political ties. He had never sought to take advantage of the fact that he was the grandson of a former president. As a young lawyer, he had taken on some of the most controversial criminal and civil cases in order to establish his ability in the courtroom. Over time, his practice centered on complex civil matters involving tax, constitutional, and corporate law. He owed his success to his hard work, mastery of the law, well-argued briefs, and masterful courtroom presentations. Even when he was in the U.S. Senate, he argued six cases before the Supreme Court, winning four of them.[73]

Even if Harrison had not served as president, in other words, he almost certainly would have continued to be a successful and prosperous lawyer taking on difficult cases, some of which might have made their way to the Supreme Court. Yet there can be no gainsaying the fact that just as there was an emergent modern presidency, there was also an emergent modern post-presidency, which shattered any barriers that might have remained as to what activities were appropriate for former presidents and offered new opportunities for them to profit from their previous service in the White House.

As the presidential office became more prominent, so did the prominence of those who held that office. As the nation's political bosses yielded to the modern two-party system, more demands were made on former presidents to campaign on behalf of party candidates. As the nation's infrastructure matured and communications and transportation wove the nation more closely together, opportunities for ex-presidents to travel and to maintain a national presence also increased. As businesses became more national (and even international), more requests were made of ex-presidents to serve on boards of directors, or as corporate officers, legal representatives, and lobbyists of these big businesses. As the readership of newspapers, magazines, and books flourished, and as publishers themselves became big businesses, so were there more opportunities for former presidents to profit financially from writing feature articles and commentary for newspapers and magazines, as well as books for national publishers. As the nation became a world power, former presidents were also called on to serve on international bodies or to arbitrate disputes between nations.

Harrison soon received various offers of employment, including the presidency of a bank and a richly endowed chair at the University of Chicago. He turned down all but two of these proposals. The first was to give a series of six lectures in the spring of 1894 at newly established Stanford University on the early legal history of the United States. Although preparing the lectures required significant work on his part, he found the stipend of $25,000 (the equivalent of about $612,000 in 2009) and the opportunities to travel to the West Coast and visit friends irresistible. Together with a number of other talks he gave during his retirement, revised copies of the Stanford lectures were later published as *Views of an Ex-President.* Harrison also contracted to write nine 3,000-word articles for the *Ladies' Home Journal* on the machinery of government; for each of the articles, he received $5,000. Later they were turned into a book, *This Country of Ours,* which, much to his delight, became a best seller in the United States and was translated into five languages. His publisher, Charles Scribner's, paid him a 20 percent royalty, the highest it had ever given to an author. The former president was pleased, he later remarked, that his writings had "promoted an interest in our public institutions."[74] Undoubtedly, he was also delighted at the income that they and his Stanford lectures generated.

Harrison's income from his lectures and writings only supplemented the income he received from resumption of his law practice. Like Cleveland, Harrison was highly selective in the clients he chose to represent. Unlike Cleveland, however, a significant part of his legal career occurred after he left office. He continued to practice law until his death in 1901 and reportedly averaged $150,000 a year in fees. In at least one high-profile case, the opposing attorney maintained that he was disadvantaged by the fact that the plaintiff was being represented by an ex-president. Harrison refused even to consider withdrawing from the case. "I assert there is no ex-President in this case," he told the presiding judge. "I am here to discharge the sworn duties of my profession as I see them. If the people of this country have seen cause to honor me, it is no reason why I should not appear in the capacity of counselor nor a reason why I should be driven from this court."[75]

Although Harrison continued to argue a number of cases before the Supreme Court, his most significant representation was as chief counsel for Venezuela in a boundary dispute with British Guiana, which Cleveland had persuaded Britain to settle through arbitration during his second administration. Venezuela turned to Harrison after Cleveland declined its offer to serve as lead counsel. That

Venezuela should turn to former presidents to represent it in an arbitration case indicated their growing prominence on the world stage, along with that of the United States as a global power.

In agreeing to represent Venezuela, Harrison insisted on a retainer of $20,000 and quarterly payments of $10,000 until the International Tribunal in Paris, which had been agreed upon by London and Washington, decided the case. By the time it handed down its decision in 1899, the former president's fees added up to $80,000. He also obtained a fee of $50,000 for his former navy secretary, Benjamin Tracy, who shared the caseload with him, and undisclosed amounts for Tracy's partner, James B. Soley, and the internationally respected authority on boundary disputes, Severo Mallet-Prevost, both of whom also assisted in preparing the case. Harrison worked hard for his fees. Over a fifteen-month period, he devoted his full time to preparing his written argument, setting up a law office at home to avoid any distractions and mastering the complex history and legal issues in question. When completed in early 1899, his brief ran about 800 pages in two volumes with additional appendices and an atlas.[76]

Responses and counterclaims followed. The final printed material submitted at the end of February totaled twenty-three volumes. Three months later, oral arguments began. The British legal team argued for fifty-two hours. After a three-month adjournment, Harrison presented the case for Venezuela, speaking for twenty-five hours over a five-day period. Although he thought he had made a compelling case in support of Venezuela, he feared that the five-member tribunal hearing the case would "decide on some compromise line . . . instead of the line of right."[77]

The former president was correct. On 8 October 1899, the tribunal, composed of two Americans, two Britons, and the president of the tribunal, Baron Frederick F. de Martens, a Russian jurist and professor of international law, handed down its decision. British Guiana was awarded about 90 percent of the land in question, making it appear that the British had prevailed. The 10 percent awarded to Venezuela, however, included the valuable gold-bearing region of the disputed territory and control of the Orinoco River, which served as the commercial gateway to the northern third of South America.

Harrison was indignant at the unanimous decision and at first wanted the two American jurists on the tribunal to file dissenting opinions. He was persuaded by Mallet-Prevost that the Americans had agreed to vote with the majority to assure that Venezuela would at least receive the mouth of the Orinoco River; if they dissented, Venezuela would lose everything. "If it should ever be known that we had it in our power to save for Venezuela the mouth of the Orinoco and failed to do so," the former president remarked, "we should never be forgiven."[78]

The Venezuela–British Guiana boundary dispute represented the milestone of Harrison's long legal career. He continued to argue important cases before the Indiana and U.S. supreme courts. Completely exhausted by the case, however, he no longer devoted himself so fully to his profession, finding more time to spend with his family or to vacation.

Somewhat against his will, the former president also remained active in politics. Unlike Cleveland, Harrison had no interest in running again for president, although his supporters, including a number of party leaders, urged him to seek the Republican nomination in 1896. "I do not see anything but labor and worry and distress in another campaign or in another term in the White House," he explained in May 1894. He continued to maintain this position, later describing the White House in an article for *Ladies' Home Journal* as "an office and a home combined—an evil combination [that afforded] no break in the day—no change of atmosphere" between public and private life.[79] Although he showed no interest in seeking another term as president, he agreed in 1894 to make two speeches on behalf of Republican candidates in Indiana. He proved to be such an effective speaker that soon the two speeches mushroomed into forty. He also agreed to campaign in New York on behalf of his former vice president, Levi Morton, who was running for governor of New York.

Addressing what was billed as a "great mass meeting" at Carnegie Hall, Harrison delivered a blistering attack on the Cleveland administration, blaming it for the nation's economic depression. He also spoke out strongly in support of commercial expansion in South America as a partial solution to the nation's economic problems and tied the nation's ability to compete there with the need for the same banking facilities, steamship service, and product lines that European countries had already established on the continent. "We should come into many [of the nations of South America] as a new trading country in many branches of commerce," he remarked. "Already English and German and French and other agents have sought out the peculiar demands of these countries," he continued. "Already they have established banking institutions, so that exchange is easy between these foreign ports and London. This has not yet been done by us, though I hope it may be, and New York may stand in such relations to many of these great South American nations."[80]

Another point Harrison emphasized in his speech was the need for lower wages for American workers in order to compete with Europe. "If we are to compete in the markets of the world, selling our goods at the same price with the nations of Europe," he told his Carnegie Hall audience, "we must get our labor as cheap as they get theirs. And yet our friends are always shy of admitting that."[81]

The former president's remarks indicated the tension that existed, even among socially conscious Republicans of genteel background, between their call for lower wages and their argument that a protective tariff was needed to assure higher wages for American labor. The same may be said about their attacks on corporate greed. As an attorney specializing in tax and corporate law, Harrison emphasized in particular the need for the wealthy to pay their proportionate share of taxes. This included not only real estate taxes but also intangible property taxes, such as stocks, bonds, notes, and mortgages. "The plea of business privacy has been driven too hard," he remarked when speaking later on "The Obligations of Wealth." "The men who have wealth must not hide it from the tax gatherer, and flaunt it in the street. Such things breed a great discontent."[82]

Harrison even supported inheritance taxes as long as they were permitted in state constitutions and were not progressive. "A higher rate for large estates seems to me to be inconsistent with that rule of proportionate and equality which should characterize all taxation," he stated. The former president, however, was more conservative and less flexible in his views than Hayes. In contrast to Hayes, he never flirted with socialist ideas or suggested limits on the amount one could pass from one generation to the next. In fact, he deplored blanket attacks on wealth. "The indiscriminate denunciation of the rich is mischievous," he added in his speech on wealth. "It perverts the mind, poisons the heart and furnishes an excuse for crime. . . . Not what a man has, but what he is, settles his class."[83]

After Republicans nominated William McKinley for president, Harrison was urged by the nominee's campaign manager, Mark Hanna, to stump on behalf of the Republican candidate. Although Harrison preferred Senator William B. Allison of Iowa to McKinley for the nomination, he agreed to campaign on McKinley's behalf. Returning to Carnegie Hall, he made another well-received address in which he blasted the Democratic nominee, William Jennings Bryan, for his campaign on behalf of free silver. Remarking that he had "hoped to add to relief from official duties retirement from the arena of political debate," he added that he felt it was his "political duty" to speak out against free silver, which he termed "the financial and moral equivalent of a declaration that fifty-cent pieces are dollars."[84]

Even after the election, the former president continued to be much in demand by Republican candidates for office. Harrison's representation of Venezuela in its boundary dispute with British Guiana and his advancing age, however, limited what he could do—or was disposed to do—in the political arena. He was willing to support Republican candidates for office, and he continued to speak out on important issues, such as lending his support for the Spanish–American War. Indeed, he wrote an article in November 1898 advocating military instruction and drill in all schools for boys. Yet he believed that the United States' role in the world should be commercial and humanitarian, and he thought the acquisition of Puerto Rico and the Philippine Islands was a "sad mistake." He even declined to campaign for McKinley's reelection because it appeared to him that some Republicans "were arguing a bill of exceptions to the Declaration of Independence."[85]

By the time that Harrison went public in his opposition to the possession of a colonial empire, he had achieved the status of an elder statesman widely admired throughout the country. Although he was sixty-six years old and had cut back his law practice and political activities, he seemed in good health, was the father of a three-year-old, and was still practicing law and writing for literary magazines. Early in March 1901, however, he came down with the flu, which turned into pneumonia. Despite the best efforts of the doctors, his condition worsened. He slipped in and out of a coma, and on 13 March, he died at the age of sixty-seven.[86]

After the former president lay in state in the rotunda of the Indiana state capitol, a private service was held at his home. This was followed by a much larger public service, attended by President McKinley and former president Cleveland, at the First Presbyterian Church where Harrison had been a member for nearly fifty years. The former president was buried next to his first wife, Carrie, at Crown Hill Memorial Cemetery in Indianapolis.

During his post-presidency, Harrison had disdained the public spotlight. Having no further interest in public office and wanting to increase his personal wealth, he had returned to his home in Indianapolis, where he decided to resume his law practice. What made his decision so noteworthy was the fact that he saw no potential conflict of interest in being a former president and in representing clients in highly contentious legal disputes. While he did not seek to profit from the fact that he was an ex-president, neither did he see any ethical or legal dilemma in the fees he charged or in the practice he maintained. He also supplemented his highly successful law practice by the unusually generous royalties and fees he received from his writing and lecturing.

Clearly Harrison broke any remaining barrier against a former president profiting from the fact that he had served in the White House. Although not all ex-presidents after Harrison chose to follow a similar path, others did. By the time he left the White House, former presidents had become highly public figures, and the temptations for some of them to profit from their former status had become irresistible. This happened well before it became common practice in the latter third of the twentieth century for former presidents to profit by publishing their memoirs and going on lecture circuits.

7

The Post-Presidency and the Modern Presidency
Cleveland II and Roosevelt

It is hard to imagine two more dissimilar former presidents than Grover Cleveland and Theodore Roosevelt (or T.R., the first president to be known by his initials). If Cleveland was brusque, dull, not very knowledgeable, and fleshy, Roosevelt was effusive, erudite, dynamic, and charismatic. Photographs of Roosevelt show a muscular man with an engaging face, prominent white teeth, bountiful moustache, and pince-nez, his manner determined, his jaw snapping, and his arms hammering away as he addressed welcoming crowds.

In terms of the modern presidency, however, Cleveland and Roosevelt represented two bookends. Under Cleveland and the other Gilded Age presidents, the modern presidency began. Under Roosevelt, it blossomed. He brought to his office an unprecedented sense of social justice. He enlarged government. He initiated some of the most far-reaching legislation in the nation's history. He turned the press into an arm of his administration. He developed the artistry of the bully pulpit, and he held the center of the world stage. By the time Roosevelt left office in 1909, the United States rivaled the major European nations as a global leader, and the authority of the presidency had been increased proportionately.

After they left office, Cleveland and Roosevelt pursued opposite paths, reflecting their different concerns and personalities. Cleveland remained interested in politics, but he had no interest in further political office. Instead, he enjoyed his new and growing family and spent his summers at his vacation home in Buzzards Bay. Seeking to increase his wealth, he made a small fortune by serving as a corporate officer and then a lobbyist for the insurance industry. Relishing the national stage, increasingly disgruntled with his handpicked successor, William Howard Taft, and retaining his sense of civic duty and responsibility, Roosevelt became the most public former president in the nation's history. Few presidents before and since have enjoyed the cult of personality that developed around him.

I

Cleveland's second administration was a punishing one for him and a letdown for the nation. On the one hand, he was faced almost as soon as he took office by a financial panic that had far-reaching consequences, including the nation's worst depression up to that time, the destructive and bloody Pullman strike of 1894, and the growth of the free silver movement in the South and West. On the other hand, he displayed a narrowness of vision and lack of finesse throughout most of his administration that left his party badly divided—and that a more imaginative and less dogmatic president might have avoided.

During the campaign, Cleveland had intended that the first order of his administration would be repeal of the McKinley Tariff Act. Faced with the worsening financial crisis gripping the nation, however, he called a special session of Congress, which repealed the Sherman Silver Purchase Act that had resulted in a dangerous drain on the nation's gold reserves. A year later, the president turned to a banking syndicate, headed by the investment house of J. P. Morgan, to sell U.S. bonds payable in gold at a sizable profit to the syndicate.

By effectively placing the nation on the gold standard and restoring the nation's gold reserves, Cleveland helped stabilize the currency and restore confidence to the financial community. Repeal of the Sherman Act, however, drove a wedge through the Democratic Party that was exacerbated by the deal his administration made with the Morgan syndicate. Farmers and other silverites accused the president of being an agent of bankers and industrialists.

During the Pullman strike, Cleveland also seemed to favor management over labor by sending troops to Chicago to quell labor violence on the basis of the need to protect interstate commerce and to ensure delivery of the mails. By the time Cleveland turned once more to tariff reform, the once-popular president had become reviled throughout much of the country. Even his own party viewed him as uncompromising, unapproachable, and impolitic. All this came out in his badly handled efforts to reduce tariff duties without resorting to free trade. The resulting Wilson–Gorman tariff of 1894 provided so little in the way of tariff reduction that Cleveland allowed it to become law without his signature.

Yet as in his first term, the president responded to the domestic crises of his second term in ways that increased the powers of his office. His actions in the case of the Pullman strike, for example, contrasted markedly from those of Rutherford Hayes during a railroad strike in 1877, when Hayes intervened reluctantly and only at the request of state officials. Similarly, Cleveland used his control of patronage to gain repeal of the Sherman Silver Purchase Act.[1]

With a year still to go in his administration, Cleveland was bitter and despondent. During his second term, he had become the father of two more daughters. Like Baby Ruth, they brought Cleveland great pleasure and joy, but hardly enough to keep his mind away from the harsh political reality his administration was facing and the personal charges being levied against him. In the 1894 congressional elections, the Democrats were thrashed by the Republicans, who took back both houses of Congress by substantial margins. The free silver movement, led by a thirty-six-year-old former congressman from Nebraska, William Jennings Bryan, was also on the verge of taking over the Democratic Party. Considering a sound currency as much a matter of conscience as a political issue, the president could not accept losing control of his party to the silverites. "I have never felt so keenly as now the unjust accusations of political antagonists and the hatred and vindictiveness of ingrates and traitors who wear the stolen livery of Democracy," he commented in February.[2]

What Cleveland failed to understand was that the call for free silver was part of a much larger rebellion of rural America against what it considered its subservience to the corporate Northeast. Despite his effort to brand silverites renegades from the principles of the Democratic Party, in Chicago the Democrats nominated Bryan for president after the Nebraskan mesmerized the convention with his famous "cross of gold" speech. In response, a group of gold Democrats, encouraged by Cleveland, held a separate gathering in Indianapolis, where they nominated Senator John M. Palmer of Illinois for president. In November, McKinley easily defeated Bryan, receiving slightly over 7 million popular votes and 271 electoral votes to Bryan's 6.47 million popular votes and 176 electoral votes.[3]

In the months after the election, Cleveland concerned himself with finding a residence and ensuring a comfortable income for his growing family. With three infant children, he thought it imprudent to live in New York City, as he had after his first term. He had spoken at Princeton University in October, and his wife and he were impressed by the surrounding countryside. A few days after the election, he wrote to a friend and professor of classics at Princeton, Andrew F. West, asking him if he knew of a house that might be for sale. With West's help, he purchased an old colonial mansion made of stucco with a large lawn, which he then named Westland after the Princeton professor.[4]

As for his finances, Cleveland had relied heavily while president on his business friends for financial counsel. His closest adviser was the gas magnate, "Commodore" Elias. C. Benedict, on whose yacht, the *Oneida,* doctors had secretly removed a malignant tumor on his upper mouth.[5] By the time he left the White House, he had accumulated between $300,000 and $350,000 (roughly the equivalent of between $7.6 and $9 million in 2009). By almost any standard, the outgoing president was wealthy. Believing, however, that he would never again be able to find gainful employment, he worried that he might still not have enough resources to guarantee his family's financial security.

In most respects, Cleveland enjoyed an idyllic retirement after he left office. He continued to be bothered by the Bryan wing's control of the Democratic Party. His political friends and allies tried to get him to challenge Bryan for the party's 1900 nomination, but he rejected the idea, pointing to his lack of standing among Democrats, who again nominated the Nebraskan.[6]

Because the major issue in the 1900 campaign was President William McKinley's decision to acquire the Philippine Islands after the Spanish–American War, rather than free silver, and because Cleveland and Bryan were both anti-imperialists, some Democratic leaders thought Cleveland would support the Democratic nominee. However, he remained adamant in believing the Democratic Party had to be purified of those whom he regarded as charlatans.[7]

Although the former president watched politics carefully throughout his retirement, politics was not his preoccupation. Rather, he settled into the routine of a village squire. His family grew with the addition of two boys. Although he had always been shy with those whom he regarded as his intellectual superiors, he easily adapted to his new surroundings. He took daily walks through the village and could be seen on frequent carriage rides with his wife. He befriended students and faculty at Princeton and began giving lectures to the university community. In 1899, he was appointed Henry Stafford Little Lecturer in Public Affairs. Although in the past he had refused to accept honorary degrees from Harvard and Princeton, believing that he did not merit them, given his lack of a college education, in 1897 he accepted an honorary degree from Princeton. In 1901, he became a Princeton trustee. Each year he also marched at the head of Princeton's commencement procession, alongside the university's president. Because that person after 1902 was Woodrow Wilson, by a twist of fate, the nation's only two Democratic presidents between 1861 and 1933 could be seen marching side by side each June. Other than the fact that Cleveland later became caught in the middle of a struggle between Wilson and his friend West, who had become dean of the graduate school, over the school's organization and physical placement, the former president relished his relationship with Princeton.

Cleveland generally ignored the more cultural side of Princeton, however, like lectures and concerts. Except for fishing and hunting with his friend, Commodore Benedict, at Buzzards Bay or in the marshes of South Carolina, where they went duck hunting, and winter trips to Florida, he also showed little interest in travel, especially outside the United States. Beginning in 1900 and continuing through 1906, he wrote regularly for the *Saturday Evening Post* and for such other magazines as *McClure's, Collier's,* the *Atlantic,* and *Ladies' Home Journal.* Most of his articles dealt either with outdoor sports or contemporary issues. None of them were particularly insightful or memorable. Four of them, however, were public lectures he had delivered at Princeton on matters he considered among the most important of his presidential career. These included his battle with the Senate over executive appointments, the issuing of gold bonds, the Pullman strike, and the dispute with Britain over the boundary between Venezuela and British Guiana. In 1904, he decided to publish these articles in book form. His acquaintances encouraged him to publish his memoirs, but he refused, convinced he had nothing to add that was not already in the public record.

Tragedy struck the Cleveland residence on 7 January 1904 when twelve-year-old Ruth unexpectedly died of diphtheria. The former president was devastated.

At age sixty-six, he had begun to lose some of his closest friends and acquaintances, including his best friend, William Bissell. Upsetting as this was, it could not compare to the grief he felt at the unexpected death of his firstborn at such a young age. "It seems to me I mourn our darling Ruth's death more and more," he wrote in his diary on 11 January.[8] Imagining how unbearable the anguish he and his family would feel spending their summers at Gray Gables, with all its memories of Ruth, he put the home up for sale. Although he continued to make annual fishing trips with Benedict and others to Buzzards Bay, he and his family now summered in the mountains of New Hampshire, where they eventually purchased a home they named Intermount.

Cleveland mourned Ruth's death for the remainder of his life, but his sense of purpose, personal fortitude, and faith kept him from retreating into a shell of seclusion. Despite being the son of a Presbyterian minister, he had not been especially religious as an adult. Turning his back on his puritanical upbringing, he ate too much, drank too much, and found too much pleasure in other worldly things. Except when he was with his mother, he rarely attended church. He was tolerant of most religions but intolerant of evangelists.

As Cleveland grew older, he began to think of his own mortality, but he was never preoccupied with thoughts of God and the afterlife. Matters of theology bored him. "The Bible is good enough for me," he once remarked to a political ally, George F. Parker. "I do not want notes, or criticisms or explanations about authorship or origin, or even cross-references. I do not need or understand them, and they confuse me."[9] However, he believed the nation was founded on Christian principles, and he maintained an abiding faith in God. The fact that he still had four young children, including a six-month-old infant, to care for also helped sustain the former president through the crisis of Ruth's death.

Within a matter of weeks, a sense of normality began to return to the Cleveland household. Perhaps as a way of deflecting his mind from his daughter's death, his friends suggested once more that he seek a third term as president. Again Cleveland rejected the idea. His age and health were now working against a third term. He had grown perceptibly older. During his second administration, he had lost sixty pounds, which made him look drawn. He also suffered from gout, forcing him to remain in bed for weeks at a time. In addition, he had problems with indigestion and frequently used a stomach pump. Friends raised the possibility that Bryan, having lost a second time in 1900 to McKinley, might seek the Democratic nomination a third time if Cleveland did not deny it to him. The former president remained adamant against running.[10]

Cleveland's friends raised the specter of Bryan in part because they knew just how much the former president continued to despise the Nebraskan and his wing of the party. More was involved than just the issue of free silver. In Cleveland's view, free silver was merely the tip of the iceberg of agrarian radicalism that would lead to class antagonism and unchecked popular passions. It would also be a step toward government control of the marketplace that would threaten the very foundations of the free enterprise system and of American liberties. In contrast to Hayes, there was no marked shift to the left during Cleveland's second retirement—quite the opposite. Like Hayes and many reformers of the late nineteenth century, he was aware of the new industrial order transforming the nation. He also had considerable sympathy for the plight of the working class, whom he always felt deserved a greater share of the nation's wealth. Great fortunes, he believed, should be a means to that end and not the end itself. After McKinley's first victory over Bryan in 1896, he warned business interests that although they could "rejoice on their escape from threatened peril," he hoped "that in this time of congratulation it will be remembered that absolute safety will only be secured when our financial system is protected by affirmative and thorough reform."[11]

In contrast to Hayes, however, Cleveland never questioned the free enterprise system or read about alternative economic systems. Despite his acceptance of changes in American society, his core values, including his belief in a strong executive branch of government, remained fundamentally Jacksonian. Bryan and his followers, in his view, represented a departure from those principles. "I am near the point of believing them to be conspirators and traitors," he even remarked shortly after he left office in 1897.[12]

On financial and monetary issues, the former president was actually closer to McKinley than he was to Bryan. Although Cleveland voted for Palmer in the 1896 elections, he was not unhappy that the Republican won the election. On inauguration eve, the two men had dinner together. As they were eating, McKinley asked the outgoing president if there were any courtesy he could extend to him. "No, Mr. President," Cleveland responded, "but I beg you remember that the time may come again when it will be necessary to have another union of the forces which supported honest money against this accursed heresy."[13]

Soon after McKinley took office, the cordiality that existed between the new and former presidents faded. On two issues especially, Cleveland disagreed with the administration. The first was over the tariff. On no other issue were Republicans and Democrats more divided. One of the reasons why the Republican Party became the majority party after 1896, controlling both the White House and Congress for most of the next thirty-six years, was that it won the argument over protectionism. Although McKinley lent his support to reciprocal trade agreements over purely protective tariffs, Cleveland never budged from his call for freer trade, packaged by the Democrats as "tariffs for revenue only." He was greatly disturbed, therefore, when the Republicans approved the Dingley tariff of 1897, the highest tariff up to that time but one which included the reciprocity principle already contained in the McKinley tariff.[14]

The other issue on which Cleveland disagreed strongly with McKinley had to do with the annexation of Hawaii, the insurrection in Cuba leading to the Spanish–American War, and the acquisition of the Philippine Islands. When he took office for his second term in 1893, he immediately withdrew from the Senate the treaty of annexation that had been worked out by his predecessor, Benjamin

Harrison. Shortly after McKinley took office, however, the new president negotiated a new treaty of annexation. Because of Senate opposition, it had to be approved by a joint resolution of Congress.

Almost as soon as he learned that a treaty had been concluded, Cleveland
voiced in private his opposition to the agreement. By 1898, he felt concerned
enough that he went public. In an interview with the Associated Press, he called
Hawaiian annexation "a perversion of our national mission [of] build[ing] up and
mak[ing] a greater country of what we have, instead of annexing islands." After
Hawaii was officially annexed in July, he continued to express his outrage, remarking to Olney that he was "ashamed of the whole affair."[15]

By this time, the United States had gone to war with Spain over Cuba. As
president, Cleveland had favored some form of local self-government for the island and had even made threatening gestures against Spain. He opposed McKinley's decision to go to war over Cuba. "It seems to me," he wrote to E. C. Benedict
on 14 April 1898, three days after McKinley's war message to Congress, "that we
have allowed ourselves to be crowded away from [a peaceful outcome to the Cuban imbroglio] and that we face today a sad, afflictive war, that our own people
will look upon as unprofitable and avoidable, and which, in the sight of contem-
poraneous judgment and history, may seem unjustifiable."[16] This is the position
he maintained throughout the short conflict that ended on 13 August with the
capture of Manila in the Spanish-owned Philippine Islands.

McKinley's subsequent acquisition from Spain of the Philippines (along
with the islands of Puerto Rico and Guam) in the Treaty of Paris of December
1898 was, in the former president's point of view, even worse than his decision
to go to war. At least the conflict resolved a long-festering problem ninety miles
off America's shore. The Cubans received the veneer of independence, and the
United States the authority under the 1901 Platt Amendment to intervene in order
to maintain Cuba's independence and stability. The acquisition of the Philippine
Islands was an entirely different matter. Not only did it deviate from the nation's
policy of restraint and limits in foreign policy, but it was also a classic instance of
imperialism. As such, it was contrary to the nation's most fundamental ideals of
freedom and liberty.[17]

Notwithstanding Cleveland's strong anti-imperialist views and the fact that
Bryan made anti-imperialism his major campaign issue in 1900, he was happy
that Bryan had been defeated. Before the election, he had calculated that the Nebraskan's second failed attempt at the presidency might mean the end of his control of the Democratic Party and the return of the party to what he considered
its traditional sound money and conservative values. Referring to "Republican
excesses" in acquiring an empire, he even raised the possibility that Republican
sound money men and anti-imperialists might unite under the banner of "*true*
Democracy . . . promising to the country the conservation and safety of domestic
principles." Blamed by many Democrats for Bryan's loss because of his refusal to

support the Nebraskan's candidacy, he brushed these complaints aside, pointing instead to the need now to cut Bryanism and Populism out of the party.[18]

Yet the former president was not as thick-skinned as he pretended. What he seems to have regretted the most was his apparent lack of influence within the Democratic Party and the national rejection of his policies and principles. He was still hated in the South and the West because of his opposition to free silver. McKinley's election, while welcomed in certain respects, also represented a defeat for anti-imperialism. Throughout his political career, Cleveland had often expressed his conviction that the American people would do the right thing at the right time. In 1896, he believed Democrats would repudiate Bryanism and free silver. They did not. In 1899 and then again in 1900, he hoped the American people would reject imperialism. They had not. "My pride and self-conceit have had a terrible defeat. I thought I understood the American people," he remarked in January 1899. Even as McKinley's victory raised flickering hopes in his mind that it might at least lead to the end of Bryanism and the emergence of a stronger Democratic Party—perhaps even a realignment of the party following traditional Democratic principles—he was by no means certain that would happen.[19]

The former president's instinct after 1900, therefore, was to enjoy his retirement in Princeton and Gray Gables, write occasional magazine pieces, not in order to become a public commentator but for the money, and otherwise to divorce himself from the public scene. He was never entirely successful. For one thing, Bryanism continued to gnaw at him. The cleansing of the Democratic Party he yearned for did not take place immediately. For another, McKinley was assassinated on 6 September 1901 while attending the Pan American Exposition in Cleveland's former home of Buffalo. McKinley's successor, Theodore Roosevelt, proved to be an even more worrisome problem for Cleveland than McKinley.

The former president was as angered and shocked as the rest of the nation by the second assassination of a president in scarcely thirty-five years. Unlike many Republicans, who had hoped that by making Roosevelt McKinley's vice president they would be relegating him to oblivion, Cleveland had held him in high esteem. Their relationship went back to the 1880s, when Cleveland was governor of New York and Roosevelt was an insurgent young assemblyman. Although Roosevelt was a Republican, he crossed partisan lines to support Cleveland on a number of crucial measures, including a civil service reform bill. For his part, the governor signed, over the objection of Democratic leaders, several pieces of legislation sponsored by Roosevelt for reforming government in the city and county of New York. Later, Roosevelt backed Cleveland during the Venezuela boundary dispute and, as vice president–elect, commended him for his position on the currency issue.

Relations between the former president and Roosevelt remained cordial through the first years of the Roosevelt administration. In 1902, Cleveland praised the president for his handling of a national coal strike. According to George F.

Parker, who knew Cleveland well and wrote the first biography of the former president after his death, Cleveland thought Roosevelt was "the most perfectly equipped and the most effective politician thus far seen in the Presidency."[20]

While Cleveland may have admired Roosevelt's effectiveness as a politician, he grew to dislike his showmanship and had major objections to his intervention in Panama in 1902 leading to the acquisition of the Panama Canal Zone and the right to build a canal across Panama. "The American people do not undervalue the object gained," he remarked, "but they keenly appreciate the importance and value of our national honor, our national good name and, above all our national morality."[21]

Cleveland also had growing doubts about Roosevelt's ethics. He was especially angry that the president published the letter he had sent him in 1902 congratulating the Republican on his handling of the coal strike. In making the letter public, Roosevelt also claimed that the ex-president had agreed to accept an offer he had made to serve on the arbitration committee to settle the coal strike but that he was forced to rescind the offer because of the objection of the mine owners, who thought the former president was too radical. On the contrary, Cleveland claimed—he had agreed only to serve on a commission to recommend various arbitration alternatives, not to be a part of an arbitration commission. "I am amazed at Roosevelt," Cleveland wrote his friend, Richard Gilder, in March 1904. "There are some people in this country that need lessons in decency and good manners."[22]

For the former president, "decency and good manners" were not a trivial matter. They were what his character and career were all about. They were what he believed politics should be about. A strict code of personal and political ethics, respect for the Constitution and the three branches of government, honest and efficient administration of government, intolerance of unrequited wealth, impatience with radicalism or class warfare, respect for free enterprise and free markets, concern for the working class—all these were part of Cleveland's sense of what constituted decency and good manners in politics. They also dictated the extent and the limits of his concept of executive power. They were what made him an activist and reformist president: quick to veto legislation he considered improper or unconstitutional; willing to speak out against combinations of wealth and power; ready to defend the just cause of workers for higher wages but to suppress what he regarded as their illegal use of violence or their unconstitutional stoppage of interstate commerce; and prepared to defend the nation's interests and honor abroad while opposing what he considered imperialist ventures.

Here the nineteenth century met the twentieth century. Roosevelt's concept of the presidency as an agent of change will be discussed in the next section of this chapter. Suffice it to say here that what Cleveland regarded as the ends of government, Roosevelt considered as the means toward a larger purpose. Even Roosevelt's concept of efficiency was far different from that of his fellow New Yorker. As for decency and good manners, they had their place in Roosevelt's vocabulary, but they hardly defined his character and politics in the way they did for Cleveland. Roosevelt was far too complex a personality and his vision of the presidency far too creative to subordinate them to the former president's view of appropriate political behavior.

Because of their substantial differences over the role of government and the presidential office, Cleveland came to view Roosevelt's presidency as more menacing than McKinley's. Worse, his very different personality from Roosevelt's amounted to two flints being rubbed together. With Bryan on the political ropes, the ex-president also hoped that the Democratic Party might return to its traditional values and then defeat Roosevelt in 1904.[23]

A number of conservative businessmen pressed Cleveland to seek the Democratic nomination. The wealthy financier, James Stillman, told a friend that if the former president were renominated, he would guarantee a larger campaign fund for him than the $3.5 million the Ohio industrialist, Mark Hanna, had raised for McKinley in 1896. Nearing seventy and in declining health, Cleveland knew it was absurd even to consider the nomination. He allowed his name to be circulated, however, so that two other prominently mentioned candidates, Bryan and the renegade publisher William Hearst, might target him instead of other candidates more acceptable to the former president. When Alton B. Parker, the chief justice of New York's court of appeals, emerged as the leading candidate among conservatives, Cleveland threw his support behind him. Parker received the nomination on the first ballot.

Cleveland was delighted by the convention's outcome. As memories of the panic and depression of the 1890s began to fade and as Cleveland lived out his retirement mostly out of the public eye in Princeton, his popularity also began to soar. The sudden death in January of Baby Ruth generated sympathy and new respect for the aging former president, whose steadfast commitment to principle, even under trying circumstances, was increasingly viewed as a matter of courage rather than as one of indifference to the nation's beleaguered classes. Gold replaced silver as the party's banner after Parker sent a telegram to the convention insisting on the irrevocability of the gold standard. No person was more closely identified with gold than Cleveland. Repeatedly the delegates cheered his name whenever it was mentioned. Never entirely in the shadow of politics, he identified the future of the Democratic Party with Roosevelt's defeat. Although he made only two public speeches, he wrote numerous letters and opinion pieces in support of Parker. He also urged the Democratic candidate to be more aggressive in his campaign. "When I consider the alternative presented to our people in the pending campaign and realize the consequences involved in their voting power, I am almost frightened. I am so anxious to have them well informed that they may see where their safety lies."[24]

Roosevelt's overwhelming victory over the listless Democratic candidate, who lost every state outside the South, staggered Cleveland. Let down once more by the American people, he wondered whether their character had changed. What Cleveland missed, of course, was that the fundamental changes in American society over the last thirty years had led to a redefinition of reform, including greater demands on government, a reformulation of the presidency, and a presidential candidate unlike any other in Cleveland's life. Henceforth, the issues facing the American people would not be change versus the status quo, but rather the nature and pace of change. The 1904 election represented, in a real sense, the end of the status quo and the type of politics Cleveland represented. Yet for the former president, the most pressing question remained how the rehabilitation of the Democratic Party was to be accomplished. The only positive outcome of the 1904 campaign, in his view, was that the issue of free silver had been cleansed from the Democratic Party forever.[25]

Actually, an increase in the gold supply made the monetary issue moot, and while the issue of free silver may have been purged from the Democratic Party, Bryan and his followers were not. After Parker's crushing defeat in 1904, Bryan was even able to regain control of the party, then, in July 1908, to be overwhelmingly nominated on the first ballot at the Democratic convention in Denver.

Cleveland did not live to see this happen. He had died two weeks earlier. Although he understood the likelihood of Bryan's nomination, he still hoped the Democratic Party was "not doomed . . . to sink to a condition of useless and lasting decadence." He remained firm that in order for this to happen, it needed to return to its traditional values. Just a few months before he died, the New York *World* asked him for his views on the best principles and policy for the Democratic Party to follow in order to give it new life. The "party should display honest and sincere conservatism," he responded, "a regard for constitutional limitations, and a determination not to be swept from our moorings by temporary clamor or spectacular exploitation."[26]

By the time Cleveland died, however, he had slipped from his own moorings—perhaps more than he realized. In fact, he spent the last years of his life becoming a very wealthy businessman through his investments in the stock market and as a spokesman of the life insurance industry. In the process, he significantly altered his views of what he had hitherto referred to as corporate greed and the inequality between the moneyed and working classes.

Although Cleveland had been extremely comfortable financially when he left the White House, he remained worried about making more money in order to provide for his family. Undoubtedly influenced by his wealthy friends, he became obsessed with investing in the stock market. He even considered what are today the illegal practices of insider trading and fixing the market. "If you and I were speculators instead of steady-going investors," he wrote in February 1901 to his friend and financial adviser, E. C. Benedict, "I think I would suggest that one of us buy a moderate amount of something, and having thus prepared the way for a decline, that the other sell a large quantity of the same thing short, and divide the profits. It must be that such a scheme would work."[27]

By 1905, Cleveland described himself as having "grown very, very rich—beyond the dreams of avarice." Unlike his Gilded Age predecessors, however, the former president never displayed much interest in donating to charitable or other worthy causes. "I mean to hold on to my suddenly acquired wealth as tightly and as long as I can," he told Benedict. He also appears to have changed his attitude toward the working class. Although he continued to attack the inequalities of wealth and the "tremendous growth of trusts," he acknowledged after the national coal strike of 1902 his growing doubts about the working class, which he held as much responsible for the strike as the mine owners.[28]

In 1905, Cleveland accepted an offer by the financier Thomas Fortune Ryan to act as one of a board of three trustees to hold the stock of the Equitable Life Assurance Society and to select a new board of directors for the company. Like several other major insurance companies, it had been the victim of fraudulent business practices by a group of insiders. Ryan had purchased control of the company when it was on the verge of failure. The near collapse of Equitable and the other insurance companies led to a headline-making investigation of the industry. The former president took the position as a trustee of Equitable on the express condition that he and the other two trustees were "to be absolutely free and undisturbed in the exercise of their judgment." He was paid $12,000, the only trustee to accept a salary. He also served as an arbitrator in disputes between insurance companies, for which he earned an additional $12,000. Even more noteworthy, Cleveland agreed in 1907 to head the Association of Presidents of Life Insurance Companies, essentially an industry lobbying association, at a salary of $25,000. Even the former president thought his remuneration (the equivalent of about $568,000 in 2009) was out of line with his limited responsibilities.[29]

By the time the former president agreed to head the life insurance association, his health had grown steadily worse, and he was spending much of his time in bed. In addition to his gout and gastric conditions, both of which had become more serious, he was suffering from heart and kidney failure. Early in the spring, he suffered a series of gastrointestinal attacks. Most likely he suffered from a duodenal ulcer. On 24 June, he lapsed into a coma and died the same day at the age of seventy-one. The probable cause of death was coronary occlusion. His last words were, "I have tried so hard to do right."[30]

Following Cleveland's request for a simple Presbyterian funeral and burial, services were held in his home. Fewer than 100 guests attended the service. The mourners included President Theodore Roosevelt and his wife, Chief Justice Melville W. Fuller, and a number of Cleveland's cabinet members and closest friends. The entire service lasted only thirty minutes. There was no music or eulogy. Afterward, he was buried at the Princeton cemetery alongside his daughter, Ruth. Only about 5,000 spectators observed the procession.

Throughout his life, Cleveland had remained a man of character, conviction, and courage. He also understood the outlines of change taking place in the United States. As president, he continued to increase the powers of the chief executive, albeit largely in a negative way. Like most reformers, whether liberal Republicans or Democrats, he also attacked trusts and corporate power. He welcomed the

Sherman Antitrust law, and he called for a more equitable distribution of the fruits of labor.

While he understood change, Cleveland never understood complexity. He failed to comprehend the intricate and multifaceted predicates of the agrarian movements and labor strife of the last third of the nineteenth century and the financial panic and depression of the 1890s. He lacked the vision, imagination, and flexibility ever to consider deviating from his philosophy of government. He viewed the presidency as a coordinate branch of government with Congress and the judiciary. As president, he sought to protect and defend his office's prerogatives. He was also prepared to recommend to Congress needed redemptive legislation, such as repeal of the Sherman Silver Purchase Act and tariff reform. Regarding his role as president as essentially administrative, however, he did not believe he had the responsibility to lead Congress in new directions. Unresponsive to changes in the nation's sociology as it went through a period of wrenching transformation, he also had little interest in any extension of governmental administrative regulation.

Throughout the eight years after he left office, Cleveland never wavered from his core beliefs. If anything, he became more conservative and more a creature of the corporate world. The fact, however, that as a former president, Cleveland ran for and was reelected as president during his first retirement and then was the first former president to receive a large salary as a public figurehead of a major industry during his second retirement illustrates the increased public presence and prominence of former presidents in much the same way as the many philanthropic and humanitarian activities of ex-president Hayes and the legal practice and writings of ex-president Harrison.

Yet Hayes, Harrison, and Cleveland had strikingly different personalities and minds. Hayes and Harrison were intellectuals. Cleveland was not. Hayes had a measure of self-doubt, curiosity, sensibility, and vision that Cleveland and even Harrison lacked. Regardless, the tensions caused by paradigmatic change were the common denominator of the period not only in terms of events, but also of ideas and values. It is what makes generalizations about the late nineteenth and early twentieth centuries so difficult.

II

In many respects, the values that shaped the career of Theodore Roosevelt were as old-school as those of the Gilded Age reformers who preceded him. Writers have used various adjectives to describe the fundamentals of his character, ranging from egocentric, hyperactive, and impetuous to romantic, idealistic, and passionate. His huge personality included these characteristics and more. As his biographer and critic, Henry Pringle, wrote almost eighty years ago, "Theodore Roosevelt was polygonal." Essential to his character were such nineteenth-century reform ideals as a robust sense of morality, honor, and civic duty. Contrariwise, he feared anarchy, was wary of the radical left, believed in property rights, and was not averse to big business or inherited wealth. Indeed, he was class-conscious and was guided throughout his career by a strong feeling of noblesse oblige.[31]

That said, Roosevelt was the quintessential transformative figure of his time, representing a new generation of Americans born during or shortly after the Civil War whose lives were shaped by the transition taking place in the United States as it moved into the twentieth century. Like other reformers of his generation, his focus was on readjusting inherited values to changing times. While he believed in laissez-fairism and had no quarrel with big business per se, he condemned what he regarded as unfair business practices and corporate exploitation of the public. As a consequence, he endorsed a stronger regulatory role for government and enhanced presidential powers. As president, he considered his role to be the positive one of marshaling and directing the country's public and private resources in order to spread opportunity and avoid social upheaval. He was eminently successful in carrying out this mission. By force of his intellect and personality, he turned his office into a dynamic vehicle of change.

Roosevelt's post-presidency was equally illustrious. The nation's youngest ex-president when he left office in 1909 at age fifty, he became one of the two or three most active and politically influential ex-presidents in the nation's history. He helped shape the course of American politics for generations to come. In 1912, he ran for president on the Progressive, or Bull Moose, Party ticket, winning the largest vote ever given to a third-party candidate. Even after he lost the election, he remained a formative political figure, pushing for the United States' early entry into World War I after Germany invaded Belgium in 1914 and becoming President Wilson's most vocal and harshest critic before the United States entered the war in 1917. Had he not died at the age of sixty in 1919, he probably would have received the Republican nomination the next year and gone on to serve another term as president.[32]

As an ex-president, Roosevelt was also a world traveler, hunter, naturalist, and explorer whose safari to Africa was followed by a grand tour of Europe and a later trip down a tributary of the Amazon River into some of the remotest regions of Brazil. In addition, he remained a prolific writer, becoming a best-selling author, serving as an editor and commentator for several magazines and the Kansas City *Star,* and maintaining a private correspondence with the leading political and intellectual figures of his time that numbered in the thousands of pages. One of the most cerebral of the nation's modern presidents and a throwback to such intellectual giants of the early Republic as John Adams, Thomas Jefferson, James Madison, and John Quincy Adams, he commented on topics ranging from arms limitation to a critique of social Darwinism.[33]

Roosevelt was born on 27 October 1858 to a socially prominent New York family. The second of four children, he was a sickly, nearsighted, and asthmatic child who had to be homeschooled because of his ailments. Highly precocious and intellectually curious, he became an avid reader and an amateur naturalist; he collected specimens of birds and animals, which he displayed throughout his family's six-story town house in an exclusive New York neighborhood. When he was a teenager, his father decided that he needed to strengthen his body. Through bodybuilding that included weight lifting, calisthenics, and boxing, he overcame his physical problems and developed a lifelong commitment to the value of vigorous physical exercise and strenuous outdoor activities like hiking and mountain climbing.

As the child of a wealthy family, Roosevelt led a pampered youth. In 1876, he entered Harvard College. At the time, he anticipated concentrating in the sciences. However, disliking the routine of the laboratory, he turned to his other passions, literature and history. Elected a member of Phi Beta Kappa, he graduated in 1880 magna cum laude. That same year, he married Alice Hathaway Lee, a member of a prominent Boston family.

From his parents, Roosevelt developed a deep sense of duty and social responsibility, which turned his interest to politics. In 1881, just two years out of Harvard, he was elected to the New York state legislature. He quickly developed a reputation as an outspoken proponent of governmental reform. His view of reform, however, was very much within the liberal Republican tradition and had mostly to do with exposing corruption and civil service reform.

Except for the death in 1878 of his father, whom he had adored, Roosevelt had led a mostly idyllic life and seemed destined for an uninterrupted career in politics. Although he alienated a number of fellow Republicans in Albany because he was outspoken and brash, he established a reputation as a reform leader who was capable of crossing party lines to work with Democratic governor Grover Cleveland. He also published his first book, a thoroughly researched *Naval History of the War of 1812,* and invested in ranch land in the Badlands of the Dakota Territory. Suddenly, however, his world came crashing down around him. On 4 February 1884, Alice died after giving birth to a daughter, whom he named after her. On the same day and in the same house, his mother also died of typhoid fever. For Roosevelt—who loved Alice, believed a major purpose of marriage was to have many children, and looked forward to raising a large family—Alice's death was an especially crushing blow.[34]

His world turned topsy-turvy, Roosevelt gave over the raising of Alice to his sister Bamie, and escaped to the Dakota Territory. For the next two years, he divided his time between the Dakota Badlands and extended visits to the East. While in the West, he coupled a career as a cattle rancher with hunting and exploration. He lived the life of a cowboy and even served as a frontier sheriff. He also built a massive physique, read voraciously, and wrote magazine articles about his ventures. Beginning in 1885, he courted Edith Carow, a spinster and childhood sweetheart. Despite reservations about betraying Alice's memory, he became secretly engaged to Edith. Then came the famous blizzards of 1886–1887, which killed most of his cattle. His hopes of making his fortune as a rancher dashed, he returned permanently to New York. After running unsuccessfully for mayor in this Democratic bastion, he married Edith in a ceremony in London.

The newly married couple soon took up residence at Sagamore Hill, a twenty-three-room Queen Anne–style structure located at Oyster Bay on Long Island, about twenty-five miles from New York City. When he was a child, Roosevelt had spent summers at Oyster Bay and had fallen in love with the area, passing his time hiking, swimming, riding, and rowing. When he was twenty-two, he purchased 155 acres of farmland just northeast of the village of Oyster Bay. After marrying Edith, he completed construction of Sagamore Hill, which he had started before his first wife's death. He would spend the rest of his life at Sagamore Hill, making it the summer White House during his presidency.

Having already gained national notice as the sacrificial cowboy candidate for mayor of New York, Roosevelt was appointed to the United States Civil Service Commission and then in 1894 to the New York City board of police commissioners. He quickly took charge of the board. He gained notoriety because of his sleuthlike activities, including walking the streets at night to catch policemen napping while on duty or drinking at a local bar. He also became an embarrassment both to the Tammany Hall machine that dominated the city and to Republican leaders when he tried to enforce the Sunday blue laws, which were commonly ignored because Sunday was the one day the working class had off to go to bars and socialize. Fortunately for Republicans, who were anxious to rid themselves of this maverick, in 1896 William McKinley was elected president.

With the help of Congressman Henry Cabot Lodge of Rhode Island, who had become his closest friend, Roosevelt won an appointment from McKinley as assistant secretary of the navy. Soon he was running the department. A student of the navy since his own book on the War of 1812 and heavily influenced by Admiral Alfred T. Mahan's classic work, *The Influence of Sea Power in History,* he laid plans to build up the fleet and became a leading proponent of war with Spain over Cuba.

After President McKinley declared war against Spain in April 1898, Roosevelt resigned his position to join the military, As friends and family tried to tell him, there were many good reasons why he should not join the fighting forces, including the fact that he was needed in the navy department and had become the father of five children, four boys and a girl. Edith had also taken charge of Alice, the child of her husband's first marriage. How, his family and friends wondered, could he put at risk everything he held so dear by going off to fight, especially when he could serve his nation more usefully at home?

The explanation is complex and reveals the many-faceted sides of Roosevelt's personality. In simplest terms, he believed issues of duty and honor were involved in going off to battle. To remain at home, even when he could justify the decision in the name of performing a higher service to his country and out of concern for his family, would be cowardly. Besides, one could not pay higher service to country than to defend its flag in wartime. Not to fight would also be to besmirch the family's name and to set a bad example for his four boys, whom he would later send off to battle during World War I. He owed it both to his nation and to his family, therefore, to join the fight against Spain.

However, he also owed it to himself. In Roosevelt's mind, the meek might inherit the earth, but the world belonged to the mighty and the heroic. In his distinctly romantic concept of being, risking one's life for a noble cause was the highest form of physical valor and heroism. Although Roosevelt's predisposition for war has often been exaggerated, he regarded a righteous war as a cause worth fighting and dying for. From all this, it followed that he owed it as much to himself as to his country and to his family to engage in the Spanish–American War.

Leading the famous charge up San Juan Hill of the legendary Rough Riders, a unit he had formed and trained, Roosevelt took advantage of the wartime fame he gained to run successfully for governor of New York.[35] He then angered Republican leaders by his nonpartisanship and efforts at governmental reform, including increasing the regulatory power of the state over factories and sweatshops. Mostly as a way of removing him from the governorship, they helped put him on the 1900 presidential ticket as McKinley's running mate. When McKinley was killed less than a year later, Roosevelt suddenly found himself elevated to the White House.

In contrast to a common image of Roosevelt as a swashbuckling reformer, he proved to be a cautious and moderate chief executive. Concerned, however, about growing corporate power, he attacked those corporations that engaged in questionable business practices. He brought a successful antitrust suit against the Northern Securities Company, which was formed from the $400 million merger of the railroad interests of three of the richest men in the United States, E. H. Harriman, James J. Hill, and J. P. Morgan. In the bitter anthracite coal strike, he took the side of the United Mine Workers in demanding an eight-hour day and higher wages. He also established a bureau of corporations to examine business practices and supported the Elkins Act prohibiting railroad rebates.

Running for a full term in 1904 on a platform that promised all Americans a "square deal," Roosevelt easily defeated his Democratic opponent, Alton B. Parker. He used his political mandate to gain approval of some of the most far-reaching legislation in the nation's history, including the Hepburn Act, which gave the Interstate Commerce Commission (ICC) authority to set shipping rates and monitor corporate records, and the Pure Food and Drug Act and Meat Inspection Act to regulate purveyors of food and drugs. The first American president to take an active interest in conservation, he also supported the Newlands Reclamation Act, providing federal funds to build dams, reservoirs, and canals in the West, and he named the conservationist Gifford Pinchot to head the newly established Forest Service.[36]

In foreign policy, Roosevelt struck out in new directions. At the Portsmouth Conference of 1905, he negotiated an end to the Russo-Japanese War. The next year, he played a similar role in reconciling differences between France and

Known for creation of the National Park system and protection of the national wilderness, President Roosevelt is shown in this 1906 photo with the great conservationist, John Muir, on Glacier Point, Yosemite Valley, California. (Courtesy of Library of Congress, Prints and Photographs Division.)

Germany over Morocco at the Algeciras Conference of 1906. Determined to build an international waterway connecting the Atlantic and Pacific oceans through the narrow isthmus of Panama, he intrigued with Panamanians in their successful revolt in 1903 against Colombia after that country rejected a treaty giving the United States the right to build a canal through its province of Panama. To protect access to the canal, he issued the Roosevelt Corollary of 1904, giving the United States the right to intervene in Latin America to prevent intervention by foreign powers.

The key to understanding Roosevelt's presidency was his strong sense of responsibility. He considered power and responsibility to be inseparable. However, he was also a progressive who believed that government, guided by the president, had to play an expanded role in responding to the new problems of a complex corporate society. He did not reject the changes taking place in the United States. On the contrary, he accepted the existence of corporate power and distinguished between good and bad corporations on the basis of whether or not they served the national interest. Although he gained fame as a trust buster, he initiated fewer antitrust actions against American industry than his successor, William Howard Taft, and he accepted the notion of natural monopolies in such industries as utilities, which he believed should be regulated, not broken up. A captivating, magnetic, and hyperactive figure, he greatly expanded the powers of the presidency and underscored the potential of the executive branch to reform the role and purposes of government.

Roosevelt loved being president and would have preferred to remain for another term. He did not run in 1908 only to honor a pledge he had made just after being returned to the presidency in 1904 that he would not seek what he considered a third term as president (since he had served all but six months of McKinley's second term after McKinley's assassination in 1901). In this way, he would be honoring the tradition established by George Washington of presidents serving no more than two consecutive terms. Instead, he designated his secretary of war, Taft, to be his successor.[37]

Roosevelt's ten years as former president were as significant as those of his presidency. Certainly no ex-president before him, including even John Quincy Adams, was as much of a public and political figure as Roosevelt. No longer was it even common for a former president to withdraw gracefully into a quiet retirement or leave public life entirely. For a phenomenon like Roosevelt, who demanded public attention and relished power, who romanticized physical challenges and idealized the heroic, and who more often than not blurred the distinction between what best served him and best served the public, a secluded retirement at Sagamore Hill was not an option. Notwithstanding his love of reading and his bent for writing, he was a man of action in need of a grand stage and an adoring public. When asked what he thought the role of an ex-president should be, he remarked that the responsibilities of a former president were the same as those of any good citizen, namely "to do his share of the work in the common good, in whatever position he may find himself." He added, "I shall certainly fight for what I deem to be right."[38]

The former president also had practical matters to consider. Because Taft had been his handpicked successor, he felt an obligation to the new president not to appear to be dictating policy to him. Like most of the presidents before him, he also needed to earn a living. His wealth had been old and inherited, and he had lost a good part of it in his cattle venture in the 1880s. Like many of those who inherited old wealth, he spent freely without worrying very much about money matters. Before entering the White House, he had authored two biographies for a series on American historical figures and a major four-volume work, *The Winning of the West (1889–1896),* which predated the famous frontier thesis of Roosevelt's friend, Frederick Jackson Turner. Although he received considerable royalties from these books and from other writings, the money was spent almost as fast as it came in.[39]

In contrast to her husband, Edith Roosevelt worried a great deal about providing for her family. She had not been happy when her husband became vice president, which meant returning to Washington to what she considered an unimportant position, maintaining a second residence again, and living on a salary of $10,000, about half of what Roosevelt had earned as governor of New York. As president, however, Roosevelt received $50,000 a year, a salary unchanged since it was doubled from $25,000 to $50,000 in 1873 but still substantial (the equivalent of about $1.18 million in 2009). His sudden quintupling of salary relieved Edith of her marriage-long worries about money.[40]

These returned with a vengeance after Roosevelt left the White House. Even Roosevelt believed he had to earn a living. "Until you boys all get to earning your own livelihood I am exceedingly anxious to save something each year," he wrote his namesake after Taft's election. He had numerous employment offers and suggestions for employment, including one to star in a Wild West extravaganza in which he would receive $300,000 to appear mounted on a spirited mustang and then reenact the Battle of San Juan Hill.[41]

As it turned out, Roosevelt had his own idea for an extravaganza. He planned to go hunting in Africa for large game, specimens of which he would donate to the Smithsonian Museum. Roosevelt had begun to plan for an African safari in 1908 after talking with a respected naturalist and taxidermist, Carl Akeley. At first he thought of a modest venture, but it soon morphed into one of the largest safaris ever undertaken, involving trained naturalists, guides, taxidermists, and more than 250 natives to carry tons of equipment. After intense negotiations, the Smithsonian agreed to contribute $30,000 for the expedition, in return for which it would receive the specimens that Roosevelt would send back to the United States. The former president also agreed to spend $25,000 of his own money, or about half of what he was to receive from writing a series of articles for *Scribner's* and a book, *African Game Trails,* compiled from the articles. In addition, he accepted an annual salary of $12,000 to write for *Outlook,* a magazine whose progressive views, he felt, closely matched his own, and one that would give him a pulpit from which to express his political philosophy.[42]

At first, Roosevelt's African safari seemed an early version of an upscale adventure operated by a travel company for wealthy clients seeking the thrills of the wild without giving up accustomed comforts. The expedition included cooks who prepared curries and knew the art of roasting; gun bearers to spot game, reload rifles, and, when necessary, fling themselves in front of a charging lion; and thirty or forty porters for each hunter, including three porters just to carry Roosevelt's tent, which included a porch roof, canvas carpet, and a small compartment in the back of the tent outfitted as a bathroom. The personal list of foods the former president ordered for the expedition included lamb's tongue, pâté, eighteen pounds of chocolate, fifty-six pounds of dried fruit, ninety-two pounds of jam, and three dozen puddings. "My tent is so comfortable (a warm bath and a cup of tea always ready for me when I come in after the day's hunt) and the food so good that I feel rather as if I was having more luxury than was good for me," he wrote his sister Bamie. The early shooting was done in the relative comfort of massive spreads of land owned by British friends who had settled in East Africa. Except for the hunting and collection of specimens of birds and small mammals, travel was by train on the Uganda railway.[43]

As the safari moved west into the bush, with the sun so hot that that expedition had to march at night and sleep by day, the challenges and risks became greater and conditions more Spartan. Both Roosevelt and his son, Kermit, who had accompanied him to Africa, faced real danger. Roosevelt killed a charging lion. He and Kermit also looked into the open mouth of a charging hippo before the former president was able to kill it.[44]

As a naturalist who was also a hunter, Roosevelt justified hunting as a way of avoiding overpopulation of wild animals and as a means of sustenance. He also regarded his safari as a major scientific contribution to the Smithsonian. There seems little doubt, however, that he enjoyed the chase and challenge involved in hunting large and dangerous beasts and that he killed far in excess of what was needed by the Smithsonian. By the time the safari ended, nearly a year after it began, Roosevelt had alone killed nine lions, eight elephants, thirteen rhinos, seven hippos, twenty zebras, seven giraffes, six buffalo, and scores of other mammals and birds.[45]

When he was not hunting, Roosevelt passed much of the time in the bush either reading or writing his articles for *Scribner's,* which he always forwarded by courier.[46] He also found time to maintain a sizable correspondence. Although one reason he had gone on his safari was to distance himself from Washington politics, he found that impossible. Cracks in his relationship with President Taft had begun to surface even before he left the United States. They became worse after he arrived in Africa. Taft replaced a number of officials, including Gifford Pinchot, whom, according to the former president, he had promised to retain. When he learned that Pinchot had been fired, he was furious. "I cannot believe it," he wrote to Pinchot. "I do not know of any man in public life who has rendered quite the service you have rendered."[47] The former president received other news that disquieted him, such as the president's mismanagement of legislation meant to lower tariffs that resulted instead in the Payne–Aldrich tariff of 1909, a jumbled measure that reduced duties on some imports but raised them on others.[48]

Despite his growing displeasure with Taft, Roosevelt denied he had any future political plans, but he did not eliminate the possibility entirely. "The chances are infinitesimal that I shall ever go back into public life," he told Henry Cabot Lodge, "but it would be the height of folly even to talk of the subject in any way."[49]

The African safari concluded in February 1910, when Edith and his daughter Ethel met Roosevelt and Kermit at Khartoum in the Sudan. Roosevelt's journey had taken him from Mombasa on the Indian Ocean north and northwestward to Nairobi, across Lake Victoria to Entebbe, into the Congo, northward to the Nile River, and then down the Nile to Khartoum. Although he was anxious to return home, plans had already been made for a grand tour of Europe.[50]

Roosevelt's reception in Europe was tumultuous. In every city he visited, huge throngs greeted him. According to Roosevelt, he and Edith had already been treated "as if they were royalties" as they made their way down the Nile from Khartoum to Cairo. He received the same treatment throughout his European tour. Roosevelt impressed the Europeans as much as they impressed him. He was still remembered as the hero of San Juan Hill. Yet he had won the Nobel Peace Prize four years earlier for his efforts as president in ending the Russo-Japanese War. He had gained respect in academic and literary circles for his contributions to history and science. He was skilled in the romantic languages. Even to Europeans, therefore, he was more than a dynamic ex-president of one of the world's most dynamic powers; he was also a world citizen extraordinaire. Accordingly, he was invited to receive honorary degrees and deliver talks at the University of Berlin, the Sorbonne, and Cambridge and Oxford universities. He also accepted in person the Nobel Prize in Christiana and, at President Taft's request, represented the United States at the funeral of King Edward VII of Britain.

The impact on Roosevelt of his ten-month sojourn through Africa and Europe was considerable. It reinforced his curious views on racism. That the former president had strong racial views is indisputable. What seems to have determined his views on race, however, was not so much matters of skin color or racial origins as of accomplishments defined in Western progressive terms. Accordingly, the Anglo-Saxon race was, in his view, the world's superior race. Although both the Japanese and Chinese were of Oriental origins, the former were a superior race when compared to the more backward Chinese. As for Latin Americans, they were a backward and distinctly inferior race. Similarly, he described native blacks in Africa during his safari as backward, primitive, ignorant, and half-naked savages "by no means as advanced as the early paleological men of Europe." This made him appreciate the "racial advancement" of black Americans under the influence of American civilization.[51]

Along similar lines, Roosevelt became increasingly persuaded that the more advanced civilizations, in particular the British, had an obligation to govern backward civilizations incapable of governing themselves. Much to the anger of Sudanese and Egyptian nationalists, whom he dismissed as "bigoted Moslems," he admonished the British publicly for not sufficiently supporting their outposts in Egypt and the Sudan. He even suggested that he could do a better job than the British as a colonial administrator. "There are plenty of jobs for which I am not competent," he wrote to the U.S. ambassador to England, Whitelaw Reid, at the end of March 1910, "but I must say, I should greatly like to handle Egypt and India for a few months. At the end of that time I doubtless would be impeached by the House of Commons but I should have things moving in fine order first."[52]

Finally, Europe's experiments with social welfare, including maximum working hours, minimum wage laws, and even national health insurance, reinforced Roosevelt's own ideas about the need for greater social justice at home. While speaking at the Sorbonne, for example, he berated the French for their low birthrates while simultaneously lauding them for their efforts on behalf of social justice. He also reached out to French republicans with whom, he commented, he "could on the whole, and in spite of certain points on which we radically differed, feel a sympathy somewhat akin to what I felt in talking with English liberals."[53]

Roosevelt's safari and tour of Europe left him at the same time exhausted but exhilarated, confident yet conflicted. "I want to go home!" he wrote Carnegie. "I am homesick for my own land and my own people! . . . I want to see my own house, my own books and trees, the sunset over the sounds from the window in the north room, the people with whom I have worked, who think my thoughts and speak my speech." He knew he would be greeted in New York by a massive crowd. However, to those planning his return, he made clear he wanted the festivities limited. He had had enough of receptions and officialdom. He was tired.[54]

Yet the former president was also exhilarated. Several of Roosevelt's close acquaintances claim that when they saw the ex-president for the first time after he returned to a reception of more than 100,000 people, he seemed a changed person, more certain even than as president that government had to be more active in promoting social justice and more determined that he had a responsibility to be an agent of change. Even while still in Europe, the former president acknowledged that his own popularity could be used as a means to an end and that he was "eager to do [his] part . . . in helping solve problems which must be solved."[55]

At home, the former president was under intense pressure from his friend, Senator Lodge, to campaign actively on behalf of a Republican Congress in 1910, but he was reluctant to do so. How could he actively campaign for Republican candidates, he asked Lodge, when the Republican leadership in Congress did not stand for the principles of social justice that had been such an integral part of his administration? How could he campaign even for progressive Republicans (the insurgent wing of the party) who felt betrayed that he had promised them Taft would adhere to the programs and policies that had been the hallmark of his (Roosevelt's) administration? As important, he told Lodge that his campaigning would simply eliminate him as a possible factor of future usefulness.[56]

In his letters to Lodge and others, the former president emphasized that he had no interest in running again for president—that, in fact, he still hoped Taft would improve and be nominated again for a second term. There is no reason to believe that Roosevelt was being insincere. Certainly he was not prepared to break openly with the president. He was, however, conflicted. He was still a Republican concerned about the future of the party, the outlook for which he thought was bleak. His relationship with the president had also become so strained that he declined Taft's invitation to the White House after he returned from Europe. In June, Roosevelt did finally see the president at his summer home in Beverly, on Massachusetts's north shore. The reunion between the two men was polite but tense.

Over the next eighteen months, Roosevelt remained torn politically and personally about his future. His son, Ted Jr., had married, and he and his wife were expecting their first child. The former president was thrilled at the prospect of becoming a grandfather.[57] Roosevelt was never able, however, to enjoy the life of a private citizen. His greatest complaint, in fact, was that he was being harassed by invitations to speak and by the politicians who came to see him at Oyster Bay. He also drove daily into the offices of *Outlook* in Manhattan to work on his monthly articles for the magazine. Wherever he went in New York, he could not escape the crowds of people who sought to get a look at him. "They wanted to carry me on their shoulders," he told his sister Corrine.[58] *Outlook* was also housed in the United Charities Building, a mecca for social reform. There he discussed progressive causes with such reformers as Florence Kelley of the Consumers' League and Paul Kellogg of *Survey* magazine.[59]

Even had the ex-president wanted to remove himself entirely from the public and political arena, he was constitutionally incapable of doing so. Everything from his sense of civic duty, to his view of national politics, to his own sense that he would play a major role politically made that possible. Over the spring, he yielded to the pleas of Lodge and other Republicans to speak on behalf of Republican congressional candidates in the West, which was the hotbed of insurgent strength in the party. He urged his followers to unite behind the Republican Party and the president, notwithstanding his own doubts about Taft and the party's conservative wing. He also denied again any plans to challenge Taft in 1912.

What kept Roosevelt loyal to the administration was not only that he was a partisan Republican, but that he saw no better alternative to the incumbent. Moving over to the party of free trade and wild-eyed Bryanism was simply beyond the pale. He might have joined Republican insurgents in supporting a progressive candidate to challenge Taft for the party's nomination in 1912. The highly respected senator from Wisconsin, Robert La Follette, was already organizing insurgents within the Republican Party and progressives outside the party into the National Progressive Republican League. The insurgents wanted Roosevelt to join them.

The former president, however, had almost as many reservations about La Follette and the progressives as he did with Taft and the conservatives. Although

Roosevelt considered himself a progressive, he did so more in the spirit of that term rather than as part of an organized movement. There were, in fact, a number of proposals that La Follette and his supporters advocated about which he had reservations. He found the Wisconsin senator too radical and ambitious for his liking. He even described him as "an extremist" with "a touch of fanaticism." He also thought he and other progressive leaders were too focused on the means to bring about reform rather than on the ends of reform, which he described as "legislation necessary to meet changing social and industrial conditions," mainly by regulating industry in the public interest.[60]

Yet Roosevelt was clearly moving leftward politically. In August, he delivered the most famous address of his political career at Osawatomie, Kansas. Roosevelt had been invited by William Allen White to Osawatomie for a service honoring the abolitionist John Brown. Afterward, Roosevelt visited a mental asylum, where he got on a kitchen table and spoke for ninety minutes to a crowd estimated at 30,000. What was striking about the speech was not so much its now-familiar themes, but the way in which they were articulated. Calling for a "New Nationalism" in which the federal government would become the guardian of all the people and "the executive power the steward of the public welfare," he attacked those individuals who would place personal or sectional interests above the national interest. He also talked about labor being superior to capital and urged the judiciary to be interested primarily in human welfare rather than in property. After the speech, he even seemed to suggest that Taft should be put out of office. "No man is worth his salt in public life who makes on the stump a pledge and does not keep it after the election and if he makes such a pledge and does not keep it, hunt him out of public life."[61]

Roosevelt's Osawatomie address outraged conservatives. Most of their response had more to do with his attack on capital and property than with his seeming call for Taft's removal. The ideologically conservative New York *Sun* reported that "the third greatest crisis in the history of the nation has arrived." It also warned "every honest and patriotic citizen to prepare himself against this New Napoleon who deemed it his mission . . . to overthrow and destroy in the name of public opinion and . . . personal advancement." The New York *Tribune* called the address "frankly socialistic."[62]

Although Roosevelt understood well the growing division within the Republican Party, he was genuinely taken aback by the reception to his address. "It is rather a curious thing that what people think is most revolutionary in my speech should be nearly a quotation from Lincoln," he wrote to Lodge. ("Capital was the fruit of labor," Lincoln had said.) "All my other statements have already been made, or at least have in effect been made, in my messages to Congress." The ex-president seems not to have realized that at Osawatomie, he had effectively laid down the gauntlet to the president and his wing of the Republican Party. In his view, he was trying to save capitalism and the Republican Party, not destroy them. He still believed he could bring conservatives and insurgents together.[63]

All the more reason, therefore, that Roosevelt found himself throughout the remainder of 1910 and most of 1911 on the horns of a dilemma as to what course to pursue. In September, he agreed reluctantly to run for temporary chairman of the New York Republican state convention at Saratoga. His purpose was to prevent conservative Republicans from taking control of the convention and naming the Republican candidates for state office in the 1910 elections. "Twenty years ago I should not have minded the fight in the least," he told Lodge. "But it is not the kind of fight into which an ex-President should be required to go. I could not help myself; I could not desert the decent people."[64]

Roosevelt had enough support to gain the chairmanship and to win the gubernatorial nomination for his friend, Henry Stimson, a rising young star whom he had encouraged to pursue public service.[65] After the New York gathering, Roosevelt stumped throughout the state for Stimson. Despite his best efforts, his candidate lost to his Democratic opponent by about 67,000 votes. His defeat was part of a general thumping of Republicans statewide and nationwide. Roosevelt even claimed that had he not campaigned for Stimson, the Republican might have lost by an additional 200,000 or even 300,000 votes.[66]

The results of the 1910 election left the ex-president more despondent than at any time since he had left the White House and even more unsure about what political road to follow. He tried to console himself by noting that one benefit of the election was that insurgent Republicans would no longer pressure him to run against Taft in 1912. It is striking that he regarded the Republican candidate's defeat as his own and that he implied that had Stimson won, he (Roosevelt) would have been the logical candidate for the 1912 Republican presidential nomination. As early as the fall of 1910, the former president appears to have been seriously contemplating challenging Taft for the Republican nomination in 1912.[67]

Even the relief Roosevelt expressed at no longer being under pressure to run for president seems disingenuous. In the first place, he always left open the possibility that the public might yet demand that he seek the White House. Roosevelt also had a cause to defend and a party to save. He could not simply dodge his civic duty by being disengaged from politics.[68]

Another element that entered into Roosevelt's calculus about his future was his glorification of Abraham Lincoln, whom he regarded as the nation's greatest president and statesman. He even had boxwood cuttings from Lincoln's home planted at Sagamore Hill and carried a wisp of Lincoln's hair in a ring he wore. As Roosevelt's Osawatomie address suggested, he tried to fashion himself after Lincoln not only in terms of Lincoln as the heroic, egalitarian, and inspirational figure who freed the slaves, maintained the Union, and died a martyr's death, but as the resolute pragmatist who sought the wisest counsel and employed whatever means were necessary to defeat the Confederacy. Like Lincoln, Roosevelt saw himself as a consummate realist. "Lincoln was to the full as conscientious as the extremists who regarded him as an opportunist and a compromiser," he editorialized in *Outlook* at the beginning of 1911, "and he was far wiser and saner, and therefore infinitely better able to accomplish practical results on a national scale."[69]

The extremists that Roosevelt referred to were the members of the short-lived Free Soil Party of the late 1840s and 1850s, which nominated Martin Van Buren for president in 1848—good men, in his view, who were opposed to the expansion of slavery into the Western territories but whose uncompromising position was undercut by the Compromise of 1850, which led to the party's demise. Roosevelt saw a parallel between Lincoln and himself and between the Free Soil Party and a growing movement among insurgent Republicans for a new Progressive Party. "Abraham Lincoln showed as much wisdom in his contemptuous refusal to ally himself with the Free Soil Party as he did in immediately joining with the Republican Party," he wrote one insurgent Republican senator, Jonathan Bourne Jr., of Colorado, "for the one movement was in the hands of fantastic extremists, who, however good, can accomplish nothing practical and the other movement was guided by practical men who also possessed high ideals."[70]

The fundamental dilemma for the former president thus remained the same throughout 1911 as it had been for much of 1910: how to get good men to regain control of the Republican Party before a new party of extremists was organized that contained the seeds of its own destruction. Still committed to saving the Republican Party and still believing in the need to restructure the relationship between government and the private sector, he objected to what he referred to as ultradicals because they did not distinguish between honest and corrupt corporations, between justice for labor and injustice for employers, between securing genuine popular rule and proposals that had the veneer of popular rule but might be counterproductive. He regarded the views of such extremists "as foolish and wicked, as being the kind of attitude which produced the hideous excesses of the French revolution, and which thereby put back the cause of reform in England at least forty years."[71]

Throughout the first half of 1911, the former president continued to deny any interest in challenging Taft for the Republican nomination in 1912, much less in leading a third-party movement. Repeatedly he expressed contentment and even joy with his life at Sagamore Hill. At the same time, he grew increasingly restless at not being more of a factor on the political scene. He also became more and more disenchanted with Taft because of his aggressive foreign policy. He even chastised him for his decision to contest Japan's growing domination in Manchuria through a policy known as dollar diplomacy (challenging Japanese economic hegemony in the region with American investments). Unlike Taft, he believed that it served no purpose and that it was even dangerous to pursue such a strategy. "Our vital interest," he wrote the president, "is . . . to preserve the good will of Japan. The vital interest of the Japanese, on the other hand, is Manchuria and Korea. It is therefore peculiarly our interest not to take any steps as regards Manchuria which will give the Japanese cause to feel . . . that we are hostile to them."[72]

As the former president grew more restive, he dropped growing hints about running again if he determined that he had a mandate to seek another term. What he meant by a mandate was not overtures by insurgent Republicans to run again, but evidence that he could actually win the nomination.

Yet Roosevelt took growing umbrage at what he considered personal attacks against him by the conservative press and Republican Party bosses. Having traveled to the West in March, he returned home seemingly more confident about his political future. More than ever, he portrayed himself in the image of Lincoln trying to save the party of Lincoln. "I am endeavoring to work in the spirit in which Abraham Lincoln worked," he wrote to Charles Dwight Willard, a California progressive. "Lincoln was not half-hearted. His zeal was just as intense, his purpose was as inflexible, as the zeal and the purpose of the extremists who denounced him."[73]

While continuing to deny that he had any presidential ambitions, Roosevelt took a more aggressive stand toward both Taft and La Follette. One of Taft's high priorities in the summer of 1911 was winning Senate approval of arbitration treaties the United States had signed in August with Britain and France. In principle, Roosevelt supported arbitration of international disputes. During his administration, Secretary of State Elihu Root signed and won ratification of arbitration treaties with twenty-five countries. The rub was that Roosevelt was reluctant to submit to arbitration any matter that included essential national interests. The treaties thus excluded all disagreements that involved "the vital interests, the independence, or the honor of the two contracting states"—in other words, virtually anything of importance that Washington did not want to submit to arbitration.[74]

Because the treaties the United States signed with Britain and France might apply, in Roosevelt's view, even to the nation's vital interests, they were unacceptable to him, and he lashed out at Taft for agreeing to them. As Roosevelt continued to rage against the treaties, the president compared his attacks to the ravings of a madman. In the end, however, the former president had his way, forcing the president to withdraw the agreements after the Senate carved them up in a way that made them toothless.[75]

By this time, Roosevelt had all but decided to challenge Taft in 1912. Any slim chance of a rapprochement between the president and ex-president vanished in October when Taft brought an antitrust action against the U.S. Steel Company, which in 1907 had acquired a controlling interest in the Tennessee Coal and Iron Company after gaining the approval of Roosevelt, who thought the merger would be a way of stabilizing a panicking economy. Immediately Roosevelt struck back, charging Taft's antitrust policy as one more fitted for the business conditions of the eighteenth century. The trust problem, he said, could be resolved by an industrial commission. Price regulations could also protect the consumer.[76]

While Roosevelt was being pushed into running in 1912 by what he considered Taft's ineptitude, he was also being pulled into challenging Taft by La

Follette's own grassroots drive for the Republican nomination. Because of Roosevelt's repeated assertions that he was not interested in being a candidate, the Wisconsin senator's campaign gained traction even though most progressive leaders made it clear that they preferred Roosevelt over La Follette.

In October, Edith was thrown from her horse while riding with her husband and remained unconscious for twenty-four hours. Although she recovered, she remained weak for months afterward and suffered from excruciating headaches. In letters to his supporters, the former president offered Edith's health as another reason to remove himself from the presidential campaign. In the same correspondence, he then explained why La Follette was no more qualified than Taft to be president. The Wisconsin senator's "chief debit," he stated in a letter to William Allen White, is "that he has not been willing to denounce as fearlessly evil when it appears in the multitude as when it appears in the few." As for his own possible candidacy, he remarked, "If there were a necessity to sacrifice me for the greater good, I should not feel at liberty to protest."[77]

In February, he informally announced his candidacy before the Ohio constitutional convention. Referring to himself as a "Progressive," he endorsed all the major reforms that La Follette and other progressives had supported, including the direct election of senators, popular review of state judicial decisions, and preferential primaries for presidential nominations. Roosevelt's support for the direct election of senators was of long standing. The former president had also favored popular review of state court decisions and recall of judges when they protected property rights at the expense of popular reforms approved by state legislatures. Decisions by federal courts and removal of federal judges, however, should remain beyond popular reach. Even though he thought decisions in federal courts also menaced the national welfare, he commented that "an irremovable Supreme Court is a good deal better than an irremovable Senate would be."[78]

Not unexpectedly, Roosevelt's proposal for popular review of state court decisions received the most attention in the press. Regarding the courts as the last bastion of protection for property rights, conservatives choked on the possibility the judiciary might be subjected to the whim of the masses. More important for the ex-president's pending campaign, however, was his proposal for preferential primaries. Several states had already enacted presidential primaries. However, he knew that Taft controlled the party machinery. His only chance of beating the president was by making the primary system more widespread, winning enough primaries, and then gaining enough pledged delegates to go to the convention with a majority of the delegates.[79]

As Roosevelt moved closer to becoming a candidate, La Follette's support melted away. His behavior became increasingly erratic and his speeches more rambling. After he seemed especially unstable during a speech in February, newspapers reported that he had suffered a nervous breakdown. Although he refused to withdraw from the race, his candidacy collapsed as most of his supporters moved over to Roosevelt. Along with Republican insurgents, the ex-president also gained the support of George Perkins, a Morgan partner, and Frank A. Munsey, a publisher; the two men became his principal financial backers. As a result, Roosevelt was able to enter the campaign with a substantial war chest. He also enlisted thousands of volunteers who set up Roosevelt clubs throughout the country. At the end of February, Roosevelt made his candidacy official. As prearranged by Roosevelt and his advisers, seven governors wrote him asking him to enter the race. "My hat is in the ring and the fight is on," the former president responded. His purpose, he said, was to make and keep the Republican Party the party "that it was in the days of Lincoln."[80]

The campaign that followed was one of the most momentous in the nation's history. It also had all the elements of high drama: the fulsomeness of the leading characters, the intricacies of the plotting, the richness of the dialogue. The first part of the drama involved the struggle for the Republican nomination between Taft and Roosevelt. Discussion of Taft will be reserved for the next chapter. Suffice it to say here that he never wanted to be president. An honorable and decent person more fitted by temperament for the judiciary than the political world, he made a better chief justice after he left office than a president.

Roosevelt also became a tragic figure in the campaign. For all his caginess before his announcement that he would challenge Taft for the Republican nomination, Roosevelt was never entirely duplicitous. He enjoyed his retirement at Sagamore Hill. Although he was still only fifty-two years old in 1911, he felt and looked older. Still muscular and broad shouldered, he was less active physically than he had been even as president. Because he continued to have an enormous appetite, he gained considerable weight since returning from Africa, especially around the waist, which thickened considerably. He had a history of accidents and broken bones going back to his days in the North Dakota Badlands. The stresses and strains of a strenuous life caused recurring aches and pains. He also had been suffering from chronic rheumatoid arthritis for years, and, like thousands of other veterans of the Spanish–American War, he had recurring bouts of malaria. He was nearly blind in his left eye because of a detached retina, the result of a punch during a boxing match while he was president.[81]

While Roosevelt often failed to distinguish between his own ambition and a higher moral and civic purpose, in the case of the 1912 election, he seems to have been driven at least as much by the latter as by the former. He had a sense that his purpose in life had not been fulfilled and that whatever he had accomplished as president might yet be destroyed. Almost certainly he would not have run if the alternative were not what he considered the ineptitude of Taft and the extremists in both wings of the Republican Party. "My loyalty to the Republican Party is naturally very great," he wrote to Governor Augustus Willson in February, "but remember . . . my aim is to make it and to keep it the Republican party that it was in the days of Lincoln." He had promised in 1904 not to seek another term in 1908 on the basis of having already served the equivalent of two consecutive terms, implying that he did not intend to break the two-term tradition going back to George Washington. His pledge came back to haunt him. Although he tried to get around it by arguing that he had never promised not to seek another non-consecutive term, his quest for an alleged third term would be used against him throughout the campaign.[82]

The former president applied all his energy to winning the nomination, accusing the president of being an incompetent stooge of the bosses and a traitor to the progressive promises he had made to Roosevelt in 1908. The huge crowds he drew wherever he went, the pledges he received, an increase in the number of states with some form of primary from ten to thirteen, and the two-to-one string of victories he won in those states over Taft, including the president's home state of Ohio, gave him cause for hope. In the primaries, he won 281 votes to Taft's seventy-one votes and La Follette's thirty-six. Coming into the Chicago convention, Taft had 472 pledged delegates to Roosevelt's 439. The race was neck and neck, with 540 votes needed to win.[83]

The problem for the former president was that Taft controlled the credentials committee, which decided on disputed delegates. Roosevelt challenged 248 of these delegates, most from the South who had been selected even before he entered the contest. Through his control of the credentials committee, Taft was able to steamroll his candidacy through the convention. As the committee made its decisions, Roosevelt breathed fire and brimstone, even charging from Oyster Bay that "we have sent to the penitentiary election officials for deeds not one whit worse than what was done by the National Committee at Chicago yesterday." Of the 248 challenged votes, the former president received only thirty-six.[84]

As soon as it became apparent that Taft was going to win the nomination, Roosevelt, who in an unprecedented move came to Chicago to speak to his followers, held a mass meeting in a nearby theater. Twenty thousand people tried to get into a facility with room for only 5,000. In one of the great speeches of his life, Roosevelt declared that he would not allow the election to be stolen from him. After speaking for about an hour, he delivered a stirring peroration: "We fight in honorable fashion for the good of mankind; fearless of the future; unheeding of our individual fates; with unflinching hearts and undimmed eyes; we stand at Armageddon, and we battle for the Lord."[85]

The convention was a raucous affair, with wild demonstrations, noisy challenges to delegates, and growing anger on the part of the pro-Roosevelt crowd in the galleries, Realizing that Taft had won the battle, Roosevelt issued a statement in which he advised his followers "to decline to vote on any matter before the Convention." On the first and only ballot, he received 107 votes to Taft's 561. Although Roosevelt's followers had not bolted the convention, a few hours after the gathering adjourned, they held a rump meeting and nominated Roosevelt as an independent candidate. The former president accepted the nomination conditionally, pending the holding of a formal convention of a new Progressive Party. In August, the gathering of 2,000 delegates met in Chicago where, in what resembled a revival meeting with singing and loud shouts, they nominated Roosevelt.

In response to reporters' questions, Roosevelt said he felt "as fit as a bull moose." Henceforth, the party became known as the Bull Moose Party.

What made the drama of the nomination so tragic was that both Taft and Roosevelt entered the election knowing they were unlikely to win. In Taft's case, he understood how much more popular the former president was among Republicans and independents. As for Roosevelt, he hoped the Democrats would choose a conservative and that Democratic progressives and independents would migrate to the new Progressive Party. Once the Democrats chose New Jersey's reform governor, Woodrow Wilson, as their candidate, he knew he would lose.[86]

The campaign nevertheless reinvigorated the former president. He fought as hard as he had in earlier elections. Almost everywhere he went on a whistle-stop campaign, he was greeted by large crowds who responded almost on cue to his attacks on the two major parties and the political bosses that controlled them. Although he tempered his remarks on Wilson, even referring to him at one point as an "excellent man individually," he described the Democratic platform as "one of the worst I have ever seen" representing "partly an unintelligent rural toryism" despite the fact that it was filled with progressive proposals including an income tax, preferential primaries, and restrictions on the use of injunctions in labor cases.[87]

Roosevelt's campaign was interrupted on 14 October in Milwaukee when a would-be assassin, John Schrank, who had visions of McKinley's ghost accusing Roosevelt of having killed him, shot the former president at close range, piercing his chest and leaving a bullet near a rib close to the heart. Only the fact that Roosevelt had in his breast pocket a metal eyeglass case and a copy of his speech slowed the bullet enough to keep it from killing him. Instead of seeking immediate medical help, he checked to see if he was coughing up blood. Seeing none, he decided to give his address. Because he had suffered a broken rib, he had trouble breathing and suffered considerable pain. Still, he spoke for more than an hour with his blood-soaked shirt clearly visible. Only then was he taken to a hospital. Edith insisted that he return to Oyster Bay to recuperate. His narrow escape probably garnered him more votes than if the campaign had run its natural course. On election day, he came in a distant second to Wilson, gaining 4.1 million popular votes to the Democrat's 6.3 million votes and eighty-eight electoral votes to Wilson's 435 electoral votes. Taft received 3.5 million popular votes and only eight electoral votes.

Although the Progressive Party had captured more electoral votes than any third-party movement in the nation's history, the former president was nevertheless greatly disappointed—not so much because he had lost, but because he and the Progressive Party had been more soundly defeated than he had anticipated. About as many Republicans had voted for Taft as had voted for him, and he only received about 10 percent of the vote of regular Democrats. States like Oregon, Kansas, Nebraska, and Iowa, which he had expected to win, went Democratic because of the split in the Republican vote. His only consolations were that his party had had only three months to organize and run a campaign, that it lacked adequate financial resources, and that no other thirdparty candidate could have done as well as he did.[88]

The following year was mostly a dreadful one for Roosevelt. In December, he became president of the American Historical Association in recognition of his historical publications and his earlier efforts while in the White House to preserve public records. He also wrote regularly for *Outlook,* where he had become an editor, and completed several books. One of these was his autobiography—an interesting and entertaining account of his life but one that was incomplete, was not especially reflective, and often distorted major historical events as he tried to encapsulate into his own career his image of the iconic American figure.[89] So, too, he reported happily on Edith's improving health and on other family affairs, including the engagement and marriage of his daughter Ethel and the engagement of his son Kermit.[90]

Mostly, however, the president busied himself by trying to turn the Bull Moose Party into a permanent organization. As he recognized almost immediately, his base was splintered between those he considered moderates and those he regarded as ultraradicals. The former recognized the virtues of pragmatism and compromise, including the importance of working with business leaders and raising money, even if that meant having as party leaders men like Perkins, who had been the principal fund-raiser for his own campaign. The latter did not believe in compromise and wanted to drive Perkins and his ilk out of the new party. "I wish that men who desire to break up the Progressive Party," he wrote to Frances Joseph Henry, one of those who wanted Perkins out of the party, "would seriously consider Lincoln's history and the history of what was attempted by his ultraradical opponents."[91] Roosevelt also realized that while the Bull Moose Party stood for the general principle of "direct democracy" as opposed to party regularity,[92] there was no single, specific issue that bound progressives together. Finally, he was aware of the real possibility that the Wilson administration might co-opt much of the rationale for a new party.

Despite the obstacles in front of him, Roosevelt labored on after the election, writing letters, traveling and speaking throughout the country, and even contributing his own money in an effort to save the new party. He became annoyed, however, by the internecine warfare that took place within progressive ranks. The fight over Perkins as chairman of the party's executive committee was especially irksome. Even as he moved steadily leftward in his own views—taking, for example, an advanced position on feminist issues and embracing certain socialist ideas within a capitalist framework—his former supporters championed their own causes. As he feared, Wilson also undercut support for a new party by advocating many of the progressive causes. At the same time, the Republican Party had considerable success in reimposing party authority by responding to some local progressive grievances while applying punitive measures against those who had supported Roosevelt against Taft.[93]

A frustrated Roosevelt embarked in October on a speaking tour of South America, taking Edith with him. He also agreed to collect rare specimens for the American Museum of Science in return for its underwriting of some of his expenses. His trip was altered when he was persuaded by the Brazilian government to also explore an uncharted river in Brazil, aptly named the River of Doubt, which headed north from its headwaters toward the equatorial rain forest of northeast Brazil and was supposed to flow into an effluent of the Amazon River. Again accompanying him was his son Kermit. Edith returned home. For his speaking engagements and a series of articles and a book he negotiated to write on his scientific expedition, he netted about $20,000 (the equivalent of about $423,000 in 2009).[94]

The expedition nearly killed the former president. From the beginning, it was plagued by faulty charts and poor planning, dense jungle, unbearable heat and humidity, insects and predators, hostile natives, and treacherous rapids. One of the party was murdered. The killer escaped into the jungle, where the former president left him to die. While trying to save two boats full of supplies by jumping into the swiftly moving river, Roosevelt reinjured a leg that had been hurt in a 1902 carriage accident. The leg became infected. He also suffered from dysentery and a high fever, and he became delirious at times. Close to death, he contemplated suicide and ordered the expedition to continue without him. Kermit refused. The former president survived. After forty-eight days, the party, half-starved, finally reached civilization.[95]

When Roosevelt returned to Oyster Bay in May 1914, he was sixty pounds lighter than when he had embarked six months earlier for South America. He also never fully recovered from his leg injury and had recurring bouts of high fever. In his book about his venture, *Through the Brazilian Wilderness,* which he completed after returning home, he hardly referred to his brush with death but remarked, "No man has any business to go on such a trip as ours unless he will refuse to jeopardize the welfare of his associates by any delay caused by a weakness or ailment of his." In Roosevelt's honor, Brazil renamed the river Rio Roosevelt.[96]

Soon Roosevelt returned to the political arena. He campaigned actively in the fall elections for candidates running on the Progressive ticket. He was disappointed once more by the election results. Except in California, Bull Moosers running for Congress were nearly wiped out. The Republican Party swept the East. Many former Progressive loyalists had already returned to the party. After November, others followed.

Roosevelt despaired. He interpreted the pathetic returns of 1914 as a personal rebuke. He declared himself "no longer fit physically or in any other way, to continue to lead an active life." Although he did not immediately give up the Progressive cause, he clearly became more interested in defeating the Democrats than continuing his war with the Republicans. Although he thought it unlikely, his hope was to see the party of Lincoln return to its roots.[97]

By the end of 1914, other matters were also beginning to weigh on Roosevelt's mind, most notably the outbreak of World War I in Europe at the end of July and the beginning of August. An Anglophile throughout most of his life, he remained one after the war began. He also believed Britain would win if the conflict continued. He had always been impressed by German industry and the German welfare state. German power also served as an obstacle to Russian expansion in Europe and Japanese expansion in Asia. His preferred outcome for the war, therefore, was to maintain a balance of power in Europe, just as it had been as president.[98]

Meanwhile, Roosevelt had come to think increasingly ill of the Democratic president. At first, he criticized Wilson mainly for lacking the fortitude and finesse necessary for statesmanship. The president failed, for example, to show the same backbone and skill in dealing with California's effort to prevent Japanese immigrants from owning land in the state as he had used in similar discriminatory incidents against the Japanese when he was president.[99]

The former president was also critical of what he considered the administration's naive handling of the ongoing Mexican revolution and Bryan's efforts at world peace through arbitration or cooling-off treaties. In September 1913, he referred privately to Bryan as "the most contemptible figure we have ever had as Secretary of State" and remarked that he regarded Wilson "with contemptuous dislike." What turned the former president into one of Wilson's bitterest foes, however, was the treaty Bryan signed with Columbia on 6 April 1914 expressing "sincere regret" for the manner in which the United States had acquired the Panama Canal Zone and agreeing to pay $25 million in compensation. Roosevelt referred to the treaty as "a crime against the United States" and later as "blackmail."[100]

Even before the outbreak of World War I, therefore, the ex-president was engaged in a private battle with Wilson. As the Germans marched through Belgium and Luxembourg, Roosevelt's view of the war changed, and his contempt for Wilson grew. As an ex-president, his attitude had to be "one of entire impartiality," he remarked in August.[101] Privately, he was anything but neutral. If Germany conquered France, Britain would be invaded and the British empire possibly destroyed. That "would be a disaster to mankind," he remarked in October.[102]

At a time, therefore, when he was convinced the United States should be engaged in military preparedness, he regarded the administration's policy of pacifism "an act of folly which is saved from being a crime against the nation only because it is so unspeakably foolish." For a former president who also regarded war as the supreme test of heroic leadership and as the ultimate road to immortality, it must have been galling that he was not at the nation's helm. His whole career had prepared him for this moment, and he could do little but fulminate in private while the United States was being led by a pacifist.[103]

As the situation in Europe deteriorated and Roosevelt read about German atrocities against the Belgium people, he slashed out even more bitterly against

Wilson, breaking from his earlier policy of not going after the administration publicly. In a series of articles and opinion pieces, he called for the United States to "interfere" on behalf of Belgium, stopping short, however, of stating the form of this interference. He also encouraged his British friends to do better in trying to influence American public opinion. He scolded the British, however, for violating the United States' neutrality by stopping American ships on the high seas suspected of carrying contraband to Germany and removing even noncontraband goods (permitted under most interpretations of international law).[104]

His nephew by marriage, Assistant Secretary of the Navy Franklin Delano Roosevelt, also informed Roosevelt that Wilson and Secretary of the Navy Josephus Daniels were leaving the navy unprepared for war. The former president regarded this as scandalous. Should Berlin conquer the French and British, the entire western hemisphere, including the Panama Canal, would be endangered. "I do not think we have ever had an administration which I more cordially despised than I do this Wilson–Bryan–Daniels combine," he concluded by the middle of November. He ranked Wilson with James Buchanan as the nation's worst presidents.[105]

Even more criminal to Roosevelt was the administration's response to Germany's use of submarine warfare and its sinking on 7 May 1915 of the British passenger liner *Lusitania* without providing for the safety of its passengers and crew as required by international law. Before the *Lusitania* set sail from New York, Germany warned that ships would be sailing at their own peril if they went into the war zone it had established around the British islands. This did not lessen the shock to Americans when they learned that more than 1,200 passengers, including 128 Americans, had lost their lives. Although Wilson issued a series of notes to Berlin, so increasingly threatening that Secretary of State Bryan resigned in protest, the president seemed to rule out war. "There is such a thing as a man being too proud to fight," he remarked.

By chance, Roosevelt published his own response to the sinking of the *Lusitania* the next day in the magazine *Metropolitan*. The former president had resigned as an editor of *Outlook* a year earlier, allegedly to devote more time to the 1914 campaign, but also because he was increasingly out of tune with its readership. Instead, he was offered a salary of $25,000 to become a contributing editor of *Metropolitan,* which in 1918 was put on the post office's watch list for possible denial of its mail privileges because of its criticism of the president.[106]

In his editorial, Roosevelt savaged the Germans, comparing the sinking of the liner to "the wholesale poisoning of wells in the path of a hostile army, or the shipping of infected rags into the cities of a hostile country." He called for the cessation of all commerce with Germany and the seizure of German ships in American waters. He also raised the possibility of war with Germany.[107]

Roosevelt was astounded, therefore, by the administration's response to the *Lusitania,* holding Wilson and Bryan "morally responsible" for the loss of American lives. "They are both of them abject creatures and they won't go to war unless they are kicked into it," he wrote to his son Archie. He called the president's "too proud to fight" statement "the nadir of cowardly infamy." He described himself as being "sick at heart over affairs in the world at large."[108]

The former president had yet other reasons to be depressed over the next twelve months. He was concerned about Edith's declining health. He broke several ribs when he was thrown while trying to mount a horse. He suffered occasional bouts of high fever. He worried about his mortality, not because he feared death, but because he found himself increasingly unable to lead the strenuous life that was such a part of his being. He had to defend himself against charges that he had made scandalous remarks against William Barnes, one of New York's state Republican leaders (he had called him "corrupt"). Although he was vindicated, the trial, held in Syracuse, lasted a month.[109]

Then there were constant political strains on the ex-president, some self-imposed, others not. Many leaders of the women's movement, such as Jane Addams of Hull House, who had strongly supported Roosevelt in 1912, broke with him over the issue of military preparedness; Addams formed the Women's Peace Party. Despite the abandonment of these reformers, the pressure on Roosevelt to run again for president on the Progressive ticket in 1916 was intense. Some supporters even wanted him to seek the Republican nomination. Although Roosevelt remained ambivalent about his future plans, by the end of 1915, he concluded that the prospects of the Progressive Party becoming a viable national party were dim to hopeless. The party lacked the necessary organization and finances. It was too divided, with too many ultraradicals in its ranks. Republicans had grown stronger after 1912. The Democrats had undercut part of the party's purpose by enacting major economic regulatory reforms, such as the Clayton Antitrust Act and measures establishing the Federal Reserve System and the Federal Trade Commission.[110]

Yet the former president was not prepared to forsake the progressive cause. Despite his break with the women's peace movement, for example, he remained a leading proponent of women's suffrage. He also continued to advocate such measures as the abolition of child labor, the creation of old-age pensions, and improved race relations.[111]

The quandary for Roosevelt remained how best to get the nation behind his pleas for military preparedness and social justice. In 1915, Wilson responded to Roosevelt's constant jabbing and to his own concerns about the need for military preparedness by launching his own preparedness campaign. In November, he called for a ten-year program to build a navy as large as Britain's, to increase the size of the regular army, and to raise a volunteer reserve army of 400,000. He emphasized that his purpose was not to move the nation closer to war but to avoid war by strengthening the nation's defenses.

Instead of embracing Wilson's proposals, Roosevelt attacked his call for a voluntary reserve army, which he referred to as a "mere make-shift [sic]."[112] What he wanted was a much larger regular army than Wilson had in mind and universal military training. Such training would not only prepare the nation for war, but like the Boy Scout movement, which he also strongly supported, it would firm the fiber of the weak. The president was attacked, however, not only by those who believed his proposals did not go far enough, but by others who were convinced they represented a dangerous step toward war. The Democratic Party split between its pacifist wing and those who supported Wilson's program. So much opposition to the program developed on Capitol Hill that the president needed to go on a speaking tour to sell it directly to the American people before presenting it to Congress.[113]

The split within Democratic ranks offered Roosevelt an opportunity to be president again. There is no question that this is what he wanted. "Don't imagine that I wouldn't like to be at the White House this minute," he remarked in the winter. The Progressive Party's nomination in 1916 was his for the asking. He knew that he could only win as the candidate of a reunited Republican Party cleansed of old-line Republicans. The progressive cause and now the war remained his major concerns, not the Progressive Party.[114]

The former president realized the odds were against him getting the Republican nomination. Party leaders were not about to relinquish their power without a fight. Other Republicans did not forgive him for abandoning the party and running against Taft in 1912. Influential German American Republicans resented him for his pro-Allied position and for referring to them increasingly as "hyphenated Americans." He could not expect any support from pacifists.[115]

As the war continued, however, public approval of the former president also grew. Both sides in the war violated American neutrality, and for a time, Britain was the more guilty party. German plans to sabotage U.S. munitions plants were uncovered. After the sinking of the passenger liner *Arabic* in August 1915 and the merchant ship *Sussex* in March 1916, Germany pledged not to use submarine warfare provided Britain agreed to lift its blockade against northern Europe. Although Berlin abided by its pledges for the rest of 1916, the chance that Germany might resume using its most powerful weapon remained real. British ships, meanwhile, continued to stop neutral ships on the high seas and remove even noncontraband goods. The allies turned down Wilson's proposal for a conference to end the war. Angering Americans even more was the British blacklisting of American companies trading with the enemy.

The changing dynamic of the European war had a profound impact on Roosevelt's standing with the public. Early in the conflict, the former president had referred to himself as a lonely prophet preaching to unreceptive audiences. His vitriol against the president even turned the public against him. Some Americans viewed him as unstable or even deranged. Others regarded him as a warlike and power-driven egotist who sought to satiate his own presidential ambitions and Anglophile agenda by taking the United States into war against Germany.[116]

As the likelihood grew that the United States might have to enter the conflict against Germany, or even possibly against Britain, more Americans began to listen to the former president. As they did so, the political prospects for Roosevelt improved. By no means did the former president ever regard his chances at gaining the Republican nomination in 1916 more than a long shot. He thought he had enough of a chance to stir himself into action.[117]

George Perkins, whose role in the Progressive Party had helped divide the party, raised the possibility a year earlier of launching a campaign on Roosevelt's behalf for the Republican nomination. Roosevelt seemed to throw cold water on the idea. "Any such effort will not only be useless from the public standpoint but will be exceedingly detrimental to me," he responded. "The bulk of the [people] are convinced that I am actuated by motives of personal ambition and that I am selfishly desirous of hurting Taft and Wilson and have not the good of the country at heart." Given Roosevelt's ambition to be president again and his wiliness as a politician, it is not too far-fetched to suggest that there was, in his letter to Perkins, a hidden message: if public opinion changed and he could be persuaded that there was strong support among moderate Republicans for his nomination, he would consider running in 1916.[118]

Over the next several months, Roosevelt played his wily game. First, he dismissed as unacceptable the candidates most widely mentioned for the Republican nomination, former secretary of war Elihu Root and U.S. Supreme Court judge and former New York governor Charles Evans Hughes. He accused Root of giving ammunition to pacifists, while he wrote of Hughes, "I thoroughly dislike him."[119] At the same time, he made clear how public opinion had changed in his favor over the last eighteen months and left little doubt how important it was to the nation to have him in the White House. "Unless there is a popular feeling in the Republican party and in the country at large such as to make the Republican leaders feel that, not for my sake but for the sake of the party and the country," he stated, "it is imperative to nominate me, why I won't even consider accepting the nomination. . . . Unless the country is somewhere near a mood of at least half-heroism it would be utterly useless to nominate me."[120]

The sinking of the *Sussex* the following month was proof to Roosevelt of the venal foolishness and failure of Wilson's policy of peace at any price. The next month, he made it unmistakable that he was prepared to accept the Republican nomination if it were offered to him. He would not actively campaign for it by running in the primaries. If he were nominated, however, he would hold no grudges against the party conservatives and political bosses he had been assailing over the last four years. "If a cut is to be healed, it must be healed to the bone," he wrote a Republican congressman from Tennessee. "If I am nominated and accept the nomination, it will be with the determination to treat the past as completely past and to give absolutely fair play to all my supporters."[121]

In the weeks that followed, Roosevelt's supporters undertook a publicity campaign on his behalf, including a four-page spread in the *Saturday Evening Post* with the headline, "Why Roosevelt Would Be Our Best Guarantee of Peace." For his part, Roosevelt continued to disparage those individuals most mentioned for the nomination, especially Hughes, who was emerging as the leading contender even though he had shown no interest in being nominated.[122]

A complication for the former president was the question of the Progressive Party. Both the Republican and Progressive parties were to meet at the same time in Chicago. This was no coincidence. As chairman of the Progressive National Committee, Perkins intended that the Republicans would nominate Roosevelt, and the Progressive Party would then fuse with the Republicans behind Roosevelt. What if the Republicans did not follow the script? Would Roosevelt then run on the Progressive ticket?

The answer was that he would not. Seeing no future for the Progressive Party, he was not about to be a sacrificial lamb for a second time. Again, Roosevelt played a devious game. In talks that Perkins and other of his closest advisers undertook with Republican and Progressive leaders in Chicago, he allowed the possibility to be raised that he might run on the Progressive ticket if the Republicans did not make him their candidate. "I must ask . . . that my friends in the Progressive Convention no more proceed upon the assumption that I will run, than my friends in the Republican Convention proceed upon the assumption that I will not run," he wrote to his former attorney general, Charles Joseph Bonaparte. The message to the Republicans could not be clearer. If he were denied their nomination, he might split the Republican vote again by running once more as a Progressive.[123]

Despite this threat, Roosevelt never had much of a chance of getting the nomination. Republican leaders still refused to forgive him for deserting the party in 1912 and for the assaults he had made against them since then. Nor could they accept his progressive agenda or his seeming determination to take the United States into war. In May, he threw away any remaining chance for the nomination when he preached the cause of militant nationalism during a speaking tour of the Midwest, the center of German American influence and antiwar sentiment.

Hoping to bring more progressives back into the party, Republicans turned to Hughes, who had gained a national reputation as a reformer during his term as New York's governor. Despite the fact that he remained at Oyster Bay, Roosevelt's ever-looming presence helped Hughes by making him the anti-Roosevelt candidate. With the approval of Republican leaders, Roosevelt was informed that unless he agreed to back one of several other candidates for the nomination, Hughes would be nominated. When the former president replied that none of the alternatives were acceptable, Hughes received the nomination on the third ballot.[124]

The Progressive Party was waiting in Chicago to see whom the Republicans chose as their candidate. When the delegates learned that Roosevelt would not be the nominee, they rejected fusion with the Republicans and nominated him by acclamation. Roosevelt turned them down. He even suggested that the Progressives nominate his friend Henry Cabot Lodge, an arch-Republican conservative. The rage of the delegates was palpable. "For a moment there was silence," wrote

William Allen White from Chicago. "Then there was a roar of rage. It was the cry of a broken heart such as no convention had ever uttered in this land before." The Bull Moose Party was dead.[125]

Once Hughes agreed to support progressivism and preparedness, Roosevelt endorsed the bearded, austere, and taciturn nominee. Even though he disliked him intensely, he poured all his energy into the campaign. Had he not done so, he feared that Americans would believe that his quest for the Republican nomination had been a matter of ego rather than of self-sacrifice. "I could not allow any such impression to go forth," he told an acquaintance.[126]

In fact, Roosevelt would have preferred to serve the nation by raising an infantry division in case war should break out with Mexico over an expedition Wilson had sent deep into that country to capture the Mexican bandit, Pancho Villa, who had earlier crossed the border and killed a number of Americans in Columbus, New Mexico. Secretary of War Newton Baker turned down Roosevelt's request.[127]

Instead of preparing a military division to fight in Mexico, therefore, Roosevelt devoted his energy to defeating Wilson. The president ran for a second term on the slogan "He Kept Us Out of War." For Roosevelt, there could be no more cowardly and dangerous slogan than that: it promised to lull Americans into a false sense of security when what was called for was military preparedness. Roosevelt could never appreciate Wilson's patient efforts to avoid war through negotiation. Earlier, his friend, Hermann Hagedorn, had called Roosevelt "the bugle that woke America." That became his purpose in the campaign. He was acting not on behalf of Hughes or even the Republican Party; he was campaigning to rid the United States of a second Buchanan, who had almost brought about the nation's destruction fifty-five years earlier.[128]

Given how close the election was, how actively Roosevelt campaigned on Hughes's behalf, and how poor a candidate the languid Hughes proved to be, one can argue the paradox that Roosevelt did more to bring Hughes to the brink of victory and to assure his defeat than any other individual. On the eve of the election, the nation was almost evenly divided over the issue of preparedness. No person had done more to bring it to the forefront of the national debate than Roosevelt. When the outcome of the election was finally determined, weeks after the last ballot was counted, Wilson eked out a narrow victory over Hughes, gaining 9.1 million popular votes and 277 electoral votes to Hughes's 8.5 million popular votes and 254 electoral votes. The difference in the outcome was California, which Wilson carried by about 3,800 votes out of more than one million cast. Had California's thirteen electoral votes gone to Hughes, he would have been president.

Results of the election left the former president embittered. Hughes had proven totally incompetent as a candidate. The Republicans' "one chance of winning" had been to nominate him. By electing Wilson, the American people had turned their back on him and shown a total lack of character. "I am completely out of sympathy with the American people," he wrote Arthur Hamilton Lee. "This is yellow, my friend! Plain yellow!" He had fought his last battle and lost. He saw himself becoming "an elderly literary gentleman of quiet tastes and an interesting group of grandchildren."[129]

To his surprise, Germany's announcement that it would resume submarine warfare at the beginning of 1917 and Wilson's decision to break off relations with Germany in February offered Roosevelt another opportunity for the type of heroic leadership he had sought throughout his life. He wanted to raise and lead a voluntary military division "for immediate service at the front." Writing to Secretary of War Baker, he even named the person he wanted for his divisional chief of staff. Baker replied that only Congress could approve the raising of voluntary troops. Even if it gave its approval, it would determine its own conditions for the "appointment of officers for the higher commands." Angered by Baker's response, Roosevelt wrote Baker another letter reminding him that, as a former commander in chief, he was eligible for any military appointment. Again, Baker turned Roosevelt down.[130] After Wilson asked for a declaration of war from Congress on 2 April and Congress approved his request two days later, Roosevelt wrote the president acknowledging he had spent most of the past four years vilifying him, but asking to let bygones be bygones and to allow him to proceed with his plans for raising the division. Further swallowing his pride, he went to the White House to press his case directly with the president.

Wilson was pleasant enough. Reportedly, he was charmed by the former president. There was also considerable reason to take Roosevelt's request seriously, including the fact that it might be a way of getting American forces to Europe quickly. Prime Minister Georges Clemenceau of France, whom Roosevelt had earlier approached through the former French ambassador to the United States, Jean Jules Jusserand, about raising a division under French and British orders if he was turned down by Wilson, thought the former president's request should be granted. In an open letter to the American president, which he published as an editorial in his own newspaper, *L'Home Enchaine,* he remarked "in all candor . . . there is in France one name which sums up the beauty of American intervention. It is the name of Roosevelt." Send Roosevelt, he concluded.[131]

Although Wilson did not dismiss Roosevelt's request without first consulting with the War Department, the cards were stacked against Roosevelt. Not only was there the reciprocal animosity that existed between the two men, there was also the whole question of military structure and command. Furthermore, the technology and strategy of war had changed since Roosevelt led the Rough Riders in 1898. He lacked the experience to lead a division, and he was physically not in good shape.

Modern warfare was a highly technical business, Wilson explained to Roosevelt. His desk was piled high with requests to join the fighting from Indian fighters, Texas Rangers, and others. The nation, however, would rely on conscripts, not volunteers. He even asked the former president to support his bill for a draft.

Although Roosevelt agreed, he understood the gist of the president's remarks. His request to raise a volunteer force would probably be turned down. Without being given a final answer by the president, Roosevelt left the White House still not trusting Wilson. Afterward, he told the president's friend and adviser, Colonel Edward House, "After all, I'm only asking to be allowed to die." Legend has it that House responded, "Oh? Did you make that quite clear to the President?" At the beginning of April, the former president received word from Secretary Baker that, because the army was going to rely on conscripts, the administration was turning down his request to raise a voluntary force.[132]

Denied his last chance for a heroic end to his life, Roosevelt returned to his bitter attacks on Wilson. He wrote a syndicated column for the Kansas City *Star,* owned by an admirer, William Rockhill Nelson, at an annual salary of $25,000. In his columns and in speeches he gave during the war, he criticized virtually every aspect of the administration's handling of the war. Because of his denunciation of administration war policies, a band of Roosevelt haters, led by the publisher William Randolph Hearst, even proposed having him arrested under the 1918 Sedition Act and to have his columns banned from the mails.[133]

At the same time that he assailed the administration's conduct of the war, the ex-president urged the country to rally behind the war effort, to subscribe to Liberty Loan drives, and to support the Red Cross. As part of his own efforts to support the war, he traveled the Midwest to press the case for sustained Americanism, and he donated considerable sums of his own money for war-related charities like the YMCA, which was active on the front and for whom his daughter Ethel was working in France.[134]

Roosevelt also intimated himself into the conflict through the military careers of his four sons, Ted Jr., Kermit, Archie, and Quentin. There was never any question, either in the former president's mind or those of his sons, that they had an obligation to fight on the front lines. Roosevelt believed that it was better for one or more of his sons to die heroically in battle than to stay out of the war or not put their lives in danger. Between 1915 and 1917, Ted, Archie, and Quentin had undergone voluntary military training at Camp Plattsburgh in New York, which had been established by Roosevelt's good friend, General Leonard Wood. Even before the United Stated entered the war, Kermit joined the British army as captain and saw action in Mesopotamia against the Turks. After the United States entered the war, his father used his influence to have Archie and Ted sent over to Europe with the first American troops. "They are keenly desirous to see service; and if they serve under you at the front and are not killed, they will be far better able to instruct the draft army next fall, or next winter, or whenever they are sent home," he wrote in May to General John Pershing, who Wilson had selected to command the American Expeditionary Force to Europe.[135]

Roosevelt also used his influence with the British government to get Kermit transferred to the American army on the Western front. "I need hardly say that you have a heavy weight of responsibility on your shoulders," he told Kermit.

"You have an obligation to England, to America, to yourself, and to me."[136] The former president's youngest son, Quentin, opted to be a pilot in the American air service. Roosevelt was delighted when Kermit received the British War Cross, Archie and Ted the Croix de Guerre for gallantry in action (Ted also received the Silver Star), and when Quentin reported that he had shot down his first enemy plane.

During the war Ted was gassed and Archie severely wounded, but both of them survived the conflict, as did Kermit. Shortly before the armistice ending the war on 11 November 1918, however, Quentin was killed while flying behind enemy lines. News that Quentin might have been shot down had been reported several days earlier. His death was confirmed by the German government, which announced that he had been buried with full military honors. Roosevelt had always been close to his sons, but the fact that Quentin had been the youngest made his son's death especially crushing. Furthermore, the former president had wanted to be near his boys, and although he never doubted he was correct in sending them in harm's way, he worried increasingly about their survival. He even occasionally hinted to his sons to seek less hazardous service behind the lines, something he would never have imagined doing a few months earlier.[137]

For all his vaunting of the heroic nature of falling in battle, Roosevelt never fully recovered from Quentin's death. His health had already been in decline. He suffered from chronic inflammatory rheumatism. In February, he had to be hospitalized for a severe throat infection that spread to his ears, and he had an abscess that had developed on his thigh removed. Complications developed, and he nearly died. He remained hospitalized for more than a month. One of the complications he suffered was loss of hearing in his left ear. As a result, he left the hospital half-blind and half-deaf, and looking much older than his sixty years.[138]

Quentin's death just added to the physical and psychological strain the former president was under. His health continued to worsen. His rheumatism left him with constant pain in his muscles and joints. By Armistice Day, it had become so severe that he had to be readmitted to the hospital, where he remained for the next six weeks. Although he was released on Christmas Day and was able to spend the rest of the holidays with his family, he required constant attention by his former valet at the White House, James Amos. On 5 January 1919, Amos noted that Roosevelt was breathing irregularly in his sleep. He had complained earlier of having trouble breathing, but the family physician, who had been called to the house, could find nothing wrong and gave him something to help him sleep. This time, Roosevelt's day nurse was summoned. By the time she arrived, the former president was dead. Although no postmortem examination was conducted, the verdict of several doctors who had treated him was that he had died of a heart attack.[139]

Not coincidentally, on Roosevelt's bedside table at the time of his death was a note to himself to tell the chairman of the National Republican Party, Will Hays, to make certain that Republicans on Capitol Hill were united on domestic issues.

Despite his health and the blow of Quentin's death, the former president had managed in the months before his death to maintain a wall of self-control, to write his regular articles for *Metropolitan* and the Kansas City *Star,* to make speeches, and to maintain his enormous correspondence. He also laid the groundwork for another run at the Republican nomination in 1920.[140]

The scope of topics on which he wrote during his last eighteen months of life was breathtaking. He continued his bitter attacks on the Wilson administration, condemning, for example, Wilson's famous "Fourteen Points" address of 8 January 1918 as nothing more than "Fourteen Scraps of Paper," calling instead for the unconditional surrender of Germany. He was especially disturbed by Wilson's call for a League of Nations, not because he was against the concept of an international peacekeeping body, but because he had always opposed any kind of arbitrational organization that might interfere with the national interest. In his view, the national interest always trumped the idealistic quest for an international brotherhood of nations. "The man who loves other countries as much as his own," he remarked, "stands on a level with a man who loves other women as much as he loves his own wife."[141]

The former president also attacked the Espionage and Sedition Acts of 1917 as violations of free speech and almost dared the administration to arrest him for violating these acts. Yet he encouraged the persecution of socialists, pacifists, and other opponents of the war and believed that seditionists should be tried by military tribunals. Initially, he supported the Russian revolution and the overthrow of the czar, but after the government of the moderate Aleksander Kerensky fell apart and the Bolsheviks came to power, he directed his wrath at the anarchists who had gained control of the country and the administration for allowing it to happen. Contrariwise, he extolled the virtues of the British empire even while he urged his British friends to grant Ireland home rule.[142]

After Wilson decided in 1917 to enter the war, Roosevelt's popularity started on an upward trajectory that continued for the remainder of his life. Wilson's decision was his ultimate vindication. He emerged as the recognized leader of the opposition. This made him the leading contender for the Republican nomination in 1920. When it was suggested that Republicans would nominate him by acclamation, his longtime rival in New York politics, William Barnes Jr., even replied: "Acclamation hell! We'll nominate him by assault."[143]

Although Roosevelt never announced formally that he would seek the Republican nomination, he resorted to his usual tactic of making it known that he would accept it if it were offered to him and if he thought he would be serving the national interest. "By George," he remarked, "if [the Republicans] take me, they'll have to take me without a single modification of the things that I have always stood for!" In the months that followed, he laid out a series of domestic reforms that made clear his continued commitment to progressive principles and his intention to reshape the Republican Party. Among the measures he advocated were old-age pensions, sickness and unemployment insurance, public housing projects, and regulation of corporations.[144]

One can only wonder, then, how different the 1920s might have been had Roosevelt not died and instead been elected president in 1920 rather than Warren Harding. Would the boom and bust of the 1920s have taken place? Would the Depression have been avoided? Would modern reformism have been dead until another Roosevelt took office fourteen years later? Would the Republican Party have become the radical party of Lincoln as Roosevelt described it—the party that emancipated the slaves, enacted the Homestead Act, and built the transcontinental railroad even as it reunited the nation?

One thing is certain, however. Just as Roosevelt's presidency was one of the most significant in terms of defining the modern presidency, so his ex-presidency was a seminal one. As an ex-president, Roosevelt earned his living as a writer. In addition to his $25,000 salary from the Kansas City *Star*, he also received $5,000 a year from *Metropolitan,* for which he continued to write occasional articles. Together with book royalties and income his wife and he still received from their inheritances, his annual salary of $30,000 (the equivalent of about $375,000 in 2009) assured him a comfortable lifestyle. In contrast to Grover Cleveland, however, he never sought to take advantage of his former position to become enormously wealthy. From a genteel background and used to the comforts of life, he wanted to have enough funds to assure a comfortable life for his children. As he told Quentin in September 1917, while he hoped to "continue earning a good salary" until all his sons came home from the war and he could help get Archie and Quentin started in private life, he then "intend[ed] to retire."[145]

Retire from writing, perhaps, but not from public life. Even after he left the White House in 1909 and undertook his lengthy safari in Africa, he had remained a political leader of the first magnitude. According to his friend William Allen White, the period after Roosevelt left office was in fact "the ripest period of his life." His kinetic energy, his masterful mind, his encyclopedic knowledge, his very presence gave him an imperial authority that set him apart from ordinary mortals. Rather than blending in, he stood out. Rather than being yesterday's news, he remained tomorrow's headlines. No other former president before him continued to be such a powerful and influential political force and public figure as Roosevelt.[146]

8

Former Presidents as Symbols of an Era
Taft, Wilson, and Coolidge

As former presidents, William Howard Taft survived almost two decades (1913–1930), whereas Woodrow Wilson lived less than three years (1921–1924) and Calvin Coolidge lived less than four years (1929–1933). Their ex-presidencies encapsulated the changing political currents and major national issues of a period that began with the flourishing of the Progressive Movement and ended with the collapse of the age of big business; an era that also went from Wilson's efforts to make the world safe for democracy to the locking doors of political and economic nationalism.

Taft had an especially distinguished post-presidential career. As professor of law at Yale University until 1920, he taught courses on constitutional law in the undergraduate college and the law school. He also went on the lecture circuit and wrote frequent magazine articles. During World War I, he served as chairman of the National War Labor Board and supported Woodrow Wilson's efforts after the war to gain Senate approval of a League of Nations. As chief justice, he modernized the federal judicial system and overhauled outdated rules of procedure.

Wilson, who was an invalid because of a major stroke he suffered in October 1919, was only a shell of the person he had been when he took office in 1913. His stroke affected his mental acuity and personality. It also destroyed any remaining chance the Senate would approve a modified version of his League of Nations and avoid the upsurge of economic nationalism in the 1930s. However, even without U.S. membership in the league, Wilson managed in the last years of his life to get the Democratic Party to pledge itself to his New Freedom programs at home and his internationalist program abroad. Working outside the framework of the league, the United States still followed an internationalist policy in the 1920s much along Wilsonian lines.[1]

As for Calvin Coolidge, his post-presidency represented the increasing willingness of former presidents to take advantage of the new entrepreneurial opportunities available to them in the 1920s. In contrast to a common view that Coolidge spent the last few years of his life in seclusion in Massachusetts and Vermont, he remained active after he left the White House. He published his memoirs, wrote articles for a number of magazines, and even became a columnist for the McClure Newspaper Syndicate. He also served on the board of the New York Life Insurance Company.

I

Handpicked by Theodore Roosevelt to be his successor in the White House, William Howard Taft had few of Roosevelt's qualities. Weighing over 330 pounds, he was neither charismatic nor energetic. Instead, he had a contemplative, judicial frame of mind, which would be valuable in his later role as chief justice of the Supreme Court, but which did not serve him well as president. In fact, he never wanted to be president. That was the ambition of his wife, Helen "Nellie" Herron. Taft's own ambition was the one he finally achieved only after President Warren Harding nominated him in 1921 to be chief justice of the Supreme Court.

Taft was born on 15 September 1857 to a prominent Cincinnati family. His father, Alphonso Taft, helped found the Republican Party in Cincinnati. Although William was raised in a loving and nurturing family and had a mostly normal childhood, because of his chubbiness, he was called Big Lub, even by his family (albeit as a term of endearment). He was also under intense pressure, especially from his mother, to succeed.[2]

A bright student who was motivated by his parents to work hard, Taft excelled in his studies. Like his father, he attended Yale. After graduating second in his class in 1878, Taft returned to Cincinnati, where he received his law degree in 1880 from the Cincinnati Law School. During his college years, his father served in the cabinet of President Ulysses S. Grant. Through his influence, William was appointed assistant prosecutor of Hamilton County, which included the city of Cincinnati. This was followed by appointment as U.S. collector of revenue for the first Ohio district and then by a series of increasingly more prestigious positions, including Ohio state superior court judge, solicitor general of the United States (1890–1892), and judge of the Sixth U.S. Circuit Court (1892–1900).

Taft's years on the bench were some of the happiest of his life. He loved the law and would have been content to stay on the bench. His fondest hope was appointment to the Supreme Court, preferably as chief justice. However, Nellie, whom Taft had married in 1886, was not content with the relatively sedentary life of a sitting jurist. She had enjoyed the social life of Washington when Taft was solicitor general. In contrast, she found Cincinnati socially constricted and intellectually stilted. She also had grand political ambitions for her husband and herself that included being the nation's first lady.[3]

After William McKinley was elected president in 1896, Taft hoped the new president would name him to the Supreme Court. A loyal Republican who had gained an enviable reputation as a hardworking and thoughtful jurist, he was also a conservative, known for his defense of property rights and antiunion decisions. McKinley, who was looking for someone to serve as governor general of the newly acquired Philippine Islands, asked him to forgo the bench in favor of the Philippines. A disappointed Taft agreed after McKinley promised that if he had the opportunity, he would appoint Taft to the Supreme Court.

Taft proved to be an effective governor. He devised a civil government based on a legal system modeled after that in the United States to replace the harsh and arbitrary military rule that Washington had imposed on the islands. This made him popular with the local population. His wide girth, warm blue eyes, upswinging mustachios, and gentle smile also gave him an avuncular appearance. A kind and caring person, he felt so obligated to carry out his purpose of bringing the blessings of Western-style government to the Filipinos that twice he turned down President Theodore Roosevelt's offers to appoint him to the Supreme Court.[4]

Despite his desire to remain in the Philippines until he felt he had completed his work, Taft was unable in 1904 to overcome Roosevelt's insistence that he return to Washington to replace Elihu Root as Roosevelt's secretary of war. Taft and Roosevelt had first met in Washington while Taft was serving as solicitor general and Roosevelt as a civil service commissioner. They attended some of the same social circles and became good friends. Taft's calmness provided a soothing tonic for his friend's restlessness. His lack of political ambition and substantial political connections made him a potential political ally in Roosevelt's own ambitious plans. His solid record of achievement on and off the bench suggested competence as well as intelligence.[5]

Roosevelt came to rely more and more on his new secretary of war. Taft campaigned for Roosevelt's election in 1904. He supervised the construction of the Panama Canal. He continued to oversee development of civil government in the Philippines. He negotiated an agreement with the Vatican for cession of church lands in the Philippines. He also negotiated the Taft–Katsura Memorandum that effectively recognized Japanese suzerainty over Korea in return for Japanese renunciation of any designs on the Philippines. Finally, he served briefly as provisional governor of Cuba. Reluctantly, he turned down another offer of appointment to the Supreme Court by Roosevelt. "Ma wants him to wait and be President," Taft's younger son, Charles, remarked in explaining why Taft rejected the president's offer.[6]

Having taken himself out of the race for president in 1908, Roosevelt was determined to name his own successor. Taft had been loyal to the point of being almost unctuous and had carried out every assignment with intelligence and competence. Roosevelt was confident he would continue to carry out the programs and principles that he backed. As for Taft, he felt too insecure and inadequate to be the nation's leader. However, under pressure from Nellie and the president, he relented. With Roosevelt's backing, he easily won the Republican nomination in Chicago.

Much to Roosevelt's disappointment, Taft proved to be a dull, insecure, and plodding candidate. Honest to a fault, he also suffered from foot-in-the-mouth disease, making remarks that were better left unsaid. Roosevelt was forced to coach Taft and play a more active role in the campaign than he intended. Still, Taft easily defeated his Democratic opponent, Williams Jennings Bryan, receiving 7.68 million votes to Bryan's 5.08 million votes.

If Roosevelt began to have doubts about Taft before he became president, he realized soon after Taft took office that his successor's concept of the presidency differed dramatically from his own. Taft viewed his role as fundamentally that of an administrator. Accordingly, he was reluctant to mobilize public opinion behind programs of economic and social reform or otherwise provide the nation with vigorous leadership. In foreign affairs, too, Taft followed a different direction than Roosevelt. Seeking to expand American markets and investments abroad through a policy known as dollar diplomacy, he challenge existing power relationships in Asia by promoting American financing of railroad construction in Manchuria.

Taft's presidency had its achievements. The Payne–Aldrich tariff of 1909, which Taft signed into law, provided for a new 1 percent tax on corporate income. The Mann–Elkins Act of 1910 gave the Interstate Commerce Commission (ICC) authority to suspend railroad rates and brought telephones and telegraphs within the commission's jurisdiction. A system of postal savings banks, a parcel post system, and a bureau of mines were also established with Taft's support and influence. He established a commission on government efficiency. He also instituted more antitrust suits against America's largest corporations than the much-fabled trust buster, Roosevelt.[7]

On the whole, however, the Taft administration was a failure. His support of the protectionist Payne–Aldrich tariff infuriated Midwestern Republicans who believed it would benefit Eastern corporate interests while raising their own cost of living. His dismissal of Gifford Pinchot estranged conservationists, including Roosevelt. His clumsy efforts at dollar diplomacy alienated Japan and Russia.

The president decided to seek reelection in 1912 only to save his pride and prevent Roosevelt, whose brand of progressivism he rejected, from winning the nomination. "I am chiefly interested in the re-nomination," he wrote to his wife. "If we lose the election, I shall feel that the party is rejected whereas if I fail to secure the re-nomination it will be a personal defeat."[8] Taft was angered and saddened to the point of tears by the harsh charges that his former friend, whose approval had meant so much to him, levied against him during the campaign. At the same time, he was relieved after losing in November to be leaving the White House.

Taft's four years as president had been a liberating experience for him. He felt confident that he had done an able job as the nation's leader. He had bested Roosevelt for the Republican nomination and kept him from returning as president with his radical ideas. Although Nellie was distressed to be leaving the White House, he had at least satisfied her lifelong quest to be the nation's first lady. He now began to concern himself more with what he wanted than with what others intended for him.

Soon after the election, Taft delivered a speech before the Lotos Club of New York. "What are we to do with our ex-presidents?" he asked his audience, just as other presidents about to leave office had asked before him. Ruefully, he offered one possibility. "The proper and scientific administration of a dose of chloroform or of the fruit of the lotus tree, and the reduction of the flesh of the thus quietly departed to ashes in a funeral pyre . . . might make a fitting end to the life of one who has held the highest office. . . . His record would have been made by one term and his demise in the honorable ceremony . . . would relieve the country from the burden of thinking how he is to support himself and his family, would fix his place in history, and enable the public to pass on to new men and new measures."

Emphatically, Taft rejected an idea put forth by William Jennings Bryan that former presidents should be made ex officio members of the Senate with no voting rights. This had been a proposal that had been made from time to time in the nineteenth century but had never had much support, even from ex-presidents. As Taft explained, "Why Mr. Bryan should think it necessary to add to the discussion in the Senate the lucubrations [*sic*] of ex-Presidents, I am at a loss to say. I can conceive of any reform in the Senate which does not lead to a limit in their debate. . . . If I must go and disappear into oblivion I prefer to go by the chloroform or lotos method. It is pleasanter and less drawn out."⁹

As Taft indicated in his speech to the Lotos Club, his most immediate concern in leaving office was earning a living. Until he became president, he had not had an opportunity to save much money. When he accepted Roosevelt's offer in 1904 to be his secretary of war, he and Nellie were worried about how they would survive financially in Washington after having lived a princely life in the Philippines. "The expenses of living on a limited salary will make life rather hard for Nellie," he wrote his mother. Nellie's unease about penury was relieved only after Taft's older brother, Charles, who had married into great wealth, came to their aid. He gave his brother 1,000 shares of Cleveland Gas Company stock that added $8,000 a year to their income. Still, they had to live modestly before Taft became president.¹⁰

In 1909, Congress raised the annual salary of the president from $50,000 to $75,000 (the equivalent of about $1.77 million in 2009). As a result, Nellie was able to save about $100,000 while Taft served in the White House. Even with his other savings and income, however, the former president felt he needed to supplement his income. Because former presidents received no pensions and so many of them had to earn a living after leaving the White House, Andrew Carnegie offered to establish a fund that would provide Taft and future ex-presidents and their widows with a generous pension of $25,000 a year. There was an enormous outcry to the idea of a nation's former leader accepting a dole from the industrial magnate. Taft understood that "the old man" meant well. As he remarked, however, it would be impossible to escape, "if you were an ex-president, the feeling of embarrassment every time you met old Carnegie . . . it is not probable that he would ever meet you without referring in a genial way to the comfortable position in which the pension he had arranged had placed you."[11]

At the same time, Congress resisted proposals to provide pensions for former presidents, just as it had when the issue had been raised in previous years by Millard Fillmore and then in 1880 by the *New York Times* as a way of assisting former president Grant. As Taft recognized, Congress had paid presidents generous salaries in part as a means of enabling them to save sufficient funds to live "in adequate dignity and comfort thereafter." If presidents were not frugal enough to save for their retirement, or if they squandered what other resources they may have had, then that was their responsibility, not that of the federal government.[12]

Having turned down Carnegie's offer, Taft's initial thought was to resume his law practice in Cincinnati. However, he had never been comfortable arguing cases in court, and he had not practiced law since 1887. Just as important, 45 percent of the federal judiciary and six of the nine members of the Supreme Court had been appointed by him. This fact alone, he remarked to a reporter for the *New York Sun,* might lead one to sense impropriety on his part should he win a case in the federal courts.[13]

Fortunately for Taft, his alma mater, Yale, offered him a position as the Kent Professor of Law. The position was in the undergraduate college, and it would pay only $5,000 annually. Otherwise, it seemed a perfect opportunity for Taft. He would be able to offer courses in the law school. He had never cared nearly as much about money as Nellie, and his salary (the equivalent of about $107,000 in 2009), while only a fraction of what he had earned as president, would be more than enough to live the modest lifestyle of an academic. The professorship offered other advantages as well. "I do not retire to the practice of law," he explained to his brothers, Charles and Horace. "I retire to the academic shades of Yale to teach it, and this act takes me out of the maelstrom of politics. It is a dignified retirement, one which Cleveland had at Princeton. . . . I could be reasonably certain to earn more to keep the wolf from the door, especially in view of the fact that I do not expect to eat so much."[14]

The former president enjoyed his years at Yale. He had never been a great speaker, and he proved not to be a great lecturer or teacher. In May, he delivered a course of lectures on "Questions of Modern Government," which were later published as a book.[15] More regularly he taught courses on constitutional law both in the undergraduate college and in the law school. Because of the opportunity to be taught by a former president, over 100 students enrolled in his courses. As the novelty of having an ex-president as a professor wore off, however, and as his reputation as a rather dull instructor grew, his class sizes dwindled. As a novice in the classroom, he was also overly trusting; cheating in his classes became rampant.[16]

At the same time, Taft took his faculty responsibilities seriously. He attended faculty meetings regularly. He made himself available to students and even coached the freshman debating team. He also became a university ambassador to the alumni and raised funds for the Yale Medical School. As a result, he proved to be popular with students, faculty, and the administration.[17]

If there was a consistent theme to his courses on constitutional law, it was the need to respect the Constitution. Even as he accepted the Kent professorship, he made clear that reverence for the Constitution would be the premise of his lectures. "There is need that our young men should appreciate the Constitution of the United States," he wrote in a letter for the *Yale Daily News*. "And this need is especially keen in a day when that instrument is regarded so lightly by a class of fanatical enthusiasts seeking shortcuts to economic perfection, on the one hand, and by unscrupulous demagogues who to promote their own interests do not hesitate to inculcate disrespect and even contempt for the Constitution and the law enacted under it, on the other."[18] The differences between Taft and Roosevelt in these regards were profound. Taft thought of the Supreme Court—the "ultimate tribunal" of the Constitution—as a welcome brake on democracy, Roosevelt as a problematic barrier to democracy.

Yet Taft was never simply a strict constructionist who sought to limit the powers of the central government—someone who even wanted to turn back the clock on the modern presidency. In addition to his regular teaching responsibilities, the former president gave lectures on the Constitution and presidency at Yale and other prestigious academic institutions. In these talks, he made clear that he did not take as activist a view of the modern presidency as Roosevelt. Unlike Roosevelt, he also did not believe the Constitution was a living document subject to reinterpretation as national needs and priorities demanded. Rather, it was a written document that defined the powers of the three branches of government.

The Constitution, however, enumerated the powers of Congress much more narrowly and specifically than it did those of the presidency. Through his complete control over the executive branch, his veto power, his authority to convene and even adjourn Congress (when the two houses could not agree on the time of adjournment), his role as commander in chief, and his duty to faithfully execute the laws of the land, the president had almost limitless power. This authority included his ability to respond to the challenges of a changing society so long as his actions could be shown to derive from a specific grant of power in the Constitution and did not violate other parts of the Constitution.

Not only did the Constitution grant the president great power, but Taft also believed the founding fathers were correct in giving the nation's leader this authority. Indeed, he favored enhancing presidential power in a number of ways, including according the president responsibility for preparing and presenting to

Congress a detailed annual budget (something he had already started to do as president) and granting cabinet officials access to the floors of the Senate and House "to introduce measures, to advocate their passage, to answer questions, and to enter into the debate as if they were members without of course the right to vote." The president, he concluded, "is no figurehead, and it is entirely proper that an energetic and active clear-sighted people . . . having selected him, should entrust to him all the power needed to carry out their governmental purpose, great as it may be."[19]

Taft's view of the presidency explains why he was willing to take antitrust action against some of the nation's biggest corporations. It helps clarify his vigorous foreign policy. It also makes clearer his views on the president's power to act against unions, particularly when they prevented the flow of interstate commerce or threatened property rights. The point remains that Taft's concept of the presidency was a modern one notwithstanding the fact that he and his administration were less progressive and more legalistic than those of his predecessor and successor and that he lacked their strong leadership.[20]

Taft's lectures on the powers of the presidency and other lectures he gave while serving as the Kent Professor of Law were only a few of the many he delivered during his years at Yale. Former presidents were now in great demand as lecturers and speakers. Soon he was away from New Haven as much as he was at home. His private secretary, W. W. Mischler, who had gone with him to Yale from the White House, became a one-person lecture bureau. In the winter of 1914, Taft also contracted with a commercial speaker's bureau for a series of lectures throughout the Midwest.[21]

For many speaking engagements, the ex-president charged no fee, but for others that he delivered before business, civic, and professional groups, he received honoraria that ranged in size from $150 to $1,000, with $400 being the average. In addition, he wrote numerous articles for the *Saturday Evening Post,* the *Ladies' Home Journal, Cosmopolitan,* the *Spectator,* and other magazines, normally receiving a fee of $1,000 for each article he wrote. Even when he accepted the position at Yale, he anticipated keeping the wolf from the door by supplementing his income. However, the demand for his time and the money he made surprised even him. If he could continue for three or four more years to earn as much as he had by lecturing and writing, Taft remarked in 1915, he would be able to ensure an annual income of $10,000 "without work at all" and that, with his life insurance, he would leave an estate of $250,000 — more than he had ever dreamed of having.[22]

In undertaking such an exhaustive schedule of lecturing and writing, however, the former president had more in mind than supplementing his income. Although he did not intend to run again for president, he wanted to influence public opinion. Notwithstanding his humorous remarks before the Lotos Club in 1912 about humanely ending the life of former presidents, he felt his experience in the Oval Office (which had been added to the White House during his term) obligated him to comment on important issues and to participate actively in public service. In 1913, he was elected president of the American Bar Association, and the next year president of the American Academy of Jurisprudence and a member of the board of trustees of the Hampton Normal Institute. In 1915, he chaired the central committee of the Red Cross. Furthermore, Taft wanted to remain a force within Republican circles, if only to prevent Roosevelt from taking over the party. He was a republican as well as a Republican. He feared that democracy, if carried to an extreme through such measures as the initiative and referendum, judicial recall, and direct primaries, would threaten the very republican principles on which the nation was predicated. He was determined, therefore, to keep the Roosevelt wing of the party from winning the nomination in 1916.[23]

While Taft came to dislike President Woodrow Wilson nearly as much as Roosevelt, his initial reaction to the first Democratic president of the twentieth century was generally favorable. He was glad that Wilson had defeated Roosevelt. With the exception of William Jennings Bryan, who, he believed, was unqualified to be secretary of state, he thought the former New Jersey governor had appointed an able cabinet. He also found him to be an especially shrewd politician, He even accepted the progressive legislation that Wilson got through Congress in his first two years, such as establishment of the Federal Reserve System and the Federal Trade Commission—not because he supported these measures (he did not), but because they took some of the wind out of the progressive wing of the Republican Party.[24]

The outbreak of World War I in Europe in 1914 was especially disheartening to Taft because he had always been a strong advocate of international arbitration. In contrast to Roosevelt, he welcomed Wilson's efforts at neutrality and nonintervention. Even after the sinking of the *Lusitania* in May 1915, he hoped that the president would avoid American participation in the war. He took umbrage at those he regarded as warmongers, like Roosevelt and former attorney general George Wickersham, for calling for American involvement in the war. "It seems to me," he commented, "that Wickersham and Roosevelt made asses of themselves and were most boyish in yielding to the passionate expressions they uttered."[25]

The fact that Taft supported Wilson's policy toward the war did not mean that he stopped being a partisan. In 1914, he campaigned diligently for a Republican victory. He continued to confer with Republican officials and other party leaders on such matters as the tariff and banking and currency issues. He even hoped that Wilson might appoint him to the Supreme Court. Although he was not surprised or deeply disappointed that the president did not, he was outraged when Wilson, in January 1916, appointed as associate justice Louis Brandeis. As a legal counselor for *Collier's Magazine*, Brandeis had damaged Taft's reputation by revealing that the president had falsified the date on a report submitted to him. Not only did the former president feel personally insulted by the appointment, but he also regarded Brandeis as a muckracker and even a socialist. "As I think the appointment over, of course I am deeply concerned to have such an insidious devil in the Court," he wrote to Gus Karger, a reporter friend of his.[26]

Taft's anger at Brandeis's appointment only added to the vigor with which he began to attack the administration and the president. He referred to the Federal Reserve Act as a worse law replacing a bad law. The Underwood tariff, which lowered tariffs dramatically, posed a danger to the delicate balance established by the Payne–Aldrich tariff. The Clayton Antitrust Act was unnecessary because the Sherman Antitrust Act already provided enough protection against monopolies. The legislation creating the Federal Trade Commission represented a threat to the business community. Wilson's New Freedom, in fact, looked a lot like Roosevelt's New Nationalism and therefore posed the same threat to sound government. Taft even joined Roosevelt in criticizing Wilson for not preparing the United States adequately for war.[27]

Their common loathing of the president helped ameliorate some of the enmity that existed between Roosevelt and Taft. As Taft commented, their mutual dislike for Wilson was "the chief bond between" them. Yet Taft was glad at least that some of the frigidity in their relationship had been lifted before Roosevelt suddenly died in 1919. To a mutual friend, he wrote, "Had he died in a hostile state of mind toward me, I would have mourned the fact all my life." At Roosevelt's funeral, which Taft attended, he was the last to leave, and he was observed crying profusely at Roosevelt's graveside.[28]

Despite Taft's criticisms of the administration, after the United States entered the war, the former president accepted Wilson's invitation to serve as joint chairman of the National War Labor Relations Board (NWLRB), whose major purpose was to resolve such labor disputes as those having to do with wages and working conditions. It proved a valuable educational experience for him. Visiting the South, he was horrified by the working and living conditions he found in the factories and homes of the workers. Having a well-earned reputation for being hostile to labor, he gained new respect and sympathy for labor's complaints. Among the guidelines he adopted for rulings in more than 1,200 cases that came before the board were the right of labor to organize, an eight-hour working day, health and safety standards, and a living wage for all workers. Labor leaders had not welcomed Taft's appointment to the NWLRB, but the consensus after the agency completed its work was that Taft and the board had been fair-minded and judicious in their decisions and had avoided dozens of strikes and lockouts.[29]

Taft's major concern during the war, however, was promoting the goals of the League to Enforce the Peace (LEP). In response to the outbreak of the conflict a number of prominent Americans began to speak and write about ways to avoid another war. In June 1915, about 120 persons gathered at Independence Hall in Philadelphia, where they established the LEP. Two weeks later, they drafted Taft, who was known for his longtime interest in arbitration treaties, as the league's first president. The LEP's purpose was not to end the world war already under way but to avoid a second world war. According to the league's governing document, disputes between nations that were justiciable (that is, capable of being decided by law) were to be resolved by a judicial tribunal; those that were not were to be submitted to a Council of Conciliation for negotiation. Signatory nations who chose war over the judicial or arbitrary process would be subject to economic or military action by the other members of the league.[30]

This type of conservative internationalism stood in contrast to the program of progressive internationalism, which Wilson came to envision and later set forth in 1918 in his famous Fourteen Points Address. Unlike proponents of progressive internationalism, Taft and other proponents of conservative internationalism did not believe in a natural harmonic relationship among nations. They favored military preparedness over antimilitarism or pacifism. Nor were they thinking in terms of superseding the balance-of-power system and rival armies with a new world order based on the predicates of the Fourteen Points. In fact, most of them were not interested in mediating an end to the ongoing war or bringing about "peace without victory," as the president later advocated. Rather they wanted the allies to win the war.[31]

These differences notwithstanding, proponents of conservative and progressive internationalism shared several goals. They both wanted to avoid future wars. They both believed in respect for international law. Most importantly, they advocated an international league to resolve differences between signatory nations.[32]

The LEP quickly became the nation's most influential pro-league organization, with more than 4,000 branches in forty-seven states. The league's strength became so great that in 1916, President Wilson, who understood the sharp differences between his views and those of the LEP and did not want to be identified with the league's conservative Republican leadership, nevertheless agreed to an invitation by Taft to speak at its first anniversary meeting.[33]

In his speech of 27 May, which he told House might be the "the most important I shall ever be called upon to make," Wilson emphasized the common interest he had with the LEP in establishing an international body to guarantee self-determination, respect for national sovereignty, and peace. At the same time, he tried to hide his differences with the LEP by avowing that "he did not come to the meeting . . . to discuss a program." His speech was greeted with tumultuous applause by the audience. Taft later commented simply that Wilson's appearance indicated "sympathy with our general purposes." For the former president, this was enough to believe he shared a common cause with the president.[34]

The election of 1916, fought over Wilson's slogan of "he kept us out of war," revealed some of the important differences between the LEP and Wilson. Taft and other members of the LEP took the president to task for not having prepared the United States for war.[35] After the United States entered the war and Wilson gave his Fourteen Points Address in January 1918, it became impossible to hide the differences between the LEP's war aims and the president's, one punitive and the other more forgiving; in contrast to the LEP, Wilson intended to welcome

Germany into a new community of nations, which the United States would lead. Yet even after it became clearer to him how much different the president's post-war plans were from his own, Taft supported Wilson's campaign on behalf of a League of Nations.[36]

As president of the LEP, Taft had been thrust into national prominence in a way he had not been since leaving Washington in 1913. Between 1915 and 1917, he traveled extensively on the league's behalf. In 1917, he also signed a contract at a salary of $10,000 a year (the equivalent of about $166,000 in 2009) to publish a weekly column with the Philadelphia *Public Ledger,* which was trying again to become one of the nation's premier newspapers.[37]

Taft's column was quickly syndicated nationally. The ex-president welcomed the opportunity to cut back on his exhausting speaking schedule while reaching a broader audience and receiving a generous compensation. He continued to write for the *Public Ledger,* sometimes several times a week, until 1921, when he resigned after being appointed chief justice of the Supreme Court. Perhaps not coincidentally, his columns competed for readership with Roosevelt's editorials for the Kansas City *Star.*[38]

Along with his service on the NWLRB, his commentary for the *Public Ledger* also led to new business propositions for Taft from such corporations as AT&T, the New York Life Insurance Company, the Metropolitan Life Insurance Company, and leading publishing houses, and his name was prominently mentioned for the presidencies of the University of Cincinnati and Cornell University. However, he turned down all these offers to concentrate his efforts on behalf of the LEP. He also hoped he still might become chief justice of the Supreme Court if a Republican was returned to the White House in 1920.[39]

In supporting Wilson's proposal for a League of Nations, Taft was torn between a rock and a hard place. He continued to distrust Wilson, even referring to him privately as a "ruthless hypocrite . . . who had no conviction that he would not barter at once for voters." Furthermore, Wilson's peace plan, as outlined in his Fourteen Points Address, indicated to Taft just how different Wilson's vision of the postwar peace was from his own even as he found Wilson's proposal for a League of Nations vague and ill-defined.[40]

Yet Taft still regarded the president's view that the postwar peace had to be predicated on an international body capable of ensuring the peace so important that he refused to criticize the president as harshly as Roosevelt or other notables of the LEP. In some cases, he publicly backed Wilson, such as on his decision to rely on conscription for raising an army. "In every other war we have depended on the volunteer system," he wrote in the *Public Ledger.* "In every other war that system has proved to be defective."[41]

During the war, Taft talked with Wilson about going to London as president of the LEP to discuss war aims with the British government. Both times, the president made clear to Taft that he did not want him to upstage his administration by making the trip. All the more wary of the president, Taft nevertheless refused to make the issue a public matter. After the war, he thought Republican senators should have been included in the delegation to Paris, but he did not seem at all piqued that Wilson failed to include him.[42]

The LEP had in fact already adopted a resolution at the war's end, pledging "its hearty support to the President in the establishment of . . . a League of Nations," and while other Republican leaders denounced Wilson's decision even to go to Paris, Taft came to his defense. Nothing in the Constitution, he said, prohibited Wilson from leading the delegation. Indeed, it was his duty to go. "He will learn much of the European situation at first hand," he wrote. "He will have an unusual opportunity to study the possibilities of a league of nations, its practical difficulties and their solution."[43]

When the president returned from Paris in February 1919 after the Europeans approved the league as the first article of the peace treaty, Taft was delighted. Wilson had not only achieved what Taft regarded as the most important requirement for world peace, but he had also produced a covenant that contained the specifics of the international body. It provided for an assembly of nations and a permanent secretariat, provisions for dealing with justiciable questions among the signatory powers, a procedure for arbitration of nonjusticiable questions, and military and economic measures for dealing with nations in violation of their obligations—in short, the very elements Taft and the LEP regarded as essential to an international organization intended to prevent future world wars.[44]

News of the league covenant preceded Wilson's return to the United States. Taft had already set out on a speaking tour on behalf of the league. On 4 March, he appeared with the president at the Metropolitan Opera House in New York. "We are here tonight in sight of a league of peace," he told his audience. "Such a war as the last is a hideous blot on our Christian civilization. . . . If Christian nations cannot now be brought into a united effort to suppress a recurrence of such a contest it will be a shame to modern society."[45]

Wilson failed, of course, either to achieve the new world order he had envisioned after he returned to Europe in mid-March to work out the details of the peace treaty, signed at Versailles on 28 June 1919, or to get the Senate to ratify the agreement after he returned to the United States. Even many progressive internationalists deserted the president, both because the treaty violated Wilson's commitment to "peace without victory" and because he refused to release critics of the war jailed under the notorious Espionage and Sedition Acts of 1917 and 1918.[46]

Throughout the fight over the league, however, Taft remained among its most vociferous supporters. Even before Wilson returned to Paris, he helped persuade him to make changes in the covenant in response to Republican critics in the Senate. Among the changes were provisions that any member of the league could withdraw from the body after two years' notice, that domestic matters, including tariffs and immigration, were beyond the league's purview, and that the league could do nothing to endanger the Monroe Doctrine. Once these amendments were approved, he urged the senators who opposed the agreement to reconsider their position.[47]

Much to Taft's annoyance, when Wilson returned home with the final peace agreement, the president refused to agree to other amendments insisted upon by the Senate. Instead, he appealed directly to the public on behalf of the league. In September, he suffered a stroke in Pueblo, Colorado, while on a nationwide speaking tour. With Wilson incapacitated, Taft became the most ardent proponent of the league. Having always had a tenuous relationship with the president, however, he now separated his own efforts from those of the administration.

The most contentious issue in the Senate remained Article X of the league covenant, which opponents of the organization claimed mandated the United States to enter into conflicts at the behest of the league council without prior congressional approval. Like other proponents of the league, Taft denied this assertion. Nevertheless, he agreed with reservations intended to clarify this point. When the president rejected any further efforts at compromise and instructed Democrats to oppose any treaty containing additional reservations, Taft broke with him, even referring to him as "that mulish enigma, that mountain of egotism and selfishness." Just before the Senate rejected the treaty for a final time in March 1920, he made clear that failure to win Senate approval of the agreement would rest entirely with the president. "Mr. Wilson had the matter in his own hands," he wrote on 6 March, "and, in his obstinate pride of opinion and partisan unwillingness to give his political opponents the small triumph of having their form of words in the Treaty rather than his, he destroyed a great world cause."[48]

Although Taft did not much care for the Republican nominee for president in 1920, Warren Harding of Ohio, whom he correctly regarded as simpleminded and the product of political cronyism, he endorsed his nomination over that of General Leonard Wood, the choice of the Roosevelt wing of the party, who had ridiculed the proposed League of Nations. The former president made the mistake of believing that Harding would be a stronger champion of a league. Knowing better, other advocates of an international peace body believed that Taft had abandoned his sacred cause.[49]

After Harding's election, however, Taft turned his interests toward securing his dream of becoming chief justice of the Supreme Court. He had his first meeting with the president-elect at his home in Marion, Ohio, on 24 December. He was pleasantly surprised when Harding told him that he wanted to appoint him to the Supreme Court as soon as possible. Even though he was delighted that his lifelong dream might be at hand, however, he told Harding that having appointed three members of the present bench and having protested against Brandeis's appointment, "he could not accept any place, but the chief justiceship."[50]

Unfortunately for the former president, the sitting chief justice, Edward D. White of Louisiana, while in frail health, was reluctant to retire from the bench. Even after he suddenly died in office on 19 March 1921, opposition developed to Taft's appointment. Although he was only sixty-three years old and had appointed a number of men over sixty to the bench, he had once remarked that no one over that age should be appointed to the courts, and his statement was held against him. Because Taft had told the president that he would not accept appointment to the Supreme Court as an associate justice, Harding had also promised his first nomination to the Court to Senator George Sutherland of Utah. Having made this promise, he came under considerable pressure to keep it. Taft lost hope as the president delayed making the nomination. After much lobbying on Taft's behalf, however, the president announced on 30 June that he was naming the former president to be the Court's new chief justice.[51]

Jubilant at the appointment, which sailed through the Senate on 21 June with only four dissenting votes, Taft began the final and happiest part of his long public career. "The truth is that in my present life I don't remember that I ever was president," he later wrote. Immediately upon learning that his appointment had been confirmed by the Senate, he resigned all his other public responsibilities, including writing for the Philadelphia *Public Ledger* and serving as president of the League to Enforce Peace and as Kent Professor of Law at Yale. Even as chief justice, however, he accepted election to the Yale Corporation and spoke at Yale on a regular basis. He also left a good part of his large library to the university. Many of his law clerks were graduates of the Yale Law School.[52]

As chief justice, Taft proved to be an extremely effective administrator. He streamlined and made more efficient the entire federal judicial system. He also mended fences with Justice Brandeis and played a crucial role in mediating differences between the more conservative justices he had appointed and the more liberal justices Wilson had named to the Court.

The former president long believed in the need for judicial reform. In campaign speeches, special messages to Congress, law review articles, and newspaper editorials, he hammered away on the need to make the justice system more just. "Delays and Defects in the Enforcement of Law," "Inequalities in the Administration of Justice," and "Needed Reforms in the Federal Courts" were just some of the subjects on which he wrote and spoke in the thirty-five years before he became the highest jurist in the land.[53]

The major problem facing the Supreme Court after the war, in Taft's view, was that it was falling increasingly behind in hearing cases. By tradition, all manner of cases could be appealed to the Court. As a result, important cases were being delayed for years. Believing in William Gladstone's maxim, "justice delayed is justice denied," Taft wanted to cut back the Court's caseload to only those cases involving issues of constitutional import. The war mobilization effort, the seizure of enemy property during the war, and passage of the Sixteenth Amendment in 1913 allowing for a federal income tax and the Eighteenth Amendment in 1919 ushering in the era of Prohibition had already led to a flood of new cases. Unless the procedure for hearing cases was reformed, the entire justice system would come to a standstill.[54]

First, Taft argued, appeals to the Supreme Court should "generally be limited

Photo of Taft as chief justice of the U.S. Supreme Court. Date of photo and photographer unknown. What is striking is how content Taft appears in the photo. Although still overweight, the former president had lost considerable weight since being president. Both as president and chief justice, Taft chose not to offer himself for frequent photo or interview opportunities. (Courtesy of Library of Congress, Prints and Photographs Division.)

to those cases which are typical and which give an opportunity to the Court to cover the whole field of the law the subject involved." Second, codes of procedure should be "simple and effective." Third, the chief justice or a council of justices appointed by him should distribute each year the nation's judicial business among the various judicial districts in order to assure that the caseload was handled as expeditiously and equitably as possible. Fourth, two district judges at large should be added to each of the nation's nine circuits and assigned to any district in the circuit where needed. Fifth, there should be an annual conference of the senior judges in each of the circuits to assign judges and present an annual report of the circuit's business in order to make them more accountable to an executive body (the chief justice or the council of justices).[55]

In seeking to reform the Court, Taft recognized the need of the judiciary to respond to changing times. "Frequently," he wrote, "new conditions arise which those who were responsible for the written law could not have had in view, and to which existing common law principles have never before been applied, and it becomes necessary for the Court to make new applications of both." This was "not the exercise of legislative power as that phrase is used. It is the exercise of a sound judicial discretion in supplementing the provisions of constitutions and laws and custom."[56]

As a conservative, however, the sanctity of private property remained foundational to Taft's republican principles; judicial reform was a way to respond to both a real need and a major cause of popular unrest while reducing the threat to private property. Unlike Roosevelt, he would make the judiciary—and not the presidency—the ultimate arbiter for resolving disputes between political democracy and property rights His jurisprudence would elevate the protection of private property to the same level as the protection of life, liberty, and the pursuit of happiness. It would also make the judicial process the guarantor of social stability.[57]

As soon as Taft put on his robes of office, he launched a vigorous campaign to achieve his reforms, He sought the support of his fellow justices. He met with Justice Department officials. He went on the lecture circuit. He even lobbied the halls and offices of Congress and testified before the House and Senate judiciary committees—something unprecedented in the history of the Supreme Court. On Capitol Hill, he met considerable opposition from progressive legislators who did not trust Taft, felt he was trying a power grab at their expense, and regarded the courts as a barrier to reform. They found particularly objectionable the concept of judges at large, which ran contrary to the tradition of judicial localism and had the potential of increasing Taft's power enormously. They also questioned the wisdom of authorizing conferences to assign judges. One senator remarked that it was "not a judicial power and does not in the remotest manner concern the exercise of the Supreme Court."[58]

Making matters even more difficult for Taft was the fact that the judiciary committee was headed by the progressive George Norris of Nebraska, who even opposed life terms for jurists. Other members of the committee were also progressives or simply had no interest in reform. "The wretched personnel of the

Judiciary Committee," Taft remarked in 1925, had not happened by accident. The men "least fitted for the Judiciary Committee" had sought to be on it because they could not improve "their reputation as lawyers in any other way."[59]

Nevertheless, the need for reform was so pressing and Taft's lobbying efforts so effective that Congress passed the Judiciary Act of 13 February 1925, a highly technical measure, the most important provisions of which limited the Supreme Court's obligatory jurisdiction while extending its discretionary review. The chief justice hoped this legislation would allow him to reroute many cases on appeal to the circuit courts and be more selective in the cases the Supreme Court decided to review. The chief justice also secured from a fiscally conservative Congress twenty-four new federal judgeships and an appropriation to purchase the land to build the current Supreme Court building, the Court's first permanent home.[60]

Taft did not get everything he wanted. Despite his efforts, he failed, for example, to get a uniform rules-of-procedure revision for the federal courts. As the first chief justice to assume a direct role in promoting and administering judicial reform, however, Taft brought the Supreme Court and much of the rest of the federal judicial system into its modern era. Hardly a Progressive himself, he had appropriated the progressive mantra of efficiency in government as the means of resolving many of the problems of the modern state.[61]

Taft's record as a jurist was less impressive, especially during his last years on the bench. Faced with a badly divided Court and having an aversion to dissent, Taft tried hard to bring the warring factions together. Although he differed greatly with Justice Holmes on his legal and social views, he became close friends with the justice. His relationship with Brandeis remained more distant, but the ex-president was impressed by Brandeis's resplendent mind and great erudition, and he went out of his way to let bygones be bygones. The two justices were able at times even to persuade the other to change his opinion on cases. At one point, the chief justice confided to his daughter, "I have come to like Brandeis very much indeed." His regular conferences to discuss cases and to assign the writing of opinions were characterized by civility and harmony. The rates of dissent in the early Taft Court were dramatically lower than those in the waning days of his predecessor.[62]

As a jurist as well as an administrator and lobbyist, Taft was a workaholic. In his ten years as chief justice, he wrote 249 opinions of the Court and seventeen dissents, or almost 20 percent of the Court's opinions during his tenure. He often took cases that the other justices did not want. None of his decisions were memorable. Reflecting on his tenure as chief justice on the eve of his retirement, *Time* Magazine observed, "Outstanding decisions: none." Also commenting on Taft's impact on jurisprudence, one recent scholar has written: "Taft has drifted into almost total professional eclipse . . . no more known to the average lawyer or law student than are Chief Justices White, Fuller, or Waite." Leading law school casebooks and their counterparts in political science carry few if any of his decisions.[63]

In his early years on the Court, the new chief justice showed some flexibility in his decisions with respect to unions and picketing. In the so-called Tri-City case (1921), for example, Taft found that while the Tri-City Central Trades Council had illegally used intimidation during a strike against American Steel Foundries to keep nonunion workers from going through the picket line, nevertheless, unions "may use all lawful propaganda to enlarge their membership and especially among those whose labor at lower wages will injure their whole guild." It was "impossible," he concluded, "to hold such persuasion and propaganda without more, to be without excuse and malicious." Reflecting his conservative judicial philosophy, however, in almost all cases involving the protection of property rights or alleged congressional appropriation of state rights, he sided with property owners and the states and was decidedly antiunion.[64]

Taft also generally came down on the side of strong executive power and a broad interpretation of the commerce clause. In *Myers v. United States* (1926), which he considered to be his proudest, he put to bed forever the Tenure Act of 1867, limiting the power of the president to remove immediate subordinates. Over the dissents of Brandeis and Holmes, he extended the presidential removal power to include quasi-judicial and quasi-legislative appointments, such as postmasters. His opinion stood until the New Deal.[65]

Especially during the Harding administration, Taft communicated with the White House, usually through Attorney General Harry Daugherty, in an effort to assure that the president, who filled three additional vacancies to the Court before he died suddenly of a stroke on 2 August 1923, appointed conservatives ready to repel assaults on the Constitution. He was enthusiastic about two of the appointments, George Sutherland and Pierce Butler, and less enamored with the third, Edward T. Sanford. "Our views are very much alike," he told the newly appointed Justice Sutherland," and it is important that they prevail." For that reason, he lobbied hard against other possible nominees, like New York court of appeals judge Benjamin Cardozo. "Cardozo is a Jew and a Democrat," he commented to Harding. "I don't think he would always side with Brandeis but he is what they call a progressive judge."[66]

In contrast to his influence with Harding, Taft and Calvin Coolidge were not close. The chief justice became disturbed at the president for making judicial appointments on the basis of politics and ignoring his advice on nonjudicial appointments. Taft also became increasingly disappointed with Hoover. "My experience with Hoover makes me think that he is a good deal of a dreamer in respect to matters of which he knows nothing, like the judicial machinery of government," he remarked at one point.[67]

In other ways as well, Taft grew more frustrated during his last years as chief justice. His differences with Brandeis and Holmes became more pronounced, and the Court became more divided. When Taft complained to Holmes about his dissents, Holmes responded that he had no choice but to dissent from bad legal opinions. For his part, Taft came to believe that Holmes's reading of the Constitution was flawed by a questionable ethical relativity and a lack of knowledge about how the government operated. He also thought that Holmes allowed himself to be influenced too much by Brandeis. As for Brandeis, Taft had a change of heart once more. Responding to Brandeis's dissent in an important case in 1926, the chief justice put him in that "class of people that have no loyalty to the Court and sacrifice almost everything to the gratification of their own publicity." In 1925, Attorney General Harlan Stone joined the Court. His liberal leanings and frequent dissents led Taft to view him with extreme distaste.[68]

Until around 1927, Taft nevertheless continued to enjoy life immensely. His wife, Nellie, socialized a great deal, took trips by herself, and sometimes got into heated arguments with the former president over such issues as Prohibition. However, having been first lady, she was content to settle into the role of the loving wife of a former president, Yale professor, and now chief justice. Taft's eldest son, Robert, graduated first in his class from Harvard Law School and began what was to be a highly successful political career by being elected to the Ohio House of Representatives. Taft's younger son, Charles, practiced law in Cincinnati and became active in local politics. His daughter, Helen, earned a Ph.D. from Yale and became dean of Bryn Mawr College. The chief justice also maintained a summer home at Murray Bay in Quebec and traveled extensively, including a trip to England where he received three honorary degrees.[69]

Money was not a problem for the former president. By the time of his death in 1930, he managed to accumulate about $450,000 (the equivalent of about $5.8 million in 2009), and at Nellie's insistence, he agreed to accept an annual pension of $10,000 that Andrew Carnegie left him in his will. Together with his other investments, this was enough to assure his family a comfortable life.[70]

Despite two minor heart attacks in 1924 and a tendency to doze after a meal or when the weather was hot, Taft's health seemed reasonably good for someone his age. Until he became chief justice, he remained addicted to golf and played as much as possible. He also enjoyed horseback riding and took to walking to work, often with his neighbor, Justice Holmes. For someone of his great weight, he was a surprisingly good dancer. Although he gave up golfing and horses after he joined the Supreme Court, he continued to walk and exercise as much as possible. He also watched his diet and weight carefully. As a result, he shed over eighty pounds after leaving the White House; a year before his death, he weighed 244 pounds.[71]

As he approached seventy, the chief justice's health began to fail. He did not smoke or drink, but he was still overweight, and this took its toll on him. He had to have an elevator installed in his home because it had become difficult for him to climb stairs. His memory began to fail. In the first radio broadcast of a presidential inauguration in 1929, he forgot some of his lines and had to improvise while administering the oath of office to incoming President Hoover. After attending the funeral of his brother, Charles, in December 1929, he returned home so weak that he had to be hospitalized. He never fully recovered. His son Robert returned to Washington in February 1930 to announce his father's retirement from the Supreme Court. Suffering from heart disease, high blood pressure, a bladder problem, and likely renal failure and dementia, he was unable in his last days of life to recognize visitors, and he often hallucinated.[72]

On 8 March 1930, Taft died in his sleep at the age of seventy-seven after lingering for more than a month. His body lay in state at the U.S. Capitol Building. After simple services, he was laid to rest at Arlington National Cemetery, the first president to be accorded that honor and only one of two presidents (the other being John F. Kennedy) to be buried at Arlington. His funeral service was also the first presidential funeral to be broadcast to the nation by radio.

Taft had been one of that phalanx of former presidents going back at least to John Quincy Adams and including such other unexceptional presidents as Millard Fillmore, Ulysses Grant, and Rutherford B. Hayes who distinguished themselves more after they left the White House than while they served as president. In Taft's case, this was not a surprise because he had never wanted to be president.

The significance of Taft's career after he left the White House transcends his accomplishments as a former president. It makes clear once more the difficulty of trying to define in simple terms a period as complex as the Progressive era. It also underscores the fact that the era did not abruptly end in 1920 with the election of Warren Harding. Notwithstanding Taft's political and judicial conservatism, he was not a throwback to an earlier age. Rather, he was as much a product of his time as Theodore Roosevelt, except at a different end of the political spectrum. Although not a social reformer in the manner of Roosevelt, he was very much an advocate of modernization. He also believed in the gospel of efficiency that helped define the progressive movement. As a result, he advanced the most ambitious reform program in the annals of the judiciary. Even his views on the inherent powers of the presidency were extraordinarily broad for someone commonly viewed as a political conservative.[73]

As for his judicial beliefs, the former president was too much of a constitutionalist to be regarded as a pragmatist. He was, however, not a formalist who believed the law should be decided independent of its political and social context. He was instead a minimalist who was skeptical of court-led efforts at social change. He was not against social change. On the contrary, one reason he feared such proposals as the recall was because he believed they could be manipulated in a way that allowed malcontents to maintain the status quo and/or have the political process be unresponsive to the legitimate concerns of minorities and outsiders. He regarded the normal legislative process as the way that large and difficult policy questions should be decided. When that did not happen, he was prepared to have the courts become a superlegislature, deciding matters in a manner that never got too far ahead or behind public sentiment.[74]

Taft was reluctant also to deal in abstractions and was not all that concerned with consistency. Of the justices on the Court with whom he served, the one he disliked the most was Justice James McReynolds, who was anti-Semitic and whose conservatism he found too extreme. He wanted solid conservatives on the

Court, but not fanatics either of the political right or the left. "I feel as if we ought not to have too many men on the Court who are as reactionary on the subject of the Constitution as McReynolds," he told Elihu Root, "and that we need men who are liberal but who still believe that the cornerstone of our civilization is in the proper maintenance of the guarantees of the Fourteenth Amendment and the Fifth Amendment." Change, in other words, should evolve consistent with the protections of the Constitution and not simply be responsive to the whims of the moment or the oratory of demagogues.[75]

In terms of foreign policy, the former president was even something of a visionary, although not one in the Wilsonian sense of seeking to impose a new world order after World War I that was predicated on American liberal values. Rather, he accepted the existing system of nation-states and sought to avoid future wars through a League of Nations with the machinery necessary to adjudicate or arbitrate differences among its members. He also left open the threat of a collective military response to renegade nations unwilling to settle their disputes in a manner acceptable to the international body. Although he failed in his efforts to get the United States to accept membership in the League of Nations, Washington did cooperate with league members in collective efforts during the 1920s not only to enforce peace, but also to avoid the causes of war through disarmament agreements and even the outlawing of war as an instrument for settling disputes.[76]

In sum, then, Taft was a conservative who believed in free markets and the protection of private property. He worried about the danger of unchecked democracy to civic order. He placed his trust instead in an educated governing class with the wisdom to adjust old prescriptions to new conditions in a gradual and cautious manner. That was what attracted him to the judiciary and ultimately to the Supreme Court. Like Wilson, he also believed that World War I represented the failure of an old order, and he sought a new way to ensure peace through an international organization. Like the founding fathers, he was a republican. Like Theodore Roosevelt, he sought to deal with the changing circumstances of a nation in transition, but with a style and approach different from that of his former friend.

II

Few presidents have had a more lasting impact on American domestic and foreign policy than Wilson. In terms of domestic policy, his administration enacted some of the most lasting reform legislation in the nation's history, from tariff, banking, and antitrust reform to child labor laws and the eight-hour working day for railroad workers. For better or worse, his concept of a new world order predicated on American ideals has been foundational for much of the nation's foreign policy into the twenty-first century.

The common opinion among historians is that the substantive part of Wilson's presidency and public life came to an abrupt end after a massive stroke on 2 October 1919, which nearly killed him and left him paralyzed on his left side for the rest of his life. Historians even debate the nature of Wilson's mental faculties and the degree of control that his wife, Edith Bolling Wilson, had over running the administration after his stroke. Some scholars maintain that Mrs. Wilson, and not the president, was in charge of running the Oval Office. Others unwilling to go that far concede that she played a crucial role in deciding what and whom the president saw.

According to this view, Wilson's post-presidency amounted to little more than a short and tragic end to a career full of accomplishment, not only as the nation's twenty-eighth president, but also as a renowned academic, president of Princeton University, and governor of New Jersey. This assessment is based on considerable evidence. Wilson's health has probably been studied by laymen and physicians more than any other president. From this literature, it seems fairly clear that beginning in 1896, Wilson suffered strokelike incidents that affected him physically, in one instance in 1906 leaving him nearly blind in his left eye, and that they were often followed by changes in behavior, including in some cases bursts of energy and whimsical fantasies, and in other cases moods of depression and even anger.[77]

At the same time, Wilson's retirement was more than a short interlude between his presidency and his death. As a former president, he tried, with considerable success, to promote his vision for a new world order. He kept up with domestic and world affairs. He remained a force in Democratic politics. Most importantly, he stayed enough of a public person so that by the time of his death, he had become to millions of Americans a venerated figure with an enduring legacy.

There can be no question that Wilson's massive stroke on 2 October left him a shell of the man he had been. His long face drooped on the left side, his formerly tight, thin lips often sagged with drool on them, and his once thrusting jaw now hung down. Sight from his blue-gray eyes, which had never been good, deteriorated even more, and one of his eyes twitched noticeably. Although he gradually regained some use of his legs and was able to walk slowly with the help of a cane, he could not climb stairs, and his five-foot, eleven-inch frame seemed wasted. Most of the time he was confined to a bed or a wheelchair, blankets pulled high over his body, his cap turned downward when he was outside so one could barely make out his features. Emotionally, Wilson seemed a crushed man as well. The president had always had a complex personality. Affectionate and craving love privately, he had watched his first wife of twenty-nine years, Ellen Louise Axson, die of Bright's disease in the White House in 1914 at the age of fifty-four. He was so distressed at his wife's death that he told his closest adviser, Colonel Edward House of Texas, that he hoped to be assassinated. A little over a year later, however, he married again. Edith Bolling was a forty-three-year-old widow and successful businesswomen. Cheery and chipper now, the president was seen by a Secret Service man after his honeymoon, clicking his heels while gushing out the popular lyric, "Oh you beautiful doll, you great big beautiful doll." By his first wife, he also had three daughters, who, while he was at Princeton, often played with Grover Cleveland's children. He adored both his wives and was a loving father with a wry sense of humor who enjoyed clowning with his children and making those around him laugh with his droll limericks:

> There was a young monk of Siberia
> Whose existence grew drearier and drearier
> Till he burst from his cell with a hell of a yell
> And eloped with the Mother Superior.[78]

At the same time, Wilson had an unpleasant side. He was often arrogant, cold, and self-righteous. A devout Presbyterian whose father had been a minister and professor of theology, he believed according to Calvinist theology that he was one of God's elected who had a mission to carry out God's work in the world. Consequently, he tended to have a Manichean worldview. Because of his own self-confidence and even smugness, he could also be rigid, distant, and distrustful of others. Even before his stroke, while he was in Paris working to exhaustion on the covenant for the League of Nations and the peace treaty, this side of Wilson's personality was clearly evident. It stood out even more after his stroke.[79]

For the first week or so after the stroke, doctors summoned to Wilson's bedside were not certain he would survive. After it became clear he would live, he was still so totally disabled that he was unable to carry out even routine executive business. Furthermore, the extent of his illness was shrouded in deception and falsehoods, including reports from his personal physician, Dr. Cary Grayson, that his condition was improving daily. The few persons who were allowed to see him as he slowly recovered were shocked by the physical deterioration and the helplessness of an individual who, like Theodore Roosevelt, had been a charismatic figure able to arouse a crowd by his rare eloquence and by his clear tenor voice, which could be heard at the farthest reaches of large crowds. Now his speech was halting and feeble, and he often lost his thought in midsentence.[80]

As he recovered, the president started to attend to some of the nation's business, dictating to Edith replies to urgent requests and meeting with a few persons that Edith allowed to visit him in his bedroom. Among them were Attorney General A. Mitchell Palmer, the first member of the cabinet to confer with him, and Senate minority leader Gilbert Hitchcock of Nebraska, who was shocked by the thin white beard Wilson had grown.[81]

Still, most of the nation's business went unheeded, including another vote on the League of Nations, which the Senate took up again after its defeat in November. Newspapers reported that the president remained in grave condition, and there were even wild rumors that he was insane. In December, Republican senator Albert Fall of New Mexico, who on the pretext of needing to consult with him on the kidnapping in Mexico of an American consular agent, was sent by Wilson's bitterest enemy in the Senate, Henry Cabot Lodge, to check on the state of his health. Understanding the real reason for Fall's visit, Edith and Dr. Grayson propped up the president with pillows on the large bed that had been Abraham Lincoln's and made it look like Wilson had been reading a report on the kidnapping incident. Fortunately, the president was able also to carry on a conversation with Fall. He even displayed his well-known wit, responding to Fall's comment that he and his colleagues had been praying for him by remarking, "Which way, Senator?" As a result, Fall had no choice other than to inform reporters that the president was making a good recovery.[82]

Two persons who were not allowed to see the president were Colonel Edward House and Secretary of State Robert Lansing. Once Wilson's closest adviser, House had been ostracized by the president for making concessions on the peace treaty with Germany during Wilson's brief return to the United States from Paris after he had secured the allies' agreement on a covenant for the League of Nations—this despite the fact that Wilson had instructed House to carry on negotiations in his absence. Similarly, Lansing had begun to fall out with the president after the secretary of state advised against him going to Paris and differed with him over the importance of a League of Nations to the peace treaty.

After Grayson issued a bulletin on the night of Wilson's stroke stating that the president was a very sick man but without disclosing the nature of his ailment, Lansing called a meeting of the cabinet in his capacity as its highest-ranking member. According to Lansing, Grayson "gave a very encouraging report on the President's condition, which, he said, showed decided improvement and seemed to indicate speedy recovery."[83] Over the next four months, Lansing held regular cabinet meetings. Wilson knew of them, but not until February did he ask for Lansing's resignation, citing as his reason his holding of cabinet meetings without his permission. To replace Lansing, Wilson appointed Bainbridge Colby, a New York lawyer working on the shipping board. Even Colby was astonished that the president asked for someone like him, who lacked any foreign policy expertise, to serve as secretary of state.

It is hard to disassociate Wilson's behavior in the last months of his administration from the lingering effects of his stroke and from the role of his wife, Edith. Wilson's break with Lansing, with whom he had serious differences even before his stroke, seems explicable. However, for Wilson to pretend in February that he only recently discovered that the secretary of state was conducting cabinet meetings without his permission, when he knew differently, did not make much sense. "The President's irritation and jealousy, which are so manifest in his letters, makes me wonder as to whether he is mentally entirely normal," Lansing wrote in a memorandum to himself the following week. "His complaints are so childish and his tone so peevish that it is hard to believe that his malady has not affected his mind."[84]

At least that is what much of the public thought. The president had supposedly been on top of things despite his illness; this now seemed a lie. Wilson should have given policy differences as his reason for asking for Lansing's resignation. The president's secretary, Joseph Tumulty, and the president's wife tried to persuade him to base his request on these grounds. He rejected their advice, and the response was public recoil. "When the announcement of Lansing's resignation was made, the flood-gates of fury broke about the president," Tumulty later wrote. Lansing could not believe what had happened. "If I did not believe in miracles before," he commented, "I certainly would after this, for this seems like direct intervention of Divine Providence."[85]

Two days later, Dr. Dean Bevan, an ex-president of the American Medical Association and a world-renowned surgeon, gave out a statement to the press calling for the president's resignation. Earlier, Dr. Hugh Young, who had been called to the White House after Wilson's stroke, issued for the first time a frank report describing Wilson's condition. Although Young commented that the president was improving satisfactorily, Bevan was asked to respond to his diagnosis. His reply was as damaging to the president as it could be. "A patient who is suffering as the President is, from diseased arteries of his brain, and where the disease had progressed to such a point as to produce paralysis of one side of the body, should under no circumstances be permitted to resume the work of such a strenuous position as that of President of the United States," Bevan stated.[86]

Other physicians who attended Wilson made public statements of their own declaring that Wilson's mind was still sharp and that he was able to complete his term. They had to fend off reports that the president had suffered a serious relapse. Evidence seemed to mount, furthermore, that the president was not functioning normally. For one thing, he rejected all efforts by leading Senate Democrats, including the minority leader, Hitchcock, to save the League of Nations by agreeing to some of the reservations that Lodge insisted had to be included for the league and peace agreement to be approved by the Senate. Tumulty warned that the people were tired of endless Senate debate. Nevertheless, Wilson demanded that loyal Democrats vote against the peace agreement in its present form. When a final vote was taken on the pact on 19 March, enough Democrats ignored the president to win a majority for the treaty. They still fell seven votes short of the two-thirds vote necessary for approval.[87]

Even Wilson's closest adviser for most of his administration, Colonel Edward House, began to have serious reservations about Wilson's mental health. After the Paris peace negotiations, Wilson refused to see the colonel despite numerous attempts by House to get an appointment with him. Because of House's efforts to prevent Wilson from marrying Edith with an election less than a year away, Edith had never cared much for the colonel. Edith's dislike of House and his concessions at Paris while Wilson was in the United States might have been reason enough for Wilson to have rejected his overtures. Still, for the president to have turned so sharply against a person with whom he had been so close and not even extend a hand of forgiveness to him after he left the White House remains difficult to fathom.[88]

Much the same can be said about Joseph Tumulty, who had been Wilson's devoted secretary since he had been governor of New Jersey and had conspired with Dr. Grayson and Edith to camouflage the nature and seriousness of the president's illness. Despite his loyalty to the president, he was not allowed to see him until November. Although Tumulty was able to maintain his position until Wilson left office, he also ceased to be part of the White House inner circle. Edith distrusted him. His repeated memos and requests to the president were ignored, and he was to see the former president only once after he retired.[89]

Although Edith unquestionably played a crucial role in deciding whom and what the president saw, it is difficult to believe that she alone was responsible for the way in which Lansing, Tumulty, and House were treated after Wilson's stroke. Wilson's aberrant behavior was almost certainly due to a change in the president's personality. Whether this was the result of actual brain damage resulting from his stroke or simply due to the fatigue and depression that occur with such a serious illness is impossible to say. That there was a relationship between the stroke and his changed personality, however, seems beyond doubt. Most likely it was organic.[90]

Although the last months of Wilson's administration had its happier moments, they were mostly the playing out of a tragedy. The president's walking continued to improve. His stamina increased, and he was able to talk and write with coherence. He enjoyed the silent movies. Each afternoon, he would have a local theater owner come to the White House and show the latest Hollywood film. Problems developed when Hollywood's production could not keep up with the president's consumption. Other pleasures included daily rides into the countryside and the visits of his grown daughters, who were now spread out as far as California. One of his daughters, Eleanor (Nellie), had married his former treasury secretary, William McAdoo, a widower with seven children. They also had two children of their own. McAdoo was considered the leading candidate for the Democratic presidential nomination in 1920.

Wilson also seriously considered running for a third term as president. Although he was in no condition to campaign for the nomination, his intent was for the convention to deadlock. After many ballots with no winner in sight, he meant for the delegates to suspend the rules and nominate him by acclamation. Having won the nomination and then the election, he would achieve his ambition of getting the United States to enter the League of Nations. In June, Wilson granted an interview to the New York *World* that was widely interpreted to mean the president wanted the nomination. McAdoo said he would take his name out of contention if Wilson decided to run. The *Wall Street Journal* made Wilson the leading contender for the nomination.[91]

It was all whimsy and fantasy, of course, and symptomatic of the lingering effects of his stroke. Cabinet members and Democratic officials tried to talk the president out of running. When they failed, Grayson and Tumulty, who feared a campaign would kill the president, conspired with party leaders to make certain that Wilson's name was not brought before the convention. Although a deadlock ensued between McAdoo and Attorney General Palmer, after Wilson refused to endorse his son-in-law, the delegates nominated, on the forty-fourth ballot, Governor James Cox of Ohio as the Democratic candidate for president.

Wilson was dejected that his name had not even been put into nomination. The fact that both his son-in-law and his attorney general had also been denied the nomination was widely regarded as a rebuff of the president. This only added to his depression, as did Warren Harding's election in November. Most Democratic leaders realized that Americans, having endured the fight over the League of Nations, postwar race riots, strikes involving four million workers, and a red scare, were tired of Wilson and his administration and ready for a change. The president had remained convinced, however, that the country would never reject him and his call for American membership in a League of Nations, much less elect a Republican who ran on a promise of a return to normalcy and who, he thought, lacked the intelligence to be president. He took Harding's landslide victory personally and hard. Rather than being vindicated, he had been repudiated.[92]

Although Wilson won the Nobel Peace Prize in December, the president remained depressed throughout the remainder of his administration. His health improved, but he knew that he was still not a well man and had to rely on others for assistance. Walking fatigued him, and he still could not climb stairs. His speech remained feeble. His left arm hung down, functionless. He continued to lose his train of thought and had bouts of amnesia. Most important, he watched helplessly as his aspirations for a new world order and American participation in a League of Nations disappeared slowly as if into quicksand.[93]

As Wilson's administration drew near its end, he and Edith began to think about where to live after the White House. One problem was resources. Together, they had accumulated $250,000 (the equivalent of about $2.7 million in 2009). Wilson also received another $50,000 for winning the Nobel Prize. Edith was also independently wealthy from her career as a businesswomen. However, the president thought it improper for a woman to pay for a family home.[94]

The difficulty was that Wilson had grown accustomed to living in a succession of mansions, and Edith had also lived well before marrying the president. The former president had to have a place to house his large library of about 8,000 volumes. Furthermore, the Wilsons wanted the cultural opportunities of urban life. They considered a number of cities, including New York, Boston, and Baltimore, before settling on Washington, D.C. Edith intended to be her own housekeeper, but the former president needed a nurse to attend to his medical needs and an aide to assist him with his personal correspondence, especially because his eyesight continued to deteriorate.[95]

Despite his resources, in other words, Wilson was stretched to find a home that would suit him. He looked at building sites along the Potomac River but decided he could not afford them. Edith, meanwhile, searched in northwest Washington near Rock Creek, in the exclusive Kalorama area, where the city met the country. She settled on a four-story Georgian Revival townhouse on S Street

Northwest designed by a sought-after Washington architect, Waddy Wood. Although the cost of the house, $150,000, was high, Wilson paid for it by combining the $50,000 from his Nobel Prize with money raised and donated by friends. One of these friends, the financier Bernard Baruch, who had headed the War Industries Board during the war, also bought the adjacent lot to prevent a house from being built on it. Beyond the cost of their new home, the Wilsons had to move walls and build shelves to accommodate Wilson's library. They also had to install an elevator for the former president, a side entrance into which he could slip into his car, and a garage for the car, the Pierce-Arrow from the White House that friends had also purchased for him. The four-story redbrick-and-limestone home was spacious and had all the modern conveniences, including an elaborate butler's pantry supplied with hot and cold running water, a hallway of black and white marble, a large billiard room, servants' quarters, a small solarium separating the library from the living room, an office, five bedrooms, and a terrace garden bright with tulips. Following Scottish tradition, Wilson presented Edith with a piece of sod from the garden and the key to the house when they first moved into it.[96]

"Dramatic and touchingly pathetic" is the way one reporter described Wilson's last day as president. Reflecting his well-known stubborn streak, the president was determined to participate in Harding's inauguration. At the last moment, he decided to forgo the actual ceremonies because of fatigue and the stairs involved in reaching the eastern portico of the Capitol where the oath of office was to be administered. Instead, he rode in an automobile with Harding from the White House to the Capitol and remained in the president's room in the Senate wing of the Capitol, where he greeted well-wishers. "The human side of Mr. Wilson was revealed," the same reporter remarked, "when, after Mr. Harding and Mr. Coolidge [the vice president–elect] had made their farewell calls upon him, while voicing his regret that he did not feel able to witness the swearing in of Mr. Harding, he said to Senator Knox, 'Well, the Senate threw me down before, and I don't want to fall down myself now.'"[97]

Five minutes before noon, when Harding was to take the oath, Wilson left his room in the Senate wing and was helped to his waiting automobile. With only a small escort, he was taken to his new home. Thousands of well-wishers assembled in front of the house during the day and tendered a series of ovations to the now former president as they tried unsuccessfully to get Wilson to make a speech. A group of women sang "Onward Christian Soldiers." Although Wilson came to the window several times to wave to the crowd outside, he remained inside, where he hosted former cabinet members, members of Congress, and other Democratic leaders.[98]

Wilson was moved to tears by the events of the day. Before the inauguration, Harding had been extremely courteous to the president, expressing his concern for Wilson by coming to the Blue Room of the White House and personally helping the president to the White House entrance, where Wilson insisted on walking unassisted to the waiting automobile. The large crowds along the route to the

Capitol extended warm cheers to both the incoming and outgoing presidents. He was especially surprised by the several thousand people who waited outside his house to wish him well.[99]

Now a former president, Wilson was never the recluse that historians have sometimes portrayed him as being. For one thing, he remained concerned about earning a living. Although he had not enjoyed the brief time he had spent being a lawyer before becoming an academic, when Bainbridge Colby suggested to him that they open a law practice together, with Colby maintaining the partnership in New York and Wilson the practice in Washington, the former president agreed to the idea and opened elaborate offices in the nation's capital. He also kept to his habit of watching movies and taking daily afternoon drives. Beginning in April, he began attending vaudeville at Keith's Theater every Saturday, just as he had done as president before his stroke. An ardent baseball fan, he often went to Griffith Park to watch the Washington Senators play. He was allowed to park his Pierce-Arrow in the outfield grass to see the game close up.[100]

Yet the first year or so of Wilson's retirement was extremely difficult for the former president. His law practice with Colby failed within a year. Wilson and Colby could have become very rich men had they accepted even a portion of the cases that were offered to them from foreign countries and corporations wishing to have the representation of a former president. Unlike Harrison and Cleveland, who had increased their wealth substantially after returning to the private sector, Wilson refused to accept any cases from foreign countries or corporations that might involve conflicts of interest or besmirch the office he had just held. "Day after day," Colby wrote Edith Wilson, "I sit in my office and see a procession walk through—thousands and thousands of dollars—and not one to put in our pockets." Finally, in frustration, Colby suggested that the former president might want to dissolve the practice that had brought Wilson a total income during the year of $5,000. Wilson eagerly agreed to his partner's suggestion.[101]

There is no doubt that the former president refused cases that could have made him enormously rich precisely for the reasons he gave. At the same time, it is hard to square his apparent refusal to profit from the fact he had been president from his willingness to accept financial assistance from his friends in order to purchase his home and automobile. It is also difficult to imagine how, under ordinary circumstances, he could have been surprised that the bulk of the cases offered to a high-powered firm headed by a former president and a former secretary of state, with offices in New York and Washington, would be just the kind he turned down. Certainly Colby had very different expectations when he suggested partnering with Wilson and paid the expenses of setting up the new firm. He regarded Wilson's reasons for turning away from a corporate and international practice as "sublime."[102]

There seem only two explanations for these inconsistencies in the former president's behavior. With respect to not understanding the potential conflicts of interest of a former president accepting money from friends for personal use, the

Portrait of Woodrow Wilson in 1921 by Edmund Tarbell, an American impressionist painter and one of the nation's most well-known and controversial artists during the Progressive Era. Tarbell wanted Wilson to pose for this portrait that was to be part of an exhibition featuring likenesses of the political and military leaders during World War I. Wilson's poor health, however, would not permit that, and Tarbell had to paint this portrait from photographs. (Courtesy of National Portrait Gallery, Smithsonian Institution; gift of the City of New York through the National Art Committee.)

only logical explanation has to involve his state of mind: he was no longer thinking as clearly and rationally as he had before his stroke. Edith wanted the house on S Street Northwest, and he wanted the Pierce-Arrow he had loved so much as president; his friends gave him the means to buy them. He accepted their gifts merely as signs of their friendship and generosity—which was, in fact, what they intended. Potential conflicts of interest did not enter his fatigued, possibly damaged mind.

The same state of mind seems also to explain why Wilson agreed to reenter a profession he had never liked and why he did not understand the implications of the partnership he was establishing with Colby. Not wanting to live out his life in idleness, he did not fully realize that practicing law after he left the White House would inevitably conflict with what he thought was appropriate for someone in his position as an ex-president. As he came to understand the nature of the practice, he was glad to give it up.

There seems to have been a second reason why Wilson happily dissolved his partnership with Colby. He was physically incapable of handling a major load of complex cases. When Colby announced the dissolution of his partnership with Wilson, he gave as the reason the fact that the former president's health had improved to the point that he thought it best to turn his energies to things more important than the practice of law. When the former president read the statement, he responded, "I wish that it were all true."[103]

Even though his health was improving, Wilson remained a sick man, both physically and mentally. The former president was able to do more things for himself, like shaving in the morning or dictating responses to his daily mail to John Randolph Bolling, Edith's brother, whom Wilson hired as his private secretary. Soon he was able to settle into a regular routine that included breakfast with Edith in the solarium that looked out into the terrace garden, the tip of the Washington Monument in the far distance, dictation with Bolling, a nap, an automobile ride in the afternoon, usually into the Virginia countryside, dinner, a massage by his male nurse, and then to bed. Occasionally, the routine was broken by a visitor. Sometimes in the evening before bed, the former president also watched a film. Then there were the regular Saturday evenings at Keith's Theater and the ball games at Griffith Park.[104]

Nevertheless, Dr. Grayson, whom President Harding allowed to remain as Wilson's personal physician even though he was still in the navy and the former president was no longer entitled to his services, recommended bed rest as his best medicine. Despite the slow improvement in his overall health, the ex-president also remained weak, tired easily, and suffered a number of setbacks. As a result, he spent much of his time in his bedroom, lying on a replica of the Lincoln bed that had been made for him, trying to regain his strength. Even when he felt strong enough to see visitors, Grayson permitted only one thirty-minute visit a day. The former president's eyesight also continued to deteriorate so that he became nearly blind and unable to read. Instead, someone, usually Edith or Bolling, had to read to him.[105]

At one point near the end of his presidency, Wilson thought that after he retired, he would do some writing. He rejected any thought of writing a history of his administration. He was too near the events and too closely involved, he believed, to write a complete and objective assessment of his presidency. He was interested, however, in political philosophy and considered the possibility of writing a book on that subject. After he retired from the White House, he even wrote the first page of the projected book, a dedication to Edith. That proved to be the only page he wrote. He was inundated with offers from book publishers, magazines, and newspapers to write for them. The well-respected Macmillan Company even suggested that he write a "Life of Jesus." "The historical problems connected with this piece of work would make a most interesting study, while the problems of personality involved, would employ the full reflective strength of your powerful mind," W. H. Murray of Macmillan's Religious Books Department wrote the former president on 14 April 1921. The next day, Wilson replied that "under no circumstances" would he consider writing the book. It was not only that the former president found this proposal absurd; he simply lacked the stamina and strength to undertake any major writing project. Indeed, the only thing he published in his retirement was a short article that he wrote for the *Atlantic Monthly* in 1923.[106]

Indirectly, however, the former president was able to make a lucrative profit from publishing. Although he refused to write a history of his administration, soon after leaving office, he gave permission to the journalist, Ray Stannard Baker, who had impressed him with a book he wrote, *What Wilson Did at Paris,* to go through papers he had collected from the Paris peace conference and had stored in a trunk. He had not even opened the trunk, much less sorted the papers. Wilson agreed to have Baker arrange the papers and a write a history of the conference. After Baker was offered $100,000 just for the syndication rights to the book and he realized that he stood to make much more money from book sales, he worked out an arrangement with George Creel, who had headed the Committee on Public Information during the war and served informally as Wilson's literary agent, whereby the president and Baker would split the profits on a fifty–fifty basis. Although Baker had always been amendable to such an arrangement, having first suggested it, he was annoyed that Creel, who thought that Wilson should write his own history of the conference and who considered it a "bitter blow" to him that Wilson had given the assignment to Baker, tried to drive a harder bargain, including the establishment of an advisory committee. Baker insisted that *"it must be my book."* After meeting with Creel and Bolling, Baker reported in his diary: "Creel & Bolling proposed that we divide up all the proceeds of the book half and half between us, sharing my expenses half and half. I accepted without a word: but made the point that I should wish to count upon the help of all of them—to the limit—in making a good book."[107]

Creel managed to negotiate a 20 percent royalty. Wilson proved particularly helpful to Baker, answering his questions and filling in details for him. In 1923, Baker published his study in three volumes. For many years, it was the standard work about the postwar gathering of allied leaders. It proved to be a lucrative deal for all concerned.[108]

For those closest to Wilson, it was natural to attribute his reluctance to undertake any major writing project of his own to the lingering physical effects of his stroke. After all, he had been an accomplished author before he entered the world of politics. It had become common for former presidents to supplement their income with books and articles, and Wilson had even started a book, even if had never gotten beyond the dedication page. That he showed little desire to make what had been his vocation his avocation was easily attributed to the slowness of his recovery and to the fact that he continued to fatigue easily and still needed plenty of bed rest, as Dr. Grayson recommended.[109]

What was of greater concern to many of Wilson's friends and family was his mental state. A cloud of depression hung over him. He rarely smiled or spoke. He easily broke into tears. He displayed little spontaneity even in terms of his daily routine. His inner circle of friends grew smaller, and he became annoyed more easily, even with Edith and his daughters. "In all these days I have been so closely in contact with his life at the White House and in S. Street (as formerly in Paris)," Baker recorded in his diary in April 1921, "it has been astonishing to me how little human contact he craves. . . . He opens his heart to no one—scarcely I think even to his wife." Two weeks later, Senator Homer Cummings made similar comments after visiting him at home.[110]

Actually, Wilson's mental state varied from week to week and from month to month. When Cummings paid him a visit in June 1922, he commented on his improvement from the previous year. Wilson, he thought, looked better than "at any time since his illness began." He also seemed to regain some of his wit and humor. After Dr. Grayson told him that the Senate had passed a resolution congratulating him on regaining his health, he responded with one of his famous limericks:

There was an old man from Khartoum
Who Kept two black sheep in his room
To remind him, he said, of two friends who were dead
But he never would specify whom.[111]

Although Wilson was often depressed, he was rarely apathetic or indifferent to what was happening in the world. He kept a close eye on international politics. He worried especially about the spread of the Bolshevik revolution in Europe. Of Karl Marx he remarked, "I know of no man who has more perverted the thinking of the world." He also remained intransigent in his position on the League of Nations. Although Secretary of State Charles Evans Hughes undertook various efforts to work closely with the league and was responsible for the Washington naval conference, which embodied the Wilsonian principles of collective security and disarmament, Wilson dismissed these efforts as "not genuine." He continued to insist on U.S. membership in the league along the lines he had demanded as president. Convinced that time was on the side of the Democrats, he warned against "any detour from the straight road."[112]

The former president also kept abreast of domestic politics. Although he refused to speak out publicly, he made his views known privately. He denounced Harding as a "fool" who had no business being president, and his administration as stupid, irresponsible, and incapable of "making anything happen." It was better, he commented, to have a strong president like Roosevelt or himself, even if he made mistakes, than someone like Harding who did nothing. He was overjoyed in 1922 when the Democrats gained seventy-five seats in the House of Representatives. In 1923, he began to think of putting together a document of principles that would provide the platform for the Democratic Party in 1924. For this purpose, he sought the help of such individuals as Louis Brandeis, Bernard Baruch, former secretary of war Newton Baker, the journalist Frank Cobb, a former economic adviser, Norman Davis, and his brother-in-law from his first marriage, Stockton Axson. All were close friends.[113]

Writing even a preliminary essay of his own thoughts proved a painful chore for Wilson, however, and the result showed the still lingering physical and mental limitations under which he labored. Using a pencil, he spent hours just trying to jot on paper an idea or two for Edith to transcribe on a typewriter. His physical limitations alone—bad eyesight, an unsteady hand, constant fatigue—made the task excruciating. However, his mental limitations were just as serious. He often began a thought and then lost it, having to stop at midsentence. Frequently, when his wife or someone else thought he was asleep in his bedroom, he would let out with a thought and ask them to write it down. Then he would fall asleep again. His once methodical mind failed him. One sentence or one paragraph seemed to crash into another without much coherence.[114]

When Wilson completed the 1,500-word essay, "The Road Away from Revolution," he had Edith, who had already read it and was embarrassed by its superficiality and incoherence, send it to Creel for his opinion. Like Edith, Creel was horror-struck by what he read. Although he remarked that Wilson wrote with "his old facility of phrase," he thought the essay lacked body or substance. He realized that if the article were published in its present form, it would not only hurt Wilson's literary reputation, but it would also raise new questions about Wilson's mental well-being and his ability to return to active public life. "Under different circumstances," he wrote to Edith. "I would advise instantly and with all my power against its publication. What we have got to consider, however, is the effect of such advice upon Mr. Wilson. I have the feeling that it would crush the confidence that you have been at such pains to build, restoring all of the old depression with possible effects upon his physical state." Quietly, he showed the essay to friends he trusted, such as the editor of *Collier's* and persons knowledgeable about news syndication. Although several magazine editors agreed to publish it, they opposed doing so out of respect for Wilson. Creel advised Edith to forgo syndication and have it published by *Collier's*.[115]

Agreeing with Creel's assessment of the harm publication of the article would do to Wilson's health and literary reputation, Edith disagreed only with the idea of having *Collier's* publish the essay; she thought $2,000 was inadequate for someone of Wilson's stature. More important, during an automobile ride in which she was also accompanied by Stockton Axson, she told her husband frankly that Creel thought the article needed more substance. Annoyed by the advice he received, Wilson responded that he "had done all I can, and all that I am going to do." Back home, Edith broke into tears before Axson, remarking that she did not know how to help her husband anymore. Axson asked to see that article, and with Wilson's permission, he agreed to rework it along the lines the former president suggested.

By removing several paragraphs and tightening the writing, Axson turned the essay into a short and readable article that the *Atlantic Monthly* published in August. In it, the former president posed as a challenge from the Russian revolution the need for capitalism in the United States to show more regard for social peace and justice and to stop regarding labor as "mere instruments of profit." He appealed to churches, political organizations, and capitalists to follow the teachings of Christ. The world, he reminded the American people, had not been made safe against "irrational revolution." Instead of embarrassing the former president, the article was well received and contributed to a comeback in Wilson's popularity among the American people.[116]

In fact, the former president, who had been overwhelmingly rejected, along with his party in 1920, and whose very mental stability was in question at the time he left office in 1921, was making a comeback in his public popularity even before his article was published in the *Atlantic Monthly*. Part of the reason for this was the scandals and incompetence of the Harding administration, which stood in sharp contrast to the idealism and accomplishments of the Wilson administration. In addition, time had a way of allowing people to forget the bad they associated with the Wilson presidency, especially after the war, and to remember only the good Wilson had sought to achieve at home and abroad. As his health seemed to improve, Americans also applauded him for the recovery he was making.[117]

Perhaps no single event did more to win favor for the former president, however, than an address he delivered on radio for Armistice Day 1923. Despite reports of Wilson's improving health, it was actually failing, and he was extremely depressed. Exhausted from having to care for her husband, Edith went on vacation for a week, only the second time she had been away from him overnight since his retirement. Nevertheless, the former president felt abandoned. To help cheer him up, Bernard Baruch's daughter, Belle, suggested that he deliver an Armistice Day address over the newly popular radio. Notwithstanding the torment he endured in preparing his article for the *Atlantic Monthly,* Wilson, who had a special reverence for the soldiers who had fought and died during the recent war, agreed to deliver the speech.[118]

The "great war for democracy and right [had been] fought and won," the former president said in his address. However, the victory was "forever marred and embittered for us by the shameful fact that when the victory was won. . . . We turned our backs on our associates and refused to bear any responsible part in the administration of peace." Still, he concluded we had time to "retrieve the past and to render mankind the inestimable service of proving that there is at least one great and powerful nation which can turn away from programs of self-interest and devote itself to practicing and establishing the highest ideals of disinterested service and the consistent maintenance of exalted standards of conscience and of right."[119]

In delivering his speech, the former president spoke softly and haltingly. He sometimes forgot his lines. In the background, one could even hear on the radio Edith whispering the lines to her husband. After he gave his address, Wilson apologized to those around him for presenting it so poorly. In fact, his speech was enormously successful. Millions of Americans listened to the address and were heartened not only by what they heard, but by the very fact that the former president was able to reach out to them again in such a direct way. Since Wilson had moved to S Street Northwest, small crowds had been gathering nearly every day as a show of fondness for Wilson and in the hopes of catching a glimpse of him. On Armistice Day, the crowds became significantly larger.

After Wilson insisted on being in the procession for the establishment of the Tomb of the Unknown Soldier on Armistice Day 1921, as many as 20,000 people waited to greet him as he returned home. The famous journalist, Ida Tarbell, wrote an editorial for *Collier's* magazine with the title "The Man They Cannot Forget." "The persistent, mysterious, unconscious way in which men today draw around Woodrow Wilson," Tarbell stated, could only be explained by the fact that Wilson always reminded the people of their best hopes and dreams even when they did not always come true. At Keith's Theater, hundreds of persons waited on Saturday nights to catch a glimpse of their former leader when his car pulled into the side of the theater, where he was helped out. As always, he received another huge round of applause as he made his way into the auditorium.[120]

After his radio address, the crowds outside Wilson's house grew still larger, and his overall popularity among the American people skyrocketed. On the day after his talk, a crowd filled five blocks around his house. With tears rolling down his face, Wilson went outside to say a few words to those who had massed to see him. A great cheer went out from the crowd, and a band played the World War I song "Over There." After Carter Glass, who was with Wilson, talked for about five minutes, the former president spoke. "I am not one of those that have the least anxiety about the triumph of the principles I have stood for," he remarked. "I have seen fools resist Providence before, and I have seen their destruction. . . . That we shall prevail is as sure as that God reigns." Although the crowd showed no disposition to leave after the former president spoke, Mrs. Wilson gently got them to disperse by telling them that it was time for her and her husband to take their afternoon ride.[121]

In the last few months of his life, the former president, who had been a dreamer all his life, had different fantasies. Despite his health, he never abandoned the thought that he might yet become the standard-bearer of the Democratic Party in 1924, in much the same way he thought he could win the party's nomination in 1920. The party would deadlock at the convention. Meanwhile, he would present the document of principles, which he and his friends had been working on for more than a year and which was completed in January 1924. The rules would be suspended, and he would be nominated by acclamation. As in 1920, he refused to endorse any of the leading candidates, which again included his son-in-law, William McAdoo, and Governor Al Smith of New York. In an interview he held in October 1923 with James Kearney, a progressive journalist and an old friend from New Jersey politics, he remarked that "under no circumstances would he permit his intimates to commit him to any other candidacy [than his own]." He also made clear to friends that he was watching party politics carefully and that he thought he could play a singular role in leading the Democrats to victory in 1924. He even prepared notes and passages on an acceptance speech. Privately, party chieftains and potential candidates were nervous about the possibility of a Wilson candidacy, believing that the debacle of 1920 had provided an appropriate burial for American membership in a League of Nations. Thankfully, his death in February saved Wilson from having to endure another disappointment when the Democrats held their nominating convention later that summer.[122]

At the same time that Wilson imagined a third term as president, he also dreamed about establishing a new university that he would head. He believed that none of the nation's colleges and universities, including Princeton, were liberal enough or did enough to encourage freedom of thought. "There are many splendid fellows in the Princeton faculty," the former president told Kearney, "but they are allowed no freedom of thought." "Candidly," he added, "if I had a son I wouldn't know where to send him for a liberal education in America." What the ex-president hoped to establish was the type of university he had dreamed Princeton would become when he was its president. The curriculum would involve personal contact between instructors and small groups of students. Although students would work under the direction of their instructors, they would be allowed a good deal of freedom. His model was Oxford University. He looked for assistance from the Rockefeller Foundation. The foundation turned him down, remarking that his idea was too experimental. "I can honestly say that my plans are so thoroughly thought out in detail that there is nothing experimental in them," he responded in disappointment.[123]

Yet death brought an end to Wilson's dreams. The end of Wilson's life was almost a celebration of his career. By virtually all accounts, he had once more become one of the nation's most admired figures. Efforts started in 1921 by a group of Harvard students, who aspired to keep the struggle going for a League of Nations by forming a Wilson club, spread first to fifty colleges, then across campuses throughout the country. The Wilson Club at Princeton enrolled more than 600 students. Princeton alumni and faculty wrote the former president to assure him that that they had not forgotten him. Wilson's former assistant secretary of the navy and the 1920 Democratic vice presidential candidate, Franklin Delano Roosevelt, embarked on an effort that culminated in 1922 with the establishment of the Woodrow Wilson Foundation with an endowment of $1 million whose purpose was to promote the fight for liberalism and internationalism. From time to time, it would make awards "to the individual or group that has rendered within a specific period, meritorious service to democracy, public welfare, liberal thought or peace through justice." "In brief," the foundation's executive committee noted, "America is to have its own Nobel Prizes."[124]

A group of his friends established an annuity of $10,000 to supplement the former president's income. "We are doing in part only what we think Congress should do for all retiring presidents," the donors remarked in establishing the annuity, "and are prompted . . . by the possibility that in devoting his life to education, statesmanship and politics he may not have laid aside sufficient savings to provide himself properly with the reasonable necessities and comforts which he so richly deserves." Wilson accepted the annuity as a new challenge to action. "As I see it," he told Cleveland Dodge, one of the donors, "the greatest fight of all lies immediately ahead of the liberal forces of this country and of the world—the fight to conquer selfishness and greed and establish the rule of justice and fair play." He thought American popular opinion had been so turned against the League of Nations that it might take another thirty years before the United States accepted its proper role in the world, but the time would come. To hasten that day, he corresponded with various groups at home and abroad that espoused a league.[125]

To celebrate his sixty-seventh birthday, another anonymous group of donors bought Wilson a specially constructed Rolls-Royce at a cost of $15,000 (the equivalent of about $187,000 in 2009). The automobile was designed with a higher top and wider doors than the standard Rolls Royce, so that Wilson could get in and out of the car without having to stoop. It also had high, deep cushions on the wide backseat. Two days after his birthday, the former president was also elected president of the American Historical Association, the second president (the first being Theodore Roosevelt) to be granted that honor.[126]

In short, what characterized the last months of Wilson's life was not the tragedy of a dying man but tributes to an American leader whose place in history, even his contemporaries who had been critical of him while in office recognized, would stand high. Time has borne this assessment out. Even though his concept of "making the world safe for democracy" has come under increased criticism in recent years as leading the United States astray in world affairs, few historians doubt that in terms of both foreign and domestic policy, Wilson's contributions as president and as a "voice crying in the wilderness" after he left office were singular.[127]

Despite the depression that had characterized so much of Wilson's post-presidential years, Wilson sensed the change in attitude toward him in his last year or so of life. At times, he seemed to understand that he had not long to live. He was feeling weaker by the day, his memory span was growing shorter, his appetite was diminishing, and his loss of vision reached the point where he had difficulty identifying those around him. When asked by one of his former students at Princeton, Raymond Fosdick, how he felt, Wilson quoted one of his predecessors: "John Quincy Adams is all right, but the house he lives in is dilapidated, and it looks as if he would soon have to move out." His thoughts, however, were not of a dying man or even of a former leader without a stage, an audience, or a cause. Even as his life ebbed, he continued to believe he was on the verge of new service to the nation.[128]

Sadly, this did not happen. Toward the end of January, the former president seemed well enough that Dr. Grayson decided he could take a vacation at Bernard Baruch's estate in South Carolina. On 28 January, however, he was called back by telegram to the White House. Wilson's health had taken a drastic turn for the worse. His children were called to his bedside. Wilson's daughter Jessie, who was in Siam, could not return. Eleanor McAdoo started out from California but was unable to reach Washington before he died. Only his third daughter, Margaret, was able to be by his bedside. On 1 February, the former president lapsed into a coma. Although he rallied briefly, he died from massive infarction of the brain on Sunday morning, 3 February 1924.[129]

As news spread that Wilson was dying, large crowds stood vigil outside his house. Joseph Tumulty came to the house to try to talk to Wilson a last time, but Edith would not allow it. As soon as they heard word that Wilson had died, President and Mrs. Coolidge, who were in church, made arrangements to come to the house and pay their respects. Extra editions of the newspapers were published announcing the news that the former president had died. All across the country and the world, millions mourned his death.[130]

Five days later, a small, private service was held in the music room in S Street Northwest. The casket was then taken across the city to Washington's National Cathedral, which was still under construction. There had been some discussion before his death about where his body should rest after he died. However, Edith chose the National Cathedral. Although it was Episcopalian in religious affiliation, it was intended to serve as a place of worship for the entire nation. In talking with Episcopalian bishop James E. Freeman, Wilson had commented at one time that the national cathedral the bishop was planning might become "the greatest spiritual force in the country." It also stood at the highest point in the District of Columbia. At the time, one could see the Capitol from it. That would please Wilson. After a simple service, Wilson's casket was lowered into a crypt; it was later moved to the nave. Wilson is still the only president to be buried in the cathedral.[131]

III

While three U.S. presidents died on July Fourth (John Adams, Thomas Jefferson, and James Monroe), only Calvin Coolidge was born on that date, in 1872. That was altogether fitting. If the celebration of Independence Day has become associated with small-town parades, local picnics and barbecues, fireworks, and proud displays of the American flag, no former president personified better the verities of small-town America than Coolidge.

The future president was born and raised in Plymouth Notch, in south-central Vermont. After graduating from Amherst College in 1895, Coolidge read law instead of going to law school, already the more common practice. Admitted to the bar in 1897, he opened his own law office in the western Massachusetts town of Northampton. In 1905, he married Grace Goodhue, an attractive young schoolteacher. After becoming involved in Republican politics, he served in the state legislature from 1907 to 1916, except for two years (1910–1911) when he was mayor of Northampton. Elected lieutenant governor in 1916, he was elected governor three years later. Unassuming in appearance and plainspoken, Coolidge stood five feet, nine inches tall with sandy hair, pale blue eyes, a long, straight nose, thin lips pursed down, a pallid complexion, and a cleft chin. Slightly built with fine features, he weighed around 150 pounds. Modest and shy to a fault, he lacked many of the characteristics normally found in a politician. He was uncomfortable with strangers, disliked shaking hands, was a poor conversationalist, and had a stern, cold demeanor. However, he studied politics carefully, worked hard, bided his time, looked for opportunities, and seized them when they came his way. His wife Grace, who, unlike her husband, was charming, gracious, and gregarious, also offset some of his social shortcomings. Taught from boyhood the values of thrift, honesty, and public service, he was known throughout his career for his moral rectitude, frugality, and cryptic language. As governor, he gained national notoriety and a place on the 1920 Republican ticket for his action in suppressing the Boston police strike of 1919.[132]

Coolidge became president on 2 August 1923 after the sudden death of President Harding from a heart attack while he was visiting San Francisco. Hardly known outside of Massachusetts and Washington political circles, he became enormously popular as president, both because he symbolized traditional values and because he became a master at manipulating the mass media. Although Taft had been the first president to hold press conferences, Coolidge institutionalized the practice, meeting twice weekly with the press and answering preselected questions. He was seen regularly on newsreels and was the first president to use the radio to speak to the American people. He was also the first president to appoint a dedicated speechwriter, Judson Welliver, a former newspaperman, who coined the term "founding fathers."[133]

As president, Coolidge became best known for his remark, "The business of government is business." For the thirtieth president, this was more than a bromide; it was the bedrock of his philosophy of government. On the one hand, this meant that less government was good government. Greatly influenced by his treasury secretary, the wealthy banker and financier Andrew Mellon, he sought to cut federal expenditures, reduce taxes, and relax government regulation of the marketplace. On the other hand, it meant that government could assist business by partnering with it. Businessmen wanted government to encourage private and corporate pursuits, and Coolidge obliged. Under Secretary of Commerce Herbert Hoover, the commerce department fostered close private–public cooperation, especially by encouraging the establishment of trade associations and promoting American foreign commerce. The Federal Reserve Board kept interest rates low. The Federal Trade Commission became a friendly adviser to business. The Interstate Commerce Commission was staffed by railroad people. In short, many of the government agencies that had been established to regulate business became its allies. Coolidge's overwhelming election victory in 1924 over his Democratic opponent, John W. Davis, and the Progressive Party candidate, Robert M. La Follette, signified the public's approval of business ascendancy in the 1920s.[134]

Coolidge's election victory was marred by the earlier death in July of his younger son, Calvin Jr., at the age of sixteen. Calvin had been playing tennis on the White House courts wearing sneakers but no socks. One of his toes developed a blood blister. The blister became infected. Without antibiotics, the infection spread throughout his entire system. An operation at Walter Reed Hospital failed to help. On 7 July, a week after the tennis game, the otherwise healthy teenager died of the infection that had poisoned his body.

His son's death deeply affected Coolidge. He remained with his son at Walter Reed, helplessly watching him grow weaker by the day. "In his suffering he was asking me to make him well. I could not," Coolidge later wrote.[135] After Calvin Jr.'s death, the president lost interest in the 1924 election, embracing the radio in lieu of travel and speeches. He also became more disengaged from his cabinet and colleagues, grew more ill-tempered, and slept as many as twelve hours a day, including taking naps as long as four hours in the afternoons. Grace said he lost his "zest for living." His relations with Congress, which had never been good, worsened. Most important, without informing even his wife or his closest advisers, he stunned the nation by announcing in July 1927, while on vacation in the Black Hills of South Dakota, that he chose not to run in 1928 for reelection.[136]

Undoubtedly, Coolidge decided not to run in 1928 for reasons other than his son's death. After he made his announcement in 1927, he told several confidants that he thought that nearly six years as president was enough for anyone. He was also worried about Grace, who had also been devastated by the loss of Calvin Jr.

Photo of President Calvin Coolidge sometime between 1923 and 1927 shaking hands with Walter Johnson at Griffith Stadium. Coolidge became a master of manipulating the mass media. He made numerous public appearances during which he took advantage of photo opportunities. This contributed to his overall popularity as president. As a consequence, when it appeared that President Hoover was going to lose his bid for reelection in 1932 to Governor Franklin Roosevelt, he called on the former president, who had tried to distance himself from politics after he left office, to make a major address on his behalf at Madison Square Garden. (Courtesy of Library of Congress, Prints and Photographs Division.)

and who had hinted to her husband that she had had enough of the White House. Finally, Coolidge had ongoing problems with his own party over such matters as relief for agriculture and a fiasco surrounding American membership in the World Court. However, a serious, even debilitating, depression overtook Coolidge after his son's death, and with it his interest in serving a second full term. "When [Calvin Jr.] went," Coolidge later wrote in his autobiography, "the power and the glory of the Presidency went with him. . . . I do not know why such a price was exacted for occupying the White House."[137]

With Coolidge having removed himself from the Republican nomination, the party turned to Hoover as its candidate. In November, Hoover easily defeated the Democratic candidate, Al Smith. Now that he was leaving the presidency, Coolidge's disposition seemed to improve. He had been constantly running for and winning office, he told reporters in September. "This time the only thing I was a candidate for was retirement and apparently I am going to be successful in that."[138]

Despite having decided for a long while not to seek another term as president, Coolidge had not determined what he would do after he left office except to return to the modest duplex on 21 Massasoit Street in Northampton that he had been renting since marrying Grace. Always frugal despite his generous salary, he worried only that the duplex's owner might raise his rent of $32 a month while he was in the White House. (He did raise it—to $34.50 a month.) At the time he left the presidency immediately after attending Hoover's inauguration in March 1929, it never occurred to him that he would want to live anywhere else than the home he had been renting for almost a quarter of a century.

In fact, Coolidge could afford a much larger, more sumptuous, and more private residence than the duplex, had he chosen to do so. Although he had been a public servant for most of his private life, he had been able to save and prudently invest a considerable part of his income. His frugality knew few bounds. Even as governor, he had taken the trolley to work rather than own an automobile. As president, he entertained modestly in the White House, kept tabs on food and other household purchases, ate sparingly, and did not drink. When he went on daily walks with his Secret Service escort, he made cheese sandwiches consisting of two pieces of bread and a piece of cheese for both his escort and himself. His single vice was that he enjoyed smoking five or six cigars a day, for which he paid twenty-one cents apiece.[139]

As a result, Coolidge was able to add substantially to his already considerable savings and investments. When his father died in 1926, he inherited his home and property. By the time he left the White House in 1929, he was worth between $200,000 and $250,000, which he was able to increase within a year to about $400,000 (the equivalent of about $5.1 million in 2009) through inside tips from banker friends and heavy investment in the shares of J. P. Morgan at below-market price. Given his reputation for rectitude and integrity, it is simply impossible to explain his willingness to accept the favors that he did.[140]

Although the former president would have been content to remain on Massasoit Street, this proved impossible. Not only did Coolidge leave the presidency enjoying great popularity, but Americans were now prosperous enough to go on Sunday outings. Even average families traveled substantial distances in hopes of catching a glimpse of the former president rocking on the porch that fronted his home. One person even tried to sneak into the residence through the bathroom while the former president was showering. Coolidge quickly realized that he would have to move. He had also heard repeated complaints from the public and his own acquaintances that it was unbecoming for an ex-president to reside in a duplex.[141]

Accordingly, Coolidge and Grace decided that they needed to be in a more secluded area that would give them the privacy they longed for and reflect the dignity worthy of a former president. The house they bought and moved into in 1930 cost $40,000. Known as the Beeches, it was a twelve-room shingled house on nine acres of land with hundreds of trees and a meadow that swept down to the Connecticut River. The residence had an elevator, a tennis court, and a swimming pool. To make the property even more private, Coolidge had the entire property fenced in.[142]

Despite the privacy the Beeches provided the former president, he had no intention of remaining secluded on his estate. After returning to Northampton, he became quickly bored from inactivity. He established offices in his old law firm, but not to resume a law practice; as a former president, he believed that would give him an unfair advantage in litigation. Rather, he wanted a place where he could go every day to read the newspapers, handle his correspondence, and smoke a cigar. He and Grace also traveled extensively in the United States, visiting California, Louisiana, and Florida and touring the Coolidge Dam in Arizona.[143]

Coolidge believed, however, that former presidents should be employed or otherwise gainfully occupied. He did not want them to set an example for those whom he referred to as the blue bloods of the nation by establishing themselves as a leisure class. "Our country does not believe in idleness," he remarked in his autobiography. "It honors hard work." He even opposed pensions or any other special benefit for ex-presidents. "We draw our Presidents from the people," he stated. "It is a wholesome thing for them to return to the people. Fortunately, they are not supported at public expense after leaving office, so they are not expected to set an example encouraging to a leisure class."[144]

Speculation as to what Coolidge would do after he left office ranged from the obvious—a Supreme Court appointment or an executive position in some corporation—to the capricious—a proposal by Flo Ziegfield that he become a Broadway censor. One acquaintance even suggested jokingly that he teach a course on frugality at Scotland's Aberdeen University. He rejected almost all the offers that came his way, including several to be a university president or professor. He also turned down several opportunities to write for newspapers, including an offer of $75,000 from the *Denver Post* to be its editor in chief. People were "trying to hire not Calvin Coolidge but a former President of the United States," he explained. "I can't make that kind of use of the office."[145]

Coolidge's view of proper and improper ways for former presidents to earn an income was both contradictory and reflective once more of the reality that the arc of history made it impossible for an ex-president to resume the life of an ordinary citizen. Even Coolidge seemed to understand the dilemma he faced. "I cannot find any place, even writing, where there are not problems and criticisms of what I am doing," he remarked at the end of 1929.[146]

Although the former president thus saw nothing wrong in taking advantage of inside tips on the stock market or buying stock at below-market price, he believed it would be dishonest to accept positions at high salaries because that would be taking advantage of his former office. Even in this regard, he was not consistent.

Although he turned down a number of high-paying offers, he accepted other similar opportunities, including writing several articles for the *Saturday Evening Post* for which he received a stipend of $17,500, an article for *Colliers Weekly* for $7,500, and articles for *American Magazine* for $30,000 and for *Ladies' Home Journal* for $15,000. He also signed a contract to write a regular column for McClure's Newspaper Syndicate for which he was paid $203,000 before deciding after a year to give it up. The column was entitled "Calvin Coolidge Says," or sometimes, "Thinking Things Over with Calvin Coolidge." Finally, he agreed to publish his autobiography for Cosmopolitan Book Corporation, first carried in installments. He received an advance of $65,000 and considerable royalties after it was published in 1929.

Except for a lengthy explanation of why he decided not to seek reelection in 1928 and details about his boyhood in Vermont, Coolidge's autobiography added little to what was already known about the former president. Critics rightly claimed that it was generally dull and of little value to the scholar. Similarly, Coolidge's newspaper column was composed mostly of aphorisms, homilies, and platitudes about how to survive the Depression. A typical column carried the message, "We need more faith in ourselves," and another the warning that "sound finance calls for payment of debt and making the revenues of each year meet the expenditures." Essentially, the former president believed the solution to the Depression was for one to endure losses and to continue spending as much as possible. Government subsidies would do more harm than good.[147]

The point remains that Coolidge was inconsistent about not taking advantage of his former office. Still committed to the principles of frugality, propriety, and economy, he seems to have fallen victim to the phony prosperity and booming optimism of the 1920s just as the nation approached the precipice of the worst economic disaster of the twentieth century. It is significant that one reason he decided to give up his newspaper column after just one year was that he felt a degree of responsibility for the Depression and believed that it was wrong for him to be making so much money while so many others suffered.[148]

Another point that should be obvious is that the common view is false that Coolidge lived out his few remaining years after leaving office in quiet retirement, derided for his responsibility in bringing about the Depression but otherwise forgotten by the American people. Despite his drive for privacy, he remained an active, albeit prosaic, writer, authoring articles, a syndicated column, and even an autobiography. He also became a trustee for the New York Life Insurance Company for $50 a month and traveling expenses, president of the American Antiquarian Society, and a trustee of Amherst College.[149]

One thing Coolidge did not want to do after leaving office was to become active again in Republican politics. He continued to follow politics carefully, but only from the sidelines. He believed his time had passed and that he had failed as president. His only trip to Washington after retirement was to attend a ceremony honoring the proclamation of the Kellogg–Briand pact outlawing war as an instrument of national policy. As a former president, he came under considerable pressure to seek another elected office, including running in 1930 for the U.S. Senate from Massachusetts. Because of the Great Depression, there was even talk of replacing Hoover with him as the Republican candidate for president or, more seriously, of having him be Hoover's running mate in 1932. However, Coolidge wanted no part of these efforts. Except for making a major speech in Madison Square Garden in the fall of 1932 and then speaking on a radio hookup from the Beeches on the night before the election, he played no role in Hoover's campaign for reelection against his opponent, Governor Franklin Roosevelt of New York. As far as Coolidge was concerned, he was through with politics.

One reason the ex-president had no desire to return to the public arena was that he was already a sick man. He may have suffered a mild heart attack as president. In retirement, he felt increasingly weak. He also had trouble breathing, which he attributed to his asthma but which may been evidence of a more serious cardiac condition. On 5 January 1933, while he was at his office, he complained about not feeling well and was driven home to rest. Grace was away at the time. When she returned home, she found her husband dead on the floor of the bathroom, where he had gone to shave. He had suffered a major coronary thrombosis.[150]

Grace rejected a state funeral for her husband. Instead, his funeral service was held in Northampton with President and Mrs. Hoover, Chief Justice Charles Evans Hughes, governors, members of Congress, and diplomats in attendance. President-elect Roosevelt was represented by his wife, Eleanor, and his son, James. After a simple ceremony, Coolidge's body was transported to Plymouth Notch, where he was buried on the Coolidge family's plot.

9

The Modern Post-Presidency

Hoover

The emergence of the modern post-presidency began about the same time as the development of the modern presidency, around the turn of the twentieth century. However, Herbert Hoover's long and distinguished career after he left the White House (1933–1964) represents the fruition of the modern post-presidency. As we have seen, according to the original republican concept of civic responsibility, presidents were considered private citizens called to public duty for a period of time, after which they were expected to return to private life, much along the Roman model of Cincinnatus. The normal expectation was that they would pass their remaining years away from politics, overseeing the operations of their farms and plantations.

In the main, the first three presidents, George Washington, John Adams, and Thomas Jefferson, adhered to this republican ideal. Beginning with the retirement of James Madison in 1817, however, a transition began to a more active post-presidency. With the long congressional career of John Quincy Adams, even the pretense of a subdued retirement for former presidents came to an end. While not all ex-presidents stayed involved in politics and a small number lived out their lives quietly (a few in disgrace), most remained active and in the public limelight, whether that involved seeking the presidency again or running for some other political office, being a behind-the-scenes political operative, returning to a former career, becoming involved in local affairs, or merely engaging in charitable and educational activities.

As the United States became a far-flung industrial power after the Civil War, economic opportunities developed for former presidents that had not existed earlier. While Benjamin Harrison could increase his wealth simply by returning to his legal practice and demanding high retainers, most other ex-presidents made considerable sums of money through their publications, business connections, and paid lectures. Even someone like Woodrow Wilson, whose invalid status and sense of ethics kept him from engaging in most moneymaking activities, was provided for by his wealthy associates.

When taking into account inflation, presidential salaries were also substantially higher throughout most of the nation's history than the $100,000 salary that presidents began to receive in 1949, or even the $400,000 income presidents have earned since 2001. Even as late as 1949, when Congress raised the president's salary from $75,000 to $100,000 (the first pay raise since 1909), the $75,000 presidential salary still had about the same value as an income of $668,000 in 2009. As a result, frugal presidents were able to put aside considerable sums of money for their retirement years; indeed, they were expected to do so.[1]

What all this meant was that while most former presidents were concerned about earning an income after leaving the White House, only a few of them (Jefferson, Monroe, Pierce, and Grant) died destitute. When they did, it was because of their lavish lifestyles or unique personal problems. In fact, most former presidents (including Grant because of the postmortem royalties from his memoirs) were able to bequeath considerable wealth to their survivors. This became even more so as economic opportunities for ex-presidents proliferated after the Civil War.

What distinguished the post-presidency of Herbert Hoover from those of earlier ex-presidents, then, was not the considerable money he earned after he left the White House. He had already accumulated a fortune as one of the world's most successful mining engineers before he entered public service. Beyond any of the nation's earlier former presidents, however, Hoover turned the post-presidency into a dynamic vehicle for public and benevolent service. No other former president was called upon to engage in such a variety of responsibilities to the country and to the world as Hoover. No other former president responded with such willingness and effectiveness. In a sense, he turned on its head the republican ideal of an immediate and unencumbered return of former presidents from public to private life. The presidency became a springboard for further public service after leaving office.

I

Born in West Branch, Iowa, on 10 August 1874, Hoover's private and public careers personified the American success story. The second of three children, he was raised in the Quaker faith. There is no universal creed to Quakerism other than belief in an inner light or divine voice, which speaks to everyone and can be expressed through word or deed. Forms of worship include complete silence until a congregate gives witness or testimony to his or her inner light. There is also a common set of practices and principles that include equality, simplicity, community, pacifism, and humanitarianism. Although Hoover regarded himself as a secular Quaker, his strict Quaker upbringing explains much of his lifelong commitment to these values and to what he called "ordered freedom" and "ordered liberty."[2]

Although Hoover had a wry humor, he was known more often for his somber disposition. Part of his character can also be attributed to his Quaker upbringing. As he later wrote in his memoirs, "Those who are acquainted with the Quaker faith, and who know the primitive furnishings of the Quaker meeting-house . . . will know the intense repression upon a ten-year old boy who might not even count his toes." His nature was also the result of the fact that he suffered the traumatic experience of being orphaned at age eight, losing his father to a heart attack when he was six years old and his mother to pneumonia two years later. After living for awhile with neighboring relatives, he was sent from the familiar surroundings of West Branch to live thousands of miles away in Oregon with an uncle, John Minthorn. A country doctor and former Indian agent, Minthorn was also a land speculator who opened an office in Salem to sell real estate in the Willamette Valley. When Bert (as Herbert was called by his family and friends) was fourteen, his uncle took him out of school and soon had him running the office during the day while attending business college in the evening. Although it was hardly the stuff of a happy upbringing, Hoover's experience nevertheless reinforced his Quaker values and made him determined to be self-reliant.[3]

Hoover's experience in Salem was life-altering in other ways as well. While running the office, he picked up a number of skills that would be of great value to him later. He proved to be an excellent manager. He learned both bookkeeping and typing. In the evening, he excelled in courses he took in algebra and geometry. Most important, he came into contact with a number of engineers who frequented the office. Learning from one of them about plans to open a new engineering school, Leland Stanford, in California, he applied for admission. Except for his background in mathematics, he was not really prepared for a college education. His training in most subjects, including English, was rudimentary or nonexistent. Problems of syntax, spelling, and wooden verbiage would plague him for the remainder of his life. He had also not even graduated from high school. However, Stanford was looking for students, and Hoover did so well in the mathematics section of the entrance exams that the examiners overlooked other deficiencies and admitted him conditionally to Stanford.[4]

Although Hoover had a difficult time at Stanford both academically and financially, he flourished personally. Majoring in geology, he spent summers doing fieldwork in the Ozarks, the Nevada desert, and the High Sierra. He also met his future wife, Lou Henry, the only female geology major at Stanford and one of the few women in the nation to graduate with a degree in geology. They were married in 1899 and had two sons.[5]

By the time Hoover married Lou, he was already on his way to a successful career as a mining engineer. Graduating from Stanford in 1894, he had difficulty at first finding a job. Eventually, however, a British mining firm, Bewick, More-ing and Company, hired him at a generous salary of $7,500 to find and develop new mines in the hot, desolate, and dusty outback of Australia.[6]

Hoover proved to be a ruthless supervisor of the men working under him. He increased their hours, made them work seven days a week, showed little con-cern about their health and welfare, and fired them en masse when they asked for higher wages. After carefully assaying an abandoned mine, he recommended that his company purchase it. The mine proved to be a major coup for both Hoover and his bosses. From an initial investment of about $1 million, Bewick, Moreing eventually took in more than $65 million. Soon Hoover was made a partner and given larger assignments throughout the world, including one in China during the Boxer Rebellion.[7]

In 1908, Hoover left Bewick, Moreing to strike out on his own. By this time, he was already regarded in his profession as one of the world's leading mining engineers. Taking advantage of his reputation, he opened consulting offices in London, Paris, New York, San Francisco, and Saint Petersburg. However, Hoover did more than consult. He revived ailing enterprises, bought into a number of them, and even participated in pools to manipulate the stock market. By 1913, he was an extremely wealthy man, worth somewhere between $3 and $4 million (the equivalent of between $64 and $86 million in 2009).[8]

Despite his success, Hoover was by this time looking for something more meaningful to do. Success in business was not contrary to his Quaker beliefs. Ma-terialism was, and his business success no longer satisfied him. Although heavily influenced by his Quaker upbringing and living away from the United States for the last three years, he was also affected by the Progressive movement's efforts at home to adjust the nation's traditional liberal values to the economic and social inequalities caused by monopoly and the enormous concentrations of personal wealth. As an engineer and a manager of men, he viewed the nation's problems as largely technical, administrative, and managerial, and he shared the progressives' faith in professionalism and the gospel of efficiency. He was also rethinking his own views on labor, now favoring an eight-hour workday and better working conditions for employees. Finally, he was beginning to develop what he would later refer to as the American system, in which all economic sectors worked vol-untarily and cooperatively to bring about a more efficient use of the nation's re-sources as the path to a better life for the entire nation. A more efficient economy amounted, in his view, to a more moral economy.[9]

Hoover's first opportunity to engage in public service came when he agreed to serve as an overseas agent for the Panama-Pacific International Exposition, which was set to open in 1915. It was the outbreak of World War I in August 1914, however, that gave Hoover the opportunity to put on international display his administrative and managerial abilities. His efforts, first as head of food relief for Belgium after the nation was overridden by Germany, then as food adminis-trator after the United States entered the war in 1917, and finally as director of

American relief efforts in Europe after the 1918 armistice, earned him an international reputation as a humanitarian.

Before becoming director of food relief for Belgian, Hoover had been responsible for getting more than 120,000 Americans fleeing the Continent to London home to the United States. The success of the venture convinced him that even huge undertakings could be successfully carried out on a voluntary basis. What he ignored was that his organization had been given semiofficial status by the U.S. government and that Washington had provided $150,000 of the $400,000 it had raised.[10]

Hoover's success in the American relief effort led to his being asked by a group of Belgians and Americans to head the Commission for the Relief of Belgium (CRB), whose food supplies had either been destroyed or taken by the Germans. Hoover accepted the offer because it was perfect for someone with his technical skills and business acumen. It also appealed to his quest for public and humanitarian service. "The result would be a monument in American history," he later wrote, "and the greatest charity the world has ever seen."[11]

The task Hoover agreed to lead was indeed gigantic, but he carried it out with enormous success. Although he had the compliance of both the British and the Germans and the goodwill of Americans, who had been reading daily reports of Belgium's plight, Hoover had to overcome major logistical problems in collecting, buying, shipping, and distributing food and supplies. Costs had to be negotiated, scarce transportation mobilized, distrustful belligerents mollified, and infrastructures repaired and maintained. Working as many as eighteen hours a day, Hoover proved how brilliant he was as a logician, tactician, manager, and administrator.[12]

When the United States entered the war in April 1917, President Woodrow Wilson had to undertake the responsibility of mobilizing the nation's enormous economy for the war. To marshal the nation's food resources, he turned to Hoover. As director of the United States Food Administration, Hoover replicated his success as head of the CRB, except on a much larger scale. Standing about five feet, eleven inches tall, with straight brown hair, a short nose, bull terrier cheeks, hazel eyes, a plump, circular face, a heavy build, and a nasal voice, Hoover was shy, socially awkward, and a poor speaker. He had difficulty making eye contact; he read from a manuscript without looking up at his audience, and he looked at his shoes when talking to someone. As a Quaker, he dressed simply and wore high detachable collars long after they were out of fashion. However, he was meticulous, thoughtful, efficient, and demanding.[13]

Bringing to the table of the Food Administration a combination of these qualities as well as the skills and experience he had learned as an engineer, entrepreneur, and administrator of food relief for Belgium, he insisted on total control of his own agency. However, he also intruded into the affairs of other agencies involved with the long and complex food chain. In addition, he undertook a major public relations campaign at home. He asked the American people to sacrifice for the war effort, mobilizing a virtual army of volunteers who committed themselves to such practices as meatless Tuesdays and wheatless Wednesdays. *Webster's* included a new entry, "Hooverize," which meant "to economize." To head the bureaucracy under his command, he hired successful businessmen like himself willing to work for a dollar a year. Soon he was being referred to as the nation's food czar.

As he had in the past, Hoover made countless enemies because of his imperious manner. He even prepared letters expanding his powers and getting Wilson to sign them without first going to Capitol Hill for its approval. Gloom as much as persistence seemed his outstanding characteristic. The results spoke for themselves. Rationing was avoided. Wheat production actually increased at home. Prices remained stable. And food made its way to the front.[14]

Even after the war, Hoover continued to supply food to Europe, serving as head or director of the American Relief Administration and several interallied relief organizations.[15] As in the case of food relief for Belgium, the overarching lesson that Hoover took from his experience during and after the war was that voluntarism under government direction worked. In a small book, *American Individualism* (1922), Hoover spelled out this political philosophy in greater detail. After commenting briefly on the various political theories that had influenced the Western world, he explained why the best one was "American individualism," "a viewpoint, however, to be tempered by assurance to all citizens" of an "equality of opportunity" and of freedom from "frozen strata of classes."[16]

What Hoover conveniently ignored was that throughout the war, he had been literally the nation's food czar, issuing edicts with the backing of the government to assure they were instituted. Although he denied the Food Administration was a price-fixing agency, he insisted on fixed prices for necessary crops and made sure they were enforced. Testifying before Congress, he even stated on one occasion that democracy was prevailing because of "its willingness to yield to dictatorship." On another occasion, he remarked that the scale of the government's involvement in the marketplace amounted to "a sort of socialization."[17]

By 1920, Hoover was one of the best-known Americans in the world. That made him a leading candidate to run for president of the United States. Hoover was interested in being president, and both political parties were interested in him. He declared himself a Republican, but it turned out that conservative elements of the party considered him too progressive and too closely identified with Wilson. Although he received a few votes at the Republican nominating convention, Warren Harding won the nomination overwhelmingly. After Harding's victory, he insisted that Hoover be his secretary of commerce. Hoover made clear that he would accept the position only if his department's status in the cabinet were elevated and he were given the authority to expand its power and responsibilities. Harding agreed to his conditions.[18]

As secretary of commerce during both the Harding and Coolidge administrations, Hoover continued to add to his reputation by transforming his department into a beehive of activity for the promotion of public–private cooperation, good management practices, and business growth at home and abroad. Although President Calvin Coolidge never cared much for Hoover's self-promotion, the secretary of commerce became the dominant individual in the administration.[19]

As one of the most influential figures of the 1920s, Hoover was an obvious choice to head the Republican ticket in 1928 after Coolidge made clear that he would not seek another term as president. In Kansas City in June, he won on the first ballot. In the election that followed, he trounced his Democratic opponent, Governor Al Smith of New York, receiving twenty-one million popular votes and 444 electoral votes to Smith's fifteen million popular votes and eighty-seven electoral votes. He even broke into the supposedly solid South, winning in Virginia, North Carolina, Tennessee, Texas, and Florida.[20]

In October 1929, not yet eight months in office, Hoover was faced with the crash of the stock market and the Great Depression that followed. At the time, most economists believed that the Depression was part of a natural economic cycle, and that as soon as general confidence in the economy was restored, economic recovery would follow. Classical theory suggested that in order to restore economic confidence, government had to cut spending and do little else.[21]

Hoover did not reject conventional economic theory insofar as it involved economic confidence building. He also believed that most of the burden for ending the Depression had to fall on the private sector. He was convinced, however, that the Depression's magnitude was too great for the government to stand idly by. Government could undertake necessary public works projects. Even more important, it could promote cooperative ventures within the private sector and assist corporate enterprise in responding to the depression.[22]

This was the approach Hoover followed as president, bringing together business leaders in an effort to get them to cooperate in maintaining wages and levels of production. He used the radio to reassure the American people that better times lay ahead. When the crisis worsened in 1932, he established the Reconstruction Finance Corporation (RFC) to make loans to faltering banks, railroads, and insurance companies. He also speeded up public works projects, such as construction of the enormous Hoover Dam, and encouraged states to do the same. In 1933, just before leaving office, he signed the Emergency Relief and Construction Act, which provided $1.8 billion in relief loans and self-liquidating public works.[23]

The problem with Hoover, then, was not that he was a cold and uncaring do-nothing president, as his critics charged, but that he relied too heavily on the private sector to deal with the worst economic crisis in the nation's history. He seemed to care more about saving the banks than feeding the poor and unemployed. Although he did much to cope with the crisis, he did not do enough.

In 1932, Hoover fell victim to the Depression when he was resoundingly defeated in his bid for reelection by Governor Franklin D. Roosevelt of New York. Hoover had failed to deal adequately with the Depression, and he had been punished for it at the polls. Yet for all of his failures as president, his administration had been part of the evolution of the modern presidency, characterized by activist executive leadership on behalf of an expanded sense of the role and responsibility of government. In this sense, he represented a logical transition from progressiv-ism to the New Deal.[24]

Despite his rejection at the polls, Hoover tried, during the six-month inter-regnum between his defeat and the time he left the White House, to get the pres-ident-elect to pursue the course he had set down. This was characteristic of his self-confidence and his belief that his policies and programs to end the depression were working. Characteristic also of his lifelong habit of shifting responsibil-ity elsewhere when something went awry was the fact that when the Depression spread to Europe, he blamed it on the Europeans. His policies were succeeding, he claimed, until Europe's banking system collapsed, European countries went off the gold standard, and world commerce dried up. What was most needed was action to restore the gold standard, which he hoped to achieve at the forthcoming London economic conference. He asked the incoming president to support the restoration of the gold standard. He also wanted the establishment of a commis-sion to resolve the issue of war debts and reparations.[25]

Roosevelt had no intention of following Hoover's lead. When he met Hoover for the first time a few weeks after the election, Roosevelt refused to commit him-self to the gold standard. He also made clear his opposition to the establishment of a war debts commission, which, he said, had little support in the United States. When the banking system in the United States began to close down in the final days of Hoover's presidency, Hoover implored the incoming president to make a joint statement with him effectively supporting the gold standard and the need for currency stability. Roosevelt refused. Relations between the two men became bilious. Hoover began more and more to blame the Depression not only on inter-national factors but on the uncertainty caused by Roosevelt's election.[26]

The outgoing and incoming presidents met again a day before the inaugura-tion. Once more turning down Hoover's request for a joint statement, Roosevelt remarked, "Mr. President, I know it is customary to do so, but you don't have to return our call if you don't want to." Red in the face, Hoover responded, "Mr. Roosevelt, when you have been in Washington as long as I have, you will learn that the President of the United States calls on nobody." After Hoover made his remarks, Roosevelt turned around and left the room, visibly angry. He would not forget.[27]

Inauguration Day was the final time that Roosevelt and Hoover met. After the swearing-in ceremonies, the now ex-president left immediately for New York City. Roosevelt failed even to provide him normal Secret Service protection.[28]

The last three years had worn Hoover out. Photographs toward the end of his administration showed a person who was clearly stressed out. He was glad to be relieved of the heavy duties of the presidency. "We are at the end of our rope," he remarked on the morning of inauguration day. "There is nothing more we can do." After a brief stay at the Waldorf-Astoria, he traveled across the continent to rejoin his family in Palo Alto. For the remainder of the year, he read, relaxed, maintained an open house for friends and visitors, traveled, and engaged in his favorite hobby, fishing. He vowed not to comment publicly on the new administration for at least the next two years. Several reporters claimed that he had no interest in being active again in politics or writing a book.[29]

Reporters make mistakes, and this one was a dandy. There was no way that such a proud and hyperactive individual as Hoover could retreat into silence and inactivity. At the very least, Hoover sought to rehabilitate his standing among the American people. At the same time, he wanted to be recognized as the titular head of the Republican Party and to help rebuild the party that had been so badly defeated in 1932. Although he denied having any interest in running again for president in 1936, he never entirely dismissed the idea. Fifty-eight years old when he left office, he was still young enough to make another try at the presidency should he decide to do so. Before he left the White House, he even organized a new political group, the Republican Federal Associates, made up of people he had appointed to office. He intended the associates as a type of Hoover political machine within the Republican Party.[30]

The first 100 days of the New Deal, especially Roosevelt's decision to undermine the London economic conference and to have the United States go off the gold standard, infuriated Hoover. So did Roosevelt's brief closing of the banks, the passage of the Agricultural Adjustment Act (AAA), and the establishment of the National Recovery Administration (NRA). Not only did the former president think the new president's decision to emphasize a domestic solution to the Depression wrongheaded, he also believed Roosevelt was moving the country toward socialism, which was anathema to his entire concept of individualism, self-reliance, and voluntary cooperation. Privately, he also bristled at the personal slights against him by the new administration, including having the name of the Hoover Dam changed to the Boulder Dam and the Hoover Airport in Washington, D.C., to the National Airport. He even suspected the administration was behind investigating his former cabinet members and attempting to prosecute his treasury secretary, Andrew Mellon, for tax evasion.[31]

Although the former president kept his promise not to speak out against the Roosevelt administration during its first two years, as Roosevelt continued to expand the role and scope of government over the remainder of his first term, he began to lash out at his successor and encouraged others to speak out as well. He tried to get the Republican Party to put a more positive spin on its message by offering Republicanism as an alternative to the New Deal. He wanted Republicans to make clear that they opposed the New Deal because, in contrast to the Democrats, they stood as the "defender of constitutional methods" and of "real liberty, not aborted by the glitter of radical dictatorship."[32]

The former president also began to publish a series of books and articles attacking Roosevelt while defending his own administration. In 1934, he published *The Challenge to Liberty,* which he intended as a sequel to *American*

Individualism, written a decade earlier. Once more, he argued that his strategies had been working until Roosevelt's election, which "by its determination of an abrupt change in national policies naturally brought a break in the march of confidence and recovery." Even more serious was Roosevelt's decision to go off the gold standard, resulting "in vast withdrawals of gold, a flight of capital abroad, and runs upon banks, despite the solvency of the system as a whole." For the rest of his life, he remained convinced that the ebb of the Depression had been reached in the summer of 1932 and that, save for Roosevelt's election, recovery would have soon followed.[33]

Hoover also lashed out the New Deal's "regimentation" of the economy through the establishment of the AAA and NRA. "Over [the nation's small business] is now the daily dictation by Government in every town and village every day in the week . . . under constant threat of jail, for crimes which have no moral turpitude. All this is the most stupendous invasion of the whole spirit of Liberty that the nation has witnessed since the days of Colonial America."[34]

Thanks to his friend, William Allen White, *Challenge to Liberty* became a Book-of-the-Month Club selection. It was also widely reviewed in the nation's leading newspapers and magazines. More liberal reviewers condemned it as "trivial," "trite," "badly written," and even "medieval." More conservative reviewers referred to the book as "eloquent" and even "prophetic." Irrespective of the reviews, *Challenge to Liberty* sold more than 135,000 copies, made the bestseller lists, and established Hoover once more as a leading voice of his party.[35]

Throughout the next two years, the former president kept up his attack on the New Deal, even suggesting in 1935 a similarity between fascist Italy, Nazi Germany, communist Russia, and the New Deal. Whether it be those countries "or their lesser followers," he remarked, "the result is the same. Every day they repudiate every principle of the Bill of Rights. . . . Here is a form of servitude, of slavery—a slipping back toward the middle ages."[36]

Between 1935 and 1936, Hoover also made a series of major addresses before such groups as the Young Republicans of the West, the Young Republican League of Colorado, and the Nebraska Republican State Central Committee. In virtually every speech, he assaulted the New Deal while boasting of his own accomplishments as president. In 1936, he published a compilation of these speeches as *American Ideals versus the New Deal.* He even spent his own money to assure the book was widely distributed to libraries and influential Republicans.[37]

Invariably, the question arose whether Hoover was planning to seek the Republican presidential nomination in 1936. Certainly Hoover indicated a strong interest in running. His speaking tour of 1935–1936 was intended to test the waters of support for another try at the presidency and to indicate his availability for a draft, which would amount to exoneration of his presidency among Republicans. This was, however, wishful thinking on his part. As several writers have already shown, in many ways, Hoover was closer to the New Deal he attacked than to the powerful conservative wing of the Republican Party. Programs like the NRA and

AAA were predicated on his own idea of business and agricultural groups working together to set codes and limits to which they would then adhere.[38]

Even Hoover recognized the parallels between what he advocated and what the Roosevelt administration enacted into law. What he objected to was the New Deal's mandatory nature. Beyond that, he also opposed what he considered its lack of careful planning, overlapping programs, bureaucratic growth, and waste. As an engineer, he looked at problems in a more orderly, planned, rational, and technocratic manner than Roosevelt, who was more concerned with what he called the "science of human relations," including individual dignity and self-worth.[39]

Opposition to Hoover's nomination, however, was not limited to the Republican Party's extreme right. Moderates and progressives also tried to distance themselves from the former president. Republican leaders even tried unsuccessfully to keep Hoover from speaking at their convention in Cleveland in June. When the former president addressed the delegates, he delivered such a rousing attack on the New Deal that the gathering could not be gaveled to order and had to be adjourned until the next day. Even so, Hoover recognized that he had no chance of getting the nomination. Instead, he returned to New York City, where he maintained a suite in the Waldorf-Astoria Towers. The following day the delegates selected as their candidate Governor Alf Landon of Kansas.

Although Landon was a moderately progressive member of the party, the former president was not pleased with his nomination. He believed the Kansas governor lacked the experience to be president. He also resented his efforts during the primaries to steal the California delegation from him. More disappointing and hurtful to Hoover than Landon's nomination was the fact that even many of his old friends refused to support his candidacy not only because they thought he would lose in November, but also that he would take other Republicans down with him. Even Landon distanced himself from the former president, limiting him to two speeches during the campaign.[40]

Hoover's absence from the campaign circuit hardly helped the Republican candidate, who ran a lackluster campaign. In November, Roosevelt was returned to the White House in one of the most lopsided victories in the country's history. Blaming Hoover and the Republicans for the Depression and taking credit for the economic recovery then under way, the ebullient Roosevelt won in every state except Maine and Vermont, capturing nearly twenty-eight million popular votes and 523 electoral votes to Landon's nearly seventeen million popular votes and only eight electoral votes.[41]

Despite the Republican debacle and the contempt heaped upon him by his own party, the former president was still not prepared to withdraw from the political scene—quite the contrary. He continued to lash out against the New Deal and to seek vindication from his own party. He intended to have a leading voice in setting the direction of the Republican agenda and in selecting the next candidate for president, which, he still hoped, might be him. Given the nation's two-term tradition for presidents and the growing unpopularity of Roosevelt after he tried to pack the Supreme Court after his victory in 1936, there seemed an excellent chance that Republicans could retake the White House in 1940.[42]

The problem for Hoover was that he continued to be widely blamed throughout the nation for the Depression. Even moderate Republicans remained uncomfortable with him. On the day after Roosevelt announced his scheme to pack the Supreme Court, Michigan senator Arthur Vandenberg recorded in his diary, "This morning ex-president Hoover phoned me . . . eager to jump in the fray. . . . Now here is one of the tragedies of life. Hoover is still 'poison'—(the right or wrong of it does not matter)." As for the White House, he was so disliked by Roosevelt that he refused to extend him the normal courtesy of inviting him to the White House for state dinners.[43]

Although Hoover's concern about New Deal policies and his own vindication remained uppermost in his mind, he did pursue other interests and concerns besides politics. He was involved in a number of pet charities, especially those promoting the causes of youth. Perhaps because he had been orphaned at a young age, he had a particular fondness for children and their needs. Throughout his life, he gave special attention to letters he received from children and responded even in his later years to as many as he could. He was also active in such organizations as the Child Health Association and the Belgian-American Educational Fund.

His favorite charity, however, was the Boys Club of America. Founded in 1906 as the Federated Boys Club of America, it reorganized in 1931 and dropped "Federated" from its name. In 1936 Hoover became its chairman and opened 500 new Boys Clubs throughout the country.[44]

Another of the former president's favorite interests was his alma mater. For fifty years, he was a member of Stanford University's board of trustees. In 1919, he also founded the Hoover Institution on War, Revolution and Peace, the archival basis for which was an enormous collection he had amassed of official documents from World War I. The documents were later housed in the Hoover Tower that was dedicated at Stanford in 1941.[45]

In addition to his charitable and service undertakings after leaving the White House, Hoover was concerned about making money. Although by most standards he was still a wealthy man when he left office, the Depression took its toll on his finances. He continued to receive hundreds of letters from destitute families asking for assistance. Instead of ignoring these letters, he had a friend investigate their claims. To those he found worthy of help, he made small donations of $100 or less. These small amounts added up to a big drain on his resources. In November 1933, he commented that he would have to get employment "before I can take care of all the burdens that come up to this desk." In addition, he was spending more than a $1,000 of his own money each month just to retain his office staff. He also maintained an expensive lifestyle. He traveled often and maintained residencies in Palo Alto and New York.[46]

Earning a living, therefore, was an issue for Hoover, just as it had been for earlier presidents. One way he tried to earn income was by returning to his former occupation as an investor in mining ventures, although on a much smaller scale than he had before entering public service. Thanks to tips from his engineering friends, he invested in mines in Utah and Nevada. He also invested in lead and zinc mines in Guatemala, which promised at first to be his greatest find. Because of Guatemalan politics, including two revolutions, a company he formed headed by his son, Allan, a trained mining engineer, to exploit the mines never panned out. As for the ventures in Utah and Nevada, they appear to have been only marginally profitable.[47]

Aside from his investments, Hoover's greatest source of income was from his publications and speaking engagements. Although it is unclear how much he received from these sources, it was considerable. In 1936, for example, he was paid $10,000 (the equivalent of almost $153,000 in 2009) for just two articles he wrote for the *Saturday Evening Post*. He was offered even larger sums by *American Magazine*.

The focus of virtually everything the former president wrote and said remained his bitterness toward the New Deal and his resolve to be a major voice of the Republican Party. Although Republican leaders on Capitol Hill tried to dissuade Hoover from involving himself in the congressional fight over Roosevelt's plan to add new justices to the Supreme Court for every sitting justice over seventy years old, he refused to be silenced. Speaking in Chicago, he accused the president of trying to subvert the Constitution. If he could add new justices to the Court to pass constitutional muster on his legislative program, he asked, "what was to keep future presidents from following the same tactic?" Hands off the Supreme Court! he concluded. Similarly, when the economy entered a recession in 1937, the former president took special pleasure in blaming Roosevelt for the economic downturn.[48]

Concerned that his voice was going unheard even within his own party and that Landon was doing a better job mobilizing Republicans and a growing number of anti–New Deal Democrats into a new Republican Party, Hoover stepped up his own organizational efforts. Most important, he attempted to get Republicans to hold a midterm convention in order to prepare a statement of principles on which to run in 1938 and give him an opportunity to lead the rebuilding of the Republican Party. "The purpose of such a convention," he wrote, would be "to secure a declaration of the fundamental principles of genuine American Liberalism—that is, 'conservatism,' as opposed to the collectivism of the New Deal."[49]

Hoover was taking a high risk. What he won was a Pyrrhic victory. With the Roosevelt administration on the defensive because of Roosevelt's attempt to pack the Supreme Court and an economic downturn, many Republicans thought it would be foolish to distract from the White House's problems by holding a midterm meeting. Republican members of Congress chose also to run on local issues. More important, Hoover's rivals within the party, including Landon, realizing the former president's own self-interest in having a midterm conference, wanted no part of it. Landon was convinced that the former president intended the gathering as "the beginning of Hoover's campaign for the nomination in 1940." Even many of those who empathized with the stated purpose of the gathering did not want Hoover as the titular head of the party. For them, the former president represented the disgraced past of the 1920s at a time when they were looking toward the future.[50]

As a result, Hoover could not develop enough support for a meeting. Instead, the Republican National Committee established a committee to formulate a statement of party principles. What it issued was so broad and general that Chester Rowell, one of Hoover's allies on the committee, described it as a mouse that "has so little vitality that it is barely able to squeak."[51] Even so, publication of the statement of principles was followed by a huge Republican victory in the 1938 congressional elections. Republicans captured eighty-one seats in the House and seven in the Senate as well as a number of governorships. Hoover took credit for the Republican victory, attributing it to his many radio addresses, speeches, and articles since 1936 and to the statement from the Republican program committee. Believing his vision for the party's future had been vindicated, he was optimistic about a Republican victory in 1940.[52]

By the end of 1938, the former president was also becoming increasingly worried about the worsening political situation in Europe and Asia. Earlier that year, he had traveled to Europe. In contrast to his unpopularity in the United States, he received a hero's welcome from the Europeans, who still remembered his humanitarian efforts during and after World War I. In Belgium, King Leopold decorated him, crowds shouted "Vive l'Amerique," and a special stamp was issued in his honor. In France, the University of Lille presented him with the first of a dozen honorary degrees he received on the trip. A street was even named after him.[53]

Much to his surprise, in Germany, the ex-president was invited to meet with Adolf Hitler. Hoover found Hitler more intelligent and informed than he had been led to believe, but he also thought that he was "partly insane." He was especially offended by Hitler's tirade against Jews. "He seemed to have trigger spots in his mind," he later wrote, "which when touched set him off like a man in furious anger." In Poland and back in the United States, he spoke out against Hitler and condemned the Nazis' treatment of Jews.[54]

Yet the ex-president was impressed by Germany's efforts in providing low-cost housing and constructing its high-speed autobahn. He also made no objection when Germany took over Austria and later moved into Czechoslovakia. Although he had no fondness for the Nazis, he did not think Germany would move against France and England. Instead, he was convinced that Hitler had his eyes on territory to its east, where significant German populations resided. He even suggested that German control there would not be a bad thing because Germany would serve as a barrier to the westward movement of the Soviets, whom he feared more than the Germans.[55]

Most important to Hoover was that the United States not become involved in a future European war. Although he did not believe war was imminent, he did not rule it out completely. The League of Nations had failed, and Europe had returned to its old concept of the balance of power. In case of war, Washington should make clear to the Europeans that it would not become involved in the conflict even to defend the democracies. "The forms of government which other people pass through in working out their destinies is [*sic*] not our business," he told the Foreign Policy Association in New York soon after returning home. To join with Britain and France would also be to ally the United States with imperial powers, and even worse with France's friend, Joseph Stalin. Rather, the United States should encourage international economic cooperation and "keep alight the flame of true liberalism."[56]

In his speeches, the former president also drew a parallel between the dangers of Roosevelt's domestic and foreign policies, which, he was convinced, was intended to draw the United States into the war. The very struggle against fascism, he remarked, could turn the nation into "practically a Fascist state."[57]

When war finally came after Germany invaded Poland in September 1939, Hoover became a leader of the peace movement in the United States. Once more, he tied domestic to foreign policy. "In 1917, when we joined in the war," he wrote in the *Saturday Evening Post* in October, "the sense of private enterprise was unimpaired. We had no Fascist taint of planned economy. We had no Socialist taint of planned economy. We had no centralization of credit. . . . We would start another war with a weakened sense of private enterprise."[58]

At the same time, the former president led the movement to provide relief to Poland, which had also been invaded by the Soviet Union from the east shortly after the German invasion, and then to Finland, after it too was invaded by the Soviet Union in November 1939. Americans felt a special kinship for the Finns because of the courageous war they fought against the Soviets, and because Finland was the only country to repay its World War I debts to the United States.

Momentarily overcoming his dislike for his predecessor, President Roosevelt even asked Hoover to head the nation's relief effort for Europe. The former president refused, believing the president was trying to sidetrack his efforts at peace. On his own, however, he raised considerable sums for European relief. The unwillingness of the British to allow aid to pass through the blockade it imposed on the continent, the lack of support he received from the Roosevelt administration, and bureaucratic difficulties in working with the Red Cross in supplying assistance to Europe, however, limited what he could accomplish. By the time Finland fell to the Soviets in 1940, the relief effort had shrunk to a trickle.[59]

By 1940, Hoover was also actively, if covertly, seeking the Republican nomination for president. His leadership of the peace movement and his effort to provide relief to Europe made him an increasingly popular figure. He was in demand as a speaker, and he was mentioned prominently, along with Alf Landon, Ohio senator Robert Taft, and the crime-fighting New York district attorney, Thomas Dewey, as a likely candidate for the nomination. As in 1936, he had no interest in campaigning publicly for the nomination, but he made it clear to friends and political associates that if the convention should become deadlocked, he would be interested in a draft. He also supported the organization of a group known as the Republican Circles, whose ostensible aim was to revitalize the Republican Party in the Western states but whose real purpose was to act as a grassroots organization on Hoover's behalf. Gradually the Republican Circles spread throughout California and then into neighboring states.[60]

Unfortunately for the former president, his insistence on a draft, the residual dislike for him among both conservative and moderate Republicans, and his opposition to most forms of military assistance to the Western allies fighting against Germany doomed his candidacy. He had banked on a deadlocked convention that would then turn to him. Instead, a crowded field eventually gave way to the relatively unknown, but moderate and charismatic, Wendell Willkie of New York, who appealed to the party's younger and more internationalist members.[61]

Like Landon four years earlier, the Republican candidate then humiliated Hoover by drastically limiting his role in the campaign to a few speeches. Roosevelt also derided the former president's administration, just as he had done in 1936. Although Willkie conducted a vigorous campaign and cut into Roosevelt's margin of victory from four years earlier, he still lost to Roosevelt by substantial margins, winning twenty-two million popular votes and eighty-two electoral votes to Roosevelt's twenty-seven million popular votes and 449 electoral votes.[62]

Until Japan bombed Pearl Harbor on 7 December 1941, the former president continued to be a leader of the peace movement in the United States. In 1939, he supported amending the neutrality laws that Congress had imposed over the last three years to the extent that belligerent countries might buy defensive weapons on a cash-and-carry basis. The next year, he also approved the exchange of British bases in the Western Hemisphere for fifty aged American destroyers. He continued to oppose the sale of offensive weapons to the belligerents, even though the distinction between offensive and defensive weapons was never clear. He also regarded the "bases for destroyers" deal as a way of strengthening the hemisphere rather than as a step toward U.S. involvement in the European war.[63]

On other measures to aid the allies, Hoover remained a vociferous opponent. In particular, he was infuriated by Roosevelt's lend-lease proposal in early 1941 that would make American military equipment available to the British. He vowed to fight "day and night" to kill the proposal. Both in foreign as well as in domestic affairs, he believed Roosevelt was assuming greater powers than any president before him, and that his war policies would "establish further centralization of authority amounting to practical dictatorship."[64]

When, after Hitler's invasion of the Soviet Union in June, the president extended lend-lease assistance to Moscow, Hoover's fury knew few bounds. He had always believed Germany posed more of a threat to the Soviet Union than to Britain and France. Even after Hitler ordered his armies into the lowlands of France and sent German airplanes over the London skies, he thought a negotiated peace between the Western democracies and Berlin was still possible.[65] In contrast, the former president was convinced that the Kremlin was so immoral that the United States should do nothing to assist it. He would have been happy, in fact, to let the Nazis and communists kill each other off in the east. "Is the world of Stalin any better than the world of Hitler?" he asked at the end of June. War between the two totalitarian regimes could only strengthen the chances of peace in the West and lessen the odds of U.S. involvement in the war.[66]

Until 1940, most of Hoover's concern had been about the possibility that the United States might be drawn into war against Germany. After the Japanese signed the Tripartite Pact with Germany and Italy in September 1940, he also grew worried that Japan might be provoked by Roosevelt into a war in the Pacific. He always regarded the Japanese as a bulwark against Soviet aggression in the Far East, just as he considered Germany a barrier to Soviet aggression in Europe. As relations continued to deteriorate between Tokyo and Washington in 1941, he went so far as to engage in his own dangerous diplomacy. Just before Pearl Harbor, he even used intermediaries to suggest to Japan a standstill agreement and a big power conference to arrange a durable peace in the Pacific.[67]

Once Japan attacked Pearl Harbor and the United States entered World War II, Hoover supported the war effort. He was nevertheless disturbed that the president chose not to call on him to play a meaningful role while war was being waged, as he had during World War I. Bernard Baruch, whom Roosevelt had invited to the White House to discuss ways to mobilize the home front, told the president that no one would be more valuable in streamlining the domestic war effort than Hoover, but Roosevelt turned him down.[68]

Ignored by the president, Hoover busied himself during the war mostly by writing several books and numerous magazine articles in which he lamented the New Deal's failure to avoid the United States' entanglement in the war. His support of the war effort also did not keep him from criticizing Roosevelt's military strategy or the allied war effort. He had little faith in Prime Minister Winston Churchill, whom he regarded as little more than a British imperialist. "This war belongs to the God-seekers and the New Dealers. It will be ours when they lose it. . . . We can pray that new men come to leadership quickly both here and in England or we shall fail."[69]

On a more constructive note, the former president proposed a more internationalist role for the United States after the war. He outlined his vision of the postwar world in two books, *The Problems of Lasting Peace* (1942) and the much shorter *The Basis of a Lasting Peace* (1945), both of which he wrote with an old friend and veteran diplomat, Hugh Gibson. Hoover and Gibson opposed the establishment of an international body modeled after the League of Nations. However, they did favor the creation of an international institution, the specifics of which they said should be decided on not during the peace negotiations, but sometime after the difficulties of a permanent peace could be resolved by groups of experts. This would allow time to develop the structure of an institution removed from the emotions of war.

On one point, Hoover and Gibson were absolutely clear. The new organization should have no coercive powers. They were unwilling to turn over to any international body the power to draw the United States into a war; the war-making power of Congress should remain sacrosanct. "No machinery of enforcement is suggested [for this new institution]," they remarked. "It would rest solely upon good faith, world opinion, and the value of immediate discussion directly between nations rather than through the intervention of an outside body." They also opposed the dismemberment of Germany. "There can be no lasting peace in Europe," they held, "with a dismembered Germany. . . . Certainly, experience shows that no nation can be punished as a whole and at the same time leave any hope of lasting peace. We can have peace or we can have revenge, but we cannot have both."[70]

Hoover hoped *The Problems of Lasting Peace* would be a best seller, not for the remuneration it would bring him but as a way of influencing the Republican Party toward a more internationalist role in the postwar world. He even helped finance the promotion of the book and donated copies of it to libraries and various organizations. As he anticipated, the book was a best seller, becoming a Book-of-the-Month Club selection. It went through nine reprints. *Reader's Digest,* which reached into five million homes, published a condensed version. Reviewers also gave it an enthusiastic reception. Even Hoover's longtime progressive critic, Walter Lippmann, praised it.[71]

By his writings and speeches, the former president helped forge a bipartisan approach to the nation's postwar foreign policy. Notwithstanding his criticisms of Roosevelt's conduct of the war, he also supported most of the agreements Roosevelt made with the allies during the war, including even the Yalta agreement of February 1945, which was later maligned by Republicans for allegedly handing over much of Europe to the Soviets. Although he privately doubted that the Soviets would abide by their commitments at Yalta, such as to hold free elections in Poland and other countries they occupied in Eastern Europe, he went so far as to issue a press statement stating that the agreement "comprises a strong foundation on which to rebuild the world."[72]

All the more reason, therefore, why Hoover became increasingly embittered at the administration for not paying him the respect ordinarily given to ex-presidents. As late as 1958, in a memorandum reflecting on his relations with Roosevelt, he expressed his resentment at his successor's failure to seek his services during the war. "Despite the urgings of such mutual friends as Bernard Baruch and Mr. Roosevelt's Secretary of War Henry L. Stimson, he frigidly declined any association with me," he recalled in 1958.[73]

The former president also had to endure the humiliation during the war of being shunned once more by Republican leaders. At the party's convention in 1944, its candidate for president, Thomas Dewey, refused to be photographed with Hoover's two sons, who were attending the gathering. A few months later, in October, at the funeral of Wendell Willkie, after his death after a heart attack at the age of fifty-two, Dewey avoided speaking to Hoover even though they sat in the same pew. Hoover responded with disdain toward the candidate. "A man couldn't wear a mustache like that without having it affect his mind," he remarked.[74]

For the former president, however, the most crushing blow during the war came on 7 January 1944, when he found his wife of forty-four years, Lou Henry, who had a heart condition, dead on the floor of their bedroom in the Waldorf-Astoria. A brilliant woman who was ahead of her time in education and independence, she had traveled to the far distances of the world with her husband and had been his partner in virtually every way. She was his alter ego and friendly, warm, and gregarious. She played an active role in the Girls Scouts, gave interviews to the press, appeared on radio, and championed the cause of women's sports. Her death capped what had been the worst period of Hoover's life since becoming an ex-president.[75]

Like most of the nation, Hoover was shocked when, a little less than a year after his wife's death, President Roosevelt died at Warms Springs, Georgia, of a cerebral hemorrhage. Yet Roosevelt's replacement as president by the little-known vice president from Missouri, Harry S. Truman, marked a new and un-expected chapter in Hoover's life. Instead of ignoring Hoover, as Roosevelt had done, the new president invited him to the White House in May. As a matter of principle, Truman believed that ex-presidents deserved to be treated with dignity and respect. Furthermore, the pragmatic Midwesterner from Independence, Missouri, understood that Hoover's vast experience might be put to good service in the postwar world, where famine threatened the lives of millions. "I invited him to visit with me and give me the benefit of his rich experience in the field of food relief," Truman later wrote. "When he came, I had a most pleasant and satisfactory meeting with him. He helped me to review the world food-distribution problem, which he knew from one end to the other."[76]

For his part, Hoover left his meeting in the Oval Office believing "that nothing more would come of it so far as I or my views were concerned." However, he was mistaken. Responding to the need for food relief abroad after the war, Truman formed a twelve-member Famine Emergency Committee in February 1946 over the objections of many of his top aides, who still held the former president in contempt, and named Hoover its honorary chairman. He intended Hoover to do more than hold an honorary title. Instead, he asked the former president to assess the food needs of Europe and other famine-stricken areas. Over the next three months, the seventy-one-year-old Hoover traveled more than 50,000 miles visiting almost forty countries. Returning to the United States, he delivered a

grim but detailed country-by-country, month-by-month program of essential relief needs. "It is now 11:59 on the clock of starvation," he told the American
people. Hoover's message became the clarion call for an enormous relief effort
that helped save Europe from massive starvation.[77]

With Truman's support, Congress in 1947 reversed an insult the Roosevelt
administration had inflicted on Hoover by restoring the original name of the
Boulder Dam to the Hoover Dam. That same year, the president gave Hoover
another major assignment when he put him in charge of a commission that soon
came to be called the Hoover Commission. Established by Congress in 1947, its
responsibility was supposedly to make recommendations for reorganizing the executive branch. Its real purpose, though, was to rein in the expansion of presidential power. Truman supported the commission for a different reason. He wanted to
bring greater efficiency to a branch of government that had grown willy-nilly.[78]

This conflict between what Congress and Truman intended from the commission played itself out in its deliberations. According to Hoover, when it looked
like the new president after 1948 would be a Republican, its vice chairman, Dean
Acheson, who had earlier questioned Hoover's mental stability and fitness to
serve on the commission, and the body's other New Dealers (James Forrestal,
James Rowe Jr., and James K. Pollock) sought to limit the president's prerogatives. When Truman was returned to office in one of the greatest political upsets
of all time, they reversed course. Nevertheless, Hoover led the commission on the
most comprehensive study ever undertaken of any branch of government. When
the commission published its findings in 1949, it attracted major national attention, and Truman implemented the bulk of its recommendations, although often
with significant alterations that did not please Hoover. As a result, the president
was able to strengthen the resources and functionality of the executive branch in
ways that gave it significant advantages over other branches of government.[79]

Although Truman brought Hoover back from the exile imposed on him by
Roosevelt, providing the basis for a lasting friendship, the two men still remained
at odds on significant policy matters. Part of the reason for this was simply their
different political philosophies. The president remained committed to carrying
out the basic tenets of the New Deal, which the former president always thought
was dangerously intrusive in a free enterprise economy. Instead, cooperative individualism remained at the core of his political views. Although the former president also came to respect and like Truman, he believed that he remained, in many
ways, a little man, a machine politician who lacked the political deftness and
dexterity of Roosevelt, especially in his dealings with Congress. Finally, Hoover
thought the Missourian suffered from a split personality, so he could not always
be trusted. "One day I find him a devoted public servant who really comes from
the people," he remarked in 1945, "the next time I find him to be a . . . politician
who will do anything for a vote." As for the president, he also had his personal
reservations about Hoover, and, like other Democrats, attacked him repeatedly in
the 1948 campaign. "You remember the Hoover cart," he remarked, for example,

in October, "the remains of an the old tin lizzie being pulled by a mule. . . . It is the only automobile that eats oats."[80]

The differences between Hoover and Truman were most pronounced in the realm of foreign policy. While Truman and Hoover were both internationalists, their views of the role the United States should play in the world differed considerably. Essentially, Hoover renounced the use of force as a means to bring about a lasting peace. Truman saw force, even the use of nuclear power, as the only way to bring about an end to the ongoing war against Japan. Although the president sought to retain the grand coalition that had won the war in Europe, Hoover continued to regard the Soviet Union as the greatest danger to world peace and wanted to have as little to do with the Soviets as possible. While Hoover supported the establishment of an international body after the war, he never endorsed the structure and authority of the United Nations. Indeed, he preferred three regional international bodies rather than a single UN. Finally, while Hoover looked at the world in ways similar to Theodore Roosevelt, who sought to maintain a balance of power in Europe, recognized Japanese dominance in Asia, and considered the Western Hemisphere as the special provenance of the United States, Truman believed in the superpower status of the United States and its worldwide responsibility to contain communist expansionism.

These differences between the president and former president became apparent during their first meeting at the White House. Emphasizing his distrust of the Soviets, whom he referred to as Russians, Hoover remarked that "the Russians were Asiatics; that they had the characteristics of Asiatics; that they did not have the reverence for agreements that was characteristic of Asiatics." However, he was against even threatening Moscow with war. "Our position should be to persuade, hold up our banner of what we thought was right and let it go at that." As for the Far East, the United States should make a separate peace with Japan in order to prevent the Soviets from entering the war. Japan should be required to give up Manchuria, which rightly belonged to China. Beyond that, Japan should be allowed to hold on to Formosa and Korea. China had no moral right to Formosa, which was not Chinese, and "Korea had a much worse government before the Japanese had taken it over." If the United States made a declaration that the Japanese could keep these two territories, that it "had no desire to exterminate the Japanese people, had no desire to destroy the Japanese form of government," and wanted Japan to "build itself into a prosperous nation," it was possible that Japan would accept these terms. He was not optimistic that this would happen but believed it was worth the effort.[81]

When Truman ignored the former president's advice and brought the war to an end in August by dropping atomic bombs on Hiroshima and Nagasaki, Hoover made clear his frustration with the president. "The use of the Atomic bomb, with its indiscriminate killing of women and children, revolts me," he told his friend John Callan O'Laughlin. "The only difference between this and the use of poison gas is the fear of retaliation. We alone have the bomb."[82]

Once the war was over, Hoover revealed another reason that had always been in the back of his mind for wanting Japan to have a strong economy after the war. A prosperous Japan would not only stave off famine, it would also "help to develop a protection against the spread of Communism over the whole of Asia, etc." Hoover continued to emphasize the need for a prosperous Japan in order to prevent communist expansion in Asia, especially after the coming to power of the Chinese communists in 1949, followed the next year by the outbreak of the Korean War and the Chinese invasion of Korea.

After China's invasion of Korea, Hoover even seemed to move from an internationalist to an isolationist foreign policy for the United States, one in which the United States would rely on its European allies in the West and Japan and a cordon of other ocean bases in the Pacific to prevent communist expansion in Europe and Asia while limiting its own military commitments largely to the Western Hemisphere.[83] Shortly after the Chinese invasion, he delivered a speech in which he proposed turning the western hemisphere into a "Gibraltar of Civilization." According to this view, the United States should strive for hemispheric and economic self-reliance, protected only by bases in Formosa, the Philippines, and Japan in the Pacific and perhaps by England in the Atlantic. In particular, Hoover opposed Truman's proposal to build up the North Atlantic Treaty Organization (NATO) alliance by sending American ground forces to Europe without congressional approval and despite Europe's reluctance to provide for its own defense. Europe, he remarked, must establish its own military force. "It must erect a sure dam against the red flood . . . before we land another man or another dollar on their shores."[84]

Dismissed by some as the mutterings of a failed leader rapidly growing senile, Hoover's remarks were nevertheless widely disseminated and received enormous press coverage, some critical, most favorable, and set off what became known as the Great Debate over the future of American foreign policy. What especially concerned the critics of Hoover's Gibraltar address was that it appeared to represent a much broader national trend toward isolationism and against bipartisanship in foreign policy. Even President Truman referred to Hoover's comments as nothing but isolationism.[85]

Even in their most extreme iteration, however, Hoover's ideas on the role of the United States in the world were never those of a total isolationist. Indeed, he believed the malignancy of communist expansion during the cold war placed an increasingly greater burden on the United States. However, war and winning battles could not change ideas; people must do that. The United States could help by encouraging and fostering economic prosperity. It could not become the policeman of the world. Nor could it carry the entire burden for a prosperous world. Otherwise, it would bankrupt itself.

The key, then, for a lasting peace, which was core to his foreign policy rather than some abstract ideal, was the cooperation and participation of all noncommunist societies to contain communist expansion, not through military alliances or engagements but through economic prosperity, peaceful promotion of democratic ideals, and disarmament. In an address at Emporia, Kansas, on 11 July 1950, shortly after the Korean War began, he in fact rejected the idea of a Rock of Gibraltar, with which he became so closely identified a few months later. He even called the United Nations the last best hope for a peaceful world. The alternative, he remarked, would be "to crawl into isolation and defend the Western hemisphere alone. That would be less than a secure peace." As he remarked a few months later in New York, however, Europe needed to do its share. If Europe did not understand that the American economy could not carry on its shoulders the economic well-being of the entire free world, then "we had better quit talking and paying, and consider holding the Atlantic Ocean with Britain (if they wish) as one frontier, and the Pacific Ocean with an armed Japan and other islands as the other frontier."[86]

Much the same sentiments had informed his support earlier of the Marshall Plan, which he favored in principle but only if the European nations were willing, in a cooperative fashion, to share the onus of their own economic recovery. He also wanted to limit Marshall Plan aid from four years to fifteen months and to restrict American grants to the nation's surplus production in any given year. As for the organization of NATO, he strongly believed that each nation had to provide for its own defense and that the United States had no justification for committing thousands of American forces in Europe, which would strain the nation's economy and raise the chances of war. He was greatly disappointed, therefore, when the European nations, in his view, failed to live up their promises to rearm at the time the NATO pact was ratified by the United States. "We should be willing to aid but, if Western Europe wants defense from the Communist tide, they must do most of it themselves—and do it fast," he commented in a broadcast from New York on 19 October 1950.[87]

Despite their differences over foreign policy, which neither Truman nor Hoover was afraid to address to the other publicly, personally, and passionately, cordiality and respect rather than rancor continued to characterize their relationship. Hoover appreciated the fact that Truman always referred to him as "Mr. President." He was grateful when Mrs. Bess Truman unveiled at the White House a portrait of Lou Henry. He expressed sympathy for the beleaguered Truman during his last years in office, making clear that his remarks should not be interpreted "as an indelicate implication that I am seeking a recruit to my exclusive union of ex-Presidents."[88]

Even after Truman left office in 1953, Hoover enjoyed referring to him as his "fellow trade unionist." The fact that Truman and he were the only two living ex-presidents and that both enjoyed vacationing in the Florida Keys bonded them even closer. In 1953, Hoover accepted a request from his fellow former president to help with a fund-raising dinner for the Truman Library in San Francisco. In 1957, he altered his plans so that he could travel from San Francisco to Independence to be present at the dedication of the library.[89]

Hoover and Truman also found a common bond in their distrust of President Dwight Eisenhower and his secretary of state, John Foster Dulles. Although Truman's misgivings about the administration had as much to do with his personal dislike of his successor and his secretary of state as over policy differences, Hoover's qualms about the first Republican administration since his defeat in 1932 were much more policy driven. Simply stated, the emphasis the administration placed on "massive retaliation" and international economic interdependence challenged the very fiber of Hoover's view that the road to lasting peace was never through military threats, and that economic independence rather than interdependence best served the national (and world) interest. Above all else, the United States must not overcommit itself in the cold war. To do so would be to undermine a political economy predicated on the values and virtues of free enterprise, the strongest antidote to the communist threat.[90]

Along similar lines, Hoover had difficulty with the large budget deficits incurred during the Eisenhower administration. He attributed much of this to the fact that instead of rolling back the New Deal, Eisenhower seemed to expand it. Often forgotten is the fact that, as the first Republican elected to office since Roosevelt, the former supreme commander of allied forces in Europe had the opportunity to reject the basic tenets of the New Deal, with its emphasis on enhanced government power and an international foreign policy. One of Eisenhower's most significant achievements as president was the fact that, with some modification, he embraced both the domestic and foreign policy of his Democratic predecessors.

For that very reason, though, Hoover preferred a more conservative Republican candidate in the 1952 election, like Senator Robert Taft of Ohio or even his longtime friend and neighbor in the Waldorf-Astoria, Douglas MacArthur, whom he had admired ever since he had been army chief of staff during his administration. Unlike Eisenhower, whom Hoover always regarded as representing the more liberal Northeast wing of the Republican Party, they might have changed the nation's direction from that of the New Deal . . . or at least Hoover believed.[91]

Although Hoover never entirely gave up his exhausting writing and speaking schedule, he managed to eke out time for relaxation, including traveling, playing gin rummy, visiting with his grandchildren and great-grandchildren, remaining active with the Boys Clubs of America, and taking apart radios and telephones. His fondest form of relaxation, however, remained fishing, especially fly fishing. He fished for salmon in the Rockies of the United States and Canada and for trout wherever he could find a trout stream. He also enjoyed the challenge of going after large bonefish off the coast of Florida, and he spent his winters at the exclusive Key Largo Anglers Club. "Fishing is the chance to wash one's soul with pure air, with the rush of the brook, or with the shimmer of the sun on the blue water," he wrote about his favorite hobby in a manner that also described some of the core values of his lifelong political philosophy. "[Fishing] brings meekness and decency from the decency of nature, charity toward tackle makers, patience toward fish, a mockery of profit and egos, a quieting of hate, a rejoicing that you do not have to decide a darned thing until next week. And it is discipline in the equality of men, for all men are equal before fish."[92]

Much to Hoover's credit, he never engaged in the domestic anticommunism that characterized much of the late 1940s and early 1950s. "I doubt if there are any consequential card-carrying communists in the Government, or if they are, they should be known to the F.B.I.," he wrote Truman in November 1950 after the president asked him to chair a bipartisan committee he was considering establishing to examine domestic threats to the United States. He helped, however, to launch the career of one of the most notable witch-hunters of the period, U.S. representative and then senator Richard Nixon, whom he greatly admired and then supported for the vice presidency in 1952.[93]

As he grew older and focused more on foreign policy, Hoover grew even more strident in his anticommunism. For that very reason, he remained committed to his long-held belief in avoiding war and promoting economic growth at home through fiscal restraint and what he continued to refer to as nonfascist or socialist means. He continued to reject the anticommunist hysteria associated with Senator Joseph McCarthy of Wisconsin. "If our intellectuals want to continue to believe in or to sympathize with abstract Communism as being freedom, they could do so," he remarked. "That could be called academic freedom. But the moment they make a move to discuss any subversive action, they might be in the toils of the F.B.I."[94]

By the time Eisenhower was elected president, Hoover was in his late seventies. Still, he continued to work eight to twelve hours every day. When he was asked by the White House to undertake a second Hoover Commission, he again took on the assignment. Eisenhower found most of its recommendations, such as selling the Tennessee Valley Authority, outdated and buried the commission's report. This contributed to Hoover's general dislike for Eisenhower, who, he said in 1958, would rank alongside Calvin Coolidge as among the nation's least notable presidents. In 1960, Hoover supported Richard Nixon for president, and in 1964, he backed Barry Goldwater, although without much enthusiasm.[95]

During his later years, Hoover began to suffer some of the infirmities of old age. In 1949, while returning from a speaking tour, he suffered a gallbladder attack. Around the same time, he developed a case of shingles. His eyesight and hearing also began to fail, and he took to wearing a hearing aid. Yet until 1962, he remained in surprisingly good health. That year, however, the eighty-eight-year-old former president had a malignant tumor removed from his intestines. Ten months later, he developed massive gastrointestinal bleeding that almost killed him. Although his health and strength seemed to improve, in February 1964, the gastrointestinal bleeding recurred complicated by pneumonia. He lingered until October, when he suffered a massive hemorrhage. After slipping into a coma, he died on 20 October at the age of ninety. In a simple service, he was buried near his birthplace in West Branch, Iowa. Later, the casket of Lou Henry, who had been

Hoover poses in his Waldorf-Astoria Suite, 1960. Although he was nearly eighty-six years old when this picture was taken, needed to wear a hearing aid, and had cut back his public activities considerably, he remained in relatively good health. He also continued to follow politics carefully and endorsed Vice President Richard Nixon for the Republican nomination for president. (Courtesy of Herbert Hoover Presidential Library-Museum.)

buried in Palo Alto, was removed from the ground and taken to West Branch to be interred beside that of her husband.

As the longest-living former president, Hoover had brought new purpose and meaning to being an ex-president. More than any other former president, he had increased the responsibilities of those who had served in the Oval Office. He had shown that former presidents could be political either alone or in partnership with incumbent presidents or could be potent political instruments for influencing public opinion and serving the state. He was, in other words, the nation's first modern ex-president.

10

The Office of Ex-President

Truman

Herbert Hoover had made the position of ex-president a full-time career. Former presidents, however, still did not have many legal perquisites and powers that went along with that career. They received neither pensions nor funds for the office and staff necessary to assist them with the huge volume of mail and requests they received. Nor were they entitled to free mailing privileges to cover their huge correspondence or to Secret Service protection. Although they were expected to refuse any remuneration that might taint the dignity of the office they had held, that practice was not always followed. They were still free to pursue other careers or just be private citizens disengaged from the whirlwind of their previous lives. As late as 1953, Truman even thought he could take a road trip as an ordinary citizen from his home in Missouri to the East Coast.

During Truman's long tenure as former president (1953–1972), most of that changed. He extended the doctrine of executive privilege to former presidents. Congress passed legislation providing pensions for ex-presidents equal to the salary of cabinet officials. The House and Senate adopted a measure establishing a formal system of presidential libraries and museums operated by the National Archives. After President John F. Kennedy's assassination in 1963, Secret Service protection was provided to all former presidents and their families. President Lyndon Johnson also put at the disposal of all ex-presidents air force jets and helicopters. Away from Washington, Truman systematized the practice, since continued and expanded on by virtually every other former president, of receiving large advances and royalties for preparing his memoirs (usually written by teams of ghostwriters) and other works, and he was the first president to receive a substantial fee for a television interview. For all his desire to return to the life of a private citizen, free to do and to travel as he pleased, he came to realize that his life had been inalterably changed as a result of his having been president.

I

Truman's elevation to the Oval Office after the death of Franklin Roosevelt in April 1945 did not come as a complete surprise to the new president. He had shared in the widespread speculation at the time the Democrats selected him as Roosevelt's running mate that Roosevelt would probably not live out his fourth term. That did not diminish the reality of the moment for Truman. He knew that, except for his work on a special congressional committee investigating over costs in war production, he was hardly known to the American people. He realized that as vice president he had not been taken into Roosevelt's confidence. He grasped that his own interests and experience had not prepared him to be a war leader at a time when the tide of battle had clearly turned and important decisions had to be made for ending the war and securing peace. And he was fully aware of the comparisons that were inevitable between the ordinary politician from Independence and the extraordinary leader from Hyde Park who had steered the nation through depression and conflict for more than sixteen years and whose death left much of the nation in shock and tears. He did not expect the comparisons to redound in his favor. "I felt like the moon, the stars, and all the planets had fallen on me," he remarked after learning Roosevelt had died.[1]

Truman had been vice president for only three months when he assumed the presidency. He was sixty-one years old and had been in national politics for scarcely a decade. Born in Lamar, Missouri, on 8 May 1884, he later remembered his childhood fondly, especially his early years in Grandview, about thirty miles from Kansas City, where his father, a farmer and livestock trader, ran his in-laws' farm. "I had just the happiest childhood that could ever be imagined," he recalled."[2]

Yet life seemed to throw one obstacle after another before the future president. Born with poor eyesight that was not corrected until he was six years old, when he finally received a set of thick eyeglasses, he did not enter the first grade until he was eight. By this time, his father had moved the family to Independence, a bustling town of 6,000 about ten miles east of Kansas City and once the starting point of both the Oregon and Santa Fe trails. Wearing expensive glasses, shy, and ordered by his mother not to roughhouse or to take part in sports, he became the easy target of school bullies.[3]

As a young boy, Truman became an avid reader. He mostly enjoyed history and biography, especially the lives of great American and classical figures, including Cicero, Caesar, Marcus Aurelius, and Plutarch. This left him with a lifelong conviction that great leaders determined the course of history, which, he believed, was generally one of progress. The certitudes of his Baptist upbringing, the pioneering spirit that still pervaded much of the far Midwest, and the fact that he grew up in the Victorian age, with its emphasis on absolutes and advancement, only confirmed his view of history. What he lacked was an appreciation of the nuances of social development and a more ambiguous view of good and evil and right and wrong. "I saw that it takes men to make history, or there would be no history," he wrote late in his life. "History does not make the man."[4]

In striking contrast to Herbert Hoover's career as a young man, Truman's ventures were largely failures. Both men had the same determination to succeed. Both were entrepreneurial in spirit. Although Hoover excelled in mathematics and the sciences and Truman proved unexceptional in anything, other differences in their native abilities were hard to find. Whereas good fortune seemed to shine on Hoover's career, ill luck appeared to follow Truman. Although he was better prepared than Hoover for college and wanted to attend one of the military academies, his poor eyesight eliminated that possibility. Several of his friends enrolled at the University of Missouri, but Truman was also denied even that opportunity by his father, who had fallen on hard financial times. Truman, who was working in a bank in Kansas City, had to move back to Grandview to help his father once more manage his mother-in-law's farm.

Truman hated this part of his life, with its long hours, hard labor, drudgery, and financial uncertainty. Worse, he considered himself a complete failure. Writing in 1911 to Bess Wallace of Independence, whom he had known from grade school and with whom he had begun a long courtship, he remarked, "I am . . . only a kind of good-for nothing American farmer, I've always had a sneaking' notion that some day maybe I'd amount to something. I doubt it now though like everything. It's a family failing of ours to be poor financiers."[5]

In 1914, Truman's father died unexpectedly. His death proved a liberating experience. Truman felt freer to engage his entrepreneurial spirit, most notably land speculation, mining, and oil exploration. Ironically, while Hoover made his fortune in mining, often buying mining rights that others had abandoned, Truman lost money by becoming a principal investor in speculative lead, zinc, and oil ventures as far away as Oklahoma, Texas, and Mexico. On several occasions, he had to stop digging and drilling for lack of capital just short of a mother lode.

Not until Truman joined the National Guard as a lieutenant in a company that was soon absorbed by the regular army and then led an artillery battalion in France after the United States' entry into World War I in April 1917 did his latent talents as a politician and administrator of men manifest themselves. A deep sense of patriotism, a fascination with the military as a result of the many biographies of military leaders he had read, and an opportunity to prove himself were some of the reasons that drove Truman to enlist in the guard.[6]

Another may have been that he was already thinking of a political career and viewed joining the guard as a political launching pad. An interest in politics was something he had inherited from his father, a passionate Democrat. As a young man, Truman involved himself in local Democratic politics, gaining appointments as a local postmaster and a road overseer whose responsibility was maintaining the county highways. A wartime military record and the network of acquaintances he would make among his fellow guardsmen could later benefit him politically.[7]

Although Truman's battalion saw only limited action during the war, it performed admirably near Verdun and in the Vosges. At the end of the war, Truman was promoted to major. For the first time in his life, he felt a sense of achievement. He also made a number of lasting friendships that would play an important role in his political career. In particular, he had gotten to know Lieutenant James Pendergast, the nephew of Tom Pendergast, whose powerful political machine controlled Jackson County, where Kansas City and Independence were located. Without perhaps fully realizing it, he had established on the battlefields of France the basis for his later political career.

In May 1919, Truman was discharged from the army. The next month, he married Bess Wallace and then moved into the large house on 219 North Delaware Street owned by Bess's mother, Madge Gates Wallace. Although Mrs. Wallace would live to see her son-in-law become president, until the day she died in 1952, she believed that Bess had married beneath her worth.

The years between his marriage to Bess in 1919 and his election to the U.S. Senate in 1934 were mixed in terms of Truman's quest to overcome failure and to achieve the level of financial success he considered necessary to be a respected member of the community. His most notable failure was as a haberdasher in Kansas City, in partnership with Eddie Jacobson, who had helped Truman run a profitable canteen at Fort Sill in Oklahoma before their battalion was shipped overseas. In 1922, the business succumbed to recession. Truman's quest for respectability seemed even more distant than it had before enlisting in the war. Recalling his third anniversary to Bess thirty-eight years later, he remarked about his situation in 1922 as "broke and in a bad way."[8]

Truman had become good friends, however, with Tom Pendergast and a number of other city and county leaders who frequented his men's store or became involved in his other business schemes. His business also became a hangout for his former soldiers. With Pendergast's backing and that of the wide circle of friends he had made over the years, Truman was elected in 1922 a county judge (the equivalent of a county executive) for eastern Jackson County. His major responsibilities were overseeing the county budget and maintaining the county roads. Both offered enormous opportunities for graft. Although the future president obliged the Pendergast machine in giving out patronage positions and approving county contracts for the cement and oil businesses Tom Pendergast owned, Truman never solicited or accepted a bribe from the Pendergast machine or awarded contracts based on anything but the best deal for the county. Pendergast understood and accepted Truman's insistence on honest government in return for having an important ally in the eastern part of Jackson County, where the organization was the weakest. In 1924, Truman won the Democratic primary for reelection, but owing to splits in Democratic ranks and a Republican sweep that year, he lost to his Republican opponent. Once more, failure seemed to follow Truman's bid for respectability and financial security.

The year 1924 was almost certainly the low point of Truman's life. That year,

Bess gave birth to the Trumans' only child, Mary Margaret. The future president now had to worry about another mouth to feed. He was barely getting by financially, and he still had no real career. Of the nation's presidents, he was at this point in his life among the least likely to reach the Oval Office.

Two years later, Truman's fortunes changed forever. With the backing of the Pendergast machine, he was elected the presiding judge of Jackson County. Twice winning reelection, he proved over the next eight years to be an honest and capable presiding judge, although he always wondered whether he had compromised his ethics by continuing to provide patronage and contracts to feed the insatiable appetite of the Pendergast machine.[9]

By 1932, Truman, who was nearing the midcentury of his life, thought of running for higher office. His chance came in 1934 when Republican senator Roscoe C. Patterson was up for reelection. With Pendergast's backing, Truman won the Democratic primary for Patterson's seat by 40,000 votes. In November's Democratic sweep, he easily defeated Patterson by more than 250,000 votes to become Missouri's junior senator in Washington.

As a first-term senator, Truman was a backbencher. Over time, however, he became a popular member of the upper chamber among both liberals and conservatives. About five feet, ten inches tall and weighing between 175 and 185 pounds, with brown hair and blue eyes, a straight nose, and his ever-present eyeglasses, Truman would not have stood out in a crowd except for the fact that he was a stylish dresser. However, he became known for his congeniality, attention to detail, and hard work. He was also able to talk easily across ideological lines. Throughout his life, he had always regarded himself as a Jeffersonian Democrat. He viewed Jefferson, however, as representing not so much small government as the common people against the moneyed interests. As in the case of the New Deal, he also felt government sometimes had to take extraordinary actions to protect the common welfare against big finance and large corporations.

As a modern Jeffersonian, Truman was able to make friends both among Southern conservatives and Western progressives. Truman's closest friend in the Senate became Burton K. Wheeler, the well-known insurgent from Montana, who made Truman a member of a special subcommittee investigating the condition of American railroads. The committee found plenty of evidence that big investment houses had made huge profits at the expense of the railroads, but nothing criminal that could provide the basis for new legislation. When he came up for reelection in 1940, therefore, Truman could boast of no major legislative achievement. He also had little party support. His ties to Pendergast, who had been sent to prison for tax evasion, were now a liability. He was expected to lose in the Democratic primary to Missouri's popular governor, Lloyd Stark. Instead, he defeated Stark and then went on to narrowly defeat his Republican opponent in the general election in November.

Still a relatively unknown junior senator from Missouri, Truman owed his rise to national prominence, and ultimately to the Oval Office, largely to his work as chairman of the Senate Committee to Investigate the National Defense Program, at first a small committee composed mostly of other backbenchers like Truman with only a small budget. By exposing considerable mismanagement and corruption in war production, however, it made national headlines. As a result, its size, status, and budget grew, making it one of the most important committees on Capitol Hill and turning Truman into a highly respected lawmaker.[10]

Looking for a compromise candidate to replace his controversial vice president, Henry Wallace, on the 1944 Democratic ticket, Roosevelt settled on the Missourian. The kindest thing that could be said about Roosevelt's choice was that Truman was an unassuming Midwestern politician who had been picked by the president to be his running mate because he was inoffensive to either conservative Southern Democrats or to Northern liberals. Certainly Roosevelt never took his vice president into his confidence. No wonder, then, that Truman felt unprepared to replace Roosevelt after he died in 1945.

During his administration, Truman made some of the most important decisions of any recent president, beginning with dropping the atomic bomb on Hiroshima and Nagasaki in 1945. Others included the Truman Doctrine (1947); recognition of the state of Israel (1948); the Marshall Plan (1948); the Berlin airlift (1948); the Point IV program (1949); establishment of the North Atlantic Treaty Organization (1949); going to war in Korea after the North Korean invasion of South Korea (1950); and firing General Douglas MacArthur as supreme commander of United Nations forces in South Korea (1951) after MacArthur disobeyed a series of his commands.

Some of the decisions Truman made were highly unpopular at the time, particularly his firing of MacArthur, which even led to calls for the president's impeachment. Others, like the Korean War, became increasingly out of favor as the conflict dragged on. Much of Truman's unpopularity, however, had to do with his domestic policies. Soon after taking office, the new president, fearing high unemployment and deflation after the war, made known that he intended to carry on and even extend the New Deal. The problem he faced after the war was inflation, not deflation, as Americans sought to use the savings they had accumulated during the war.

The mood of the country had also become distinctly conservative. Nevertheless, liberals were angry at Truman for not pushing harder for his progressive agenda. His poor handling of demobilization and of food scarcities and rising inflation added to a popular backlash against him. So did his response to a rash of strikes immediately after the war. By seeking a middle ground between labor's demands for higher wages to cope with inflation and business's reluctance to concede some wage increases, he alienated both sides.

Truman appeared, in other words, over his head as president and incapable of dealing with the whirlwind of problems associated with economic conversion. "To err is Truman" became a popular Republican refrain. In 1946, Republicans gained control of both houses of Congress by wide margins. The election represented a massive repudiation of the president and augured a Republican return to the White House in 1948.

That did not happen. Whistle-stopping across the continent, Truman connected with the American people by attacking the "do-nothing" Eightieth Congress. "Give 'em hell, Harry" became the response of growing crowds to the plainspoken and spirited Missourian. The Republicans also ran a lackluster candidate, Thomas Dewey, in an equally lackluster campaign. As a result, the Democratic underdog once more mortified the pollsters. When the election results were tallied, Truman received slightly under 50 percent of the popular vote and 303 electoral votes to Dewey's 45 percent of the popular vote and 189 electoral votes.

In 1952, there was speculation that Truman might seek reelection. Truman even allowed his name to be entered into the New Hampshire primary. By this time, however, he was even more unpopular than he had been at the end of his first administration. The major reasons why the American people turned once more against Truman had to do with the growing unpopularity of the Korean War that had stalemated both on the battlefield and at the negotiating table. Televised hearings linking organized crime to Democratic big-city machines also hurt Truman's chances in 1952. On the advice of his advisers, Truman decided to withdraw from the race.

Although Truman had been persuaded by the reality check given to him by his advisers not to seek another full term as president, he would have preferred to remain in Washington. He enjoyed being at the fulcrum of national power. As a student of history, he also had a special reverence for the nation's capital and its temples to the nation's history.[11]

Because of his interest in remaining in Washington, the president briefly considered running again for U.S. senator from Missouri. His years in the Senate had been among the happiest of his life. He would have enjoyed being a legislator again without the enormous burdens of the Oval Office. However, Bess Truman was anxious to return to Independence, and at age sixty-eight, Truman was also feeling the strain of the last twenty years.

He looked the picture of health. Almost every day he could be seen taking a brisk two-mile walk near the White House surrounded by the Secret Service. Always well dressed, often tanned from vacationing in Key West, Florida, he was prim and trim for a man of his age, a fact that he attributed to a strict diet of wholesome foods and to his own satisfaction as the nation's leader. To his colleagues, he liked to brag that he never lost a night's sleep even over a difficult decision he had made. He seemed comfortable in his own skin, a person who could make difficult decisions and then live with them convinced he was doing his best for the nation.

The reality was something different. Truman had always been a workaholic and worrier. Both before and after he became president, he was susceptible to anxiety attacks and exhaustion that sometimes manifested themselves in nausea and stomach pains. "He slept, so he told us, as soon as his head touched the pillow, never worrying, because he could not stay awake long enough to do so," his former secretary of state and close friend, Dean Acheson, later commented about the president. His solution was to get away from Washington where he could enjoy rest and quiet. As president, he frequented Key West, visiting the nation's southernmost town eleven times for a total of 175 days. The commandant's house at the naval submarine station in Key West, where he stayed, came to be known as the Little White House.[12]

As Acheson also commented, there were two sides to Truman's personality. One was considerate, appreciative, modest, and courtly, a paradigm of traditional small-town values. This was Truman, "the captain with the mighty heart." This, too, was Truman when he was fully rested and relaxed. The other Truman was the more public figure, feisty, sometimes belligerent, peppery, often didactic, the "give-'em-hell" Harry. Truman could also be rash, insecure, easily wounded, resentful, and impulsive to the point of being self-destructive. He was the person who, from childhood, sought respect and acceptance, worked hard to achieve it, and as president was weighed down by a keen sense of being unappreciated.[13]

So it was that Truman became increasingly irascible and, now and then, even irrational. He sometimes misspoke or made public mistakes for which he was unapologetic, such as one statement in November 1950 during a press conference in which he even raised the possibility of using nuclear weapons to repulse the Chinese invasion of Korea. British prime minister Clement Attlee had to scurry to the United States to get the president to modify his statement. Lashing out at his critics, the president fixated on the press, with whom at one time he had had good relations. He even accused some newspapers of aiding and abetting the enemy by printing maps with the location of defense plants and military installations. "Stalin needs no spy system to tell him our top secrets," he told one columnist. "Some of their antics in the last campaign were next door to treason," he told another.[14]

Truman was not upset, therefore, to leave what he referred to as "the great white jail" of the White House. Besides, he also shared the republican (and Jeffersonian) view of presidential retirement after dutiful service to the nation. "In my opinion eight years as president is enough and sometimes too much," he wrote privately as early as April 1950. "This is a Republic. . . . I want this country to continue as a Republic. Cincinnatus and Washington pointed the way."[15]

The outgoing president was not pleased, however, that the person replacing him was Dwight D. Eisenhower. Truman had once admired Eisenhower and probably suggested to him in 1951 that he would like him to be the Democratic presidential nominee in 1952.[16] Even after Eisenhower announced in January 1952 that he was a Republican and declared his candidacy for the Republican nomination. Truman had good things to say about him. "I am just as fond of General Eisenhower as I can be," he later told reporters.[17]

That all changed during the campaign between Eisenhower and the Democratic nominee, Governor Adlai Stevenson of Illinois. Truman's relationship with his party's fifty-one-year-old erudite and highly articulate candidate, whose paternal grandfather had been Grover Cleveland's vice president, was an uncomfortable one. Although having decided not to seek another term in the White House, the president intended to remain head of his party and to determine its candidate in 1952. Although his first choice had been Supreme Court chief justice Frederick Vinson, he settled on the popular and well-regarded governor from Illinois after Vinson declined to seek the nomination. He did not know Stevenson well, and he thought at first that he was too much of the patrician Ivy League type (Stevenson was a graduate of Princeton and Northwestern Law School) to be a good candidate. He had been impressed by his speeches, his wit and eloquence, and his political philosophy. Just as important, he was anxious to defeat the leading candidate for the nomination, Senator Estes Kefauver of Tennessee, who had made his national reputation holding highly publicized television hearings on organized crime that linked crime bosses to prominent Democrats. Truman believed Kefauver was intellectually dishonest and could not be trusted. Kefauver had also beaten Truman in the New Hampshire primary.[18]

Truman hoped at first to make Stevenson his protégé. He became increasingly distressed by Stevenson's indecision about seeking the nomination until three days after the nominating convention met in July. When Stevenson asked the president whether he would be "embarrassed" if he announced he would be the candidate, the president expressed his frustration with the governor. "Has your head been so much in the clouds as not to have understood that I have been trying to get you to run for the last six months?" was the essence of Truman's response to Stevenson. Nevertheless, he gave the governor his full support, and with his backing, Stevenson was nominated on the third ballot.[19]

What followed was even more frustration with Stevenson and growing anger at Eisenhower. Stevenson tried to distance himself from the unpopular Truman as much as possible. Not only did he replace the president's friend, Frank McKinney, as chairman of the party's national committee with his own person, Stephen Mitchell, but he also established the campaign's headquarters at Springfield, Illinois, instead of Washington, D.C. Truman regarded both decisions as unwise. More than that, he was enraged by Mitchell's appointment, which he considered a personal insult. "I have come to the conclusion," he wrote to Stevenson in a letter he had the good sense not to send, "that you are embarrassed by having the President of the United States in your corner in this campaign. Therefore I shall remain silent and stay in Washington until November 4th."[20]

Stevenson made other mistakes that also offended Truman, such as indirectly acknowledging that a mess existed in Washington. Believing, nevertheless, that the election represented a referendum on his presidency and that it was too important for him to remain on the sidelines, the president campaigned vigorously for the Democratic nominee throughout the country, replicating his whistle-stop campaign of 1948. Still, he found Stevenson a poor candidate, whose appeal was to the intellectual elite rather than to the common citizen. He considered him wooden, mealy-mouthed, and too remote from the public.[21]

If Truman was distressed by Stevenson, he became increasingly infuriated by Eisenhower, beginning with Eisenhower's choice of the red-baiting senator from California, Richard Nixon, as his running mate. From the beginning of the campaign, he lashed out at the Republican. The GOP, he said, stood not for the Grand Old Party but for the General's Own Party. "The Republicans have General Motors and General Electric and General Foods and General MacArthur and General [Albert C.] Wedemeyer. And they have their own five-star general who is running for President . . . [but] general welfare is with the corporals and the privates in the Democratic Party."[22]

As the campaign continued, Truman's comments became rougher and tougher. In part this was a reaction to Republican attacks on his administration, which the GOP accused of "K_1 C_2" (Korea, communism, and corruption). It was also an expression of his boiling anger with Eisenhower, who, according to Margaret Truman, had always agreed with the president's foreign policy "to the point of obsequiousness." The president knew that Eisenhower would be a popular candidate. What he did not comprehend until after the campaign got under way was the extent of his popularity and his effectiveness as a candidate, especially in contrast to Stevenson. While the Democrat resorted to the airplane and selected speeches to deliver his message to the American people, the Republican surpassed Truman in his use of the train, conducting a 53,000-mile campaign that took him into virtually every nook and cranny of the country. What struck observers was his personal attraction that seemed to overpower the crowds, who rapturously chanted, "I like Ike." Often forgotten about Eisenhower, who was later accused of fumbling the English language, was that even as a general, he had been an effective mass communicator.[23]

Angry at Eisenhower and befuddled by his popularity, Truman fired salvo after salvo against the Republican candidate, accusing him of being "a stooge of Wall Street" who was "owned body and soul by the money boys." He was also furious when Eisenhower's running mate, Senator Nixon, accused him, Stevenson, and Dean Acheson of being "traitors to the high principles in which many of the nation's Democrats believed." Truman interpreted this statement to mean that Nixon had called him a traitor.[24]

The final straw in shaping Truman's attitude toward Eisenhower was a much-anticipated speech that Eisenhower made in Milwaukee in which he failed to defend George Marshall against attacks by Joseph McCarthy. Truman considered the former army chief of staff and his secretary of state and secretary of defense as a true American hero. He also believed that Eisenhower, who owed his rapid rise to five-star general to Marshall, had an obligation to come to his defense. A well-publicized advance text of the Milwaukee speech included a tribute to Marshall. Seated on the same platform as the Wisconsin senator, however, Eisenhower excised that part of his speech. To Truman, his decision was disgraceful, and he never forgave him for it. "It was one of the most shameful things I can ever remember," he later said.[25]

Nor did Eisenhower forgive Truman for his harsh remarks during the campaign. Eisenhower became so incensed at the president that he threatened, if elected, to break the custom since 1801 of driving down Pennsylvania Avenue with the outgoing president on Inauguration Day.[26]

Truman was greatly disappointed but not surprised when Eisenhower won in November an overwhelming victory, receiving almost thirty-four million popular votes and 442 electoral votes to Stevenson's 27.3 million popular votes and eighty-nine electoral votes. He indicted the Democratic candidate for the mistakes he made, including firing McKinney, moving the campaign headquarters from Washington to Springfield, and distancing himself from the president.[27]

Even Truman acknowledged, however, that while Stevenson may have been able to pick up more votes if he had run a better campaign, the Democratic candidate never had much chance of defeating his opponent. More than anything Stevenson did, Eisenhower owed his victory to his immense popularity, the voter's displeasure with Truman, especially over the Korean War, and a promise he made toward the end of the campaign to go to Korea if elected to put an end to the war. Truman called Eisenhower's pledge little more than a campaign ploy that might actually have delayed the end of the conflict.[28]

Although Truman despaired over the fact that Eisenhower would soon be moving into the White House, he offered the presidential airplane to Eisenhower for his trip to Korea and invited the incoming president to the White House for meetings with him and his cabinet. In seeking a smooth transition of power, Truman remembered his ordeal and that of earlier presidents when they were catapulted into power. The result was a model for all future transitions.

Later the president-elect wrote Truman to thank him for his graciousness during the transition. Yet he never had the same respect for the president that Truman had for him. He was also resolute against making any commitment that might seem to tie him to the outgoing administration's policies. Although Truman was generous in making himself and his entire administration available to Eisenhower, Eisenhower met only once with the president during the transition.

The transition left Truman with a bitter taste toward the new president that would remain with him for the next fifteen years. Compared to Hoover, the president-elect seemed a petty man. He still stewed over Eisenhower's pledge to go to Korea and, after he returned from Korea over his announcement that he planned to meet with Truman's mortal enemy, Douglas MacArthur. At a press conference after Eisenhower returned from Korea Truman denounced MacArthur and called Eisenhower's trip to Korea "a piece of demagoguery." The outgoing president also claimed later to have been surprised at his November meeting with Eisenhower by how unprepared he found him to be for the office he was about to assume. "When the general and his aides left," he wrote in his *Memoirs,* "I was troubled. I had the feeling that, up to this meeting in the White House, General Eisenhower had not grasped the immense job ahead of him."[29]

After the inauguration, the Trumans attended a luncheon hosted by Dean

Acheson for the now ex-president. Five hundred people surprised them by waiting outside the Acheson house and cheering them when they arrived. After the luncheon, they went to Union Station for the train ride back to Independence. Thousands of well-wishers again surprised Truman by turning out to bid him, Bess, and Margaret a fond farewell. As the train left the station, the crowd burst into a thundering chorus of "Auld Lang Syne."[30]

The greeting Truman received as he left the nation's capital and the crowds that turned out to see him gave him an enormous boost. At each train stop on the way to Independence, crowds of as many as several hundred waited to greet the former president. At Independence, a huge gathering that Margaret later estimated exceeded 10,000 welcomed him home.

On the train, Margaret referred to her father as "Mr. Truman." Her purpose was to remind her father that he was, once more, an ordinary citizen. The former president laughed at being called by his surname rather than as "Mr. President." (Etiquette did not yet provide for continuing the name "Mr. President" for ex-presidents, although Truman always referred to Hoover as "Mr. President.") Being called by his last name resonated well with him, however, because he had little use for titles. "I don't care what people call me," he said when asked how he wanted to be addressed. "I've been called everything."[31]

Once home, the former president expected to conduct himself as an ordinary citizen. He intended to remain active in Democratic politics and to express his views on political matters. "As long as I live I'll never retire from politics," he wrote in August 1958 to Marvin Gates, a longtime friend. At the same time, he felt that former presidents should not offer their advice to incumbents unless asked for it and should be circumspect in their public comments, especially on foreign policy. He believed it was essential to the nation's safety to avoid making foreign policy a political football. For the most part, Truman followed his own advice, but he still managed to be less than bipartisan in attacking the administration even on matters of national security.[32]

As for his personal life, Truman saw no reason to behave much differently than his neighbors. When he was asked by a reporter after returning home about what he intended to do now, he replied, "Take the grips [suitcases] up to the attic." The former president anticipated, of course, that he would be the object of attention and have crowds of spectators gather outside his house. Because former presidents and their families were not yet entitled to any Secret Service protection, crowd control soon developed into a serious problem. Fortunately, the chief of police in Independence assigned a detachment outside the Truman home. On the advice of former president Hoover, Truman also retained the iron fence the Secret Service had installed around his home while he was president. Even then, protection for the former president and his family remained an issue. The iron fence was not much of a restraining barrier, and the local police could not offer full-time security. Touring buses and a parade of cars passing the house remained a constant nuisance. One time, a man was able to walk up to the front door and demand to see Truman. Margaret, who answered the door and thought the individual was deranged, called the police, and the stranger was arrested. At the station house, he was found to have been recently released from a mental institution and was carrying a loaded .45 caliber revolver.[33]

The crowds gradually dissipated, however, and neighbors tried to protect Truman's privacy. The former president continued to take daily strolls, walking with one of more than a hundred canes he owned, usually within a circumference of a mile or two of the house, accompanied by a bodyguard and a police car made available to him by Missouri's governor. Occasionally he was stopped on the street by someone who recognized him and wanted his autograph or just to chitchat with him. One time, a small boy dressed as a cowboy jumped out of the bushes and pretended to shoot the former president with a toy gun. Truman smiled and patted the boy on the head. Today, even if the Secret Service allowed Truman to take his daily walks, the young boy might well have been killed in a hail of gunfire. Since the ex-president woke up at dawn and normally began his brisk walks around 6:30 in the morning, he was usually able to enjoy them without much interruption.[34]

The house in which the Trumans lived was the same two-and-half-story ramshackle Victorian in which Bess and Harry had lived all their thirty-four years of marriage. They had purchased the home from the estate of Bess's mother, Madge Wallace, after her death in 1952. It was the only home they ever owned. Much of its wallpaper was stained. Most of its furniture was old and dilapidated. The kitchen set was made of red Formica. An inexpensive Proctor-Silex toaster stood atop the table. Bookshelves in a small reading room sagged under the weight of the histories, biographies, and mysteries that the Trumans read over the years. Although they fixed up the house and gave it a new coat of paint, it remained in such disrepair that it cost the government several hundred thousand dollars to make repairs after it was deeded to the National Park Service in 1983.[35]

Even after the former president returned to Independence, he was not entirely certain how he would spend his retirement. One issue that he immediately faced was financial. As he told Martin Stone, a lawyer and television mogul, before he left Washington, he would be needing money when he returned home. As a former government employee, he was not entitled to Social Security. Because he had not served in Congress long enough to receive a congressional pension, and because presidents did not receive pensions or money for office expenses, his only income was a pension of $111.96 a month (the equivalent of about $888 in 2009) for his army service in France during World War I.[36]

As president, Truman had been able to save some money. How much is unclear. Estimates ran as high as $250,000, but it was almost certainly more modest than that. The Grandview farm that he and his two siblings had inherited was also increasing in value as a site for commercial development.[37] However, like many of the nation's earliest presidents, Truman was cash poor and land rich. The president had even been forced to take out a loan during his last weeks in office.

Undated photo by Sammie Feeback of former President Truman taking his daily constitutional in Independence, MO, and stopping to talk with journalist Randall Jessee, far right, whom he first met in 1948 when he was news director for a Kansas City radio station, and a photographer, Bill Birch. Roosevelt was always a dapper president. Notice his black and white patent leather shoes. (Courtesy of Harry S. Truman Library.)

Making matters still more difficult for Truman was that he had rented offices in the Federal Reserve Bank Building in Kansas City and hired several staff members to help him with the enormous correspondence he had received after leaving office (70,000 letters in the first two weeks alone) and to prepare the files of presidential papers that were being temporarily housed at the building and at the county courthouse.[38]

As was now common for a former president, Truman was offered lucrative business opportunities, including the vice presidency of a clothing store for a six-figure annual salary and an eight-year contract at a salary of over $500,000 a year requiring only an hour's work a week. Truman refused all such offers. Under no circumstances would he be a party to the commercialization of the office he regarded with such reverence. "I could never lend myself to any transaction, however respectable, that would commercialize on the prestige and dignity of the office of the Presidency," he commented later.[39]

One moneymaking venture that Truman was prepared to undertake, however, was writing his memoir. A number of earlier presidents, beginning with

John Adams and including Thomas Jefferson, James Monroe, Martin Van Buren, James Buchanan, Ulysses Grant, Theodore Roosevelt, and Herbert Hoover, had begun or even completed their autobiographies. Most of them were unfinished, overly argumentative, self-serving, unpublished, or otherwise of little use to the scholar or the general reader. By almost all accounts, the finest memoir by a former president was Grant's, written while he was under a sentence of death from throat cancer. In terms of narrative style, detail, accuracy, and personal insight and observation, it remains the template of excellence in presidential autobiography. Unfortunately, its narrative ended before Grant assumed the presidency.[40]

By the time Truman left the presidency, the publishing world had become keenly aware of how profitable the written word of former presidents could be. Not only Grant but also Roosevelt and Hoover had proven that point. Even Buchanan's memoir had sold several thousand copies. The enormous commercial success of Dwight Eisenhower's *Crusade in Europe* (1948), while written by a national hero rather than by a former president, had also underscored how potentially profitable were the recollections of well-known national figures.

As a student of history who believed strongly that former presidents had an obligation to preserve a factual history of their administrations, Truman had planned to begin writing his memoir as soon as possible after he left office. Instead of commercializing the presidential office, he regarded the preparation of his autobiography as a duty to future generations. That he would profit from the venture was secondary to his larger purpose.[41]

A month after Truman left office, he negotiated a contract with Time-Life to write a one-volume memoir of his presidency to be completed in two years. For the rights to the book, he was to receive an advance of $600,000. Although a handsome figure (the equivalent of about $4.8 million in 2009), it by no means resolved Truman's financial problems. He was not to receive the first installment of the advance until 30 June 1955, when he was supposed to deliver the completed manuscript. Meanwhile, the president was responsible for all his expenses, which were substantial. Furthermore, unlike Eisenhower, who was allowed to claim his income from *Crusade in Europe* as capital gains, the former president had to claim his as ordinary income at a substantially higher tax rate. Since Truman was taxed at 67.5 percent, he paid most of the income from his memoirs for expenses related to the publication or for taxes. The former president claimed later that his income after these were deducted from his advance and subsequent royalties was about $37,000 (the equivalent of about $300,000 in 2009).[42]

Truman managed to supplement his income by selling a few acres of the Grandview land he had inherited with his siblings. Together with other money Truman had saved and borrowed, it allowed him, Bess, and Margaret to take a vacation in Hawaii. Truman enjoyed his month on the islands. He traveled by train to San Francisco to meet the ship for Hawaii on the private car of Averell Harriman, son of the railroad baron and a high-ranking diplomat during Truman's presidency as well his secretary of commerce after he fired Wallace. In Hawaii, the former president was the guest of Edwin Pauley, a millionaire oilman and longtime political ally and member of his administration. Apparently Truman saw no conflict between accepting perks from the well-heeled and his concern for preserving the dignity of the presidential office even as a private citizen. Earlier presidents, including Grover Cleveland, Theodore Roosevelt, and Woodrow Wilson, had done the same. Also, Truman regarded Harriman and Pauley as friends.[43]

One wonders, just the same, whether the ex-president was not drawing too fine a distinction between his concern for avoiding the commercialization of the presidential office and accepting favors from his wealthy and well-connected friends. Was he compromising, perhaps without even realizing it, his Jeffersonian principles? In doing so, was he helping to make the presidency a stepping-stone to something that the founding fathers could never have imagined or wanted and that was far different from his own ideal of the citizen-president? Certainly the line he seemed to draw between what were legitimate and reasonable activities for ex-presidents or what kinds of offerings, gifts, or special treatments were or were not acceptable would be crossed even more blatantly by future ex-presidents.

Apparently unconcerned by the implications of accepting costly courtesies from his friends, Truman returned from Hawaii with two major projects in mind. The first was preparation of his memoirs. The former president dreaded the undertaking and even wondered whether he should have agreed to it. Unlike Hoover, he had no experience as a professional author. "I'm not a writer," he exclaimed many times over the course of the next two years. Because he intended his volume to be a factual history of his lengthy administration rather than a story about himself, he also faced the daunting task of going through and organizing the thousands of documents being stored in fifty large metal file cabinets lining the walls of his suite of offices at the Federal Reserve Bank Building in Kansas City.[44]

Obviously the former president needed professional help in organizing his papers and preparing what turned out to be two volumes instead of the one agreed to in his contract. Truman had begun to assemble a staff almost as soon as he returned to Independence. Leading the team of researchers and ghostwriters were two of Truman's best and most loyal former speechwriters, William Hillman and David Noyes. The person most responsible for completing the project was Francis Heller, a political scientist from the University of Kansas. Truman hired Heller after Hillman and Noyes employed and then dismissed two earlier academics because they made little progress on the manuscript and because the former president hated what he saw. "Good God, what crap!" he scribbled at the top of one draft.[45]

Initially Truman's role in preparing his memoirs was to respond into a dictating machine to questions prepared for him by the scholars involved in the project. His answers were transcribed and then checked for accuracy by several researchers. The scholars wrote the manuscript on the basis of Truman's dictation. Finally, the former president and members of his White House staff, whom he invited to Kansas City to assist him, read the manuscript and made whatever changes they felt were needed.[46]

Writing the manuscript proved tremendously time-consuming and tedious. The researchers became overpowered by the sheer volume of material they had to process and check. As for the former president, he became overwhelmed by the daily grind of sitting for hours before a dictating machine trying to reconstruct from memory a detailed history of his administration as viewed from the Oval Office. Just as he did as president when he felt tense and weighed down, he sought escape from the rigors of his daily routine by getting out of town. "I like to take trips—any kind of trip," he later acknowledged. What was unique was that he sought relief by undertaking with Bess an unescorted three-week road trip, first to Washington, D.C., to see friends and supporters, then to Philadelphia in order to deliver a speech to the Reserve Officers Association Convention, and finally to visit Margaret, who was living in New York, and to do a little sightseeing before driving back to Independence.[47]

"When it got out that Mrs. Truman and I were going to drive to Washington by ourselves . . . the news nearly bowled our friends over," Truman later recounted. "They organized a regular filibuster, telephoned me at home and the office, stopped me on the street and got at me over the lunch table trying to talk me out of the trip." The former president simply could not understand why he and Bess could not travel incognito across the country just as long as he did not divulge the travel plans he had already mapped out. Besides, ever since he had been a young man, he loved automobiles, having bought his first one in 1915 while courting Bess.[48]

Learning that he had checked with a local dealer soon after returning to Independence about buying a Chrysler, the Chrysler Corporation offered to give Truman an Imperial, its most expensive model, outfitted with the latest technology. The former president deemed the Imperial "too swanky" for him, and he refused as a former president to accept such a gift. Instead, he bought the next less expensive model, the New Yorker, also outfitted with the latest features. How much he paid for the New Yorker is unclear, but a Chrysler official familiar with the matter speculated that the price might have been as low as a dollar. Chrysler even sent an engineer to Independence to help Truman get the hang of driving his new automobile.[49]

After packing the trunk and backseat of the big New Yorker with eleven suitcases, Harry set out with Bess on 23 June on their cross-country trip. It proved to be the last effort by a former president to be just an ordinary citizen. Either stubbornness or naivety led Truman to believe he could travel over a thousand miles to Washington without being recognized along the way. Virtually everywhere he stopped, he was identified. As word got out that he was eating at a nearby restaurant or staying at the local hotel or motel, he was mobbed by crowds of people seeking his autograph or a picture with him. In the age of the modern presidency and growing telecommunications, the very idea of a former president driving his wife and himself across the country was news. At the very least, the trip was too good a human interest story for reporters to pass up.[50]

From the viewpoint of the Secret Service, the trip was also dangerous. Aside from the fact that the former president and his wife were easy targets for some crazy man to shoot them, there were the dangers all drivers experienced at the time, except they were exaggerated by the diminishing reflexes of a sixty-nine-year-old driver; these included poor roads, lax law enforcement, lack of speed limits on some roads, lack of safety features in cars, and little vehicle inspection. Before becoming president, Truman was also known for driving fast. He had a record of minor accidents and at least one serious one. No wonder, then, that when the director of the Secret Service learned about the road trip, he expressed regret that his agency could not provide protection for ex-presidents.[51]

As it turned out, the trip went off without incident, beyond the attraction it received. Bess made her husband promise not to drive faster than fifty-five miles an hour. She watched the speedometer carefully to make sure he kept to that limit. The only problem the former president encountered was on his way back to Independence from New York, when he was stopped on the Pennsylvania Turnpike by a state trooper, who pulled him over for going too slow in a passing lane. After Bess's ultimatum, Truman was cruising at fifty-five miles an hour while a long line of automobiles followed behind him, unable to pass. After Truman put his window down to ask the reason for being stopped, the trooper recognized him immediately. Privately, the trooper cursed under his breath. Trying to maintain his demeanor, he explained patiently to the driver that while he was not going to ticket him, he could not drive so slowly in a passing lane and asked him not to do it again.[52]

On 8 July, the Trumans arrived safely back home. Realizing it was virtually impossible to travel incognito, they never took another long road trip. Still, the former president had enjoyed it immensely. He loved trying out his new car. He had been away from the pressures of Independence. He enjoyed seeing the countryside. He even mostly enjoyed the people coming up to him and asking for his autograph or a picture. His five-day stay at the Mayflower Hotel in Washington, whose manager had completely redecorated his two-bedroom suite and charged the president a special rate of $15 instead of the normal $36 a night, was a special treat for him. "As soon as we arrived in Washington, the calendar seemed to have been turned back a year," he recalled. "My old staff was there to meet me, as were most of the members of my Cabinet, and many judges, senators, and congressmen. . . . It seemed like a dream to relive such an experience."[53]

While in Washington, Truman had use of a Packard limousine shipped from Detroit especially for him as a courtesy, complete with a smartly uniformed chauffeur. The limousine was identical to two others Packard sent to the White House for Eisenhower's use. Truman made clear that he had no plans to see the president, and the Eisenhower administration pretended he was not even in town.

Instead of visiting the president, Truman spent a lot of time on Capitol Hill, where the highlight was a visit onto the Senate floor. Because Nixon was president of the Senate, protocol dictated the former president pay a courtesy visit on one of the few men he hated.[54]

That formality over, the former president was escorted to the upper chamber, where he was greeted with huge rounds of applause both before and after he made his few comments. Sitting at his old desk, he remarked: "I think I have told you before that the happiest ten years of my life were spent on the floor of the Senate."[55]

Truman's address to the Reserve Officers Association in Philadelphia, the next stop on his itinerary, was his first major one since leaving the Oval Office. Speaking before an audience of more than 1,000 former and present military officers, he delivered a broadside aimed at Eisenhower's recent cuts in defense spending. Despite having talked about the need for former presidents not to speak out publicly against an incumbent's foreign policy, Truman launched into an attack on the right-wing elements of the Republican Party. He then added, "There can be no doctrine more dangerous than the notion that we cannot afford to defend ourselves. And no doctrine quite so foolish either. . . . The greatest danger period of the 'cold war' is not necessarily behind us as some seem to think. . . . Big talk does not impress the rulers of the Soviet empire. . . . What impresses them are planes, and divisions, and ships."[56]

Truman's speech in Philadelphia was the capstone of his road trip as "Mr. Citizen." The response to his address followed the usual partisan lines, and it had no major impact on the size of the defense budget. The very next day, in fact, the Republican-controlled House Appropriations Committee slashed defense by another $1.3 million. The address nevertheless represented a statement by the former president to both Democrats and Republicans that he planned to remain a major player on the national political scene.[57]

In New York, the last leg of his trip before returning home, Truman was a guest of the Waldorf-Astoria Hotel. After visiting with Margaret, and taking in the sights and a show, he set off on his return trip to Independence, arriving home a few days later, tired but refreshed.[58]

Once back, Truman's highest priority became completing his memoirs. With a manuscript due in about eighteen months at Time-Life, which had planned all along to publish only excerpts from the memoirs and which had already sold the book rights to Doubleday and Company, the former president had to concentrate almost all his efforts on meeting his deadline. The task was not easy. Not until 1954, when Truman hired Heller, was real progress made in completing the project.[59]

Even then, unforeseen problems arose. In June, Truman was rushed to the hospital with a severe gallbladder attack. Complications set in, and for a time Truman's condition became critical. More than a 100,000 get-well cards and letters and enough flowers, as the former president said, "to supply every customer," flooded the hospital. Nearly three weeks passed before he was able to leave the hospital in order to recuperate at home.[60]

Fortunately, Heller brought considerable skill to writing the draft and overseeing the entire project full-time. Representatives from Time-Life and Doubleday also came to Independence to add their expertise. Acheson flew in from Washington to help. Despite his illness, Truman increased his participation, not only responding to questions but playing a more active role in editing and annotating what Heller wrote and adding entire paragraphs and sections of his own to the draft. By the beginning of 1955, the manuscript had become so huge that the publishers renegotiated their contract with Truman, agreeing to double the number of words to 650,000 and consenting to two volumes instead of one. The first volume, *Years of Decision,* which briefly covered Truman's early career and his presidency through 1946, was rushed into publication in the fall of 1955. The second volume, *Years of Trial and Hope,* which dealt with the rest of his presidency, came out the next spring.[61]

Both volumes sold well and received a few favorable reviews from such distinguished journalists and historians as Richard Rovere and Allan Nevins. Most reviewers, however, were less enthusiastic. Acheson, who would later win a Pulitzer Prize for his own memoirs, hit on the major problem with the manuscript when he accused it of being too impersonal and tepid on the one hand, and too didactic and instructive on the other. "The material is more interesting and gripping," he commented in one critique in June 1955, "when you are talking about your own life and your own ideas than it is when you are giving lists of callers at the White House and the activities of the Truman Committee which do not reveal much about you as a man."[62]

Still, the publication of Truman's two volumes marked a landmark in terms of presidential memoirs. Henceforth, every future president but one would sign a lucrative contract to prepare a presidential memoir. Unfortunately, with a few exceptions, they followed the model Truman established. They were prepared by ghostwriters rather than by the former presidents themselves; their major tasks were responding to questions and editing and annotating drafts. The completed books also tended to be lifeless attempts at self-justification and vindication.[63]

Other than completing his memoirs, Truman devoted most of his time in his first few years after leaving office to raising funds and selecting a site for the Truman Library and Museum. Although he made a number of speeches and appearances during these years, most were fund-related events. Whatever fees he received, he donated to an endowment established for the construction of the library and museum.

Like the publication of Truman's *Memoirs,* the dedication of the Truman Presidential Library and Museum on 6 July 1957 marked a milestone in terms of the ex-presidency. In the first place, it was the first library to be created under provisions of the 1955 Presidential Libraries Act. More important, it was the first one operated by the federal government the primary purpose of which was more archival and historical than commemorative.

The honor of establishing the first presidential library belonged to Webb Hayes, the son of Rutherford B. Hayes. Because presidential papers were regarded as the personal property of the president who created them, the fate of these historical documents was determined by the former presidents and their descendants. "I suppose if I desired to take them into my custody I might do so with entire propriety," Grover Cleveland remarked about his papers while he was president, "and if I saw fit to destroy them no one could complain." Cleveland had no great interest in preserving his papers, and most of his prepresidential papers were lost. Fortunately, his wife, Frances, gave most of the documents that had been willed to her to one of his first biographers, Robert McElroy. Eventually they made their way to the Library of Congress, as did other presidential papers. Still other collections were donated to or purchased by state or private depositories. Too often, the papers were simply destroyed or lost, either by accident or intentionally. Most of John Tyler's papers were destroyed in the burning of Richmond in 1865. Millard Fillmore and Chester Arthur ordered that their papers be burned.[64]

Seeking to preserve the memory of his parents and to avoid the loss or destruction of his father's presidential papers, Webb Hayes in 1910 deeded his parents' twenty-five-acre estate to the state of Ohio, provided "that a suitable fireproof building [be constructed] for the purpose of preserving and forever keeping" the records and relics of his mother and father. The legislature and family provided the funding for the construction of a neoclassical building, which, since its opening in 1916, has been privately administered by the Ohio Historical Association and the Hayes Foundation.[65]

The first presidential library administered with public funds was the Franklin D. Roosevelt Library, which opened in 1941. Even after the establishment of the Hayes Library, the legacy of presidential papers remained checkered. Mindful of their historical responsibility, Theodore Roosevelt and William Howard Taft deposited their large collections of papers in the Library of Congress. Surprisingly, Woodrow Wilson declined to do anything with his papers during his lifetime, but eventually most of them were also sent to the Library of Congress. Warren Harding's widow, Grace, destroyed many of his personal papers and bequeathed the rest to the Harding Memorial Association. Calvin Coolidge destroyed his personal files; the remainder were eventually deeded to the Library of Congress. Although Herbert Hoover had established the Hoover Library on War Revolution and Peace at Stanford University, he still had made no final decision about his presidential papers when Franklin Roosevelt first began to think about the home for his papers and memorabilia.[66]

Concerned about his legacy, and sensing that the Hayes Library might serve as a model for the construction of his own library, Roosevelt drew a sketch in

1937 of the library he envisioned, a two-story Dutch colonial building faced with stone, a full-length porch, small windows, and a steeply pitched roof, which blended in with his Hyde Park estate where the library was to be constructed. After commissioning Henry J. Toombs, a close friend, to draw up a design based on his sketch, he raised private funds for its construction and then issued an order to have the library federally administered, using as his model the recently completed National Gallery of Art, privately built but operated by the National Archives. By joint resolution of Congress in 1939, the library and the land on which it was erected were deeded to the government.[67]

There can be no question that in constructing the Franklin D. Roosevelt Library and deeding it to the federal government, Roosevelt was concerned with a more orderly procedure than earlier presidents for preserving and making available to the nation the historical record of his administration. The method he chose—constructing the library with private funds and then turning over its operation to the National Archives—became the model for all future presidential libraries and led directly to the Presidential Libraries Act of 1955. This measure provided for the orderly transfer of presidential papers and memorabilia to the federal government. The law also allowed ex-presidents to build presidential libraries with private funds and then to transfer these facilities to the government, which agreed to maintain both the property and the buildings at public expense. Supporters raised more than $400,000 to build the library.[68]

There can also be no question that Roosevelt's primary purpose in constructing his library was more one of commemoration than preservation. Although he summoned some of the nation's leading historians to the White House to gain their support for the library, he intended it mostly as a temple glorifying his presidency, just as the Washington Monument, the Lincoln Memorial (dedicated in 1922), and the Jefferson Memorial (completed in 1943) were intended by a grateful nation as shrines to three of the nation's most renowned presidents. Indeed, in 1937, Roosevelt complained to Toombs that in planning the structure, he had not taken into sufficient account the number of tourists that would be visiting the building and proposed that the planned research room be converted into a comfortable display room for sightseers that he could also use when the library was closed. He estimated that as many as 3,000 tourists might visit the library in the summers.[69]

Although the library opened in 1941, Roosevelt's papers were not even turned over to it until 1947. Despite the fact that the library was deeded to the government, Roosevelt also still thought of it as his personal property. Supreme Court Justice Felix Frankfurter even had to talk him into choosing a professional archivist, Fred Shipman, to be director of the library rather than his close adviser, Harry Hopkins. Roosevelt insisted also on going through his confidential files and "select[ing] those which are never to be made public."[70]

Truman's concept of his presidential library was substantially different from Roosevelt's. Certainly, he intended it to be commemorative. Like his predecessor, he also wanted to have control over his own papers. Unlike Roosevelt, however, he did not want it to be primarily a museum of relics celebrating the achievements of his administration—a shrine devoted to the eternal memory and exaltation of his presidency. Rather, he meant it to be an active center of research and scholarship. "If the Truman Library in Independence had been conceived as a memorial to me personally, I would have done everything I could to prevent its establishment during my lifetime," he later wrote. "I encouraged the building of the Library only because it was to be a center for the study of all Presidents and the Presidency as well as the history of the United States."[71]

Not only did the former president intend that his library be a repository for his papers, where researchers could come to study his presidency, he also wanted it to have a regional purpose. In a memorandum to Truman in 1952, his administrative assistant, David Lloyd, pointed out that besides being a place where his papers would be "permanently available to "scholars [and] students," the library should become "a center of research and study which will stimulate scholarly activity in the institutions of learning in Missouri and surrounding states."[72] Lloyd's concept for the Truman Library resonated with the president, who had long been dismayed by the fact that most of the nation's great historical memorials and documents and most of the nation's leading institutions of higher education were located on the East Coast. He considered those who want to "keep all the centers of learning out of the reach of the Midwest and West" as provincial elitists. He hoped that the Truman Library might begin to correct the imbalance by encouraging the nation's leading scholars to come to the Midwest and increasing scholarly prospects for students and faculty in the region's colleges and universities. More than that, he envisioned a place where students at all levels of learning might gain an appreciation of history through the visual materials on display. The displays were an opportunity to experience history. It was no accident, therefore, that the museum side of the library did not overwhelm the archival side, or that the two most prominent features for visitors entering the main doors of the library were a huge mural by the Missouri artist, Thomas Hart Benton, "Independence and the Opening of the West," depicting the westward movement of settlers from Independence, and a nearly full-size replica of the Oval Office while Truman was president.[73]

The former president had first begun to think about building a presidential library as early as 1950. Like Roosevelt, he was shocked to learn how much of the presidential record had been destroyed. Soon a group of friends established a nonprofit corporation to raise funds for the library. At first Truman intended that it be built on twenty acres of the family farm in Grandview. However, that would be inconvenient both for him and for future scholars wanting to use his papers. Because the real estate was increasing in value, devoting substantial acreage for a presidential library also meant a considerable financial sacrifice both for his siblings as well as for himself.[74]

Fortunately, the city of Independence, understanding the financial boom and prestige that would come to Independence should the library be located there, donated part of a park about a mile away from Truman's home. For Truman, this meant that he would be able to maintain an office in the library to which he could walk or drive in a few minutes each day, saving him both the cost of having to rent a suite of offices and the trouble of daily trips to Kansas City.

Once the former president finished his *Memoirs,* he traveled the country to raise money for his library. "The pace he set absolutely terrified me. It would have killed a man half his age," Margaret Truman later wrote. In 1955, members of an advisory committee that had been formed even before Truman left office spoke on Capitol Hill in support of the Presidential Libraries Act. Significantly, they emphasized the advantages of regional presidential libraries over a plan that would store the presidential papers in Washington, D.C. The historian Henry Steele Commager, a member of the committee, remarked "that the career and character of a historical figure can best be studied and understood in the environment in which he grew to maturity." Arguments along these lines and Truman's personal lobbying were instrumental in the passage of the legislation later that year.[75]

By the time the library opened in 1957, more than 17,000 individuals and organizations had donated $1.75 million to cover the construction costs of the facility, officially known as the Truman Presidential Library and Museum. A plain but still impressive structure (perhaps reflecting Truman's own sense of himself) with a limestone exterior, it became his pride and joy. Prominent public officials, including former president Hoover—but not President Eisenhower, even though he had been invited—attended the dedication ceremonies. Chief Justice Earl Warren gave the principal address. At about the same time, the Harry S. Truman Library Institute was organized, the purpose of which was to sponsor scholarly conferences, especially on international relations, and to provide financial assistance to scholars using the library.[76]

Almost from the first, the former president intended to be available to scholars and other visitors to the library, and even to participate in programs for visiting groups of students. Whenever he was in town, he would arrive at his office even before the library opened. Not only did he meet with scholars using the facility, but he also gave impromptu lectures to groups of students assembled in the library's auditorium followed by question and answer sessions. He talked to as many as five groups a day when he was at home. No former president made himself as accessible to the public as Truman.[77]

Indeed, Truman considered one of his roles as a former president to be that of an educational missionary, proselytizing the importance of historical knowledge, especially of the American presidency. One of his greatest pleasures was meeting and talking with groups of young people. He preferred to go to high schools and small colleges. Yet he also gladly accepted opportunities to be a visiting lecturer at such prestigious universities as Yale, Cornell, and Columbia. Typically, he spent a few days at a college or university delivering a lecture and then devoting the rest of his time to small seminars with selected groups of students and faculty.[78]

Another important part of his mission to spread the gospel of historical knowledge was to win passage of legislation providing funds for the indexing and microfilming of all presidential papers housed at the Library of Congress. In 1957, he went to Washington to testify in support of a measure that House majority leader John McCormack of Massachusetts had introduced for this purpose. Congress approved the legislation by voice vote. Eventually microfilm copies of these papers were made available to libraries across the country.[79]

Although completing his memoirs and raising funds for construction of the Truman Library consumed most of Truman's time in his first years after leaving office, he kept busy with other matters as well, including politics. Although he was not able to play a significant role on the campaign circuit during the 1954 congressional elections, he managed to deliver several addresses attacking the Eisenhower administration, just as he had at the Reserve Officers Association in Philadelphia in 1953. Careful not to assail the White House's foreign policy directly, he aimed his guns at the perceived shortcomings of the administration's domestic and national security policies—in failing to increase the minimum wage, for example, and in cutting money for the air force.[80]

Truman was also the first ex-president to use executive privilege in refusing to appear before the House Un-American Activities Committee (HUAC) in a case involving Harry Dexter White, an assistant treasury secretary during his administration. Truman appointed White to the board of directors of the International Monetary Fund (IMF) even though White had been publicly accused of being a Soviet agent, a charge White falsely denied. Although the case had been long forgotten by 1953, Eisenhower's attorney general, Herbert Brownell, raised it again when he accused Truman of having appointed White to the IMF despite evidence against him from the FBI. Instead of replying that he had been given no *persuasive* evidence, the former president denied receiving any warning from the FBI. This led to a subpoena for Truman to appear before HUAC. In a televised address, he accused the Eisenhower administration of "McCarthyism," "shameful demagoguery," and "cheap political trickery" aimed against him. Claiming entitlement to the same constitutional privileges as sitting presidents, he then stated that he would not honor the subpoena. Rather than trying to drag a former president into a committee hearing room, the administration allowed the matter to be quietly dropped. While not being entirely truthful in his counterpunching against the administration, Truman had nevertheless defended the institution of the presidency and established an important precedent to be used, for better or worse, by future presidents and members of their staffs.[81]

Eisenhower thought it "inconceivable" that Truman knowingly promoted a Soviet agent. Truman fumed nevertheless at the White House, which, he believed, was duplicitous in the red-baiting of its first years in office. In particular, he was furious at charges that Roosevelt and he had given away Eastern Europe and made too many concessions to the Soviet Union during the Yalta and Potsdam conferences. These charges, he said, "were without foundation in fact. Had the agreements made at Yalta and Potsdam been carried out by the Russians, there would have been no 'cold war.'"[82]

Truman was ready, therefore, to help bring down the administration in the 1956 presidential campaign. Beyond his disagreement with the administration's policies, he deeply resented being cold-shouldered by President Eisenhower, and he was even more venomous in his attitude toward Nixon, who had been the White House's front man in red-baiting the Democrats. Although he had refused to engage in most political campaigning before 1955, Truman made it clear to the chairman of the Democratic National Committee, Paul Butler, that he would soon be ready to go wherever the party wanted. Although he was aware of Eisenhower's personal popularity, he believed, on the basis of the 1954 congressional election in which the Democrats won a majority in both houses of Congress, that the Republicans would be highly vulnerable in 1956.[83]

Beginning in early 1955, the former president began traveling the country. Despite his promises not to speak out publicly against the administration's foreign policy, he delivered what he described as "a bald statement" in Chicago attacking the administration for not taking a stronger stand against a Mideast arms deal recently concluded between Moscow and Cairo. The next spring, he went even further. In a speech in Des Moines in April 1956, he attacked Eisenhower's "betrayal" of the farmer and compared Eisenhower's leadership to the do-nothing Eightieth Congress. Not stopping there, he added that the administration had "made a mockery of bipartisanship in foreign affairs by putting politics ahead of the national interest."[84]

The immediate problem concerning the former president was selecting a Democratic nominee to oppose Eisenhower. The leading candidate was again Adlai Stevenson, but he was not Truman's choice. The former president had not forgotten Stevenson's campaign of 1952. He was also disturbed about some of the Illinois politician's recent statements, especially a call he made in 1956 for the United States to unilaterally stop testing the hydrogen bomb. "In that speech, it seemed to me that he did not fully grasp the implications and the danger of the proposal he made," Truman later stated.[85]

If not Stevenson, then who? Certainly not Estes Kefauver, Stevenson's closest challenger, whom Truman continued to distrust. Only one person, Governor Averell Harriman of New York, seemed worthy of the nomination. Although aristocratic and distant in manner, Harriman had an enviable record as a diplomat during both the Roosevelt and Truman administrations. He also supported the domestic programs of the two administrations and had been able to eke out a narrow victory two years earlier to become governor of the nation's most populous state. Although Truman realized that Harriman did not have much popular support, he decided to lead the effort on his behalf. In May, he asked not to be a delegate to the party's national convention because, as he said, he wanted "to be a completely free agent" at the Democratic conclave being held again in Chicago.[86]

At the convention, the former president announced his support for Harriman and issued a statement attacking the front-runner's "counsel of moderation" and lack of a "fighting spirit." He also remarked that he did not think Stevenson could win in 1956. Truman's endorsement, however, did Harriman little good. Stevenson easily won the nomination on the first ballot. Already annoyed at the Democrats' choice of Stevenson, Truman was further irritated when the nominee decided to throw open the choice of his running mate to the convention—another instance, in Truman's view, of Stevenson's indecisiveness. The delegates then narrowly nominated Kefauver for vice president over the handsome young senator from Massachusetts, John F. Kennedy. Truman had little use for either Kefauver or Kennedy, whose father, Joseph Kennedy, he despised because he had maligned Roosevelt and supported Joseph McCarthy.[87]

Bent on beating Eisenhower, however, Truman hid his displeasure with the Democratic ticket. In a show of unity, he went to the podium just before Stevenson delivered his acceptance speech to pledge his strong support for the nominee. During the fall campaign, he traveled the country on Stevenson's behalf, warning that if it reelected Eisenhower, it was also reelecting his running mate, Richard Nixon. "Remember this and remember it well," he cautioned, "you cannot elect Ike without electing Tricky Dicky."[88]

Stevenson never had much of a chance of defeating Eisenhower. The Republican incumbent was too popular. Almost as crucially, he understood and masterfully used the medium of television to deliver his message to the American people. In November, Eisenhower won 35.5 million popular votes and 457 electoral votes to Stevenson's twenty-six million popular votes and seventy-five electoral votes. Eisenhower garnered a greater percentage of the popular vote (57 percent) than he had in 1952 (55 percent).[89]

Although the Democrats managed to hold on to their control of Congress, Truman was deeply disturbed by Eisenhower's reelection. An unrepentant liberal, he believed that for all his talk about a new Republicanism, the president was becoming increasingly a creature of his party's right wing and was trying to undermine the social and economic gains achieved under Democratic leadership. At the end of November, he wrote a letter to the president that he never sent in which he vented his frustrations. After listing some of the most prominent right-wing Republicans (and Democrats) in Congress, he concluded, "With that crew you should be able to wreck T.V.A., give away the balance of our national resources, completely ruin our foreign policy and set the country back to 1896 and 1919. Best of luck and may the honest Democrats and Liberal Republicans save you from disaster."[90]

Yet the next fifteen years were the happiest and most fulfilling of Truman's retirement. In 1956, his only child, Margaret, married E. Clifton Daniel, a *New York Times* correspondent (and later managing editor) after her singing career had dead-ended. Shortly thereafter, she published her autobiography to highly favorable reviews. The next year, she gave birth to Clifton Truman Daniel, the first of four boys she had over the next nine years.

Having his thirty-two-year-old daughter begin what turned into a highly successful writing career, marry so well, and then start what became a large family brought a sense of personal fulfillment to an individual whose own life at Margaret's age seemed destined to failure. The marriage and birth of his first grandson happened, moreover, about the same time that Truman published his *Memoirs* and hosted the dedication of his library and museum, the two great projects of his retirement.[91]

During these years, Truman also obtained the financial security he had longed for his entire life. In 1958, Congress passed the Former Presidents Act (FPA), providing for a generous pension and other expenses for ex-presidents and their widows. Throughout the country's history, there had been occasional efforts to provide for the financial security of former presidents. One reason Congress raised, over considerable opposition, the salary of presidents in 1873 from $25,000 to $50,000 (the equivalent of $885,000 in 2009) was so that the president, in the words of one group of lawmakers, "could save enough money to retire [after leaving office] from all active or at least from all money-making pursuits."[92]

From time to time, private donors had also offered to provide former presidents with financial assistance or pensions. It will be recalled that in 1912 Andrew Carnegie tried to embarrass Congress into providing ex-presidents with pensions by offering to pay former presidents and their widows an annual pension of $25,000 (the equivalent in 2009 of about $550,000) funded by the Carnegie Foundation. However, members of Congress believed it was inappropriate for private parties to fund annual pensions for ex-presidents, and the outgoing president, William Howard Taft, publicly declined Carnegie's offer.[93]

Carnegie's gesture, however, brought attention to the financial plight that some former presidents faced after leaving office. On Capitol Hill, legislation was introduced to provide ex-presidents with a pension of $2,000 a month. Other legislation would have provided a former president a $10,000 annual pension in his capacity as commander in chief of the army. Neither of these measures made its way out of committee, and the idea of pensions for former presidents was largely forgotten for the next forty years.[94]

In 1953, after Truman, who was known to have limited financial resources, hired an office staff to handle his mail and requests for speeches, his friends in Congress began to consider once again granting compensation to previous presidents. In 1955, Senator Lyndon Johnson introduced legislation providing retirement benefits for former presidents in order "to maintain the dignity of that great office" and to prevent an ex-president from engaging "in business or [an] occupation which would demean the office he has held or capitalize upon it." It died in House committee.[95]

In response to a letter he received from House majority leader John McCormack inquiring about lifetime compensation for former presidents, Truman wrote to McCormack and House Speaker Sam Rayburn describing his financial situation and acknowledging that his income was based largely on the sale of his farmland in Grandview. In 1955, he and his siblings sold fifty acres of their Grandview farm for $220,000. Eventually the former president received nearly $90,000 plus interest as his share of the sale. "Had it not been for the fact that I was able to sell some property that my brother, sister, and I inherited from our mother," he wrote to McCormack, "I would practically be on relief, but with the sale of that property, I am not financially embarrassed."[96]

The former president stated to the majority leader that he was not asking for pensions for former presidents. "I do not want a pension and do not expect one," he remarked. At the same time, he made clear his view that he and other ex-presidents should be compensated to cover part of their unusually high overhead expenses. "My total overhead for the period from February 1953 until about November of last year, 1956, amounted to a sum over $153,000," he pointed out. "I would say 70 percent of the $153,000 that I have put out for office help, rent, postage, telephones and everything else that goes with the expense of an office for a former president should be paid." Noting that all five-star generals and admirals received three clerks and "all the emoluments that went with their office," he added that ex-presidents should be treated no differently.[97]

After receipt of Truman's letter, McCormack and Senator Mike Monroney of Oklahoma introduced identical legislation to provide former presidents an annual pension of $25,000 (the equivalent in 2009 of about $188,000), clerical assistance, and free mailing privileges. The amount of the pensions was based on comparable pensions for five-star generals. Senate majority leader Johnson strongly supported the legislation. The House committee reporting out the measure stated that it would "avoid the possibility of indignities and of deterioration in public and world regard for the office of the President of the United States." McCormack stated that the proposed pensions would also provide recognition and gratitude for previous presidents' service to the country, which was ongoing even after they left the Oval Office. Other lawmakers made similar comments. Opponents of the legislation, mostly House Republicans, argued that there was no justification for the pensions and other benefits and that they would establish a new entity with the appearance of official standing, unwarranted and undefined by the federal government.

Despite these grumblings, which proponents of the legislation complained were directed mostly at Truman, the legislation easily passed both the Senate and House with bipartisan support and was signed into law by President Eisenhower on 25 August 1958. The historic measure provided an annual taxable allowance of $25,000 for the president and $10,000 for his widow. It also authorized the General Services Administration (GSA) to provide and fund an office staff and suitable office space "appropriately furnished and equipped" at a location in the

United States designated by the former president. Truman was clearly delighted by passage of the measure, the main impetus for which had been to relieve him of any financial concerns. Writing on 26 August to Lyndon Johnson, who had spearheaded Senate approval of the legislation, he remarked: "I will never be able to thank you enough for everything you did in connection with the Presidential retirement bill. Some time or other I hope to see you and express more personally exactly how I feel."[98]

Even before the measure was enacted into law, however, Truman had entered into negotiations with ABC to prepare a pilot for a possible television series on the American presidency. The negotiations fell through, but in 1958 he became the first former president to be interviewed on television for "a substantial sum" when he appeared on *See It Now,* a popular program hosted by Edward R. Murrow. In 1961, he signed a contract with Talent Associates–Paramount to film twenty-six one-hour programs on the major events during his presidency, for which he was to be paid $7,500 an episode. He also agreed to write a regular column at $1,500 apiece for the North American Newspaper Alliance. In addition, he wrote paid articles for various popular magazines and journals, including two articles for *Look,* the first on his views on the presidency and the second on his decision to drop the atomic bomb during World War II. For each article, he received $5,000.[99]

After a bidding war between several book publishers, the former president signed a contract with Bernard Geis Associates to write two books, one on his post-presidential years and another a history text for young readers. Geis guaranteed Truman $20,000 a year for ten years regardless of how well the first of the two books sold. After ten years, he would receive additional royalties if the earnings exceeded the minimum guarantee. Truman never wrote the second book, but the first, *Mr. Citizen* (1960), which represented a far more revealing and interesting self-portrait of Truman than his earlier *Memoirs,* went through a number of printings and was eventually picked up by Popular Library. Although Geis verged on bankruptcy and Truman's literary agent and lawyer had to threaten legal action before the former president received his royalties, eventually he collected in excess of the $200,000 he was guaranteed.[100]

In 1956 and 1957, the Trumans also traveled extensively, including a seven-week trip to Europe. Its main purpose was to accept an honorary degree from Oxford University, but he also used the occasion to tour England and the continent. Although hobbled much of the time by a sprained ankle (a result of slipping on stairs while carrying suitcases down from the attic) and by poor weather, the former president enjoyed himself thoroughly. To the greatest extent possible, he tried to act just like another tourist visiting Europe that summer. He sipped coffee at a small outdoor French café, strolled the Place de L'Opera, visited the Louvre, saw Capitol Hill and the ancient monuments of Rome, and visited Florence, Naples, Venice, Salzburg, Vienna, Bonn, Brussels, and Amsterdam.

Trying to be an ordinary tourist proved impossible, of course. Wherever he went, he was greeted by large crowds, who fondly remembered the former president as the person most responsible for ending World War II and helping Europe recover from the war through the Marshall Plan. While in England he visited with Winston Churchill and his family, the last time the two statesmen were to meet. While in Rome, he toured the sites with his longtime political foe, Henry Luce, publisher of *Life* and *Time*. In Bonn he met with Chancellor Konrad Adenauer of West Germany. In Holland, he and Bess had lunch with Queen Juliana at the royal palace.[101]

The most interesting call the former president made while on the Continent was a luncheon visit with the ninety-year-old Bernard Berenson, the preeminent authority on Renaissance art and one of the most celebrated and respected intellectual figures of his time. Berenson's famous villa outside of Florence, with its many art masterpieces and 55,000-volume library, was a virtual shrine that drew the world's most famous intellectual and cultural figures. All the more remarkable, then, was Berenson's impression of the former president, which he later recorded in his diary. "In my long life," he wrote, "I have never met an individual with whom I felt so instantly at home. He talked as if he had always known me, openly, easily, with no reserve (so far as I could judge). Ready to touch on any subject, no matter how personal. I always felt what a solid and sensible basis there is in the British stock of the U.S.A. if it can produce a man like Truman. Now I feel more assured about America than in a long time"[102]

Despite his many other activities in the fifteen years after 1956, politics remained central to Truman's life. Trying to assure that his party remained true to its liberal heritage, he became active in the Democratic Advisory Committee (later renamed Democratic Advisory Council, or DAC) formed after the 1956 elections to prepare a liberal agenda for the 1960 presidential elections. He also continued to maintain close relations with such party notables as House Speaker Sam Rayburn, majority leader Lyndon Johnson, and Senator Hubert Humphrey of Minnesota, who regarded Truman as a party icon. Both Humphrey and Johnson were seeking their party's presidential nomination in 1960 and hoped to have Truman's backing.[103]

In reality, Truman's support was no longer worth all that much. After the 1956 Democratic Convention, his influence within party circles went into an irreversible decline. As even the former president realized, his intemperate language with respect to Adlai Stevenson before he received the nomination, especially his comment that Stevenson could not beat Eisenhower, was not easily forgiven by many party loyalists. "There was even a suggestion that my days of usefulness, in Democratic politics were over," the former president acknowledged after the convention. At the time, he did not take such comments seriously. As the journalist James Reston remarked, however, "Harry Truman, the Goliath who set out to slay David, had succeeded only in knocking out himself."[104]

Besides shooting himself in the foot in 1956, a new generation of politicians born in the twentieth century was coming to power in both the Republican and

Democratic parties. In the Republican Party, the transition was best personified by Richard Nixon, the odds-on favorite to lead the Republican ticket in 1960. In the Democratic Party, the change was most clearly embodied in the presidential aspirations of its glamorous star, Senator Kennedy, who was about to take on Humphrey, another of the new generation, in the most crucial series of primary contests in the nation's political history up to that time.

For reasons not entirely clear, Truman refused to endorse either Humphrey or Kennedy in their primary struggle for the Democratic nomination. Kennedy had asked the former president in January 1960 not to endorse any candidate, and he may have decided simply to honor the senator's request. More likely, he did not sense how important the primaries would be in deciding the nominee. In 1952 and 1956, Kefauver had not been able to win the nomination even though he had won more delegates in the primaries than any other candidate. Probably Truman thought the nominee would again be decided at the convention. That was Johnson's strategy, and Truman still hoped to play the role of kingmaker at the Los Angeles convention.

Although the ex-president did not endorse either Kennedy or Humphrey, he clearly preferred Humphrey over Kennedy. He believed Kennedy was too young and inexperienced to be president. He regarded him as part of the Ivy League–educated elite that had never impressed him. The fact that Kennedy was a Catholic also bothered Truman. He had never been openly prejudiced against Catholics, but he did not want a repeat of the 1928 election when Catholicism was an issue that helped defeat Al Smith. Furthermore, he maintained doubts as to whether Kennedy could always act independently of church leaders. Finally, he continued to resent Kennedy's father, Joe Kennedy, who, he believed, was using his personal fortune to buy the Democratic nomination for his son. "It's not the pope I'm afraid of; it's the pop," he said.[105]

Despite his warm relationship with Johnson and the majority leader's mentor, Sam Rayburn, the former president was not even all that taken by Johnson. The Texan had refused to join the DAC, and as majority leader, he was one of the Democratic leaders in Congress who tried to work with the Eisenhower administration. Truman urged Johnson after the 1956 election to pursue an aggressive liberal program, including a tough civil rights measure, repeal of the Taft–Hartley legislation, and a strong farm bill, as well as to hold a series of hearings on foreign policy. "I do not believe that the Executive Department understands national finance, international relations, or national defense," he told Johnson.[106]

In response, Johnson indicated to Truman that he while he intended to go along with much of what the former president recommended, he planned at the same time to pursue a more cautious approach. "My long range hopes," he wrote him in December 1956, "are that we can pass enough good legislation in the 85th Congress to convince voters that they return even stronger Democratic majorities in 1958."[107]

As the Democratic Convention approached in July, Truman faced a dilemma.

Kennedy had defeated Humphrey in the primaries and came into the convention as the favorite to win the nomination. His strongest rival was now Johnson, who had substantial support among Southern delegates, party leaders from Congress, and others who, like the former president, wanted to stop the Kennedy bandwagon. Among the latter was a group of Stevenson loyalists led by another Democratic icon, Eleanor Roosevelt. Truman was not about to turn once more to Stevenson, who had spent the last eight years distancing himself from the former president.[108]

Still believing he could be a kingmaker, and intent above all to keep Kennedy from getting his party's nomination, the former president repeated some of the same mistakes he had made in 1956. In May, he announced that he was supporting for president a native son of Missouri, his former air force secretary and now a Missouri senator, Stuart Symington. Although Symington had been mentioned as a possible presidential candidate in 1956 and was well liked among those who knew him, he was not well known nationally and never had much of a chance of winning the nomination. Truman would probably have had more influence if he had thrown his support behind Johnson. That may have been his strategy all along, but if it was, it did not work. By the time the Democrats assembled in Los Angeles, the Kennedy bandwagon had gained too much momentum to be stopped.

On the eve of the convention, the former president stunned Democrats by announcing at a news conference that because he had no desire to participate in what appeared to be "a prearranged affair," he would resign as a delegate to the gathering. He also questioned Kennedy's qualifications to be president. "Senator, are you certain that you are quite ready for the country, or that the country is ready for you in the role of President in January 1961?" he asked as if addressing Kennedy. Then he listed ten other Democrats who "had earned the right" to be considered for the Oval Office. By demeaning the presumptive nominee in this way, Truman appeared little more than a querulous and cantankerous old man who was out of tune with the new generation of Democratic leaders.[109]

Always a party loyalist, however, Truman announced his support for Kennedy after he received the nomination. To his surprise, Kennedy then responded by flying to Independence in August and making clear that he wanted the former president to play an important role in the campaign. Truman, who had been delighted at Kennedy's selection of Johnson as his running mate and was struck by the nominee's obvious charisma, warmed to him almost immediately.[110]

The fact that Kennedy's opponent for president was Richard Nixon provided all the incentive Truman needed to work for the Democratic ticket in the fall. At age seventy-six, he was not able to campaign as vigorously as he had in previous elections. As he had grown older, however, he had become looser with his tongue, and this was reflected in the campaign. Addressing a Democratic dinner in San Antonio, he remarked: "If you vote for Nixon, you ought to go to hell." Later, at a news conference, he added that the Republican presidential candidate had "never told the truth in his life." A Baptist, Truman also addressed a number of churches in the Bible Belt in order to assure them that, contrary to his earlier comments, he had no problem with Kennedy's religion.[111]

Truman was elated by Kennedy's victory over Nixon. After eight years under a Republican leader, who, he believed, would rank among the nation's worst presidents, the Democrats had recaptured the White House. "I believe that not only our own people but people everywhere can expect a new surge of dynamic, decisive, and productive leadership from this country," he wrote in his syndicated news column.[112] As president, Kennedy also continued to show his respect to the former president. He invited the Trumans to the White House, where he and his striking wife, Jacqueline, charmed the elderly couple with their youth and elegance. He also consulted frequently with the former president before his assassination in 1963, news of which left Truman visibly shaken.[113]

Future presidents also continued to treat Truman with deference. President Lyndon Johnson maintained an ongoing correspondence with the former president, offered him an air force jet or helicopter and a military aide whenever he wished to travel, and made sure that the Defense Department kept him abreast of the United States' growing involvement in the Vietnam War. After Kennedy's murder, Johnson signed legislation authorizing Secret Service protection for life for ex-presidents. In 1965, he traveled to Independence to sign the Medicare bill and to present Truman and Bess with Medicare card numbers one and two. Truman had taken the lead in pushing for a plan of comprehensive national health insurance ever since he had been in the White House. The Medicare and accompanying Medicaid programs, which covered seniors over sixty-five years old and the indigent, were far less than what the former president had wanted. At the same time, they were giant steps in providing a social safety net to those most likely to need health care and most in danger of not being able to pay for it.

Even Truman's archenemy for so many years, Richard Nixon, showed deference to the former president after he narrowly defeated Hubert Humphrey in the 1968 election. In fact, as Truman entered the evening of his life, he healed his wounds with many of his old political rivals, including both Nixon and Eisenhower. The reconciliation with Eisenhower had begun even while Eisenhower was still president and Truman was lashing out against his administration. The former president never relented in impeaching Eisenhower's overall conduct of the Oval Office. Yet on numerous occasions, such as when Eisenhower issued the Formosa Doctrine pledging the United States to defend Formosa against attack from the mainland, or when the president issued the Eisenhower Doctrine pledging to prevent communist expansion in the Middle East, Truman issued statements and wrote the president letters congratulating him for his actions. Eisenhower reciprocated by arranging for Truman to be briefed by the CIA on major foreign policy issues.[114]

After Eisenhower left office, he asked to see the Truman Library and Museum. After giving Eisenhower a personal tour of the library, Truman had a long conversation with the new member of the former presidents club. That broke the ice between the two men. The next spring, Eisenhower invited Truman to attend the dedication of his library.[115] In subsequent weeks, the two former presidents were together at the memorial services for House Speaker Sam Rayburn at Bonham, Texas, and of Eleanor Roosevelt at Hyde Park. By the end of 1961, one of Truman's longtime friends, Abe Feinberg, was expressing his delight at the growing rapprochement between Truman and Eisenhower. "Now that there are three members of the Ex-Presidents Club, two of whom are Republican," Feinberg remarked, "I think you must be careful not to be outvoted or worse still voted out."[116]

In 1963 Eisenhower and Truman sat next to each other at the memorial service in Washington, D.C., for President Kennedy and then at his burial in Arlington National Cemetery. The deaths of two of the older generation of national leaders and the assassination of the nation's youngest elected president within a period of about two years left the seventy-nine-year-old Truman and the seventy-three-year-old Eisenhower, who had already suffered a serious heart attack, with a sense of their own mortality and a natural inclination to let bygones be bygones. From 1961 until Eisenhower's death in 1969, they exchanged letters at birthdays, holidays, or when one of them suffered from an illness. In the second volume of his memoirs, *Waging Peace* (1965), Eisenhower listed Truman as one of "the towering governmental figures of the West." In his public tribute after Eisenhower's death in 1969, Truman was equally gracious: "General Eisenhower and I became political opponents but before that we were comrades in arms. . . . He led the great military crusade that freed Western Europe from Nazi bondage, and then commanded the allied forces that stood guard over the liberated lands until they regained their strength and self-reliance."[117]

By the time Eisenhower died in 1969, Truman was nearing his eighty-fifth birthday and was in failing health. He still continued to follow politics carefully. He supported Lyndon Johnson for reelection in 1968 despite the growing opposition to his administration because of the Vietnam War. "It doesn't make any difference what the rest of them do. . . . The present man in the White House is the man we'll vote for," he remarked in April. Eleven days later, however, Johnson announced he would not seek another term. Truman then threw his support to Humphrey. However, Truman's endorsement hardly mattered anymore. Despite the deference shown to him by presidents Kennedy and Johnson, he had been virtually without political influence within his own party for the last decade.[118]

The former president was no longer able to attend the Democratic convention or to campaign on Humphrey's behalf. He had suffered a major fall in his bathroom a few years earlier from which he never fully recovered. He had also lost considerable weight and walked slowly with his back crouched over. He was hard of hearing, and his thick glasses looked even thicker and larger than they were because of his slim face. He rarely went to his office in the Truman Library anymore. Nor did he take his daily constitutionals.

In early December 1972, the former president was taken to the Research Hospital and Medical Center in Kansas City with lung congestion. Over the next twenty-two days, he battled an internal infection. His heart became unstable, and he slipped into a coma. On 26 December 1972, he died at the age of eighty-eight. Bess Truman declined a state funeral. After a small and simple funeral in the auditorium of the library he loved so much, he was buried on the library grounds. When Bess died ten years later, she was buried next to him.[119]

More than any other ex-president before him, Truman established the fact that no matter one's personal desires, it was not possible for a former president to retire from view and become an ordinary citizen again. In the global world of the mid-twentieth century, at a time when the United States was the most powerful nation in the world, former presidents were simply too visible to withdraw easily from the public stage even if they wanted to. In the case of Truman, he wished to have it both ways: to be known as "Mr. Citizen" rather than as "Mr. President," but to remain active in politics. His road trip from Independence to the East Coast soon after he returned to Missouri underscored how impossible that would be. What remains surprising, in fact, is how much latitude he still had to take his daily walks, to travel extensively, and to spend his days at the Truman Library and Museum with only a modicum of protection.

Truman's importance as a former president, however, extends beyond putting to bed forever the republican concept of ex-presidents even as he still tried to cling to it. The literary contracts he signed, the television appearances he made, the funds he raised for the Truman Library and Museum, the public role he played as an educator and teacher, all established in ways that had not been defined before the full menu of activities for future presidents. In none of them did Truman believe he was straying from his convictions that former presidents should not use their celebrity and influence for personal gain. Whatever profit he made from his writings and television appearances he considered ancillary to his larger civic purpose. However, he did accept free vacations and heavily discounted prices that bordered on commercializing the ex-presidency. It was also virtually impossible to disassociate the large royalties and fees he made for his writings and appearances from the educational benefit and public service they were intended to provide.

Finally, and perhaps most importantly, a quasi-official office of ex-president was established during Truman's career as ex-president. Many of the perks and powers that went with this office, such as arrangements for federal operation and management of presidential libraries and museums, funds for office and staff, free mailing privileges, and even pensions for former presidents and their widows, were due in significant measure to Truman's own lobbying. Others, like the availability of aircraft and military aides when traveling, and Secret Service protection, were not.

11

The Limits of the
Office of Ex-President
Eisenhower and Johnson

Compared to the long ex-presidencies of Herbert Hoover and Harry S. Truman, those of Dwight David Eisenhower and Lyndon Baines Johnson were short. Both men had serious heart conditions even before they left the Oval Office. Heart failure took Eisenhower's life within eight years after he retired from the presidency and Johnson's life within four years.

After he left the White House, Eisenhower divided most of his time between his farm in Gettysburg, Pennsylvania, and playing golf and bridge with his rich friends in Palm Desert, California, and Augusta, Georgia. Johnson retired to his Stonewall ranch in the hill country of Texas, about seventy miles outside Austin. Contrary to a common view, however, neither of the former presidents withdrew from the public scene or the national political arena.[1]

Besides playing golf and bridge and dividing his time between the East and West coasts, Eisenhower wrote his memoirs, attended to the opening of his library and museum in Abilene, Kansas, did a series of paid television interviews, served as an informal adviser to presidents John F. Kennedy and Johnson, and stayed highly involved in Republican politics. Johnson also stayed busy. Like Eisenhower, he indulged himself by overseeing the ranch he loved so much, entertaining friends, spending time with his family, and taking regular vacations. He also busied himself with his memoirs, involved himself in the planning and construction of his library and museum on the campus of the University of Texas in Austin, did a series of paid television interviews on his administration, consulted with President Richard Nixon on the Vietnam War, and maintained an extensive correspondence with the leading political figures of both parties. His retirement, in this sense, was not all that different from Eisenhower's.

Eisenhower's and Johnson's retirements were similar in another way. Even in those instances when their advice was requested or, in the case of Eisenhower, when he tried to determine the direction of the Republican Party, they were politely but largely ignored by those in power. This put in sharp relief the fact that while the office of the ex-president was established under Truman, its influence remained limited. Whatever remnants of power went with the retiring president, the real power was gone.[2]

I

Dwight Eisenhower (or Ike, as he was called from childhood) was the archetypal youngster growing up in small-town America around the turn of the century. He was born in Denison, Texas, on 14 October 1890, the third of seven boys (one boy died in infancy). After a series of business failures, his father moved to Abilene, Kansas. Although Dwight's parents always had to struggle financially, he came from a close-knit and loving family in which honesty, hard work, ambition, fear of God, and character were the guiding principles. It was a testimony to their upbringing that, in addition to Dwight, three of his other brothers graduated from college, and Eisenhower's youngest sibling, Milton, became prominent in his own right in government and academia.

Like Harry Truman, Dwight loved to read history as a young boy. While many of his heroes were the same as those of Truman, unlike the Missourian, he did not try to learn lessons from history. "For me, the reading of history was an end in itself, not a source of lessons to guide us in the present or to prepare me for the future," he later wrote.[3] Studies came easy to him, and he graduated with high grades. However, he was not especially studious or deeply intellectual. More than anything else, he enjoyed sports, especially football and baseball, in which he displayed his natural abilities as a leader and organizer on and off the field. He later remarked that sports also taught him teamwork.[4]

Like most of his other brothers, Dwight was determined to go to college. Money was always a problem. After graduating from high school, Dwight worked for two years to help his brother, Edgar, through the University of Michigan. The expectation was that Edgar would do the same for his brother. One of Eisenhower's close friends, who was hoping to attend Annapolis, convinced him to join him at the Naval Academy. Eisenhower was attracted more to the idea of a free education and of playing sports than to a military career. Because Annapolis restricted the entering class to those aged nineteen or younger and Dwight was twenty, he had to accept an appointment to the U.S. Military Academy at West Point, whose cutoff age for admission was twenty-two.[5]

When he matriculated in 1911, Eisenhower stood about five feet, eleven inches tall, and weighed around 150 pounds. Muscular and a natural athlete with broad shoulders and large hands, he was also a fun-loving, self-confident, optimistic, and good-looking youngster, with a fair complexion, brown hair, blue eyes, wide mouth, and, his most famous characteristic, a broad grin. He became almost as well known among his closest acquaintances for his fiery temper, a life-long problem.[6]

At West Point, Eisenhower remained more interested in playing football than in his studies. Even though he was considered too small for the team, he made the varsity team through a regimen of body building and sheer grit on the field. His greatest disappointment came when he suffered a leg injury that made him ineligible to play football any longer. He graduated sixty-first in a class of 164. Even at the time of his graduation, when he was told that his leg injury might keep him from being given a commission, he did not seem all that bent on a military career.[7]

After graduation, Eisenhower was assigned to Fort Sam Houston in San Antonio, Texas, where he served as an inspector instructor of a National Guard unit. He found his stay at Fort Sam Houston "in the main uninteresting." While in San Antonio, however, Eisenhower met a debutante from Denver, Mamie Doud. After a quick courtship, they became engaged and married on 1 July 1916.[8]

When the United States entered World War I in 1917, Eisenhower sought a combat assignment in Europe. Having already gained a reputation for his skills as a teacher and organizer of men, he was given various assignments stateside to train the vast civilian army that was being created for wartime. In February 1918, he went to Camp Meade in Maryland to put together the formation of the first tank battalions. Eisenhower's performance evaluations were good enough that within a short time he was given charge of the army tank corps training center at Camp Colt near Gettysburg. By July 1918, he was in command of more than 10,000 men and 600 officers. In October, he was promoted to the temporary rank of lieutenant colonel. Just when it seemed that he would be sent overseas, the war came to an end. With the downsizing of the army, his temporary rank of lieutenant colonel was reduced to his permanent rank of captain. A few days later, he was promoted to major, a rank he held for the next sixteen years.[9]

In the years between World War I and World War II, Eisenhower received various assignments in the United States, in the Panama Canal Zone, in Europe, and at the War Department in Washington, where he served on the staff of General Douglas MacArthur. Throughout his twenty-five-year career in the army, Eisenhower never had any battle experience. Nor had he had an active command above a battalion. As late as 1941, he was still only a lieutenant colonel. Ordinarily this would have placed strict limits on his future advancement. Yet in important respects, he had an advantage over more senior officers with battle experience. As a staff officer, he had gained a university-level education in organization, administration, leadership, and tactics. In the Panama Canal Zone, he became the protégé of the commanding general, Fox Conner, an intellectual who was regarded by many as the brains behind the American Expeditionary Force (AEF) in Europe. His relationship with Conner was crucial. In January 1921,

Eisenhower's three-year-old son, Icke, died of scarlet fever. His death crushed Eisenhower and left him inconsolable. At work, he just seemed to go through the motions.

Although Eisenhower never fully recovered from Icke's death, his relationship with Conner and the birth of a second son, John Sheldon, in August 1922, pulled him out of his lethargy. Conner had Eisenhower read and discuss with him the works of leading military theorists. Through Conner, Eisenhower also came to the attention of General John Pershing and through Pershing to his aide, Colonel George C. Marshall, who would be chief of staff of the army when the United States entered World War II. All the while, he devoted years of study to becoming an expert in his craft. Besides strategy, he mastered both tact and tactics.[10]

In 1925, Eisenhower was assigned to the Command and General Staff School at Fort Leavenworth, a stepping-stone to higher command. Eisenhower was able to put to good use the experience and training he had received without having served as a combat officer. At the end of the yearlong course, he finished first in his class of 275 officers.

In 1941, Eisenhower had an opportunity again to show off his ability as a commander and to begin his rapid rise through the ranks. By this time, he had been promoted to colonel and was back at Fort Sam Houston as chief of staff of the Third Army. During maneuvers in Louisiana, his display of tactical skills won him promotion to brigadier general and brought him to the attention of Army Chief of Staff Marshall. After Pearl Harbor, Marshall summoned Eisenhower to Washington. After just a few months, he made him chief of the war plans division and put him on the fast track for even more important assignments. In March 1942, he promoted him to major general; in July, he was given his third star as a lieutenant general. At the same time, he was also given charge of Operation Torch, the Allied invasion of North Africa, his first field command. The North African campaign, followed by success in Sicily and then the invasion of Italy, prepared the way for the invasion of Europe. In February 1944, Eisenhower was officially designated Supreme Commander of the Allied Expeditionary Force (SHAEF), with responsibility for planning and carrying out the successful invasion of Normandy on 6 June 1944 (D-day). From then until the end of the war, he had supreme command of all allied forces in Europe. As recognition of his senior position, he was promoted in December 1944 to the five-star rank of general of the army. He proved to be an effective leader and a skillful diplomat, negotiating successfully with military and world leaders, many of whom were known for their supreme egos.

The victory over Germany less than a year after Normandy turned Eisenhower into a world celebrity. In 1948, he retired from the army to become president of Columbia University. Unhappy in that position, he assumed command in 1950 of NATO forces in Europe. By this time, a movement was under way in both major parties to draft Eisenhower for president. A confirmed internationalist, he was persuaded in 1952 by a group of moderate Republicans to head the Republican ticket after he became convinced that the leading Republican candidate for the nomination, Senator Robert Taft of Ohio, would follow an isolationist policy. Winning the nomination on the first ballot, he then went on to an easy victory over his Democratic opponent, Governor Adlai Stevenson of Illinois.

Although Eisenhower had been the candidate of moderate Republicans, once in office, he proved to be a fiscal conservative. He also believed in limiting the role of the federal government. Yet he also accepted the basic outlines of the New Deal. Thus he signed into law a measure providing for the biggest single expansion of the Social Security system in history, fought successfully for an increase in the minimum wage, and favored limited expansion of federal activity in housing, medical care, and education. In addition, his administration established the Department of Health, Education, and Welfare, and it obtained legislation providing for the construction with Canada of the Saint Lawrence Seaway and for the building of a 42,000-mile interstate highway system, the biggest program of its kind in the nation's history. This was all part of Eisenhower's vision of what he called modern Republicanism, or what historian Robert Griffith later referred to as a corporate commonwealth—a cooperative and harmonious society in which popular passions and group conflict were avoided by reconciling the needs and objectives of business, labor, and agriculture, of the well-to-do and the needy, all pursuing enlightened long-range goals rather than immediate self-interest.[11]

Eisenhower's foreign policy also followed the international lines of his Democratic predecessors. Believing that the Democrats had relied too heavily on the costly buildup of ground forces to contain Soviet expansion, he predicated his containment policy on the threatened use of massive retaliation with nuclear weapons. In Korea in 1953, he let the Chinese know that he might use nuclear weapons. In 1954, he considered using atomic weapons in Indochina where French troops, fighting the communist Vietminh forces, were on the verge of a major defeat at Dien Bien Phu. That same year, he considered bombing mainland China if the Chinese invaded the offshore islands of Quemoy and Matsu, which were under the control of Chinese Nationalists.

The difficulty with massive retaliation was that by reducing conventional ground forces, it seriously limited U.S. foreign policy options, leaving little but total war or inaction as policy choices. As presented to the American people by Secretary of State John Foster Dulles, moreover, massive retaliation was overtly provoca-tive and confrontational, raising the level of cold war rhetoric several decibels.

Eisenhower was the first American president who was barred from running for a third term by the Twenty-Second (or "two term") Amendment to the Constitution (1951). Given his popularity, he probably could have won a third term in 1960 had he been allowed to run. According to his son, John, he would like to have run for a third term even though he was already suffering from serious health problems.

Throughout his presidency, Eisenhower had had an ambivalent relationship with his vice president, Richard Nixon. He selected Nixon mainly to satisfy the more conservative wing of the Republican Party and to balance the ticket. Because of revelations that donors had established a secret fund for Nixon's private use, Eisenhower was prepared to drop him from the ticket. Nixon saved himself only by going on national television and pulling at the nation's heartstrings by stating that his wife wore a plain cloth coat and that he refused to return a dog named Checkers, which had been given to his children.[12] Even then, the relationship between Nixon and Eisenhower was never close. In 1956, Eisenhower tried unsuccessfully to remove him from his ticket for reelection by offering him a cabinet appointment. Nixon, Eisenhower felt, "just hasn't grown. People don't like him." However, Nixon was wise enough to turn down the offer, and Eisenhower felt he had no choice other than to keep him on the ticket.[13]

When it became clear in 1960 that Nixon would win the nomination, the president gave him only lukewarm support. In response, the Republican nominee refrained from asking Eisenhower to campaign actively for him until near the end of the campaign.[14] Because Eisenhower drew huge crowds wherever he went and Nixon lost by only 119,000 votes out of sixty-five million cast for his opponent, John F. Kennedy of Massachusetts, Nixon's decision not to use the president earlier in the campaign might have cost him the election.[15]

Eisenhower was deeply upset by Kennedy's victory. What bothered Eisenhower almost as much as the fact that the Republicans had lost, which he interpreted as a repudiation of his own administration, was the dim view he had of the president-elect. He considered Kennedy, at age forty-three the youngest man ever elected to the White House, weak and inexperienced, a second-term senator with an undistinguished record on Capitol Hill who, he remarked, had "no idea of the complexity of the job." "I will do almost anything to avoid turning my chair and country over to Kennedy," the outgoing president had also commented during the election. For his part, Kennedy viewed Eisenhower almost as an antique, the oldest president ever to leave office, who was out of step with the American people. Privately he referred to him as "that old a-hole." He also campaigned on an alleged missile gap between the United States and the Soviet Union, which Eisenhower knew to be untrue, and on what the Democrat claimed was the nation's general drift under his leadership. Although Kennedy was careful never to attack the president directly, Eisenhower regarded these charges as personal affronts. After the election, the president was also upset by the uncritical way the press treated the president-elect, extolling his virtues and treating him almost as a savior.[16]

Yet both Eisenhower and Kennedy worked hard to bring about a smooth transition. At Eisenhower's invitation, Kennedy met with the president at the White House on 8 December 1960. Much to Eisenhower's surprise, the president-elect came alone rather than with a retinue of staffers. Their meeting went an hour longer than scheduled. During their get-together, the two men discussed the gamut of foreign policy issues facing the new president, including an ongoing crisis over the future of Berlin and the threat from Fidel Castro in Cuba. They also discussed the structure of decision making in the Oval Office. Eisenhower urged Kennedy to follow the command and staff organization that he had adhered to while in the Oval Office, but the president-elect, who had other ideas, remained noncommittal. Throughout the meeting, Kennedy listened carefully to what the president said and asked intelligent questions that hinted at the seriousness with which he approached the meeting. Toward the end of discussion, Kennedy asked the outgoing president if he would continue to serve the country in a manner appropriate to a former president. Eisenhower responded that "the answer was obvious," just as long as he was not being asked to carry out ceremonial and frivolous errands.[17]

Before Eisenhower left office, Congress restored him to his rank of five-star general, which he had given up when he resigned from the army in 1952. He also made what many scholars regard as the most important farewell address since George Washington's Farewell Address of 1796. In it, the outgoing president spoke in stirring language about the dangers of communism. More important than the communist threat, he said, were the dangers at home of the "unwarranted influence, whether sought or unsought[,] by the military-industrial complex," which he described as the development of an insidious relationship between a scientific–technological elite and the nation's military establishment. Such a complex, he feared, might become so powerful as to set the direction of the nation's public policy. After the president's speech, the concept of a military-industrial complex became part of the nomenclature of critics of the nation's military and industrial policy.[18]

After Kennedy's inauguration, the Eisenhowers drove to their home in Gettysburg, Pennsylvania. Until 1950, the president and Mamie had never owned their own home. That year, they bought a 246-acre farm adjoining the Gettysburg battlefield. Although Eisenhower did not care for the winter climate of Gettysburg and spent most of his winters in the desert of California, he and Mamie found Gettysburg attractive for other reasons. The battlefield itself was of great interest to Eisenhower. He had first visited Gettysburg with his class at West Point in 1915. He found himself back at Gettysburg three years later as commander of Camp Colt. His ancestors came from the region, and its rolling fields and hills in the distance reminded him of Abilene. Gettysburg was also close enough to Washington, D.C., and New York for occasional visits to those cities and for friends to visit them for the weekend.[19]

Eisenhower's retirement was delayed, of course, when he assumed command of NATO and then served two terms in the White House. In the interim, he tore down most of the old farmhouse and built a spacious and handsome two-story, twenty-room Georgian-style mansion. Construction began in 1952 and was not completed until March 1955. The residence contained eight bedrooms, eight baths, a living room, dining room, kitchen, and glass-enclosed sun porch that looked out on the Gettysburg battlefield. Just outside were a putting green and sand trap, a gift of the Professional Golfer's Association in recognition of Eisenhower's love of the game. The property also included a guesthouse, barn, and skeet range. It was elegantly decorated with the memorabilia and gifts Eisenhower had received over his career.[20]

Once the home was completed, it became an essential retreat for the president, a place where he entertained family, friends, and world leaders. After he retired, he became a gentleman farmer, routinely checking on the crops grown on the farm and on his herd of Angus show cattle. He also played golf at the Gettysburg Golf Club, shot skeet, and oil painted. On weekdays, he went to his office, the former home of the president of Gettysburg College, where he met business and political associates and worked on his memoirs.[21]

The columnist Drew Pearson later claimed that some of Eisenhower's wealthy acquaintances, including three Texas oilmen who contributed $500,000, had helped pay for the farm. Eisenhower emphatically denied the charge. "Nobody has ever built any part of my farm," he told newsmen. In truth, after World War II, Eisenhower made friends with some of the nation's richest and most powerful men. They enjoyed spending time with a national hero. These friendships continued through Eisenhower's presidency and retirement. His gang, as he called them, reinforced his views on fiscal conservatism, wisely managed his investments as president in a blind trust, and spent time with him, either as a golfing partner or by joining in some of his other pastimes, including fishing, hunting, and playing bridge. Just before leaving office, he prepared a list of names of twenty-two persons, who, he insisted, were to call him Ike after he left office. Most of them were his gang of friends.[22]

That he accepted gifts from a variety of sources, including the gang, which added to the value of the farm is beyond doubt. Like Truman, he made an oblique distinction between using his former position for personal profit and accepting gifts and favors. Among the many gifts he accepted for the Gettysburg farm were the putting green and sand trap, a prize Black Angus calf, a tractor, two flower gardens, an orchid greenhouse, a power-tool shop, a fireplace that had once been used at the White House, a Grandma Moses painting, and fifty white pine trees that lined the driveway, one from each state Republican Party. However, the former president seems to have paid for the farm fully from the lucrative royalties he made from *Crusade in Europe*.[23]

Money never seems to have been a major problem for Eisenhower. Although *U.S. News and World Report* estimated his income at the time of his retirement, mostly from his presidential pension and investments, at about $30,000 (the equivalent of about $213,000 in 2009), he was able to spend his winters golfing in Palm Desert, California, and at the famous Augusta National course in Augusta, Georgia, virtually for free. He and Mamie almost never traveled at their own cost; either the Republican Party or some corporation picked up their expenses. His friends also took care of most of his expenses in Palm Desert; at Augusta, they even built a cottage for him before he became president that became known as Mamie's Cabin and put in a fishpond stocked with bass. He also accepted honorary memberships in other golf clubs and had the use of hunting lodges or fishing camps whenever he hunted or fished. He often spent time in Georgia hunting quail as the guest of Robert Woodruff, chairman of the Coca Cola Company, or at the plantation of his former treasury secretary, the Ohio industrialist George Humphrey.[24]

Eisenhower's income at the time he left the Oval Office was also soon supplemented by other earnings from television interviews, an advance for his memoirs, and occasional newspaper and magazine articles he wrote. He refused, however, to accept any honoraria for speeches. "I have made it a practice for years never to accept an honorarium for any talk: this policy I adopted right after World War II," he told his older brother, Edgar, who lived in Tacoma, Washington, after Edgar asked him to speak at the University of Puget Sound for a $1,000 honorarium.[25]

Shortly after he left office, the now ex-president did a series of interviews on CBS with Walter Cronkite for which he received a handsome fee. In 1963, he traveled to Normandy with Cronkite for another program, *D-Day Plus 20,* for which he again received a lucrative sum. The program was televised the next year. It showed Eisenhower driving a jeep across the beaches of Normandy while answering questions that Cronkite posed to him.[26]

Besides his interviews for CBS, Eisenhower worked diligently on his memoirs. Although all the major publishing houses wanted to publish them, he signed with Doubleday and Company, which had published *Crusade in Europe* and gave him a $1 million advance (the equivalent of about $7 million in 2009). His son, John, a West Point graduate, retired from the army and lived at a home he had earlier built on the farm in order to oversee the writing of the memoirs and take care of his father's business affairs.[27]

When Truman wrote his memoirs, he said his purpose was to let the facts speak for themselves. Like most memoirs, the facts turned out to be a defense of his administration. Eisenhower was more forthcoming about his purpose. He deeply resented the accusations of his critics against his presidency. He was offended by charges, widely accepted at the time, that he had been a passive, do-nothing president who preferred a game of golf to the duties of his office and had never been in charge of his administration. He was all the more offended by comparisons to Kennedy, supposedly surrounded by a group of the best and brightest minds in the country, who were determined to alter the country's course from one of drift to one of dynamic leadership. By writing his memoirs, he hoped to set the record straight. "One thing this book is going to demonstrate," John remarked as work began on the memoirs, "is that Dad knew what was going on, and was the person in charge."[28]

Eisenhower, who was a better writer than Truman, insisted that his memoirs be his own work. Yet like Truman, a good part of the memoirs, published in two volumes in 1963 and 1965, *Mandate for Change: 1953–1956* and *Waging Peace: 1956–1961,* was, in fact, written by committee. In addition to John, who took responsibility for much of the research and wrote many of the first drafts of chapters, others involved in the project included William B. Ewald Jr., one of Eisenhower's early speechwriters, and Samuel S. Vaughan, a senior editor at

Doubleday. Eisenhower's role was first to read the drafts of chapters written by his son and Ewald, then rework them, refining the language and sometimes adding whole sections or passages. In this sense, Eisenhower kept his promise to make his memoirs his own work.[29]

Yet both volumes lacked the warmth, the insight into Eisenhower's own personality, his honest evaluation of the individuals with whom he came into regular contact, the drama, that Eisenhower displayed in *Crusade in Europe* and the storytelling ability he showed in his 1967 more personal, autobiographical volume, *At Ease: Stories I Tell Friends.* He skimmed over embarrassing details about his administration. He was also reluctant to criticize other individuals still living, like Truman and Nixon. As most reviewers of the two volumes commented, they read more as a sphinxlike apologia for the defense than a sprightly affirmation of the administration.[30]

Sales of the memoirs were strong but not overwhelming. The first volume, *Mandate for Change,* had an initial printing of 125,000 copies, and early sales were brisk. Unfortunately, the book came out about the same time as Kennedy's assassination occurred, which eroded public interest in the Eisenhower administration. When *Waging Peace* was published two years later, it was overshadowed by two prize-winning volumes on the Kennedy administration, Theodore Sorensen's *Kennedy* and Arthur Schlesinger Jr.'s *A Thousand Days.* As a result, the volume failed to sell as well as *Mandate for Change.* In a sense, the alleged Kennedy curse, so often associated with Richard Nixon, seemed also to follow Eisenhower.[31]

One can extend this analogy further. The former president's relations with Kennedy remained overtly cordial. Certainly he never shared Nixon's paranoia toward his successor. Eisenhower supported the White House on such matters as foreign trade expansion, civil rights, and the Cuban missile crisis of October 1962, about which Kennedy kept him fully informed. He also backed Kennedy's policy in Southeast Asia, where the situation in Vietnam was deteriorating and where Kennedy was trying to end a civil war in Laos that he believed threatened Thailand.[32]

Nevertheless, the former president continued to harbor resentment toward his successor, especially toward the free ride he thought the media was giving him— this despite serious mistakes he believed his administration was making both in its foreign and domestic policies. He appreciated, for example, that Kennedy consulted with him at Camp David after the Bay of Pigs debacle in April 1961 and that Kennedy took full responsibility for the disaster. Rather than acknowledging that plans for the debacle began under his watch, he blamed the Bay of Pigs on Kennedy's failure to have a well-structured organization in the White House through which information on major issues could be filtered before it reached the Oval Office. He was dismayed to learn that the president had not even had a full meeting with the National Security Council before going ahead with the Cuban invasion. He thought the president's spoke-and-wheel approach to decision making, in which unfiltered information came directly to the Oval Office and the president relied on small groups of advisers, was a mistake.[33]

Similarly, when the Soviets cut off access to West Berlin in 1961, he believed Kennedy's initial response was too timid. "I would like to write about . . . what I believe organization can do constructively for the nation and the destructive effect of disorganization is almost certain to be," he wrote to his former aide, Major General Andrew Goodpaster, during the developing Berlin crisis in August.[34]

Even with respect to the more serious Cuban missile crisis of 1962, Eisenhower was not entirely satisfied with Kennedy's handling of the matter. He approved of the president's decision to impose a blockade and to warn the Soviets of air strikes and an invasion of Cuba if they did not remove the missiles. He was unhappy, however, with the president's promise to Moscow not to invade Cuba in return for the Soviet pledge to dismantle all its bomb sites in Cuba and return the missiles to the Soviet Union. "I observed, since we make a point of keeping our promises that I thought our government should be very careful about defining exactly what was meant by its promises," he recorded in his diary after Kennedy called him on 28 October to explain his agreement with the Soviet leader, Nikita Khrushchev. "It would be a mistake," he went on to say, "to give the Russians an unconditional pledge that we would forever and under all conditions not invade regardless of changing circumstances."[35]

As for the new president's economic and fiscal policies, known as the New Frontier, Eisenhower accepted the view among other Republicans that Kennedy was a big spender whose domestic program would lead to serious inflation. "I feel that our most serious internal problem today is that of adopting long term policies that will avoid the debasement of our currency and assist in combating every cause of inflation," Eisenhower remarked in July. Similarly, he thought Kennedy's decision to establish the Peace Corps and his announcement in the fall of 1961 to send a man to the moon by 1969 at a cost of as much as $40 billion the "height of folly."[36]

If Eisenhower was not already annoyed enough by what he regarded as the unfair comparisons being made between his administration and Kennedy's, especially in light of what he considered serious blunders on the inexperienced president's part, he was even more disturbed when he grasped how limited his influence was at the White House. As he came to realize, the president's supposed outreach policy toward his predecessor was largely a sham. According to Bobby Kennedy, in fact, his brother consulted with the former president primarily so he "wouldn't hurt the Administration by going off at a tangent." "Not that Eisenhower ever gave him any advice that was very helpful," Bobby added. Kennedy's adviser, Arthur Schlesinger Jr., later acknowledged that after the Bay of Pigs fiasco, Kennedy consulted Eisenhower and other Republican leaders mainly as a way of protecting himself against bipartisan attack in the wake of the disaster. As for Kennedy's fiscal policy, one of his purposes was to convince the American people to reject Eisenhower's connection between the inevitability of increased federal spending and inflation. "That is the one thing Eisenhower has put over to the American people," he once told Schlesinger Jr.[37]

The fact that Kennedy ignored his recommendations and seemed to be taking the country down the road of fiscal irresponsibility gave the president all the more reason to lead the Republicans to victory in the congressional elections in 1962 and the presidential election two years after that. The problem was that with Nixon's defeat in 1960, he saw no heir apparent. Certainly he did not want Nixon to run again. In August 1961, he wrote his vice president, encouraging him to run for governor of California. "My judgment," he told Nixon, "is that it would be highly valuable experience for you, for such later political activity on the national scene as you aspire to, to administer the affairs of a great and complex state like California. Your rich and varied career has not provided you so far with this kind of essential opportunity."[38]

Other than Nixon, the two most prominent Republicans nationwide were Governor Nelson Rockefeller of New York and Senator Barry Goldwater of Arizona. He considered both too extreme in their political views, and he had questions about Rockefeller's character and intelligence going back to the time when the governor worked for him in the White House.[39]

Out of concern for the future of the Republican Party and as a reflection of his resentment toward the Kennedy administration, Eisenhower followed his predecessor's course of delving into the political arena. As the nation's most admired and popular individual according to all polls, he was flooded with requests by Republican officeholders and candidates asking for his endorsement or help in fund-raising. He had anticipated a flood of mail for the first month or so after he left the presidency. Instead, the mail continued unabated. He became increasingly exasperated by the demands on his time and even more by a sense that he was being used by the very political extremists to the left and right of the middle course he sought for his party.[40]

The former president was worried especially by the ultraconservative movement led by Senator Goldwater, who, he believed, posed the most imminent threat to his brand of moderate Republicanism. He revealed his displeasure with Goldwater when, in September 1961, the Arizona senator, who was eager to have the former president's support even though he had a record of blasting his administration as reminiscent of the New Deal, sent him a copy of an article he had written for the *Northern Virginia Sun* in which he again denounced his administration and Kennedy's for not having taken more aggressive action against the worldwide communist threat. "The inept handling of the Cuban situation by the Eisenhower administration, and the tragic indecision of the Kennedy administration, has encouraged our enemies to test our will once more in Berlin," he wrote in the article that he forwarded to the Gettysburg farm.[41]

The former president was flabbergasted by what he read. As taken aback as he was that Goldwater had even sent him the article, in his cover letter, he told Eisenhower not to "worry, it is only for your eyes." "Over a fairly long lifetime,"

Photo of 25 March 1962 of Eisenhower with President John F. Kennedy at Palm Desert, CA, where Ike spent his winters playing golf and bridge. Although relations between Eisenhower and Kennedy were publicly cordial, privately, Ike did not much care for Kennedy. For his part, Kennedy kept in contact with all the former presidents, but he very rarely paid much attention to their advice. (Courtesy of Dwight D. Eisenhower Library.)

Eisenhower responded to Goldwater, "I have found it dangerous to criticize without being in full possession of the facts—all the facts."[42]

In hopes of stemming the growing extremist tide in the Republican Party, he sought out more moderate candidates for office. More out of a sense of obligation than anything else, he campaigned in California for Nixon, who had followed his advice and ran—unsuccessfully, as it turned out—for governor. In his own state of Pennsylvania, he persuaded the Republican leadership, headed by U.S. senator Hugh Scott, to throw its support for governor behind a forty-five-year-old first-term congressman, Williams W. Scranton.

The congressman had come to Eisenhower's attention while working in the State Department during his administration. Handsome, a graduate of Yale Law School, a successful businessman, and from one of the state's patriarchal families, Scranton was also one of the most progressive Republicans on Capitol Hill. Although he had reservations about running for governor after having served only one term in Congress, Eisenhower persuaded him that it was his duty to run. After winning a landslide victory against his Democratic opponent, he emerged as a possible contender for the Republican nomination in 1964.[43]

While supporting moderate Republican candidates for office, Eisenhower helped form the Republican Citizens, another attempt by the former president to break the grip of the old guard. "What we are trying to do," he explained in a letter to a Cleveland businessman, "is to build a bridge between the Republican Party on the one hand and the Independents and the dissatisfied Democrats on the other so that these latter people may eventually find themselves more comfortable living with Republican policies and personalities." Yet the organization had little support either from the Republican National Committee (RNC) or from the Republican leadership on Capitol Hill, which seemed more interested in controlling the party than in taking control of government. In November, the Democrats gained the most impressive victory of any party in power since 1934, and the Republican Citizens simply went out of business.[44]

Despite this setback, Eisenhower labored on. While in Washington the next year for President Kennedy's funeral after his assassination, Eisenhower met with the new president, Lyndon Johnson. The two men had worked together closely in the 1950s when Eisenhower was president and Johnson was Senate majority leader. Although Eisenhower respected Johnson's political skills, he found him devious and privately referred to him as a phony. Even as late as the 1968 presidential campaign, when Eisenhower was living out his final months at the Walter Reed Hospital, he wrote in his diary about Johnson: "He calls Republicans [the] 'party of fear.' When I recall his . . . cowardly actions when a Senator I could laugh except that it is all so false."[45] At their meeting, Johnson asked for and received Eisenhower's promise of support and counsel. Probably neither man took this exchange as more than a formality—or anticipated how often Johnson would be consulting Eisenhower in the coming years over the Vietnam War.

After a short moratorium on all political activities out of respect for the fallen president, the 1964 campaign for president resumed in earnest. On the Democratic side, Johnson was the uncontested candidate for the Democratic nomination. On the Republican side, matters were less certain. Goldwater was the golden boy of the party's right wing and the leading contender for the Republican nomination. However, Rockefeller remained a formidable opponent.[46]

Both Goldwater and Rockefeller remained unacceptable to Eisenhower. On 24 May, the Arizona senator appeared on ABC's *Issues and Answers* and called for defoliation of Vietnamese forests by low-yielding atomic weapons. He even suggested crossing into China to end the war in Vietnam. The next day, Eisenhower responded with an 1,100-word statement published in the New York *Herald Tribune*. Describing what he expected of the Republican candidate for president, Eisenhower wrote that he should pledge himself "to responsible, forward-looking Republicanism" and dismissed as unacceptable anyone who was prone to "impulsiveness" in the conduct of foreign policy.[47]

Although the former president's statement was clearly aimed at the Arizona senator, he backpedaled after Rockefeller used it to suggest he had the former president's blessing. In response, Eisenhower remarked that he was not leading any stop-Goldwater effort. In reality, he was looking for an alternative to both Rockefeller and Goldwater and settled on Governor Scranton of Pennsylvania as his candidate.[48]

Unfortunately, the former president completely bungled his handling of Scranton's candidacy. After Goldwater's victory in the California primary, Eisenhower, who now thought the Arizona senator was "nuts," invited Scranton to Gettysburg to press him to announce his candidacy for president. As Scranton later recalled, "He never said that he would support me . . . but he made it very clear that he wanted me to run." With Eisenhower's implicit endorsement, the governor attended the Republican governors' conference in Cleveland in order to round up support and to announce that he was running on CBS's *Face the Nation* that Sunday morning.[49]

Before making his announcement, however, Scranton received a telephone call from his Gettysburg patron informing him that he had no intention of joining a "cabal" against Goldwater. What had happened was that the Goldwater forces had learned of Eisenhower's conversation with Scranton and then persuaded the former president's friend and staunch Goldwater supporter, George Humphrey, to have a talk with Eisenhower. During their conversation, Humphrey convinced Eisenhower to remain neutral by pointing to the danger of ripping the party apart if he came out openly against Goldwater. Dumbfounded by Eisenhower's phone call, Scranton delayed his announcement. "My God," the governor later remembered thinking, "how am I going to run for president if it's a yes, no, yes, no?"[50]

The Pennsylvania governor was ready to give up his undeclared candidacy when Goldwater joined Southern Democrats in opposing the 1964 Civil Rights Bill. Once more, Eisenhower called Scranton to tell him how "sick" he was about Goldwater's vote and to encourage him to run. Again, he failed to offer him his unequivocal support. Even without it, Scranton was so dismayed by the prospect of a Goldwater candidacy that he decided to run anyway, and on 11 June, he officially announced his candidacy. He tried to appeal to all wings of the party by calling himself a liberal on civil rights, a conservative on fiscal matters, and an internationalist on foreign affairs — in other words, an Eisenhower Republican. He also sought to persuade even conservative Republicans that Goldwater could not win in November.[51]

Unfortunately for Scranton, his candidacy amounted to too little, too late. The right wing controlled the party. Goldwater had proven he could win even in such a large and diverse state as California. He avoided any serious blunders in the remaining weeks before the convention. The Pennsylvania governor had almost no organization, and perhaps most important, Eisenhower refused to announce his support despite pleas from the candidate and the urgings of Hugh Scott, Lodge, Nixon, and his brother, Milton, who later delivered the nominating speech for Scranton. When the delegates met at the Cow Palace in San Francisco, they overwhelmingly nominated Goldwater on the first ballot.[52]

In his speech accepting the party's nomination, the Arizona senator confirmed his radical reputation with his remark about "extremism in the defense of liberty [being] no vice" and "moderation in the pursuit of justice [being] no virtue." The former president was enraged by Goldwater's acceptance speech and by the unbending attitude of his delegates toward moderation, including an especially savage outburst of jeering when Rockefeller took to the podium. The day after Goldwater delivered his speech, the former president called the Republican nominee to his hotel room and, still in his pajamas, vented his anger. "Barry, what the hell did you mean last night about extremism?" he asked Goldwater. "I couldn't make any sense out of it and I thought it was a damn silly thing to say."[53]

The senator tried to mollify Eisenhower, and the former president agreed to go to a unity gathering in Hershey, Pennsylvania, attended by Scranton, Rockefeller, and Nixon. Later he participated in an obviously scripted half-hour televised "conversation" from his farm with the Republican candidate, in which he said it was "a silly notion" that Goldwater was a right-wing extremist.[54]

Eisenhower limited his participation in the campaign to the minimum he believed needed to avoid appearing derelict in his duty to the party. Privately, he continued to express his dismay with Goldwater. After the Hershey gathering, he remarked, "You know, before we had this meeting I thought that Goldwater was just stubborn. Now I am convinced that he is just plain dumb." He also expressed contrition that he had not been more forceful in pushing Scranton's nomination. "If the Lord spares me for 1968," he later remarked, "I am going to come out for somebody at least 18 months ahead of time. This year I tried to do what was decent."[55]

After Goldwater's humiliating defeat—he received only 38.5 percent of the popular vote and only fifty-two electoral votes to Johnson's 60.7 percent of the popular vote and 520 electoral votes—Eisenhower and Nixon convinced Goldwater to replace the Republican Party's national chairman, Dean Burch, whom Goldwater had named to the position, with a more pragmatic politician, Ray Bliss. The next summer, the former president hosted a picnic at his Gettysburg farm attended by 400 leading Republicans in an effort to bring the various factions of the party closer together. In 1968, he also endorsed Nixon from his bed at Walter Reed Hospital, where his heart was failing him, three weeks before the Republicans held their nominating convention. From Walter Reed, he also delivered short remarks to the gathering. After 1964, however, he withdrew from politics as much as it was possible for any former president to do.[56]

Goldwater's nomination marked the end of the Eisenhower era of the Republican Party. Despite the senator's embarrassing defeat and the nomination for president of the more moderate Nixon in 1968 and Gerald Ford in 1976, more conservative elements at all levels of the party were slamming the lid on Eisenhower's middle-of-the-road Republicanism. Had the former president openly supported an alternative to the senator much earlier, he may have been able to delay this swing toward the right. There was still strong resistance to a Goldwater candidacy from more moderate elements. Goldwater had defeated Rockefeller in the California primary by only 58,000 votes out of more than two million cast. Eisenhower still remained the most popular living American. Had he indicated his concern about Goldwater or even remained silent before the primary, the New York governor may very well have beaten his opponent and stopped the Goldwater bandwagon. He had recently won the Oregon primary. On the eve of the California primary, he was still leading in the state polls, although the Arizona senator was closing what had been a large gap. The former president's statement of neutrality may have been just enough to carry the day for Goldwater.[57]

As for Scranton's candidacy, it turned out to be a comedy of errors choreographed and directed by the former president. Scranton was himself a victim of Eisenhower's incompetence. He had no great interest in running for president, saying that he would accept his party's nomination only if he were drafted. Eisenhower had persuaded him, however, to run and gave him every reason to believe he would support him openly. Then he undermined his candidacy by refusing to endorse him.

All that said, it still seems unlikely the former president could have delayed for long the whirlwind of change Goldwater's candidacy represented. A group of young conservative activists that included members of the Young Republicans and Young Americans for Freedom and conservative intellectuals like William Buckley Jr. and William Rusher of the *National Review* were changing the dynamics of the party. In contrast, such moderates as Rockefeller, Governor George Romney of Michigan, and Nixon each had their own competing political ambitions and agendas. Romney also did not like Rockefeller, and neither cared much for Nixon.[58]

Like Truman's inability to influence the nominating process of his party, Eisenhower's failure to lead the Republican Party down the middle of the road toward modern Republicanism underscored the limits of the office of ex-president. Strong and popular presidents, as far back as Andrew Jackson and as recently as Theodore Roosevelt, were able to name their own successors and remain determinative political forces within their parties for years after they left the White House. Increasingly, however, the impact of organization, the importance of money, and the influence of the media—all aspects of the modern political process—outweighed the personal popularity, private ties, political skills, and fundraising abilities of former presidents. They had the privileges and entitlements of a political office but not the power. With passage of the Twenty-Second Amendment limiting presidents to two terms, they could not even hold over the heads of political opponents the threat of running again for the White House.

Even though it became routine after Kennedy took office for former presidents to be given regular, even daily, briefings on major national policy issues and to be consulted on a regular basis by their successors in the White House, their influence in the decision-making process also remained limited. Presidents listened, but rarely deferred, to former presidents. Why should they? The evolution of the modern presidency meant the development of an extensive executive apparatus supported by a massive bureaucracy, with teams of advisers and reams of reports offering an exhaustive array of presidential options. At most, former presidents, even those with particular expertise on pressing issues of lasting consequence, were lonely voices among choruses of experts holding the reins of power.

Kennedy had acted independently of Eisenhower during the Cuban missile crisis, although their views coincided on not invading Cuba immediately. Similarly, Lyndon Johnson sought out Eisenhower's advice on Vietnam, and their views coincided insofar as escalating the war was concerned. In only one instance, however, did the former president's counsel appear to have played any consequential role in the decision-making process.

No president was more respectful of former presidents than Johnson. He was the first president to make available to ex-presidents as a matter of policy military aides and aircraft when they were traveling. He also pushed successfully for Secret Service protection for former presidents and their families, and he extended both to Truman and Eisenhower every small courtesy he could. Rather than being grateful for Johnson's thoughtfulness, however, Eisenhower held to his view of Johnson as untrustworthy and regarded his gestures as sycophantic.[59]

The former president was not wrong in his judgment. The president was doing more than giving Eisenhower the famous Johnson treatment. Bent on a policy of escalating the war in Vietnam, he wanted Eisenhower's unique moral authority and military prestige behind his policy. At Johnson's request, he met at the White House on 17 February 1965 with the president and his national security advisers to discuss Vietnam. This was a week after the Vietcong had attacked the U.S. Air Force base and barracks at Pleiku, killing nine Americans and wounding more than a hundred. Reflecting Eisenhower's own growing hawkish views, he warned the president and his advisers of the importance of saving Southeast Asia from the communists and urged Johnson to do whatever was necessary to win the war, including bombing North Vietnam.[60]

Eisenhower's conclusion that a bombing campaign would weaken Hanoi's resolve buoyed Johnson's decision to launch in March Operation Rolling Thunder, the bombing of North Vietnam. Even without his input, however, it seems certain that Johnson would have gone ahead with the bombing. Johnson was already being pressured by his own national security team to launch regular air attacks against North Vietnam. By the end of November, the administration had formulated concrete plans for a two-phase program of escalating air attacks. On 1 December, the president gave his approval in principle to the first phase. In January, he moved to implement the entire program, and in February, even before he met with Eisenhower, he began retaliatory strikes across the seventeenth parallel dividing South Vietnam from North Vietnam. A week after his meeting with the former president, he approved what became Rolling Thunder. Eisenhower's rec-ommendation for an air campaign against North Vietnam, in other words, seems only to have reaffirmed a decision Johnson and his advisers had already made.[61]

Increasingly, the former president grew critical of Johnson's Vietnam policy. He feared the war was dragging on too long. He criticized the administration for its defensive strategies, for "acting by driblets" and taking "piddling steps" in Vietnam. He was also worried about the "disregard for law and order, and weakening of the morals" he associated with the growing antiwar movement and the leftist culture of the 1960s. He believed the White House needed to be more transparent with the American people. Until Johnson was able to explain and to justify the war to the American people, he foresaw the possibility of a domestic disaster.[62]

Eisenhower was also concerned about the unfavorable impact the war was having on U.S. relations with its European allies. He thought Johnson needed to put more demands on South Vietnam to make the reforms needed to assure a stable government. "We should keep constant pressure on bringing the South Vietnamese to the point where they will be strong enough, both in Saigon and the countryside, to govern themselves effectively," he advised the president.[63]

None of this kept the former president from backing Johnson's expansion of the war. At one point in 1967, he even stated that he would not "preclude" using nuclear weapons against North Vietnam. Although he backtracked a few weeks later, calling the idea "silly," he remained committed to an intense bombing cam-paign against the North. His growing disagreements with the administration over the particulars of its war strategy highlighted the limits of his influence within the White House. It also left Eisenhower increasingly frustrated and angry, especially since the Democrats tried, as the war dragged on, to tie the country's commitment in Vietnam back to his own administration, a position he emphatically rejected.[64]

Eisenhower, of course, did not live to see the end of the war. He did live to see Richard Nixon eke out a narrow victory over his Democratic opponent, Hubert Humphrey, in the 1968 presidential campaign. He also lived to see his grandson, David, marry Nixon's youngest daughter, Julie. Too sick to attend the wedding, he was able to watch it through a closed-circuit television hookup at the hospital.

Eisenhower had been in poor health for years. Easily irritated, with a type A personality and erratic blood pressure that often reached levels of mild hyper-tension, Eisenhower had smoked as many as four packs of cigarettes a day until 1949, when, on the advice of his doctors, he went cold turkey. He had also been under intense pressure since at least his commanding role during World War II. For years, he had suffered from a pattern of severe abdominal pains, the cause of which the doctors were not able to diagnose but which his personal physician, Dr. Howard Snyder Jr., who sought always to emphasize Eisenhower's good health, referred to as a relatively minor gastrointestinal problem.[65]

On 27 September 1955, while in Denver visiting his in-laws and after a day playing golf, Eisenhower suffered a major heart attack. Dr. Paul Dudley White, widely regarded as the nation's preeminent cardiologist, was summoned from Boston to Denver to head a group of cardiologists and radiologists caring for the president. Mindful of a presidential election only a year away, Dr. Snyder played down the seriousness of the coronary. Soon Eisenhower was waving to crowds from the hospital's sundeck. On 11 November, he was able to walk out of the hospital and return to Washington. Over the next several months, he recuperated at Gettysburg and Key West, Florida.[66]

While the public felt relieved over the president's recovery, the attending physicians were divided on his fitness to live through a second term should he decide to seek reelection. Among those who believed he should not run again were doctors White and Thomas Mattingly, Eisenhower's cardiologist at Walter Reed Hospital. Given White's national prominence, he carried with him the fate of Eisenhower's political future. Realizing this, the president made clear to him that he expected to decide his own future. His advisers, who were anxious for him to run again, also applied pressure on the team of doctors caring for him. White, who had been promoting the idea that a person who had suffered a heart attack could still lead a productive life with proper diet, exercise, and rest at a time when it was common to believe that death usually followed a heart attack within a few years, bowed to this presidential pressure. Despite his doubts about Eisenhower's health, he declared on 14 February that "medically, the chances are that the President should be able to carry on an active life satisfactorily for another five to ten years."[67]

Eisenhower's health continued to be an ongoing issue throughout the remainder of his presidency. In 1956, he suffered an intestinal blockage, which finally led to the diagnosis that he had been suffering from chronic ileitis, an inflammation of the lowest portion of the small intestine (Crohn's disease) for a number of years. The surgery necessary to remove the blockage delayed his slow recovery from his earlier heart attack. More serious was a mild stroke the president suffered in November 1957.[68]

When Eisenhower left office in 1961, he seemed in good health, especially for a person who had had two heart attacks and a stroke within the last dozen years and had been suffering from Crohn's disease throughout his presidency. The fact that he could maintain such a full schedule, travel extensively, and play at least one, and sometimes as many as three, rounds of golf every time he had a chance, was testimony both to his natural athleticism and stamina even though, at age seventy, he was the oldest president to leave office.

Yet Eisenhower was not in good health. In September 1965, while in Augusta, he suffered another heart attack. After recuperating for two weeks at a local army hospital, he was transferred to Walter Reed. After a slow recovery, his doctors determined he was fit enough to play golf again, but he was ordered to use a cart and was limited to a par-three course. Realizing that his heart was failing, the former president began to put his affairs in order. He sold his prized herd of Angus cattle and deeded his farm to the government.[69]

The former president also decided that he wanted to be buried in Abilene, where the Dwight D. Eisenhower Library and Museum were located. Eisenhower had not been heavily involved with the construction of his library. In the 1940s, a nonprofit group, the Eisenhower Foundation, had been established under a state charter. It raised most of the funds needed to build the thirteen-acre Eisenhower Center encompassing, on a campuslike setting, the museum and library (two separate sandstone and granite buildings located across from each other), the president's boyhood home, and a small meditation chapel. In April 1960, the foundation transferred the still privately endowed library to the National Archives. After Eisenhower left office, most of his papers were transferred immediately to the handsome three-story library, which was formally dedicated on 1 May 1962.[70]

In March 1967, the former president suffered his third heart attack in Palm Springs. After a month of recovery, he was transferred to Walter Reed, where he lived out the remaining eleven months of his life. At the hospital, he suffered three more heart attacks and several episodes of cardiac fibrillation. He also had to undergo abdominal surgery in February 1969 to relieve another intestinal blockage. Given his weakened heart and a bout of pneumonia that followed the operation, it was a medical surprise that he managed to survive the surgery. He grew increasingly weak. Finally, on 28 March 1969, with Mamie, John, and David at his bedside, his heart gave out. His final words were, "I want to go: God take me."[71]

After his death, Eisenhower was given a state funeral. His body was flown to Washington, where his body lay in state at the Capitol rotunda. An estimated 100,000 persons passed by the casket. President Richard Nixon gave the eulogy during a service at the rotunda, the first time a president gave the eulogy for a former president. After a funeral service at the National Cathedral, his casket was returned by train to Abilene for final burial at the meditation chapel of the Eisenhower Center. He was laid to rest in an army coffin in full military uniform. Thousands of people lined the railroad tracks to pay their final respects. Thousands more flooded Abilene to bid their farewells to one of the most beloved leaders of the twentieth century.[72]

II

One of the most complicated individual ever to serve in the Oval Office, Lyndon Johnson was a whirlwind of emotions and a contradiction of opposites. At different times, he could be coarse or courtly, humorous or humorless, inspiring or insufferable, insecure or self-assured, sinister or well-intentioned, overbearing or deferential, miserly or generous.

One aspect of Johnson's personality that engendered no opposite, however, was his ambition. He set out to be the greatest president in history. His Great Society programs were the most far-reaching of any president. Ambition of a different sort—a determination not to be remembered as the only president to lose a war—led ultimately to the expansion of the Vietnam War and to the downfall of his administration. That was both the great national and personal tragedy of his presidency.

Johnson was born in a small farmhouse—really a shack—on 27 August 1908, along the Pedernales River between Stonewall and Johnson City, Texas. Growing up in the hill country of Texas around the turn of the century was far different from growing up even in a small rural town like Abilene. During Eisenhower's youth, Abilene paved its streets, built cement sidewalks, installed an electric generator, added running water and a sewerage system, and acquired a telephone network. The hill country offered few of these amenities. Johnson's high school was not even accredited. His mother had to carry heavy buckets of water each day from an outdoor water pump. An outhouse substituted for in-house plumbing. Homes were lit by kerosene lamp. After a rain, the unpaved streets and pathways were often impassable. The lack of such an infrastructure helped shape Johnson's later views on the responsibilities of government.[73]

The conflicted personalities of Johnson's parents also explain many of the contradictions of Johnson's own personality. In contrast to Eisenhower's stable home, where according to the former president his parents shared similar values and never argued, Johnson's parents had different upbringings and interests. A graduate of Baylor University, Rebekah Baines Johnson had refined tastes that included a love of music, dance, poetry, and literature. She tried to pass these interests on to Lyndon, always her favorite child. However, she qualified her love for him. When he was disobedient or failed to live up to her expectations, she refused to talk to him or even to acknowledge his existence.[74] In contrast to his mother, Lyndon's father, Sam Early was crude, gruff, and self-righteous. He swore, drank, engaged prostitutes, and often did not come home at night. He was also a harsh disciplinarian who could become nasty when drinking.

Johnson sought to please both his father and mother but feared rejection by both. Johnson was also torn between the frailty and sensitivity of his mother and the rudeness and roughness of his father, by his mother's insistence on refinement and his father's rejection of what he considered an effete intellectualism, and by a need for attention and a sense of loneliness resulting, in part, from the fact that as the firstborn, he was the complete center of attention of his parents until, in relatively short order, he had to share it with four siblings.[75]

Johnson always felt closer to his mother than his father. Rebekah regarded him as extraordinarily gifted and taught him to believe he could accomplish anything. Yet his father had the greater influence on him. His father was a state legislator for much of the time that Lyndon was growing up. As a boy, he loved campaigning with his father. During legislative sessions, he often stayed on the

House floor, observing the lawmakers and learning the tricks of the political trade. As a lawmaker, his father fought against corporate interests and introduced legislation to help his largely poor constituency. Sam also hated bigotry, even speaking out against the Ku Klux Klan, which for a time dominated Texas politics. All this had a lasting impact on Lyndon. So did his father's sense of manly bravado and anti-intellectualism.[76]

Graduating high school at age fifteen, Johnson went through a rebellious period, traveling to California with a group of friends and then working on a road gang in Texas, before enrolling at Southwest Texas State Teachers College in San Marcos (now Texas State University). More interested in becoming one of the most influential students on campus than in the college's curriculum, he established a pattern that he followed throughout his political career.

The key to success, Johnson wrote in a college editorial, "was to train the mind on the essentials and discard the frivolous and unimportant." He spent his first month studying carefully the structure and dynamics of the college and its small 700-member student body. By the time he graduated in 1930, he had ingratiated himself with the college's faculty, staff, and president, Cecil Evans. First working for Evans as a gofer, he eventually took on the responsibilities of an administrative and legislative assistant. He also organized the student body to gain control of the student council, which had traditionally been controlled by the athletes and dispensed most of the student activities budget to the athletic program.[77]

Before his senior year, Johnson took a teaching job in the small town of Cotulla, about sixty miles north of the Mexican border. Most of his students were the children of poor Mexican farmworkers. According to Johnson, they were treated by the Anglos in the town "just worse than you'd treat a dog." Although he taught in order to pay for his senior year at San Marcos, he spent much of his salary on the students. His experience in Cotulla added a further dimension to his lifelong yearning to assist the deprived, neglected, and helpless.[78]

After graduating from San Marcos in 1930, Johnson taught briefly in Houston before gaining a position as the administrative aide to Richard Kleberg, an heir to the King Ranch fortune, who had recently won a special election for an open congressional seat.

As administrative aide to Kleberg, Johnson followed the pattern he had already established as a college student and schoolteacher. He threw himself totally into his job and mastered his environment. He observed, studied, and picked the brains of other, more senior, aides in order to learn how Congress worked and where the centers of power rested. He ingratiated himself with the rising stars on Capitol Hill, including the three senior members of the Texas delegation, Sam Rayburn, Wright Patterson, and Maury Maverick. Johnson also ran Kleberg's office with ruthless efficiency, typically making the staff work late hours and even on weekends answering inquiries that came into the office. Within a short time, he became one of the best-networked and respected congressional aides on Capitol Hill.[79]

Johnson spent so much time vanquishing his surroundings and furthering his agenda that he seemed to have little time for a personal life. While on a short trip to Austin, however, he met and immediately fell in love with Claudia Taylor, known since childhood as Lady Bird, the shrewd but shy daughter of a prominent family from Karnack, Texas. In typical fashion, Johnson wasted no time in proposing to her. After a brief courtship, they were married in November 1934. Throughout Johnson's political career, she became a stable counterweight to his tumultuous personality. Notwithstanding his numerous extramarital affairs, she was totally supportive of him. Together they had two daughters, Lynda (b. 1944) and Luci (b. 1947).[80]

Except for a two-year stint as director of the National Youth Administration (NYA) in Texas, Johnson remained in Washington for the next thirty-nine years. In the short time he served in the NYA, he was also one of its most successful state leaders. He did so well that he came to the attention of Franklin and Eleanor Roosevelt. His forty-member staff at the NYA also became the basis for his future political machine. In 1937, he began his long career in elective politics when he won a special election for Congress. Scarcely known outside his home of Blanco County, he won the election by traveling to more places and delivering more speeches than his opponents and by being a stronger backer of the New Deal.

Johnson served six terms as a member of the House. As his future vice president, Hubert Humphrey, said about him, "Politics was not an avocation with him. . . . It was *the* vocation. It was his life. It was his religion, it was his family . . . it was his totality." Or as his future secretary of health, education, and welfare, Wilbur Cohen remarked, he was a man "larger than life."[81]

Cohen's comment described Johnson almost as well physically. Standing six feet, four inches tall and weighing about 210 pounds with brown, narrow eyes and black hair, he had a large nose, oversized, jutting ears, a long, lined face, and equally long arms, legs, and hands. However, it was not his size alone that made him so physically awesome. The Johnson style was to overwhelm an individual by standing within inches of that person's face, grabbing an arm or a collar, and staring directly into his eyes, all the while overpowering him with his forceful, often curse-laden arguments. As president, he was known even to stand on a chair so that he could look down on those whom he was trying to persuade.

In 1948, Johnson decided to run for the U.S. Senate. He had made an earlier run for the Senate in 1941 against the popular governor "Pappy" O'Daniel. He seemed to have won the race, until enough "new" votes from counties controlled by O'Daniel were found to throw the race to the governor. In 1948, Johnson once more faced formidable opposition from a popular governor, Coke Stevenson. Unofficial results from the Democratic runoff had Stevenson beating Johnson by a narrow margin. But Johnson had learned his lesson well from 1941. Enough "new" votes were suddenly found in the counties Johnson controlled that in the official tally, he was declared the winner by eighty-seven votes. From that time forward, his political enemies in the state and on Capitol Hill often mocked him as "landslide Johnson."[82]

Johnson's rise to majority leader of the Senate was meteoric. Instead of using the Senate as a forum for reaching a broader national audience, like other members of his entering class, such as Humphrey or Estes Kefauver, he sought to dominate the Senate. How he did this was complicated but illustrative of his political shrewdness. First he focused his attention on the inner circle of senior Democrats, almost all from the South, who, rather than the formal senatorial leadership, controlled the Democratic side of the chamber. He became especially close to Richard Russell, the ranking member of the Armed Services Committee and perhaps the most powerful Democrat in the Senate. Then by getting himself elected part of the Senate's leadership, first as minority whip, then as minority leader, and in 1955 as majority leader, he transferred control of the Senate to himself. The key to his success was his intimacy with all aspects of senatorial life, from the chamber's rules to his knowledge about each senator through personal conversation and an elaborate intelligence network he developed. He carved out what seemed a special relationship with each senator. To the extent possible, he responded to their preferences for committee assignments. He called up or held back bills as they requested, and he shared "confidential" information with them. He also won changes in the seniority rules to allow new senators at least one important committee assignment. In such ways, he put them in his debt. When necessary, though, he applied the Johnson style he had perfected.[83]

Of course, there was much more to Johnson's leadership of the Senate than the power he came to control. Committed to the principle that bargains could always be made between reasonable people, he worked successfully with the Republican leadership on Capitol Hill and with the White House in such matters as civil rights legislation without alienating his fellow Southern Democrats and the establishment of the National Aeronautics and Space Administration (NASA). As a result of his leadership in the Senate, he became the nation's most powerful elected official next to the president himself.[84]

Johnson was already eyeing the White House for himself. On 2 July 1955, however, he suffered a severe heart attack that almost cost him his life and required months of recuperation before he could resume his duties as majority leader. Although he had been a chain-smoker and a heavy eater and drinker, he quit smoking and cut back on his eating and drinking. By the next year, he considered himself healthy enough to seek the presidency four years hence. However, he made the mistake of avoiding the primary route, so that by the time the delegates assembled, it was too late to stop the Kennedy juggernaut. After easily defeating Johnson by a two-to-one margin, the Democratic nominee surprised the convention by offering the vice presidential spot to Johnson. Seeing the vice presidency as the only avenue for a Southerner to win the White House, he agreed to be Kennedy's running mate. With Johnson on the ballot, Kennedy was able to carry Texas and win the election by the narrowest margin in the nation's history.

The most miserable years of Johnson's political career were the thousand days he served as Kennedy's vice president. Although he hoped he might play a powerful role in the administration, he was denied that opportunity, remaining mostly a figurehead who contributed little to the decision-making process. After Kennedy's assassination, however, he found himself suddenly holding the office he was only able to dream of winning perhaps in 1968.

The new president made the most of the opportunity before him. In order to satisfy the Kennedy wing of the Democratic Party and to establish his own legitimacy, Johnson asked the Kennedy cabinet not to resign. Then he went before Congress to ask it to pay the dead president the highest tribute it could by passing two measures that Kennedy had failed to get it to approve—a $13.5 billion tax cut and a civil rights bill banning discrimination in public accommodations. In addition, he used his political wizardry to gain congressional approval of federal funds for mass transportation and an $800 million war on poverty.

After his landslide victory in 1964 against Senator Barry Goldwater of Arizona, Johnson pushed through an overwhelmingly Democratic Congress a legislative agenda that included a $1.3 billion program of federal aid to primary and secondary education, national health insurance for the poor and elderly, an additional $1.6 billion for the war on poverty, a manpower training bill, college scholarships, environmental legislation, and measures to establish the Department of Housing and Urban Development and the National Endowment for the Arts and Humanities. Perhaps the greatest legacy of the Great Society program was the Voting Rights Act of 1965, which authorized federal examiners to register voters and banned literacy tests for voting. For the first time, blacks in the South were able to vote in large numbers.

About the same time that Congress was approving the Voting Rights Act, Johnson was taking a series of steps that would entrap the United States in the Vietnam War. Never an acute student of foreign policy, he blamed the civil war in Vietnam on North Vietnamese and Chinese aggression, which, if not stopped, would lead to further aggression. In August 1964, after informing the nation that North Vietnam had attacked American warships in the Gulf of Tonkin, Johnson got Congress to approve a resolution authorizing him to wage a presidential war in Vietnam. After an attack by Vietcong guerrillas on U.S. military advisers at Pleiku in February 1965, Johnson instituted an air war against North Vietnam. He also decided to increase the number of American ground forces in South Vietnam. By the end of 1965, he had committed more than 180,000 American troops to the fighting. Three years later, the United States had more than 500,000 troops in Vietnam with no end of the war in sight

The war destroyed Johnson's presidency. Despite the Great Society programs that he had pushed through Congress, he never won the trust of Democratic liberals, who disliked his often crude behavior and his reputation for wheeling and dealing. The war turned many of them openly against the administration. More important, as Johnson expanded America's commitment in Vietnam, opposition to the war grew on college campuses. The antiwar movement reached a crescendo in 1968 after the January Tet offensive, in which communist forces attacked all the major cities in South Vietnam and even penetrated the American embassy in Saigon. Although the offensive was a military defeat for the North Vietnamese and Vietcong, the fact they had been able to launch such an extensive and well-coordinated attack seemed to belie the administration's claim that it was winning the war.

The political fallout of the Vietnam War was manifested in the New Hampshire presidential primary in March 1968, when a relatively obscure political figure, Senator Eugene McCarthy of Minnesota, almost upset the president. Four days later, a more formidable opponent, Senator Robert Kennedy of New York, entered the race. On 31 March, Johnson went on national television to announce that he was restricting the bombing of North Vietnam to a small area and to invite the North Vietnamese to begin discussions on ending the war—an invitation they quickly accepted. Then Johnson startled the nation by declaring that he would not seek or accept the Democratic presidential nomination. By then, lawmakers of his own party were in open rebellion against him. Because of his unpopularity, he declined to attend the riotous Democratic convention in Chicago later that year, which nominated for president his vice president, Hubert Humphrey.

Humphrey and Johnson had not been on good terms for most of Humphrey's vice presidency. Johnson considered Humphrey a quintessential bleeding-heart liberal who substituted verbosity for achievement, and he thought Humphrey would have a difficult time making tough decisions. During the election, Humphrey tried to distance himself from Johnson without renouncing his Vietnam policy. He had wanted to deliver a speech before the convention making clear that, if elected, he would be more willing to compromise on Vietnam than Johnson. When the president read a draft of the speech, he forced Humphrey to backtrack by warning his vice president that if he delivered the speech, he (Johnson) would destroy his chances of becoming president.

At the end of September, however, the vice president dared do what he wanted to do earlier by delivering a speech in Salt Lake City in which he promised to stop the bombing of North Vietnam if he were elected president. After the speech, his poll numbers began to rise dramatically. Had he made that speech earlier, some political pundits believe he might have won the election. In November, he lost to Nixon by the slim margin of 43.4 percent of the vote for the Republican to Humphrey's 42.7 percent.

Johnson was greatly disappointed by the results of the election, notwithstanding the fact that he felt betrayed by Humphrey because of his Salt Lake Center speech. Toward the end of the election, he learned of a plot by the Nixon campaign to undermine a peace initiative he had undertaken involving a bombing halt and the willingness of South Vietnam to negotiate with the enemy. Because he could not link Nixon directly to the plot, he refrained from making it public.

Johnson was nevertheless deeply troubled that a man whose actions were, in his view, treacherous, if not treasonable, was now president-elect. Equally disturbing was the fact that he considered Humphrey's defeat a personal repudiation. He could never understand how the public could turn on him the way it had. Reasonable people, he always believed, would act reasonably, not irrationally. He wanted—needed—the appreciation, if not the love, of the American people. Notwithstanding the Vietnam imbroglio, he thought he had earned it.[85]

Rejection was a legacy Johnson carried with him back to Texas. Another was his total mistrust of Nixon. Publicly, relations between the outgoing and incoming presidents could not have been better. Determined to have as smooth a transition as possible, Johnson informed Nixon that he was available to meet with him as soon as he wanted. He also instructed his staff to extend as much assistance to Nixon's staff as possible. On 11 November, Nixon received a full briefing at the White House on Vietnam and on a Nuclear Non-Proliferation Treaty (NPT) that the United States had signed in July along with fifty-six other countries, including the Soviet Union. Nixon assured Johnson he would do nothing on Vietnam without his approval. "We must be a united front," he told Johnson. He also indicated that he would encourage Saigon to come to the peace table and would support Johnson's efforts to get Congress to approve a one-year extension of the income surtax he had finally asked and won from Congress to help pay for the war. Similarly, he stated he would help the president win Senate approval of the NPT (which had been held up because of the Soviet Union's invasion of Czechoslovakia at the end of August).[86]

The president-elect proved less accommodating than he promised. He equivocated on his assurance to Johnson about maintaining continuity of policy toward Vietnam, stating that first there would have to be "prior consultation and prior agreement" on what policy to pursue. In response, the president issued a statement making it clear that until he left office, only he and his advisers would make foreign policy. Nixon also reneged on his promise to help the president win Senate approval of the NPT or congressional approval of an extension of the income surtax.[87]

Although the president-elect finally sent a strongly worded letter that convinced Saigon to go to the Paris talks, Johnson continued to distrust him. On his last day in office, at a small White House dinner, he suggested to his outgoing secretary of health, education, and welfare, Joseph Califano, that he pay an extra $500 every year he owed on his income taxes. "It's not enough for Nixon to win," he remarked. "He's going to put some people in jail."[88]

In the months and years that followed Johnson's return to the ranch, his displeasure with his successor only grew. As in the past, relations between the two leaders appeared cordial enough. Just as the former president went out of his way to accommodate his living predecessors, so Nixon did the same with the two remaining living presidents, Truman and Johnson. He provided Johnson with the same intelligence briefings he read. He even sent the director of the CIA, Richard Helms, and his national security adviser, Henry Kissinger, to the ranch for special briefings. At their first briefing, Helms told Johnson that the president instructed him to give Johnson anything he wanted. Nixon also had the former president to the White House. He attended the opening of the Lyndon Baines Johnson Library. He extended special courtesies to Johnson's daughter and son-in-law, Lynda and Charles Robb, who lived in Virginia.[89]

For his part, Johnson made clear at his first meeting with Helms that, recalling from 1964 the problem of new men taking over the government, he wanted to do everything he could to help the president. He even came out against an organized effort led by his former defense secretary, Clark Clifford, soon after Nixon took office, to get out of Vietnam as quickly as possible. On special occasions, like birthdays, he gave the president gifts and exchanged frequent pleasant notes with him.[90]

Privately, Johnson grew increasingly angry with the president. Especially bothersome to him was Nixon's apparent efforts to dismantle or limit the programs of the Great Society. He was disturbed, for example, at the administration's concerted effort in 1970 to block congressional renewal of the Voting Rights Act and to delay implementation of court-ordered desegregation of urban school districts. Likewise, he resented Nixon's proposal to substitute revenue sharing for his administration's welfare state policies. "I figured when my legislative program passed the Congress," he told Doris Kearns in 1971, "that the Great Society had a real chance to grow into a beautiful woman. . . . But now Nixon has come along and everything I've worked for is ruined. . . . It's a terrible thing for me to . . . watch someone else starve my Great Society to death."[91]

As significant as Johnson's distrust of Nixon, however, was the fact that instead of removing himself from the national political scene and retreating into a lonely retirement on his Texas ranch, as some writers have claimed, the former president kept himself fully informed about national and international affairs. Not only did he ask thoughtful questions to those who came to brief him on foreign policy, but he also read carefully the briefing papers he received from the administration. He also had his former national security adviser, Walt Rostow, read and comment on them. A brilliant international economist and former faculty member at MIT, Rostow was widely known as one of the architects of Johnson's Vietnam policy. A target of antiwar sentiment because of his own unrepentant hawkish views and acerbic comments about foes of the war, he followed Johnson back to Texas as a faculty member at the Lyndon B. Johnson School of Public Affairs. It would have taken a total transformation of character in the short span of one or two years for a person who had spent two-thirds of his life in Washington and believed, with good reason, that he had done so much to enhance the nation's welfare to become a recluse.[92]

In truth, Johnson was terribly conflicted as he returned home on 20 January. On the one hand, he mentioned frequently how relieved he was that he would no longer have to carry the burdens of leadership on his shoulders.[93] Almost anyone freed from the awesome responsibility of presidential power was bound, of course, to feel at least fleeting satisfaction that a heavy weight had been removed from his shoulders, even someone like Johnson, who had always relished having that authority. If for no other reason than his health, however, there seems considerable substance to Johnson's claim of relief at being able to leave the weight of the Oval Office behind him. Throughout his political career, he had a long history of stress-related health problems, including indigestion, pneumonia, severe rashes on his hands, and, in July 1955, the heart attack that nearly killed him. After his attack, he became convinced he would die at an early age. Not only did he lose weight and give up his chain-smoking and heavy drinking, but he also became a hypochondriac. In 1964, he had a secret actuarial study conducted to determine how long he was likely to live. It predicted that he was probably not going to live beyond the age of sixty-four. In 1968, Lady Bird encouraged him not to seek another term as president because of the stress he had been under during the last two years over the Vietnam War.

The stress was reflected in his appearance. He looked tired and haggard. The wrinkles in his face became more obvious. He began to tell or hint to a number of his friends and administration officials that he was not going to run for reelection in 1968 because of his health.[94] After the assassination of Bobby Kennedy in June, however, Johnson began to reconsider his decision. There was still the unfinished business of Vietnam and the Great Society. Poverty had not been eliminated. Urban blight continued to be an eyesore everywhere there were cities. Millions of Americans were still without health care. The assassinations of Martin Luther King Jr. in April and Kennedy in June showed that bigotry and race, violence and hatred, stayed sores on the American character. There also remained the loss of power and control, the quest for which had always been such an integral part of Johnson's personality.

The president hoped, therefore, that the nominating convention in Chicago might become deadlocked and that the delegates would draft him to run for another term. He was deeply hurt when it became apparent that he lacked the support, even among Southern governors, for a draft movement. He was also mortified that strife between the police and antiwar protesters became so serious that Democratic leaders asked him not even to come to the Windy City.[95]

The pleasantries of his last days in office and the crowd of 5,000 that awaited Johnson and Lady Bird at Bergstrom Air Force Base to welcome them home could not dispel the despair that Johnson had felt since at least the convention and that had grown only worse with Nixon's victory in November. After returning to the ranch and looking at the luggage in the carport without aides to carry them into the house, Lady Bird commented: "The coach has turned back into a pumpkin and the mice have all run away." For Johnson, that was no joke.[96]

During his first three or four months at the ranch, Johnson seemed a lost soul. As Elizabeth Goldschmidt, who served the president in several capacities, later recounted

> We went to the Ranch—it was the Easter following [Johnson's] departure from Washington. [Lady] Bird urged us to come, I think because she was trying desperately to find a way to pull Johnson out of what was clearly a depression. And he absolutely refused to discuss anything that was less than twenty-five years old. We talked about things from our youth, and he remembered so-and-so. But nothing relating to the presidency. Bird was obviously frantic about his state of mind.[97]

Bouts of depression recurred on a regular basis throughout Johnson's retirement years. Never one to suffer in silence, he cursed, complained, and lashed out at those around him with growing regularity. It took all of Lady Bird's patience, love, and understanding to remain level-headed with him. He remained close to the ranch, even more so as his health deteriorated. After making himself available to the press the week after he returned to the ranch, he rarely had anything to do with reporters. He spoke out with more frequency against Eastern elitist intellectuals, especially after they panned his memoirs. His heart conditioned worsened, and he began to have painful attacks of angina and shortness of breath, causing him to rely on nitroglycerin pills to relieve his pain and to keep an oxygen tank next to his bed. He began again to smoke heavily and to ignore his diet. Sometimes it seemed he had a death wish. He also allowed his hair, which turned completely white, to grow long and curl up in the back. Hitherto a snappy dresser who wore well-tailored suits and spit-polished shoes and boots, he appeared to care less and less about how he looked. His face seemed more crinkled and his appearance shabby. It was easy, therefore, even for those who spent considerable time with him, to analyze his idiosyncratic behavior as that of a defeated, angry, and exhausted man with diminished physical and even mental capacity, knowing he did not have long to live and passing his last years in lonely semiseclusion. Those holding this view were not entirely inaccurate.[98]

Neither were they entirely correct. Johnson was indeed exhausted and glad to be rid of the problems and the press that had hounded him during his last years in office. He looked forward to being able to do whatever pleased his fancy. "By God," he told his former press secretary, George Christian, "I'm going to do what I want to do. If I want to drink a glass of whiskey, I'm going to drink a glass of whiskey. And if I want to have some bad manners, I'm going to have bad manners." After a few months of adjustment, Johnson became less melancholy and more in control of his life.[99]

Johnson had always been a consummate storyteller, a tradition passed down from his grandfather. With great effectiveness, he had mastered the art of caricature. Folksy mimicry and parody were as much part of the Johnson style as his ability to cower his foes. For one always in need to control, the intimacy of both manners of persuasion worked brilliantly. Johnson's outbursts of anger, then, were often proceeded by his well-crafted style of humor, just as gift giving often followed his flashes of fury. Control over his situation remained the compelling factor of his retirement, just as manipulation remained part of his shrewdness.[100]

A few days after leaving office, Johnson sold the rights to his memoirs, and Lady Bird received a contract for a White House diary she had kept for $1.2 million (the equivalent of about $7.3 million in 2009). The former president also opened an office in Austin. To help with his memoirs and with the large correspondence all former presidents were now receiving, Johnson hired a staff of twelve, half as consultants. Heading it was Tom Johnson, his twenty-seven-year-old former deputy press secretary, whom he appointed as his executive assistant. Johnson and the others were paid with funds from the Presidential Transition Act of 1963, which Congress had passed upon Johnson's recommendation to promote the orderly transition of power after the election of a new president and vice president. As a result of the legislation, Johnson received a onetime allotment of $375,000, which he had to use within eighteen months after leaving office. After that, he received $80,000 annually for office expenses.[101]

Among those whom Johnson hired on a part-time consultancy basis was Doris Kearns, an assistant director of the Kennedy Institute of Politics at Harvard, who, as a graduate student completing her Ph.D. in government, had been appointed as a White House fellow. Kearns quickly took charge of assisting the former president in preparing his memoirs, and she became Johnson's most intimate confidante.

The relationship between Kearns and Johnson was unique. Even though Kearns admired Johnson for his Great Society programs, as a graduate student she had been a vocal, street-marching opponent of the Vietnam War. She did not keep this secret from the committee. It nevertheless selected her for the prestigious fellowship program. A month before her selection was to be announced in a White House ceremony, she coauthored an article for the *New Republic,* "How to Remove LBJ in 1968." In it she raised the possibility of a third-party movement of "the poor, the black, and the young" to prevent Johnson's election.[102]

At the White House ceremony, Kearns danced with the president, who seemed fascinated by her Ivy League background. Although he intended to have her serve on his staff, once her article appeared in the *New Republic,* Johnson's advisers decided it would be inappropriate to have her in the White House. Instead, she was assigned to Labor Secretary Willard Wirtz. However, she was told that Johnson did not want her to withdraw from the fellowship program.[103]

At a White House meeting with the president for the fellows, Johnson turned to Kearns and remarked angrily, "Don't you understand—how can you possibly not understand—how deep and serious the country's opposition to the war in Vietnam is?" Then he walked out of the room. Although Kearns believed that would be the last time she would be invited back to the White House, she was asked back several times more. The last time was after Johnson made his announcement that he would not run again for president. Meeting with Kearns in the Oval Office, the president told her that he wanted her to work for him in the White House. "I've decided to do some teaching when I leave office," he stated. "I should have been a teacher, and I want to practice on you. I want to do everything I can to make the young people of America, especially you Harvards, understand what this political system is all about."[104]

So began an arrangement where Kearns became Johnson's sounding board. Although her official duties were to work on manpower projects, her main role was to sit with Johnson in the evening while he recounted the details of his day. As Kearns and others close to Johnson have commented, he could not stand to be alone. He always kept three televisions on in the Oval Office and in his bedroom, each one tuned to one of the three main networks. He also kept wire tickers from AP, UP, and Reuters. "These tickers," he later said, "were like friends tapping at my door for attention. . . . They made me feel that I was truly in the center of things." His evening sessions with Kearns also helped lift some of his loneliness, especially in the evenings.[105]

A month after Johnson left office, he asked Kearns to come to the ranch to work full-time on his memoirs and the establishment of the LBJ Library and School of Public Affairs. Although she turned him down, saying she liked Cambridge and wanted to pursue an academic career, the former president persisted, even lining up a position for her at the University of Texas, offering to give her a huge salary, and promising to introduce the twenty-nine-year-old unattached academic to a different millionaire each weekend. "Now," he said, "what girl in her right mind wouldn't come and work with the President of the United States under these conditions?"[106]

Kearns agreed to spend weekends and vacations at the ranch, but not to give up her career at Harvard. For the next four years, she came regularly to the ranch. Because the former president and Kearns were together so much, rumors spread that Johnson was having an affair with her. The fact that Johnson had a number of affairs throughout his marriage gave these rumors the semblance of truth. Lady Bird even became jealous, acknowledging that she let Kearns come to the ranch too often. Both Kearns and the former president, however, emphatically denied the rumors, and there is no reason to believe otherwise. "He talked to me simply because I was there, present, as he moved knowingly, terrified, toward death," Kearns later wrote.[107]

Working with Kearns on the memoirs were a number of former White House staffers, including two former speechwriters, Harry Middleton, who would later become the director of the LBJ Library, and Robert Hardesty, who became president of Southwest Texas State University. Theoretically, Middleton and Hardesty were in charge of the project, and their responsibilities, along with the other staffers, included doing research for the memoirs. Kearns's main role was to work with Johnson in writing and fashioning the manuscript. In fact, everyone involved in the project, which came to include a host of former administration officials who came to the ranch for short visits, undertook a variety of overlapping responsibilities.[108]

One thing became immediately clear. Despite his best intentions, Johnson lacked the personality and the motivation to involve himself heavily in the preparation of his manuscript. As president, Johnson had been his own best editor, insisting from his speechwriters simple language, simple sentences, and short speeches, with a clear news lead that even a "charwoman" would understand. However, he never regarded himself as a wordsmith. He lacked the discipline and the personality to sit in solitude, spending hours laboring over a paragraph or a page. He had an even harder time sitting in front of a tape recorder in order to tell the story of his presidency. He had to have an audience. He had to lead a conversation, and there had to be a response.[109]

As a result, Johnson spent hours with Kearns and, to a lesser extent, with his other ghostwriters, allowing them to take notes as he spoke to them rather than trying to put something on paper or dictate into some inanimate machine. Because Johnson was such a consummate storyteller, Kearns liked this arrangement. When it came time to write the manuscript, she hoped to bring out the personal, folksy, humorous, and human side of Johnson's career in a manner lacking in the memoirs of earlier presidents. She also expected to incorporate the hundreds of incisive anecdotes he had stored in his mind over the years. The memoirs would then be as much Johnson's personal story as an impersonal account of his presidency.[110]

That did not happen. Perhaps reflecting his own insecurities, Johnson insisted that his memoirs be dignified and that anything that might make him appear vulgar, crude, or less than presidential be removed from the manuscript. There would be none of the homespun storytelling or folksiness, which, he feared, might become the object of Eastern intellectual derision—but which might have made the book all the more attractive to reviewers.[111]

Precisely because Johnson's memoirs, *The Vantage Point: Perspectives of the Presidency, 1963–1969,* seemed almost formulaic, both in how it was written (by ghostwriters) and in content (a rehash of the major events of the Johnson presidency carefully checked for accuracy of detail), most critics reviewed the book harshly, adding it to the growing list of failed presidential memoirs. Even Kearns, who begged the president to allow her to keep the anecdotal material that provided insights into the former president's personality and could have given the book more color and flavor, was disappointed by the final outcome. "In the last couple of days I have read the entire book," she wrote the president on 30 July, when the manuscript was nearing completion. "The purpose of this memo is to develop a series of questions for you in the hope that your answers to them can be woven into the book and in so doing, enrich and personalize the entire effort."[112]

Advance sales of *Vantage Point* reached 120,000 copies. The Book-of-the-Month Club printed an additional 190,000 copies. The *New York Times,* which syndicated the book on a fifty–fifty profit-sharing arrangement with Holt

Rinehart, received more than $200,000 from the serialization of the book in a number of European and other newspapers. Despite the best efforts of Holt Rinehart to get Johnson to promote the book, he refused. His failure to market it and its generally poor reviews held sales back. Johnson was himself annoyed by the reviewers. "I guess you were trying to be nice when you urged me to write another book—but if you had to read all the reviews of the *Vantage Point* that we suffered through, you might not wish that on me again," he wrote Wilbur Cohen in February 1972.[113]

In addition to preparing his memoirs, Johnson's other major efforts after he left the White House were completing a series of tapes with Walter Cronkite about his presidency and finishing the construction of the LBJ Library and School of Public Affairs. Like former president Eisenhower, Johnson was paid a handsome fee ($300,000) for doing the interviews with the highly respected journalist and television anchorman. The former president hoped to showcase the record of his administration. Unfortunately for him, CBS had final control over the editing of the tapes. The result was a less than flattering portrayal of his presidency.[114]

The twenty-two hours of tapings concentrated on three issues: Vietnam, Johnson's announcement on 31 March to resign the presidency, and Kennedy's assassination in 1963. The first of the edited interviews, "Why I Chose Not to Run" was shown on 27 December 1967. It went poorly for the former president, many of whose assertions seemed dubious. He had never been an ambitious man who wanted power more than anything else, he claimed. Because of his disadvantaged background, he did not think he was even qualified to be president. "I have never really believed that I was the man to do that particular job. I have always felt that every job that I had was really too big for me." Until Lady Bird Johnson encouraged him otherwise, he had serious reservations about running for president in 1964 and had more doubts about his chances for winning in 1964 than he did in 1968. He had decided long before his 31 March announcement not to seek reelection in 1968. Humphrey lost the election because of his September speech in Salt Lake City.[115]

Throughout the interview, Johnson appeared nervous, self-pitying, and self-delusional. Even many of his former colleagues conceded how poorly he came across to the media and the public. On 2 January 1970, George Christian told Tom Johnson that the press on Capitol Hill thought "the CBS show was a minus." Christian did not elaborate, Johnson added, "except to say that most of the Capitol Press (nameless) with whom he talked did not believe the 1964 story that you were more concerned about winning in 1964 than in 1968 and that they found it hard to believe that you never wanted the power of the nation's top job."[116]

The last two segments, shown on 6 February and 2 May 1970, were hardly more satisfying. On the Vietnam War, the former president remained defensive. He claimed he had never deceived the American people about Vietnam because, in passing the Gulf of Tonkin resolution, Congress knew he was being given unlimited authority to carry on the war. Instead of highlighting the achievements of his administration, the segment on Vietnam amounted to little more than a rehash of what Johnson had been saying throughout the debate over his Vietnam War policy. Certainly it did nothing to assuage the antiwar movement.

The final segment, on Kennedy's assassination, irked Johnson even more than the first two. It made it seem that Johnson disagreed with the Warren Commission's conclusion that Lee Harvey Oswald acted alone in murdering Kennedy. In fact, Johnson added nothing new to the report except his comment that after hearing Kennedy was dead, his first thought was that the assassination might be "an international conspiracy [in which America's enemies] were out to destroy our form of government and the leaders in that government." After weeks of negotiations with CBS, during which the former president threatened to do no more interviews unless his comment on the assassination was removed, the portions dealing with the Warren Commission report were eliminated. Even then, leaks about the original script forced the president to issue a statement reiterating his belief that the report accurately reflected all available data.[117]

The final project that consumed Johnson's time after he left office was the LBJ Library and Museum and the LBJ School of Public Affairs, which catty-cornered each other on thirty acres of land on the easternmost part of the University of Texas–Austin campus. Unlike Truman and Eisenhower, Johnson did not have to worry about raising funds for either structure. The university donated both the land and most of the construction funds, thereby becoming the first university to be home to a presidential library. Johnson and his wife also gave their advances from Holt Rinehart and the $300,000 from CBS to the LBJ Foundation established to support both institutions. Other donors also contributed funds to the foundation and for furnishing the two buildings.

Not surprisingly, given Johnson's enormous ego, he intended "to have the best Presidential Library in the world." It would be a paean to the Great Society. More than that, it would be the most stunning and functional building of its kind in the country, an edifice that would attract huge crowds and be admired in the architectural world for years. In thinking in these terms, the former president had more in mind than those presidential libraries already completed, which he considered architecturally bland. Rather, he saw his library in competition with the John F. Kennedy Library. Planning for the Kennedy Library had already begun. The Kennedy family wished to have it built on a twelve-acre site adjacent to the Harvard campus. Construction was postponed when the Harvard University faculty objected to the huge crowds and congestion it feared the library would generate. Jacqueline Kennedy had nevertheless chosen I. M. Pei to design the building. Pei's initial plan to build a striking glass pyramid flattened at the top set the creative world abuzz. Pei was even featured on the front page of the *New York Times*.[118]

Johnson was determined, therefore, not only that his library be the biggest presidential library and the first tied to a public university, but that it also be architecturally more stunning than the Kennedy Library. This was part of his long-standing rivalry with the Kennedy family and the whole Eastern intellectual elite. Not all that different from Harry Truman's desire to use the Truman Library as the basis of a nationally recognized center of higher learning that would challenge the East's grip on top-flight higher education, Johnson wanted his library and the adjacent school of public affairs to outshine the best institutions the East had to offer. They would provide his fellow Texans with the intellectual opportunities then seemingly only within the grasp of Harvard intellectuals and their ilk.[119]

This meant a search for the nation's best architectural firm and scrupulous attention to every detail in the construction of the library. Leading the search was Lady Bird Johnson. Not only was she more comfortable talking with the creative community, but she also had a better taste for design than her husband. As a graduate of the University of Texas, she had already convinced him to donate his papers to her alma mater rather than to establish his library in Johnson City, near the ranch.[120]

In 1965, Lady Bird undertook a lengthy architectural tour, visiting all the presidential libraries as well as noteworthy buildings at Yale University, in New York City, and at Princeton University. She was impressed by the work of several architects. Two other architects with whom she was consulting settled on the high-profile architect Gordon Bunshaft, who was best known for the Lever House in New York. This twenty-four-story skyscraper with curtain walls of green glass melded size with design and set the standard for hundreds of similar skyscrapers throughout the world. Although Lady Bird was skeptical of the design Bunshaft presented to her and the president, Johnson was won over.[121]

The library, built at a cost of $18 million, was dedicated on 21 May 1971. From that time until the present, it has been variously described as a pyramid reminiscent of the great pyramids of the Egyptian pharaohs, as a mausoleum, and as a shrine to Johnson's presidential ego. There is truth in all these characterizations, as there was in Lady Bird Johnson's initial response to Bunshaft's design as "monolithic, massive, unrelieved, and forbidding." The architectural critic Ada Louise Huxtable called the library a "pharaonic pomposity." The cartoonist Herblock sketched Johnson seated as pharaoh, labeling his work "Opening of the Great Pyramid of Austin." Johnson's biographer, Robert Caro, described the library as a "huge, monolithic windowless structure that said quite a bit about the man."[122]

Despite this criticism, the library still remains an imposing structure and a striking piece of architecture. The library stands eight stories high with side walls that flare a little at the top as it gravitates toward the upper cantilevered level, which overhangs both sides. Three-foot windows wrap around the entire seventh floor, giving the upper floor a floating appearance. With its great hall, its polished marble throughout, its five-story glass wall behind which are the depository's manuscript holdings neatly housed in red archival boxes, and its replica of the Oval Office, the interior of the building is welcoming, functional, and elegant.

Sitting atop the crest of a hill, the library can be seen throughout much of the Texas campus and in downtown Austin. The sun that shines most of the time in the capital city gives its unencumbered tan travertine walls almost an incandescent look.[123]

If Johnson intended his library to be a structurally imposing monument to his presidency, he also meant it to be a center of historical scholarship.[124] When the building was dedicated, it contained more than thirty-one million pages, the largest collection by far of any presidential library up to that time. Even while the library was still under construction, Johnson's staff organized an oral history project, whose purpose was to interview more than 1,300 persons. The president also requested additional staff from the administration to declassify material at the library so that it could be open to scholars when the facility opened.[125]

"It's all here: the story of our time—with the bark off," Johnson remarked at the library's dedication. "There is no record of mistake, nothing critical, ugly, or unpleasant that is not included in the files." In making these remarks, Johnson anticipated that as scholars studied and wrote the history of his administration, the documents at the library would become as much a monument to the greatness of his presidency as the building itself. Regardless, his purpose was to encourage scholarship. The less imposing three-story, block-long LBJ School of Public Affairs, with its dark glass windows recessed within a grip of concrete bays, was meant to serve a similar scholarly purpose as well as to prepare future generations for public service. To assist scholars often conducting research for many weeks away from home, and to provide scholarships and fellowships for students at the School of Public Affairs, Johnson raised money for the LBJ Foundation, one of whose major functions has been to provide financial aid to researchers at the library and students at the school of public affairs.[126]

The library's dedication in May 1971, attended by President Nixon and scores of public dignitaries, was a singular day for the former president, marred only by a group of loud antiwar protestors who were kept at a distance from the ceremonies. One of Johnson's political friends in Texas, Monk Willis, remarked that for Johnson, it "was the greatest day in the world."[127]

In the remaining years of Johnson's life, the former president had his problems with the library. He was disappointed with its first director, Chester Newland, whom Tom Johnson described as almost "too much of a librarian and a professional." The former president replaced him with Harry Middleton, whom Tom Johnson described as having "the magic touch with President and Mrs. Johnson." Even then, Johnson had issues over the release of documents. Johnson wanted all the papers released as soon as possible, while Middleton delayed opening those he thought might be injurious or embarrassing to living persons.[128]

For the most part, however, Johnson was able to set policy and to plan the library's programming and even exhibits. He had his way, for example, in dictating a liberal policy for the opening of archival materials. Wanting the library to be a living educational institution, he also had it sponsor a regular schedule of public symposia. A week after it opened, he asked Middleton what the library was going to do in the way of programming now that it was open to the public. Middleton suggested that each time a group of papers was opened for research, a conference should be held to discuss initiatives that the government might take on the topic of the papers. Since the first set of papers was on education, Middleton suggested a symposium on that topic. "We'll do that," Johnson responded, "let's do that. Then right after that we'll open the civil rights papers and we'll have a conference on civil rights." The former president then pressed Middleton to go with Lady Bird the next day to see the president of the university in order to form a planning committee of the most distinguished Texas faculty. The group became the planning committee for a series of substantive conferences that have continued to the present.[129]

Because the former president was able to control much of the planning and programming of the library and the adjacent museum, he took an abiding interest in the library throughout the remainder of his life. A month before his death, when he knew he was dying of congestive heart failure, he insisted in participating in a symposium on civil rights even though he was advised not to attend because the day was extremely cold, and the road from the ranch to Austin was icy and dangerous. At one point, the conference almost broke up when a group of radical black spokesmen, dissatisfied that the symposium had turned into a celebration of the Johnson administration's civil rights accomplishments and anxious to denounce the racism of the Nixon administration, insisted on being heard. Johnson, who had already spoken earlier, went to the podium again and urged that the group be allowed to be heard. Using all his political skills, and interjecting folksy stories with a deliberate but passionate delivery, he saved the conference from disaster. If they made demands of Nixon "without starting off by saying he's terrible because he doesn't think he's terrible," he told his audience, they might surprise themselves. Personally, there was not much he could do to help their cause given the state of his health, except to "provide a lot of hope and dreams and encouragement." He might even "sell a few wormy calves now and then and contribute." Then he concluded, "Until every boy and girl born into this land, whatever state, whatever color, can stand on the same level ground, our job will not be done." His remarks brought even the dissidents to their feet and then to the podium to shake Johnson's hand.[130]

What Johnson was unable to control, except in a limited way, was the selection of faculty, the programming, and the direction of the LBJ School of Public Affairs. As it became apparent to the former president that the university's administration considered the new school an integral academic part of the Texas institution under the firm control of the faculty and administration, Johnson lost further interest in its development.

Once again, in matters on which he could be in charge, he took charge and participated actively in them. In matters he could not control, he lost interest and left them to others. The same applied to politics. It is simply false to maintain that Johnson lost interest in national political affairs. As we have seen, President Nixon kept him fully informed about developments in Vietnam and elsewhere. During his retirement, Johnson also came to Washington several times to confer with old political allies. He visited with the president at least twice. Virtually every prominent political leader, including the president, conferred with Johnson at least once at the ranch.

In 1972, the former president even planned to attend the Democratic National Convention in Miami. That he did not and failed to play a more prominent role in the Democratic presidential campaign was a result mainly of his failing health and his realization that he could do little to dictate the nominee. He would have preferred Senator Edmund Muskie of Maine, Humphrey's running mate in 1968, as the Democratic candidate. The Muskie campaign imploded in 1972 after an incident in Manchester, New Hampshire, in which, at a press conference, Muskie cried over editorials in the famed conservative newspaper, the *Union Leader,* attacking his wife. As the campaign of the antiwar candidate, Senator George McGovern of South Dakota, gained unstoppable momentum, he lost interest in the selection process. In fact, Johnson preferred Nixon's reelection to a McGovern victory. After McGovern visited the former president at the ranch, Johnson issued a lukewarm endorsement of McGovern, but otherwise, he remained uninvolved in the campaign.[131]

Johnson's retirement, therefore, was not all that much different from Eisenhower's even though Eisenhower lived longer than the former Democratic president. There is no doubt that Johnson was often morose and depressed in the years after he left the White House. Yet considering his failing health throughout most of his retirement years, he enjoyed a full and robust retirement, just as Eisenhower did. Like Eisenhower, he took annual vacations — in Johnson's case, to Acapulco, Mexico, every February, where he was the guest at the sprawling villa of Mexican president Valdes Aleman, with its private beach and a breathtaking view of its mountain-ringed bay, vermillion sunsets, and tropical jungle foliage. He was always accompanied by a large contingent of friends. While at Acapulco, he enjoyed large, long, and sumptuous meals during which he would show off his gift for gab and storytelling. His mind remained sharp, enthusiastic, and generally optimistic.[132]

Although not a golf buff like Eisenhower, Johnson enjoyed an occasional round and could occasionally be found at a local golf course in Acapulco or in other places where he liked to vacation, including the desert land of Southern California. Even as he found time for leisure, he also did considerable charity work for his local community, including gaining federal support for a nursing home named after his mother and launching a Head Start program for poor Mexican children. He made sure that the children received hot meals every day and regular physical examinations.[133]

As enjoyable to Johnson as his philanthropic work were his business dealings. Money was never a problem for Johnson. In addition to vast holdings of ranch land, he had multimillion-dollar investments in radio and television and in bank holdings. His many rich Texas friends had helped him invest in promising land and other ventures. As a senator, he had also used his influence with the Federal Communications Commission to benefit his broadcast stations. With the help of her husband, Lady Bird ran the family's radio and television properties and invested in cable properties, which were still in their infancies.[134]

Johnson's greatest pleasure, however, was operating his ranch, which he ran much as he had run his presidency. Most mornings he was up six o'clock. Soon thereafter, he was handing out the orders for the day and expecting them to be carried out perfectly. To assure perfection, he used the Johnson method of demanding the best of his ranch hands, lashing out at them when they disappointed him, always urging them to produce the finest chickens, eggs, and cattle of any ranch, and sometimes awarding them with generous gifts—in some cases with new cars—to show his appreciation for their efforts. He even had two-way radios installed in all the ranch vehicles and in the rooms of the residence so that he could be kept constantly informed about ranch business and be able to bark out new orders. His ranch manager, Dale Malecheck, felt so harassed at times that he wished Johnson was still back at the White House.[135]

Unfortunately for Johnson, his health began to deteriorate after he returned to his ranch from the White House. He began to suffer attacks of angina that became more frequent and severe. He was seen frequently taking nitrogen pills to relieve his pain. The fact that he returned to his earlier habits of eating, drinking, and smoking too much did not help. In March 1970, he was taken to Brooke Army Medical Center with severe chest pains but released a few days later, after tests indicated that he had not suffered another heart attack. The next January, he returned to Brooke, this time with pneumonia. After a few days, he was again released without any apparent damage to his heart.[136]

In April 1972, however, the former president suffered a major heart attack while visiting his daughter and son-in-law in Charlottesville. Dr. Willis Hurt, who had treated Johnson when he had suffered his first heart attack, flew up to Virginia to care for his patient. Privately, he told Mrs. Johnson that her husband's arteries were so blocked that he could suffer a fatal attack at any moment. Although Johnson was warned that it could kill him, he insisted after a week in the Virginia hospital on returning to Texas. If he was going to die, he told Lady Bird, he wanted to die in Texas. Back at the Brooke Army Medical Center, he suffered a series of irregular heartbeats that indicated he had congestive heart failure.

For the last few months of his life, Johnson was in constant pain that left him scared and breathless, and in constant need of nitroglycerin pills and oxygen. Yet he hoped to live for a few more years. As late as December, he told an old friend that he hoped to become active again in politics in 1973. "After the inauguration," he said, "we'll have four years behind us and I think I can speak up a little more." He continued to smoke and eat heavily, however. His weight shot up to 235 pounds. He developed stomach pains and diverticulosis. His doctors

Photo of Johnson on his ranch, near Stonewall, Texas, by Frank Wolfe. The photo was taken on 18 September 1972, just four months before his death in January 1973. Although Johnson was in constant pain from congestive heart failure, he was always happiest in his role as a rancher. In this photo he seems content, with little indication that he was already very sick. (Courtesy of Lyndon Baines Johnson Library and Museum.)

recommended surgery, but the famed cardiologist Dr. Michael DeBakey, whom the former president consulted, determined that any surgery, including a coronary bypass, would kill him.

The end came on 22 January 1973. In the morning, Johnson seemed well enough that Lady Bird decided to drive to her office in Austin. After spending the morning checking the fencing on the ranch and having lunch, Johnson went to his bedroom for a nap. Shortly thereafter, he summoned the Secret Service. By the time they arrived, they found the former president lying on the floor and not breathing. Efforts to revive him failed. He was flown to Brooke Army Medical Center, where he was declared dead on arrival. An autopsy later determined that death had been caused by a large coronary occlusion. Johnson was only sixty-four years old.[137]

After his death, Johnson's body was taken to the LBJ Library in Austin to lie in state. Because Johnson never liked to be alone, Lady Bird asked that friends and colleagues stand vigil during the night before the library doors were open to the public. On 24 January, the body was flown to Washington, D.C., for a state funeral and then to the Capitol rotunda, where it lay in state again for another seventeen hours. The nation's top leaders, including President Nixon, passed by the coffin, as did thousands of ordinary citizens. Then the body was flown back to the Texas hill country for the last time, where, to the singing of "The Battle Hymn of the Republic," Johnson was buried next to his parents and grandparents in the family plot beneath a large oak tree on the banks of the Pedernales River.[138]

As one of a number of dignitaries to offer eulogies while Johnson's body lay in state at the nation's capital, former vice president Humphrey remarked, "He could take a bite of you bigger than a T-bone steak and the very next day, he would put his arm around you like a long-lost brother." That was an accurate observation about this most complicated man from Stonewall, Texas. These mood changes applied as much to his retirement as his entire political career.[139]

Yet like Eisenhower, the significance of Johnson's retirement was the limits of influence he could exert out of power. Indeed, that is why he never fully adjusted to being a former president. When asked if he would support a candidate for the 1972 Democratic presidential nomination, he explained why he would not: "All I could accomplish would be to make a fool of myself. I don't hold public office. I don't have a party position. I don't have a party platform. I don't have any troops." Then he added, "The only thing more impotent than a former president is a cut dog at a screwing match."[140]

12

The Mass Marketing of
the Post-Presidency
Nixon and Ford

Mass marketing is a strategy to sell or promote a product or service to a broad consumer market or audience through various forms of mass promotion. Ordinarily its object is financial gain, but it can be used in other ways, such as to promote candidates in political campaigns.

In varying degrees, all the former presidents after World War II engaged in mass marketing to sell their memoirs and other books. Harry Truman and Dwight Eisenhower were more willing mass marketers than Lyndon Johnson. Each of these presidents signed lucrative contracts with his publisher. However, profit was never their only motive. They also wanted to offer the view from the Oval Office of the most difficult and/or controversial issues they had had to deal with as president, and to establish what they regarded as their rightful places in history.

No former presidents tried to mass markets themselves more than Richard Milhous Nixon and Gerald R. Ford. Ford's purpose was primarily financial. Through his writings, corporate directorships, and appearances on the lecture circuit, he became a multimillionaire with homes in Palm Springs and Rancho Mirage, California, and Vail, Colorado. Mainly through his writings and television interviews with David Frost, Richard Nixon also became a wealthy man after he left the White House. Unlike Ford, personal profit was not his main purpose. Rather, he sought to market himself as an elder statesman instead of a disgraced ex-president.

I

During the 1970s, the post–World War II presidency reached its low point. Richard Nixon was forced out of office in disgrace; Gerald Ford, the United States' first nonelected president, was defeated in 1976 by Jimmy Carter, who had been unknown to most Americans a year earlier; and Carter was in turn resoundingly defeated in his own bid for reelection in 1980 by Ronald Reagan. Although some of the prestige of the office was restored under Reagan, the history of American politics since the 1970s has increasingly been one of gridlock between a weakened presidency and a reinvigorated Congress.

If the 1970s represented the nadir of the American presidency, the person most responsible for that development was undoubtedly Richard Nixon. Commenting on his resignation in 1974, the *London Spectator* observed that the presidency in the United States had come full circle: George Washington could never tell a lie, Richard Nixon could never tell the truth. The liberal spokesman Arthur Schlesinger Jr. remarked of Nixon's resignation that the presidency had been saved "from the man who did more to discredit and endanger it than any other President in our history." On the opposite side of the political spectrum, Senator Barry Goldwater of Arizona stated that he had lost all sympathy for the disgraced president.[1]

Besides the stain on the American presidency caused by the Watergate affair and Nixon's forced resignation as president, Watergate is important because of the insights it offers into the president's character. Probably no president has had his personality subjected to more psychological inquiry than Nixon. Biographers have described his personality as follows: "compulsive liar," "narcissistic," "masochistic," "criminal," "inner-conflicted," "insecure," and "maladjusted." Not surprisingly, most of these same authors trace these personality flaws back to his childhood and family.[2]

The second of five sons of Frank and Hannah Milhous, Richard was born in Yorba Linda, California, on 9 January 1913 and raised in nearby Whittier, where his father owned a small grocery store and gas station. Although a devoted parent, his father was cold, demanding, and argumentative, as well as a harsh disciplinarian. As a boy, Richard spent most of his free time working in the store. While Nixon later described his Quaker mother as a saint, she was shy, undemonstrative, and remote. Along with her many chores as a housewife, she had to care for Richard's oldest and second youngest siblings, both of whom died of tuberculosis. After Harold, the oldest son, contracted the disease, Hannah spent three years nursing him in the dry climate of Prescott, Arizona. Richard saw his mother mostly in the summers, when he joined her in Arizona and took on numerous odd jobs to help with family finances.

Nixon attributed his own work ethic, scholarly drive, and aversion to personal confrontation to his quarrelsome father, who often engaged in loud shouting matches with his customers and sons.[3] Yet not all of Nixon's later character and personality can be attributed to his family. In fact, his childhood and adolescence were not all that different from those of Lyndon Johnson or Dwight Eisenhower. Both former presidents came from poor families with stern, loving, but often remote parents (more in the case of Johnson than Eisenhower). There were also raised in small towns and had to work hard even while going to school.

The impact of their early years, however, was quite different for Nixon than it was for Eisenhower and Johnson. Eisenhower left for West Point well-adjusted, gregarious, and self-confident. Johnson shared some of Nixon's insecurities, including his resentment of those who had been born privileged. He also had Nixon's drive and determination to succeed. Unlike Nixon, who was shy, socially awkward, and, by his own admission, a loner, Johnson feared being alone, but despite his insecurities, he was enormously self-confident. Instead of emphasizing his distaste of the well-heeled, he stressed his concern for the poor and underprivileged.

What Nixon took away from his early years was disappointment and bitterness at the fact that while he had the intelligence and ability that, he believed, should have opened early opportunities for success, he was denied them. Although accepted to Harvard with a scholarship, his parents were not able to afford the remaining expenses of living away at an expensive college. Instead, he attended Whittier College, a local Quaker school. Although on scholarship, he worked throughout his college years. He loved sports, and his natural competitiveness led him to try out for Whittier's football team. However, he lacked the coordination of an athlete, and as a result, he had to settle for being a bench warmer.

Nixon was also shy and socially ill at ease. Standing nearly six feet tall and weighing about 150 pounds, he was thin with brown, curly hair, brown eyes, slightly protruding jowls, and a ski nose that became even more prominent as he grew older. Although certainly not unattractive, he did not stand out in a crowd. Until he met his future wife, Pat, he dated the same girl for six years.

What was surprising was how much Nixon was able, through sheer perseverance, to overcome his shyness and lack of social skills at Whittier. He became a star debater, performed in plays, and organized the Orthogonian Society, a group of "have-not students," in Nixon's words, to challenge the Franklin Club, a fraternity of more well-off students, who controlled student life at Whittier. The Orthogonians helped elect Nixon as student-body president. He also managed to graduate second in his class. He then attended Duke University's new law school on a scholarship. Even at Duke, he had to live his first two years in a $5-a-month room and then to share with three friends a one room-shack. Although graduating third in his class of twenty-five, he was denied an entry position with all the leading New York law firms.

By almost all accounts, these rejections and disappointments tormented Nixon and left a lifelong bitterness toward the advantaged and what he regarded as the Eastern elite. "When you come from privilege, as [H. Walker George] Bush did," he later reflected while assessing his successors, "well, you just don't have to try as hard. When you come from a much more modest background, like [Harry] Truman's, you have to fight for everything you get."[4]

After failing to find a position with a New York law firm, Nixon returned to Whittier, where he took a position with a small law firm and quickly became a partner. In 1938, he met Thelma "Pat" Ryan while both of them were performing for a local acting group. After a two-year courtship, they were married. Later, they had two daughters, Tricia (b. 1946) and Julie (b. 1948).

From 1937 to 1942, Nixon practiced law in Whittier. During World War II, he worked in Washington, D.C., at the Office of Price Administration (OPA). Bored and turned off by the bureaucracy he witnessed at the OPA, he stayed only a few months before joining the navy. Assigned to the South Pacific as an operations officer, he saw just limited action.

After the war, Nixon decided to enter politics. Why such a shy and introverted person should decide on a political career remains a mystery, but clearly he was driven by the same ambition and determination to overcome personal limitations that had characterized his entire life. He also thought in Darwinian terms. Life, he believed, was a constant struggle (a series of crises) in which victory went to the toughest—those with the greatest fortitude and strength of mind to overcome obstacles and defeat opponents. Not surprisingly, he titled the first book he published, after narrowly losing the presidency in 1960, *Six Crises.* "When a man has been through even a minor crisis," he wrote in *Six Crises,* "he learns not to worry when his muscles tense up, his breathing comes faster, his nerves tingle, his stomach turns. . . . Far from worrying when this happens, he should worry when it does not. Because he knows from experience that once the battle is joined, all these symptoms will disappear." Politics offered the perfect arena for Nixon's combative spirit.[5]

Nixon also wanted more than being a small-town lawyer. So when the local Republican Party went looking for a candidate to challenge the five-term liberal Democratic incumbent in Congress, Jerry Voorhis, Nixon leapt at the opportunity. A young war veteran who had volunteered for the service, fought against the Japanese in the South Pacific, and was a new father, Nixon made an attractive candidate and was chosen over five others for the office.

In the Republican sweep in the 1946 election, Nixon easily defeated Voorhis. Nixon's political foes later accused him of defeating Voorhis through a smear campaign of red-baiting and guilt by association, charging his opponent with having the endorsement of the CIO-PAC, which, he maintained, had a large number of "Communists and fellow-travelers." But Nixon maintained it was his political values, which mirrored the increasingly conservative views of his congressional district rather his attacks on Voorhis, that accounted for his victory.[6]

As a new member of the Eightieth Congress, he was appointed to the already infamous House Un-American Activities Committee (HUAC). As a member of HUAC, Nixon spearheaded the investigation of Alger Hiss, a former State Department official who was later found guilty of perjury for denying under oath that he had been a communist. The Hiss case galvanized the nation and turned Nixon into a rising star within the right wing of the Republican Party—and into a target of liberals who accused Nixon of having conducted a witch hunt against Hiss.

In 1950 Nixon ran successfully for the Senate in a campaign whose signal issue was anticommunism. Nixon maintained that the voting record of his Democratic opponent, Congresswoman Helen Gahagan Douglas, was almost identical to that of Vito Marcantonio, the self-proclaimed Marxist congressman from New York. His campaign against Douglas solidified his reputation among his foes as an unprincipled opportunist with a cutthroat political style. Henceforth, his political foes referred to him as Tricky Dick.[7]

In 1952, Dwight Eisenhower, seeking to balance the Republican ticket and mollify the party's right wing, selected Nixon as his running mate. For the next eight years, Nixon served dutifully as Eisenhower's vice president. When Nixon narrowly lost to John F. Kennedy in the 1960 presidential election and then ran unsuccessfully for governor of California two years later, it seemed that his political career was over. Instead, Nixon spent the next six years quietly cultivating the support of Republican leaders. In 1968, he was rewarded for his efforts with the Republican presidential nomination. In the November election, he narrowly defeated his Democratic opponent, Vice President Hubert Humphrey, by about 500,000 votes.

During the campaign, Nixon had indicated that he had a secret plan to get the United States out of Vietnam. In fact, he had no plan, but, sensing the growing antiwar tide in the United States, he began a phased withdrawal of American forces from the country. Nixon was not abandoning Vietnam; at the same time that he announced the withdrawals, he intensified the bombing of North Vietnam and, in a policy known as Vietnamization, increased military aid to the South Vietnamese army. He coupled Vietnamization with the Nixon Doctrine, which called for the reduced presence of American forces in Asia generally, and until 1970, when he appeared to widen the war by sending American forces into Cambodia, he was able to quell the antiwar movement in the United States.

Although the invasion of Cambodia reignited the antiwar movement and led to the fatal shooting of four students at Kent State University by the Ohio National Guard, most Americans were satisfied with Nixon's performance as president. When he ran in 1968, the country seemed on the verge of consuming itself by a spasm of violence. The baby boomer generation had morphed into a new youth movement demanding not only an end to the war, but also a cluster of reforms from civil rights to gay rights to women's rights. Other alienated youth displayed their disaffection by challenging traditional cultural and social norms. Appealing to what he called the Silent Majority, Nixon promised to end the war in Vietnam with honor and to restore law and order to the nation. On the eve of the election, the White House announced that peace was at hand in Vietnam. That proved to be a false promise. Still, most American troops had already been withdrawn from Vietnam. The antiwar movement and mayhem of the 1960s had largely dissipated.

Even in domestic matters, Nixon surprised many of his liberal critics by seeming to practice what he had termed in 1946 "practical liberalism." He lobbied for the establishment of an Environmental Protection Agency (EPA) and a Department of Natural Resources. He supported a proposal that would have guaranteed a family of four an annual income of $1,600 plus $800 in food stamps. He adopted the Philadelphia Plan, which set aside jobs for minorities in the construction industry. He also strengthened the Equal Employment Opportunity Commission (EEOC) and supported an Equal Rights Amendment (ERA) to the Constitution.

American voters saw no reason, therefore, to vote Nixon out of office, especially because he was running against a weak Democratic candidate, Senator George McGovern of South Dakota. In November, he won an overwhelming victory, beating McGovern by 61 percent to 38 percent and losing only in Massachusetts and the District of Columbia. In giving Nixon such an overwhelming victory, American voters ignored news stories of White House involvement in the arrest of five persons for burglarizing the Democratic National Committee headquarters in Washington's Watergate complex.

In January 1973, Nixon was able to announce that after the heaviest bombing yet of North Vietnam, the Hanoi government had signed a cease-fire. The agreement allowed the North Vietnamese to keep their forces in South Vietnam but permitted the South Vietnamese government to remain in power. Unfortunately for Nixon, this was the last time he would be able to win public favor. Soon thereafter, his administration began to unravel.

Nixon himself took a sharp turn toward the political right, even dismantling the Office of Economic Opportunity. Balance of payment deficits led to a further weakening of the dollar in international markets. Oil prices and inflation skyrocketed as a result of an Arab oil boycott after the administration's decision to resupply Israel with military equipment during the so-called Yom Kippur war of October 1973.

What led to Nixon's undoing as president, however, was the Watergate affair. It is now known that the president tried to cover up the involvement of the White House staff and reelection campaign with those arrested for the attempted Watergate burglary. As evidence of the attempted cover-up mounted, it was revealed that Nixon had been secretly tape-recording meetings in the Oval Office and in other White House locations. Despite the president's best efforts to hold on to the tapes, the Supreme Court required him in April 1974 to make all of them available to a special prosecutor, Leon Jaworski. One tape arrived with an 18.5-minute gap that experts determined had been deliberately erased. Other tapes showed the more sinister side of Nixon—conspiratorial, vulgar, and even anti-Semitic. However, a tape of a 23 June 1972 meeting in the Oval Office revealed clearly that Nixon had tried to use the CIA to cover up the Watergate burglary. Once this smoking gun became public, even most Republicans gave up trying to save the president. Impeachment and removal from office seemed inevitable. Under pressure from the Republican leadership, Nixon announced on 8 August 1974 that he would resign the next day, becoming the first American president ever to leave office voluntarily before the end of his term.

Nixon had fallen victim to the demons that had never left him since he entered politics. In a long conversation at San Clemente with his former communications director, Ken Clawson, shortly after he resigned from office, he opened a window into the deepest recesses of his mind. He stated more clearly than ever before his obsessive belief that life was an ongoing conflict. In the end, he would always win over his adversaries because he was shrewder and tougher. Even in this worst period of his life, when he had been ostracized from public life and was subjected to endless calumny and censure, he hinted at his intention to emerge victorious over those who sought to destroy him.

In his conversation with Nixon, Clawson expressed concern about his future and those with whom he had worked at the White House. "I know you are feeling bitter," Nixon responded. "You've got to keep control. You know—discipline your mind to keep from taking on the whole thing now. How long has it been? It seems just yesterday, and then, sometimes, it seems like years ago. We . . . I've got to let time go by, put some distance between then and now." When Clawson responded by pointing to all the good things that the former president had accomplished, Nixon snapped back: "They'll never give us credit for that. . . . We're out now, so they try to stomp us . . . kick us when we're down. They never let up, *never,* because we were the first real threat to them in years."

Then, ruminating back to his childhood, he continued,

I knew what it was like. I'd been there before. . . . What starts the process, really are the laughs and snubs and slights you get when you are a kid. Sometimes, it's because you're poor or Irish or Jewish or Catholic or ugly or simply that you are skinny. But if you are reasonably intelligent and if your anger is deep enough and strong enough, you learn that you can change those attitudes by excellence, personal gut performance, while those who have everything are sitting on their fat butts.

"You were a good athlete," Nixon went on, "but I was not, and that was the very reason I tried and tried and tried. To get discipline for myself and to show others that here was a guy who could dish it out and take it. Mostly, I took it," Nixon concluded. "You've got to be tough. You can't break, my boy, even when there is nothing left. . . . Some people think I should go stand in the middle of the bullring and cry, *'mea culpa, mea culpa'* while the crowd is hissing and booing and spitting on you. But a man doesn't cry. I don't cry."[8]

Nixon did not cry as he returned to his estate, Casa Pacifica, in San Clemente after his resignation. In fact, when his plane landed at El Toro Marine Base, he told a waiting crowd that he had no intention of just sitting back and enjoying the blissful climate of California. That this was more than idle talk became apparent a few days later, when the now ex-president assembled his staff of twenty assistants, aides, and secretaries, many of whom he had taken with him to San Clemente.[9] Dressed in a business suit and tie despite the already oppressive heat, and irritated that he had to awaken some of his staff for the 7:30 A.M. meeting, he made clear that nothing had changed as a result of his resignation. Within the week, he called another meeting of his senior staff. After berating one of the staff for wearing Bermuda shorts, he acted as if he were conducting a cabinet meeting. "I've called you here to discuss an important topic," he told them, "and that is, what are we going do about the economy in the coming year?"[10]

The former president was determined to be in charge of his own history. The overarching theme of his post-presidency became restoration of his proper place in history. Throughout his political career, he believed he had been characterized, caricatured, and criticized by the entire liberal elite. That included the media, academia, and the talking circles of others who passed themselves off as the nation's intellectual elite. Contrary to what they had to say about him, he was convinced he deserved to be ranked among the nation's great presidents.[11]

For Nixon, then, it became essential to have his papers and tapes shipped to San Clemente, both in order to be able to write his own version of his political career and to prevent his enemies from accessing them for their own purposes. Tradition was on his side. Since Franklin Roosevelt, former presidents had established their own presidential libraries to house their papers, which were gifted to the National Archives and opened over time to researchers. Nixon had promised at one time to follow that tradition. However, until Congress changed the law in 1978, all official presidential papers were considered the private property of the president who generated them.

Nixon's first act as a former president, therefore, was to gain control of his papers and tapes. On the same day he returned to California, Master Sergeant Bill Gulley, director of the White House Military Office responsible for overseeing Nixon's transition to San Clemente, had secretly removed twelve sealed cartons from the family quarters and accompanied them back to California on an unmarked air force Jetstar.[12]

At Casa Pacifica, Gulley met with Steve Bull, Nixon's appointments secretary, and Jack Brennan, a marine officer who had been the former president's military aide at the White House. Gulley told them about the cartons he had returned to Casa Pacifica and pointed out that there were still a "shitload" of Nixon's papers back in Washington. In fact, 400,000 pounds of Nixon materials had already been shipped to San Clemente. Three trucks, parked outside the basement of the West Wing, were loading more boxes for shipment. Only after one of Ford's young aides, Benton Becker, got wind of what was going on was he able to get Haig to order the trucks unloaded until President Ford decided their fate. Haig told Becker that he had not known about the removal of the documents, but he may actually have arranged for their confiscation.[13]

Arguing rightful ownership of the papers, Nixon demanded that the embargo be lifted. However, his papers and tapes contained evidence that could be used in the pending trials of his top White House advisers, John Ehrlichman, Bob Haldeman, and former attorney general James Mitchell for their involvement in the Watergate affair. Nixon might also be indicted for obstruction of justice in the cover-up. Although President Ford was leaning toward pardoning him, he had not made a final decision. A Gallup Poll in August showed that 56 percent of Americans favored a criminal trial for the disgraced former president.[14]

Special prosecutor Leon Jaworski had strong objections to indicting and trying a former president. Until he, too, made a final decision, he did not want Nixon to have control over the papers and tapes, which he might destroy. The public also had the right to know what happened in the Nixon administration. At the very least, the issue of ownership of the papers might be used as a bargaining chip by Ford to get the former president to admit guilt in the Watergate cover-up before granting him a pardon.[15]

Although Ford's attorney general, William Saxbe, advised him that the former president was entitled to his papers, the White House decided to hold on to them pending further discussion. Nixon was furious. "They're after your ass," Gulley told him. Ford's aides were even referring to him as a crook. "Goddamn," Nixon responded, "you know what I did for Johnson, and you know what I did for Ike and Truman, and goddamn it, I expect to be treated the same way. . . . And goddamn it, you tell Ford I expect it."[16]

Despite the bravado he had displayed after returning from Washington to California and his determination to carry on as usual, Nixon was still a broken man. The very foundation of his life had crumbled beneath him. In his mind, he was not being treated fairly by the president who should have been beholden to him for the office he now held. His future remained uncertain. Would he be indicted and even have to go to prison? He had earlier been named as an unindicted coconspirator by a Watergate grand jury. He also had serious financial problems. Because he had had to pay more than $1 million in lawyers' fees for matters related to Watergate and because he owed the federal government hundreds of thousands of dollars in back taxes, he was financially strapped when he left office. If he went to trial, he would have additional legal expenses. He had already received two subpoenas, the first to testify as a defense witness for Erlichman and the second for his deposition in a civil suit involving the exclusion of Nixon foes at a campaign rally.

As vice president and then president, Nixon had also become accustomed to the good life. He enjoyed fine food and wines. In addition to Casa Pacifica, a twenty-eight-acre estate that included a fourteen-room hacienda-style home overlooking the Pacific, he owned two homes in Key Biscayne that he had purchased in 1969 for $250,000. Just the upkeep of his properties was enormous. The federal government expected him to pay for improvements it had made to the homes that did not involve his safety and security as president. There were even reports that it planned to bill him for use of Air Force One from Kansas City (where it was in flight at the time his resignation went into effect) to El Toro. "Well, if that's what the bastards want I'll pay," he burst out angrily after Gulley told him what was being said in Washington.[17]

Nixon's financial problems seemed resolved for the moment after he signed a contract with Warner Books for his memoirs with a $2.5 million advance. On 20 August, he also received his first call from President Ford since leaving office. Ford told him that he intended to nominate New York governor Nelson Rockefeller to be his vice president. Although Nixon was upset by the nomination of a man who represented the liberal Eastern elite he so despised and was unhappy that the president remained mum about a pardon for him, he nevertheless appreciated the courtesy of the call and expressed his support for Rockefeller's nomination. Ten days later, Gulley, who had just returned from Washington, was able to report to him that Ford had decided to have briefing papers, intelligence evaluations, and similar materials sent to Casa Pacifica every two weeks. He would not, however, have use of military aircraft. Again, the former president was not happy that he was being denied what he had done for Johnson and what Johnson had done for Truman and Eisenhower. However, at least he was being extended most of the courtesies recently given to former presidents.[18]

Still, Nixon was depressed. The very fact that in the first two weeks after returning to Casa Pacifica he tried to act as if he were still president suggested he was out of touch with reality. He was also unable to concentrate for a more than a few hours at a time. He kept to himself. He refused to answer the telephone. He looked worn down. His earlier combativeness gave way to listlessness and lethargy. Family members called the White House about Nixon's health. Julie's husband, David, telephoned Ford. If something was not done soon (meaning granting him a pardon), he told the president, Nixon "might go off the deep end."[19]

At the beginning of September, Ford's counsel and his aides, Phil Buchen and Benton Becker, informed Nixon's lawyer that the president was planning to grant Nixon a pardon. He expected the former president first to reach an agreement on the papers and tapes and to make a statement of contrition, preferably an acknowledgment of his guilt in the Watergate cover-up. Even Jaworski, who believed he could make a criminal case against Nixon, made clear that he would not oppose a pardon. Besides the absurdity of bringing a former president to trial, he did not believe Nixon could get a fair trial anywhere, given public opinion.[20]

At first, Nixon balked at making any statement of contrition, much less an admission of guilt. He still believed that while he may have made mistakes, he had done nothing wrong or illegal. Johnson and Kennedy had been guilty of worse campaign violations than his administration. "People accused me of abusing power during Watergate," he later recalled, "but . . . *real* abuse of power involves malicious intent. Watergate was a series of blundering mistakes, but not a grand scheme driven by malicious intent. Great leaders know the potential of power and use it wisely, but they know its limits and obey it." Besides refusing to make any statement of contrition, he remained adamant about having complete control of his papers.[21]

Ford was prepared to announce to the American people that he was granting a pardon to Nixon unconditionally. He delayed the announcement while negotiations continued in San Clemente. Probably having learned from Haig of Ford's intentions, Nixon bargained with the administration from a position of strength.

After much tough talk on both sides, he finally agreed to a settlement on the papers that gave him virtually everything he desired. Ownership of the papers and tapes would be shared by Nixon and the government. Third parties, such as scholars and journalists, would have to subpoena to see them. The former president could reject the subpoenas on various grounds. After five years, he could destroy whatever document or tapes he wanted.

Nixon also agreed to a statement prepared by his former press secretary, Ron Ziegler, who was now serving more as his personal aide, that omitted any reference to criminal wrongdoing on his part but acknowledged he was wrong in not acting more decisively and forthrightly in dealing with Watergate. That was "a burden I shall bear every day of the life that is left to me," he concluded. Satisfied he had gotten as much from Nixon as possible, and still determined to put Watergate behind him, Ford announced on a Sunday morning, 8 September, that he was granting Nixon an absolute pardon for all offenses he may have committed prior to 9 August 1974. Simultaneously, Nixon released his statement of contrition.

Ford had failed to prepare the American people for the pardon—quite the opposite. After taking office, he had indicated that he would not pardon the former president. Throughout the country, therefore, condemnation of the president was immediate and almost universal. A common feeling was that the pardon was part of a deal Ford had made earlier with Nixon. The president's popularity in the polls dropped overnight by 2 percent.[22]

Undoubtedly, the pardon came as a relief to Nixon, who seemed more worried about the costs of defending himself than of actually going to prison—an unlikely possibility even if he were found guilty. If Nixon was comforted by the president's decision, his behavior did not show it. That he felt forced into issuing a statement of contrition in exchange for the pardon depressed him even further. Although he expected Ford would be criticized, he was genuinely surprised by the political firestorm the pardon created.[23]

Not only was Nixon's mental state worrisome, but his physical condition remained no better. Just before returning to Washington, Becker met with the former president. He was shocked by Nixon's appearance. Back at the White House, he told Ford that he had real questions about whether Nixon would still be alive at the time of the next election. "Well," Ford answered, "1976 is a long time away." "I don't mean 1976," Becker responded, "I mean 1974."[24]

Shortly after receiving his pardon, Nixon secluded himself at Sunnylands, the massive and magnificent estate near Palms Spring of Walter Annenberg, a media mogul whom Nixon had named as ambassador to the Court of Saint James's. While at Sunnylands, he developed phlebitis, a serious vein inflammation in the legs that could lead to blood clots and death. His leg had swollen to three times its normal size. Despite a doctor's orders, he refused to go to the hospital or even to wear a support stocking. When he returned to San Clemente, the swelling became even worse. Doctors again urged him to go to the hospital, and once more he refused. "If I go to the hospital," he said, "I'll never get out of there alive."[25]

Making matters even worse for Nixon was the national resentment that continued over his pardon. The *Washington Post* fed into this anger when it published a report that Nixon had planned to ship to San Clemente more than $2 million worth of gifts he had received as president from foreign leaders, including diamond and ruby jewelry from Saudi Arabia; the law provided that any gift received from a foreign government worth more than $50 remained the property of the federal government.

Special prosecutor Jaworski was upset at the agreement that had been reached over the disposition of the Nixon papers and tapes. When he failed to get Ford to repeal it, he helped persuade an already angry Congress to pass legislation that voided the agreement by stating that all of Nixon's presidential papers and tapes belonged to the federal government and were to be stored in the National Archives and released to the public "at the earliest reasonable date." In addition, the special prosecutor announced that he planned to call Nixon as a prosecution witness in the upcoming Watergate cover-up trial.

The White House also distanced itself from the former president. It refused even to take telephone calls from San Clemente. In September, Ford decided to remove Haig from his administration by naming him commander of NATO forces in Europe. The president's staff had resented Haig, who, many believed, had been serving as a conduit to Nixon through Ziegler.[26]

Nixon's ex-presidency reached its lowest point during the fall and winter of 1974–1975. Dr. John Lungren, who had first urged Nixon to go to the hospital when he was at the Annenberg estate, arrived at Casa Pacifica on 16 September for a follow-up exam. He found that Nixon's physical condition had deteriorated dangerously since he last saw him. The swelling in his foot had increased, and he was in terrible pain. He warned the former president again that he could die if he were not immediately hospitalized and the phlebitis properly treated.

This time, Nixon agreed to enter Long Beach Memorial Hospital. A chest scan revealed that a large clot had traveled from his leg to just outside his right lung, Had it been larger, it could have clogged a central artery and killed him. Although the doctors were able to dissolve the clot and the former president was able to return to Casa Pacifica after a few weeks, his recuperation was extensive. In constant pain, his fury knew few bounds. The Watergate cover-up trial was about to begin, and Judge Sirica expected him to testify. Even after Dr. Lungren said he was still too sick to travel to Washington, Sirica remained dubious. He ordered a full medical evaluation and warned that if he were not persuaded to the contrary, he would insist that Nixon testify. When Nixon filed a motion demanding that his prior agreement with the Ford administration on his papers and tapes be upheld, his motion was denied. In testimony before Congress on Nixon's pardon, Ford promised that the Nixon papers would "not be delivered to anybody until a satisfactory agreement is worked out with the special prosecutor."[27]

Nixon was convinced that he was being victimized just because he was Nixon. Other presidents, like Johnson, whom he characterized "as an astonishing creature, a piece of work," had committed worse offenses than he, but they had always gotten away with them. People judged him differently, like the Jews, who always hated him. "Christ," he said, "if it weren't for me there wouldn't be any Israel."[28]

All the issues preying on Nixon's mind took on secondary importance when, on 31 October, Dr. Lungren checked on Nixon only to find that his leg was swelling again. After consulting with specialists, he ordered that the former president be hospitalized immediately. At the hospital, a venogram of his leg revealed that one of the main veins leading to his heart was almost completely blocked, nearly shutting off the blood supply to his thigh. Other smaller clots threatened to break off and possibly kill him. Despite intensive drug therapy, the former president's condition worsened. Doctors discovered a new clot, eighteen inches long, that was about to break off from the wall of the vein, requiring immediate surgery.

Although the surgery went well, internal bleeding developed. Nixon slipped into a coma. He was unconscious and in cardiovascular shock. His blood pressure dropped dangerously. He was given four pints of blood before he regained consciousness. Feverish and tied to life-support machines, he feared he was going to die. With his family by his bedside, he asked for a notebook so that he could dictate his final thoughts.

Gradually, the former president's condition stabilized. After two days, he was out of danger. A visit from President Ford, who was in Los Angeles, lifted his spirits. Further complications, including a bout with pneumonia and a collapsed lung, delayed his recovery, but after three weeks, he was able to leave the hospital. Judge Sirica was finally convinced that he was still too sick to testify or even to give a deposition.[29]

Nixon's brush with death left the former president more determined than ever to restore his reputation and be respected once more as a world leader. Speaking with his aides, he told them that the experiences of the past few weeks had left him more aware of what others in similar situations had undergone. "You mean religiously?" one of them asked. No, he responded, intellectually. In his private diary, he wrote,

> We've had tough times before and we can take the tougher ones that we will have to go through now. That is perhaps what we were made for—to be able to take punishment beyond what anyone in this office has ever had before particularly after leaving office. This is a test of character and we must not fail the test.[30]

A few days later, he added, "Some way there must be a way to come back." The transition did not happen all at once. The former president remained a sick man who fatigued easily, needed constant care, and brooded frequently. One immediate consequence, however, was an improvement in his marriage with Pat. Watergate had been a particularly difficult period for her. She blamed much of the scandal on Haldeman, Erlichman, and Mitchell. In contrast to her husband, who was devastated when they were found guilty in January, she displayed little sympathy for them. Although in typical fashion she always kept her emotions to herself, she also resented how distracted her husband had been in the eighteen months the scandal unfolded and how he had seemed to go out of his way to slight her.[31]

Throughout Nixon's past hospitalization, however, Pat stood vigil at his bedside. When he returned home, she took on responsibility for his convalescence. She even arranged a small dinner party with his closest friends to celebrate his sixty-second birthday. All this brought the couple closer together. As she looked at her husband when he almost died, Pat also reflected about the past—and the future. "I used to resent the fact that Dick's time with his family was so limited," she told a friend. The she added, "His work is what's important now—we can wait."[32]

Still in poor health, Nixon continued to think about the future. Although Barry Goldwater had lost all respect for Nixon after he learned the extent of his involvement in the Watergate cover-up, he visited the former president in late January. During their conversation, Nixon began discussing his future. At the right time, he would like to become a spokesman for the Republican Party and speak out on world issues, he told the Arizona senator. According to Goldwater, he even remarked that he would make a fine ambassador to the People's Republic of China.

Afterward, the senator repeated his conversation with Nixon to reporters. The next day, it was headline news across the country. The former president was incensed. "It's a goddamn lie," he told Gulley about Goldwater's statement. "I never told Goldwater a goddamn thing about wanting to be an ambassador to China or anyplace else." Probably the senator made the statement after getting drunk at the San Clemente Inn, he added. "Christ, I know how the American public would never accept a thing like that. Not in any foreseeable future can I see being able to participate in any way in government."[33]

While denying that part of Goldwater's statement about his interest in an ambassadorship to China, the former president did not deny the other part of the senator's account of their conversation: Nixon's desire to become a spokesman again for the Republican Party and to speak out once more on world affairs. In early 1976, the former president traveled to the People's Republic of China (PRC) at the invitation of the Chinese government in order to celebrate the anniversary of his landmark trip to the country four years earlier, a role he enjoyed playing. He met with all of China's major leaders, including Chairman Mao. He also issued a number of statements in which he called for building on the opening to the PRC that he had begun in 1972. The future of the world depended on good relations between the United States and the PRC, he said. The trip did much to lift Nixon's spirits and to make him forget his troubles at home.[34]

In the United States the reaction was entirely different. The former president had not informed President Ford of his planned trip until just before making it.

Although Ford had no choice except to express his best wishes to Nixon, privately, he and his foreign advisers fumed. In the middle of a fight with Governor Ronald Reagan of California for the Republican nomination for president, he feared Nixon's trip would remind voters of the Nixon pardon and hurt him badly in the upcoming New Hampshire primary, which was only two days away. Nixon had also promised him just a few weeks earlier that he would not be traveling to China in the near future.

Ford felt like he had been double-crossed. Because of overtures he had made to the Soviet Union, the president had also been coolly received when he made his own trip to China the previous November. At best, Nixon was being used by the Chinese to express their displeasure with Ford. At worst, the former president was purposely interfering in the nation's foreign policy, especially after his many statements while in China that seemed to identify relations with Beijing as being more important than those with Moscow.

On Capitol Hill, Barry Goldwater suggested that the Justice Department consider prosecuting Nixon for violating the Logan Act prohibiting private citizens from negotiating with foreign countries. "If he wants to do this country a favor," he said on the Senate floor, "he might stay over there." Similar feelings were expressed on all sides of the political spectrum.[35]

Although Nixon delivered a report on his China visit to the administration, the White House quietly ignored it. If anything, Nixon became more of a persona non grata in Washington and among the American people after he returned to the United States than before he had left for China. When the Republicans held their nominating convention in Kansas City, his name was not mentioned even once from the podium. During the campaign, the Democratic nominee, Governor Jimmy Carter of Georgia, linked Ford to the Nixon administration, remarking in his final campaign address in Boston: "We don't like their betrayal of what our country is."[36]

The reception his trip received in the United States had to be demoralizing to Nixon. Certainly it was counterproductive to his plans to be recognized once more as a leading authority on foreign policy. Returning from China, however, he faced two more pressing problems. The first was regaining his strength and making sure he remained healthy. He put himself on a regular regimen of exercise that included walking, swimming, and playing golf. He came to enjoy golf and became a good amateur player for his age, one time even breaking eighty.

Nixon's sporting companion was his former military aide, Jack Brennan. Like all former presidents now, he was given funds—at first $200,000, but then cut by Congress to $60,000—to pay for transition staff not already on the federal payroll and other expenses for a six-month period. That ended in February. Brennan was ordered to the next class at the Naval War College, a stepping-stone to becoming a general officer. Because he had struck up a close relationship with Nixon and felt responsible for his health and welfare, he retired from the service in order to work for the former president as his administrative assistant. He replaced Ziegler, who left San Clemente hoping to find a high-paying position in the private sector.[37]

The end of the transition raised the second serious problem for Nixon. He was broke. Although the former president had signed a contract providing for a $2.5 million advance for his memoirs, the advance was to be paid in installments as the manuscript was written and approved for publication. The first installment, made at the time the contract was signed, was for only $175,000. His congressional and presidential pensions amounted to around $80,000 (the equivalent of about $345,000 in 2009). Together with his advance, that should have been sufficient to meet his expenses, but it was not. Because of his large staff after returning to San Clemente, the $60,000 he received during the six-month transition period was not enough even to cover those expenses, and he had to let most of his staff go even before February.

Given Nixon's other expenses, including his heavily mortgaged homes and the staff he retained, he had a negative net worth. He also faced increased costs of litigation. In the four years after he left office, over sixty lawsuits were filed against him. Most were spurious and were dismissed, but they all had to be defended. More serious ones were Watergate related. He was faced with legal bills of $750,000, and he still owed back taxes of over $200,000.

The former president became overdue on his Casa Pacifica mortgage, which was costing him as much as $226,000 a year in addition to the $37,000 a year he paid in property taxes. He also had to pay $23,000 in hospital expenses because he neglected to take out medical insurance after leaving the Oval Office. After paying the hospital, he had less than $500 in his bank account. Because he could not pay for gardeners to care for the extensive grounds of Casa Pacifica, they became seedy looking and overgrown with weeds. The neighbors even complained that Nixon was violating the area's zoning laws and hurting property values.[38]

To become solvent again, the ex-president had to complete his memoirs as soon as possible. In the interim, he needed another large source of income. He recalled that Eisenhower and Johnson received substantial sums for interviews with Walter Cronkite of CBS after they left office. The same network was paying Bob Haldeman $100,000 to talk for two hours about his White House years. Maybe the networks would pay him even more to talk about his presidency. The problem was that CBS was getting hammered for paying Haldeman for his interviews.[39]

Fortunately for the former president, David Frost, a British talk-show host/entertainer whose own career was in flux after losing his New York–based talk show, was shopping around the idea of doing a series of interviews with Nixon on his presidency. "For me, he was without doubt the most intriguing man in the world to interview," Frost later wrote, "and in this moment of ignominy, probably the least likely to make himself available."[40]

Nixon was interested. Frost had interviewed candidate Nixon in 1968. Having been thrown softballs by his host, he believed he could easily handle a series of interviews from the genial but not deeply probing celebrity. Frost made contact with the former president's literary agent, Irving "Swifty" Lazar, one of Hollywood's leading agents, who was already in talks with NBC. Lazar asked for $750,000 for a maximum of four one-hour shows. Having failed to line up any financial support from the networks, advertisers, or other investors, Frost was prepared to offer as much as $500,000 for a maximum of four hours. He also wanted complete editorial control of the content and editing.[41]

A series of negotiations followed, carried out largely between Frost, Lazar, and Jack Brennan. In the end, Frost got most of what he wanted in terms of editorial control and an exclusivity clause. According to the contract, the interviews were to be shown as four ninety-minute shows. As many as twenty-four hours of interviews would be required before editing. In return, Frost agreed to pay Nixon $600,000 plus 20 percent of the profits, with $200,000 paid to the former president at the time the contract was signed.[42]

Frost was taking a major financial gamble. None of the major networks wanted to carry the paid interviews featuring a former president, whom many advertisers still regarded as radioactive. He also had difficulty lining up advertisers, financial backers, and independent stations willing to broadcast the interviews. The costs of production would be at least $2 million. Other problems included the number of hours of interviews, a final date for finishing the interviews, and even the approach to the interviews. One by one, Frost and his production and legal team were able to work out these problems. Frost got the financial backers and advertisers he needed. He also established his own independent network of stations.[43]

The initial tapings did not go well for Frost. Nixon was able to dominate the discussions. He went into long monologues that frustrated Frost. Because the former president was writing his memoirs, he had a mastery of detail that Frost lacked. When it came to Watergate, however, Frost gained the upper hand. Pointing to conversations, which had never been brought up during the unfolding of the Watergate drama and which Nixon claimed not to have remembered, Frost pushed Nixon into going farther than he had ever before in acknowledging remorse for his participation in the Watergate cover-up. He had "let down the country" and brought himself down, he acknowledged. However, his remorse was qualified by the bitterness he still felt toward his unnamed enemies. "I gave them a sword and they stuck it in. And they twisted it with relish." The former president also refused to admit that he was guilty of obstruction of justice. (He did not even seem to understand what constituted that crime.) Quite the opposite; he denied criminal intent or criminal wrongdoing. "You're wanting me to say that I participated in an illegal cover-up," he remarked to Frost. "No!"[44]

The Nixon–Frost interviews paid off in a big way for both Frost and Nixon. The four ninety-minute shows, which were carried worldwide, were seen by more than fifty million viewers in the United States alone—the largest audience ever for a show of this kind. Frost made an estimated $2 million from the interviews.

He was also elevated into the front rank of serious interviewers, and his career was given new life. In subsequent years, he interviewed virtually every major political leader as well as scores of celebrities. He became the producer/star of a series of successful franchises. His assets, including his own production company, David Paradine Productions and its affiliates, was estimated to be worth more than £200 million. He married into royalty and in 1993 was knighted by Queen Elizabeth.[45]

The interviews were equally beneficial to Nixon. Although much of the media and the public still criticized the former president for not owning up to his guilt in the Watergate cover-up, he was lauded by others for how far he had gone in acknowledging his involvement. Others praised him for his obvious expertise in foreign affairs. Still others believed he had outperformed Frost, especially in those parts of the interview not involving Watergate. Many of these views were reflected in a Gallup Poll taken shortly after the interviews were televised. Seventy-two percent of the American public still thought Nixon was guilty of obstruction of justice, and 69 percent even thought he had lied during the interviews. However, 44 percent were now more sympathetic to Nixon, while only 28 percent felt less supportive. The interviews also began Nixon's rehabilitation from the Watergate scandal. Although his purpose in agreeing to be interviewed had been to pay his bills, the interviews turned out to be the beginning of the mass marketing of Nixon as a world statesman.[46]

The money Nixon received for the interviews, most of which went directly to pay off his legal obligations, was also a major step in getting out of debt. Another was the completion of his memoirs. Nixon had begun to work on his memoirs soon after signing with Warner Books. Before his trip to China, he had already assembled a team in San Clemente to begin working on them.

From the beginning of the project, Nixon laid down the guidelines he expected his staff to follow: "We won't grovel; we won't confess; we won't do a *mea culpa;* but we will be one hundred percent accurate." These guidelines were mostly meaningless because the former president had preset interpretations, especially of the Watergate affair. Nevertheless, the staff indexed an astonishing chronology of every significant day in Nixon's political career based on interviews, thousands of photocopies of documents from the Nixon papers, an extensive diary that Nixon had kept while at the White House, and a huge collection of newspaper clippings the former president had compiled since first running for Congress in 1946.[47]

Twenty-eight-year-old Diane Sawyer was responsible for the Watergate section of the memoirs. She spent six months compiling a massive compendium of material in an effort to answer definitively the famous question posed about Nixon during the Ervin hearings by Tennessee senator Howard Baker: What did he know, and when did he know it? She also spent long stretches of time alone with Nixon in an effort to get his recollection of what had transpired. Her sessions with the president left her emotionally exhausted because she had to deal with the same problem that Frost later faced: Nixon's habit of going into extensive monologues that often were tangential to the issues at hand.[48]

More than any other former president before him, however, Nixon was involved in the actual preparation of his memoirs, working nine or ten hours most days for nearly three years. The only extended times he took off were when he visited China in 1976 and the three months he spent on the Frost interviews in 1977. Often working alone in his office at home, he dictated and carefully edited and annotated the text his staff had prepared.

Eventually the size of the manuscript became unmanageable. Nixon's dictation alone amounted to 1.5 million words. Warner Books, which was a paperback reprint house, lacked the editorial and managerial experience to handle an original manuscript of this size. Realizing it needed outside help, it sold the hardcover rights for $225,000 to Grosset and Dunlap, a respected publishing house, which brought in its own team of editors to make the manuscript less unwieldy. Nixon and his staff also completed work on the Watergate section of the memoirs that, for various reasons, had yet to be written. Tempers often flared between Nixon and Sawyer, with Nixon sticking close to what he had said in the Frost interviews and Sawyer trying to correct some obvious inconsistencies in his account. One major issue was over responsibility for the eighteen-and-a-half-minute gap in one of the tapes. Nixon maintained his own innocence and that of his secretary, Rose Wood. He also offered a number of explanations for the gap, most of them implausible. Although these went into the final text, the former president included a paragraph stating his awareness "that my treatment of the gap will be looked upon as a touchstone for the candor and credibility of whatever else I write about Watergate."[49]

Reviews of *RN: The Memoirs* were mixed. As Nixon had predicted, most academic reviewers panned the book as a familiar rehash of the former president's defense of his policies from the bombing or Cambodia and Hanoi during the Vietnam War to his refusal to admit to obstruction of justice during the Watergate affair. Many reviewers made the same point as David Frost about the inconsistencies between what Nixon said and knew during the cover-up. Others questioned how anybody could believe even the new material in *RN*, supported by the 10,000 pages of diary pages that Nixon allegedly kept while he was president.[50]

Despite the size of *RN* (1,090 pages), the volume remains mainly a restatement of familiar arguments in defense of Nixon's entire political career. Yet it is also one of the more important of the presidential memoirs. Regardless of the factual content or soundness of *RN*, it provides penetrating insights into Nixon's character, psychology, and views on leadership. For those reasons alone, it remains perhaps the best single book for understanding the Nixon years.

A consistent theme throughout the volume was victimization. A question Nixon raised repeatedly was why acts deemed acceptable when perpetrated by others were viewed as monstrous and even illegal when committed by him. Indeed, he asked whether it was he or the Democrats, with their bitter anticommunist rhetoric in defense of their foreign policy, who were more responsible for the vicarious anticommunism of the 1940s and early 1950s. Was it he or the Hollywood liberals who engaged in blacklisting, or was it President Truman, who pushed for loyalty oaths? Yet they were never accused of red-baiting. As for Watergate, both John Kennedy and Lyndon Johnson engaged in bugging, secret taping, the use of the IRS, and various conspiracies, including the attempted assassination of Fidel Castro, to strike back at their enemies. Their actions were never questioned, however, whereas he was accused of criminality and forced out of office.

Nixon found no easy answer to this central question of why he could not get away with what were really normal practices in Washington except to suggest an ongoing conspiracy against him and the middle American values he represented. It was the press and other forms of the media, joined by the federal bureaucracy and the privileged Eastern establishment, with their liberal values, that conspired against him.

The irony, in Nixon's mind, was that he regarded himself as a moderate conservative who combined principle with pragmatism. He did not consider himself part of the Republican right wing, even though his enemies labeled him as such. He struggled as much with archconservatives as he did with liberals. As president, he even seriously considered establishing a new party of moderate conservatives. The 1968 election had revealed what he termed the New Majority or the Silent Majority. After his landslide reelection victory in 1972, he planned to revolutionize American politics.

"At the beginning of my second term," the president wrote in his memoirs, "Congress, the bureaucracy, and the media were still working in concert to maintain the ideas and ideology of the traditional Eastern liberal establishment that had come down to 1973 through the New Deal, the New Frontier, and the Great Society. Now I planned to give expression to the more conservative values and beliefs of the New Majority throughout the country and use my power to put some teeth into my New American Revolution."[51]

The question for Nixon then became one of exerting presidential leadership to achieve his goals. Given the strength of the opposition against him, he could not be a timid leader or try to find some middle ground. What was required was bold, assertive leadership that tested the bounds of executive power. In Nixon's mind, the president had enormous powers. When the Watergate break-in became one of the obstacles to his American revolution, he had to manage it, just as he had to manage other obstacles and institutional barriers: by reform, replacement, or, in the case of Watergate, circumvention. "In this second term I had thrown down a gauntlet to Congress, the bureaucracy, the media, and the Washington establishment and challenged them to engage in an epic battle," he stated. "Now, suddenly, Watergate had exposed a cavernous weakness in my ranks, and I felt that if . . . I admitted any vulnerabilities, my opponents would savage me with them. . . . Given this situation and given this choice . . . I decided to answer no to the question as to whether I was also involved in Watergate."[52]

It was this epic struggle for survival, not just his own but the nation's, against entrenched enemies that became Nixon's ultimate justification for the Watergate cover-up. It was also why it was impossible for him to admit to any criminality or to feel especially guilty about the whole affair. The ends justified the means. That the former president told his readers nothing factually new about Watergate in *RN,* as his more critical reviewers maintained, was not what was important about *RN.* It was what *RN* had revealed about Nixon.

Publication of *RN* helped Nixon get out of his financial hole. Within six months, it sold more than 330,000 volumes, the best-selling presidential memoirs up to that time. Jack Brennan also negotiated several overseas business deals that resulted in substantial commissions for Nixon. Together with the sale of his Key Biscayne properties for an estimated $750,000 to a nonprofit organization that his friends Bebe Rebozo and Bob Abplanap had helped organize, Nixon was able to pay off his debts and to begin the road to becoming a rich man.[53]

In 1980, the ex-president and Pat decided to move to New York. In 1978, Julie had given birth to their first granddaughter, and in 1979, Tricia gave birth to a grandson. Pat had also suffered a stroke in 1976. Both grandparents wanted to be closer to their grandchildren. By this time, they had also grown tired of San Clemente and wanted to be nearer to the nation's major metropolis.[54]

Nixon was able to sell Casa Pacifica in 1979 for a reported $2.5 million (the equivalent of about $6.7 million in 2009). Nixon's profit of about $2 million from the sale to a group of conservative businessmen raised eyebrows. The sale seemed to Nixon's enemies just another instance of his shady character. Democrats in Congress voted to withhold $60,000 from his allowances as a former president unless he repaid the government for improvements at San Clemente, reported to be around $700,000, including $2,300 for a flagpole. Nixon responded that all the improvements, except for the flagpole, were made at the request of the Secret Service. He then demanded that the items in question be removed and the estate be restored to its original condition. One exception was the flagpole, for which he sent the U.S. Treasury his check for $2,300. A former poker player, Nixon successfully called the Democrats' bluff.[55]

The Nixons had trouble buying a co-op or condominium in New York City. Residents of the buildings where they tried to make a purchase complained that given Nixon's security needs and the public attention the Nixons would generate, their residence would be too disruptive. However, the lingering dislike of the former president also played a part in their rejection. Finally, the Nixons were able to purchase a town house in New York's fashionable Upper East Side. Ironically, living directly behind them and sharing a fence that divided their backyards was Arthur Schlesinger Jr., whose most recent book, *The Imperial Presidency* (1973), was an unabashed attack on Nixon's conduct of the Vietnam War.[56]

By the time Nixon moved to New York, he was already on his way to returning to public life and establishing his reputation as an elder statesman. The same year *RN* was published, Nixon signed a contract to write another book analyzing power in the world through the end of the century. Published in 1980, *The Real War* was a hard-line critique of American foreign policy that took President Jimmy Carter to task for being naive in his conduct of foreign policy.

Nixon had been critical of Carter even before he took office. He found it difficult to understand how a one-term governor of a small Southern state, with no experience in foreign policy, could be elected to the White House. By emphasizing during the campaign his moral integrity, Carter called attention to Nixon's own moral deficits. The former president also resented what he perceived as purposeful personal slights on the president's part, like not extending an invitation to Nixon to stay at Blair House in 1978 when Nixon decided to attend the funeral of Hubert Humphrey, or pressuring the Australian government that same year not to extend an official invitation to Nixon to visit Australia. The Australian prime minister said he would receive him only as a private citizen. As a result, Nixon canceled his planned trip. Although his relationship with Carter improved after Carter left office, Nixon remarked as late as 1992, "Carter is one of those types who tries to be morally superior but does such small petty things that it becomes almost hypocritical."[57]

Although Nixon supported Carter's foreign policy publicly during his first three years in office, particularly the Camp David accords of 1978 between Israel and Egypt, he became more outspoken against the president because of his handling of the Iranian hostage crisis and his refusal to give the shah of Iran, whom he considered a close friend and ally of the United States, permanent residence in the country. He also objected to Carter's moralism in foreign policy, such as his emphasis on human rights and his call for a north–south dialogue. Nixon's own views on foreign policy hardened as he moved away from his policy of détente with the Soviet Union toward a more confrontational policy. In *The Real War,* he declared that the United States was at war with the communist world. What was needed was full mobilization of the nation's economic, diplomatic, and military resources, including beefing up the United States' military.

In the book, Nixon mentioned the Carter administration by name only a few times. He criticized, for example, the president for his decision to cancel construction of the B-1 bomber in the summer of 1977. Yet *The Real War* amounted to a scathing attack on Carter's entire foreign policy. When a paperback edition of the book was published in 1981, after Ronald Reagan had defeated Carter's bid for reelection, Nixon remarked in a new introduction, "When I first wrote this book, I did so in a mood of short-term alarm. . . . I believed that unless the United States changed its policies, the West faced a catastrophe: either defeat in war or surrender without war." Since that time, however, "the most important world event has been the American election. The results of that election have substantially increased my optimism."[58]

Like *RN, The Real War* was a national and international best seller. The *New York Times* Syndicate bought the serial rights to the book and gave it wide distribution. Published at a time when the nation had suffered an embarrassing setback in Iran after the overthrow of the shah of Iran, when hope for a Middle East settlement generated by the Camp David accords was turning into dismay, and when the Soviets were invading Afghanistan, *The Real War* struck a chord with the American people. As even Nixon critic Ronald Steele noted in his review of *Real War,* "Here as in the rest of his career, [Nixon] has shown both his intelligence and his deviousness, his claim to statesmanship and his unerring instinct for the unscrupulous. Certainly this is the time for a knowledgeable polemic on foreign policy . . . and Nixon is certainly qualified to undertake such a polemic."[59]

No sooner had *The Real War* been published than the former president signed a contract for another book, *Leaders,* with a scheduled first printing of 100,000 copies. As Nixon remarked before the book hit the market at the end of 1982, he sought to explain in *Leaders* what set great leaders apart and "what account[ed] for that particular, indefinable electricity that exist[ed] between the leader and the led." The book focused on leaders from World War II whom Nixon admired. They ranged from such well-known figures as Winston Churchill, Charles de Gaulle, Konrad Adenauer, and Douglas MacArthur to lesser-known leaders such as Shigeru Yosdhida (the prime minister who led Japan toward economic recovery after World War II) and Kwame Nkrumah (the first president and prime minister of Ghana and a leading advocate of Pan-Africanism). Obviously reflecting his own view of himself as a great leader who had been ostracized after Watergate, a theme of the book was "years in the wilderness" when Churchill, de Gaulle, and others were out of power. The book was another best seller and was syndicated internationally by the *New York Times.*[60]

Publishing was only one mass-marketing venue for Nixon. Two others were his speaking engagements and frequent trips abroad. Even when he was in semi-seclusion at Casa Pacifica, Nixon received hundreds of invitation for speaking engagements. Until 1978, he refused them all. That year—the same year that *RN* was completed and his health fully restored—the former president decided he was ready to get into the public arena again. The occasion was an invitation to speak in the small town of Hyden, Kentucky (population 500), deep in Kentucky's Appalachian mining region and solidly Republican. The local county had built a $2.7 million recreation center, complete with a swimming pool and gym, using funds from Nixon's revenue-sharing program. Having named the center after Nixon, it invited the former president to speak at its dedication. Much to the surprise of county officials, Nixon accepted their invitation.

Speaking from a lectern decorated with the message THANKS FOR COURAGE UNDER FIRE, Nixon talked for over forty minutes denouncing reporters, Cubans, and communists and extolling Republicans, the military, and the CIA. Some "have given up on America," he said. "But let me tell you of another America . . . of people who believe America should have the kind of leadership that will persist in the struggle with foreign aggressors . . . who believe America should be strong . . . and who believe that America should have the kind of leadership which will prevail." It was vintage Nixon, and the crowd loved it.

Despite the remoteness of Hyden and the fact that the state's governor and two senators were noticeably absent, the former president was delighted by the reception he received. He was ready for more speeches. He even wrote Republican leaders indicating he was prepared to take a more active role in the next congressional elections. Afraid that the American public might still not be ready for the return of the former president to politics, they made clear that was not a good idea. "To hell with them," was his essential response. He had paid his time in purgatory.[61]

Nixon had also planned a six-week world tour in which he intended to meet with world leaders in the Pacific Rim, the Far East, the Middle East, and Europe. Again he was dissuaded from making the trip, even by his former secretaries of state, William Rogers and Henry Kissinger, and by a number of world leaders who were still reluctant to see him, much less to engage in meaningful talks with him. The time was still not propitious for the type of world trip that Nixon had in mind. Maybe later.[62]

Still determined to make a political comeback, Nixon decided to concentrate on finishing *The Real War*. Even that did not keep him from accepting more invitations for speaking engagements and becoming more of a public figure. Among the speaking engagements he accepted was a Veterans' Day address in the Mississippi Gulf Coast, hit hard in 1969 by Hurricane Camille. Nine thousand party faithful filled the Mississippi Coast Coliseum to hear the former president. This time, every Republican of importance was present and delighted to have their picture taken with Nixon. Not a word was mentioned about Watergate. "You've come back [from Camille], and I've come back," he told his audience. His speech was received with the most boisterous outburst he had gotten since leaving the White House.[63]

Meanwhile, the former president received an invitation from the centuries-old Oxford Union, a debating society at Oxford University. He accepted both that invitation and another long-standing one to go to France to appear on a television call-in show. His appearance in France was a smashing success. The call-in questions he received from the audience were mostly friendly and afforded him the opportunity to display his knowledge of world affairs. At a reception afterward, he was buoyant and upbeat. He even exchanged pleasantries with Pierre Salinger, John F. Kennedy's former press secretary and Nixon antagonist, who was living in Paris. The reviews of his appearance were euphoric. An American journalist wrote to his editor in the United States: "It's too bad he can't run for President of France. He would win hands down."[64]

In accepting the invitation to the Oxford Union, the former president was taking a major chance: the organization was bound to bring up the Watergate affair and had a reputation for heckling its guests. Also, there was strong opposition among leftist trade unionist and expatriate American students to his visit. All the government's ministers, with one exception, refused to meet with him or to attend any of his speeches. The foreign office made clear that it still regarded

Nixon as unwelcome. Jonathan Aitken, a former foreign office official, who had interviewed Nixon a number of times for a biography he was writing, arranged for him to meet a number of high-ranking officials, including the leader of the Conservative Party, Margaret Thatcher, and a large delegation from the House of Commons.

Despite a small crowd of taunting demonstrators when he arrived at Oxford, the former president put on another bravo performance, speaking for fifty minutes before a skeptical audience and then answering questions. Asked whether he regretted bombing Cambodia in 1971, he replied he should have done it earlier and then added: "Accusing the United States of invading the North Vietnamese occupation zones in Cambodia is the equivalent of accusing the Allies of invading German Occupied France in 1944." Of Watergate he responded: "Some people say I didn't handle it properly and they're right. I screwed it up and I paid the price. *Mea culpa.* But let's get on to my achievements. You'll be here in 2000 and we'll see how I'm regarded then." After his speech, the former president received a fifty-second standing ovation. After the question-and-answer period, he received a second standing round of applause. He was jubilant.[65]

The rest of Nixon's trip to England went equally as well. Over the next two days, he spoke to a gathering of conservative academics, intellectuals, and politicians, many of whom had come to bury him but left the meeting praising him. He also met with Robert Blake, the author of *Disraeli,* one of his favorite biographies. He capped off his trip with a lavish dinner hosted by the former labor prime minister, Harold Wilson.

Typically, the former president had prepared carefully for each engagement during his visits to France and England. He seemed to have fun, but as Aitken later wrote, "to those who spent many hours of his visit in his company, one of the principal impressions was how unrelaxed he remained. He was obviously not on some retired politician's junket down memory lane." Although he told everyone he met that he could not run for president again, "he seemed to be winding himself up as if he was running for some new office."[66]

Of course, the former president was—just not a political one. Before he left for home, he asked Aitken if he thought his trip had been a success. Aitken assured him it had been. Then, offering Aitken some advice, he repeated what had by now become his mantra: "You have to be ready to fight through all life's ups and downs. . . . Disappointment doesn't finish you. . . . You have to stay in the arena. . . . If the cause is great enough, it's always worth fighting back. . . . That's what makes a politician."[67]

After returning from Europe but before moving to New York, Nixon had a final party at Casa Pacifica to celebrate John Mitchell's birthday. Despite spending nineteen months in prison, Mitchell had never criticized the former president, and they remained close friends. Noticeably absent from the gathering of Nixon's former aides at the White House, however, were John Ehrlichman and Bob Haldeman, both of whom had also recently been released from prison. They believed

Nixon should have pardoned them instead of letting them be incarcerated. Haldeman had already written a book harshly critical of his former boss, although he later apologized for his remarks and mended fences with the former president. Ehrlichman, who remained less forgiving, was in the process of writing his own account of the Nixon years. Despite their absence, it was a nostalgic event. The guests heaped praise on the former president for what he had accomplished and generally dismissed Watergate as a skid on the road.[68]

Yet the Watergate affair remained more than a skid on the road for the former president. Because of Watergate, the Republican Party refused for a second time to invite him to speak at its nominating convention in Detroit. He still faced legal problems stemming from Watergate. About fifty lawsuits had been brought against him because of Watergate, some for damages, others for access to the Nixon papers and tapes. Although the Justice Department and private contributors paid for some of the litigation, the former president had already forked over $1 million of his own money. Furthermore, Nixon continued his fight for sole ownership of his presidential papers and tapes. Even after Congress enacted the Presidential Records Act of 1978, which provided for public ownership of all presidential papers, he asked the federal courts to award him unspecified damages as a result of the government's continuing control over his papers and tapes. He asserted that no other ex-president had been subjected to such a practice and that it was in violation of his constitutional rights to privacy, speech, and freedom of association.[69]

By 1980, however, Nixon's efforts to market himself as a wise elder statesman who had come out of exile were bearing fruit. When reporters questioned the ex-president after he returned from France and Britain, the questions they asked had nothing to do with Watergate but were about his future plans. In the months that followed, Nixon could be seen everywhere. In January 1979, a reluctant President Carter invited Nixon to a state dinner at the White House for Chinese deputy prime minister Deng Xiaoping after the Chinese insisted that he be there. His visit to the White House was the first since his resignation. The next morning, he met for two hours with Deng. Afterward, it was announced that the former president would visit Beijing in the summer.

In September, Nixon made his second trip to China since leaving office. Although his trip was more low-key than the first visit in 1976, the former president was nevertheless treated as if he were an official representative of the United States. The Chinese held two banquets in his honor, and Nixon had long conversations with Deng, who tried to get the former president to acknowledge that "hegemonism" (a code word for the Soviet Union) threatened world peace. Nixon was too coy to fall into that trap.[70]

The next year, Nixon visited Europe again and then flew on to the Ivory Coast to attend a golf tournament as a guest of President Felix Houphouet-Boigny. In July, he flew via commercial jet to Cairo to attend the funeral of the shah of Iran. The former president was furious that President Carter had refused to send even a representative to the funeral. He believed Carter's failure to have the United States represented at the funeral epitomized the administration's shabby treatment of someone who deserved the nation's respect rather than its disdain.[71]

In September, Nixon was invited by NBC to be a guest for a week on its morning *Today Show*. His role was to answer questions on the pending presidential campaign from the authority on recent presidential elections, Theodore White. Although he predicted that Reagan would win the election, he warned that Carter was tough and "shrewd with a ruthless staff," so that a Republican victory could not be taken for granted.[72]

In his new town house, Nixon started a practice that he continued for most of the rest of his retirement. He began hosting dinner parties with important journalists, political figures, academics, and other opinion makers—the very Eastern elite establishment he had spent most of his life attacking. The dinners always followed the same format. They began with cocktails, followed by the main meal, almost always Chinese, served with different wines. After dinner, the party adjourned to the living room, where Nixon served glasses of mao-tai (a 106-proof Chinese brandy) and demonstrated the Chinese manner of toasting. The evenings ended promptly at 10:30 P.M., when Nixon joked irreverently, "Well, I promised to get so and so to the local house of ill repute by eleven, so I guess we ought to call it a night."

Throughout the meals, Nixon regaled his guests with personal stories and little anecdotes about the world leaders he had met, from de Gaulle to Mao Zedong. Always he tried to impress those around the table with his mastery of global issues. He usually succeeded. Hugh Sidey, the White House correspondent of *Time,* who in 1974 had said that Nixon had relegated himself to the "sloughs of history," now remarked that he would rather sit at Nixon's table than at any other, and he called the former president "a strategic genius."[73]

For a person who had developed a well-deserved reputation as being a loner, who had always been in the habit of limiting access to himself as much as possible, and who did not like even to mix with crowds and shake the hands of his supporters, it must have taken an astonishing amount of sheer grit and determination to market himself the way he did, especially after coming to New York City. However, it was the road he chose as he sought to redefine his place in history. "People who want a quiet life, unchallenged, should not live here," he remarked about his move to New York. "It's the fastest track in the world."[74]

Nixon promoted himself not only through his books and dinners. He remained constantly on the move. He allowed himself to be interviewed frequently on television with all the well-known media personalities. He accepted speaking engagements before prestigious audiences, both at home and abroad. He wrote newspaper columns and op-ed pieces, and he gave backgrounders to editorial boards for all the major media outlets, commenting mostly on foreign policy matters and always cultivating the statesman aura. He even mediated a contract dispute between major league baseball and the umpires' association.[75]

By the 1980s, Nixon's effort to define himself as "an *homme serieux,*" in the words of his former speechwriter, Ray Price, was working. "Richard Nixon is back," wrote Julie Baumgold in a cover story on Nixon for *New York Magazine* in 1980. Six years later, *Newsweek* ran almost a nearly identical headline— "He's Back: The Rehabilitation of Richard Nixon"—for its own cover story on the former president. What made the feature so important was that *Newsweek* was owned by the *Washington Post,* which had broken the Watergate scandal. In addition, its publisher was Nixon's old nemesis, Katherine Graham. Impressed by the reception Nixon received after delivering a speech at an Associated Press luncheon, she shook hands with the former president and suggested that her reporters interview him for a story. Nixon granted the interview on the condition that he appear on the magazine's front cover.[76]

Columnists like Hugh Sidey, David Broder of the *Washington Post,* and younger writers like R. Emmett Tyrell, editor of the *American Spectator,* were also writing and quoting the former president again. At the urging of Alexander Haig, then President Ronald Reagan's secretary of state, Reagan included Nixon, along with former presidents Gerald Ford and Jimmy Carter, as part of the nation's official delegation to the 1981 funeral of Egypt's slain leader, Anwar Sadat, the first time Nixon represented the country in any official capacity since his resignation. Appearing on the CBS *Morning News* the next year, he remarked that as far as the country was concerned, "the Watergate syndrome [had] probably run its course, [and] that was good."[77]

For Nixon, though, the Watergate syndrome would never be over. A survey by *Newsweek* in the spring of 1982 found that 75 percent of Americans still believed his actions regarding Watergate warranted his resignation—more than thought so at the time he stepped down. However, the number of persons who opposed Ford's pardon of him and his return to public life had also eroded considerably. He also received a growing number of requests from Republican officeholders to speak at fund-raising events. Even more impressive, the Gallup Poll ranked Nixon as one of the ten most admired men in the world.[78]

Although Nixon had twelve more years to live, these trend lines continued through the remainder of his life. In 1990, the former president acknowledged that the decade between 1978 (when he began his comeback) to 1988 (when ground was broken for the Nixon Library) was the happiest of his life. During his 1980 presidential campaign against Carter, Ronald Reagan asked for Nixon's advice, and the former president readily gave it. During his presidency, Reagan remained solicitous of the former president. Nixon responded by providing him with a regular stream of advice, some solicited, most not. Although there is serious question as to how much Reagan listened to the former president, just the fact he felt he had renewed influence with the White House gave him great satisfaction.[79]

After publishing *Leaders* in 1982, the former president published three more books in the 1980s: *Real Peace: A Strategy for the West* (1983), *No More Vietnams* (1985), and *1999: Victory without War* (1988). In them, Nixon covered

mostly familiar ground. *Real Peace* was full of pithy phrases and broad generalizations without much substance or insights. Nixon's conclusion was that "to
keep the peace and defend our freedom, we need to adopt a policy of hard-headed
détente." He then defined "hard-headed détente" as a "combination of détente
with deterrence." For a volume that purported to define a new strategy for the
West, the former president substituted sweeping statements for strategy.[80]

No More Vietnams was a book in two parts. The first was a self-serving analysis of what went wrong in Vietnam that largely repeated arguments Nixon had
made in *RN*. By failing to finance U.S. air support and supplies to sustain South
Vietnam after 1973, Congress was responsible for its fall to the communists in
1975. The second part was a plea by Nixon to combat communism in third world
countries through trade and aid. It also amounted to a backing of the Reagan administration's policy of supplying the noncommunist regimes of Central America
with the material needed to put down communist insurrections.[81]

Of the three books, *1999: Victory without War* was the most thoughtful.
Nixon seemed more optimistic than he had in his previous works. He welcomed
the reforms the Soviet Union's leader, Mikhail Gorbachev, was making in his
country. He also predicted that Eastern Europe would soon undergo fundamental
change, but he also warned that the "United States and the Soviet Union have
foreign policy objectives that are diametrically opposed," and that a "structure of
real peace can only be founded on the bedrock of nuclear deterrence."[82]

The books Nixon wrote in the 1980s not only contributed to his growing reputation as a foreign policy expert and skilled diplomat, but they also continued to
make him a lot of money. How much he received in royalties is unclear, but they
were all best sellers. In his next book, *In the Arena: A Memoir of Victory, Defeat
and Renewal* (1990), a strange volume that was part memoir of the years since *RN*
was published and part homilies on various unrelated topics ranging from time
and memory to wealth and television, the former president made clear that he had
become a wealthy man. He had never sought wealth, he said, but he admired men
of wealth because they represented the entrepreneurial spirit that had made the
United States so successful. Obviously paraphrasing a line made famous by the
character Gordon Gekko in the movie *Wall Street* (1987), he remarked: "Greed
is not good. But wealth is, if it used to good purposes." Good purposes could include a good lifestyle and having "fun." Although in his view "struggle . . . [was]
better than fun" because those "who welcome and enjoy it will get something out
of life far more rewarding than those who do not," he recognized a place for relaxation. "We should not go overboard," he commented, "and make life so grim,
so tough, that we take all the joy out of living."[83]

Nixon found relaxation in a number of ways. Most important was being with
his grandchildren. While Tricia and Ed Cox had only a single child, a son, Julie
Eisenhower gave birth in 1980 to her and David's second child, a boy, and, in 1984
to their third child, a second daughter. For someone who considered overcoming
life's obstacles more enjoyable than what most people regarded as relaxation, he

took no greater pleasure than playing with and entertaining his grandchildren. As they grew older, he also liked to take the boys to baseball, football, or basketball games. Going to games or watching them on television, especially football, was another form of leisure for the former president.

To accommodate the growing Nixon clan while also giving the former president more privacy and Pat more opportunity to enjoy her love of gardening, the Nixons decided after eighteen months to sell their town house and to move to a four-and-a-half-acre wooded estate in the exclusive community of Saddle River, New Jersey, about fifty minutes outside of New York City, where Nixon still commuted daily to his office. Their new fifteen-room fieldstone and redwood home, located at the end of cul-de-sac and surrounded by woods, came with a tennis court, pool, guest quarters, and a large wine cellar. Nixon paid slightly over $1 million for the estate. He sold his town house in what the *New York Daily* News called "the sweetest real estate deal since the Indians sold Manhattan Island for $24," to the Syrian Mission to the United Nations for $2.6 million—more than three times what he had paid for it.[84]

Even though the former president no longer lived in the city, New York's intellectual, business, and cultural elite made the nearly hourlong trek to Saddle River when invited by the former president for the dinners that he continued to hold at his new home. Although they served the ulterior purpose of self-promotion and Nixon did most of the talking, he enjoyed engaging in interesting conversation. In fact, he regretted what he believed was the decline of conversation, attributing it in large part to the "hours of video-induced catatonia" as a result of television.[85]

A final form of recreation for Nixon was extensive travel abroad. During the ten years between 1978 and 1988, the former president made four more trips to China. He also visited two dozen other countries, including the Soviet Union, most of the rest of Europe, Northern Africa, and parts of the Middle East, South Asia, Southeast Asia, and the Pacific Rim. When he traveled, it was not to engage in sightseeing or to be entertained. Rather, his purpose was to meet with heads of state and other national leaders to discuss world affairs, usually without any aides present.[86]

Less a form of recreation than a major project for Nixon was the construction of the Richard Nixon Library and Museum in Yorba Linda, California. A Nixon Library Foundation had been established as early as 1971. At the time, Nixon planned to amend the tax laws to allow him and his associates, including Henry Kissinger, to take a tax deduction for donating their papers to the projected Nixon Library. Nixon's papers alone were valued at about $3 million.

Watergate killed these plans, and the Library Foundation went into limbo. However, plans for a library went forward. At first, Nixon wanted to build the Library at Pat's alma mater, the University of Southern California (USC). USC was not interested in having the library on its campus without possession of the Nixon papers, whose fate remained uncertain. Then in 1981, Terry Sanford, the president of Duke University, proposed building the library at Duke, where Nixon had gone to law school. When the Duke faculty learned of Sanford's offer, they rebelled. Led by the eminent Duke political scientist James Barber and other prominent figures in Duke's political science and history departments, who might have profited the most in terms of scholarship by having the papers at Duke, large elements of the faculty protested that they had not been consulted in advance by Sanford. More to the point, they did want not want Duke's good name muddied by having on its campus the papers of the most disgraced president in the nation's history. "I don't want to spend the rest of my life at this place correcting the record regarding Nixon," Barber remarked in an open letter to the faculty. "As of now, I say it's broccoli and I say to hell with it." The acting head of the history department even compared having the Nixon Library on campus to having an Al Capone building at Duke.[87]

Although other faculty supported construction of the library on the basis of academic freedom and the scholarly benefits it would bring Duke, the university's academic council voted against the library by a single vote. While the board of trustees still approved its construction, faculty discontent remained so pervasive that the next February, Duke officials announced that because of a poor economy and an "unfavorable political climate," the university had decided to drop plans for the Nixon Library.[88]

With Duke having taken itself out of contention, Nixon's aides looked for a nonacademic—and presumably less controversial—place to build the facility. A number of towns, including Independence, Missouri, home of the Truman Library, offered space for the library. Eventually, the reconstituted Nixon Archives Foundation settled on Nixon's birthplace, Yorba Linda.

The original 81,000-square-foot structure was considerably smaller than the Ford or Kennedy libraries, which both ranged around 100,000 square feet. Located adjacent to Nixon's birthplace, it was built in Spanish colonial style with a red tiled roof and white stucco walls. Because it did not house the Nixon presidential papers and tapes, which were still in Washington, the library was not made part of the presidential library system operated by the National Archives. Accordingly, the Nixon Archives Foundation had to raise $25 million to build and operate the facility, which was more a museum than a library.[89]

Construction was started in 1988 and completed in 1990. The facility and Nixon's birthplace were dedicated on 19 July 1990. More than a thousand reporters were present for the dedication. Most of the former leaders of Nixon's administration were also in attendance, as were such celebrities as Bob Hope, Gene Autry, Billy Graham, and Norman Vincent Peale. Present on the podium were President George H. W. Bush and former presidents Gerald Ford and Ronald Reagan, as well as their spouses. Notably absent was former president Jimmy Carter, although he had been invited to the dedication. With the president and two of the three living former presidents on the podium, Nixon's return from the cavernous depths of Watergate seemed complete. Speaking before a crowd of

50,000, the former president might have been commenting metaphorically when he remarked, "Nothing we have ever seen matches this moment—to be welcomed home again."[90]

Nixon lived four more years after the dedication of his library. During this period, the former president remained busy. The same year the Nixon Library was dedicated, his book *In the Arena* was published. He also hired Monica Crowley, a graduate student working on her Ph.D. in international relations at Columbia University, to be his research assistant and later his foreign policy assistant. She worked for Nixon from 1990 until his death in 1994. Not unlike Doris Kearns's relationship with Lyndon Johnson, Crowley became Nixon's confidante and sounding board. For hours at a time, he talked to her about a variety of topics, from Watergate to former presidents and leaders he had met throughout his long career. Crowley kept a diary in which she recorded his comments as she recollected them. She later published them in two volumes, *Nixon Off the Record* (1996) and *Nixon in Winter* (1998).[91]

Crowley intended to highlight Nixon's human side and his brilliance as a politician, notwithstanding the Watergate fiasco. Instead, the ex-president came off in Crowley's two volumes as an individual who still harbored bitter personal resentments and who rarely had anything good to say about any of the presidents during his long political career. In contrast to these other presidents, he continued to regard himself as one of the nation's great presidents. As even Crowley acknowledged,

> He was . . . not particularly generous with his assessments of the American presidencies that came before and after his own. . . . America had had few truly great presidents according to Nixon; Washington, Jefferson, Lincoln, Theodore Roosevelt, Woodrow Wilson, Franklin Roosevelt, and implicitly Nixon himself. These men met the test of great leadership: great men in a great country, encountering and directing great events. His inclusion of himself on this list was driven less by determined historical revisionism than by a genuine belief that he belonged in their ranks.[92]

Oddly enough, after Clinton was elected president, Nixon developed a closer relationship with him than he had with his Republican successors, Reagan and Bush. At one time he had regarded Clinton with total contempt—a person who represented the worst of his generation, an antiwar draft dodger who smoked pot and had extramarital affairs. Even after Clinton took office, Nixon still had reservations about the new president. When the Whitewater scandal developed, he thought Clinton and his wife, Hillary, were guilty of obstruction of justice and should pay the price, just as he had paid the price for Watergate. The former president also found the new president equivocal, directionless, and lacking in personal character.

Even so, Nixon warmed up considerably to Clinton after he took office. Much of this had to do with the fact that Clinton went out of his way to cultivate a close relationship with him. Soon after he took office, Nixon made another trip

Photo of Nixon at the dedication of the Nixon Library on 19 July 1990, speaking before a crowd of more than 50,000, including all the former presidents except Jimmy Carter. The former president believed the dedication of his library marked the culmination of his long campaign to rehabilitate his reputation since the Watergate scandal. He was only partially correct. (Courtesy of the Richard Nixon Foundation.)

to the Soviet Union. To Nixon's relief, when he informed the White House of his plans, Clinton approved them and stated that he would request a debriefing after he returned to the United States. Soon after Nixon returned home, Clinton called him, and, as Crowley later wrote, from that time, "their unexpectedly close relationship was born." "He was very respectful but with no sickening bullshit," the former president told Crowley about his long talk with Clinton.[93]

In the 1990s, Nixon wrote two final books, *Seize the Moment: America's Challenge in a One-Superpower World* (1992) and *Beyond Peace* (1994). The major theme of both works was the new responsibilities the end of the cold war and the collapse of communism imposed on the United States. Washington had "a moral imperative to use [America's] awesome capabilities as the world only superpower to promote freedom and justice," he said in *Seize the Moment.* Although he said the same thing in *Beyond Peace,* his emphasis in that book was on the need for American domestic renewal. "Today America must be a worthy example for others to follow, but our example is tarnished with every deepening domestic problem." These problems ranged from "rampant crime and violence" to "the spread of a spiritual emptiness."[94]

Although the former president remained busy in his final years and kept a full schedule, including a two-mile walk each morning at 5:30 A.M., a practice he had been following for many years, he slowed down considerably as he grew older. He gave fewer interviews, accepted fewer speaking invitations, wrote fewer op-ed pieces, and became more reflective. He also spent more time with Pat, who had been in declining health for more than a decade. In 1983, she suffered another stroke. Although she made nearly a full recovery, it left her considerably weakened.

The next year, Pat was admitted to the hospital for a pulmonary infection from which she never fully recovered. She attended less to her gardening and finally gave it up entirely. As she became more frail, she became more secluded and rarely went out. Concerned that the house was becoming too much for her, the former president decided to move into a smaller home in a gated community in Park Ridge, New Jersey. Shortly thereafter, Pat was diagnosed with emphysema, and then in 1992 with lung cancer. She died on 22 June 1993, the day after her fifty-third wedding anniversary. She was eighty-one years old. She was buried on the grounds of the Richard Nixon Library. The former president sobbed openly at her funeral.[95]

Ten months later, the former president died. Until very near the end of his life, Nixon had been in good health. He seemed to have overcome his problem with blood clots in his legs. On Monday, 18 March 1994, however, he suffered a major stroke. He had been working on the page proofs of *Beyond Peace,* which had arrived just that day. Taken by ambulance to the Cornell Medical Center in New York, he appeared to improve. However, the next night, he developed symptoms of cerebral edema (swelling of the brain), which caused his condition to worsen. He had already made clear that he did not want to be placed on a respirator if he were incapacitated. On Thursday, he slipped into a coma and died on Saturday, 23 April, at the age of eighty-one, with his family at his bedside.

Having declined a state funeral, the former president was buried beside his wife at the Nixon Library after lying in state in the library's lobby. Despite heavy rain, police estimated that 50,000 people waited in lines up to eighteen hours to file past his casket. All the former presidents attended his funeral. Among those who eulogized him was President Clinton. Commenting on Nixon's accomplishments, especially in foreign affairs, he concluded, "May the day of judging President Nixon on anything less than his entire life and career come to an end."[96]

Despite Clinton's advice that Americans judge Nixon by the entirety of his career, this has never happened. More than anything Nixon had said or done during his long political career, his name had become indelibly associated with Watergate.[97] A March 2002 Gallup poll revealed, for example, that 54 percent of the American people still disapproved of Nixon's performance as president, while 34 percent approved. A Quinnipiac Poll of 2006 asked 1,534 registered voters to rank the worst American president of the last forty-six years. They listed Nixon as the second worst president behind only George Bush, who was at the lowest point of his presidency because of the war in Iraq.[98]

The fact that the American people still regarded the Nixon presidency unfavorably does not undermine the point that beginning around 1978, the former president made a concerted effort to mass market himself as one of the nation's leading experts on foreign policy. One of his purposes was, of course, to sell books. It is no coincidence that many of his television appearances took place about the same time that one of his books was being published. However, selling books to make money was never his primary purpose.

Rather, Nixon's aim was to reach the summit of the mountain he saw himself so often having to climb: to put Watergate behind him; to gain the respect of the very groups he had always regarded as his enemies; to become once more a person of influence nationally and globally; and most important, to establish what he still believed was his rightful place as the nation's best post–World War II president and one of the nation's great presidents, deserving inclusion in the same pantheon of leaders that he wrote about in *Leaders*.

That Nixon was guilty of hubris in believing he could achieve so much is beyond question, especially because the problem he faced was not so much restoring what he believed was his rightful place in history but establishing it in the first place. That said, it is remarkable how much he did achieve. The sales of his books, the demands on his time, the fulsome praise he received even by those who just a few years earlier would have sent him to jail—all these indicated the degree of redemption he had achieved by the time of his death.

II

Gerald Ford's highest political ambition before being appointed vice president in December 1973 was to be Speaker of the House of Representatives. Ford had spent most of the 1972 campaign season traveling the country on behalf of Republican congressional candidates. However, the White House, including the president, had made the campaign a personal one—Nixon against McGovern—rather than a campaign of Republicans against Democrats. Worse, the president ended his own campaign with millions of dollars left over, which he never considered sharing with his party's candidates for Congress.

Ford had always considered himself a good friend to Nixon ever since the California congressman had first introduced himself to the freshman from Michigan shortly after he arrived in Washington in 1948. He had supported Nixon's nomination for president in 1960, and he was delighted that he had been elected president in 1968. Nevertheless, Ford had been disconcerted by some of the actions Nixon had taken over the years, especially Nixon's neglect of Congress after he became president and his utter unwillingness to campaign in 1972 for Republican congressional candidates. He blamed Nixon for his party's failure to capture either the House or the Senate despite the president's landslide victory over McGovern.[99]

Having lost his last, best chance to fulfill his lifelong ambition of becoming House Speaker, Ford told both his family and friends that he intended to run one more time for Congress and then to retire in 1977. He would be almost sixty-four years old, and he wanted to spend part of each week on the golf links. He also needed to resume his law practice part-time in order to earn enough money to be able to retire full-time. Although he owned a home in Alexandria and a condominium in Vail, Colorado, he had little in savings. The only retirement income he would have was his congressional pension, which, he estimated, would be $26,000 a year (the equivalent of about $91,000 in 2009)—a decent amount but not enough to maintain two homes, to finish putting his children through college, to be able to take vacations, and to otherwise enjoy a leisurely retirement.

While playing golf with his friend, House Speaker Tip O'Neill, Ford even urged O'Neill to help get a pay raise through Congress. O'Neill asked the minority leader what he had in mind. "Well, I'd like to get my pension up to thirty thousand dollars," Ford responded. "Then I can go back to Grand Rapids. I want to practice law three days a week and play golf the other four. I figure I can make around twenty-five thousand dollars in my practice, and together with the pension I'll have a good living."[100]

Ford's life was turned around, of course, when in quick succession he was nominated by Nixon to replace Spiro Agnew as his vice president, approved as vice president by the Senate in December, elevated eight months later to the presidency after Nixon's resignation, and then defeated by Jimmy Carter in 1976 in his bid for election to a full term as president. The Former Presidents Act of 1958, which provided pensions, transition expenses, staff and office benefits, and related expenses for ex-presidents, was amended over the years to provide increases in presidential pensions and allowances for office space and staff. When Ford left office in 1977, his annual presidential and congressional pensions totaled approximately $100,000 a year—more than enough to retire comfortably. By the time he died in 2006, his presidential and congressional pensions amounted to just over $300,000. In addition, he was receiving around $500,000 for staff and office allowances. He maintained two offices, one in Rancho Mirage, California, which had become his permanent residence, and another in Vail, where he still had his condominium.[101]

Ford has also become a multimillionaire. More than any other president before him, after he left the White House in 1977, and especially after 1980, when he finally gave up any interest in returning to the Oval Office, he took advantage of his former office to merchandise himself. When correspondents and even Nixon later questioned the way he was selling himself as a former president, he maintained that he was doing nothing wrong or unethical. He had extended the bounds of what was deemed appropriate for an ex-president. What makes his former presidency so surprising was that he was the least likely ex-president to commercialize himself the way he did. His whole biography before becoming president was characterized by his reputation for honesty and integrity and his seeming disinterest in making money.

The first American president not to have to face a national electorate, Ford was born Leslie Lynch King Jr. in Omaha, Nebraska, on 14 July 1913. His father was physically abusive to his mother, Dorothy Gardner. Shortly after they were married, she left him; she divorced him three years later. Meanwhile, she moved to Grand Rapids, Michigan, where she met and married Gerald Rudolf Ford Sr., a paint store owner. Although he never formally adopted Dorothy's boy, he raised him as his own son. He and Dorothy renamed him Gerald R. Ford Jr. In addition to Gerald Jr., the Fords had three other boys, Thomas, Richard, and James.

Although the Fords lost their home during the Great Depression, Gerald Sr. maintained his store and eventually recovered from the Depression. He bought another home in a comfortable middle-class section of Grand Rapids, which at the time was one of the nation's most flourishing cities, prospering from its furniture-making business and increasingly from the auto industry, which built several major plants in the city and surrounding area.

Gerald Jr. was raised in what can only be described as a solid Midwestern middle-class family. In contrast to Nixon's upbringing, his parents were open in their affection for each other and for their children. Although they were strict disciplinarians, they insisted only that their children tell the truth, work hard, and come to dinner on time. Yelling and corporal punishment were not part of the normal family routine. Raised as an Episcopalian, Gerald was expected to go to church with the rest of the family on Sunday and to be guided by the Ten Commandments. Religion was not central to his upbringing. Although his father worked long hours, he found time to throw a football or baseball around with the boys, to vacation on nearby Lake Michigan, and to take the boys fishing. Ford remembered, "Neither of my parents could be described as 'secure' economically; but emotionally, both were very secure, and if I retain that characteristic today, I owe it to them."[102]

Ford's sense of security from childhood was only one trait that differentiated him from Nixon. In personality, they were polar opposites. While Nixon always regarded himself as a loner, Ford was an extrovert. In contrast to Nixon, he genuinely liked people and made few enemies even during his political career. As a teenager, he became an Eagle Scout, and in his senior year, he even won a contest as the most popular high school student in Grand Rapids. His prize was a trip to Washington, D.C. While Nixon brooded about life's unfairness, Ford felt as if the sun always shone on him. In contrast to Nixon, Ford was also a gifted athlete on the football field. In high school, his team won the state championship, and he was chosen captain of the all-state team. At the University of Michigan, he made All–Big Ten and was offered contracts by the Green Bay Packers and the Detroit Lions after his graduation in 1935.[103]

Ford turned down professional football to become an assistant football coach at Yale. His hope was to win admission to the university's prestigious law school. Although Ford had always been a solid student in high school and at the University of Michigan, he was not as gifted intellectually as Nixon or John F. Kennedy. His interest in the law and politics had been whetted by his visit to Washington as a high school senior. Knowing he could not get into Yale through the regular admissions process, he hoped to use his position at Yale to become a part-time student in the law school and to prove himself worthy of becoming a full-time student. Eventually he was given permission to enroll in several courses, where he earned good enough grades to be admitted full-time.

In 1941, Ford graduated from Yale in the top third of his class. Although he was offered positions with prestigious law firms in New York and Philadelphia (something Nixon had failed to achieve), he decided instead to return to Grand Rapids and open his own law firm with a good friend, Phil Buchen. Their practice grew quickly, but then came World War II.

In 1942, Ford enlisted in the naval reserves and was soon called to active duty as an ensign. During the war, he served as a gunnery officer on the U.S.S. *Monterrey*. By the time the war was over, he had won ten battle stars. He had a close brush with death, however, when he was almost thrown into the sea by a typhoon off the Philippines, which left the *Monterrey* so badly damaged that it had to return to the United States for repairs. For the remainder of the war, Ford was posted in the United States. After being honorably discharged in 1946, he spent the next two years practicing law in one of Grand Rapids's more venerable law firms, where Phil Buchen, now a partner in the firm, helped secure him a position.

Even before the war, Ford had begun to take an interest in politics. Raised as a Republican in a solidly Republican region, where the virtues of individualism, limited government, and the free enterprise system were embedded, the future president never doubted the truth of these essential principles. He was by nature, however, moderate and considerate of other viewpoints. A committed isolation-ist before the war, he became a lifelong internationalist after the war because of his admiration for Michigan's senator, Arthur Vandenberg. His internationalist outlook and his distaste for the local Republican boss, Frank McKay, led Ford in 1948 to challenge long-term congressman Bartel J. Jonkman, an isolationist aligned with McKay. In the Republican primary, he overwhelmed Jonkman and then easily beat his Democratic opponent in November in this safe Republican district.

Ford had double cause to celebrate his election to Congress. Not only was he going to Washington as a new congressman, he was going as a newly married man. As a star athlete with a pleasant personality and handsome features, Ford had always been popular with women. He stood about six feet tall and weighed 195 pounds. He was trim at the waist and broad shouldered, with blue eyes and blond hair, a square jaw, straight nose, and a generous mouth that allowed him to show off his broad grin and straight teeth. He dressed modestly but comfortably, often in a sports jacket and matching pants. While at Yale, he had what he later described as a "torrid four-year love affair" with a coed, Phyllis Brown, who was so striking that she was signed by a leading modeling agency and appeared on the cover of some of the nation's most prominent magazines. Phyllis introduced Jerry to skiing, the theater, and even to modeling. In 1940, they appeared together on the cover of *Look* and in 1942 on the cover of *Cosmopolitan*. Although they talked about marriage, after the war, Ford decided to move back to Grand Rapids, and Phyllis continued her modeling career in New York. They remained good friends.

By the time Ford returned to Grand Rapids, he was already in his thirties, and his parents feared he might remain a bachelor. Then he was introduced to Eliza-beth "Betty" Bloomer Warren, a former model and dancer with the famed Martha Graham Dance Company, who had just divorced her first husband. After dating for a while, Ford proposed to her in February 1948. Without telling her about his plans to run for office, he insisted that they not get married until the following October (after the Republican primary). They were married on 15 October 1948. She was thirty, he was thirty-five. Together, they had four children.

Ford was reelected twelve times to Congress, always by large majorities. Although he never introduced a single piece of major legislation, he worked hard and was well liked by fellow legislators on both sides of the aisle. Unlike his predecessor, he always flew home on weekends to attend to his constituents. By establishing a reputation as one of the hardest-working congressmen and ingrati-ating himself with party leaders, he soon became a rising star in the Republican ranks. After the drubbing the Republicans received at the polls in 1964, he suc-cessfully challenged Charles Halleck of Indiana for House minority leader. As the Republican leader in the House, he became a strident opponent of President Lyndon Johnson's Great Society programs, which he regarded as government gone awry. Although he supported Johnson's expansion of the war in Vietnam, he objected strenuously to his policy of "butter and guns," and he worked hard for Nixon's election in 1968.

Although Ford became angry at Nixon for not lending more support to Republican candidates in 1972, he remained loyal to the president even as the Watergate affair unfolded. He accepted Nixon's assertion that he was not involved in the cover-up. When Vice President Agnew was forced to resign in 1973, Nixon decided to replace him with Ford after congressional leaders stated that he would be the easiest to confirm, and the minority leader made clear that he had no intention of challenging Nixon's choice for the Republican nomination in 1976, Treasury Secretary John Connally of Texas. Ford still planned to retire in 1977.

For most of the eight months between Ford's appointment and Nixon's resignation, the new vice president remained in the background, continuing to believe in Nixon's innocence and thinking that the president would serve out his full term. When it became apparent that Nixon would be forced to resign or face impeachment, most political analysts anticipated that Ford would be a caretaker president, serving only until a new president was elected in 1976. Instead, he signed into law a $25 billion aid to education measure, a campaign reform act, consumer protection legislation, an extension of unemployment benefits, and a $4.8 billion measure to improve mass transit facilities. He also used his veto power sixty-six times and had only twelve of them overturned by a two-thirds vote in Congress.

Yet the Ford presidency was characterized by political miscalculation, bad judgment, and lack of vision. By merely adding Nixon's senior staff to his own staff, he almost assured the administrative disarray that encumbered his presidency. More detrimental were his decision to offer clemency to Vietnam-era draft evaders and deserters and his handling of the Nixon pardon, which were part of his effort to end two of the nation's most nightmarish events. Despite later charges to the contrary, no political deal was involved in Ford's decision to pardon Nixon. He decided on the pardon because, as he said, he felt Nixon had been punished enough, and, more important, he wanted to get on with the nation's other business. Nevertheless, Ford handled the pardon issue poorly, failing even to insist that Nixon give up his presidential papers and tapes or issue a statement of contrition. The pardon also destroyed Ford's honeymoon with the American people, millions of whom were already infuriated by his decision to grant clemency to Vietnam-era draft evaders.

In a period of both high unemployment and high inflation, Ford also vacillated between a tax cut to promote economic growth and budgetary restraints to curb inflation. He also badly mishandled the so-called *Mayaguez* incident, in which fifteen marines were killed and eight U.S. helicopters were downed when rescuing the crew of the merchant ship *Mayaguez,* which had been captured by the Khmer Rouge when it allegedly sailed into Cambodian waters. Not only were more lives lost in the rescue mission than the number of crew rescued, but the administration rejected the option of negotiations before the rescue mission.

Despite his promise not to seek the presidency when he agreed to become

Nixon's vice president, he changed his mind. After narrowly beating off a major challenge from Governor Reagan for the Republican nomination, he lost in a close election to the Democratic candidate, Jimmy Carter of Georgia. His pardon of Nixon and a major gaffe during his first debate with Carter, in which he maintained that Eastern Europe was not under Soviet domination, probably cost him the election. In November, he received 39.1 million popular votes and 240 electoral votes to Carter's 40.8 million popular votes and 290 electoral votes.

Ford toyed with the idea of challenging Carter again in 1980, but he gave the idea up when it became apparent that he could not win his party's nomination. Instead, he almost concluded a deal with the Republican nominee in 1980, Governor Reagan, to be his running mate after Reagan indicated a willingness to give Ford vast powers as his vice president, in effect establishing a copresidency. The deal fell through when Reagan decided that Ford's demands were excessive. After 1980, the former president expressed no further political aspirations.

While Ford had not ruled out another run for the White House after he left office in 1977, politics was not uppermost in his mind. Rather, he was concerned with making money.[104]

Exactly how much Ford was worth when he left the presidency is not entirely clear. At the time of his nomination for vice president in 1973, he listed his net wealth at $261,000, of which only $1,281 was in bank accounts. Most of his other assets were in the three residencies he and Betty owned: their residence in Alexandria ($70,000), their condominium in Vail ($65,000), and their Grand Rapids home, which they rented out ($25,000). Other investments included $49,000 in the congressional retirement system, $8,500 in life insurance policies, $9,000 in the Ford family paint company, and about $4,500 in stocks and mutual funds. The Fords had been able to pay off their three properties by using money from savings, borrowing against their and their children's life insurance policies, taking an advance against Ford's congressional salary, using a small inheritance Betty received from her parents, and earning between $12,000 and $15,000 a year for speeches the congressman gave. Even assuming Ford was able to save part of his $62,500 annual salary as vice president and his $200,000 annual salary as president, it is unlikely he would have been able to save much in three years.[105]

When he left the White House, in other words, Ford was comfortable. Just before leaving the White House, he was able to sell his Alexandria home, for which he had paid $34,000 in 1955, for $137,000, adding a substantial amount to his nest egg. He was not, however, a wealthy man, and most of his wealth was still in fixed investments. Although he could rely on a comfortable income (the equivalent of about $350,000 to $375,000 in 2009), as president, he had expanded his horizons, making wealthy new acquaintances, playing golf with celebrities in some of the nation's most expensive golf courses, and traveling extensively. Unlike another Midwesterner, Harry Truman, he was not content to return to Grand Rapids and live in his old house. He had gotten used to vacationing and golfing in sunny Southern California. He had grown especially fond of the exclusive

Rancho Mirage golf course near Palms Springs. He still had strong ties to Michigan, but not strong enough to want to experience its harsh winters.[106]

Ford's interest in making money did not mean that was his only concern. Like a number of former presidents before him, including Truman, he wanted to lecture and engage college students. After leaving the White House, he joined a conservative think tank, the American Enterprise Institute, which arranged for a series of twenty or so campus visits for him each year. In the following three years, he visited fifty-eight campuses, where he talked to students and faculty about national defense, American politics, and the domestic economy. Nevertheless, the former president's highest priority was earning enough so that he could move to California, enjoy an affluent lifestyle, and provide for his family after he died.[107]

On the day after the 1976 election, Ford asked his military aide, Robert F. Barrett, to be his executive assistant after he left office. Barrett accepted the offer, resigned his commission, and began the task of organizing the president's post-presidential career. At first, this involved mainly fending off such offers as a professorship, positions at think tanks, various investment opportunities, requests from television producers for paid interviews, and memberships on boards of businesses and charities. "Ford comes out and everybody likes him," recalled Barrett. Even the former president was astonished by the number of requests he received for his services. "I never had that experience before," he remarked.[108]

The most intriguing offer came from Norman R. Brokaw of the William Morris Agency. Brokaw had been introduced to Ford through Don Penny, one of the president's speechwriters, who had also been one of Brokaw's former clients, "I had gotten very close to the Ford family since I came to the White House," Penny later told Ron Brownstein of the *National Journal*, "and I became very concerned that he had a high falutin' job but he didn't have any money in the bank. So I said to him: 'I've got this friend in California named Brokaw who has got a tremendous talent . . . the bottom line is, after you meet Norman you won't be worth this $300,000 but $9 million, and that's a much better number.'"[109]

Ford did not forget his conversation with Penny. After he left the White House, the former president decided to move to Rancho Mirage. "We had some friends in Southern California who we could get together with," he later explained. "We would rent a place and spend about a week playing golf, relaxing, and we figured this was an ideal spot for Betty's health—she has arthritis. I like to play golf and there are a lot of golf courses here." However, living in one of the nation's most exclusive resorts cost a lot more than Ford could afford, even with his pensions and other investments.[110]

One of Ford's friends at Rancho Mirage was Leonard Firestone of the Firestone Tire family. The former president had Penny arrange another meeting with Brokaw at Firestone's home. There Ford told Brokaw that he was not interested in any full-time job or anything that lasted more than six months. He had had enough of that in Washington. He wanted the flexibility to pick and choose what he wanted to do. He was also not interested in being associated with any business enterprise in case he should decide to run for president again in 1980. He did not want to have to explain his business ties to the electorate.

Brokaw then put together for Ford the most elaborate money-making plan of any former president. First, he arranged for the publication of the former president's memoirs by Harper and Row and *Reader's Digest*. The arrangement included a contract for the publication of Betty Ford's memoirs with a combined advance of $1 million.[111] Ford also signed a $1 million contract with NBC to appear in documentaries and be available for interviews over the next five years. He even endorsed a series of collectors' medals commemorating great presidential moments—a new low point for former presidents. He also went on the lecture circuit. For each lecture, he received $10,000 to $15,000. "I saw it as an extension of the office of the presidency," Brokaw commented in explaining the plan he had prepared for the former president. "Before, Presidents didn't go out and get a network deal or necessarily go out and lecture. I don't recall Harry Truman going out and lecturing or doing some broadcast deal, but I felt time had moved on."[112]

Brokow was not accurate, of course. Truman lectured to students and other groups, although usually at the Truman Library. Eisenhower was well paid for the series of interviews he conducted with Walter Cronkite in 1961 and 1964, and Johnson received $300,000 for his own interviews with the CBS correspondent. Nixon was paid even more handsomely for the Frost–Nixon interviews. All these presidents were also were paid large advances for their memoirs. In writing their memoirs and other books and engaging in their other activities, these ex-presidents were as much concerned with their place in history as with their advance and royalties.

Not so Ford. His former press secretary, Jerald terHorst, who had resigned his position over Ford's decision to pardon Nixon, was so appalled by his former boss's commercialization of the post-presidency that he wrote an article in the *Washington Post,* "President Ford, Inc.," in which he condemned Ford's activities as an extraordinary example of "the huckstering of an ex-president." Ford, he remarked, had transformed "the former First Family into something of a conglomerate."[113]

Once Ford announced in 1980 that he would not seek a full term as president, he felt free to pursue the corporate ties he believed it would have been politically unwise to follow while still pondering running again for president. He became a member of the board of directors, and in some cases a well-paid adviser, to a number of mostly moderate-sized corporations. Because of his extroverted personality, his outspoken commitment to the free enterprise system, and the many friendships and connections he had developed throughout his political career, corporate leaders wanted to have him on their boards of directors. Besides giving them cachet, they would have an individual who enjoyed mixing with influential figures from throughout the world. As a paid board member, he could be more than a useful figurehead. He could lend his expertise on domestic and foreign affairs and open doors that might not otherwise be open to them.

Ford was not naive. He understood as well as anybody how valuable a commodity he was. Part of his justification in joining the companies he did was that he could be selective and associate himself only with those corporations he respected and whose leadership he knew. He also shied away from defense contractors, almost all of whose business was with the government. "I've never asked to join a company: I've always responded to a request," he remarked. "I was very scrupulous in picking those where there was no conflict of interest. I was very careful to be affiliated with companies that I think had a good reputation. I probably turned down three [offers] for every one I accepted."[114]

The first corporate board he joined was an international oil drilling company, the Sante Fe International Corporation, whose chairman, Roderick M. Hills, had worked for Ford in the White House and who then served as chairman of the Securities and Exchange Commission. In September 1981, the company was acquired by Kuwait Petroleum Corporation, but Ford remained on the board until 1986. Besides the drilling company, Ford accepted invitations to be a board member from a number of other companies, including G. K. Technologies; Shearson Loeb Rhodes, later bought by the American Express Company; Tiger International Inc.; Texas Commerce Bank; Beneficial Corporation of New Jersey; the Charter Company, an oil, insurance, and communication conglomerate; AMAX, a land resources concern; and the Pebble Beach Corporation, a subsidiary of 20th Century Fox Film Corporation. In all, Ford became a board member of nine companies and a consultant to five of them and to three others, including two not-for-profit organizations.[115]

By all accounts, the former president was a diligent and hardworking member of the boards on which he served, not merely a figurehead. He read carefully the materials he received ahead of the board meetings. Although he normally deferred to other board members who knew more about the business than he, he was not reluctant to ask questions and offer suggestions. Several of the companies said they valued especially his ability to analyze trends in government policy and world affairs. His pay for serving on the boards varied, but $25,000 to $35,000 annually from each company was not unusual.[116]

Ford made more money as a consultant than he did as a corporate director. In addition to his director's stipend, for example, he received $100,000 a year for his advice to AMAX and $120,000 annually from the American Express Company. His activities as a business consultant varied considerably. Although the former president denied lobbying for a firm he represented, he did acknowledge assessing how best to approach officials in government. For the Charter Oil Company, he played an even more important role. Charter sent him on an eleven-nation trip to the Middle East and Europe to secure long- and short-term crude oil supplies and to confirm credit arrangements made in Europe.[117]

The former president did not limit his business ties to consultancies and corporate directorships. He also joined into a number of business relationships with his wealthy friends, including part ownership of two Colorado radio stations and various real estate ventures. As early as 1979, even before he announced that he would not seek the Republican nomination for president, he joined with his friend and now neighbor at Rancho Mirage, Leonard Firestone, to form Fordstone, a company that invested in a $90 million hotel and residential project called the Mirada, which a Houston-based development firm wanted to build in the hills surrounding Rancho Mirage. In 1983, the former president helped to defeat a referendum by local environmentalists to stop the project.[118]

By 1983, the *New York Times* was reporting that the former president had an annual income of about $1 million (the equivalent of about $2.3 million in 2009). In addition, he owned three homes: his principal residence at Rancho Mirage valued at nearly $1 million; a spectacular ten-room ski chalet that he had built in Beaver Creek along the ski slopes high above the Vail valley, valued at $2.5 million; and a large new condominium apartment in Los Angeles valued at more than $500,000. "The happiest politician in the United States today, without question, is Gerald Rudolph Ford, the 38th president, who lives and works on a golf course here in the beautiful Coachilla Valley between the San Jacinto and Little San Bernardino Mountains," wrote the famed columnist James Reston from Rancho Mirage in March 1982. "Jerry has it all figured out," Reston continued. "He will be 69 on July 14—Bastille Day—and looks like 60, or even younger in his slacks, light blue sweater and fire-engine red shirt: no pretense, no books he wants to write, no advice he wants to give. He's not mad at anybody, and nobody's mad at him." In his view, "the best job in America was not President but ex-president, with many of the advantages of the White House and none of the disadvantages."[119]

By the time Reston wrote his article, Ford had already completed most of the obligations that he had agreed to after leaving the White House. Because his occasional appearances on NBC did not attract much interest, the network and former president agreed mutually in 1979 to cancel the remainder of his five-year contract. In 1979, Ford also published his memoirs, *A Time to Heal: The Autobiography of Gerald R. Ford,* which had been mostly ghostwritten by Trevor Armbrister, a respected reporter and journalist. Ford had spent several hundred hours being interviewed by Armbrister and checking and annotating drafts of chapters. A number of other people, including archivists at the Gerald R. Ford Library in Ann Arbor, Michigan, helped with the research and fact-checking.[120]

Ford did not, however, devote nearly as much time preparing his memoirs as his predecessors. Certainly he did not assemble teams of researchers, as Nixon or Johnson did, to reconstruct the major events of his administration. The volume had all the earmarks of a ghostwritten work by a talented journalist. It was well written and the narrative flowed easily, but it provided few revelations and insights of a personal or historical nature. Although the former president offered a strong and reasoned argument for his pardoning of Nixon, his justification of the *Mayaguez* rescue mission and his effort as House minority leader to impeach Supreme Court Justice William Douglas seemed disingenuous. Too much of the book was also wasted on trivia, and it offered little of importance that could not be garnered from the public record.

Another important piece of unfinished business that Ford completed before Reston wrote his article was the construction and dedication in 1981 of the Gerald R. Ford Library and the Gerald R. Ford Museum. Ford was the first and only president to separate his library from his museum. The library was constructed on the new North Campus of the University of Michigan in Ann Arbor, while the museum was built in Grand Rapids, 133 miles to the west. As the place where researchers would come to view Ford's presidential papers, it made sense to have them in one of the nation's most vital university towns and within easy driving distance to Detroit. Locating the Ford Museum in a newly revitalized part of Grand Rapids was intended by the former president to give a boost to his hometown's economy by making it more of a tourist attraction. According to a Ford Library archivist, the split of the two institutions was also an attempt by the president to shield them from growing complaints about the excessive growth of presidential libraries.[121]

Funds for building the library and museum were raised through the efforts of the Gerald Ford Commemorative Committee established in 1977, the University of Michigan, which had donated the land for the library, and local and county officials in Ann Arbor and Grand Rapids. Like his predecessors, Ford also actively solicited funds for the two structures, determined that "when the last tree is planted, all the bills will be paid." Construction of the $4.3 million, 50,000-square-foot library was completed in 1981. Intended to harmonize with the neighboring Bentley Library and other buildings on the North Campus, it was a highly functional but nondescript two-story low-lying structure with pale red brick and tinted glass. It was dedicated in April 1981 with former president Ford and members of his administration in attendance. The former president appeared tan and, at 192 pounds, slimmer than he was when he left the White House. According to reporters, he looked younger than his sixty-seven years.[122]

The Ford Museum was more costly and architecturally more striking than the library. Built at a cost of $11 million, the sleek, 44,000-square-foot, two-story glass-and-concrete triangular museum was also the central attraction in a twenty-acre park complex along the west bank of the Grand River that meanders through Grand Rapids's downtown area. Besides the former president and most of his cabinet, those in attendance at its dedication in September included President Reagan, Vice President George Bush, leaders of the Democratic and Republican parties, and several foreign leaders. "They say you can't go home again," Ford commented before a crowd of several thousand. "Well, they're wrong." The high point of his life, he continued, "is here today, in my hometown among my friends."[123]

One of those not present at the dedication of the Ford Museum was former president Jimmy Carter. Part of the reason was that he was still nursing the scars of his defeat by President Reagan and was not prepared to share a platform with a person he believed was unfit to serve in the Oval Office. Another reason was the ill will still left over from the 1976 campaign and the fact that Ford had been highly critical of Carter's presidency, even though he had supported Carter on such important matters as the normalization of relations with the People's Republic of China, the transfer of the Panama Canal and Canal Zone to Panama, and the sale of F-15 bombers to Saudi Arabia.[124]

A month after the dedication of the Ford Museum, however, President Anwar Sadat of Egypt was assassinated. Because President Reagan, who had also been nearly murdered in 1981, and Vice President George Bush were advised for security reasons not to attend Sadat's funeral, the president asked the three living ex-presidents, Nixon, Ford, and Carter, to be part of a large delegation representing the United States at the funeral. The three former leaders agreed. The coolness between them, both at a meeting at the White House before the flight to Egypt and then on the long flight itself, was palpable. "Oil and water, you know," Carter said of Ford while on the flight. Curiously enough, Nixon broke the ice between the two men. They found they actually shared common views on a number of matters, especially on the urgent need to find a solution to the Palestinian question before the Arab–Israeli problem could be resolved.[125]

On their return flight, Carter and Ford held a joint news conference during which they agreed on the need for Israel to give up the remaining territories it had occupied since the Suez war of 1967, including the Golan Heights and the West Bank, and to negotiate with the Palestinian Liberation Organization (PLO). "At some point, this has to happen," Ford remarked with respect to negotiations with the PLO. "I would not want to pick the date today, but in a realistic way that dialogue had to take place." Carter added, "There is no way for Israel ever to have assured permanent peace without resolving the Palestinian issue, so I think these discussions have to be done." What made these statements by Ford and Carter so striking, and so annoying to the Reagan administration, was that U.S. policy was not to recognize the PLO until it recognized the existence of the state of Israel. For the first time in the nation's history, two former presidents were stating publicly a foreign policy position contrary to existing policy.[126]

The flight home began a friendship between the two former presidents that lasted until Ford's death in 2006. Although they disagreed on most domestic issues, they found that they had much in common. Both of them had served in the navy, were outdoorsmen, loved skiing, and shared almost identical views on foreign policy. On the plane, they agreed to collaborate on future projects. "We've made an agreement never to discuss domestic policy issues because the gulf between us is so wide," Ford explained. "But on foreign policy our views are similar, so we can work together on joint projects very effectively."[127]

As the years passed, the two former presidents found that they moved closer together on domestic matters. Ford, who had always considered himself a moderate Republican, in the manner of Eisenhower and Nixon rather than of Goldwater and Reagan, became increasingly disenchanted by the right-wing capture of the Republican Party and increasingly critical of the Reagan administration's policies on such matters as the environment, health issues, and opposition to the Equal Rights Amendment (ERA). Like Ford, Carter always regarded himself as a fiscal conservative and a moderate on most domestic issues. He was even more of an environmentalist than Ford, and his antipathy toward Reagan only increased during his two administrations. So while Ford remained loyal to the Republican Party and Carter continued to support Democratic candidates for president, they discovered that the chasm between them philosophically and politically was not all that insurmountable. Both men even criticized Reagan for his increases in the defense budget. "I don't know of any basic philosophical differences between me and President Ford," Carter even remarked in 2005.[128]

Sustaining the growing friendship between the two former presidents was the comradeship that developed between their two wives, Betty and Rosalynn. One problem that caused Ford considerable grief during his presidency was his wife's growing addiction to alcohol and pain pills. In 1974, doctors had discovered a lump on her breast, causing her to undergo a full mastectomy. Fortunately, later tests revealed that the cancer had not spread. Unfortunately, her brush with death made her increasingly dependent on drugs and drinking. She had started to drink while her husband was still in Congress. As he climbed the political ladder, her drinking became worse. "I was resentful of Jerry's being gone so much," she said. "I was feeling terribly neglected. . . . The loneliness, the being left to yourself at night, is what makes marriages crack, makes liquor more attractive." Making matters worse was a pinched nerve in her neck, causing her considerable pain, which she tried to relieve with pills and alcohol.[129]

Mrs. Ford was able to keep private her addiction problem while her husband was in the White House. After they moved to California, the former president and her children, who also sensed the seriousness of her problem, persuaded her to enter the dependency program at the U.S. Naval Hospital in Long Beach.[130] After successfully completing the program, she spoke to her friends about the need for a center that emphasized the special needs of women. She also went public with her addiction problem, just as she had after her mastectomy at a time when the nation was still reluctant to talk about breast cancer. Together with Leonard Firestone, a recovering alcoholic, she established in 1982 the nonprofit Betty Ford Center on a twenty-acre campus in Rancho Mirage. It has since become one of the premier dependency treatment centers for both men and women.[131]

Rosalynn Carter had made mental health issues one of her priorities as first lady. She and Betty were also outspoken supporters of the ERA. Because they shared similar concerns and took up causes in which they believed deeply, they became good friends and soon found themselves lobbying together on such issues as substance abuse prevention, mental health, and the ERA. Their friendship nourished the ties between their husbands.[132]

Although Carter did not attend the dedication of the Ford library or museum, he agreed to cohost a two-day conference in February at the Ford Library on public policy and communication; in return, Ford agreed to cochair a gathering at the Carter Center. "To my knowledge this was the first time two former presidents ever cooperated in such a tandem fashion," Ford remarked in opening the meeting on public policy and communication. Subsequently, Ford cochaired several conferences at the Carter Center and at Emory University on such matters as arms control and the Middle East, both of which received considerable attention in the media.[133]

Ford and Carter also coauthored a number of articles that appeared in mainstream newspapers and magazines. An article they published in *Reader's Digest,* in which they criticized Israel for not living up to the Camp David accord, stirred a hornet's nest of controversy, especially within the American Jewish community. Israel, they wrote in February 1983, "has shown little inclination to grant real autonomy to the Palestinians in the West Bank and Gaza areas. It has continued to confiscate properties in the occupied territories and to build settlements as if to create a *de facto* Israeli ascendancy there. . . . This has caused both of us deep disappointment." Other articles they coauthored covered the gamut from support of free trade and the ERA to criticism of the tobacco lobby.[134]

At the request of two former senior White House aides, James Cannon, who was domestic policy adviser to President Ford, and Stuart Eizenstat, who served in the same position under President Carter, the two former presidents worked together in 1988 with a bipartisan panel of twenty-five experts, including such prominent government alumni as Henry Kissinger, Edmund Muskie, and Brent Scowcroft, to prepare *American Agenda: Report to the Forty-First President of the United States of America.* In the report, they set forth a series of proposals for balancing the federal budget, which, they commented, was the nation's most pressing concern. Among their recommendations for reducing the budget was to raise taxes. They also recommended slowing down increases in the defense budget and cutting the cost of Medicare. Although President George H. W. Bush had vowed as a candidate not to raise taxes and allowed the report to gather dust, it was presented to him in a high-profile ceremony at the White House. It was even chosen by the Book-of-the Month Club as a main selection.[135]

Ford and Carter also lobbied together in 1993, during President Bill Clinton's administration, for the North American Free Trade Zone (NAFTA), for the China Trade Bill, and against initiatives in 1996 to legalize drugs in California and Arizona. Interestingly enough, Clinton had a much closer relationship with Ford, with whom he often conferred from the White House and with whom he played golf in Vail while vacationing in 1993, than with Carter, whose personal diplomacy sometimes conflicted with the administration's foreign policy.[136]

During the Senate trial after the impeachment of Clinton for lying under oath and other charges, Ford and Carter issued a joint statement in the *New York Times* calling for a censure rather than for his removal from office by the Senate. "In the wake of President Clinton's impeachment by the House of Representatives,

Caroline Kennedy and Senator Ted Kennedy present Ford with the John F. Kennedy Foundation Profile in Courage Award, 21 May 2001. The former president was especially touched by this award, regarding it as final vindication of his highly controversial decision to grant Richard Nixon a pardon for his cover-up of the Watergate Affair. (Courtesy of Gerald R. Ford Library.)

America once again suffers from a grievous and deepening wound. Our people are angrily divided. Our political institutions are called into question. . . . It is with this in mind that we personally favor a bipartisan resolution of censure by the Senate."[137]

In August 1999, Clinton awarded Ford the Presidential Medal of Freedom for holding the nation together during the Watergate scandal. At the time he received the medal, the former president had just turned eighty-six. He was still, however, in relatively good health. He had had to give up skiing years earlier because of two joint replacements in his knees. He was also doing less traveling and had stopped making speeches. He still gave occasional interviews, swam a quarter mile in his pool both morning and night, golfed, and watched his weight carefully. He and Betty divided their year between Rancho Mirage and Vail at Christmastime and in the summers when temperatures in the California desert topped the century mark. Three of their four children were married. The former president enjoyed being with his children and ten grandchildren during annual family reunions at Christmas in Vail.[138]

In 2000, the former president went to Washington for the 200th birthday celebration of the White House. In August, he also attended the Republican presidential convention in Philadelphia. While at the convention, he suffered two mild strokes caused by atherosclerosis, fatty deposits in the blood vessels that impair blood flow. However, he recovered fully, and the next year, he was able to travel to the Kennedy Library in Boston to receive from Caroline Kennedy Schlossberg the Profile in Courage Award for his pardon of Nixon.

Being named recipient of the prize was one of the highlights of Ford's post-presidency. For the former president, the award represented final vindication that he had acted correctly—indeed, courageously—in pardoning Nixon. Although the pardon had led to his defeat in 1976, the nation had slowly come around to his explanation that pardoning Nixon was necessary to bring closure to the Watergate affair. "I myself contributed to the din [of cynicism about the pardon] with a series of screeds about unequal justice," wrote the highly respected columnist for the Washington *Post* Mary McGrory in commenting about Ford's receipt of the award. "But almost 27 years later, it looks a little different. What seemed then to be cynicism now looks more like courage."[139]

Almost to the year he died, Ford remained vigorous and active. Four months after he received the Profile in Courage Award, the terrorist bombings of 11 September 2001 occurred. Despite their age, the Fords flew to Washington, where, holding hands, they participated in the National Day of Remembrance Ceremony. Ford also participated in various charitable golf tournaments, including his own Jerry Ford Invitational Golf Tournament in Vail. Also in Vail he enjoyed watching the American Ski Classic, featuring the Jerry Ford Celebrity Cup. In July 2004, a year into the war with Iraq, Ford gave an interview to Bob Woodward, the investigative reporter of the *Washington Post,* in which he discussed his views on the war. In the interview, which was embargoed at Ford's request until after his death, the former president commented that he disagreed "very strongly" with President George Bush's decision to invade Iraq. "I don't think I would have gone to war," he remarked. He was also critical of Vice President Dick Cheney, who had been his chief of staff when he was president, and Defense Secretary Donald Rumsfeld, who had also served as his chief of staff before moving over to the Pentagon. He was especially hard on Cheney. "He was an excellent chief of staff," he said about the vice president. "But I think Cheney has become much more pugnacious" as vice president.[140]

The former president's health had begun to decline at the beginning of the year. In January, he spent eleven days at the Eisenhower Medical Center in Rancho Mirage recovering from pneumonia. In July, while vacationing at Vail, he was hospitalized for shortness of breath. The next month, he was admitted to the Mayo Clinic in Rochester, Minnesota, where he underwent an angioplasty procedure and was fitted with a pacemaker. In October, because of poor health, he was unable to attend the dedication of the Gerald R. Ford School of Public Policy at the University of Michigan. Confined to bed at his home in Rancho Mirage and suffering from end-stage coronary artery disease, he died on 26 December 2006 at age ninety-three. At the time of his death, he was the longest-lived U.S. president.

13

Citizen/Politician of the World

Carter, Reagan

Historians and the public alike have broadly acclaimed Jimmy Carter as one of the best—if not the best—ex-presidents. Working through the Carter Center, which he established after he left the White House, Carter has sought to help the poor, stop the spread of disease, support human rights, and bring about world peace through conflict resolution and the monitoring of democratic elections. He has also become inextricably associated with Habitat for Humanity, an organization that builds homes for families in need.[1]

There has, however, been an aspect of the Carter post-presidency that has been largely ignored. As a former president, he redefined the role and expectations of former presidents. A theme throughout this book has been the transition of the ex-presidency from one defined by the republican ideal of the citizen president returning to private life after fulfilling his civic responsibility to former presidents assuming an increasingly more active public life, even marketing themselves for personal gain.

The precise role that ex-presidents should play, however, was never entirely resolved. In his classic study, *The American Commonwealth* (1888), the British jurist Lord Bryce proposed following the Roman practice and inviting them to become members of the Senate. William Jennings Bryan made a similar proposal, and it remained a recurring idea throughout much of the twentieth century. As late as 1960, former president Harry Truman proposed making ex-presidents ex officio members of both houses of Congress. According to Truman, he had been considering this proposal since being in the U.S. Senate. In his book *Mr. Citizen* (1960), he devoted an entire chapter to the topic. "Congress," he wrote, "should pass enabling legislation designating former presidents of the United States as *Free members of the Congress*. . . . They would have the right to take part in debate . . . and the right to sit [in] on any meetings of any committee, subcommittee or joint committee of both houses and take part in discussion. They would not, however, have the right to vote." Truman concluded, "My proposal would not only utilize men of talent and experience who could render valued public service but would also cushion the shock when an abrupt change in administration takes place."[2]

For the most part, however, the proposal to give former presidents a role in government was dismissed even by the former presidents. Their opposition ranged from the lighthearted remarks of Grover Cleveland that ex-presidents should be shot and William Howard Taft's stated preference to be poisoned rather than be made an ex officio member of Congress to former president Rutherford B. Hayes's comments that the Senate had already become a "rich man's place" and that making a former president a member of Congress would undermine the principle of popular government. Seventy years later, former president Herbert Hoover also threw ice on the idea, remarking that he didn't "look at the prospect of sitting on a hard cushion for several hours a day and listening to speeches as being attractive." In January 1954, Democratic senator William G. Magnuson of Washington proposed legislation to add former presidents to the National Security Council. However, his proposal failed to gain any traction even in the Senate.[3]

This lack of definition about the role of ex-presidents continued throughout most of the twentieth century. As late as 1990, former president Gerald Ford commented at a conference on former presidents, "I have known seven former presidents personally. . . . If you look at their activities after leaving office, you will be hard put to find a common pattern. What we do as former presidents is very much a matter of personal choice."[4]

At the same conference, the eminent historian Daniel Boorstin proposed a new national council composed not only of former presidents but of prominent members of the other branches of government. Although Boorstin was vague on specifics, he suggested that each of the former presidents might name three members of what he also referred to as "A House of Experience," modeled in part on the British House of Lords.[5]

A few speakers at the conference showed a polite interest in Boorstin's proposal, but most of them thought that while presidents could use their influence on behalf of certain causes and/or serve on committees and commissions, it should be up to them to decide on how best to spend their years as emeritus presidents. The former news anchor for CBS Roger Mudd even went so far as to remark, "It seems to me that the day a president becomes a former president he becomes a former president—not a former president without a portfolio, or a former president at large or a former president in loco presidentis."[6]

Former president Jimmy Carter had a different concept of the role of ex-presidents. Although he retired to private life in his home in Plains, Georgia, after being defeated in his 1980 bid for reelection, he still believed he had a Christian obligation to use the influence he had as an ex-president to serve mankind. As to how, he was not exactly sure. However, in his farewell address of 14 January

1981, he laid out some of his ideas. Although often neglected by historians, the message proved to be one of the most important that Carter gave during his presidency. "In a few days," he began, "I will . . . take up once more the only title in our democracy superior to that of president, the title of citizen." In making this unremarkable comment, Carter appeared to be speaking in the vernacular of traditional republicanism. As he soon made clear, that was not his intention. "I want to lay aside my role as leader of one nation," he continued, "and speak to you as a *fellow citizen of the world* about three issues: The threat of nuclear destruction, our stewardship of the physical resources of our planet, and the preeminence of the basic rights of human beings" (my italics).[7] In effect, Carter turned the republican definitions of a good citizen and the role of former presidents on their heads. A good citizen was a citizen of the world engaged in ongoing public service. It followed that his role as an ex-president was to use the influence bestowed on him by having served in the Oval Office for the welfare of mankind.

Carter was, of course, not the first former president to attempt to redefine the role of ex-presidents or to view his responsibility after leaving the White House as one of engaging in worldwide humanitarian efforts. Millard Fillmore believed that presidents leaving office should not return to private life as common citizens. Hoover spent much of his post-presidency in the same way he had before becoming president: engaging in public service and humanitarian efforts. Carter was also not offering a template that he believed other presidents had to follow. Nevertheless, by the multitude of his own activities as a citizen of the world, Carter was able to go beyond anything ever conceived by his predecessors, including even Hoover. Furthermore, he reached out to Republicans, like Gerald Ford, and to the private sector to join him in his work.

Carter's outspoken views on such issues as the Middle East and his sometimes brazen efforts at diplomacy, even against the wishes of incumbent presidents, led to a backlash of criticism by some American officials and segments of the American public. The fact, however, that he appeared to gain the attention and respect of most Americans seemed to speak to what they valued about, and even expected from, their former presidents. With the exception of Carter's successor, Ronald Reagan, who regarded himself as a citizen/politician and who was diagnosed with Alzheimer's disease after he left the White House, each former president following Carter has engaged in different forms of well-publicized philanthropic activity.

|

Like President Barack Obama, Carter's rise to the presidency was meteoric. At the time he decided to run for president, however, he was even less well known than Obama, and his chances of winning the White House were far slimmer. Born on 1 October 1924 in Plains, Georgia, a community of about 500 people in the state's southwestern part, he was the first president to be born in a hospital. The oldest of four children, he grew up on the family's 350-acre farm in Archery, a predominantly black community a few miles from Plains. His father, Earl, was a successful local businessman and farmer who owned a considerable amount of real estate and operated a warehouse and brokerage in peanuts. His mother, Lillian Gordy, was a registered nurse.

Carter had a typical childhood for a white youngster growing up in the rural South whose father was a successful member of the community. Like other youngsters of the rural South, Jimmy had his daily chores. He was also obsessed with hunting and fishing. It was not only the outdoors and the challenges of the two sports he loved, but also the opportunity to be with his father, whom he adored. He also loved his mother, Lillian, but she was more unconventional than her husband and more distant from her children. Although she never quite crossed the bounds of traditional Southern mores—she was never, for example, a foe of segregation or a champion of civil rights—she tried their outer limits. As a working mother, she was not always home, and when she had free time, she preferred reading to household or maternal chores.

It would be easy to overemphasize the formative impact of Jimmy's upbringing on his later political career and presidency. Certainly it had an important bearing: Jimmy's father was a stern disciplinarian who worked his son hard and who expected him to be obedient and follow the Golden Rule. President Carter's own commitment to hard work and sense of discipline can clearly be traced to his father. So can his love of outdoor sports and the environment.

From his mother and one of his high school teachers, Carter also developed a lifelong commitment to learning and a love of reading, which was carried out even at the supper table. President Carter's concern for the poor and the underprivileged and his commitment to racial and gender equality were also unquestionably influenced by his mother's work with African Americans. The importance of faith in Carter's life can be traced back to the fact that he came from a devoutly religious family and was expected to attend Sunday school and services on Sundays. Most important, Carter's personal sense of self-confidence and commitment to doing what he believed was right, regardless of its political consequences, was traceable to the fact that his upbringing was a rooted one—rooted in a mentoring father, nurturing and loving parents, and a sense of place and certitude.

The formative elements of Carter's later political career and presidency were, however, not so much his rural childhood but rather what came after he left Plains. In terms of personality, he fit neither the gregarious mode of his father nor the curmudgeon-like qualities of his mother. Nor was there anything in his boyhood that set him apart from other relatively privileged and bright children of the rural South or that hinted at a political career. In physical appearance, he was good-looking, but not strikingly so. He stood just five feet, six inches tall at the end of his senior year in high school (he would grow three inches over the next year) and weighed about 130 pounds; his only memorable features were his pale blue eyes and broad, toothy smile. Indeed, convention, rather than a lack of it, characterized Carter's younger years.

After finishing high school in 1941, Carter spent the next two years boning up on his science background at Georgia Southwestern College and the Georgia Institute of Technology before being admitted to the U.S. Naval Academy, which had been his goal since he was six years old. The challenge of his studies at Georgia Tech and the discipline he endured at the academy had a lasting impact on him, forcing him to focus his attention and leaving him with a determination to achieve and a sense of vulnerability he had never experienced before. He also turned inward, becoming a very private person. He worked hard, excelled in his studies, and received high grades, finishing in the top 10 percent of his class. Aside from his good academic record, however, there was little else that made him stand out at the academy.

After graduating from Annapolis in 1946, Jimmy married Rosalynn Smith, whom he had known since childhood but did not begin dating until after he returned from Annapolis. Like Jimmy, Rosalynn had set high standards for herself, graduating high school as class valedictorian. She also shared Jimmy's desire to see more of the world beyond Plains.

Carter spent the next seven years in the navy. In 1951, he was assigned to the development of the first atomic submarine. Before he received the assignment, he had to be screened by the person most responsible for the navy's atomic submarine program, Captain (later Admiral) Hyman Rickover, a brilliant but demanding naval officer. Rickover asked the junior officer whether he had done his best at Annapolis. After reflection, Carter said he had not, to which Rickover countered, "Why not?" The interview had a profound and lasting impact on Carter. "Why Not the Best?" would be the theme of his drive for the presidency and the title of his campaign autobiography.[8]

Rickover put the young officer to work on the *Seawolf,* one of the prototypes of the nuclear submarine. Carter's future now seemed settled. He was a seasoned submariner and lieutenant senior grade, working on the latest submarine technology. He had been selected to be the chief engineer of the *Seawolf* when it put to sea. He was also the father of three boys. Both Rosalynn and he loved the navy life—the work, the new experiences, the camaraderie that existed among the officers. He would therefore pursue his career in the navy.

Then word came from Plains that Carter's father was dying, and his life abruptly changed. After his father's death, Carter went through a crisis. "I began to think about the relative significance of his life and mine," Carter later remarked. "He was an integral part of the community. . . . He was his own boss, and his life was stabilized by the slow evolutionary change in the local societal structure." The more he compared his life with his father's, the more he was convinced his father's way had been the more satisfying one. In 1953, he, Rosalynn, and their three boys came home to Plains to stay.[9]

Carter's first years back in Plains were difficult as he and Rosalynn tried to readjust to rural living and rebuild his father's faltering warehouse peanut business. Things soon improved. After a few years, Carter's business was prospering. Active in community affairs, he had become by 1960 one of the town's most respected business and civic leaders.

Although Carter had shown little interest in politics to this point, when some of his friends encouraged him to run for office, Carter responded favorably. The ambition that had made him so determined and competitive was still a driving force of his personality, but it is undeniable that he also had a real commitment to civic duty. As his first bid for public office, Carter ran for a seat in the Georgia senate in 1962. As in future races, he made personal character—his compared with that of his opponents—the central campaign issue. It was an "amateurish and whirlwind" effort, Carter later remarked. Although he lost the primary by 139 votes, the election involved a tampered ballot box, forcing a new election, which Carter won by a comfortable margin.[10] Carter's campaign for the senate had a profound impact on the way he looked at politics. He was especially offended by the gerrymandering, cronyism, and special interests that were part of Georgia politics.[11]

Carter served two terms in the state senate, where he established a record as a moderate progressive who supported good-government measures and educational reform. By 1965, he was named in a Georgia newspaper poll as one of the state's most influential legislators. Spurred by this to seek higher office, the next year he announced he was running for governor. Virtually unknown outside his own district, Carter conducted a grueling gubernatorial campaign. On the eve of the election, he fully expected that he would be in a runoff against either former governor Ellis Arnall or Lester Maddox, a restaurant owner who had gained national notoriety for defying integration by standing in the doorway of his establishment holding an ax handle. The next morning, however, Carter learned that he had finished a close third. He fell into a deep depression, which was lifted only by the solace he found as a born-again Christian.

Although religion had always been an important part of his daily life, it was not at the core of his very existence. Now Carter went through a second experience of conversion, and his renewed Christian faith only intensified his commitment to public service. Although he never thought that his faith provided unerring answers to contemporary problems, he was more convinced than ever that his purpose was to serve God's will, and he interpreted this to mean serving humanity. As a result, his secular sense of public duty became firmly wedded to a gospel of service based on his strong religious convictions.

At peace with himself and convinced that he had good work to do, Carter decided to run for governor again in 1970 and to win whatever the cost. The result was a campaign in which he appealed to segregationists and white supremacists that even his own advisers later regretted. He went on to win the primary and then an overwhelming victory in the general election.

Considering his campaign pitch, almost no one could anticipate that, as governor, Carter would promote racial moderation, yet that is precisely what happened. His main goal as governor, however, was to reorganize state government in order to make it more efficient. At times he was his own worst enemy, committing many of the same strategic and tactical mistakes he would make as president, such as resisting efforts at compromise and coalition building when the reorganization proposal was finally submitted to the Georgia general assembly. Yet Carter succeeded in getting most of his program passed by the legislature.

By the end of his second year in office, Carter appeared to typify a new group of Southern governors known for their moderate racial views and progressive response to economic and social change in the South. He was even featured in a cover story in *Time* as part of a political renaissance taking place in the South.[12]

So it was that in 1972, after only two years as Georgia's governor, Carter turned his attention to the nation's top political prize: the White House. Even though he was virtually unknown outside of Georgia, he was encouraged to seek the Democratic nomination by his young aide, Hamilton Jordan, who recognized what more seasoned politicians missed: the significance of changes that had taken place in the Democratic Party's guidelines for selecting delegates to the national convention, and the shift in the nation's political temper. He also sensed a real advantage in the fact that Carter was not part of the Washington establishment. Chalking up victories in the Iowa caucuses and the early primaries in 1976, he was able to gain the Democratic nomination and then to defeat President Gerald Ford narrowly in November.

Elected president mainly because he offered the American people new leadership, Carter almost immediately alienated Congress by cutting from the budget a series of popular water projects. He also presented Congress with an overly ambitious legislative agenda, which included welfare reform, a comprehensive energy program, hospital cost containment legislation, tax reform, and Social Security reform. By August 1977, every one of these initiatives had become stalled on Capitol Hill. Meanwhile, a sluggish economy and the fact that the president was more concerned with attacking inflation than with dealing with high unemployment alienated many Democratic constituencies.

Besides domestic issues, Carter devoted considerable attention to foreign policy. In March 1978, he won a major victory when the Senate ratified the Panama Canal agreement turning over ownership and control of the canal to Panama by the year 2000. Six months later, Egyptian president Anwar Sadat and Israeli prime minister Menachem Begin signed the Camp David accords ending their nations' long conflict and providing the framework for a settlement of the entire Arab–Israeli dispute. The next month he won an important legislative victory when lawmakers finally approved his long-stalled energy program

The considerable political capital that Carter gained as a result of Camp David and his success on Capitol Hill was short-lived. As the nation experienced slow economic growth, high unemployment, and high inflation, the president's approval ratings spiraled downward. Carter fell so low in the polls that many political observers thought the Democrats would turn to Senator Edward Kennedy of Massachusetts as their presidential nominee in 1980.

The political landscape was then dramatically changed by the seizure in November 1979 of the American embassy in Tehran and the taking of fifty American hostages and the Soviet invasion of Afghanistan. Carter reacted to the hostage crisis by trying to gain the hostages' release through diplomatic means. He responded to the Afghan invasion by imposing a grain embargo on the Soviet Union and asking the Senate to delay consideration of the SALT II agreement, which he had signed with Soviet leader Leonid Brezhnev. As a result of his handling of these two crises, Carter was able to fend off the Kennedy challenge and win the Democratic presidential nomination.

Yet the hostage crisis, together with the slumping economy, ultimately helped defeat Carter's bid for reelection. A failed military mission in April 1980 to rescue the hostages became another entry in the list of failures that many Americans attributed to the president. On 4 November, Reagan was able to win an overwhelming victory over Carter, receiving 51 percent of the popular vote to Carter's 41 percent and 7 percent for an independent candidate, Republican congressman John Anderson of Illinois.

During his last days in the White House, the president reflected on his four years in office. Although he conceded that he had made mistakes as president, he attributed most of his problems not to his errors but to his willingness to tackle politically difficult issues. Only after thirty years did he acknowledge that such missteps as not paying enough attention to the concerns of lawmakers and "overburden[ing] Congress" with his legislative requests might have affected the election's outcome. "It is not easy for me to accept criticism, admit my mistakes, or revise my way of doing things," he wrote in an afterword to published excerpts from the daily diary he kept as president.[13]

Immediately after Reagan's inauguration, Carter, Rosalynn, and their young daughter, Amy, returned to Plains. The next day, at Reagan's invitation, Carter flew to Wiesebaden, Germany, to welcome back to freedom the Iranian hostages. It was an exhilarating moment for Carter, but it was followed by a difficult period of transition from president to private citizen. Carter had not recovered fully from the shock of his defeat. He was also faced with personal financial problems. Before taking office in 1977, he had put his assets into a blind trust, only to discover as he was about to leave office that his principal asset, the Carter peanut warehouse business, was $1 million in debt. For Rosalynn, the return to Plains was even more traumatic. "There was no way I could understand our defeat," she later wrote. "It didn't seem fair that everything we had hoped for, all our plans and dreams for the country could have been gone when the votes were counted on election day."[14]

During their first few months in forced retirement, the Carters spent most of their time out of the public spotlight. By the end of the summer, many commentators were already dismissing Carter as a forgotten vestige of the past. In late

August, Godfrey Sperling Jr., chief of the *Christian Science Monitor's* Washington bureau, asked, "Is there for Jimmy Carter no way back to the center of the political stage?" "Political experts," Sperling continued, "deride even the slightest suggestion that Carter might be able to rise from the ashes."[15]

In fact, Carter was never as far removed from the public arena as Sperling and others suggested. Earlier in August, Egyptian president Anwar Sadat paid him a visit in Plains, where they discussed the Camp David accords. This gave the former president the opportunity to attack the new administration for not building on the accords. At the end of the month, he and Rosalynn made a two-week trip to China and Japan. Meeting with Chinese leader Deng Xiaoping, he was warned of a "retrogression" in Sino-American relations if President Reagan went through with his plans to sell arms to Taiwan. Carter tried to reassure the Chinese that the new president was not as pro-Taiwanese as his campaign rhetoric seemed to suggest.[16]

The former president's desire to help the poor and bring about world peace led him to continue to travel around the world. In doing so, he demonstrated his determination—just as he did as president—to speak out and act in support of what he believed was right, even when it met with disapproval at home and abroad. In 1983 and again in 1987, the former president traveled to the Middle East, where he held consultations with the leaders of Israel, Saudi Arabia, and Jordan and the head of the Palestinian Liberation Organization (PLO), Yasir Arafat, to discuss regional peace. In 1986, he and his wife went to Central America, where he held talks with the Sandinista leadership in Nicaragua. He also continued to criticize President Reagan's administration for its military buildup and denounced Reagan's policy of "constructive engagement" with South Africa, by which the administration kept close ties with the nation despite its adherence to apartheid. Such a policy was a "disaster," Carter said, "because of the general presumption of the world that [it] in effect means approval of apartheid."[17]

Beginning with a bus trip in 1984 to the Lower East Side of New York to help renovate a dilapidated building, he and Rosalynn also became the public face of Habitat for Humanity, a charitable organization founded in 1973 to provide housing for the poor. The former president and Rosalynn were often seen swinging hammers at construction sites in New York, Philadelphia, and Chicago.

With increasing frequency, the former president made speeches on such issues as the depletion of world resources, conditions in Central America, the arms race, and the threat of nuclear war. He also granted interviews to reporters. In one interview in November 1982, he took a stand against Israeli settlements on the West Bank that would become even harsher over the years as Israeli continued to expand its settlements. On an entirely different subject, he defended his apolitical approach to the presidency "No way could I [have done] it differently," he told Tom Wicker of the *New York Times* in 1984.[18]

While Carter remained a presence at home and abroad even during his first years in retirement, he still managed to spend much of his time writing, teaching at Emory University, and trying to raise funds for a Carter Presidential Center to be part of the Carter presidential complex that would also include the Jimmy Carter Library and Museum and be located in Atlanta. According to Rosalynn, he had come up with the idea for the center in an epiphany he had in 1982. In fact, it also stemmed from his commitment in his farewell address to be a citizen of the world and his intention after he left the White House to establish a Carter complex that would be more than a monument to his presidency.[19]

The former president envisioned the Carter Center as a place where international disputes could be mediated in a nongovernmental and academic setting, and where world experts could discuss and even take action on such important world issues as nuclear arms control, human rights, the environment, world hunger, and health care. Notwithstanding his good intentions, he had difficulty raising the funds needed to construct the center and the rest of the $27 million Carter complex. As he later explained, it was "not an easy thing for a defeated Democratic candidate who has no further political ambitions" to find donors.[20] Since opening in 1986, however, the center has become a locus of research and social and political activism. The former president has been intimately involved with all its endeavors.[21]

Despite his humanitarianism, Carter was still held in low public esteem during the first half of the 1980s. Reagan's success in getting his budget, tax cuts, and military spending increases through Congress seemed to highlight Carter's ineptitude as the nation's chief executive and to prove what Carter's critics had said—that the nation was governable if the right leader was at the helm. Even his own party distanced itself from him. "House Speaker Thomas P. ("Tip") O'Neill . . . does not talk about Jimmy Carter. . . . He doesn't want to hear about Jimmy Carter. He wants to forget that Jimmy Carter ever existed," Mary McGrory of the *Washington Post* reported at the end of June 1983. Walter Mondale, the Democratic candidate for president in 1984, did not even seek his former boss's endorsement. Although Carter spoke at the Democratic National Convention, the party was not enthusiastic about his appearance.[22]

Starting in the second half of the 1980s, however, the former president's reputation began to show signs of rehabilitation. While he was excoriated by Reagan's supporters for challenging the president's policies, Americans praised him for his work with Habitat for Humanity and for his world health initiatives. His 1986 trip to Central America received widespread media coverage and praise from opponents of Reagan's policy of providing military support to the Contras in their war against the Soviet- and Cuban-supported Sandinista government. Between 1989 and 1991, Carter and other Carter Center officials also monitored elections in Panama, Nicaragua, the Dominican Republic, Zambia, and Haiti. "It is as if Carter had decided to take the most liberal and successful policies of his failed administration—human rights, peacemaking, and concern for the poor—and make them the centerpieces of a campaign for his own political resurrection," the *Nation* commented.[23]

Even so, Carter remained a lightning rod for controversy. His courting of Arafat, his declarations that Israel was an impediment to peace in the Middle East, and his opposition to the use of force in the Persian Gulf in 1990–1991 were widely criticized. Furthermore, many Americans had not forgotten his record as president. Among them was President Bill Clinton, elected in 1992, who had held a grudge against Carter since 1980 when he sent 18,000 Cuban refugees from the Mariel boatlift to Arkansas, many of them criminals or mentally ill. At the time, Clinton was seeking reelection as governor. He later blamed Carter for his defeat.

The former president presented the Clinton White House with difficult choices. Although Clinton disliked Carter personally and believed that he often acted recklessly in carrying out his global agenda, the president also recognized that his growing reputation as a man of peace could be used to defuse world crises. On several occasions, he sent the former president on missions abroad or gave his unofficial approval to one of his overseas undertakings. In 1994, for example, Carter went to North Korea on a four-day visit. The president, who had reservations about the trip because of increased tensions on the peninsula as a result of North Korea's efforts to develop nuclear weapons, decided to give it his blessing. As the president told reporters, he hoped Carter would "reaffirm our position [against developing nuclear weapons and] get a better sense from [the Koreans] about where they are." The alternative to not dropping their nuclear program, he should make clear, would be sanctions against the North Koreans.[24]

After four days of negotiations, the former president declared that the crisis was over: North Korean president Kim Il-sung had assured him that his nation was not building nuclear weapons and had offered to freeze its nuclear programs so long as high-level talks were begun with Washington. Instead of warning Kim Il-sung that the resumption of his nuclear program would lead to sanctions, Carter, who opposed sanctions, told Kim the sanctions effort would be suspended. He even expressed his hope that his mission to North Korea might set the administration on a wiser course. "If I had thought the sanctions were a good idea, I would never have gone over there," he remarked to CNN from Pyongyang.[25]

The White House was incensed, believing that Carter had undermined the possibility of using sanctions or other options to get the North Koreans to continue negotiations. Upon his return from North Korea, Clinton refused to meet with the former president, assigning his chief foreign policy adviser, Anthony Lake, and Assistant Secretary of State Robert L. Gallucci to debrief Carter. "I would not call [Carter] naïve or gullible," a senior administration official said. "But let's just say that we are a lot more skeptical than he is about whether the North Koreans mean what they say."[26]

The former president's trips to Haiti and the former Yugoslavia in 1994–1995 also created controversy. In Haiti, the former president was able to restore to power President Jean-Bertrand Aristide, who had been elected in 1990 but overthrown in a military coup in 1991. Yet Carter undid much of the credit he received for that successful mission when he went on CNN and defended the leader of the outgoing junta and criticized the sanctions the Bush and Clinton administrations had imposed on the Haitian military government. White House officials accused him of "glory-hogging on CNN"; even Carter's attorney, Terence Adamson, advised him to stop giving interviews, telling him that he "was talking away his accomplishments."[27]

In the former Yugoslavia, Carter succeeded in arranging a cease-fire between warring Serbs and Muslims. However, his willingness to meet with Radovan Karadzic, a Serbian warlord accused of the ethnic cleansing of Muslims, prompted the *New Republic* to declare that the former president "provides tyrants with the thing that tyranny cannot provide, which is legitimacy."[28] The Clinton administration, doubtful that Carter's cease-fire would be any more effective than nearly a dozen previous ones, kept its distance from him. Relations between Clinton and Carter remained strained even after Clinton left the White House in 2001.

The former president did not allow criticisms or brush-offs to stop him from promoting his agenda. "His technique?" Steven Goldstein of the *Philadelphia Inquirer* asked after Carter achieved a cease-fire in Bosnia, "A throw-out-of-the-textbook form of diplomacy that employs patience, empathy, tenacity, moral suasion and, what U.S. Rep. Robert G. Toricelli (D., N.J.) calls 'a unique ability not to be troubled by the scorn of others.'" Carter's efforts were assisted by his friend from Atlanta, Ted Turner, owner of the pioneering cable news station CNN, who used CNN to aggrandize the former president's efforts, creating the prototype of telediplomacy.[29]

In 1995, the former president traveled to Rwanda to try to end a tribal conflict between Tutsi and Hutu tribesmen. The following year, he journeyed to Jerusalem to monitor the Palestinian elections. In 2002, he went to Cuba and met with Fidel Castro, becoming the first U.S. president to go to that island since Castro seized power in 1959. In 2003, he condemned President George W. Bush's decision to launch a war against Iraq, declaring that that nation posed no threat to the United States and that invading Iraq would destabilize the Middle East. In 2005, he called on the Bush administration to close down the prison at Guantánamo Bay, Cuba, contending that charges of prisoner abuse at the facility were damaging the United States' reputation. As he continued his personal diplomacy, Carter's critics continued to assail him for being too willing to cozy up to dictators and to act as an independent agent.[30]

Yet by the turn of the twenty-first century, Carter had established his reputation as one of the world's great peacemakers. In 2002, he received what many commentators believed should have been given to him following the Camp David accords of 1977, the Nobel Peace Prize. For many Americans, this was merely an additional testament to what they had already come to believe—that Jimmy Carter was the nation's greatest ex-president. Since 2002, his reputation in this regard has only continued to grow despite the controversy that he has continued to generate by his outspoken remarks. An NBC–*Wall Street Journal* poll even ranked Carter "as having the highest moral character of any president."[31]

Besides his peacemaking efforts, Carter has been a prolific author. As of 2010, he has written two dozen books. Although most of them have been on current events (more on the Middle East than on any other subject), they have included his memoirs, his White House diary, a novel, a children's book, a book for teenagers, and a book of his poems. Two have been illustrated by his daughter, Amy. Others have varied from the very personal (his experience growing up in the rural South and an homage to his mother) to matters of aging, faith, hunting, and fishing.[32]

Unlike Nixon, Carter's main purpose as an author has not been one of redemption or exculpation. Although he later acknowledged he made mistakes as president, he also believed that he had had nothing for which to apologize. Given his record of good works after leaving office, he went so far as to declare in 2008 that he had "moral authority—as long as I don't destroy it." He regarded himself, in fact, more of a "missionary than . . . a politician." "I never really liked the political world," he commented in 1994.[33]

Rather than vindication, Carter's purpose as a writer has been to supplement his income. Finding himself in debt when he left the White House, he needed another source of income besides his pension. In what he conceded as "a somewhat weak moment," he told reporters soon after leaving office that he would not try to take advantage of his former position by going on the lecture circuit or sitting on corporate boards. "Others have wanted to make a lot of money," he said of his fellow ex-presidents in 2008. "Which I don't criticize. . . . That doesn't appeal to me." He had always had an interest in writing, however, and thought that was a more admirable route to follow. Whether he anticipated that he would become a millionaire several times over from his books is unclear, but he did expect to make a good income.[34]

Carter's library of books has varied as much in quality as in content. His first book after leaving the White House was his memoirs, *Keeping Faith* (1982). In contrast to his recent predecessors in the White House, who were offered sizable advances for their memoirs, Carter had difficulty finding a publisher willing to make him a substantial offer. Because of his unpopularity, the lack of a Watergate-like incident during his administration, and the mixed financial success of earlier presidential memoirs, most established publishers were concerned that his autobiography would not sell well. In order to gain credence within the publishing world, however, Bantam, a paperback publisher trying to become a publisher of serious hardcover titles, reportedly offered Carter a multimillion-dollar contract. "They took a chance on us, and we took one on them," Jack Romanos, a former Bantam executive, later recalled.[35]

Unlike most of his predecessors, Carter did not rely on a staff of researchers or ghostwriters in preparing his memoirs. He employed just one research assistant. Even as president, he had written much of his own prose and had developed a reputation among his staffers for his exacting writing standards. He also described himself, correctly, as a fast writer. Under the Presidential Records Act of 1978, he was the last president to retain the records he had created while in the Oval Office. Relying on these papers, even more on his diary while in the White House, and on his exceptional recall of data, and working eight to ten hours a day, he was able to complete *Keeping Faith* a year after signing with Bantam.[36]

It quickly became apparent to Bantam executives that bookstores were cool to purchasing *Keeping Faith* in large volume. The executives were so worried, in fact, that they persuaded the former president to address the annual booksellers' convention in hopes of generating excitement for the forthcoming volume. "Mr. Carter spoke for 20 minutes without notes about his desires and expectations for the book, what he planned to put into the book, and why he was taking it as seriously as any aspect of his presidency," Stuart Applebaum, then the public relations director for Bantam, recounted in 2006. "It was the single best motivational speech I've heard in more than 30 years in this business." After Carter's presentation, Bantam sent out 6,000 cassettes of his address to a list of Carter supporters supplied by the former president's office. The cassettes were accompanied by a pitch for two luxury models of the book, one a $300 leather-bound edition and the other a more modest $60 deluxe edition in blue buckram. Twenty-five hundred copies of the more expensive edition were personally signed and numbered by Carter.[37]

Reviews of *Keeping Faith* were mixed. About a third of the 600-page volume recounted the thirteen-day meeting at Camp David between Sadat and Begin. Another large section was on the Iran hostage crisis, while the remainder of the volume dealt briefly with the other important issues of Carter's administration. Although the former president recounted in exquisite detail his own contribution to the Camp David accords, he offered little substantively new. Although his prose was clear and straightforward, and the volume did not have the hallmarks of being written by committee, it also lacked any sparkle and was overly preachy and moralistic in discussing the issue of human rights. "*Keeping Faith* ought to be taken more as a warning for the future than as an illuminating assessment of the recent past," concluded Richard Barnet in his review for the *New Yorker*.[38]

Nevertheless, *Keeping Faith* became a best seller and a Book-of-the-Month Club selection. Bantam took the chance of approving an original printing of 100,000 copies. It eventually sold more than 300,000 copies. The former president proved to be its best salesperson. "No presidential author had ever made himself so available to the media," the historian Douglas Brinkley has commented. To spark interest in purchasing his books, Carter purposely stoked the flames of controversy with inflammatory comments, including insulting remarks about his past and present political foes. At book-signing events, thousands of his fans often turned up to have their copies autographed. The former president mastered the ability to use a shorthand signature "J Carter" while speaking to everyone who came through. Yet he managed to sign as many as 800 copies an hour. "Book retailers love him," reported the *Wall Street Journal* in 2006, "in part because he works so hard at book signings and understands the 'retail politics' of the publishing business."[39]

Another of Carter's best-selling volumes and undoubtedly his finest literary effort was *An Hour before Daylight* (2001). One of three finalists for the Pulitzer Prize in 2002 in the category of biography and autobiography,[40] *An Hour before Daylight* was an eloquent, vivid, and illuminating account of a young boy (Carter) growing up in the rural, segregationist South of the Great Depression era. Carter was able to capture the rhythms of farm life, where the typical day began an hour before sunrise and ended at dusk, where hard work was expected of every family member, where there was still time to explore and fish and hunt, and where during quail season, it was permissible for a boy to accompany his father on a hunt even if that meant being tardy at school. Reviewers rightfully criticized Carter for overromanticizing the rural South, and certainly there was more than a whiff of nostalgia for a bygone way of life. *An Hour before Daylight* remains a classic, however, a paean to a time and place rich in values. As of 2006, the book had sold around 400,000 hardback copies and an unknown number of the paperback edition.[41]

Among Carter's other successful books have been two of his most recent and most controversial, *Our Endangered Values* (2005) and *Palestine: Peace Not Apartheid* (2006). *Our Endangered Values* is an attack on the fundamentalist Christian right for abandoning the humane values of Christianity in order, Carter believes, to advance its own narrow agenda. The work was the eighteenth book Carter published since leaving the White House. Having debuted at number one on the *New York Times* best-seller list, following on the success of five of his last six books that also made the list, *Our Endangered Values* sold 750,000 hardback copies within just a few months. The former president correctly predicted it would top more than one million copies, making it his best-selling book. Although a spokesman for his publisher, Simon & Schuster, refused to give out any financial information, one industry veteran anticipated that Carter and his publisher stood to earn more than $2.5 million in the first year alone.[42]

Carter's most provocative work, however, has been *Palestine: Peace Not Apartheid*. One of Carter's overarching concerns throughout his post-presidency has been fulfilling the promise of the Camp David accords. Essential to a peace in the Middle East is the establishment of a Palestinian state carved out of the West Bank and the Gaza Strip. Also is the need for an agreement between Israel and the Arab countries on the future of Jerusalem. As president, Carter had been offended by Prime Minister Begin's persistent reference to the West Bank as the ancient Jewish provinces of Judea and Samaria, his insistence on Jerusalem as the rightful capital of Israel and not subject to any division or international authority, and his ongoing policy of building Jewish settlements on the West Bank.

In *Palestine: Peace Not Apartheid*, Carter criticized Israel for its refusal to stop building settlements on the West Bank and its treatment of Palestinians, which, in his view, violated their basic human rights, He was also persuaded that Israel was purposely building settlements on the West Bank's choicest areas and connecting them with highways, on and across which Palestinians could not go. Even worse was what he referred to as the "segregation barrier"—a huge concrete and razor-wire barrier built to protect Israeli settlements from attack. According to Carter, the wall allowed Israel to seize large patches of Palestinian land while cutting off whole Palestinian communities and separating Palestinian farmers from their fields.

More than any other development, the construction of this wall justified, in Carter's view, his reference to the Israelis' policy as one of apartheid. "Their presumption is that an encircling barrier will finally resolve the Palestinian problem," he wrote. "Utilizing their political and military dominance, they are imposing a system of partial withdrawal, encapsulation, and apartheid on the Muslim and Christian citizens of the occupied territories."[43]

The former president was careful to distinguish between the Israeli and South African policy of apartheid—the first based on the acquisition of land and the second on racism. Despite the title of the book, Carter used the word *apartheid* only once in the text. Like all his books on the Middle East, his views were also reasonably restrained. He acknowledged, for example, that there was plenty of blame to go around in the Arab–Israeli dispute. Along with Israel's "confiscat[ion] and coloniz[ation] of Arab lands," the second major obstacle to a Middle East settlement was, in his view, that "some Palestinian react by honoring suicide bombers as martyrs to be rewarded in heaven and consider the killing of Israelis victories."[44]

The former president's unremarkable view of the problems in the Middle East was obfuscated, however, by a sense among American Jews and the influential pro-Israeli lobby in Washington that his attitude toward Israel and the Arab world had been irredeemably influenced by his close friendship with Sadat, his dislike of Begin, and his willingness to accept at their word the promises made by Arab despots and terrorists. Carter's use of such terms as "colonization" and "inhumane" in describing Israeli treatment of Palestinians in the occupied territories and his decision to meet with leaders of the militant group, Hamas, added to their concern about Carter's lack of impartiality.

After the publication of *Palestine: Peace Not Apartheid,* Kenneth Stein of Emory University, the first executive director of the Carter Center, resigned as a fellow of the center. In a letter explaining his action, Stein criticized the book as being "replete with factual errors, copied materials not cited, superficialities, glaring omissions and simply invented segments." Law professor Alan A. Dershowitz of Harvard University called the book "ahistorical" and later challenged Carter to a debate. The Simon Wiesenthal Center issued a statement accusing Carter of harboring bias against Israel.

The next month, fourteen of Atlanta's business and civic leaders resigned in protest from the Carter Center's advisory board. "It seems you have turned to a world of advocacy, even malicious advocacy," they wrote Carter. "We can no longer endorse your strident and uncompromising position. This is not the Carter Center or the Jimmy Carter we came to respect and support."[45]

The fierce reaction to *Palestine: Peace Not Apartheid* caught the former president completely off guard. At the end of January, he accepted a speaking invitation from Brandeis University, a nonsectarian university founded by Jews, where 50 percent of the student population was Jewish.[46] Addressing an overflow crowd of 1,700 students and faculty, the former president acknowledged that he chose the title of his latest book "knowing that it would be provocative." He also apologized for a sentence that seemed to suggest the Palestinians would not have to end their suicide bombings and acts of terrorism until Israel withdrew from the territories. He remarked that his comment "was worded in a completely improper and stupid way" and that he had written to his publisher "to change that sentence immediately."[47]

At the same time, Carter told his audience that he stood by his book and title, and that he had been greatly disturbed by the accusations that had been levied against him. "This is the first time that I've ever been called a liar and a bigot and an anti-Semite and a coward and a plagiarist," he remarked. "This is hurting me." He also stated that he meant to describe conditions not in Israel but in the occupied territories, and that he did not mean to equate Zionism with racism. Rather, he intended only to point out "that this cruel oppression [was] contrary to the tenets of the Jewish religious faith and contrary to the basic principles of the state of Israel."[48]

Although some of the audience left still unhappy with Carter, his reception was overwhelmingly favorable. He was greeted with a standing ovation when he appeared on the stage and after he completed his remarks and answered questions from the audience. A number of students commented later that they agreed with his position that Israel was treating Palestinians inhumanely and needed to withdraw from the occupied territories. Even Dershowitz, who was in the audience and spoke afterward, commented that what Carter said was "terrific." Unfortunately, he added, his remarks were belied by comments elsewhere.[49]

Carter's appearance at Brandeis lowered the level of discord caused by his use of the term *apartheid*. It was raised again after his latest foray into Middle East diplomacy. In 2008, he agreed to join a group of former statesmen, known as the Elders, formed in 2007 by Nelson Mandela to promote peace and assist in conflict resolution. The group was funded by British entrepreneur Sir Richard Branson and musician Peter Gabriel. Besides Mandela, the Elders also included Archbishop Desmond Tutu and Mary Robinson, former president of Ireland and subsequently United Nations high commissioner for human rights. Many Jews wondered how Carter could embrace a group known as the Elders when *The Protocol of the Learned Elders of Zion* was widely regarded as the biggest-selling book among bigots and anti-Semites.[50]

The Elders asked to consult with all the principals involved in the Middle

East dispute, including the leaders of Hamas and the PLO, in order to "probe for the possibilities of reconciliation." Although Israeli prime minister Ehud Olmert made clear that he would not cooperate with the Elders, Carter went ahead with the mission under the auspices of the Carter Center. He met with the leaders of the Palestinian authority in the Gaza Strip, with Egyptian president Hosni Mubarak and lower-ranking officials of Hamas in Cairo, and with Syrian president Bashar Al-Asad in Damascus. He also met in Israel with several former Israeli leaders and peace activists, but with only one member of the Israeli cabinet.

Undoubtedly, the most contentious aspect of the mission was Carter's meeting while in Damascus with Hamas leader Khaled Mashaal. "There he goes again!" wrote the editor in chief of *U.S. News and World Report,* Mort Zuckerman, in response to news of the meeting. "Former President Jimmy Carter acting out his stubborn, self-righteous moralism and his stunning vanity, persists in legitimizing terrorism."[51] About the same time, Democrats decided to downgrade Carter's profile at their national convention, relegating him to speaking early on Monday, when audience attention was expected to be at a minimum. Party leaders also lined up a number of prominent Jewish politicians to speak at the convention and included seven rabbis in convention-related events. The presumptive party nominee, Barack Obama, publicly disagreed with Carter's attitude toward Israel. Earlier Obama and his leading opponent for the nomination, Hillary Clinton, said they would never meet with Hamas.[52]

Republicans hit back. The Republican Jewish Coalition attacked Carter's inclusion at the Democratic gathering, accusing him of displaying "a troubling anti-Israeli" bias for his recent meeting with Mashaal and for his "error-filled, egregiously biased book" (that is, *Palestine: Peace Not Apartheid*). A senior foreign policy official for the Bush administration remarked, "Carter is an idiot savant. But hold the savant." At their national convention, the Republicans also lined up their own group of Jewish speakers, including independent senator Joseph Liebermann of Connecticut, who supported the presumptive Republican nominee, John McCain of Arizona.[53]

Despite the criticism against him from both Democrats and Republicans, Carter remained convinced that the Israeli government posed the greatest obstacle to peace, and he has continued to speak out harshly against its treatment of the Palestinians in the occupied territories. In June 2009, he made yet another trip to the Middle East in which he visited Gaza and met again with Hamas leaders. Although he urged them to try to resolve the conflict with Israel, he emphasized the destruction inflicted on the Palestinians by Israel's three-week military offensive against Hamas in January. "Tragically, the international community largely ignores the cries for help, while the citizens of Gaza are treated more like animals than human beings," he remarked. Visiting the site of the American International School, which had been destroyed during an air attack, he held himself partially responsible for the destruction because the school had been "deliberately destroyed by bombs from F-16s made in my country."[54]

On the basis of his earlier visit to the Middle East as one of Elders, however, the former president concluded that the time was propitious for another effort at peace. The outlines of a peace agreement had become clearer. Hamas had shown flexibility with respect to Israel and the PLO, and the desire for peace enjoyed broad international support. Although he continued to criticize the Israeli government, he distinguished between the government and the Israeli people. There was, he said, "an overwhelming common desire for peaceful and prosperous lives among the *citizens* of Israel, Palestine, Lebanon, Syria, Jordan, and Egypt" (my italics).[55]

All this he described in a new book, *We Can Have Peace in the Middle East* (2009). In fact, he assumed a softer position with respect to Israel, even apologizing for using the term *apartheid* in describing Israeli policy toward the Palestinians. "I learned a lot from the reaction to the publication of my book *Palestine: Peace Not Apartheid*," he wrote. In retrospect, "I should have realized that the previous use of the word *apartheid* during the spirited debates in Israel had already aroused the sensitivity of many Israeli supporters in America about Israel being equated with the racist regime in South Africa."[56]

In December, the former president wrote an open letter to the American Jewish community in which he again apologized for any of his "words or deeds" that might have upset American Jews and expressed his hope that the new year would bring peace between Israel and its neighbors. "We must not permit criticisms for improvement to stigmatize Israel," he said. "I offer an Al Hetfor [a prayer of forgiveness said on Yom Kippur, the Jewish day of atonement] for any words or deeds of mine that may have done so."[57]

There remains considerable suspicion about Jimmy Carter's position on Israel, especially within the American Jewish community. There are also a number of Americans who, like Zuckerman, have continued to criticize Carter for being sanctimonious, self-serving, naive, full of starchy pride, and inept—many of the charges made against him when he was president. Even more serious have been accusations that Carter has overstepped the bounds for ex-presidents by meddling into foreign affairs, even against the wishes of the incumbent administration.[58] "Eighty-three years old, he should by now be entitled to national treasure status," commented Jonathan Freedland in June 2008. "Instead, Jimmy Carter remains as controversial a figure today as he was when he sat in the Oval Office. He is denounced on op-ed pages and in the blogosphere, even as armies of activists regard him as perhaps their most prestigious advocate."[59]

Carter's response has always been that the Carter Center has only undertaken missions not normally undertaken by Washington or official international organizations, that he has always informed the White House before personally undertaking any venture and then kept it updated during the mission, and that he has always desisted when requested to do so by the Oval Office or the State Department. Furthermore, he has repeatedly made the point that negotiation, even with despots, is almost always preferable to violence and conflagration.

For that reason, and also because of its policy, according to Carter, of ignoring the Middle East, the former president has been outspoken in his criticism of the Bush administration, which he has labeled "the worst in history." In an interview on BBC at the end of 2007, he called Vice President Dick Cheney a "disaster" and a "militant" with undue influence over foreign policy. He has also attacked the administration for using mercenary groups like Blackwater USA, the private firm handling security in Iraq. He has accused Blackwater of recklessly killing civilians and operating without private oversight, leading to waste, corruption, and incompetence.[60]

Now in his mideighties, Carter still has the ability to stir controversy. In September 2009, for example, the eighty-four-year-old ex-president told NBC news that much of the criticism of President Obama was driven by racism. "I live in the South, and I have seen the South come a long way," he remarked. "But that racism inclination still exists and I think it has bubbled up." He also asserted that South Carolina Congressman Joe Wilson's "You lie!" outburst when Obama addressed Congress on health care earlier that month was "based on racism." His remarks set off a war of words. The African American chairman of the Republican National Committee, Michael Steele, hit back, remarking that Carter's comments were "a pathetic distraction by Democrats to shift attention away from the President's wildly unpopular government-run healthy care plan." Even the White House, which tried hard to project a postracial view of the world, sought to separate itself from the former president's comments. "The President does not believe that criticism comes based on the color of [Obama's] skin," press secretary Robert Gibbs said, adding that the president had not discussed the matter with Carter.[61]

Despite the controversy Carter continues to generate, he remains a much admired—as opposed to beloved—ex-president. Most Americans still appreciate his many efforts over the years to resolve international conflict and achieve world peace, just as they marvel at his efforts and those of his wife in building homes for Habitat for Humanity. Carter's work for Habitat, which began in 1984, has evolved into an international "Jimmy and Rosalynn Carter Work Project" held in various cities in the United States and abroad. In 2009, the 26th Carter Work Project—also called the Mekong Build—took place in five countries in Asia: Thailand, Cambodia, Vietnam, China, and Laos. That brought to thirteen the number of countries in which housing has been built under the auspices of the Carter project. In 2010, the Carters helped put the final touches on twenty-eight houses in Birmingham, Alabama. Houses were also built in Maryland, Minnesota, Annapolis, and Washington, D.C.[62]

One undertaking of the Carter Center that may have received less attention in the media than the former president's other enterprises has been the center's health initiatives, including its efforts to eradicate diseases that have devastated some of the world's poorest populations, particularly in Africa, because of toxic drinking water and poor (or nonexistent) sanitary facilities. The Carter Center has had major success in mobilizing a massive and largely voluntary effort to eliminate these human scourges, and the former president has been heavily involved in the effort. The elimination of several of these blights is one of his proudest achievements.

Especially successful has been the near eradication of dracunculiasis, or guinea worm (*Dracunculus medinensis*), a horrible parasitic infection caused by untreated water leaving worm larvae inside the body, which then develop into worms. Known as the "fiery serpent," the worms then grow up to three feet long before extricating themselves through the skin. If the worm is accidentally broken, the dead and rotting part often leads to infection and even death. The easiest solution for dealing with the disease, which has affected millions of people living in the most isolated and poorest areas of Africa, India, Pakistan, and Yemen, is by a process of filtering water through cloth that did not rot quickly when repeatedly used. The problem was getting an appropriate cloth to the inhabitants of the inflicted areas and then teaching them to use it properly. Through the Carter Center, the guinea worm has been nearly eradicated, with only 4,100 cases being reported in Ghana in 2006 and another 497 cases in seven other countries. In May 2010, Nigeria announced that it was now guinea worm free, and its claim was accepted by the World Health Organization. In 1988 there had been 680,000 reported cases of guinea worm in the country.[63]

Another success, which has extended to countries not only in Africa but in South and Central America and South Asia, has been the near eradication of onchocerciasis ("oncho," or river blindness), the second leading infectious cause of blindness. The disease is caused by worms transmitted through the sting of tiny blackflies that breed in turbulent streams replete with oxygen. The regeneration of microscopic worms results in skin rashes, debilitation, and serious visual impairment and blindness. To end this blight in the Western Hemisphere, the Carter Center became the sponsoring organization for the Onchocerciasis Elimination Program of the Americas. Working with the Carter Center, Merck Pharmaceutical Company donated more than 560 million doses of a drug, which has virtually eradicated the disease throughout Latin America. They are in the process of attempting the same in Africa.[64]

Other health programs in the underdeveloped world in which the former president has been heavily involved include the prevention of elephantiasis, or lymphatic filariasis, which causes hideous swelling of the arms, legs, and sexual organs; the deterrence of trachoma, the leading cause of preventable blindness; the eradication of malaria through chemical spraying and the use of insecticidal bed nets to prevent bites from malaria-infected mosquitoes; and vaccination programs against measles. In addition, the president has raised millions of dollars to develop new strains of seeds for sustainable agricultural growth and to provide agricultural education in the world's most impoverished areas. By any measure, these initiatives in health and agriculture deserve to stand along Carter's other humanitarian efforts in the political and diplomatic arenas.[65]

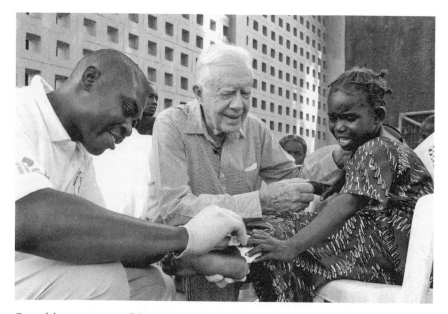

One of the most successful aspects of the Carter Center has been its programs to eradicate some of the worst, yet most curable, health blights in sub-Sahara Africa and other third-world regions. In this 2007 photo, taken by Louise Gubb, one of the 100 photojournalists who participated in the "A Day in the Life of Africa" project, shows the eighty-two-year-old president trying to comfort six-year-old Rhuhama Issah at Saveluga Hospital in Ghana as a Carter Center technical assistant dresses Issah's extremely painful Guinea worm wound. (Courtesy of the Carter Center/L. Gubb.)

Now in the twilight of his career, Carter has been helping to raise a $400 million endowment for the Carter Center in order to continue its work after he and Rosalynn are no longer involved in its activities. Without ignoring the fact that, like other former presidents, Carter has used his fame as a former president and his skill at promoting himself and his books to amass a small fortune, estimated as high as $18 million, that is not how he will be remembered. Instead, his legacy will almost certainly be the achievement of what he promised in his farewell address to the nation in 1980: to be a citizen of the world. Beyond that, he has become the model against which future former presidents will most likely be evaluated.

II

Was Ronald Reagan, the former actor, merely following a script as president prepared by his staff, the cabinet, his political advisers, and his wife? Or was he "*the* great conservative politician of the twentieth century"? Was he cerebral or intuitive? Was he the most malleable or the least movable of presidents? Was he transparent (what you saw is what you got) or a mystery even to his wife and closest confidante, Nancy Reagan? These are just some of the questions that have been asked of the nation's fortieth president since he left the White House in 1989—and will probably continue to be asked of him for generations to come.[66]

A tentative answer seems to be "all of the above." As a movie actor and star for twenty-five years, he was noted for sticking to his scripts, which he memorized with what seemed to many a photographic memory, and for following the lead of his directors and studio executives without complaint. By almost all accounts, this was the way he also conducted himself as president. He delegated most responsibilities to his staff. He worked from a carefully prepared agenda. He rarely commented or asked questions during his daily meetings. Much of what he contributed was anecdotes drawn from his days in Hollywood. He was closely protected by his staff. His days were relatively short, certainly in contrast to the long hours that Carter had devoted to the job.[67]

At the same time, Reagan adhered religiously to a number of firmly held principles, the most important of which was that government was the cause of most of the nation's problems. The solution to these problems, he thought, was through the free-enterprise system and the protection of individual freedoms. To Reagan, the United States was truly an exceptional country, a consecrated land and a beacon of light for the rest of the world, and communism was destined to the ash heap of history.

When he expressed these beliefs, it often appeared that Reagan was reading from prepared lines written by trolls, full of clichés, conventions, and other chestnuts. Sometimes when he went off script, he fumbled for words. If the Great Communicator, as he came to be known, seemed to be playing a role, he was always the same person on or off stage. Because he believed in the lines he chose to act out, what you saw was, in fact, what you got.

Certainly Reagan was not a person of keen intellect, deep curiosity, or catholic interests. Born on 6 February 1911 in Tampico, Illinois, but raised in Dixon, about eighty miles west of Chicago, he attended Dixon High School and then Eureka College, a small liberal arts college about a hundred miles south of Dixon, from which he graduated in 1932. He loved sports and played football both in high school and college. He was also an excellent swimmer and worked summers as a lifeguard at a beach on the Rock River near Dixon. During those years, he reportedly saved seventy-seven swimmers, making him a local legend.[68]

Besides sports, Reagan often played the leading man in student plays. Standing six feet, one inch tall, weighing about 165 pounds, with blue eyes and thick, wavy brown hair, and having the brawny frame of an athlete and a husky voice, he looked and sounded like a movie star long before he was one. Soft-spoken, easily approachable, and imperturbably cheery, he was popular with students. He was never more than a middling student. By his own account, he studied little. When he later returned to Eureka for an honorary degree, he joked, "I thought my first Eureka degree was an honorary one."[69] If his college experience had expanded his interests or aroused his intellectual curiosity, it was not immediately apparent. "I have no definite plans for the future outside of trying to get a position in some business, probably as a salesman," he wrote on a student loan application. Later he remarked that if he had gotten a job he wanted at Montgomery Ward, he probably would never have left Illinois."[70]

Reagan was, however, intellectually more lazy than obtuse. He learned to read before entering school and even skipped a class in elementary school. Describing himself as "already a bookworm of sorts," he enjoyed especially books about nature, adventure, boyhood heroes, and gridiron rivalries. At an early age, he became a proficient letter writer, a practice he continued as president. When in the Oval Office, he kept an extensive diary.[71]

If Reagan lacked the intellect or the energy of a Theodore Roosevelt or Woodrow Wilson, he knew how to put his message forward simply, sincerely, and forcibly. The great philosopher Isaiah Berlin once divided mankind into the hedgehogs and the foxes. The latter devoured knowledge, and the former knew one big thing.[72] Reagan was the consummate hedgehog. Long before it happened, he sensed that communism was doomed and that the Soviet Union's efforts to keep up with the United States militarily would result in the nation's inevitable collapse. Rather than trying to distinguish between his intellect and his intuition, like some of his critics have done, it seems more accurate to say that Reagan was both intuitive and intelligent.[73]

While Reagan seemed entirely transparent and straightforward, he always remained mysterious in his seemingly uncomplicated completeness. In 1998, his son, Ron, remarked, "You're not going to figure him out. I don't think he's figured himself out." Even Nancy Reagan found that there was always "a wall around him" that simply could not be breached. "You can get just so far to Ronnie, and then something happens," she remarked after his death.[74]

One mystery about Reagan was why he always seemed so upbeat. His own youth was filled with more than its share of pain and anguish. His father, Jack, a transient shoe salesman and alcoholic, was always grappling to find work. "Our family didn't exactly come from the wrong side of the tracks," Reagan recalled, "but we were certainly always within the sound of the train whistles."[75] His mother, Nelle, was an especially patient and caring woman. Because his family moved so often, he was always the "new kid in school." Also, he was small as a young boy and so nearsighted (although he didn't realize it until he was a teenager) that he had trouble in sports and in making close friends. As a result, he grew up reserved and self-consciousness. "In some ways I think this reluctance to get close to people never left me completely," he later commented. "I've never had trouble making friends but I've been inclined to hold back a little of myself, reserving it for myself."[76]

Yet Reagan's recollections of his early years were not those of an unhappy childhood and adolescence. "As I look back on those days in Dixon, I think my life was as sweet and idyllic as it could be, as close as I could imagine for a young boy to the world created by Mark Twain in *The Adventures of Tom Sawyer.*" He viewed his entire career, in fact, as one of good fortune. While acknowledging that he was highly disciplined and that some of this "good fortune" was of his own doing, he felt far more often that God had a plan for him.[77]

Good luck seemed to follow Reagan's career. After losing the job at Montgomery Ward, he looked for a position in radio. Unsuccessful in finding work in Chicago during the Depression, he presented himself at radio stations in smaller markets. A station in Davenport, Iowa, had a temporary opening to broadcast several Iowa University football games. Before being offered the position, he had to audition by broadcasting an imaginary game. Drawing on his own experience as a Eureka football player, he brought enough imagination and color to his reporting that he got the job. Eventually the Davenport station was absorbed by its Des Moines affiliate, a clear channel station reaching much of the Midwest, where he eventually became chief sports announcer. As part of his duties, he fleshed out telegraphic accounts he received of Chicago Cubs and White Sox games. Instead of just reading what he received, he announced the games as if he were actually there. He became a big hit and was soon one of the best-known sportscasters in the Midwest. During this time, he also became an avid horseman. To improve his skills, he enlisted in a local army reserve cavalry unit.[78]

Reagan got into the film industry in 1937. While in Southern California to cover the Cubs during their spring training, he auditioned for an opening at Warner Bros. and was signed to an acting contract at a salary of $200 a week. He was only twenty-six years old. During the next twenty-five years, he played in more than fifty B movies, which, as Reagan later said, "the studio didn't want good, they wanted 'em Thursday."[79] He usually starred in roles that physically embodied All-American values—youth, athleticism, boundless optimism, and absolute trustworthiness. He began to make a few A movies, the most famous of which was playing the role of the dying Notre Dame football player, George Gipp, in the film, *Knute Rockne—All American.* On his deathbed, Gipp tells Rockne to "win just one for the Gipper." After that, his name became synonymous with the Gipper, and he became one of Hollywood's highest-paid actors.[80]

In 1940, Reagan married Jane Wyman, an actress who had also been signed by Warner Bros. After the outbreak of World War II a year later, he was called to active duty. Instead of being sent overseas, he was assigned for the entirety of the war to making training films in California for new enlistees.[81] In 1945, he was discharged from the service, but by this time, his acting career had hit a wall. In his midthirties, he was given few roles. Meanwhile, Jane Wyman became a star. Friction developed between them, and in 1948, they divorced. They had two children, Maureen (b. 1940), and a son by adoption, Michael (b. 1945).[82]

With his acting at a standstill, Reagan became active in union politics. His parents were loyal Democrats. During the Great Depression, Jack and Nelle had been saved from the unemployment rolls by getting work with several New Deal agencies. Like his parents, the future president supported the New Deal. Even after he moved to the political right, he continued to admire Franklin Delano Roosevelt. His involvement in union politics soared as his marriage to Wyman soured. He became president of the Screen Actors Guild (SAG). During the famous investigation by HUAC into communist infiltration of the film industry, he tried to find a moderate position. Reflecting his Midwestern and small-town values, he had little empathy for communist sympathizers. At the same time, he thought the industry could police itself.[83]

After being released from his exclusive contract with Warner Bros., Reagan was still not able to find much work. Then television offered him a new start. General Electric (GE) was looking for an affable and well-liked individual whom television viewers would welcome into their home in order to host its new television production, *General Electric Theater*. GE also wanted someone to tour its factories for pep-rally speeches to its workers. Reagan seemed to fit the bill, and from 1954 to 1962, he became a household name once more.

Around this time, his politics began to change. He became increasingly concerned about what he regarded as the worldwide communist movement and by radical leftists within SAG. Influenced by the business executives with whom he frequently came into contact and by his new wife, Nancy Davis, the daughter of a doctor and an aspiring actress, he grew more conservative and politically more active. In 1964, he gave a nationally televised speech in support of Barry Goldwater. After Goldwater's defeat, he became the new hope of conservative Republicans. In 1966, he shocked political analysts by running for governor of California and defeating the popular two-term incumbent, Pat Brown, by a million votes.

Reagan served two terms as governor. During this time, he became widely regarded as the nation's leading conservative spokesman. He became so popular among conservatives that he nearly defeated President Ford for the Republican presidential nomination in 1976. Four years later, he won the nomination. His landslide over President Carter followed in November.

As president, Reagan made the most wholesale changes in the nation's political landscape since the New Deal. He also became the same iconic figure to conservatives that Franklin Roosevelt was already to liberals. Adopting the theory of supply-side economics—the view that tax cuts stimulated economic growth and actually led to increased tax revenues—he got through Congress a five-year $750 billion tax cut. He also won congressional approval for reductions in domestic programs such as Medicare and Medicaid, school lunches, welfare, and food stamps. Aided by the Federal Reserve Board, which adopted a tight-money policy, he succeeded in bringing down the rate of inflation, although at a cost of higher unemployment. To unleash private enterprise, he instituted a program of federal deregulation in areas such as banking, natural gas, and environmental protection.

In foreign affairs, Reagan followed a firmer and more consistent policy than his predecessor. Taking a tough stand against the Soviet Union, which he referred to as "the evil empire," he increased defense spending and ordered the production of the B-1 bomber that Carter had canceled. He gave aid to anticommunist forces in Nicaragua (the Contras) and in El Salvador, and in 1983 he sent forces to the Caribbean island of Grenada to depose a leftist government. Finally, he took a strong stand against Israel after its invasion of Lebanon in 1982. He also sent marines into Beirut in an effort to restore peace to that city.

That decision proved to be a major blunder. In October 1983, a terrorist bomb exploded near the marine compound, killing 241 American troops. As a result of the carnage, Reagan was forced to withdraw the remaining American forces to ships stationed off Lebanon's coast. Nevertheless, the president remained enormously popular. In November 1984, he was overwhelmingly reelected to a second term, gaining 54.2 million votes to 37.5 million for his Democratic opponent, former vice president Walter Mondale of Minnesota.

During Reagan's second term, he succeeded in getting through Congress a major tax reform bill, which provided for the lowest tax rates since the 1920s. In December 1987, he and Soviet leader Mikhail Gorbachev signed the Intermediate-range Nuclear Forces (INF) treaty, in which they agreed to eliminate whole classes of nuclear weapons. A year later, Gorbachev announced that that he was reducing the size of the Soviet military as well as its presence in Eastern Europe. This thawing of the cold war seemed to justify Reagan's earlier tough stance toward the Soviet Union.

Yet much of Reagan's second term was dominated by the so-called Iran-Contra affair, involving the sale of arms to Iran in return for Iran's promise to help free American hostages held by Islamic fundamentalists in Lebanon. What made the arms-for-hostages agreement so embarrassing to the administration was Reagan's earlier vow never to deal with terrorists and his efforts to keep other nations from selling arms to Iran. What turned it into a scandal were the efforts by White House officials to cover up the swap, along with the revelation that the funds received from Iran had been secretly diverted to the Contras in Nicaragua. A special commission headed by former Texas senator John Tower condemned the administration for secretly trading arms for hostages. Although it pinned the blame on Reagan's advisers rather than on the president, the Tower commission criticized Reagan for his loose management style. Televised congressional hearings into the Iran-Contra affair confirmed what many people already suspected—that the president was not in control of his own administration.

Despite the Iran-Contra affair, Reagan had shown what a determined president with a well-defined legislative program and a mandate from the voters could accomplish. When he took office in 1981, he had faced the difficult task of reversing the decline in presidential authority that had occurred in the 1970s. To his credit, he enjoyed considerable success in achieving that goal. As a result, when he left office, his popularity, as measured by the Gallup Poll, was at 63 percent, the highest of any president since Franklin Roosevelt. His final approval rating in the CBS–*New York Times* poll was 68 percent.[84]

Former president Reagan sitting in the cockpit aboard SAM 27000 during his return to California on 20 January 1989 following the inauguration of President George H. W. Bush. At the time he left the White House, Reagan's public popularity stood at over 60 percent, the highest since Franklin Roosevelt. Within a short time, it would begin to drop precipitously. (Courtesy Ronald Reagan Library.)

Within a few months, however, the former president's popularity began to diminish. In March 1990, a NBC–*Wall Street Journal* poll found that Reagan had appreciably higher negatives than Jimmy Carter. When during the *Phil Donahue Show,* a popular television talk show in the 1990s, Donahue mentioned the name "Reagan," the audience responded with a chorus of groans. "What's this? How can this be?" Donahue responded in amazement.[85]

Reagan's popularity, although still high, continued to fall over the next year. In November 1991, the Los Angeles *Times* reported that 52 percent of Americans approved of Reagan's presidency and 42 percent disapproved. Only 28 percent of those surveyed rated him above average as president.[86] The former president's reputation was hurt by ongoing revelations within months after he left office of scandals that underscored his critics' earlier charges that he was out of touch with what was going on within his administration. The disclosures had already begun with the Iran-Contra scandal. Although most Americans believed the president when he denied having any knowledge of the arms-for-hostages deal, the scandal did not go away. In 1990, John Poindexter, Reagan's national security adviser, was found guilty on several counts of conspiracy, obstruction of justice, lying to Congress, and destroying important documents. Testifying during Poindexter's trial, Reagan appeared confused, inattentive, and forgetful. He was hazy on meetings, remarking at one point, "I don't recall these meetings."[87] Commenting afterward, the respected columnist Haynes Johnson concluded that the former president's "stumbling Iran-Contra revisited appearance leads to two conclusions: He never knew what was going on, or he did and isn't telling the truth. Either way, he loses."[88]

The next year, Oliver North, a marine colonel assigned to the National Security Council and a central figure in the entire affair, wrote that "Ronald Reagan knew of and approved a great deal of what went on with both the Iranian initiative and private efforts on behalf of the contras and he received regular, detailed briefings on both."[89] A few months later, Reagan's former defense secretary, Caspar Weinberger, was indicted on two counts of perjury and one count of obstruction of justice related to his involvement in the scandal. Whether North's charges against the former president were true or not, they—along with the guilty verdict of Poindexter, Reagan's poor performance as a witness in Poindexter's trial, and Weinberger's indictment—raised disturbing Watergate-like questions about what the president knew about Iran-Contra and when did he know it. If he did not know about the arms-for-hostages deal, why not?

Further hurting Reagan were a series of recently published books that portrayed him and Nancy Reagan in an unfavorable light. The most notorious was a scathing attack on Nancy written by Kitty Kelley, known for unauthorized biographies of famous people and for making scorching accusations often based on sloppy reporting, poor fact-checking, and inaccurate quotes taken out of context. Although Kelley called herself a journalist, most respected journalists regarded her as a hack. Nevertheless, she sold millions of copies of her books.

In 1991, Kelley published *Nancy Reagan: The Unauthorized Biography*. As Maureen Dowd of the *New York Times* remarked, Kelley portrayed Nancy as a "cold and glittering icon for a morally vacuous era [who] reinvented herself with a tissue of fabrications about her background, age, and family . . . ; that she had her nose fixed and her eyes lifted . . . and that Mrs. Reagan had a long-term affair with Frank Sinatra."[90]

While Kelley's characterization of Nancy was based largely on gossip and innuendo, some of her accusations seem to be substantiated when in 1992, Nancy's daughter, Patti, who had a troubled relationship with her mother, published her autobiography in which she savaged her mother, accusing her, among other things, of being hooked on tranquilizers and of abusing her. She repeated her charges on national television. According to Patti, her mother struck her "every day for a while." After she told her father about the beatings, "he said . . . I was crazy." Interviewed about Patti's autobiography, the former president called it "interesting fiction." Later he and Nancy issued a statement in which they remarked that they had "always loved all our children, including our daughter, Patti. We hope the day will come when she rejoins our family." Nevertheless, Patti's autobiography was fodder for Kelley, who said that she was not surprised. "There's no question she had an excruciating childhood."[91]

One charge that Kelley made that seemed to have more than a nugget of truth was that Nancy Reagan ruled the White House with an iron fist. When, for example, Reagan was given the agenda for his first meeting with Soviet leader Gorbachev in Geneva, he asked, according to Kelley, whether the agenda had been cleared with Nancy. When he was told it had not, the president said to his aides to get back to him after she had passed on it. Whether this incident actually happened, a number of administration officials, including Reagan's former chief of staff, Donald Regan, whom Nancy had worked to force out of the White House, had already drawn a similar picture of a passive president dominated by a controlling and demanding wife.[92]

Also in 1991, Gary Sick, who as a member of President Carter's National Security Council had been intimately involved in the Iran hostage crisis, published *October Surprise,* in which he elaborated on a startling assertion he had made in the *New York Times* a year earlier. In the 1980 presidential election, wrote Sick, Reagan's campaign manager, fearing that the early release of the American captives would assure Carter's victory, arranged with the Tehran government to keep the hostages until after the election. According to Sick, the Iranians were promised large quantities of arms once the new Reagan administration took office. Sick based his allegations on a computerized database, which, he claimed, revealed a "curious pattern" that suggested such a bargain had been struck.[93]

Sick admitted he had "no smoking gun" and could not "prove exactly what happened at each stage" of the arms-for-hostages deal. The director of the Ronald Reagan Library, Ralph Bledsone, said he could find no evidence in the Reagan campaign files to substantiate Sick's claims. No member of the Carter campaign in 1980 appears to have suspected the Republicans were maneuvering to delay the release of the hostages until after the election. Nevertheless, Carter stated publicly that there might be substance to Sick's charges, and a number of Democratic lawmakers on Capitol Hill even called for an investigation into the matter. In October 1991, the Senate voted to conduct an inquiry. The next month, Senate Republicans blocked the needed funding.[94] Nevertheless, Sick's charges further undermined Reagan's legitimacy with the American public."[95]

In 1991, Lou Cannon, a highly respected journalist who had already written extensively on the former president, published *President Reagan: The Role of a Lifetime,* which proved the most damaging to Reagan's reputation. Although reaching a far smaller audience than Kelley or even Sick, his was the most comprehensive account of the Reagan presidency up to that time. Comparing Cannon's biography with Kelley's work on Nancy Reagan, one reviewer remarked, "Cannon is kinder and gentler than Kelley, but in his thorough and careful way, he serves up a Ronald Reagan who for eight years played—gracefully and artfully and with feeling and nuance—a role he didn't understand. Cannon is not unsympathetic. He is not unkind. He is not cruel. He is merely devastating."[96]

Cannon's premise was that throughout his political career, Reagan remained a performer following a script and that his biggest role—"the role of a lifetime"—was being president of the United States. He took with him to Hollywood and then to the White House the small-town values and humble personality he had developed growing up in Dixon. In many ways, Cannon found this admirable. He respected Reagan's commitment to his core values, his humility, self-depre-cations, small kindnesses, perennial optimism, and ability to transfer this opti-mism to the American people. Like Franklin Roosevelt, he understood the need for inspirational leadership. His success "in reviving national confidence at a time when there was a great need for inspiration," he found, was "his great contribu-tion as president."[97]

Cannon did not conclude, however, that Reagan was a great or even good president. Quite the contrary. His presidency was mostly stage-managed. He spoke from cue cards. He confused fact with fiction, reality with Hollywood fan-tasy. He approached his presidency as if it were a series of productions. He re-sisted introspection and was easily distracted. He lacked a technical grasp of most issues and left it up to others to deal with them. As a result, he knew little about what was going on within his administration, resulting in a series of scandals and resignations. His lack of attention to detail and his commitment to deregulation without recognizing the need for some watchdog authority over such crucial in-dustries as banking and finance led to the savings and loan debacle of his second administration. Even leaving aside the Iran-Contra scandal, his may have been the most scandal-ridden presidency since the Harding administration. Cannon concluded, "In the end [the presidency] proved too big for his talents."[98]

Scandals in the news, scandals about the Reagans by a widely read scandal-monger, their daughter, and a respected biographer undermined Reagan's reputa-tion in the first years after he left office. Making matters worse was the size of the national debt Reagan left to his successor, George H. W. Bush. What may have been as important as anything else in Reagan's declining favorable ratings, how-ever, were unfavorable comparisons of his post-presidency with Carter's in the eighteen months after he left office.

In contrast to his predecessor in the White House, Reagan never laid out for himself an ambitious agenda in retirement. In fact, Reagan's farewell address to the nation on 11 January 1989 was a valedictory on his achievements as president rather than a statement about the future. Blandly familiar in its characterization of the United States as the shining city on the hill, it contained none of the warnings of previous farewell addresses, such as Dwight Eisenhower's caveats about a mil-itary-industrial establishment or Carter's admonitions about the threat of nuclear destruction, dangers to the environment, and the need for basic human rights. Instead of projecting into the future, the outgoing president spoke almost exclu-sively about the past. In contrast to Carter's intention to become a "citizen of the world," Reagan referred to himself simply as a "citizen politician" who "went into politics in part to put up my hand and say 'Stop' to increased government bureaucracy and 'confiscatory taxes.'" "I think we have stopped a lot of what needed stopping," he went on to say. "And I hope we have once again reminded people that man is not free unless government is limited."[99]

In other words, Reagan left the Oval Office not with an eye on using his influence to carry out a humanitarian agenda, but basking in his past achievements. As for the future, his ambitions were limited and mostly self-serving. Aside from raising funds to build a Ronald Reagan Library, he intended to deliver speeches in what he often referred to as the "mashed potato circuit,"[100] write his memoirs, and ride horses and clear trails and brush at the 688-acre ranch he had purchased in 1974 in the Santa Ynes Mountains, thirty miles northwest of Santa Barbara, California, which he named Rancho del Cielo ("heavenly ranch"). He also planned to divide his time between his ranch and his home in Bel Air, a wealthy suburb of Los Angeles. When in Bel Air he meant to spend a couple of days a week working at his spacious penthouse office in Century City, about five minutes from his home.[101]

One of Reagan's first interests after leaving office was to complete construction of the Ronald Reagan Library. A foundation to raise funds for the library and a Center for Public Affairs had been established immediately after Reagan's landslide victory in 1984. Reagan planned the library primarily as a shrine to his administration. He intended the center to be a conservative think tank not all that different from the Hoover Institution at Stanford University. He had already made the institution the repository of twenty-five tons of his gubernatorial and campaign records, and many of his closest advisers had close ties to the institution when they joined Reagan's first presidential administration. Reagan was highly receptive, therefore, when he received an invitation from Glenn Campbell, the institution's director since 1960, who had long burned over losing possession of the Hoover presidential papers to the Hoover Library in West Branch, Iowa, to establish the Ronald Reagan Library and Center for Public Affairs at Stanford.[102]

The proposal, however, encountered the same opposition that plans to establish the Richard Nixon Library at Duke were to face a few years later. Relations between the conservative Hoover Institution and the more liberal Stanford faculty and student body had never been good. At first, the issue was as much over the semiautonomous nature of the institution as it was over ideology. After more than a year of study, a university committee, appointed by President Donald Kennedy, agreed to allow the Reagan Library and a small museum to be built on the Stanford campus, but it insisted that if the Reagan Foundation wanted to establish a think tank at the Hoover Institution, it had to be governed according to the rules of Stanford and not those of the institution. This stipulation applied even to faculty-level appointments. The Hoover Institution adamantly resisted this condition.[103]

The way to building the Reagan Library at Stanford seemed to be cleared when the Reagan Foundation and Hoover Institution decided to establish the think tank off campus, thereby sidestepping the need to be governed according to Stanford rules. But by this time, the talks had so soured that when Stanford raised additional questions about the proposed location and design of the library, they broke down completely. Although efforts were made by the Stanford board of trustees to save the negotiations, President Reagan himself decided to situate the library elsewhere.[104]

Numerous proposals were offered for the site of the Reagan Library, but the president accepted an offer to build it on a 100-acre parcel in the Simi Valley, in Southern California's Ventura County, forty miles west of Los Angeles, a bastion of Reagan support. The site was donated by a local real estate developer who had wanted to build a 300-room hotel and conference center on 540 acres near the library. However, because part of the land was within a greenbelt, the project had to be scaled back to just the library, with some conference rooms and a second-story work space for the president. The original mission-style design for the library, intended to blend into the Stanford campus, was retained.[105]

Because of the delay in locating a site for the library, construction of the building did not begin until 1988—too late to be opened by the time Reagan left office. Initially the Library Foundation had hoped to raise about $80 million for both the library and the think tank. Because the Center for Public Affairs was eliminated and fund-raising slowed, the budget was scaled down to about $50 million. After he left office, Reagan had to spend more time raising money for the library than he had originally intended.[106]

The library was completed in 1991 at a cost of $57 million. It was the most expensive and largest of any of the nine libraries operated at the time by the federal government. Two-thirds of the 153,000-square-foot building, housing more than fifty-five million documents and millions of visual and audio materials, were built underground. The Spanish mission-style structure with a red tile roof commanded a panoramic view of the dust-brown hills that were often used as a backdrop for Hollywood westerns. On a clear day, spectators could even see the Pacific Ocean.[107]

At the library's dedication, President Bush and the fraternity of the four living presidents were present, as were other presidential family members, including Lady Bird Johnson and Luci Johnson, and John Jr. and Caroline Kennedy. Carter, who came despite his feelings about Reagan, quipped that the Republicans had an advantage over him because "at least all of you have met a Democratic president. I've never had that honor yet." During the ceremonies, Reagan gave a typically sentimental speech in which he accepted credit for having helped win the cold war and noted that the United States' best days were still ahead.[108]

Besides raising funds for the Reagan Library, the other big project that consumed the former president's time was writing his memoirs. In contrast to his predecessors, the former president's decision to write the book caught the publishing industry by surprise because Reagan had shown little interest in undertaking the project.[109] Unlike other presidents before him, Reagan did not need the royalties his memoir would generate. A frugal person, the former president had carefully saved and invested much of the high salary he had been earning since he had become an actor in the 1940s. He had done especially well in the burgeoning land market of California. In 1951, he purchased two parcels of land totaling 290 acres in the Santa Monica Mountains north of Los Angeles for $85,000. In 1968, he sold most of the land, which abutted 2,500 acres owned by 20th Century Fox, for nearly $2 million. When Fox decided not to exercise an option it had to purchase the remainder of the land (54 acres), Reagan used it as a down payment on a 778-acre ranch in Riverside County, south of Los Angeles, for which he paid $347,000. In 1976, he sold that land for $856,000.[110]

Nancy Reagan, however, wanted her husband to write his autobiography, and the contract the former president received was simply too good to turn down. Apparently without his knowledge, his literary agent, Morton J. Janklow, had been negotiating a deal with Simon & Schuster, which agreed to pay the former president $5 million for his memoirs and a book of speeches.[111]

When announcement of the deal was made, Janklow said that the former president planned to write his memoirs by himself. Janklow was only partially correct. Much of *An American Life* (1990) appears to have been written by a ghostwriter, Robert Lindsey, an accomplished author.[112] Like most presidential memoirs, it disappoints. The majority of the volume is little more than an extended version of Reagan's farewell address, which itself was an abbreviated and sterile account of his presidency. Indeed, the most fascinating part of the memoir is its earlier chapters, which deal with events prior to Reagan's entrance onto the national political scene in 1964. Especially interesting are the chapters on his boyhood years in Dixon, which capture the insecurities he felt as a boy — but even more the joy he experienced growing up in small-town America. The remainder of the volume is vintage Reagan: a fable of how a young boy was able to overcome his insecurities, apply the verities he learned in Dixon, go on to fame and fortune, become president of the United States, and change the direction of both the nation and the world. Throughout, the former president is homespun, optimistic, unpretentious, self-assured, and unabashed in his moralism and belief in American exceptionalism.

Because the autobiography is so sanitized, however, it is neither good history nor good autobiography. Analysis and insights are wanting. Reagan remains elusive, distant, and unfathomable. Key figures of the Reagan presidency are barely mentioned. Unpleasant experiences are ignored, dismissed, or, as in the case of the Iran-Contra scandal, papered over with selective choice of facts. Hardly an unkind word is said of even his most inveterate political foes. The result is one of the more charming and readable of the presidential memoirs, but it is also one of the most inconsequential in terms of information or insights into the man and his time.

After *An American Life* went on sale, the former president did the circuit of morning talk shows and appeared with his close friend William Buckley on his show, *Firing Line,* to promote the book. For the most part, Reagan was treated gently, even by Buckley, who was known for both the gentility and brutality of his line of fire with his guests. Like the polished performer he was, Reagan was almost always able to finesse a difficult question or one he did not want to answer with one of his store of anecdotes going back to his days in show business. On several occasions, he was asked to comment on his divorce from Jane Wyman, which he had dismissed with one short sentence in his memoir: "Our marriage produced two wonderful children, Maureen and Michael, but it didn't work out, and in 1948 we were divorced." Reagan refused to elaborate.[113]

In the year after he left office, the former president and Nancy also traveled a lot, including a visit in the summer of 1989 to Buckingham Palace, where he was knighted by Queen Elizabeth.[114] In September, he and Nancy went to the Soviet Union as guests of President Mikhail Gorbachev, with whom he had developed a warm relationship as president. Speaking before the Soviet parliament, he recounted the folktale about Rip Van Winkle waking up from a twenty-year sleep. "Nowadays," he commented, "if Rip Van Winkle were to fall asleep in the Soviet Union, he would only have time for a very short nap before finding that everything had changed."[115]

Most of Reagan's travel had to do with making the rounds of the speaking circuit. The ex-president normally received $50,000 for each speech he delivered. In October, however, Nobutaka Shikanai, a Japanese multimillionaire and owner of the Fujisankei Communications Group, a media conglomerate, paid Reagan $2 million for two speeches and some media interviews in Japan. Shikanai's motivation in paying Reagan such an astounding amount almost certainly had to do with his desire to create goodwill for his conglomerate by hosting the former president. Not only was he regarded as a heroic figure by the Japanese, but also Fujisankei was seeking to expand its business in the United States at a time when American commentators were already talking about a Japanese "invasion" of America because of Japan's investments in the country. At least one other Japanese megafirm, Shuwa Corporation, which had extensive real estate holdings in major American cities, reportedly offered Reagan $5 million for his services but was turned down. "I did not regard that as a serious offer," Charles Wick, the head of the United States Information Agency, who represented Reagan in negotiations with the Japanese, told the *New York Times*.[116]

News of the $2 million fee created an uproar in the United States. Just recently a Japanese prime minister had been toppled from office for his involvement in a payoff scandal. To many Americans, the $2 million Reagan received seemed just another influence-peddling payoff by another Japanese firm seeking to gain influence in Washington through its close relationship with a former president.[117]

Even those who regarded Reagan as a decent and honorable man, someone who would never peddle his influence for money, were appalled by the symbolism of Reagan's decision to accept so much money for so little effort. "The hiring of Ronald Reagan by Japanese business to serve as their glad-handler and front man for a festive week in Tokyo—within one year of his leaving office—strikes the nostrils with the force of week-old sushi," wrote William Safire, who had been a speechwriter for Richard Nixon. "Let us grant our former leaders the right to make money in great fistfuls, especially in memoirs—it's a free country, and they are private citizens. But there is such a thing as seemliness, decorum, respect for high office once held. . . . For a former President with a hot agent and no sense of sleaze, the profit opportunities are endless."[118]

Invariably, Reagan's $2 million deal with Fujisankei led to further unfavorable comparisons between him and Carter. "It is hard for foreigners to realize how much and how many Americans despised Jimmy Carter," wrote the Sydney *Morning Herald* in July. "Now Carter is bouncing back. People contrast him with Reagan, who now rolls around in money like a hog in slop. . . . He earns $50,000 a speech, he's accepted $5 million for his memories and he's being paid $2 million to spend a week in Japan."[119]

Reagan sensed the backlash he was creating. Even as he arrived in Japan, he tried to nudge the Japanese to open more of their markets to American goods in order to redress the growing trade imbalance between the two countries. "Japan has responsibility for more than its own success," he remarked at an arrival ceremony at Haneda Airport.[120] As he continued his nine-day tour, he became even firmer in urging the Japanese to be better trading partners with the United States. He even spoke of the harm Japan's policies were causing the world environment and warned of a possible boycott of its products unless it corrected these policies. "As a friend," he remarked, "I tell you Americans are not as patient as the Japanese."[121]

Despite talking tough to the Japanese, Reagan could not stop the unfavorable comparisons being made between his post-presidency and Carter's. "Former President Jimmy Carter is back in the capital for an informal reunion with staffers from his Administration and for a symposium in which he'll report on his mediation efforts in eastern Africa, Central America and elsewhere," Terence Smith, a correspondent for CBS, wrote in November. "Ronald Reagan, fresh from the Orient is back in his Bel Air counting house going over the receipts from his multi-million–dollar visit to Japan."[122]

Yet Reagan still remained a highly popular former president. A black-tie dinner in Beverly Hills to celebrate his eightieth birthday, which cost $10,000 a ticket to attend, raised $2 million for the Reagan Library and attracted well-known figures from the two worlds of politics and entertainment. At the dinner, Reagan shared top billing with former British prime minister Margaret Thatcher, with whom he had developed a special relationship when the two held office at the same time. Lou Cannon, who covered the event, described it as "a lavish flag-waving affair suffused in the glow of past glories and the mist of present patriotism." In her remarks, Thatcher praised Reagan for setting out and succeeding in "enlarg[ing] freedom the world over," while Reagan, in reviewing his life, remarked that "most of [his] dreams [had come] true."[123]

Reagan was also in great demand on the campaign trail. During the 1990 congressional campaign, he made twenty-nine appearances or videotapings for Republican candidates. In 1992, he spoke at the Republican National Convention in Houston, where he showed that he had not lost his ability to deliver a rousing speech. After reviewing his accomplishments and laying out a stirring view of America's future, he thrilled the audience by borrowing from Lloyd Bentsen's zinger in his vice presidential debate with Dan Quayle in 1988. Alluding to his old age, the former president said of the Democratic presidential candidate, Governor Bill Clinton of Arkansas, "This fellow they've nominated claims he's the new Thomas Jefferson. Well, let me tell you something, I knew Thomas Jefferson. He was a friend of mine. And governor, you're no Thomas Jefferson."[124]

Until he was diagnosed with Alzheimer's disease in 1994, Reagan kept a busy schedule. He even wrote an occasion editorial, such as one calling for approval of the so-called Brady bill, named after his former press secretary, James Brady, who suffered permanent brain damage as a result of being shot by John Hinckley Jr. during an attempt to assassinate President Reagan in 1981. The Brady bill called for a seven-day waiting period for handgun purchases. "Every year, an average of 9,200 Americans are murdered by handguns, according to Department of Justice statistics," Reagan wrote in the *New York Times*. "This does not include suicides or the tens of thousands of robberies, rapes and assaults committed with handguns. This level of violence must be stopped."[125]

Although the former president was not diagnosed with Alzheimer's until 1994, there is considerable evidence that he had been suffering from dementia for a number of years. In *The Reagan I Knew* (2008), the last book he wrote before his death, William Buckley, one of Reagan's greatest admirers, recollected an incident involving Reagan as early as 1967, when, after delivering a speech at Yale University, he was shaking hands with a line of faculty and students. "What happened was that at a certain moment a faintly detectable glaze fell over his eyes," Buckley recalled.

> *Nothing else was noticeable.* . . . About the twenty-third guest came by, and I knew that Reagan was no longer distinguishing between them. Then an electric moment. A particular guest had grabbed Reagan's hand firmly and was leaning just slightly toward him, a summons to that extra little intimacy often seen on receiving lines. . . . suddenly the guest withdrew his hand. "Ronnie," he said, in a voice just a little strained. "This is me, George Bush." The glaze lifted and there was some lively patter between the Chubb Fellow who thirteen years later would become president and the man who would become his vice president and successor.[126]

Writing about his father, Ron Reagan claimed that he began to worry about his mental acuity as early as 1984, when he seemed to flounder in his first presidential debate with his Democratic opponent, Walter Mondale. "Watching the first of his two debates with . . . Mondale, I began to experience the nausea of a bad dream coming true. . . . My heart sank as he floundered his way through his responses, fumbling with his notes, uncharacteristically lost for words. He looked tired and bewildered." Although Reagan rebounded by dominating the second debate, his son continued to worry about his father's mental well-being. "Something I couldn't quite put my finger on wasn't right."[127]

Even when Reagan was governor of California, his aides noticed that he did not remember what he had said or done. By the time of the Iran-Contra scandal, members of his family other than Ron were also beginning to wonder about his mental state. At his daughter Maureen's request, Ron arranged a meeting with the president. When he met with his father, Ron expected to find him deeply immersed in the details of the Iran-Contra mess. "Instead, I found my father lost in a fog of depression and denial." "I don't want to give the impression when I recall my concerns about him, that my father was catatonic or mumbling incoherently during this or any period. [But] I could not shake my feeling, though, that something was amiss."[128]

Reagan's appearance before the Tower Commission, in which he denied remembering many of the details about the Iran-Contra affair, including the decision to supply the Contras with arms, shocked the members of the commission. "The Tower Board," Lou Cannon later reported, "had been exposed to the real Reagan, as he was seen at close range every day by the handful of aides with personal access to him. And neither Tower nor his colleagues Brent Scowcroft and Edmund Muskie knew what to make of Reagan's performance. They had not imagined that he would be devoid of any independent recollection or so mentally confused, and they thought it useless to question him further."[129]

In July 1989, while riding in Mexico, the former president fell off his mount—in itself something unusual—and suffered a sizable contusion that required medical attention. According to Ron Reagan, when surgeons opened his skull to relieve pressure on his brain, "they detected what they took to be probably signs of Alzheimer's disease." No formal diagnosis was made, however, and for the next several years, Reagan carried on a normal schedule, including his stirring appearance at the Republican National Convention in 1992. However, even the former president sensed that something was wrong. His speech at the Republican National Convention turned out to be his last major national address, and he cut back sharply his schedule of public appearances. In 1993, he went to the Mayo Clinic to be examined and tested. Doctors gave a preliminary diagnosis of Alzheimer's disease, pending further examination a year later.[130]

When after another year Reagan returned to the Mayo Clinic, doctors found sufficient further deterioration to make a final diagnosis of Alzheimer's. Instead of keeping secret the dreaded diagnosis, the family decided it would be best if Reagan informed the public of the disease. On 5 November, the former president issued a short but eloquent statement that he had written himself:

I have recently been told that I am one of the millions of Americans who will be afflicted with Alzheimer's Disease. . . . At the moment I feel just fine. I intend to live the remainder of the years God gives me on this earth doing the things I have always done. I will continue to share life's journey with my beloved Nancy and my family. I plan to enjoy the great outdoors and stay in touch with my friends and supporters.

He ended with a final note that was pure Reagan. "I now begin the journey that will lead me into the sunset of my life. I know that for America there will always be a bright dawn ahead. . . . May God always bless you."[131]

Despite a series of maladies that the former president had suffered in recent years, including colon cancer in 1985, prostate cancer in 1987, and increased problems hearing, Reagan still had the cardiovascular system and strength of a man twenty years younger. As a result, he was able to live another ten years, but his mental faculties declined rapidly. In 1995, the former president had to be told by his Secret Service agent and riding partner, John Barletta, that he could no longer be trusted on the back of his horse. "I know, John," said Reagan.[132] Soon thereafter, Nancy, who always preferred Bel Air to the ranch, sold Rancho del Cielo. In 1996, she hoped that the former president would be able to attend a party planned to celebrate his eighty-fifth birthday, but she had to tell friends that he was not up to facing crowds. In 1997, Reagan's son, Michael, reported that his father often could not identify members of his family or carry on a conversation. When evangelist Billy Graham visited him, he remarked afterward that he was shocked by how profoundly the disease had ravaged his mental faculties.[133]

The former president was still able to go for daily walks during the first years after he was diagnosed with Alzheimer's. He even went to his office at Century City for a few hours most days, where he looked at a daily schedule that contained nothing on it, nibbled on chocolate truffles, or just sat quietly, unable to speak. He swam regularly but was soon reduced to the mortification of having to use water wings. He also played an occasional round of golf as part of a foursome that always included his doctor. When leaves fell into the water from the magnolia trees near his swimming pool at home, he got so much pleasure in plucking them from the water that his Secret Service agents made sure there were always enough leaves for him to take out of the pool.[134] Alzheimer's soon limited even these physical activities. He found it increasingly difficult to walk or even stand up. In January 2001, he was rushed to the hospital with a broken hip. He was nearing ninety years of age, when a third of all hip fracture patients died within a year of the injury. But he recovered.[135]

The end came finally on 5 June 2004. "My family and I would like the world to know that President Ronald Reagan has passed away after 10 years of Alzheimer's disease at 93 years of age," Nancy Reagan said in a statement. Although few were surprised by the announcement, which had been anticipated for years, news of his death made headlines throughout the world. As planned, a state funeral was held for the former president before his burial at the Reagan Library. In Washington, the lines of people waiting to walk past his coffin in the Capitol rotunda stretched for miles. The rotunda's hours had to be extended so that everyone could be accommodated. Hundreds of thousands of people lined the streets of Washington to watch the state funeral, and millions more watched on television.

Despite the controversy that Reagan's presidency stirred, and that will continue as historians and others evaluate the impact of his administration on the United States, there seems little doubt that more than any other president since Franklin Delano Roosevelt, Reagan changed the direction of the federal government in a way that affected both political parties. In a real sense, the challenge Reagan presented to the view of government associated with the New Deal has been the basis of the national political dialogue that constitutes the modern version of the ongoing dialogue first set forth between Hamiltonians and Jeffersonians at the birth of the new nation.

Reagan's five years as a former president before being diagnosed with Alzheimer's disease were also a further illustration of the mass marketing of the post-presidency that still continues. It makes clear that not all former presidents intended to buy into Jimmy Carter's concept of former presidents as "citizens of the world." Yet one wonders what path Reagan might have followed had he been younger and unafflicted with dementia—perhaps years before he was diagnosed with Alzheimer's disease. Would the force of events, public pressure, and concern about his future place in history have led Reagan to pursue a course more along the lines that Carter followed? Certainly the two presidents that succeeded Reagan into the White House, George H. W. Bush and Bill Clinton, whose post-presidential ambitions were very different from each other, suggest that Carter's impact on the post-presidency has been as indelible as Reagan's was on the presidency.

Epilogue
Bush and Clinton

After being defeated for reelection in 1992, President George H. W. Bush was not entirely certain what he wanted to do as an ex-president, but he had some ideas. Like all recent former presidents, he planned to raise funds for his presidential library and museum to be built at Texas A&M University in College Station, Texas. He also wanted to make money. In contrast to every former president since Harry Truman, however, he had no interest in writing his memoirs; he regarded memoirs or autobiographies as largely self-serving.[1] Nor was he interested in remaining in politics. For all his efforts to the contrary, he had never been fully accepted even within the Republican Party, certainly not by the diehard Reaganites, who still regarded him as part of the hated liberal Northeast establishment. Even had he been interested in remaining politically active, he lacked the base of support needed to make that happen.

Unlike former president Jimmy Carter, Bush also had no intention of becoming an activist ex-president. In fact, as he told Hugh Sidey of *Time,* one of the first reporters to interview him after he left office, he had spent the past year purposely trying to avoid what he regarded as the supercilious traditions of ex-presidents. "Deimperializing" the role of former presidents was the way he put it.[2] Yet even Bush found himself playing a more activist role at home and abroad than he imagined when he left the Oval Office.

In contrast to Bush, former president Bill Clinton adopted the Carter model of ex-presidents. Television commentator Chris Matthews even produced a documentary on former president Clinton in 2010 in which he went a step beyond Carter's reference to himself as a "citizen of the world" by characterizing Clinton as "*president* of the world." While Matthews may have been guilty of hyperbole, there seems little doubt that Clinton has become the world's most popular and respected American ex-president and that his name carries with it a cachet that no other president, including Carter, can claim.

I

Although Bush rejected the Carter model of an activist ex-president, it was not because he was uncaring or unmindful of world needs. On the contrary, he was a considerate and compassionate individual who had a gift for creating friendships and inspiring loyalty and confidence. A key to his success in business and politics was the long list of influential and trusted friends he developed over the years. As a former president who had held a variety of elected and appointed government positions, including being chief of the U.S. Liaison Office in communist China before being elected president in 1988, he was also well aware of the needs of poor people throughout the world. At the same time, Bush did not believe former presidents should be involved in crafting programs to deal with an imperfect world, just as he did not think the role of government was to attempt to resolve all the nation's economic and social ills.

A member of a New England patrician family, Bush was born in Milton, Massachusetts, on 12 June 1924, the second son of Prescott Bush Sr. and Dorothy "Dottie" Walker. Both his parents came from old and well-connected families.[3] From an early age, the future president was taught by his parents that the more advantaged a person was, the more obligation he had to give back to his country and to others. As he later put it, privilege meant "turning the American ideal into reality by making life better not only for ourselves but for those less fortunate."[4] Duty and responsibility were values that Bush held throughout his life.

At the same time, Bush's Republican lineage meant he was raised to believe in the principles of free enterprise, individualism, self-reliance, and limited government. His parents made clear to him from an early age that while he could look to them for assistance, he would have to succeed through his own efforts. He was also taught a number of personal values that included humility, lack of pretension, good manners, sportsmanship, grace, and loyalty to friends and family—in short, a basic sense of civility and integrity. That he sometimes did not practice what he had been taught—that, for example, he might not have told the entire truth in explaining his involvement as vice president in the Iran-Contra scandal, or that in his ambition to be president he sometimes aimed for the jugular—should not detract from his essential decency.

Bush attended Phillips Andover Academy and was accepted to Yale University. Instead of enrolling immediately at Yale, however, he enlisted in the navy after the bombing of Pearl Harbor. At the age of eighteen, he received both a commission and his wings as the navy's youngest commissioned aviator. During the war, he saw action in the South Pacific. In 1944, he had to parachute from his plane after it was shot down by antiaircraft fire. He managed to land in the sea and to stay afloat on a raft until he was rescued by a U.S. submarine. In all, he flew fifty-eight missions before being ordered home in December 1944. For his bravery in action, he received the Distinguished Flying Cross.[5]

Three weeks after his return home, Bush married Barbara Pierce of Rye, New

York, whom he had met three years earlier. Barbara's family were descendants of President Franklin Pierce. Her father, Marvin Pierce, was vice president of the McCall Corporation, the publishers of such women's magazines as *McCall's* and *Redbook*. A married man and veteran now, Bush returned to Yale and quickly developed a large network of close friends and acquaintances. He was active in fraternity life and was elected captain of his baseball team. Although a good student (he graduated Phi Beta Kappa), with a great capacity for remembering names, faces, and places, he displayed little talent for conceptualization or abstraction. He was never singled out either at Andover or Yale by any of his instructors or fellow students as being either deeply intellectual or imaginative. While at Yale, he and Barbara celebrated the birth of their first boy, George W. Bush.

After graduating from Yale in 1948, Bush had the option of going to work on Wall Street for his father's firm, Brown Brothers and Harriman, or his father-in-law's private Wall Street bank, George H. Walker and Company. He turned both opportunities down. He wanted to be successful in his own right. Like a number of his friends from Yale and elsewhere, he was attracted to the oil frontier of west Texas. Leaving Barbara and his toddler at the family compound in Kennebunkport, Maine, on the rocky southeast coast of Maine, he set off for Odessa in the booming Permian Basin, where rich new oil fields were being developed.

Lest it be thought that Bush was cutting his ties from his family's wealth and connections, he left for Odessa in a new red Studebaker his father had given him, with a job in hand working for Dresser Industries, a Texas oil-drilling supply company, whose president, Neil Mallon, was an old friend of his father and became, as Bush later put it, a "surrogate uncle and father-confessor" for young George and his siblings.[6] Although he went through the indoctrination of starting as a lowly clerk at Ideco, a Dresser subsidiary, and living in half a shotgun house whose single bathroom the Bushes had to share with their neighbors, a mother-and-daughter pair of prostitutes, he was soon promoted to a sales job in California.

After working in California for two years, Bush was transferred back to Midland, Texas. Although Midland was only thirteen miles from Odessa, they might have been in two separate worlds. Odessa was still a working-class town of around 35,000, while Midland was transforming itself into the white-collar center of the Permian Basin, growing from about 25,000 in 1940 to almost 60,000 by 1950. It had become the epicenter of the oil business in the Permian Basin and the headquarters for independent oilmen in Texas. Two hundred fifteen oil companies had offices in Midland. Like Bush, many of those living in Midland came from upper-class homes in the East. Midland even boasted separate Harvard, Yale, and Princeton clubs.[7]

While they lived in California, Barbara had given birth to a second child, their first girl, Robin. Once they moved back to Midland, Barbara had three more boys, John Ellis Bush (Jeb, b. 1953), Neil Mallon (b. 1955), and Marvin Pierce (b. 1956). Tragedy struck the family in 1953 when three-year-old Robin died after being diagnosed with leukemia. Both Barbara and George pined for another girl, and in 1956, Barbara gave birth to Dorothy, known as Dora.

While in Midland, Bush's neighbor, John Overby, an independent oil operator, persuaded him to form a partnership, the Bush–Overby Oil Development Company, to engage in the risky but profitable business of buying and selling oil leases. To be successful, large amounts of capital were needed. To get the funds, George turned to his family and its network of friends. They invested generously. Although Bush–Overby enjoyed moderate success, Bush became increasingly convinced that the real money to be made in oil was in exploration. After a short time, he and Overby teamed up with two lawyers, J. Hugh and William C. Liedtke, who were more interested in the oil business than in practicing general law. Together they formed Zapata Oil Company, named after the Mexican revolutionary, Emiliano Zapata.

The company struck oil in the very first hole it drilled. Within a year, Zapata had drilled 130 successful wells that produced nearly 2,000 barrels a day. Soon the company formed a subsidiary, Zapata Off-Shore Company, to drill in the Gulf of Mexico. Afraid of the risks involved in offshore drilling, Overby withdrew from the partnership. The relationships between the Liedtkes and the Bush family also became strained to the point where the partners decided to split. The Liedtkes took ownership of Zapata Petroleum, while Bush took control of Zapata Off-Shore Oil, which he had already transformed into a multinational operation with offices and operations in the Persian Gulf, Trinidad, Borneo, Mexico, and Colombia. Despite their split, the former partners remained good friends. Hugh played an instrumental role in raising Texas oil money to finance Bush's and his sons' later political careers.[8]

By the 1960s, Bush had moved his company's operations to Houston. Now independently wealthy and looking for new opportunities, he decided to enter politics. What drove Bush to make this decision remains a mystery. Hitherto he had never shown much interest in politics. However, there has always been within the Bush family a sense of competition, akin to the one that always existed within the Kennedy family. In 1952, George's father, Prescott Sr., had been elected U.S. senator from Connecticut after having decided to leave the private sector. It is possible that the younger Bush decided to enter politics as a way of showing his father that he could be as successful as him in politics. He also regarded politics as a public duty, and he was concerned that the extreme John Birch Society would gain control of the fledging Republican movement in Houston unless it was challenged by more moderate Republicans.[9]

Whatever the reasons, Bush was persuaded by a group of leading Harris County (Houston) Republicans to run for chairmanship of the county party. After being easily elected, he proved to be the most effective chairman that the county Republicans had ever had, even getting the first Republican ever elected to the Houston city council. His appetite for politics now whetted, in 1964, he challenged the vulnerable Democratic incumbent, Ralph Yarborough, for his seat in the U.S. Senate. Unfortunately for Bush, he tied himself too closely to the extreme right-wing views of Barry Goldwater and lost the election.

In losing, however, Bush gained 44 percent of the vote. This was enough to make him the favorite to win the new Seventh Congressional seat carved out of some of Houston's most affluent and conservative neighborhoods. Running as a moderate conservative, he easily won the race. In 1968, he was returned unopposed to a second term in Congress and might easily have been reelected every two years had he not set a higher goal for himself.[10]

What kept Bush from seeking a third term was the attraction of again challenging Yarborough in 1970. His chances seemed good. Texas was becoming more conservative, and the Democratic Party could scarcely tolerate the aging populist senator. National Republicans, including President Richard Nixon, encouraged him to challenge Yarborough. The senator was defeated in his party's primary, however, by the conservative former congressman, Lloyd Bentsen. A more effective campaigner and speaker than Bush, who had a high-pitched voice and spoke with a slight lisp, Bentsen defeated the Republican in November.

Although it seemed that Bush's political career was over, Nixon had promised him a government position if he lost the Senate race. True to his word, Nixon appointed him ambassador to the United Nations. At the UN, he proved an able spokesman for the administration's policy. Typically, he also easily made friends with other delegates. Bush felt used by the White House, however, when it allowed him to defend vigorously Taiwan's membership in the UN at a time when the administration was secretly planning a rapprochement with the People's Republic of China (PRC). When it was announced that Nixon was planning a trip to Beijing, the news undermined whatever support remained for Taiwan. Bush felt he had been betrayed.[11]

The same thing happened a second time during the Watergate scandal. As Watergate began to unravel, the White House replaced the acerbic chairman of the Republican National Committee (RNC), Senator Robert Dole of Kansas, with the more amiable Bush. Almost until Nixon resigned from office in August 1974, Bush spent most of his time defending the president against charges of a cover-up reaching into the Oval Office. He was outraged, therefore, when he learned on 4 August that the president had known about the break-in shortly after it had taken place. He joined with other Republicans in urging Nixon to resign.[12]

Hoping that the new president, Gerald Ford, would name him as his choice for vice president, he was disappointed when Ford settled on Nelson Rockefeller of New York, whose own liberal views he did not share. As a consolation prize, he was given, at his own request, the post of chief of the U.S. liaison office in China. Why he chose China is not entirely clear, although he was anxious to participate in forging the new relationship with Beijing and might have sensed the future importance of China's mineral resources.[13]

Bush remained only thirteen months in China. Much to his disappointment, President Ford recalled him to take over the scandal-ridden CIA. For someone who by now was aiming either for the vice presidency or presidency and who believed his years of loyalty to his party and his experience in a series of difficult jobs made him qualified to be president, heading such a fractured and discredited agency seemed to put him off track.

When Jimmy Carter was elected president in 1976, he replaced Bush with Admiral Stansfield Turner. As Carter's popularity with the American people spiraled downward over the next two years, Bush decided to challenge Carter in 1980 by winning the Republican nomination for president. However, he underestimated the political skills and potency of his strongest opponent, Ronald Reagan, who thrashed him in the primaries. Because Bush, who had run as a moderate, had angered Reagan during the campaign, even accusing him of endorsing "voodoo economics," the former California governor was reluctant to have him as his running mate. He decided, however, to put him on the ticket as vice president as a way of balancing the ticket and because Bush had been his strongest opponent in the primaries, even winning the Iowa caucuses and carrying several important states.

As vice president, Bush logged more than a million miles visiting foreign capitals. He also headed a number of task forces and, despite his later denials, was probably involved in the decision to sell weapons to the Iranians. For the most part, however, he maintained a low profile, biding his time until 1988, when a new president would be elected. Although he did poorly in the Iowa caucuses, he won the New Hampshire primary and then went on to a series of primary victories that left him without opposition at the Republican convention in New Orleans. In his acceptance speech in New Orleans, he made a pledge that would come back to haunt him: "Read my lips. No new taxes." Resorting to negative campaign tactics, he defeated his Democratic opponent, Governor Michael Dukakis of Massachusetts, who ran a poorly conceived and desultory campaign, by a margin of 53 percent to 46 percent.[14]

Three matters dominated the Bush administration: the economy, the collapse of communism, and the Persian Gulf war. Although inflation declined to less than 3 percent during the Bush administration, the economy remained stagnant. Unemployment and bankruptcies rose, while the number of newly created jobs declined. The annual federal debt doubled to about $350 billion. To combat the growing deficit, Bush reversed the pledge he had made not to raise taxes by agreeing to a series of tax hikes on everything from boats and luxury automobiles to gasoline and cigarettes. His broken promises on taxes caused a backlash within Republican ranks, which contributed to his reelection defeat in 1992.

As president, Bush also had to deal with a major crisis in the savings and loan industry. Hundreds of savings and loan institutions became insolvent as a result of their involvement in risky real estate ventures and generally poor lending practices. To bail out the industry, Bush signed into law a package of reforms that included the establishment of a new federal agency, the Resolution Trust Company Corporation, to close failed institutions and sell their assets at a cost to the federal treasury expected to reach $500 billion by the year 2030.

For much of the Bush's administration, domestic concerns were overshadowed by events abroad. In Eastern Europe, all the communist governments collapsed after Soviet leader Gorbachev made it clear that they could no longer rely on Soviet military forces to save them. Even more spectacular was the sudden disintegration of the Soviet Union in August 1990. Events in the Middle East were also dramatic. In August 1990, Iraq invaded Kuwait after the tiny but oil-rich sheikdom refused to pay for a greater share of Iraq's recent war with Iran. Although the invasion took the administration by surprise, Bush responded by mobilizing a major international operation, known as Desert Shield, to prevent Iraq from moving into Saudi Arabia and to pressure Iraq's leader, Saddam Hussein, to withdraw his forces from Kuwait. When Saddam refused to leave, Bush approved a two-stage military operation against Iraq known as Desert Storm. It began on 17 January 1991 with the bombing of Iraq's military infrastructure and culminated on 24 February with a ground offensive against Iraqi forces that routed them in less than five days at a cost of fewer than 150 Americans killed in action. As a result, Bush's public approval rose so high, reaching 91 percent in one poll, that few Democrats were willing to challenge him in 1992.

Yet Bush's popularity quickly began to fall. One reason was that he allowed Saddam to stay in power. A more fundamental reason was the economy, which continued to be plagued by high unemployment and huge budget deficits. In a three-way race for the presidency in 1992, which included the independent candidacy of Texas billionaire Ross Perot, Bush's Democratic opponent, Bill Clinton, was able to use the economy to defeat him, gaining 43 percent of the vote to Bush's 37 percent and Perot's impressive 19 percent.

Bush was shocked and angry that he had been so roundly rejected by the American people in favor of a politician who came to the White House already followed by a series of scandals. Barbara Bush was especially angry at Clinton for what she regarded as shameful charges against her husband. Both she and her husband just wanted to get out of Washington and return to Houston, where they had rented a home while a new house was being built for them. "Well, this is the day," she recorded in her diary on Inauguration Day 1993. "Both of us are ready. . . . We need to get out of here."[15]

The former president and his wife spent the remainder of the winter and the spring unpacking in their rented house, learning to live without the perks of high office, and doing a considerable amount of traveling. Much of their travel involved speaking engagements in Europe and elsewhere. Barbara, whom the American people admired for her frankness and lack of pretension, was paid between $40,000 and $60,000 an appearance, while George received as much as $100,000 a speech. Barbara also signed a contract to write her autobiography.[16]

Of one thing Bush was certain. His role as an ex-president would be significantly different from what Carter had planned for himself. He intended to engage in public service and give back to his country. He did not see it as his duty to devote the remainder of his life to a series of world causes, however well intended they were. From a strictly selfish point of view, he was already sixty-eight years old, which made him one of the oldest former presidents in history, and twelve years older than Carter when he left office. For another, he had spent most of his adult life serving his country. With such a legacy of service, he felt no pressing need to do more. Perhaps because of his patrician upbringing, he also experienced a degree of self-confidence and contentment that other former presidents did not. He lacked the same need for the further self-fulfillment that President Carter did.

Instead, Bush was very much a family man with thirteen grandchildren. As a former president, he intended to divide his time between Houston and the Bush compound at Kennebunkport with his friends and family, and especially his grandchildren. As he told Hugh Sidey, "I really meant it when I said I wanted to get active with the grandchildren," teaching them how to fish and to use safely one of his high-speed boats that he so loved.[17]

Beyond personal reasons, Bush had philosophical and practical motives for not wanting to be an activist former president. While sympathetic to the world's economic and social needs, he placed greater stress on trying to solve the nation's own pressing problems. Throughout much of his political career, he had also come to believe that the solution to these problems was not through massive government programs but through the mobilization of volunteers on a community level—or, as he put it most memorably in his 1989 inaugural address, through the mobilization of a "thousand points of light." "I have spoken of a thousand points of light, of all the community organizations that are spread like stars throughout the Nation doing good," he remarked after taking the oath of office in 1989. "We will work hand in hand, encouraging, sometimes leading, sometimes being led. . . . I will ask every member of my government to become involved. The old ideas are new again because they are not old, they are timeless: duty, sacrifice, commitment, and a patriotism that finds its expression in taking part and pitching in."[18]

Although most closely associated with his Inaugural Address, Bush had used the "thousand points of light" metaphor when accepting the Republican nomination for president in August. In that speech, he called for a "kinder and gentler nation" to be achieved through the voluntary efforts of America's heterogeneous population. Americans, he said, must not wait indifferently "while Washington sets the rules." They were the potential sources for establishing "a new harmony, like stars, like a thousand points of light in a broad and peaceful sky."[19] He continued to use the same phrase after he took office. Volunteerism and public service remained at the core of Bush's politically conservative ideology during his presidency, just as they had throughout his life.[20]

They were also the core principles of Bush's retirement. He believed the nation's biggest problem was the disintegration of the family. "I talked about it in the [1992] campaign," he told Sidey in 1994. "We were written off as 'rabid right-wingers' for saying so."[21] The solution to this problem, in his view, was not massive programs of government intervention and assistance, but volunteerism—neighbors helping neighbors, community members helping other community members, the privileged and the famous assisting the deprived and the forgotten.

That is was what he meant when he talked of being the "Grandfather in Chief" during his interview with Sidey. "He would grandfather the entire population if he could," Sidey wrote. "He is just back from the bedside of a child dying from brain cancer. 'Might brighten his life,' he says. . . . Next he worries about a Kentucky kid who wants Bush to come for his Eagle Scout ceremony. . . . These are little things compared with the power equations at the White House, but to him they are 'points of light' that answer his call for volunteerism from those old days."[22]

In response to his inaugural speech of 1989, an independent, nonpartisan, nonprofit Points of Light Foundation was established "to encourage and empower the spirit of service." After going through a period of reorganization and mergers with similar nonprofit organizations, the Points of Light Foundation merged with the Hands on Network to become the Points of Light Institute, creating the largest volunteer management and civic engagement organization in the nation.[23]

Bush's "thousand points of light" approach to humanitarianism contrasted sharply to Carter's laserlike efforts. Carter's programs were largely institutionally based and project oriented. Bush's were not. Carter sought to raise massive amounts of money on a national and international basis and to employ the world's leading experts in order to tackle some of the world's most difficult problems. Bush had no such ambitions. Most important, while Carter intended to devote most of his remaining years as a driving force in helping to organize and promote his causes, Bush envisioned a much more limited role for himself. His highest priority being his own family, he intended to be a participant rather than a leader and to remain out of the limelight. He would be just one of his thousand points of light.

Even that proved impossible. After returning to Houston, the former president and Mrs. Bush joined a group from a private relief organization, started in 1982 by one of Bush's former classmates at Andover, Bob MacAuley, to take medicine and other supplies to Guatemala. Expecting to be put to work once they arrived in the country, the Bushes dressed in old clothes. When word got out, however, that the former president was flying to Guatemala, top government officials, "dressed to the teeth" according to Barbara Bush, were at the airport to meet the plane and then to have them tour the local area.[24]

This type of small-scale charitable activity was characteristic of the Bushes' humanitarian pursuits. As Mrs. Bush later noted, about half the speeches they gave each year were for pay. The others were unpaid fund-raisers in support of a local charity or Republicans running for office. In 1994 alone, she gave forty luncheon or dinner speeches for charities, and thirty-nine for which she was paid. "At every talk," she remarked, "I tried to urge people to support their local literacy programs, libraries, hospitals, schools, etc." That same year, her husband gave 111 speeches divided between paid and unpaid appearances.[25]

In their charitable work, the Bushes were especially supportive of the Mayo Clinic in Rochester, Minnesota, and the M. D. Anderson Cancer Center in their

hometown of Houston. Not widely known until Barbara Bush published her book
in 2003 was the fact that in the ten years after they left the White House, the former president and his wife had undergone ten operations between them, including
two hip replacements for Mrs. Bush and one hip replacement for her husband, as
well as two toe amputations for Mrs. Bush, also performed at the Mayo Clinic.
While Bush was president, he and Barbara were also treated for Graves' disease
(hyperthyroidism) by doctors from the clinic. As a result of the service they received at the Mayo Clinic, the Bushes made it one of their favorite charities, not
only donating generously themselves, but also participating in numerous fund-
raising events. In addition, Barbara served on the Mayo Clinic board from 1993
to 2001. Because of the loss of their daughter, Robin, to leukemia in 1953 and
the fact that the M. D. Anderson Cancer Center was widely known as one of the
nation's best hospitals for the treatment of cancer, the Bushes also donated generously to the facility. The former president also served on its board.[26]

The most ambitious project undertaken either by the former president or his
wife, however, was raising funds for the Barbara Bush Foundation for Family
Literacy. An avid reader herself, with a special fondness for mystery novels, Mrs.
Bush had established the Bush Foundation in 1989. Convinced that illiteracy was
a major national problem that doomed the illiterate to lives of poverty and single-
parent families, she felt these problems could only be resolved by making reading
and learning a family and community affair. As first lady, she placed the problem
of illiteracy at the top of her agenda. One of her first acts after her husband became president was to hold a White House Conference on Literacy.[27]

The purpose of the Family Foundation was to raise money and make grants
"to support the development and expansion of family literacy programs in set-
tings where parents and children read and learn together—across the United
States." By 2007, the foundation had awarded $30 million to 650 programs. In
keeping with its purpose of awarding grants on a local basis, it also started several
statewide literacy programs. In 1996, fourteen literacy programs were funded in
eleven Maine cities. Since then, statewide programs have been launched in Texas,
Florida, and Maryland. As a way of raising the funds and highlighting reading at
the same time, the foundation has also held a series of programs in which small
groups of best-selling authors visited a city to discuss and read from their works,
then mix informally at a reception with invited guests. George and Barbara Bush
hosted these receptions, usually with other members of the Bush extended family. In addition, both Bushes traveled extensively throughout the country, raising
money for the foundation.[28]

At the request of his son, President George W. Bush, the former president
also teamed up with former president Bill Clinton to raise funds for the victims
of the great tsunami of 26 December 2004 that ravaged much of Southeast Asia.
In August 2005, they did the same for the victims of Hurricane Katrina that damaged so much of New Orleans and the Gulf Coast. The fact that Bush and Clinton
teamed together to help the tsunami victims surprised many. "Can anyone recall a

more unlikely partnership than that of George Herbert Walker Bush and William Jefferson Clinton?" asked Michael Duffy of *Time*. In addition to their dissimilar backgrounds, there was a major difference in their ages. Bush was eighty-one-years old, while Clinton was only fifty-nine—young enough to be his son. Beyond the fact that Bush already had a son in the White House while the other had a wife with an eye on his job, relations between the two former presidents had remained strained since the 1992 presidential campaign, which had been an especially heated one with lots of negative campaigning on both sides. No wonder that Barbara Bush nicknamed Clinton and Bush "the Odd Couple."[29]

Despite their lingering dislike for each other, Bush and Clinton decided to ignore their differences. "I am an old-fashion[ed] guy," Bush explained. "I still think politics is a noble calling. I believe most people in politics are honorable people that are serving for the right reasons." Clinton's reasons for working with Bush represented his more activist view of the post-presidency. "I think that if someone gives you the White House and gives you the most wonderful job in the world, you ought to spend the rest of your life trying to give back to the American people whatever you can."[30]

As the two former presidents traveled to Southeast Asia and to Sri Lanka (formerly Ceylon), located at the tip of India's southwest coast, a bond developed between them similar to the close friendship that developed between former presidents Gerald Ford and Jimmy Carter. Clinton's gregarious personality and efforts to please worked as well with Bush as it did with the American public. Their common shock at the massive damage done by the tsunami in Thailand, Indonesia, and Sri Lanka also drove them together. Sigmund Freud's theories may even have played a role. Remarking that Clinton had not been raised by his biological father and noting their age difference, Bush remarked, "Maybe I'm the father he never had."[31]

The two former presidents established the Bush–Clinton Tsumani Relief Fund and appeared together on television appealing for donations. The fund raised more than $1 billion, which was then distributed among various relief organizations without much oversight on their part. When Hurricane Katrina struck the Gulf Coast in August, Bush and Clinton repeated their efforts of less than a year earlier, traveling together throughout the area stricken by the hurricane and once more appearing together on television to ask for money for hurricane victims. This time they took more control of the $130 million they raised by establishing the Bush–Clinton Katrina Fund and then awarding grants for Gulf Coast colleges and universities, churches, and state governments. In terms of the amount of money raised, the fund was exceeded only by the Red Cross and Salvation Army. For their efforts, *Time* named Bush and Clinton "Partners of the Year" as part of its annual "Person of the Year" presentation. In October 2006, the Philadelphia Foundation also awarded the two ex-presidents the prestigious Liberty Medal, which carried a stipend of $100,000. "These men have raised the bar on the obligation of public officials," Mayor John F. Street said at a news conference announcing the recipients of the award.[32]

The warm relationship between George H. W. Bush and Clinton was extended to the entire Bush family. Neil Bush has even described the former president as "a brother from another mother."[33] While not as effusive as his younger sibling, George W. Bush also expressed kind feelings toward Clinton. They still remain political rivals who campaigned hard for their respective parties in the 2004 presidential election. However, after Senator Hillary Clinton voted for the war against Iraq in 2003 and decided not to seek the Democratic nomination for president in 2004, these differences appeared less important. "These men belong to a tiny and extremely exclusive club," Larry Sabato, the director of the Center for Public Politics at the University of Virginia, observed about the relationship between Clinton and the two Bushes. "They have so much in common with one another than anyone else."[34]

The warm relationship between Clinton and the two Bushes has continued to grow. In 2009, Clinton and George W. even went on a speaking tour. At one event, 6,000 people paid between $200 and $2,500 to see them together. Expecting to hear the two former presidents square off at each other, they got instead a love feast. "[As] they settled into overstuffed chairs," one reporter described the scene, "Mr. Bush and Mr. Clinton became something of an ex-presidents' support group, avoiding direct critiques of each other, or, for that matter, their future club member, President Obama."[35]

As for the more private side of George H. W. Bush's life—what a grand life it has been! His flock of grandchildren, which numbered thirteen at the time he left the White House, had expanded to seventeen by 2010. He also increased his wealth substantially since he left the White House. Although the exact size of Bush's fortune remains unknown, it has been estimated to be well in excess of $20 million, compared to about $3.2 million when he left the Oval Office. He has made his money from his and Barbara's speeches—"pay the bill speeches," as he called them[36]—and from the two volumes of memoirs his wife wrote, *Barbara Bush: A Memoir* (1994), which covered the first sixty-eight years of her life and sold more than 750,000 copies, and *Reflections: Life after the White House* (2003), which dealt with the ten-year period since the former president and she left the White House. The former president has also lent his name to a number of corporations to open doors for them in China and the Middle East, where he still maintains a large network of friends and acquaintances. Of particular note has been his role as a paid senior adviser on Asia for one of the nation's largest equity firms, Carlyle Group, which has large investments in sectors ranging from telecommunications to technology. Since leaving the Oval Office, he has made twenty-two trips to China and numerous other trips to Saudi Arabia and the Persian Gulf. According to the *Washington Post,* he has encouraged numerous members of the royal family, with whom he has close ties, to make investments in Carlyle.[37]

In recent years, the former president has suffered the infirmities of old age. After having undergone a second hip replacement and back surgery, he has had to walk with a cane and to give up golf and tennis, two of his favorite activities.

More recently, he was diagnosed with a form of Parkinson's disease, which has slowed him down even more and led him to use a scooter at the Kennebunkport compound. "My legs don't move when my brain tells them to," he remarked during an interview in April 2011. "But I am in no pain, and I have discovered the amazing scooter, which Barbara accuses me of driving like I drive my boat." However, for a man approaching ninety years of age, he is generally healthy, exercises frequently, and still keeps an active schedule. He also retains a healthy sense of humor. When asked what advice he had for George W. Bush about life after the White House, he responded, "Make the coffee in the morning, and don't forget it's your job to take the garbage out now." Always known for his good looks and youthful appearance, he continues to appear considerably younger than his years.[38]

An indication of Bush's vitality has been the fact that since 1997, he has made four parachute jumps with the help of the army's Golden Knights. He got the idea to make the first jump after speaking to the annual meeting of the International Parachute Association in Houston in 1996, during which he described his terrifying experience during World War II when, parachuting into the Pacific, he pulled his chute too early. Both in order to prove that he was still able to complete a parachute jump and to inspire senior citizens to remain physically active, he decided to make a jump. Although his family was strongly against it, he convinced them when he told them it was "something I must do." George W. Bush, who was then governor of Texas, responded, "Just don't tell anyone about your eighteen-year-old-girlfriend."[39]

Bush successfully completed his first jump on 25 March 1997 over the Arizona desert. To celebrate his seventy-fifth, eightieth, and eighty-fifth birthdays, he subsequently completed three more skydives. None of them was a solo effort because he parachuted in tandem with the Golden Knights. His third jump, made near the Texas A&M University campus in College Station, almost ended in tragedy. During the jump, Bush spun out of control. Although the former president was saved by two of the Golden Knights, who were able to get him straightened out at the last moment, they were all ashen when they landed. After his last jump in 2009, Bush stated his intention to celebrate his ninetieth birthday with another jump. "You don't want to sit around just because you're an old guy, drooling in the corner," he stated before the dive. "You want to send a message around the world. . . . Old guys can still do stuff." However, he is no longer certain. "I have three more years to decide," he remarked in 2011. "My legs' not working properly might be a deterrent." His jumps remain a testimony to his vitality.[40]

Bush's near-tragic jump in 2009 was made near the Texas A&M University campus because it had been selected as the site of the George H. W. Bush Presidential Library and Museum. The jump was part of a combined fund-raiser for the library, the M. D. Anderson Cancer Center, and the Points of Light Institute, with tickets for the benefit costing between $5,000 and $1 million. The former president would have liked to have had the library built at Yale, but according to

Former president Bush during a tandem parachute jump with the U.S. Army Golden Knights at his birthday celebration at the George Bush Presidential Library on the Texas A&M University. This jump almost ended in tragedy. One of the reasons why Bush jumped every five years was to encourage senior citizens to remain physically active. (Courtesy George Bush Presidential Library.)

Marlin Fitzwater, the university snubbed him. "They just couldn't wrap themselves around a Republican," Fitzwater commented.[41]

Wasting little time, Bush decided to build his library at Texas A&M University, which he selected because the university offered him a ninety-acre site on its west campus and promised to help raise funds for the library. Furthermore, it agreed during negotiations with the Bush Library Foundation to incorporate as part of the presidential library complex the George Bush School of Government and Public Policy. Also, many of the Bush's closest friends and allies, including the chairman of the foundation, Michael Halbouty, a legendary Texas oilman, had either graduated from Texas A&M and/or sat on its board of trustees. Finally, College Station was only ninety miles away from Bush's home in Houston.[42]

The Bush Library and Museum was the first presidential library constructed under the Presidential Libraries Act of 1986 that required private foundations building presidential libraries to raise an endowment equal to 20 percent of the costs of the buildings in order to support their maintenance. At the time the legislation was enacted, Senator Lawton Chiles of Florida, who was leading the charge on Capitol Hill to rein in the cost of support for ex-presidents, claimed that the costs of operating the facilities had "ballooned" to about $15 million. Although over \$4.5 million was raised as an endowment, its proceeds have hardly been sufficient to cover the operating costs, and the government still has to provide the majority of this support.[43]

The library and museum were built at a cost of \$40 million raised by the Library Foundation. The School of Government and Public Policy, which was built and is maintained with funds from Texas A&M, cost an additional \$43 million, making the three-building limestone complex more costly than its Reagan Library predecessor. Ten thousand donors contributed to the library and museum, including the former president of the United Arab Emirates, the Kuwaiti Foundation for the Advancement of Sciences, and the longtime Saudi ambassador to the United States, Prince Bandar, an old friend of the Bush family. Sixteen other donors made seven-figure contributions. Over 20,000 people attended the dedication on 6 November 1997, including former presidents Ford, Carter, and Clinton and former first lady Nancy Reagan.[44]

A week after the dedication of the Bush Library, the former president's son, Jeb Bush, announced that he would run a second time in 1998 for governor of Florida. Jeb's decision to enter Florida's gubernatorial election in 1998 came as no surprise to his parents. In 1994, both Jeb and his elder brother, George W. Bush, had run for governor in their home states of Florida and Texas. Of their two eldest sons, the former president and Barbara had expected that Jeb, not George, would be the most likely to follow in his father's footsteps. George had shown little interest in politics, and until he was reborn as an evangelical Christian in midlife, he had led a reckless life, including having a serious drinking problem. Jeb, on the other hand, had always been regarded as the more serious of the two brothers and had been active in his father's campaign for election in 1988 and for reelection in 1992. He had also been chairman of the Dade County Republican Party and played an important role in the successful 1986 election of Bob Martinez as governor of Florida. Barbara even tried to dissuade George from running because she believed he would have little chance against the popular Democratic incumbent, Ann Richards, who at the 1988 Democratic convention had accused her husband of having been born with a silver foot in his mouth.

Although Bush had been reluctant to reenter the political arena after leaving the White House, he worked hard on behalf of both his sons, but especially for Jeb, who was more eager to have his father's help than his elder brother. Referring to his father, George W. commented, "He knows I can handle my own self. But I hope he raises me a whole bunch of money." The former president did just that. Taking advantage of his large and wealthy network of family, friends, and political connections, the elder Bush made sure his sons had plenty of cash on hand. He also tried to turn the off-year elections into a referendum on the Clinton administration, hitting it hard for lacking a consistent and reasoned foreign policy. "And whether we are talking about Haiti or [North] Korea or the former Soviet Union," he remarked in one address, "the current administration's biggest problem is this: There doesn't seem to be a coherent plan."[45]

Although the outcome of the election was a major victory for the Republican Party—and in one sense a repudiation of the Bush administration because it brought into Congress a group of young radicals who rejected Bush's tax hikes as president—the results were mixed for the Bush family. George W. surprised even the political pundits by easily defeating Richards, while Jeb, the more seasoned speaker and campaigner, lost in an extremely close race to Childs. However, because Jeb was defeated by less than 2 percent of the vote, he began to prepare almost immediately for a second bid in 1998.

The former president had been nervous throughout both his sons' campaigns, the results of which, the polls had predicted, would be close. He was, of course, pleasantly surprised by how well his eldest son did in Texas. However, he was deeply distraught by Jeb's defeat. Although he was close to all his children, he had developed a special bond with Jeb. "The joy is in Texas," he remarked as he watched the returns in Houston. "My heart is in Florida."[46]

The results four years later, therefore, could not have been more gratifying for the former president. Instead of remaining in Houston as he had in 1994, he traveled with Barbara to Florida to be with Jeb and his family when the election results came in. As the polls had indicated, Jeb won by a landslide, gaining over 55 percent of the ballots cast. His elder brother, who had proven to be highly effective in getting his programs through the legislature, walked away in his bid for reelection with over 68 percent of the vote. As a result, he emerged as one the leading contenders for the GOP nomination in 2000.[47]

Jeb Bush, of course, went on to serve two terms as governor of Florida and is still mentioned prominently as a future presidential candidate (something his father wants to happen),[48] while George W. easily won the Republican nomination for president in 2000. In an election that ultimately had to be decided by the U.S. Supreme Court, he then defeated his Democratic opponent, Vice President Al Gore, by capturing the majority of the electoral votes even though Gore received over 500,000 more popular votes.

In 2004, Bush defeated his Democratic rival, U.S. senator John Kerry of Massachusetts, in another close election. This time, though, Bush won both the electoral and popular vote. Although initially popular because of his response to the terrorist attack on the United States on 11 September 2001, the president became increasingly unpopular mainly because he led the country into a war with Iraq in 2003 under false pretenses. As opposition mounted against the administration, the president was widely accused of being one of the nation's most disastrous presidents.

It is beyond the scope of this book to evaluate either the Bush presidency or its critics. What is appropriate to consider is the relationship of the father (often referred to as Bush 41 to distinguish him from the forty-third president, Bush 43) with his elder son. On this subject there has already been considerable discussion in the media. A number of writers have alleged an Oedipus-induced effort by Bush 43 to distance himself from his father. According to this view, during his formative years, the former president turned his back on the New England patrician upbringing of his father, purposely playing the role of the prodigal son by his reckless behavior until his midforties and exaggerating his Texas roots and customs. Commentators even attribute Bush 43's decision to go to war against Iraq as a means of proving that his father had made a mistake during the gulf war in not removing Hussein from power. The son has also purposely ignored the advice of his father and those who counseled him when he was president, such as Brent Scowcroft, his former national security adviser and a highly regarded expert on foreign policy, who opposed the war in Iraq.[49]

Bush 41 probably did not think invading Iraq was any better an idea in 2003 than it had been in 1991, when he decided against a similar invasion. In *A World Transformed* (1998), which the elder Bush agreed to write with Scowcroft, the two authors discussed Bush's decision not to march to Baghdad during Desert Storm: "Had we gone the invasion route, the United States could conceivably still be an occupying power in a bitterly hostile land," they wrote.[50] Not having changed his view about the folly of invading Iraq in the seven years since Desert Storm, there is no reason to suppose he did so in the years that followed.

Whether the former president actually advised his son against invading Iraq before 2003, however, is a different matter. Hugh Sidey, who had more access to the Bushes than any other political reporter, raised this very question with Bush 41 in September 2002. According to Sidey, the elder Bush's response was that he did not advise his son. "In the first place," Sidey wrote, "George H. W. Bush does not voluntarily tell his son George W. Bush what he should do on Iraq or anything else more profound than a dockside suggestion like 'Try this new lure to hook the stripers.' The father would consider it an insult to his son's abilities."[51]

After President Bush's decision to invade Iraq, the official line from the White House was that the former president only gave his son advice when he asked for it. According to the *Washington Post*'s Bob Woodward, the president remarked in an interview about his father, "You know, he [Bush 41] may have been the wrong father to appeal to in terms of strength. There is a higher father that I appeal to."[52] The relationship between father and son seems, however, to have been more nuanced than that. A number of the president's aides, including his first chief of staff, Andrew Card, and family members, maintain that Bush 43 and Bush 41 talked to each other virtually every morning. The president even acknowledged that he briefed his father frequently. Although the former president studiously avoided saying anything critical to his son and made clear that he should act according to what he believed was right, at times the elder Bush apparently expressed irritation with some of the younger Bush's advisers and urged him to seek outside advice.[53]

Although the precise relationship between the father and son during Bush 43's presidency will not be known until their papers are made available to scholars, one aspect of that relationship is already clear: how much the elder Bush anguished over the criticisms and barbs against his son. "It wears on his heart," one of his former aides, Ron Kaufman, commented in 2007. "Personally, I think he's dying inside," another remarked. President Bush himself became so concerned about the emotional state of his father that he even urged him to turn off the television. "I am actually more concerned about him than I have ever been in my life, because he's paying too much attention to the news."[54]

Notwithstanding the anguish the war in Iraq has caused the elder Bush, the former president has still been able to reap the rewards of a full and fulfilling life. There were, of course, the opening of the Bush presidential complex at Texas A&M University, his extensive travel throughout the world, and the pride he took in having one son as president and another a successful governor of Florida and potential presidential candidate. There were also the many visits he made to Washington to visit with his son at the White House, the pleasure he received from his skydiving and the publicity surrounding it, his charitable work, and, of course, the annual family reunions at the Kennebunkport compound he loves so much. At the compound, he not only had the opportunity to play the role of granddad, but also the chance to play host to a number of foreign dignitaries, who his son or even the former president invited for a visit and a round of informal diplomacy. "There is nobody who can match up with this life, bolstered by being a member direct and indirect in the Presidents' club," Hugh Sidey wrote of Bush in June 2004.[55]

In March 2011, a country music charity gala was held in Washington to honor the former president for his life of volunteerism and to raise funds for the Points of Light Institute. Besides Bush 41, the other three living former presidents—Carter, Clinton, and Bush—were in attendance. Although President Barack Obama, who a few months earlier had awarded Bush with the Presidential Medal of Freedom, the nation's highest civilian honor, was not able to attend, he met the former president at Texas A&M a year earlier for a similar celebration of his commitment to community service. "He didn't call for one blinding light shining from Washington," the president remarked. "He didn't just call for a few bright lights from the biggest nonprofits. He called for a vast galaxy of people and institutions working together to solve problems in their own backyards. Twenty years later, I think for a minute about that impact he's had."[56]

This was a fitting tribute to a life of public service that continued even after Bush left the White House. Although the former president was never the activist former president or "citizen of the world" that Jimmy Carter became, he and Barbara devoted much of their time, effort, and money to humanitarian activity, especially to promoting the cause of voluntary community efforts. Part of his approach to philanthropy had been purposely to avoid making the major commitment of time and effort that Carter has made. Bush wanted to enjoy the life of a private citizen. He also believed that charity began at home and that the key to dealing with the nation's problems was through voluntary efforts and community action. Even so, his charitable activities and work with Bill Clinton in response to the Southeast Asian tsunami made his former presidency closer to the Carter model of an ex-president than he might have realized.[57]

II

Like Bush, Bill Clinton had not entirely decided how he wanted to spend his time after he left office. But one thing was certain. At age fifty-four, he was the youngest former president since Theodore Roosevelt. Like Roosevelt and Carter, Clinton had no intention of retiring into oblivion.

In many ways, Clinton incorporated the best and worst of America's most noteworthy twentieth-century presidents. He ranks only with Teddy Roosevelt in terms of native intelligence. He stands alongside Franklin Roosevelt, John F. Kennedy, and Ronald Reagan in terms of sheer charisma. He needs to be included with Roosevelt, Dwight Eisenhower, and Reagan as among the nation's most popular presidents. His mastery of Washington politics was matched or surpassed only by Lyndon Johnson, and of retail politics only by Franklin Roosevelt. He shares with Harry Truman the trophy as the president with whom the common man most easily identified. His ability to deliver blockbuster speeches was equaled only by Wilson, Franklin Roosevelt, Kennedy, and Reagan. Like Nixon and to a lesser extent Johnson, however, he had a flawed personality. Intently ambitious, he was considerate but manipulative, caring but narcissistic, diplomatic but predatory, intently focused but chaotic, good-natured but hot-tempered, and unguarded to the point that it almost cost him his office.

Born on 19 August 1946, in Hope, Arkansas, Clinton came from a highly dysfunctional family. His father, William Blythe III, had died in an automobile accident three months before Clinton was born.[58] Soon after Blythe was killed, Clinton's mother, Virginia Cassidy Blythe, married Roger Clinton, a car salesman who opened a branch in Hope of his brother's Hot Springs Buick dealership. Bill had a rocky relationship with his stepfather, a gambler, philanderer, and alcoholic who, when drunk, was abusive with Virginia and their children, including Bill's half-brother, Roger Clinton Jr. (b. 1956). At one point, Virginia divorced Roger, then, against Bill's advice, remarried him. Nevertheless, at the age of sixteen, Bill, who had gone by the name Clinton since his mother married Roger, legally changed his surname from Blythe to Clinton. High-spirited and rebellious, Virginia had a reputation, even as a teenager, as a flirt. Treated as a social pariah by her fellow students, she felt the stings of rejection and longed to belong. The more she was rejected, the more she refused to play the role of a wallflower. Even as an adult, she wore loud clothes and lots of makeup, sought the companionship of men, and enjoyed going to nightclubs and gambling. Yet she was intelligent and the breadwinner of her family. She became a nurse anesthetist. Needing to be loved, she went through two more marriages after Roger's death from cancer in 1967. However, her son Bill was the love of her life. His intelligence and talents brought her the special pride common to parents of high achievers.[59]

Much of Virginia's rebellious nature was directed against her mother, Edith Cassidy. Edith, a strong-willed, temperamental, and unhappy woman, competed with Virginia for the love and custody of her grandson. Only when Roger's dealership failed and they moved to Hot Springs did Virginia finally feel able to raise Bill without interference. She loved Hot Springs, known at the time not only for its restorative springs, but also as a den of iniquity because of its racetrack, strip clubs, and illegal gambling.

Growing up in such a dysfunctional family had a lasting impact on the future president. He shared his mother's craving for affection and feared rejection or being alone. Having to intercede between his stepfather and mother and between his mother and grandmother during sometimes violent arguments, his natural disposition was to mediate disputes. The fact that his mother was a free spirit may also help explain why he became such an uninhibited, gregarious, and promiscuous adult.[60]

It was not just his family life, however, that shaped Clinton's character. Attending school in Hot Springs, he was singled out at an early age as a gifted student with an exceptional mind. Determined to remain first in his class, he had difficulty coping with reversal or accepting defeat. At Hot Springs High School, he became the protégé of the school's principal, who mentored him and helped him gain a place in Arkansas's Boy's Nation summer retreat, a training ground of future leaders. There he was elected one of the state's two senators.[61]

Clinton's election as a senator assured him a trip to Washington, where he mingled with congressional leaders from his home state and went to the White House to hear President John F. Kennedy, already one of Bill's heroes. A snapshot taken of the president shaking the hand of a sixteen-year-old future president has since become an icon.

Clinton's experience in Washington was formative. Already leaning toward a career in public service, he decided to master the art of politics and run one day for high public office. In Washington, he also had an opportunity to impress Senator J. William Fulbright with his knowledge and quick mind. The senator later became another of his mentors.

Clinton wanted to spend his college years in Washington. He applied only to Georgetown's School of Foreign Service. At first, Clinton was shunned by his fellow students. Georgetown was an elite Catholic university; most of its students came from upper-middle-class families and had graduated from the best Catholic high schools. Many of them looked down at this oddity from a rural, backward state, still best remembered for the 1957 incident over the integration of Little Rock Central High School.

Yet Clinton established himself quickly as a student leader. The east campus, where the School of Foreign Service and several other schools were located, was separated by a few blocks from the main campus. Unlike the main campus, the east campus enrolled female students. It was also more of a melting pot, with many foreign students and more religious and cultural diversity. With his insatiable curiosity, charming modesty, and gregarious personality, Clinton thrived. Standing six feet, three inches tall, a little pudgy with his weight ranging north of 200 pounds, a full head of thick, curly brown hair, intense blue-gray eyes, and a slightly bulbous nose, Clinton had a boyish look and a welcoming smile that made him easily approachable. He made friends effortlessly. One of his great gifts was an ability to listen to people with such an intensity and curiosity as to totally disarm them. In his first two years at Georgetown, he was elected president of his freshman and sophomore classes.

In order to help pay for his education, Clinton gained a staff position on Senator Fulbright's Committee on Foreign Relations. He seized the opportunity to meet lawmakers, network, and learn the craft of insider politics. He also began to learn more about the Vietnam War. Under the influence of Fulbright and the committee staff, he moved from supporting the war to opposing it. However, he never became a part of the growing antiwar movement.

Clinton's four years at Georgetown represented a first step in his political career. What Clinton gained from Georgetown came not so much from the class-room. Although he was a voracious reader, what he read was not so much his class assignments as what caught his fancy. His interests ranged from George Orwell's metaphorical *Animal Farm* to William Faulkner's dense Yoknapatawpha cycle, to Theodore White's *The Making of the President: 1960* and the essays of Montaigne and Rousseau. If there were common themes to his reading, they were to understand the culture of his native South, to learn more about human nature, and to find lessons applicable to a political career.[62]

Clinton began more and more to skip classes, preferring the education he received on Capitol Hill to the education offered on the Georgetown campus. During Fulbright's successful run for reelection in 1966, he spent most of the first semester of his junior year in Arkansas, working on the campaign. Until Fulbright got tired of his constant chatter, he even served as the senator's driver. Yet he excelled in his classes. An international studies major, he charmed his fellow students into borrowing their notes and then crammed for exams, easily passing them with high grades. He wrote papers in a similar way, reading on his subject with great concentration and then quickly writing a paper that dissected a problem in clear and well-reasoned prose.

Fulbright encouraged Clinton to apply for a Rhodes scholarship at Oxford University. Needing little persuasion, Clinton won one of the thirty-two spots available for 1968. In the fall, he sailed to England with the other Rhodes scholars. Among those with whom he became friends were Robert Reich, a graduate of Dartmouth, who later served as Clinton's secretary of labor, and Strobe Talbott of Yale, whom he later appointed an ambassador at large and then a special adviser to the secretary of state on the newly independent states of Eastern Europe.

The two years that Clinton spent at Oxford were two of the happiest and yet the worst of his life. On the one hand, he took advantage of the light demands Oxford placed on its students to do what he enjoyed most—making new and fascinating friends, spending hours at a time reading, being the master inquisitor, and soaking up the ideas of those with whom he engaged in conversation. He also toured much of Europe, visiting as far away as Moscow. As at Georgetown, he found these extracurricular aspects of his Rhodes opportunity the most reward-ing. Unlike many of his colleagues, he never even received a degree from Oxford.

Hanging over Clinton, however, were the Vietnam War and the draft. An is-sue that followed him into the White House was whether he attempted to avoid the draft. Despite his denials, it is reasonably clear that Clinton did by gaining a coveted place in the ROTC program at the University of Arkansas at Fayetteville after receiving his draft notification with the understanding that he would attend the university's law school in the fall. He then changed his mind when it became less likely that he would be drafted.[63] Determined on a political career, Clinton was not as interested in academics as the credentials that came with graduation from esteemed schools and being a Rhodes scholar. Graduating from the Univer-sity of Arkansas Law School did not fit into his calculus for success. Yale Law School did.

In 1970, Clinton was able to enter Yale with the Vietnam War behind him. In the three years he was there, he followed the same pattern he had at Georgetown and Oxford. He increased his circle of friends, engaged frequently in all-night talk sessions, missed classes regularly—even working in the 1970 senatorial campaign in Connecticut for the Democratic candidate, Joe Duffy, and taking off most of the fall semester in 1972 to serve as a state coordinator in Texas for presidential candidate George McGovern—and then spending the last few weeks of the semester getting the notes of more diligent students, writing papers, and studying for his exams.

While at Yale, Clinton met his future wife, Hillary Rodham, a graduate of Wellesley. The relationship between Bill and Hillary was complex and tempes-tuous, and it remains controversial.[64] Bill and Hillary had complementary abili-ties and personalities. While both of them were extremely bright, Hillary was more disciplined, self-directed, and detail oriented than Bill. She had the focus, businesslike acumen, and managerial skills that he lacked. At the same time, she was temperamentally colder, harder, more aggressive, and less imaginative and sociable than him. Whereas those who knew or met Bill often talked about how he exuded compassion, those who were acquainted with Hillary referred to her inability to relate to people on a personal level except as they might be needed to further her interests; when they were of no more use to her, she discarded them. Counterintuitively, Bill and Hillary were a perfect match.[65]

Before meeting Hillary, Clinton said that he had no intention of getting married. After dating her, he told his mother and friends that there was no other woman he would marry. For her part, Hillary made a number of sacrifices to be with him, including delaying her own graduation by a year to be able to graduate with him (because Bill had spent two years at Oxford, she was in the class ahead of him) and giving up a promising career in Washington.

After graduating from Yale in 1973, Clinton took a position teaching law at the University of Arkansas. Shortly thereafter, he announced that he would run for Congress against the popular Republican incumbent, John Hammerschmidt.

During the campaign, Hillary moved from Washington to Fayetteville, where she also took a job teaching law at the university. In 1975, she married Clinton. Although Clinton narrowly lost the race, he ran a brilliant campaign. As a result, he became a rising political star in Arkansas. Two years later, he ran unopposed in the general election for attorney general after easily knocking off his opponents in the Democratic primary.

Clinton used the office of attorney general as a stepping-stone to the governorship in 1978. At age thirty-two, he was the youngest governor in the nation. Defeated in his bid for reelection two years later, largely because he had raised taxes and offended the trucking industry, he was returned to office in 1982 after asking the voters for a second chance and running an effective television ad campaign. He was reelected three times (beginning in 1986, the gubernatorial term was extended from two to four years) before deciding to seek the Democratic presidential nomination in 1992.

In deciding to run for president, Clinton had the advantage that Bush's high approval ratings after Desert Storm had scared off some of his strongest potential opponents. Even before his campaign had started, however, Clinton was nearly forced out of the race by allegations of a twelve-year extramarital affair with Gennifer Flowers, a model and singer. His campaign was saved when Clinton and his wife, Hillary, went on the popular television show *60 Minutes*. Clinton denied the allegations, and Hillary made it clear that she stood by her husband. After winning important primaries in New York and in the South, Clinton gained the Democratic nomination in July. Although starting the presidential campaign with a substantial lead over Bush, he saw his margin dwindle as questions were raised about his draft deferment during the Vietnam War, his opposition to the war, and his general character. However, helped by the candidacy of Ross Perot and making the economy his major campaign issue, he was able to defeat Bush by a margin of 43 percent to 37 percent, with Perot getting 19 percent of the vote.

As president, Clinton had a difficult time during his first two years in the Oval Office. To his credit, he passed a number of important pieces of legislation, including the Family and Medical Leave Act of 1993, the Brady Bill of 1993 requiring a five-day waiting period on the purchase of handguns, and an economic package combining tax cuts for low-income families and small businesses with tax increases on the wealthiest and spending cuts that lowered the deficit.

Yet the new president found himself repeatedly on the defensive. In 1994, he suffered a major setback when his highest legislative priority, a comprehensive program of national health insurance, was defeated on Capitol Hill. In foreign policy, he was also roundly criticized for a lack of consistency, or for having no policy at all. He was even charged with allowing rhetoric to drive policy, as in the case of Bosnia, once part of Yugoslavia, where he was accused of embracing themes of high morality but of failing to back them up with military power.

Complicating matters for the president were the beginnings of an investigation into a land deal gone bad along the White River in the Ozarks. The Clintons were partners with their friends, James and Susan McDougal. Questions about conflict of interest arose because Hillary Clinton's law firm did business with Jim McDougal's savings and loan, Madison Guaranty, while Clinton was serving as governor. McDougal later died in jail after being convicted of fraud. Although no charges were brought against the Clintons, a special prosecutor, Ken Starr, was appointed to investigate the so-called Whitewater affair. Starr later broadened the investigation to embrace a host of other matters, such as the tragic suicide of Vincent Foster, the president's personal attorney, who worked at the White House and handled Clinton's personal and financial matters. His death sparked more suspicions about the character and conduct of the president. Making the failures and practices of the president and his administration a major campaign issue and proposing a "Contract with America" that included major budget cuts, reduced taxes, and a balanced budget amendment to the Constitution, Republicans captured both houses of Congress for the first time since the Eisenhower administration.

Having already labeled himself the "comeback kid" after placing second in the New Hampshire primary in 1992 after a distant third-place finish in the Iowa caucuses a few weeks earlier, Clinton made another comeback. He put the Republicans on the defensive by refusing to sign their budget, which called for drastic cuts in Medicare and other popular programs while cutting taxes disproportionately for the wealthy. He then ordered the shutdown of the government, closing it briefly in November 1995 and then again in December. The public largely blamed overreaching Republicans for the shutdowns. The Republicans were forced to back down and pass a temporary agreement that reopened government offices.

Clinton also brought into the White House a brilliant but unscrupulous political strategist, Dick Morris, whom he had used while governor in Arkansas. Morris crafted a program that preempted the Republicans on such issues as crime and welfare reform. The president increased the number of police on the street by 100,000 and cut the welfare rolls by limiting to two years the time that a welfare recipient could receive welfare checks. In his State of the Union Address in 1996, Clinton declared in almost Reaganesque terms that "the era of big government is over." The president also conducted a campaignlike round of travel and appearances that kept him in the public eye. In April 1995, he delivered a particularly moving speech that rallied the nation after the bombing of a federal office building in Oklahoma City that took 168 lives, including nineteen children under the age of six. In foreign policy, he became more aggressive in the war in the Balkans by authorizing air strikes against the Serbs in Bosnia that led to a cease-fire.

As Clinton co-opted the political center, his popularity in the polls shot up, helped by an increasingly robust economy. In 1996, he easily defeated his Republican opponent, Senator Robert Dole of Kansas, who looked his age of seventy-three and who seemed inarticulate and wooden. In contrast to Dole, who talked more about the past than the future, Clinton emphasized ways to move forward and emphasized that his next administration would be a bridge into the twenty-first century. Although the president was still unable to gain a majority of the votes in November because Ross Perot decided to run a second time, he came close, gaining 49 percent of the vote to Dole's 41 percent and Perot's 9 percent. The Republicans lost seats in both the House and Senate but managed to retain both majorities.

The euphoria of victory proved short-lived. In 1997, the president negotiated a deal with the Republicans that included tax cuts, limiting increases in Medicare spending, and a promise to balance the budget in five years. In foreign policy, he helped stop the ethnic cleansing of Albanians by Serbs in the former Yugoslavia by a bombing campaign and eventually the employment of a UN peacekeeping force. His special emissary to Ireland, former senator George Mitchell of Maine, negotiated an accord to end the ongoing conflict between the Republic of Ireland and Northern Ireland. He also persuaded Moscow to accept the expansion of NATO, and he prevented an impending implosion of financial markets in Asia (just as he had done in Mexico two years earlier). He even came closer than any president in arranging a peace agreement between Israel and the PLO, although those efforts ultimately failed.

At the same time, the special Whitewater prosecutor, Ken Starr, began an investigation into every aspect of Clinton's life, looking for evidence of crimes or cover-ups committed by the president. As the investigation continued, it morphed into the Lewinsky scandal, which Starr made the target of his investigation.

The scandal involving Monica Lewinsky began when Linda Tripp, a supposed friend of Lewinsky, a young intern at the White House, leaked a series of conversations she had with Tripp, in which Lewinsky told her that she had had sex with Clinton beginning in late 1995. The revelations followed a lawsuit brought by Paula Jones, a state employee in Arkansas accusing Clinton of making an unwanted sexual advance against her while he was governor of Arkansas.

Under oath, Clinton denied he had ever had sex with Lewinsky, but her accusations were later supported by DNA from Clinton found on one of her dresses. Faced with this evidence, Clinton apologized to the nation for his "inappropriate behavior" but maintained that he had not lied about his relations with Lewinsky. He took the position that oral sex did not constitute sex as defined by the courts. Nevertheless, Starr sent a report to the Congress stating that there were grounds for impeaching Clinton for perjury, obstruction of justice, abuse of power, and other related charges.

The Republican-controlled House responded by impeaching Clinton on the grounds of perjury and obstruction of justice. Once more, the Republicans overreached. During the seven months in which the Lewinsky scandal unfolded, the public became convinced the Republicans were interested not so much in justice as in destroying Clinton. Democrats also came to the president's defense, expressing deep regret that Clinton had engaged in such tawdry behavior but arguing he had not committed the "high crimes and misdemeanors" needed to sustain the charges against him. On 12 February 1999, the Senate easily acquitted him on both charges.

Clinton emerged from the Lewinsky scandal and his impeachment trial with his popularity intact. His rating in the polls reached an all-time high of 70 percent. Although the public believed that what he had done was shameful and thought he should be censured or condemned for his actions, they were not persuaded that his private behavior justified impeachment. They also approved of Clinton's record as president and took umbrage at the fact that the Republicans seemed to be using a personal matter for partisan purposes.

The Starr investigation and the Lewinsky scandal had taken so much oxygen out of the air that Clinton was unable to accomplish much else during the remainder of his administration. Just before leaving office, however, Clinton issued 140 pardons, a number of which drew considerable criticism even from Democrats. Several of them involved Clinton's half-brother, Roger, who sought clemency for ten friends and associates. Two others implicated the president's brother-in-law, Hugh Rodham, who received nearly $400,000 for lobbying for the clemency and pardon of two of his acquaintances. When the fee was reported in the press, Clinton issued a statement that he and Mrs. Clinton were "deeply disturbed" by the news reports and demanded that Rodham return the money. At the end of February, he agreed to do so.[66]

The most questionable pardon that Clinton gave, however, was to Marc Rich, a notorious billionaire commodities trader accused of multiple crimes. To avoid a possible prison term, Rich had fled in 1983 to Switzerland. A number of high-profile figures, including Rich's former wife, Denise Rich, a big Democratic donor who had also given $450,000 to the Clinton Presidential Library, and members of the Israeli government urged Clinton to grant the pardon. Israeli officials said Rich had supported Israeli intelligence operations around the world. The deputy attorney general responsible for reviewing pardon requests was Eric Holder. Holder had a close relationship with Rich's lawyer, Jack Quinn, who also had been a former White House counselor and trusted aide to Clinton. In the waning hours of the administration, Holder delivered a lukewarm but crucial endorsement of the pardon. That was good enough for the president, who signed it on the last day of his administration.[67]

The response in the press was blistering. The *Washington Post* denounced Clinton's "scandalous present to Mr. Rich," which it said "diminished the integrity and grandeur of the pardon power," while the *New York Times* condemned what it called Clinton's "shocking abuse of presidential power." Clinton tried to defend himself in an op-ed article in the *New York Times,* pointing to the pleas from Israel and maintaining that Rich's case should have been treated as a civil rather than a criminal action. Congressional and federal investigations were launched to determine whether efforts had been made to buy pardons from the White House.[68]

The Clintons were also accused of "a last minute effort to cash in on the presidency" by taking from the White House $196,000 in gifts, including art, furniture, and other furnishings, of which $86,000 had been given to them in

Photo of President Bill Clinton golfing in 1999, a year away from the end of his administration. Like many other presidents, Clinton found golfing one of his favorite pastimes, although he was not nearly as good a golfer as some other presidents, such as Eisenhower and Ford. Having survived the Lewinsky scandal and attempts by the Republicans to remove him office, Clinton's popularity stood an all-time high. In this photo, he appears totally relaxed. (Courtesy William J. Clinton Presidential Library.)

Clinton's last year in office. Most of the gifts had to do with Hillary's recent election as U.S. senator from New York and the need to furnish two new homes, one in New York and one in Washington. To establish residency in New York, the Clinton's purchased a $1.5 million home in the upper-scale Westchester community of Chappaqua, north of New York City. After her election, Hillary purchased a second lavish home in the Embassy Row section of Washington, using as a down payment part of a generous $8 million advance she had received to write her memoirs.

To help furnish her new homes, her friends gave her gifts valued at $86,000. The question was whether these gifts and the balance of the $196,000 in property she and Bill had taken from the White House had been registered as personal gifts to the Clintons or were part of the White House collection. In an effort to settle the matter, the former president agreed to reimburse the twenty-seven persons who had given Hillary and him the $86,000 in gifts over the last year. Clinton refused to return or pay for the $104,000 in gifts received before last year. "As have other presidents and their families before us," the former president explained, "we received gifts over the course of our eight years in the White House and followed all the gift rules." Nevertheless, the Clintons were accused of trashing the White House, especially after two donors were quoted as saying that the Clintons had taken $28,000 of furnishings that were intended to become part of the permanent White House collection. Finally, the Clintons stated they would return any items found to be White House property.[69]

Another issue that followed Clinton after he left office was his decision to rent his presidential offices on the fifty-sixth floor of the Carnegie Hall Tower. Annual rental for the offices, which took up the entire floor, was estimated to be $650,000. Hitherto, the most expensive rent for a former president was $285,000 for Ronald Reagan's offices. Republicans on Capitol Hill and even his friends criticized Clinton for his profligacy. The former president had his Presidential Library Foundation pick up $300,000 of the annual cost. This hardly satisfied his critics. "Even if he got people to donate $300,000 a year, he's still asking taxpayers to pay $400,000 every year for his presidential penthouse," remarked Republican representative Ernest Istook of Oklahoma, who headed the House subcommittee that handled the budget of former presidents. The pressure on the former president became so great that he decided in February to find offices elsewhere. On the advice of Charlie Rangel, he moved his offices to a building in the heart of Harlem. Already referred to in 1998 as "America's first black president" by the prize-winning writer Toni Morrison, Clinton's decision to move to Harlem only tightened the bonds he enjoyed with African Americans.[70]

Despite finding a solution to the controversy over office space, Clinton still left office dogged with scandal and faced with attorney fees estimated at over $11.3 million from having to defend himself during the impeachment proceedings against him. He had to pay Paula Jones $850,000 to settle the suit she had brought against him.[71] Clinton was also ordered to pay $91,000 for additional expenses resulting from his dishonest and misleading statements during the Lewinsky affair. Making matters worse, on the day before he left office, his license to practice law in Arkansas was also suspended for five years.[72]

Other women with whom the former president was alleged to have had sex also brought lawsuits that were still making their way through the courts.[73] A legal defense fund established on behalf of the president and Hillary paid off all but $3.9 million of their outstanding legal bills. That still left a considerable debt. Clinton's greatest concern after leaving office, therefore, remained paying off his legal bills and earning a substantial income beyond his pension of $191,000 as a former president. He resolved his financial concerns in the same way that other recent ex-presidents had assured their financial future: he sold his memoirs and went on the lecture circuit. Because of the controversial nature of Clinton's administration, especially the Lewinsky scandal, publishers realized the potential gold mine that his autobiography presented them. In August, 2001, Alfred A. Knopf Inc. agreed to pay Clinton more than $10 million for the worldwide rights to publish his memoirs. It was largest nonfiction advance ever given to an author.

Together with a similarly astonishing $8 million recently paid to now-senator Hillary Clinton for her memoirs, this meant that the Clintons could pay off their legal bills and still be multimillionaires.

The advance was not even the most significant part of Clinton's potential cash cow. He had already proven his ability to connect on a personal level with individuals or with large audiences. Although soft-spoken with a voice that tended to be raspy, he had nevertheless worshipped frequently at black churches and had mastered the natural moves and cadences that were the genius of the best of the black preachers. Yet Clinton was flexible in his delivery and had had the gift for gab and storytelling. Charismatic, with an overpowering physical presence, he did more than charm his audiences; he mesmerized them. "I . . . saw Clinton perform before a variety of audiences, large and small," James Fallows of the *Atlantic,* wrote in 2003. "Simply as an experience, this was like coming across a champion athlete who had retired in his prime . . . and seeing that he still has the old stuff. No one else in modern politics has matched Clinton's ability to speak with equal poise at every level of class, education, and sophistication."[74]

Enjoying star power on par with even the most popular celebrities, Clinton was able to demand fees as high as $250,000 an appearance. His speaking engagements were sometimes arranged like a touring concert, where he went from city to city, raking in huge sums of money. In just his first year out of office, Clinton made $9.2 million from giving fifty-nine speeches to investments banks, Jewish and Israeli organizations, public relations companies, advertising agencies, and other organizations. On one particularly good day in Canada, Clinton made $475,000 for two speeches. By the end of 2008, he had earned $52 million in speaking fees since leaving office.[75]

A final source of income that Clinton enjoyed as a private citizen came from his role as senior adviser at two investment funds, the Yucaipa American Fund and the Yucaipa Corporate Initiatives Fund. Like other former presidents, Clinton was inundated with job offices after leaving the White House. He turned them all down except for being an adviser to the Yucaipa funds started by the billionaire Ronald W. Burkle, a former grocery store magnate. Burkle was interested in having Clinton serve as an adviser to the fund because of the prestige his name would add to the Yucaipa family of funds. The former president had his own reasons for accepting Burkle's offer. In the first place, he and Burkle had become good friends over the years. Burkle contributed to Clinton's legal fund and was a significant benefactor of the Clinton Presidential Library.[76]

Second, the Yucaipa funds specialized in investing in minority-owned businesses in lower-income urban and rural communities that traditional funds and banks were reluctant to serve. These types of investments fitted in nicely with Clinton's philanthropic plans. As an adviser to the funds, Clinton also had no day-to-day responsibilities over how the more than $1 billion in the funds was to be invested. This allowed him to spend most of his time meeting his other commitments. Finally, Clinton did not have to put up any of his own money, but he stood to make millions of dollars depending on how well the funds did. "If we make money, he makes money," Burkle said without being more specific.[77]

In fact, the Yucaipa funds did very well. In 2005, one fund reported a 51.3 percent gain and the other a 25.8 percent gain. In 2006, a third fund was added that invested overseas. Instead of being an adviser to the fund, Clinton was made a partner. He received regular payments and stood to receive one-third of the profits when the fund was dissolved. Reportedly, he earned from the Yucaipa funds between $12 and $15 million and stood to receive a final $20 million payout.[78]

Five years out of office, Clinton, who throughout his career had never been much interested in making money, had made more money after leaving the White House than any other former president. In 2004, he published his memoir, *My Life*. The former president wrote the book himself in longhand. He said the book would be doomed if he used a ghostwriter. The stilted tone would give it away. His main help in preparing the manuscript came from a historian, Ted Widmer of Washington College in Maryland, who had been a speechwriter on Clinton's national security staff. Meeting once or twice a month with the former president, Widmer asked him questions to draw out his recollection. The sessions were recorded on eighty tapes, which were then transcribed. The former president worked almost exclusively from the transcripts. He wrote the large sections on his term as president in just three months. "Some of this has been painful for me," Clinton confessed to James Fallows as he was completing the manuscript, "but it's all been widely instructive. And it convinced me that nearly every person over fifty should find time to sit down and engage in the same exercise, even if you never intend to publish anything. You need to think about what really meant something to you. Who did you really love. Who made you what you are."[79]

Publication of *My Life* was preceded by an extraordinary publicity campaign. In many ways, Clinton was his own best salesman. Knopf arranged for a host of news media outlets to interview the former president, including all the major news programs. Clinton also gave a rousing speech to 2,000 booksellers in Chicago. "One thing we know for sure," the caustic columnist Maureen Dowd commented, "Bill Clinton is going to do what it takes to sell more books than the best-selling author he refers to as 'my senator.'"[80]

Despite the high expectations surrounding the release of *My Life,* the memoir was generally a disappointment, and it was panned by most reviewers. A ponderous volume of 957 pages, promising to provide its reader with new insights into the personality and presidency of Bill Clinton, *My Life* only partially succeeded. On the positive side, Clinton exposed a childhood that was more frail than he had ever acknowledged. Indeed, his journey back to his childhood was almost psychoanalytical testimony to how a drunken stepfather and a mother whom Clinton always loved dearly, but whose free spirit, gambling and drinking, and relationships with unsavory men left permanent scars on an obviously brilliant and gifted child. "I came to accept the secrets of my house as a normal part of my life," Clinton wrote in a series of revealing paragraphs. "The question of secrets," he continued,

> is one I've thought about a lot over the years. We all have them, and I think we're entitled to them. They make our lives more interesting. . . . Still secrets can be an awful burden to bear, especially if some sense of shame is attached to them. . . . I know only that it became a struggle for me to find the right balance between secrets of internal richness and those of hidden fears and shame, and that I was always reluctant to discuss with anyone the most difficult part of my personal life. . . . I know this struggle is at least partly the result of growing up in an alcoholic home and the mechanisms I developed to cope with it. It took me a long time just to figure that out. It was even harder to learn which secrets to keep, which to let go of, which to avoid in the first place. I am still not sure I understand that completely. It looks as if it's going to be a lifetime project.[81]

Some reviewers praised *My Life* precisely because of its introspective nature and gave the volume high marks. Dan Rather, who interviewed Clinton on *60 Minutes*, compared the book to the memoirs of Ulysses S. Grant. Walter Isaacson remarked that the autobiography "captures and conveys, in ways that are sometimes brilliant and at other times unintentional, the essence of [Clinton's] personality and presidency: fascinating, undisciplined, deeply intelligent, self-indulgent and filled with great promise alternately grasped and squandered."[82]

Most reviewers, however, rightly panned *My Life* as being dull, sprawling, and even poorly edited. Clinton seemed to remember and felt the need to record even the tiniest detail of his early life. Even the more analytical parts ran for pages on end. *My Life* was also unfocused and self-indulgent. He spent only one paragraph on the first bombing of the World Trade Center but two pages justifying a well-publicized haircut he took while on Air Force One on the runway of the Los Angeles International Airport, holding up traffic at the busy airport for hours. Similarly, there were other purposeful gaps on such key matters as his relationships, from the political to the sexual. If the reader expected to learn much more beyond what was already covered in the press about his relationship with congressional leaders, like House Speaker Newt Gingrich, or with the women with whom he had sexual relationships, like Gennifer Flowers or Monica Lewinsky, they were sadly disappointed. Even Isaacson in his review described Clinton's coverage of his administration as a "hastily-disgorged data dump on the day-by-day chronology of his presidency that features stretches of unrelated paragraphs." The reviewer for the *New York Times*, Michiko Kakutami, wrote that "*My Life* reads like a messy pastiche of everything that Mr. Clinton ever remembered and wanted to set down in print. . . . There are endless litanies of meals eaten, speeches delivered, voters greeted and turkeys pardoned."[83]

Yet *My Life* was a huge commercial success, selling 606,000 copies in the first week it was released, with advance orders reported to be as high as two million. Even in its first weeks on the market, it far surpassed in sales any other previous presidential memoir. It remained on the *New York Times* best-seller list for forty-six weeks. By 2010, it had sold more than 2.2 million copies in the United States alone and had been published in more than thirty countries.[84]

Although the former president's greatest concern after leaving office was paying off his legal bills and making money, he also devoted considerable time to raising funds to build his presidential library. Clinton had begun making plans for his library while he was still president. Like other presidents before him, he first established a foundation, the William Clinton Foundation, to raise money for the library. With his roots still in Arkansas, he decided that he would build the structure in Little Rock on twenty-seven acres along the banks of the Arkansas River, making it the anchor of a successful redevelopment of the Little Rock riverfront. The library would be part of a complex that would also include a policy center to advance themes that he considered essential to his presidency, a public policy school affiliated with the University of Arkansas, parkland, and a restored pedestrian bridge between Little Rock and North Little Rock. He intended his library "to be more than a little shrine to me," he told James Fallow in 2003. Instead, it would be "America's first museum about our transition into a new millennium—about a new way of working, of relating to each other and the rest of the world."[85]

From the beginning, Clinton was intimately involved in planning the library complex. "I had thought a lot about the library and its exhibits," he later wrote. "I wanted the exhibit space to be open, beautiful, and full of light, and I wanted the material presented in a way that demonstrated America's movement into the twenty-first century." He approved plans by a well-known New York architectural firm for a glass-and-steel structure that would extend over the river. He also hired an exhibit designer who had worked at the Holocaust Museum in Washington. The Clinton Foundation had the task of raising $200 million to pay the estimated $165 million needed to build the project with the balance going to the endowment now required by law. It would be the largest private-sector project in Little Rock's history.[86]

Immediately the proposal ran into a number of problems. Clinton's last-minute pardon of Marc Rich promoted a congressional subpoena for the library foundation's donors to see if there were any conflicts of interest. There were local lawsuits and petition drives challenging the city's condemnation of the land for the library. Although Arkansas was a right-to-work state with union members making up only a very small percentage of the construction labor force, national labor leaders insisted that the library be built exclusively by union members. The local unions boycotted the project until their demands were met. All these issues delayed construction of the library complex for about a year. However, by June 2002, enough of them had been resolved to get the bulldozers clearing brush and excavating the site.[87]

Over the next two years, the former president spent much of his time raising funds for his library complex. Donors had already pledged close to $145 million for the library, although only $21 million had actually been collected. By the time the Clinton Presidential Library and Museum was dedicated in November 2004, however, most of the $200 million goal had been raised. Part of the money may have been tainted because some of the largest donations were believed to have been made while Clinton was still president and had come from foreign corporations or sovereign governments doing business with the White House; the emirs in Dubai alone gave $30 million, while the Saudis contributed $10 million. Other donations, like the one from Denise Rich, came from those seeking a pardon at the end of the administration for a relative, friend, or acquaintance. A few known donors were accused in the media of using Clinton's influence after he left office in questionable deals with foreign governments.[88]

The library was dedicated on 18 November 2004. A 150,000-square-foot structure of cantilevered steel and glass that included atop the building an all-glass, 2,000-square-foot penthouse for the former president, the building was described by one writer as a "trailer on stilts." At a time when architecture had joined other art forms as marketing sites, another critic called the building "architecture as politics, played skillfully to please a large constituency and accommodate a range of perspectives." One result of the Clinton Presidential Library was that it led to the redevelopment of a run-down area of abandoned warehouses, which were replaced by new restaurants, hotels, and apartment buildings. The purpose of the design, however, was to evoke Clinton's bridge to the future.[89]

Despite cold, rainy weather, it was a joyous day for the former president. Just a few months earlier, Clinton had had quadruple bypass surgery at New York Presbyterian Hospital. After spending almost three weeks in the hospital, he had been released with a clean bill of health. He had then gone on the campaign trail for the unsuccessful Democratic candidate for president, Massachusetts senator John Kerry.

The dedication of the Clinton Presidential Library afforded the former president the chance to lay aside the setbacks and disappointments of the past few months. Despite the weather, moreover, a crowd estimated at around 40,000 turned out for the dedication celebrations. Among those present on the speaker's platform were President Bush and former presidents Jimmy Carter and George H. W. Bush. Whatever hard feelings that might have existed from the past or surfaced during the election were gone. Former president Carter even expressed his regrets for the Mariel boatlift. Former president George H. W. Bush, who referred to Clinton as "the Sam Walton of national retail politics," acknowledged how he had been outclassed by Clinton during the 1992 presidential debates. "You know, to be very frank with you, I hated debates. And when I checked my watch at the Richmond debate, it's true, I was wondering when the heck Ross Perot would be finished and how the heck I can get out of there. But it was also clear that President Clinton . . . was in his element that night." President Bush made the former president burst into laughter when he talked about Clinton's renowned political skills: "A fellow in Saline County was asked by his son why he liked Governor Clinton so much. He said, 'Son, he'll look you in the eye, he'll shake your hand, he'll hold your baby, he'll pet your dog, all at the same time.'"[90]

The dedication of his library marked a turning point in Clinton's post-presidency. After he left the White House, the former president had not been certain what he wanted to do with the rest of his life except to write his memoirs, plan and raise funds for his presidential library, and engage in some undefined humanitarian endeavors. In fact, he felt depressed, uncertain about the future, and alone in his Chappaqua house. By 2004, he had published his autobiography, become wealthy, and watched over the dedication of his library. By this time, he too had decided to devote most of his energy to humanitarian work, using Jimmy Carter as his model.

Within months after departing the Oval Office, Clinton had already begun to give clues as to what he was most interested in pursuing in his retirement. In April 2001, he traveled to India as chairman of the new American India Foundation (AIF), which was formed by a group of wealthy Indian American entrepreneurs and doctors in response to a massive earthquake that had killed more than 20,000 people and destroyed more than a thousand villages in the western state of Gujarat. The AIF established for itself the goal of raising $50 million to rebuild at least a hundred of the destroyed villages. During the week that followed, he visited the devastated area as well as Bombay (now Mumbai), Calcutta, and New Delhi. Wherever he traveled, he was greeted with chants of "Clinton, Clinton, Clinton," indicating how popular he remained despite his no longer being president. The former president was moved by the mountains of rubble he found in the devastated area. At one village, he lay a bouquet of roses in a lane where 150 schoolchildren were buried. At each of the places he toured, he vowed to return to India on a regular basis. "I'm just trying to find something useful to do in a place I care about," he remarked.[91]

Another project on which Clinton embarked soon after leaving office was the prevention of the spread of AIDS, which was ravaging much of sub-Saharan Africa and other underdeveloped areas. To fight the AIDS epidemic, Clinton agreed in 2001 to head the board of advisers of the International AIDS Trust. By this time, he had also begun to stitch together an array of causes that interested him: combating AIDS, economic empowerment of the poor, and racial, ethnic, and religious reconciliation. He realized that he could not look solely or primarily to the government to deal with these problems. He would have to depend on private philanthropy, using the assistance of nonprofit organizations and corporate leaders with deep pockets. "There is no way government can do this alone," he said about tackling the AIDS crisis. Using the power of the bully pulpit and his extensive network of influential individuals, he held a fund-raising event in New York in August for AIDS that brought together 100 power brokers, including real estate celebrity Donald Trump; entertainment mogul Harvey Weinstein; Dr. Samuel D. Waksai, chief executive of ImClone, the city's largest biotech employer; and Jerry Inzerillo, executive vice president of Sun International.[92]

In 2001, Clinton extended the purpose of the William J. Clinton Foundation to include a commitment to humanitarian work. Although the foundation has evolved over the years into a massive organization with offices in the United States and abroad undertaking a number of worldwide humanitarian efforts, its new mission statement was vague: to be "a nongovernmental organization that could leverage the unique capacities of governments, partner organizations, and other individuals to address rising inequalities and deliver tangible results that improve people's lives." The following year, the foundation undertook its first major project when, at the request of South Africa's leader, Nelson Mandela, the former president began the Clinton HIV/AIDS initiative, which eventually evolved into the independent nonprofit Clinton Health Access Initiative, to improve global access to care and treatment.

The Clinton Foundation's most ambitious undertaking, however, has been the Clinton Global Initiative (CGI), which the former president launched with a conference in New York in September 2005, attended by 800 wealthy and influential people, each paying $15,000 to be at the gathering. As a result of the foundation and CGI, the former president has been able to raise billions of dollars to deal with pressing world needs from global poverty and disease to religious strife and information technologies.[93]

Invariably, questions were raised after Clinton left the White House as to his motives in undertaking such an ambitious program of humanitarian activity. According to the former president, his intent was simple and clear-cut. He had done a considerable amount of soul-searching about what he hoped to accomplish in his retirement from office. He even analyzed what other former presidents had done and concluded that Jimmy Carter was "the only person who'd done anything that remotely resembled what I thought I could do." Skeptics, however, continued to raise doubts as to his real motivation. "Everyone was worried," said Richard Marlink, who led Harvard's AIDS Institute. "Is this a campaign with photo ops and press releases or a long-term commitment?" Even as president, Clinton had not made AIDS a high priority, never budgeting more than a $141 million to deal with the pandemic until the last two years of his administration, and then more than tripling that amount to $540 million in his last budget. But even this figure paled against the $15 billion, five-year global AIDS plans instituted by his successor, George W. Bush. In fact, for most of his presidency, Clinton's trade office had fought to protect the patent rights of pharmaceutical companies against attempts by poverty-stricken countries to make or import cheaper generic drugs. "I think it was wrong," he admitted in 2006.[94]

Indeed, the skepticism about Clinton's motives behind his charities extended well beyond the issue of whether he was seeking photo ops and redemption for some of the scars of his administration. Questions were even raised whether the former president was working his global ties both to assist his business associates as well as to benefit his charities. In February 2008, for example, the *Wall Street Journal* ran a long story in which it suggested that Clinton had helped a wealthy Canadian businessman and generous donor to the CGI, Frank Giustra, acquire an interest in Colombian oil fields and a major uranium deal in Kazakhstan. "The relationship with Mr. Giustra is part of a sprawling business and charitable empire that the former president has created," the newspaper commented."[95]

That Clinton should still be asked questions about the motivation behind his humanitarian actives so long after leaving the White House indicates the degree of cynicism, at least within the media, that has continued to follow the former president. Yet given the effort that the former president has devoted to his charitable and humanitarian activities since leaving office, his concern throughout his political career to help the destitute and others in need, and his belief as president in the power of government to lift up, it is hard to doubt Clinton's sincerity. "The reason I do this work I do is that I really care about politics and people and public policy," he responded, with a flash of anger, to a question more than five years after leaving the White House as to whether he was merely seeking redemption for the Lewinsky scandal. "I'm 60 years old now, and I'm not running for anything, so I don't have to be polite anymore. I think it's a bunch of hokum." He said much the same thing in a book, *Giving: How Each of Us Can Change the World*, that he published in 2007. "When I left the White House, I knew I wanted to spend the rest of my life giving my time, money, and skills to worthwhile endeavors where I could make a difference. I didn't know exactly what I would do, but I wanted to help save lives, solve important problems, and give more young people the chance to live their dreams."[96]

Beside his humanitarian activities, there have been other matters that have commanded Clinton's attention since 2004. The most important by far involved the former president's efforts to get the 2008 Democratic nomination for president for Hillary, who had begun the primary season as the presumptive front-runner but who quickly found herself in an uphill battle against the charismatic U.S. senator from Illinois, Barack Obama. In an effort to save the nomination for his wife, the former president began campaigning alongside Hillary, but he soon found himself putting his foot in his mouth, even seeming to question Obama's patriotism. The most notorious incident occurred after Obama's decisive victory in the South Carolina primary at the end of January, when the former president compared Obama's victory in the state to the Reverend Jesse Jackson's South Carolina victories in 1984 and 1988, suggesting that they had won because they were black in a state with high African American vote. The implication seemed to be that Obama could win the black vote but not the general election. Immediately critics attacked the former president, who noted that his remarks were at the least racially insensitive, and at worst an effort by Clinton to insert the race card into the election—something Obama had assiduously avoided.[97]

Clinton tried to defend himself by going on all the morning talk shows and stating that his remarks had been distorted. "They made up a race story out of that," he responded about his critics. "There was no disrespect to Senator Obama in that. So I think our side got a bum rap." Nevertheless, his comments did serious damage to the campaign and to the former president personally. They turned many black officials and African American voters against Hillary, who cited them repeatedly as the reason why they had coalesced behind Obama. According to an NBC–Wall Street poll released in March, 45 percent of respondents now viewed the former president negatively, while 42 percent viewed him positively. A year earlier, the respective numbers had been 35 percent and 48 percent.[98]

Once Hillary conceded the nomination to Obama, it took a while for Clinton to get over his wife's defeat and the slurs he believed the Obama camp had made against him. In an interview in August, just before the Democrats held their convention in Denver, he even refused the opportunity to affirm Obama's readiness to be president. However, after Obama was formally selected as the Democratic candidate, he and the Democratic candidate appeared together at Clinton's Harlem office, and the former president offered to campaign on Obama's behalf. Although Obama believed there were only a few places where he could help him, in October, they made a joint appearance in Florida, a key state where Clinton was popular within the important Jewish community of south Florida.

Once Obama was elected and looked to Hillary to be his secretary of state, Clinton, who still remained distant from the president-elect, did everything demanded of him by the vetting team to assure her selection, including agreeing not to make paid speeches overseas and to distance himself from fund-raising projects abroad. Although the chemistry between the former president and the incumbent president still leaves room for improvement, Clinton has been supportive of the president. After the Democrats' drubbing by the Republicans in the 2010 midterm elections—not dissimilar from the one Clinton suffered in 1994—Obama met with Clinton at the White House for a postelection conversation. Increasingly the president has turned to Clinton for political advice.[99]

In 2009, the former president was instrumental in gaining the release of two American journalists, Laura Ling and Euna Lee, who had been held captive by the North Koreans for allegedly crossing North Korea's border with China. When the Pyongyang government made it clear that their release depended on a personal appeal for clemency by a high-ranking American, the former president agreed to deliver the request. After meeting with North Korea's leader, Kim Jong-il, he secured their pardons and brought them home.[100] With acts such as these, Clinton has recovered whatever popularity he lost during his wife's campaign. All the polls indicate he is the most popular living Democrat.[101]

Clinton has therefore pursued an activist role as a former president. By force of his highly publicized annual CGI conferences and his own personality, he has almost compelled some of the world's wealthiest individuals to take the initiative in developing programs for the world's indigent and to commit the resources to carry them out. If referring to Clinton as "president of the world," as Chris

Matthews did in his 2010 documentary, was an overstatement, certainly referring to Clinton as a "citizen of the world" is not. Even former president George H. W. Bush, who rejected the Carter model of the post-presidency in favor of a more private and less active retirement, thought it his duty, both as a privileged private citizen and an ex-president, to pursue his own humanitarian agenda as part of his "thousand points of light." That fact alone is testimony to the evolution of the post-presidency since the time of George Washington, John Adams, and Thomas Jefferson more than two centuries earlier.

Notes

PREFACE

1. Nancy Gibbs and Michael Duffy in *The Presidents Club: Inside the World's Most Exclusive Fraternity* (New York: Simon and Schuster, 2012), which covers the relationships between incumbent presidents and former presidents from Truman to Obama, maintain a somewhat different view. Two highly respected editors for *Time* magazine, they argue that the nation's more recent former presidents, in particular Eisenhower and Nixon, have had considerable influence on incumbent presidents, certainly more so than I argue here. They also maintain that there has been an exclusive "club" between former and incumbent presidents, beginning with Truman's relationship with Herbert Hoover, drawing upon the natural empathy that only men who have gone through the unique common experience of being the world's most powerful person can appreciate. Gibbs and Duffy base their argument on considerable research and interviews with the presidents and former presidents. As a result, their book is a major contribution to the history of the presidency and former presidency. That said, I adhere to my contention that the influence of former presidents on incumbent presidents, including Eisenhower and Nixon, has been limited and largely on the margins and that most certainly it has not "changed the course of history" as their publishers maintain. Indeed, I dispute the very notion of a "club." Certainly the former presidents exchanged frequent pleasantries, kept each other abreast of important national and international developments, and were often together for social occasions, from the opening of presidential libraries to funerals. Sometimes they developed close, and often surprising, relationships, such as those between Carter and Ford and Clinton and the Bush family. But as even Gibbs and Duffy acknowledge, Carter and Nixon were generally regarded as the black sheep of the "club" and were never treated as full members of the so-called "club." Also, enmity, distrust, and even deception characterized the relationship of members of the "club" as much as friendship and admiration for each other. Because *The President's Club* was published after the manuscript for this book was in the late stages of production and was about to be sent to the typesetters, I have had to limit my references and comments about the book to the notes. For an early review of *The President's Club*,

see Janet Maslin, "The Knotty Ties Binding America's Ex-Leaders," *New York Times,* 18 April 2012.

2. *Wall Street Journal,* 23 January 2008. See also *Wall Street Journal,* 20 December 2007.

CHAPTER 1: THE REPUBLICAN IDEAL OF THE POST-PRESIDENCY

1. Quoted in "The Sheila Variations 1797—John Adams Inauguration," http://www .sheilomalley.com.

2. Washington to James McHenry, 3 April 1797, in *The Papers of George Washington: Retirement Series,* ed. W. W. Abbott, 4 vols. (Charlottesville: University Press of Virginia, 1998), 1:33n1.

3. My understanding of republicanism is drawn from extensive literature on the subject. See especially Jack Rakove, *Original Meanings: Politics and Ideas in the Making of the Constitution* (New York: Vintage Books, 1997); Drew McCoy, *The Elusive Republic: Political Economy in Jeffersonian America* (New York: Norton, 1980); Lance Banning, *The Jeffersonian Persuasion: Evolution of a Party Ideology* (Ithaca, N.Y.: Cornell University Press, 1978); Stanley Elkins and Eric McKitrick, *The Age of Federalism: The Early American Republic, 1788–1800* (New York: Knopf, 1993); Joyce Appleby, *Liberalism and Republicanism in the Historical Imagination* (Cambridge, Mass.: Harvard University Press, 1992); Isaac Kramnick, "The Great National Discussion: The Division of Politics in 1787," *William and Mary Quarterly* 45 (1988): 3–32; Robert E. Shalhope, "Douglas Adair and the Historiography of Republicanism," in *Fame and the Founding Fathers: Essays by Douglas Adair,* ed. Trevor Colbourn (New York: Norton, 1974), xxv–xxxv; Gary Ward Sheldon, *The Political Philosophy of James Madison* (Baltimore: Johns Hopkins University Press, 2001); and Drew R. McCoy, *The Last of the Founding Fathers: James Madison and the Republican Legacy* (New York: Cambridge University Press, 1989). On the colonial fascination with ancient Rome in particular and the ancient republics in general, see Gordon S. Wood, *The Radicalism of the American Revolution* (New York: Knopf, 1992), 100–109.

4. Elkins and McKitrick, *Age of Federalism,* esp. 489–528; Sean Wilentz, *The Rise of American Democracy: Jefferson to Lincoln* (New York: Norton, 2005), esp. 3–98.

5. The full text of the message can be found in Victor Hugo Paltsits, *Washington's Farewell Address* (New York: New York Public Library, 1935), 139–169.

6. Quoted in Joseph J. Ellis, *His Excellency: George Washington* (New York: Knopf, 2004), 171.

7. Quoted in ibid., 149.

8. Quoted in Richard Norton Smith, *Patriarch: George Washington and the New American Nation* (New York: Mariner Books, 1997), xvi.

9. Paltsits, *Washington's Farewell Address,* 139–169.

10. Quotes are in Eric Burns, *Infamous Scribblers: The Founding Fathers and the Rowdy Beginnings of American Journalism* (New York: Public Affairs, 2006), 1–15, 304–311, 317, 322–326. See also John Tebbell and Sarah Miles Watts, *The Press and the Presidency: From George Washington to Ronald* Reagan (New York: Oxford University Press, 1985), 16–19; James Flexner, *George Washington: Anguish and Farewell (1793–1799)*

(Boston: Little, Brown, 1972), 245; Barry Schwartz, *George Washington: The Making of an American Symbol* (New York: Free Press, 1987), 56–69, 431–449.

11. Washington to John Jay, 8 May 1796, in *The Writings of George Washington from the Original Manuscript Sources, 1745–1799,* ed. John C. Fitzpatrick, 39 vols. (Washington, D.C.: Government Printing Office, 1931–1944), vol. 39. I cite from the online version (http://etext.virginia.edu/washington/fitzpatrick/).

12. Quoted in "George Washington's Mount Vernon—Creating Identity," http://www.mountvernon.org.

13. "George Washington's Mount Vernon," http://www.mountvernon.org. See also Ron Chernow, *Washington: A Life* (New York: Penguin, 2010), 76–78, 162–163, 476–478; and Marcus Cunliffe, *George Washington: Man and Monument* (New York: Mentor Books, 1982), 104–105.

14. Of the land and slaves from the marriage, he also managed as legal guardian of Martha's two children from her first marriage an additional 15,000 acres and between 200 and 300 slaves. See Chernow, *Washington,* 79–80, 100, 156. See also Ellis, *His Excellency,* 48; and John McGregor Burns and Susan Dunn, *George Washington* (New York: Times Books, 2004), 14.

15. Washington to Law, 7 May 1798, and Washington to Lear, 26 June 1798, in Abbott, *Papers of George Washington,* 2:257–258, 2:358.

16. Washington to Hamilton, 15 May 1796, in Fitzpatrick, *Writings of George Washington,* vol. 35. Interestingly, Hamilton had argued in another celebrated document, *The Federalist Papers,* defending the new Constitution, that it would be dangerous to set term limits on presidents because of what they might do once out of office. "Would it promote the peace of the community, or the stability of the government," he argued in *Federalist* 72, "to have half a dozen men, who had had credit enough to raise themselves to the seat of the supreme magistracy wandering among the people like discontented ghosts and sighing for a place which they were destined never more to possess?" However, although there were no term limits in the Constitution, most of the founding fathers thought differently. Benjamin Franklin, for example, regarded it as a promotion for a president to return to the people as a private citizen. *The Federalist Papers,* ed. Clinton Rossiter (New York: Mentor Books, 1961), 438.

17. "Farewell Address [First Draft]" enclosed with Washington to Hamilton, 15 May 1796, in Fitzpatrick, *Writings of George Washiington,* vol. 35.

18. Quoted in Clinton Rossiter, *The American Presidency,* 2nd ed. (New York: Harcourt, Brace and World, 1960), 232.

19. Washington to Oliver Wolcott Jr., 15 May 1797, in Abbott, *Papers of George Washington,* 1:142–143.

20. Quoted in Flexner, *George Washington,* 392.

21. Schwartz, *George Washington,* 44–45. See also Gordon S. Wood, *Revolutionary Characters: What Made the Founders Different* (New York: Penguin, 2006), 41–42, 60–61.

22. John Meacham draws the distinction between public and civil religion in *American Gospel: The Founding Fathers and the Making of a Nation* (New York: Random House, 2006), esp. 3–105. But also consult Benjamin Hufbauer, *Presidential Temples: How Memorials and Libraries Shape Public Memory* (Lawrence: University Press of Kansas, 2005), esp. 6–9, 25–26, 121.

23. Quoted in John Alexander Carroll and Mary Wells Ashworth, *George Washington: First in Peace* (New York: Charles Scribners and Sons, 1957), 493–494.

24. Joseph J. Ellis, *Passionate Sage: The Character and Legacy of John Adams* (New York: Norton, 1944).

25. On these points, see especially David McCullough's best-selling *John Adams* (New York: Simon & Schuster, 2001); Richard Alan Ryerson, "John Adams and the Founding of the Republic: An Introduction," in *John Adams and the Founding of the Republic,* ed. Richard Alan Ryerson (Boston: Massachusetts Historical Society, 2001), 1039; Ellis, *Passionate Sage;* and John Ferling, *John Adams: A Life* (Knoxville: University of Tennessee Press, 1992). But see also the following earlier works: Ralph Adams Brown, *The Presidency of John Adams* (Lawrence: University Press of Kansas, 1975); Peter Shaw, *The Character of John Adams* (Chapel Hill: University of North Carolina Press, 1976); and Page Smith, *John Adams,* 2 vols. (Garden City, N.Y.: Doubleday, 1962).

26. Quoted in Shaw, *Character of John Adams,* 79. Shaw has written one of the most perceptive accounts of Adams's personality.

27. On these points, see especially Joyce Appleby, "John Adams and the New Republican Synthesis," in Appleby, *Liberalism and Republicanism,* 188–209; Banning, *Jeffersonian Persuasion,* 278–290; Elkins and McKitrick, *Age of Federalism,* 529–537.

28. Adams to Richard Cranch, 30 May 1801, John Adams Papers (hereafter Adams Papers), Massachusetts Historical Society, Boston, microfilm edition, reel 359.

29. Quoted in Tebbell and Miles Watts, *The Press and the Presidency,* 28.

30. Quoted in Shaw, *Character of John Adams,* 285.

31. Quoted in Ferling, *John Adams,* 426.

32. Quoted in Shaw, *Character of John Adams,* 286.

33. John Adams to Richard Rush, 24 November 1814, quoted in ibid., 312.

34. "Adams National Historical Park—Places (U.S. National Park Service)," http://www.nps.gov.

35. Quoted in Ellis, *Passionate Sage,* 58.

36. John Adams to Thomas Boylston Adams, 18 December 1800, in Adams Papers, reel 118. "President John Adams: Health and Medical History," http://www.doctorzebra.com. Smith, *John Adams,* 2:1113–1115; Ferling, *John Adams,* 417 and 426–430.

37. *Diary and Autobiography of John Adams,* ed. J. L. H. Butterfield, 4 vols. (Boston: Harvard University Press, 1961), 2:253. The autobiography is available online as *Adams Papers: An Electronic Archive,* Massachusetts Historical Society, http://www.masshist.org/digitaladams/.

38. Lester H. Cohen, introduction to Mercy Otis Warren, *History of the Rise, Progress and Termination of the American Revolution, Interspersed with Biographical, Political and Moral Observations, in Two Volumes* (1805), available at the Online Library of Liberty, http://oll.libertyfund.org/.

39. Adams to Mercy Otis Warren, 20 July 1807, and Mercy Otis Warren to John Adams, 28 July 1807, in Charles Francis Adams, ed., *Correspondence between John Adams and Mercy Warren,* in *Collections of Massachusetts Historical Society,* vol. 4, 5th ser. (1871), 353 and 480.

40. Wilentz, *Rise of American Democracy,* 76.

41. Adams to Jefferson, 30 June and 13 July 1813, in *The Adams–Jefferson Letters: The Complete Correspondence between Thomas Jefferson and Abigail and John Adams,*

ed. Lester J. Cappon (Chapel Hill: University of North Carolina Press, 1988), 2:348, 2:355.

42. Jefferson to Adams, 28 October 1813, and Adams to Jefferson, 15 November 1813, in ibid., 2:391, 2:401.

43. On Adams's failing health, see John R. Bumgarner, *The Health of the Presidents: The 41 United States Presidents through 1993 from a Physician's Point of View* (Jefferson, N.C.: MacFarland, 1994), 14.

44. Adams to John Quincy Adams, 13 March 1813, in Adams Papers, reel 413.

45. In fact, Adams had tried to dissuade Quincy Adams from engaging in a political career. On this point, see Mary W. M. Hargreaves, *The Presidency of John Quincy Adams* (Lawrence: University Press of Kansas, 1985), 253. See also Donald H. Stewart and George P. Clark, "Misanthrope or Humanitarian? John Adams in Retirement," *New England Quarterly* 28 (March 1955): 216–236. In his highly praised biography of John Quincy Adams, Paul C. Nagel makes no mention of any role that John Adams played in forwarding his son's career. In fact, he states that Quincy Adams's appointment as secretary of state was not well received by his wife, Louisa, because it would distract him from the recent attention he had been giving to his family. Paul C. Nagel, *John Quincy Adams: A Public Life, A Private Life* (Cambridge, Mass.: Harvard University Press, 1997), 232.

46. Adams to Jefferson, 17 April 1826, in Cappon, *Adams–Jefferson Letters,* 2:614.

47. John Murray Allison, *Adams and Jefferson: The Story of a Friendship* (Norman: University of Oklahoma Press, 1966), 274–276, 278–283, 285–287; Bumgarner, *Health,* 14.

48. My interpretation of Jefferson's interest in the political world differs somewhat from that found in Alan Crawford's recent study of Jefferson's years after the White House. Crawford argues that Jefferson "kept abreast of political developments" largely through his friends in Albermarle County. But our differences are mostly ones of emphasis. In fact, we both agree that the issues that most concerned Jefferson were those related to the country's future, such as the development of the economy and the future of republicanism itself, rather than daily politics. See Alan Pell Crawford, *Twilight at Monticello: The Final Years of Thomas Jefferson* (New York: Random House, 2008), especially xxi.

49. The first two quotes are in Tebbell and Miles Watts, *The Press and the Presidency,* 41. For Jefferson's remarks about advertisements, see Crawford, *Twilight at Monticello,* xx.

50. The issue of Jefferson's position on slavery is complex and the literature is large and heated just as it is for the founding fathers in general. But see especially Lucia C. Stanton, "'Those Who Labor for My Happiness': Thomas Jefferson and His Slaves," in *Jeffersonian Legacies,* ed. Peter S. Onuf (Charlottesville: University Press of Virginia, 1993), 147–180; Paul Finkelman, "Jefferson and Slavery: 'Treason Against the Hopes of the World,'" in Onuf, *Jeffersonian Legacies,* 181–221; Howard Tempereley, "Jefferson and Slavery: A Study in Moral Perplexity," in *Reason and Republicansim: Thomas Jefferson's Legacy of Liberty,* ed. Gary McDowell and Sharon I. Noble (New York: Rowman & Littlefield, 1997), 85–99; Robert G. Kennedy, *Mr. Jefferson's Lost Cause: Land, Farmers, Slavery, and the Louisiana Purchase* (New York: Oxford University Press, 2003), esp. 2, 19, 29–30, 36, 39, 73–83, 213–214; Joseph Ellis, *American Sphinx: The Character of Thomas Jefferson* (New York: Vintage Books, 1998), 20, 60–61, 65–66, 101–106, 171–180, 233, 313–326, 329, and 356; Dumas Malone, *The Sage of Monticello* (Charlottesville: University Press of Virginia, 2006), 316–327; Merrill D. Peterson, *Thomas Jefferson and*

the New Nation: A Biography (New York: Oxford University Press, 1975), 44, 91–92, 260, 779–785, 997–998; Andrew Burstein, *The Inner Jefferson* (Charlottesville: University Press of Virginia, 1996), 278–281; Crawford, *Twilight at Monticello,* 194–200.

51. The standard account of the Jeffersonian image in American history remains Merrill D. Peterson, *The Jefferson Image in the American Mind* (Charlottesville: University Press of Virginia, 1998). But see also Ellis, *American Sphinx,* 349–362; and Douglass Adair, "The New Thomas Jefferson," in Colbourn, *Fame and the Founding Fathers,* 235–245.

52. One of his biographers has even characterized him as the American sphinx. Ellis, *American Sphinx.*

53. Quoted in Crawford, *Twilight at Monticello,* 48–49.

54. Jefferson to Benjamin Rush, 22 September 1809, in *A Jefferson Profile as Revealed in His Letters,* ed. Saul K. Padover (New York: John Day, 1956), 187–188.

55. The classic study of the agrarian myth is Richard Hoftsadter, *The Age of Reform: From Bryan to F.D.R.* (New York: Knopf, 1955), esp. chap. 1.

56. Ellis, *American Sphinx,* 36–41, 47. See also Iain McLean, "Before and After Publius: The Sources and Influence of Madison's Political Thought," in *James Madison: The Theory and Practice of Republican Government,* ed. Samuel Kernell (Stanford, Calif.: Stanford University Press, 2003), 18.

57. On these points, see especially Appleby, *Liberalism and Republicanism,* 253–276. See also Crawford, *Twilight at Monticello,* 72–73.

58. Jefferson to Pierre du Pont de Nemours, 2 March 1809, quoted in Wilentz, *Rise of American Democracy,* 135.

59. James Morton Smith, introduction to *The Republic of Letters: The Correspondence between Thomas Jefferson and James Madison, 1776–1826,* ed. James Morton Smith, 3 vols. (New York: Norton, 1995), 1:27–29. On the Jefferson–Madison relationship, see Adrienne Koch, *Jefferson and Madison: The Great Collaboration* (New York: Oxford University Press, 1964), esp. 3–14, 33–61; and McCoy, *Last of the Founding Fathers,* 45–64.

60. Aside from the issue of the Constitution, perhaps the most important incident in which Madison's advice prevailed over Jefferson's instincts was his warning to Jefferson not to agree to Adams's offer of a political concord between the two men after Adams's presidential victory in 1796. Merrill D. Peterson, *Adams and Jefferson: A Revolutionary Dialogue* (New York: Oxford University Press, 1974), 67–68.

61. Jefferson's Circular Letter about His Relations with President Madison, March 1809, in Smith, *Republic of Letters,* 3:1574.

62. Jefferson to James Madison, 25 May 1810, and Jefferson to John Tyler, 26 May 1810, in *The Papers of Thomas Jefferson: Retirement Series,* ed. Jefferson Looney, 2 vols. (Princeton, N.J.: Princeton University Press, 2004–2005), 2:416–417, 2:420–421; Malone, *Sage of Monticello,* 66.

63. Jefferson to James Madison, 30 March 1809, in Looney, *Papers of Thomas Jefferson,* 1:92–93; Jefferson's Conversation with James Monroe: Editorial Note, Thomas Jefferson to James Madison, 30 November 1809, James Monroe's Account of a Conversation with Thomas Jefferson, 30 November 1809, Smith, *Republic of Letters,* 2:42–46; Smith, *Republic of Letters,* 3:1563–1564.

64. Malone, *Sage of Monticello,* 14–15, 65.

65. Jefferson to Madison, 27 April 1809, in Smith, *Republic of Letters,* 3:1585–1586.

66. Quoted in Peterson, *Thomas Jefferson and the New Nation,* 931.

67. Jefferson to William Duane, 4 April 1813, in Padover, *Jefferson Profile,* 206–207. For useful summaries of letters between Jefferson and Madison before and during the War of 1812, see Smith, *Republic of Letters,* 3:1561–1563, 3:1614–1623. See also Crawford, *Twilight at Monticello,* 92–93, and Marie B. Hecht, *Beyond the Presidency: The Residue of Power* (New York: Macmillan, 1976), 6–11.

68. Thomas Jefferson to Monsieur le Comte Diodati, 29 March 1807, quoted in Crawford, *Twilight at Monticello,* 60.

69. On Jefferson's assets and liabilities, see also Malone, *Sage of Monticello,* 34–42; Peterson, *Thomas Jefferson and the New Nation,* 926–927 and 938–939; Crawford, *Twilight at Monticello,* xxiii, 59–60, 110–112, 122, and 172–173; Burstein, *Inner Jefferson,* 249–253. On Jefferson's frequent hospitality, see also McLaughlin, *Jefferson and Monticello,* 4 and 9–10.

70. Jefferson to Madison, 22 May 1809 and 13 May 1810, in Smith, *Republic of Letters,* 3:1588–1589 and 3:1628–1629.

71. Peterson, *Thomas Jefferson and the New Nation,* 922–923.

72. Thomas Jefferson to Joseph Priestley, 18 January 1800, quoted in Crawford, *Twilight at Monticello,* 152.

73. Quoted in Peterson, *Thomas Jefferson and the New Nation,* 961–964.

74. Jefferson to Madison, 1 February 1825, in Smith, *Republic of Letters,* 3:1923–1924.

75. Madison to Jefferson, 8 February 1825, in ibid., 3:1924–1925.

76. Jefferson to Adams 11 January 1816, in Cappon, *Adams–Jefferson Letters,* 2:458–461.

77. Jefferson to Adams, 10 December 1819, in ibid., 2:548–550.

78. Jefferson to Adams, 27 June 1822, in ibid., 2:580–581. In a fascinating, albeit speculative and controversial study, Andrew Burstein has argued that until his post-presidency, when he was flooded with letters seeking his advice and counsel, letter writing had been a passion for Jefferson and the lock to understanding his seemingly imperturbable personality. See Burstein, *Inner Jefferson,* esp. 273–275.

79. After Jefferson's daughter, Martha, left Monticello penniless, the legislatures of South Carolina and Louisiana each voted her $10,000, but Jefferson's native state of Virginia did nothing. Hecht, *Beyond the Presidency,* 189–193.

80. Jefferson to John Holmes, 22 April 1820, in *The Writings of Thomas Jefferson,* ed. Paul Leicester Ford, 10 vols. (New York: G. P. Putnam's Sons, 1899), 10:157–158; Peterson, *Thomas Jefferson and the New Nation,* 997. See also Malone, *Sage of Monticello,* 328–231.

81. Jefferson to Adams, 27 June 1822, in Cappon, *Adams–Jefferson Letters,* 2:580–581.

82. Jefferson to Madison, 24 December 1825, and Madison to Jefferson, 28 December 1825, in Smith, *Republic of Letters,* 3:1943–1951.

83. Quoted in Peterson, *Thomas Jefferson and the New Nation,* 1001. See also Allison, *Adams and Jefferson,* 288–289.

84. Jefferson to Madison, 26 February 1826, in Smith, *Republic of Letters,* 3:1964–1967.

85. Peterson, *Jefferson Image.*

CHAPTER 2: FROM THE REPUBLICAN TO THE DEMOCRATIC IDEAL OF THE POST-PRESIDENCY

1. *The Diary of John Quincy Adams, 1794–1845,* ed. Allan Nevins (New York: Scribner), 360; Ellis, *Passionate Sage,* 210–211.

2. On the coincidence of Monroe's death on 4 July, following the death exactly five years earlier of Adams and Jefferson, as an act of providence, see Harry Ammon, *James Monroe: The Quest for National Identity* (New York: McGraw Hill, 1971), 572. On the reports about trying to keep Madison alive until 4 July 1836, see Virginia Moore, *The Madisons: A Biography* (New York: McGraw Hill, 1979), 477.

3. Wood, *Revolutionary Characters,* 4.

4. There is some disagreement as to Madison's exact height. Virginia Moore insists that he was five feet, six inches tall, although most other sources place his height at five feet, four inches. Regardless, there is little disagreement that Madison was frail, sickly, and slight of stature. Moore, *Madisons,* 35.

5. Robert Allen Rutland, *The Presidency of James Madison* (Lawrence: University Press of Kansas, 1990), esp. 186–189 and 209–213; Jack N. Rakove, *James Madison and the Creation of the American Republic* (Glenview, Ill.: Scott Foresman, 1990), 159–169; Garry Wills, *James Madison* (New York: Times Books, 2002); McCoy, *Last of the Founding Fathers,* 10–11.

6. McCoy, *Last of the Founding Fathers,* 40–42 and 49–50; McLean, "Before and after Publius," 16–19; Wilentz, *Rise of American Democracy,* 42–45.

7. Irving Brant, *The Fourth President: A Life of James* Madison (Indianapolis, Ind.: Bobbs-Merrill, 1970), 143–196; Robert Rutland, *James Madison: The Founding Father* (New York: Macmillan, 1987), 16–19; McCoy, *Last of the Founding Fathers,* 43–45 and 52–61.

8. "Report on the Virginia Resolutions," in *The Mind of the Founder: Sources of the Political Thought of James Madison,* ed. Marvin Meyers, rev. ed. (Hanover, N.H.: University Press of New England, 1981), 229–273; Brant, *Fourth President,* 283–296; Wilentz, *Rise of American Democracy,* 106–107.

9. Rutland, *Presidency of James Madison,* 193–195 and 203.

10. Ibid., 205–206; McCoy, *Last of the Founding Fathers,* 92–101.

11. Madison to Gallatin, [?] March 1817, in U.S. Congress, *Letters and Other Writings of James Madison: Fourth President of the United States,* 4 vols. (Philadelphia: J. B. Lippincott, 1865), 3:37–39.

12. Ralph Ketcham, *James Madison: A Biography* (Charlottesville: University Press of Virginia, 1990), 614–621; McCoy, *Last of the Founding Fathers,* 74; Stanley Elkins and Eric McKitrick, *The Age of Federalism: The Early American Republic, 1788–1800* (New York: Oxford University Press, 1993), 79–92.

13. Ketcham, *James Madison,* 427–428 and 613–614; Hecht, *Beyond the Presidency,* 193–194.

14. Rutland, *Presidency of James Madison,* 242–243; Ketcham, *James Madison,* 621–625.

15. Ketcham, *James Madison,* 660–664. Hecht, *Beyond the Presidency,* 195.

16. Madison to William T. Barry, 4 August 1822, in *The Writings of James Madison,* ed. Gaillard Hunt, 9 vols. (New York: G. P. Putnam's Sons, 1900–1910), 9:103–109.

17. Madison to Robert J. Evans, 15 June 1819, in Meyers, *Mind of the Founder.*

18. Madison to Robert Walsh, 27 November 1819, in Hunt, *Writings of James Madison,* 9:1–13.

19. McCoy, *Last of the Founding Fathers,* 113; Kenneth M. Stamp, "The Concept of a Perpetual Union," *Journal of American History* 65 (Spring 1978): 30.

20. McCoy, *Last of the Founding Fathers,* 123–126.

21. Madison to Jefferson, 17 February 1825, in Smith, *Republic of Letters,* 3:1927–1928; McCoy, *Last of the Founding Fathers,* 117–118 and 138–139. See also Madison to Joseph C. Cabell, 22 March 1827, in Hunt, *Writings of James Madison,* 9:284–287.

22. Madison to Robert Y. Haynes, [3 or 4] April 1830, in Hunt, *Writings of James Madison,* 9:383–396n1. See also McCoy, *Last of the Founding Fathers,* 135.

23. Madison to Joseph C. Cabell, 22 March 1827, in Hunt, *Writings of James Madison,* 9:284–287.

24. Madison to Edward Everett, 28 August 1830, in U.S. Congress, *Letters and Other Writings of James Madison,* 4:95–106.

25. Madison to Haynes, [3 or 4] April 1830, in Hunt, *Writings of James Madison,* 9:383–386n1. See also Ketcham, *James Madison,* 643.

26. Madison to Nicholas Trist, [?] May 1832, in U.S. Congress, *Letters and Other Writings of James* Madison, 4:217–218; McCoy, *Last of the Founding Fathers,* 143–148; Wills, *James Madison,* 162–164.

27. Quoted in Ketcham, *James Madison,* 641. Surprisingly, Wilentz, in his extended discussion of the nullification crisis, does not mention Madison's important role in the crisis. See Wilentz, *Rise of American Democracy,* 374–389.

28. The quotes are in Moore, *Madisons,* 450–451.

29. Both quotes can be found in Armin Rappaport, ed., *The Monroe Doctrine* (New York: Holt Rinehart and Winston, 1966), 59–61. But see also James Monroe to Thomas Jefferson, 17 October 1823, in Stanislaus Murray Hamilton, ed., *The Writings of James Monroe,* 7 vols. (New York: AMS Press, 1969), 6:323–325; James Madison to James Monroe, 19 October 1823, and Monroe to Richard Rush, 13 November 1823, in Hunt, *Writings of James Madison,* 9:157–166.

30. McCoy, *Last of the Founding Fathers,* 240–252; Ketcham, *James Madison,* 636–640; Wilentz, *Rise of American Democracy,* 42–45.

31. Bumgarner, *Health,* 4–30; Ketcham, *James Madison,* 669.

32. Quoted in Wilentz, *Rise of American Democracy,* 202.

33. Ammon, *James Monroe,* 76, 79, 131, 163; Noble E. Cunningham Jr., *The Presidency of James Monroe* (Lawrence: University Press of Kansas, 1996), 1–13.

34. Ammon, *James Monroe,* 66, 352–354; Cunningham, *Presidency of James Monroe,* 15–19.

35. Congress later appropriated an additional $30,000 for furnishings. For a full account of the furniture fund, see Lucius Wilmerding Jr., *James Monroe: Public Claimant* (New Brunswick, N.J.: Rutgers University Press, 1960), 11–15. See also Cunningham, *Presidency of James Monroe,* 145–147. On Monroe's deference to Congress, see Ralph Ketcham, *Presidents above Party: The First American Presidency, 1789–1829* (Chapel Hill: University of North Carolina Press, 1984), 127–128.

36. Monroe to Jefferson, 31 October 1824, in Hamilton, *Writings of James Monroe,* 7:42–43.

37. Ammon, *James Monroe,* 115–116.

38. W. P. Cresson, *James Monroe* (Chapel Hill: University of North Carolina Press, 1946), 104 and 471; Ammon, *James Monroe,* 163–164, 205, 230, 293, and 347.

39. Ammon, *James Monroe,* 408; Cresson, *James Monroe,* 471–472; Christopher

Fennell, "An Account of James Monroe's Land Holdings," 1998, http://www.histarch
.uiuc.edu/highland/ashlawn0.html; "Ash Lawn-Highland—Home of James Monroe,"
http://www.ashlawnhighland.org.

40. During his presidency, Jefferson even urged him to cut back almost completely
on the lavish entertainment that was part of the Monroe White House, but Monroe did
not follow the former president's recommendation. On this point, see Cunningham, *Presidency of James Monroe*, 136. See also Wilmerding, *James Monroe*, 126–127.

41. Ammon, *James Monroe*, 546–553; Cresson, *James Monroe*, 477.

42. Monroe to General Jackson, 3 July 1825, in Hamilton, *Writings of James Monroe*, 7:546–549; Wilmerding, *James Monroe*, esp. 53–77 and 116–117; Stuart Gerry
Brown, ed., *The Autobiography of James Monroe* (Syracuse, N.Y.: Syracuse University
Press, 1959), v; Hecht, *Beyond the Presidency*, 196–197.

43. Those historians who have scrutinized Monroe's claims have generally concluded that although he had a basis for some of them, most were overinflated, duplicative,
or without legal merit. They have raised the question, therefore, why Monroe pursued
his case with such vigor, especially because he refused an offer of financial assistance
from the Marquis de Lafayette, who ironically had been in similar financial straits until
given a generous grant of money and land from Congress. Although recognizing that his
compelling financial needs were one reason, Wilmerding suggests that other factors were
involved. These included his belief that he had never received adequate credit for his public service and grievances going as far back as his relief as minister to France in 1796 by
George Washington because of his pro-French views. He also resented personal attacks
made against him while he was president. Other writers have insinuated more sinister reasons for Monroe's action, even his alleged embezzlement of the furniture fund during the
refurbishing of the White House. "The President," Henry Graff wrote, "was by a curious
mental inversion, turned into a permanent plaintiff in order to aver to himself and to the nation a Founding Father's equivalent of 'Well, I am not a crook.'" Wilmerding, *James Monroe*, 121–123; Henry F. Graff, "What Was Bugging James Monroe," *American Heritage
Magazine*, December 1990, http://www.americanheritage.com; James Madison to James
Monroe, 21 April 1831, and James Monroe to James Madison, 11 April 1823, in Hamilton,
Writings of James Monroe, 7:231–236.

44. Ammon, *James Monroe*, 556. See also Monroe to Thomas Jefferson, 23 February
1826, in Hamilton, *Writings of James Monroe*, 7:69–70.

45. Monroe to Madison, 11 April 1831, in Hamilton, *Writings of James Monroe*,
7:231–234.

46. Bumgarner, *Health*, 34–35; Ammon, *James Monroe*, 572–573.

47. Wilmerding, *James Monroe*, 115–116.

48. On this latter point see, for example, Nagel, *John Quincy Adams*, 296–323; Wilentz, *Rise of American Democracy*, 257–280; Stephen Skowronek, *The Politics Presidents Make: Leadership from John Adams to George Bush* (Cambridge, Mass.: Harvard
University Press, 1993), 117–127; Merrill Peterson, *The Great Triumvirate: Webster, Clay,
Calhoun* (New York: Oxford University Press, 1987); Hargreaves, *Presidency of John
Quincy Adams*, esp. xiii–xv and 308–323.

49. Samuel Flagg Bemis, *John Quincy Adams and the Union* (New York: Knopf,
1965), 121; Leonard L. Richards, *The Life and Times of Congressman John Quincy Adams*
(New York: Oxford University Press, 1986), 29; Nagel, *John Quincy Adams*, 309–310.

50. Quoted in Samuel Flagg Bemis, *John Quincy Adams and the Foundations of*

American Foreign Policy (New York: Knopf, 1949), 253. See also Wilentz, *Rise of American Democracy,* 256–257.

51. John Quincy Adams to Charles Francis Adams, 29 January 1828, John Quincy Adams Papers (hereafter JQA Papers), Massachusetts Historical Society, Boston; microfim edition, reel 148.

52. Nagel, *John Quincy Adams,* 142–156, 173–180, and 300; Wilentz, *Rise of American Democracy,* 240; Michael F. Holt, *The Rise and Fall of the American Whig Party: Jacksonian Politics and the Onset of the Civil War* (New York: Oxford University Press, 1999), 2–7.

53. According to the historian Ralph Ketcham, Adams was, in fact, "the last president, before the triumph under [Andrew] Jackson of a conception of leadership tied to a positive idea of party, who aspired to embody all the dimensions of a patriot leader." Ketcham, *Presidents above Party,* 130. By the "first modern party system" I mean merely to distinguish the Democratic and Whig parties of the mid-nineteenth century from the post–Civil War Democratic and Republican parties that have constituted the second modern party system.

54. His election to the U.S. Senate in 1803, for example, was the result of a backroom bargain between his supporters in the Massachusetts Senate and backers of his opponent, Thomas Pickering, whom Adams detested but said he would gladly support for a second open Senate seat. Nagel, *John Quincy Adams,* 138–140.

55. Quoted in Wilentz, *Rise of American Democracy,* 259.

56. Holt, *Rise and Fall,* 8; Wilentz, *Rise of American Democracy,* 250–253, and 307–310; Skowronek, *Politics Presidents Make,* 117–127; Robert V. Remini, *The Life of Andrew Jackson* (New York: Harper & Row, 1977), 157–171.

57. Diary of John Quincy Adams, 11 December 1828, JQA Papers, reel 39; Marie B. Hecht, *John Quincy Adams: A Personal History of an Independent Man* (New York: Macmillan, 1972), 481–482; Bemis, *John Quincy Adams and the Union,* 154–155.

58. Quoted in Hecht, *John Quincy Adams,* 496. See also Nagel, *John Quincy Adams,* 329–332, and Bemis, *John Quincy Adams and the Union,* 178–180.

59. Quoted in Nagel, *John Quincy Adams,* 322.

60. *Memoirs of John Quincy Adams, Comprising Portions of His Diary from 1795 to 1848,* ed. Charles Francis Adams, 12 vols. (Philadelphia, 1874–1877) (Standford, CA: Hoover Institution Press, 1983), 8:431.

61. Daniel Walker Howe, *The Political Culture of the American Whigs* (Chicago: University of Chicago Press, 1984), 51–57; Richards, *Life and Times,* 37–43.

62. Adams, *Memoirs of John Quincy Adams,* 8:379; Howe, *Political Culture,* 54–59; Holt, *Rise and Fall,* 13–15; Richards, *Life and Times,* 38–51; Bemis, *John Quincy Adams and the Union,* 273–304.

63. Quoted in Nagel, *John Quincy Adams,* 337. See also Bemis, *John Quincy Adams and the Union,* 163 and 215–217.

64. Adams, *Memoirs of John Quincy Adams,* 29 November 1820, 5:210. See also Howe, *Political Culture,* 63; William Lee Miller, *Arguing about Slavery: John Quincy Adams and the Great Battle in the United States Congress* (New York: Vintage, 1998), 185–193.

65. Nagel, *John Quincy Adams,* 339.

66. Adams, *Memoirs of John Quincy Adams,* 9:162.

67. Ibid., 8:546.

68. Ibid., 8:304.

69. Robert V. Remini, *John Quincy Adams* (New York: Times Books, 2002), 138.

70. Howe, *Political Culture*, 1–42. For a somewhat different view than Howe's on the potential longevity of the Whig Party, see Holt, *Rise and Fall*, ix–xiv. On the Whigs and the Antimasons, see also Holt, *Rise and Fall*, 37–38.

71. Howe, *Political Culture*, 9–10; Holt, *Rise and Fall*, 28–32; Wilentz, *Rise of American Democracy*, 482–493.

72. Bemis, *John Quincy Adams and the Union*, 297–305; Hecht, *John Quincy Adams*, 524–529.

73. Nagel, *John Quincy Adams*, 344–346.

74. Richards, *Life and Times*, 22; Nagel, *John Quincy Adams*, 361, 372, 376.

75. Adams to Charles Francis Adams, 5 March and 8 April 1835, JQA Papers, reel 152.

76. Wilentz, *Rise of American Democracy*, 403–412.

77. *Register of Debates* 13, Part 2, 6 February 1837, 1588; Nagel, *John Quincy Adams*, 356; Bemis, *John Quincy Adams and the Union*, 340–348; Miller, *Arguing about Slavery*, 339–370.

78. Quoted in Nagel, *John Quincy Adams*, 356–357. See also Bemis, *John Quincy Adams and the Union*, 345–346, 349, 375–376; Remini, *John Quincy Adams*, 141.

79. *Congressional Globe*, 27th Congress, 2d Session (1841–1842), 168–215; Adams, *Memoirs of John Quincy Adams*, 12:70–88; Richards, *Life and Times*, 139–145; Nagel, *John Quincy Adams*, 385–386.

80. Adams, *Memoirs of John Quincy Adams*, 12:115–116; Richards, *Life and Times*, 177–178; Nagel, *John Quincy Adams*, 402–403; Wilentz, *Rise of American Democracy*, 554–555 and 557–558.

81. Nagel, *John Quincy Adams*, 395–398; James E. Lewis Jr., *John Quincy Adams: Policymaker for the Union* (Lanham, Md.: Rowman & Littlefield, 2001), 129.

82. Bemis, *John Quincy Adams and the Union*, 354–359; Hecht, *John Quincy Adams*, 538–541.

83. Register of Debates, 12, part 4, 25 May 1836, 4027–4031; Bemis, *John Quincy Adams and the Union*, 339.

84. Adams, *Memoirs of John Quincy Adams*, 12:171; Richards, *Life and Times*, 178–182; Lewis, *John Quincy Adams*, 130; Bemis, *John Quincy Adams and the Union*, 364–371.

85. Adams to Branzt Mayer, 6 July 1847, and Adams to Albert Gallatin, 26 December 1847, JQA Papers, reel 155. See also Lewis, *John Quincy Adams*, 136; Richards, *Life and Times*, 190.

86. Richards, *Life and Times*, 182–185.

87. Ibid., 183–184; Bemis, *John Quincy Adams and the Union*, 487–495; Lewis, *John Quincy Adams*, 137.

88. Nagel, *John Quincy Adams*, 379–381; Bemis, *John Quincy Adams and the Union*, 384–415; Wilentz, *Rise of American Democracy*, 477–478 and 521–522.

89. Hecht, *John Quincy Adams*, 560–565; Nagel, *John Quincy Adams*, 403–404, 408–409.

90. Quoted in Richards, *Life and Times*, 198–200.

91. Adams, *Memoirs of John Quincy Adams*, 12:279; Bumgarner, *Health*, 41; Nagel, *John Quincy Adams*, 414.

92. Quoted in Miller, *Arguing about Slavery*, 167; Nagel, *John Quincy Adams*, 415–416.

CHAPTER 3: FORMER PRESIDENTS AS PARTISAN POLITICIANS

1. H. W. Brands, *Andrew Jackson: His Life and Times* (New York: Doubleday, 2005), 399–401; Marvin Meyers, *The Jacksonian Persuasion: Politics and Belief* (Stanford, Calif.: Stanford University Press, 1957), 7–12. See also chap. 2, 43–44. Peterson, *Jefferson Image*, 70.

2. Skowronek, *Politics Presidents Make*, 133–134. See also Sean Wilentz, *Rise of American Democracy*, 487–493 and 507–518.

3. Peterson, *Jefferson Image*, 75; Meyers, *Jacksonian Persuasion*, 8; James Roger Sharp, *The Jacksonians versus the Banks: Politics in the States after the Panic of 1877* (New York: Columbia University Press, 1970), 3–24. In the case of a change of ideology, the earlier books of Peterson, Meyers, and Sharp are challenged by the renowned political historian Joel Silbey, who refers to a "striking" ideological shift in American political thought. However, even Silbey seems to qualify this ideological shift by recognizing that even in the mid-1830s, it was still "incomplete and ambiguous." See Joel Silbey, *The American Political Nation, 1838–1893* (Stanford, Calif.: Stanford University Press, 1991), 19–21. In the matter of a major shift in ideology, I find Peterson, Meyers, and Sharp more persuasive.

4. Ketcham, *Presidents above Party*, 141–161. See also John Meacham's recent biography, *American Lion: Andrew Jackson in the White House* (New York: Random House, 2008), 76, 123, and 132–133.

5. Compare, for example, Robert V. Remini, *Life of Andrew Jackson* (New York: Harper Perennial, 2001), with Andrew Burstein, *The Passions of Andrew Jackson* (New York: Knopf, 2003). Remini's work is an abridgement of his three-volume biography of Jackson. For a more balanced view, see Sean Wilentz, *Andrew Jackson* (New York: Times Books, 2005), 2.

6. Bumgarner, *Health*, 43–49.

7. Silbey, *American Political Nation*, 29; Wilentz, *Andrew Jackson*, 39–40; Skowronek, *Politics Presidents Make*.

8. The number of officials removed from office was much larger than previous presidents but still fewer than 1,000 of about 10,000 officeholders. Glyndon G. Van Deusen, *The Jacksonian Era, 1828–1848* (New York: Harper & Row, 1959), 35. See also Donald Cole, *The Presidency of Andrew Jackson* (Lawrence: University Press of Kansas, 1993), 38–39. Meacham, *American Lion*, 82.

9. Peterson, *Jefferson Image*, 82; Meyers, *Jacksonian Persuasion*, 16–32; Brands, *Andrew Jackson*, 373–376 and 400–401; Wilentz, *Rise of American Democracy*, 315; Cole, *Presidency of Andrew Jackson*, 39–42 and 269–277.

10. Silbey, *American Political Nation*, 42–44; Lynn Hudson Parsons, *John Quincy Adams* (Madison, Wis.: Madison House, 1998), 189; Wilentz, *Rise of American Democracy*, 516–518.

11. Quoted in "Agriculture at the Hermitage," http://www.thehermitage.com. See also Arda Walker, "Andrew Jackson, Planter," *East Tennessee Historical Society Papers* 15 (1943): 20.

12. Jackson to Andrew J. Hutchins, 4 April 1837, in John Spencer Bassett, ed., *Correspondence of Andrew Jackson*, 7 vols. (Washington, D.C.: Carnegie Institution of Washington, 1931), 5:473–475.

13. Jackson to Donelson, 10 December 1839, in Bassett, ed., *Correspondence of*

Andrew Jackson, 6:41–42; Brands, *Andrew Jackson,* 533–534; Hecht, *Beyond the Presidency,* 198–199.

14. Jackson to President Van Buren, 6 June 1837, in Bassett, ed., *Correspondence of Andrew Jackson,* 5:486–489; Robert V. Remini, *Andrew Jackson and the Course of American Democracy, 1814–15* (New York: Harper & Row, 1984), 450.

15. Quoted in Hecht, *Beyond the Presidency,* 200.

16. Stanley F. Horn, *The Hermitage: Home of Old Hickory* (Nashville, Tenn.: Ladies Hermitage Association, 1950), 37–42; Hecht, *Beyond the Presidency,* 200–201.

17. Jackson to Andrew J. Hutchings, 5 September 1839, in Bassett, ed., *Correspondence of Andrew Jackson,* 6:25–26; Burstein, *Passions,* 216.

18. Van Deusen, *Jacksonian Era,* 119–120; Sharp, *Jacksonians versus the Banks,* 8–19; Holt, *Rise and Fall,* 105–111.

19. Jackson to President Van Buren, 6 June 1837, in Bassett, ed., *Correspondence of Andrew Jackson,* 5:486–489; Brands, *Andrew Jackson,* 534–535.

20. Burstein, *Passions,* 210, 231; Brands, *Andrew Jackson,* 537–538 and 544.

21. Silbey, *American Political Nation,* 29.

22. Jackson to Antonio Lopez De Santa Anna, 1 March 1844, in Bassett, ed., *Correspondence of Andrew Jackson,* 6:268–269.

23. Francis P. Blair to Jackson 2 May 1844, in ibid., 6:281–282.

24. Jackson to Francis P. Blair, 11 May 1844, in ibid., 6:285–286.

25. Jackson to the editors of the Nashville *Union,* 13 May 1844, in ibid., 6:289–291. See also Jackson to Blair, 7 May 1844, in ibid., 6:283–285; Remini, *Andrew Jackson and the Course of American Democracy,* 496–503; Brands, *Andrew Jackson,* 550–551.

26. Jackson to Andrew J. Donelson, 18 November 1844, in Bassett, ed., *Correspondence of Andrew Jackson,* 6:329–330.

27. Jackson to James K. Polk, 28 February, and Jackson to Francis Blair, 11 April 1845, in ibid., 6:372–373 and 6:394–396.

28. Bumgarner, *Health,* 53–54; "President Andrew Jackson: Health and Medical History," http://www.doctorzebra.com; Remini, *Andrew Jackson and the Course of American Democracy,* 518–525. Remini attributed the cause of death to kidney failure; Bumgarner attributes it to heart failure. What seems likely is that Jackson had so many illnesses and had been sick for so long that his vital organs simply failed him.

29. Quoted in Joel H. Silbey, *Martin Van Buren and the Emergence of American Popular Politics* (Lanham, Md.: Rowman & Littlefield, 2002), 218; see also 46–54. Nagel, *John Quincy Adams,* 301, 356, 360, and 380.

30. John Niven, *Martin Van Buren: The Romantic Age of American Politics* (New York: Oxford University Press, 1983), 525; Ted Widner, *Martin Van Buren* (New York: Times Books, 2004), 149; Silbey, *Martin Van Buren,* 11–13, 32–33, and 54–57.

31. Donald B. Cole, *Martin Van Buren and the American Political System* (Princeton, N.J.: Princeton University Press, 1984); Silbey, *Martin Van Buren,* xii–xiii and 218–220.

32. Wilentz, *Rise of American Democracy,* 448–507; Silbey, *American Political Nation,* 49–52; Cole, *Martin Van Buren,* 372–373.

33. Quoted in Silbey, *Martin Van Buren,* 157.

34. Martin Van Buren to Benjamin Butler, 21 December 1840, Martin Van Buren Papers, Library of Congress, reel 37. (Microfilm edition published by Chadwyck-Healy, Inc.) See also Silbey, *Martin Van Buren,* 156–158.

35. Niven, *Martin Van Buren,* 478 and 482–487; Cole, *Martin Van Buren,* 381–382; Silbey, *Martin Van Buren,* 159–160 and 208.

36. Wilentz, *Rise of American Democracy*, 527–528, 533–538, 544–546; Niven, *Martin Van Buren*, 501–510; Cole, *Martin Van Buren*, 388–390; Silbey, *Martin Van Buren*, 156, 162–163, and 172.

37. Silbey, *Martin Van Buren*, 178–179; Niven, *Martin Van Buren*, 542–548; Cole, *Martin Van Buren*, 398–399.

38. Van Buren to Benjamin Butler, 20 May 1844, Van Buren Papers, reel 42. See also Niven, *Martin Van Buren*, 532.

39. Niven, *Martin Van Buren*, 550–553.

40. Cole, *Martin Van Buren*, 400–404; Silbey, *Martin Van Buren*, 180–182; Niven, *Martin Van Buren*, 549–565; John Siegenthaler, *James K. Polk* (New York: Times Books, 2003), 106–108.

41. Niven, *Martin Van Buren*, 556.

42. Cole, *Martin Van Buren*, 407; Niven, *Martin Van Buren*, 231, 273, 291–292, 343, 486–487, 512–513.

43. "Address of the Democratic Members of the Legislature of the State of New York," 12 April 1848, Van Buren Papers, reel 45; Cole, *Martin Van Buren*, 409–411; Niven, *Martin Van Buren*, 567–569, 574–577; Silbey, *Martin Van Buren*, 194–195; Eric Foner, *Free Soil, Free Labor, Free Men: The Ideology of the Republican Party before the Civil War* (New York: Oxford University Press, 1995), 60–61.

44. Van Buren to John Van Buren, 3 May 1848, Van Buren Papers, reel 45.

45. Quoted in Cole, *Martin Van Buren*, 413.

46. Quoted in ibid., 414–415.

47. Quoted in Paul H. Bergeron, *The Presidency of James K. Polk* (Lawrence: University Press of Kansas, 1987), 252–253.

48. Niven, *Martin Van Buren*, 597–598 and 608.

49. Ibid., 600–603.

50. "Autobiography of Martin Van Buren," *Annual Report of the American Historial Association*, 2 vols. (Washington, D.C.: Government Printing Office, 1920), 2:7.

51. Bumgarner, *Health*, 56–58.

52. Widner, *Martin Van Buren*, 165–166.

53. Milo M. Quaife, *The Diary of James K. Polk during His Presidency, 1845 to 1848*, 4 vols. (Chicago: McClurg, 1910), 4:372–373.

54. Bergeron, *Presidency of James K. Polk*, 258–259; Bumgarner, *Health*, 59–63 and 67–76.

55. Wilentz, *Rise of American Democracy*, 525–526.

56. Norma Lois Peterson, *The Presidencies of William Henry Harrison and John Tyler* (Lawrence: University Press of Kansas, 1989), 45–56.

57. Robert Seager II, *And Tyler Too: A Biography of John and Julie Gardiner Tyler* (New York: McGraw Hill, 1963), 294–295; Oliver P. Chitwood, *John Tyler: Champion of the Old South* (Newtown, Conn.: American Political Biography Press, 1990), 409–411; "Sherwood Forest Plantation: Home of President John Tyler," http://www.sherwoodforest .org.

58. Chitwood, *John Tyler*, 414–417; Seager, *And Tyler Too*, 296–300, 310, 361–375, 389, 415, and 515. Chitwood claims that Tyler had inherited the Kentucky property from his father. Seager states that Tyler purchased it himself in the 1830s. Seager's documentation is more persuasive.

59. Lyon G. Tyler, *The Letters and Times of the Tylers*, 3 vols. (Richmond, Va.: Whittel and Shipperson, 1884, 1885, and 1896), 2:463–464.

60. Seager, *And Tyler Too,* xiii, 268–269, 313–315, and 322–323; Edward P. Crapol, *John Tyler: The Accidental President* (Chapel Hill: University of North Carolina Press, 2006), 225 and 233; Chitwood, *John Tyler,* 423–424. On Webster's use of the secret fund with Tyler's approval, see Robert V. Remini, *Daniel Webster: The Man and His Time* (New York: Norton, 1997), 540.

61. Tyler to Gardiner, 17 June 1847, in Tyler, *Letters and Times,* 2:426.

62. Crapol, *John Tyler,* 225–230; Seager, *And Tyler Too,* 320–322, 324–327.

63. The first quote is from Tyler, *Letters and Times,* 2:478; the second is from Chitwood, *John* Tyler, 429; and the third is from Seager, *And Tyler Too,* 402–406. See also Hecht, *Beyond the Presidency,* 12.

64. Chitwood, *John Tyler,* 428–430; Seager, *And Tyler Too,* 331–332, 395–397, 400, and 407–409; Holman Hamilton, *Prologue to Conflict: The Crisis and Compromise of 1850* (Lexington; University of Kentucky Press, 1964), 74.

65. Seager, *And Tyler Too,* 428–432; Chitwood, *John Tyler,* 428–450.

66. Howard Cecil Perkins, ed., *Northern Editorials on Secession,* 2 vols. (Gloucester, Mass.: Peter Smith, 1964), 2:1002–1003; Crapol, *John Tyler,* 259–262; Chitwood, *John Tyler,* 436–447; Hecht, *Beyond the Presidency,* 15–18.

67. Tyler, *Letters and Times,* 2:694.

68. Chitwood, *John Tyler,* 452–455.

69. Bumgarner, *Health,* 64–66; Seager, *And Tyler Too,* 423–424 and 469–471; Chitwood, *John Tyler,* 464–465.

70. Seager, *And Tyler Too,* 471–472; Chitwood, *John Tyler,* 465.

CHAPTER 4: DOUGHFACE FORMER PRESIDENTS

1. The full text of Whitman's "Dough-Face Song" is available at http://www.bartleby.com. See also David S. Reynolds, "Politics and Poetry: Whitman's Leaves of Grass," http://www.thehamptons.com.

2. Leonard L. Richards, *The Slave Power: The Free North and Southern Domination, 1780–1860* (Baton Rouge: Louisiana State University Press, 2000), 85–86.

3. Robert J. Rayback, *Millard Fillmore: Biography of a President* (Buffalo, N.Y.: Buffalo Historical Society, 1959), 12–13, 36.

4. Hamilton, *Prologue to Conflict,* 107–108, 136, 157–158, 161, 185; Elbert B. Smith, *The Presidencies of Zachary Taylor and Millard Fillmore* (Lawrence: University Press of Kansas, 1988), 95–122; Wilentz, *Rise of American Democracy,* 643; Rayback, *Millard Fillmore,* 95–11, 206–267, 238–252.

5. Quoted in Rayback, *Millard Fillmore,* 252.

6. Fillmore to Robert Collins, 19 November 1850, in Frank H. Severance, ed., *Millard Fillmore Papers,* 2 vols. (Buffalo: Buffalo Historical Society, 1907), 2:304. The two volumes are available at http://ebooks.library.cornell.edu/n/nys.

7. Rayback, *Millard Fillmore,* 332–348; William Elliot Griffis, *Millard Fillmore: Constructive Statesman, Defender of the Constitution, President of the United States* (Ithaca, N.Y.: Andrus and Curch, 1915), 120–124.

8. Quoted in Hecht, *Beyond the Presidency,* 78.

9. It is impossible to overemphasize the important role that Abigail played in

Fillmore's entire career. Certainly other presidential spouses, including Martha Washington, Abigail Adams, and Dolley Madison, left more indelible marks in the nation's history than Abigail Fillmore. Like her, they were also tremendous assets to their husbands' political careers. However, from the time Abigail first met Fillmore, she remained an essential intellectual and political force in his life. Throughout their marriage, they read and studied books constantly; in effect, she provided the future president with an ongoing class in self-improvement. When the Fillmores entered the White House and found no books in the mansion, she obtained a congressional appropriation to begin the White House library. Although she left many of the social activities in the White House to her daughter, Margaret, she was also Fillmore's most trusted adviser. He consulted her on almost every vital matter. Whatever success he enjoyed in politics was due in considerable measure to her good political instincts. On only one important matter did he go against her advice; that was to sign the Fugitive Slave Law, which she had correctly predicted, would cost him the 1852 Whig presidential nomination. Many historians believe that had Abigail not died, she would have been able to keep him from aligning himself with nativist elements after he left the White House and from seriously damaging his standing in history by running as the presidential candidate of the American or Know-Nothing Party. Smith, *Presidencies,* 251.

10. Quoted in Robert J. Scarry, *Millard Fillmore* (Jefferson, N.C.: McFarland, 2001), 246–247.

11. The interview can be found in Severance, ed., *Millard Fillmore Papers,* 2:39–40. See also Rayback, *Millard Fillmore,* 385–386; Hecht, *Beyond the Presidency,* 203.

12. Ibid.

13. Quoted in Scarry, *Millard Fillmore,* 237–238.

14. Severance, ed., *Millard Fillmore Papers,* 2:v.

15. *Richmond Daily Whig,* 11 May 1854, as quoted in Scarry, *Millard Fillmore,* 253.

16. Ray Allen Billington, *The Protestant Crusade, 1800–1860: A Study of the Origins of American Nativism* (Chicago: Quadrangle Books, 1964), 380–430; Humphrey J. Desmond, *The Know-Nothing Party: A Sketch* (Washington, D.C.: New Century Press, 1905), 49–125; Rayback, *Millard Fillmore,* 378–381, 389–392; Scarry, *Millard Fillmore,* 278; Smith, *Presidencies,* 251–252; Wilentz, *Rise of American Democracy,* 679–684.

17. Billington, *Protestant Crusade,* 429–430; Holt, *Rise and Fall,* 911; Rayback, *Millard Fillmore,* 156 and 379–380; Hecht, *Beyond the Presidency,* 115–116.

18. Fillmore to Dix, 29 August 1854, in Charles M. Snyder, ed., *The Lady and the President: The Letters of Dorothea Dix and Millard Fillmore* (Lexington: University of Kentucky Press, 1975), 215.

19. Fillmore to Maxwell, 10 March 1855, in Severance, ed., *Millard Fillmore Papers,* 2:351–354.

20. "Acceptance of the Nomination for President by the American Party," 21 May 1856, in Severance, ed., *Millard Fillmore Papers,* 2:358–360.

21. Albany Union Speech, 26 June 1856, in Severance, ed., *Millard Fillmore Papers,* 2:19–23.

22. Quoted in Hecht, *Beyond the Presidency,* 82.

23. Severance, ed., *Millard Fillmore Papers,* 1:xxxi–xxxiv; Scarry, *Millard Fillmore,* 332–330; Rayback, *Millard Fillmore,* 417–418; Griffis, *Millard Fillmore,* 138–139.

24. Quoted in Rayback, *Millard Fillmore,* 420–421.

25. Severance, ed., *Millard Fillmore Papers,* 2:62.

26. Fillmore et al. to Secretary of War Simon Cameron, 10 January 1862, in Severance, ed., *Millard Fillmore Papers,* 2:402–406; Rayback, *Millard Fillmore,* 426–427; Griffis, *Millard Fillmore,* 139–140.

27. "On the Death of Lincoln," 9 May 1865, in Severance, ed., *Millard Fillmore Papers,* 2:131–141.

28. "History of an Interview," 16 September 1873, in Severance, ed., *Millard Fillmore Papers,* 2:131–141.

29. Bumgarner, *Health,* 77–78; Rudolph Marx, *The Health of the Presidents* (New York: G. P. Putnam's Sons, 1960), 160; "The Health and Medical History of President Millard Filllmore," http://www.doctorzebra.com.

30. Severance, ed., *Millard Fillmore Papers,* 2:7.

31. On the anniversary of Pierce's 200th birthday, *Boston Globe* reporter Alex Beame even referred to Pierce as "America's handsomest president." *Boston Globe,* 16 November 2004, http://www.bostonglobe.com.

32. Peter A. Wallner, *Franklin Pierce: New Hampshire's Favorite Son* (Concord, N.H.: Plaidswede Publishing, 2004), 16–92; Roy Franklin Nichols, *Franklin Pierce: Young Hickory of the Granite Hills* (Newtown, Conn.: American Political Biography Press, 2003), 9–27, 175; Larry Gara, *The Presidency of Franklin Pierce* (Lawrence: University Press of Kansas, 1991), 30.

33. Wallner, *Franklin Pierce,* 168.

34. Nichols, *Franklin Pierce,* 202–203; Wallner, *Franklin Pierce: New Hampshire's Favorite Son,* 192–201; Gara, *Presidency of Franklin Pierce,* 32–35.

35. Michael S. Green, *Politics and America in Crisis: The Coming of the Civil War* (Santa Barbara, Calif.: Praeger, 2010), 65.

36. Quoted in Nichols, *Franklin Pierce,* 481.

37. Quoted in Hecht, *Beyond the Presidency,* 230.

38. Quoted in Peter A. Wallner, *Franklin Pierce: Martyr for the Union* (Concord, N.H.: Plaidswede Publishing, 2007), 331; Nichols, *Franklin Pierce,* 513.

39. Nichols, *Franklin Pierce,* 514.

40. Wallner, *Franklin Pierce: Martyr for the Union,* 325, 333–334.

41. On Holt, see Philip Gerald Auchampaugh, *James Buchanan and His Cabinet on the Eve of Secession* (Lancaster, Pa.: privately printed, 1926), 84; George Ticknor Curtis, *Life of James Buchanan, Fifteenth President of the United States,* 2 vols. (New York: Harper and Brothers, 1883), 2:456–464; Jean H. Baker, *James Buchanan* (New York: Times Books, 2004), 135–136 and 142.

42. Quoted in Wallner, *Franklin Pierce: Martyr for the Union,* 342.

43. Quoted in Nichols, *Franklin Pierce,* 520–521.

44. Quoted in Wallner, *Franklin Pierce: Martyr for the Union,* 349.

45. Ibid., 343 and 352–335.

46. Quoted in Nichols, *Franklin Pierce,* 526.

47. He may have been drinking even as president. After accompanying Pierce to New York in the summer of 1853, where the president attended the World's Fair, John W. Forney, the clerk of the House of Representatives and one of Buchanan's longtime associates, wrote the Pennsylvania politician a letter in which he remarked that Pierce "drinks deep." The presidency "overshadows him," Forney added. "He is crushed by its great duties." Still, the evidence that Pierce was a heavy drinker as president remains scant. Ibid., 284.

48. Quoted in Wallner, *Franklin Pierce: Martyr for the Union*, 370.

49. Bumgarner, *Health*, 83–84; Marx, *Health of the Presidents*, 168.

50. Address of Buchanan to Lancaster Gathering, 6 March 1861, in John Bassett Moore, ed., *The Works of James Buchanan: Comprising His Speeches, State Papers, and Private Correspondence*, 12 vols. (New York: Antiquarian Press, 1960), 11:161–162.

51. For a useful introduction to the historiography on Buchanan, see Michael J. Birkner, "Introduction: Getting to Know James Buchanan, Again," in *James Buchanan and the Political Crisis of the 1850s*, ed. Michael J. Birkner (Selinsgrove, Pa.: Susquehanna University Press, 1996), esp. 17–19, 24–25, 27, 29–32. See also William E. Gienapp, "'No Bed of Roses': James Buchanan, Abraham Lincoln, and Presidential Leadership in the Civil War," in ibid., 93–120, and "The Presidency of James Buchanan: A Reasssessment," in ibid., 171–202. The latter is a discussion on the Buchanan presidency by a group of leading authorities on the middle period of the nineteenth century, including Kenneth Stampp, Donald Fehrenbacher, Robert Johannsen, and Elbert Smith.

52. Philip Shriver Klein, *President James Buchanan: A Biography* (University Park: Pennsylvania State University Press, 1970), 206–211; Baker, *James Buchanan*, 16, 47.

53. James Buchanan, *Mr. Buchanan's Administration on the Eve of the Rebellion* (New York: D. Appleton and Company, 1866), 24 and 28.

54. Baker, *James Buchanan*, 141; Wilentz, *Rise of American Democracy*, 706–719; Donald E. Fehrenbacher, *The Dred Scott Case: Its Significance in American Law and Politics* (Oxford University Press: New York, 1978), esp. 307–314.

55. Some historians have tried to defend Buchanan by pointing out that had he taken more decisive action, he might have hastened the secession of the Upper South and put the federal government in the awkward position of provoking a civil war. Certainly Buchanan believed this to be the case. Even his successor, Abraham Lincoln, recognized that it would have been imprudent for the United States to strike first against the South. The fact remains, though, that Buchanan based his refusal to act against the South on the constitutional grounds that he had no authority to use force against the South. Yet he did not feel limited by the Constitution from using military force against the Mormons in Utah when they defied federal law. There also seems little question that Buchanan decided to leave it to his successor to deal with the nation's most serious crisis since its establishment eighty-five years earlier. Birkner, "James Buchanan and the Political Crisis of the 1850s," in Birkner, ed., *James Buchanan and the Political Crisis of the 1850s*, 29. For a contrary view, see Baker, *James Buchanan*, 75–141.

56. Mark W. Summers, "Dough in the Hands of the Doughface? James Buchanan and the Untameable Press," in Birkner, ed., *James Buchanan and the Political Crisis of the 1850s*, 68, 77, 80–82.

57. Mark Summers, *The Plundering Generation: Corruption and the Crisis of the Union, 1849–1861* (New York: Oxford University Press, 1987), 249–259; Elbert B. Smith, *Presidency of James Buchanan* (Lawrence: University Press of Kansas, 1975), 98–99.

58. Buchanan to James Bennet, 11 March 1861, quoted in Birkner, "James Buchanan and the Political Crisis of the 1850s," 3.

59. Klein, *President James Buchanan*, 410–412; Tebbell and Miles Watts, *The Press and the Presidency*, 165; Hecht, *Beyond the Presidency*, 23.

60. On this latter point, see, for example, Edwin M. Stanton to Buchanan, 16 March 1861, in Moore, ed., *Works of James Buchanan*, 11:170; Klein, *President James Buchanan*, 404–407.

61. On this latter point, see, for example, Buchanan to Dr. Blake, 21 November 1864, in Moore, ed., *Works of James Buchanan,* 11:377.

62. Quoted in Michael Birkner, "Buchanan's Civil War," address delivered at Wheatland, 20 September 2005, 6–7, 11, http://www.wheatland.org. See also Klein, *President James Buchanan,* 420.

63. Birkner, "Buchanan's Civil War," 8.

64. Baker, *James Buchanan,* 131–137; Gienapp, "No Bed of Roses," 102–103. For Floyd's mismanagement of the War Department and the broader problem of corruption in the Buchanan administration, see Summers, *Plundering Generation,* 240–248.

65. Birkner, "Buchanan's Civil War," 8; Buchanan, *Mr. Buchanan's Administration,* iii.

66. Black to Buchanan, 5 October 1861, in Moore, ed., *Works of James Buchanan,* 11:224.

67. Buchanan to Judge Black, 4 March 1862, in ibid., 11:260–261. See also Black to Buchanan, 1 March 1862, in ibid., 11:258–259.

68. Buchanan, *Mr. Buchanan's Administration,* 11.

69. Ibid., 28, 37.

70. Ibid., 153.

71. Ibid., iii.

72. Buchanan to Mr. Johnston, 14 November 1867, quoted in Curtis, *Life of James Buchanan,* 2:657–648; Marx, *Health of the Presidents,* 171; Bumgarner, *Health,* 87.

73. Quoted in Klein, *President James Buchanan,* 427.

74. Marx, *Health of the Presidents,* 172.

75. Nevins's full sermon can be found in Curtis, *Life of James Buchanan,* 2:681–686.

CHAPTER 5: FORMER PRESIDENTS IN AN AGE OF TRANSITION

1. Mark Twain and Charles Dudley Warner, *The Gilded Age: A Tale of Today* (New York: Doubleday, 1969). See also Nancy Cohen, *The Reconstruction of American Liberalism, 1865–1914* (Chapel Hill: University of North Carolina Press, 2002), 18.

2. Morton Keller, *Affairs of State: Public Life in Late Nineteenth Century America* (Cambridge, Mass.: Harvard University Press, 1977), 66–67, 148–153, and 366–370.

3. The historian Nancy Cohen believes, in fact, that modern liberal reform, often associated with the Progressive Movement of the early twentieth century, had its origins in the period of Reconstruction and in the conflict that ensued between an expansive vision of democracy as first promulgated by the radical Republicans, and efforts to assure civil order and protect emergent corporate capitalism from democratic challenges. "The Gilded Age," she states, "was the era of reconstruction of the North, and it too began with the end of the Civil War." "Just as the Civil War had unsettled ingrained ideas about who was rightfully a citizen," she adds, "so too had the exigencies of war violently recast the relationship of the individual American to the vastly more powerful national state." Cohen, *Reconstruction,* 18 and 27. Without necessarily disagreeing with the thrust of Cohen's argument about liberalism in the Gilded Age, journalist Jack Beatty writes: "This book tells the saddest story: How having redeemed democracy in the Civil War, America betrayed it in the Gilded Age." Beatty, *Age of Betrayal: The Triumph of Money in America* (New York: Knopf, 2007), xi. See also Eric Foner, *Reconstruction: America's Unfinished Revolution, 1863–1877* (New York: Harper & Row, 1988), xxvi and 18–25.

4. There are numerous historiographical articles on Johnson and Reconstruction, but a good introduction to the literature to the mid-1960s can be found in Eric McKitrick, ed., *Andrew Johnson: A Profile* (New York: Hill and Wang, 1969), vii–xxii. On the more recent literature, see also Foner, *Reconstruction,* xix–xxvii. The best biography of Johnson is Hans L. Trefousse, *Andrew Johnson: A Biography* (New York: Norton, 1989), which reflects the current scholarship on Reconstruction. See also Eric L. McKitrick, *Andrew Johnson and Reconstruction* (Chicago: University of Chicago Press, 1960), 3–14; Brooks D. Simpson, *The Reconstruction Presidents* (Lawrence: University Press of Kansas, 1998), 1–6 and 67–130; Albert Castel, *The Presidency of Andrew Johnson* (Lawrence: University Press of Kansas, 1979), 218–230; Max Skidmore, *Presidential Performance: A Comprehensive Review* (Jefferson, N.C.: McFarland, 2004), 135–142. The C-Span 2009 Historians Presidential Leadership Survey (http://www.c-span.org) ranks Johnson the second worst out of forty-two presidents, just ahead of James Buchanan and behind Franklin Pierce. The United States Presidency Centre's U.K. Survey of Presidents Results (http://americas.sas.ac.uk) places him a little higher, at thirty-sixth out of forty presidents, behind Millard Fillmore and Benjamin Harrison but ahead of John Tyler and Warren Harding.

5. Trefousse, *Andrew Johnson,* 34, 45, 54, 73.

6. Ibid., 44.

See, for example, Glenn Porter, *The Rise of Big Business, 1860–1920,* 2nd ed. (Arlington Heights, Ill.: Harlan Davidson, 1972); and Walter K. Nugent, *Money and American Society, 1865–1880* (New York: Free Press, 1968).

8. *Fourth Annual Message,* 9 December 1868, in LeRoy P. Graf, Ralph W. Haskins, and Paul H. Bergeron, eds., *The Papers of Andrew Johnson,* 16 vols. (Knoxville: University of Tennessee Press, 1967–2000), 15:284–289. See also Johnson to Thomas Ewing Jr., 24 October 1868, in ibid., 169–172; Kenneth M. Stampp, *The Era of Reconstruction, 1865–1877* (New York: Vintage, 1967); Trefousse, *Andrew Johnson,* 260, 262–263, 346–348.

9. Johnson to Thomas Ewing Jr., 24 October 1868, in Graf, Haskins, and Bergeron, *Papers of Andrew Johnson,* 15:169–172.

10. For economic issues during reconstruction, consult Martin E. Mantell, *Johnson, Grant, and the Politics of Reconstruction* (New York: Columbia University Press, 1973), 104–112. For a more detailed analysis, see Irwin Unger, *The Greenback Era: A Social and Political History of American Finance, 1865–1879* (Princeton, N.J.: Princeton University Press, 1964), esp. 41–162. Surprisingly, Unger makes only passing reference to Andrew Johnson. See also Gretchen Ritter, *Goldbugs and Greenbacks* (New York: Cambridge University Press, 1997), esp. 62–109. Ritter mentions the Johnson administration only once.

11. Trefousse, *Andrew Johnson,* 355.

12. Ibid., 168, 229, 240, 259, 348, 358, 360, 378.

13. Ibid., 337–339; Castel, *Presidency of Andrew Johnson*, 198–202.

14. Absolom A. Kyle to Johnson, 16 January 1869, in Graf, Haskins, and Bergeron, eds., *Papers of Andrew Johnson,* 15:389; Natus J. Haynes & Sons to Johnson, 8 February 1869, in ibid., 15:423–424; Johnson to Natus J. Haynes & Sons, 15 February 1869, in ibid., 15:443. See also Francis H. Gordon to Johnson, 4 February 1869, in ibid., 15:421–422; Castel, *Presidency of Andrew Johnson,* 207–209; Trefousse, *Andrew Johnson,* 339–343.

15. Interview with *New York World* correspondent, 28 February 1869, in Graf, Haskins, and Bergeron, eds., *Papers of Andrew Johnson,* 15:490–491.

16. Speech in Lynchburg, Virginia, 18 March 1869, in ibid., 15:530–532; George

Fort Milton, *The Age of Hate: Andrew Johnson and the Radicals* (New York: Coward-McCann, 1930), 654–655; Mantell, *Johnson, Grant,* esp. 3–4; Trefousse, *Andrew Johnson,* 293–298, 350–355.

17. Dickens's description of Johnson is in Trefousse, *Andrew Johnson,* 34; Castel, *Presidency of Andrew Johnson,* 214.

18. Speech at Knoxville, 3 April 1869; speech in Nashville, 7 April 1869; speech in Memphis, 15 April 1869, in Graf, Haskins, and Bergeron, eds., *Papers of Andrew Johnson,* 15:565–574 and 15:579–582. On Tennessee politics, see Foner, *Reconstruction,* 413–414, 439–440; Trefousse, *Andrew Johnson,* 554–555 and 594–561.

19. Interview with New York *Herald* corespondent, 27 June 1869; speech at Washington, D.C., 1 July 1869, in Graf, Haskins, and Bergeron, eds., *Papers of Andrew Johnson,* 16:39–45 and 16:50–63.

20. Speech at Knoxville, Tennessee, 17 August 1869, in ibid., 16:102–106.

21. Speech in Memphis, 15 April 869, in ibid., 15:613.

22. Johnson to Andrew Johnson Jr., 11 May 1869, in ibid., 10:6.

23. Johnson to William M. Lowry, 13 February 1870, in ibid., 15:168. On the relationship between Reeves and Johnson, see especially Lloyd Paul Stryker, *Andrew Johnson: A Study in Courage* (New York: Macmillan, 1929), 781–783. Stryker interviewed Reeves, who was still alive, in 1927. See also Milton, *Age of Hate,* 636 and 661–662; Trefousse, *Andrew Johnson,* 358.

24. Johnson to Malcolm Hay, 31 January 1871, and Johnson to Edgar Cowan, 13 February 1871, in Graf, Haskins, and Bergeron, eds., *Papers of Andrew Johnson,* 16:223–231.

25. Speech at Knoxville, Tennessee, 27 May 1871, in ibid., 16:235–263.

26. Trefousse, *Andrew Johnson,* 361–363; Milton, *Age of Hate,* 665.

27. Trefousse, *Andrew Johnson,* 364–367; Castel, *Presidency of Andrew Johnson,* 34 and 216. See also Giddeon Elles to Johnson, 5 November 1873, and Johnson to the editor of the *Washington Chronicle,* 11 November 1874, in Graf, Haskins, and Bergeron, eds., *Papers of Andrew Johnson,* 16:471–489.

28. Castel, *Presidency of Andrew Johnson,* 117–118. See also Tebbell and Miles Watts, *The Press and the Presidency,* 213. In addition, see interview with New York *Herald* correspondent, 27 September 1872 and 12 September 1873; interview with Washington *Star* reporter, 13 October 1873; interview with Knoxville *Press and Herald* correspondent, 10 January 1874, in Graf, Haskins, and Bergeron, eds., *Papers of Andrew Johnson,* 16:277–290, 16:443–451, 16:454–457, and 16:500–503.

29. Interview with Knoxville *Press and Herald* correspondent, 10 January 1874, and Speech at Memphis, Tennessee, 16 May 1874, in Graf, Haskins, and Bergeron, eds., *Papers of Andrew Johnson,* 16:500–503 and 16:549–552. It is not entirely clear what Johnson meant when he talked about interest-bearing national banknotes. Like greenbacks, national banknotes were irredeemable paper currency. Before the resumption of the gold standard in 1879, their value was tied to that of greenbacks because greenbacks were used in the reserve funds of banks issuing the notes. See Ritter, *Goldbugs and Greenbacks,* 74–77.

30. Johnson to Lewis P. Dayton and Ebenezer P. Dorr, 11 March 1874, and Johnson to Richard M. Edwards, 20 July 1874, in Graf, Haskins, and Bergeron, eds., *Papers of Andrew Johnson,* 16:517–518 and 16:576–577; Trefousse, *Andrew Johnson,* 367–368; Stryker, *Andrew Johnson,* 805–806.

31. On Johnson's comments about "extreme Democrats," see Johnson to John P.

White, 30 January 1874, in Graf, Haskins, and Bergeron, eds., *Papers of Andrew Johnson,* 16:10–12.

32. Quoted in Trefousse, *Andrew Johnson,* 371.

33. Quoted in ibid., 373.

34. Milton, *Age of Hate,* 670–672; Castel, *Presidency of Andrew Johnson,* 217; Stryker, *Andrew Johnson,* 809–810 and 820–822.

35. Still feeling the effects of the illness at the time of his inauguration as vice president in March 1865, he made the mistake of gulping down some whiskey to bolster his strength. Instead, it aggravated his condition and left him inebriated and incoherent at the time of his swearing-in ceremony, embarrassing the president and providing future ammunition to be used against him by his enemies in Congress. He was branded unfairly and forever as a drunkard. Trefousse, *Andrew Johnson,* 188–190.

36. Bumgarner, *Health,* 98–101; Marx, *Health of the Presidents,* 195–196 and 202.

37. Bumgarner, *Health,* 102; Marx, *Health of the Presidents,* 202.

38. The comment about Grant's dislike of music can be found in Brooks D. Simpson's introduction to *Personal Memoirs of U. S. Grant* (Lincoln: University of Nebraska Press, 1996), xi. See also Geoffrey Perrett, *Ulysses S. Grant: Soldier and President* (New York: Modern Library, 1998), 19.

39. Jean Edward Smith, *Grant* (New York: Simon & Schuster, 2002), 13–19.

40. Ibid., 464–465, 480–481, and 576–582.

41. For the rise of investigative reporting during the Grant administration, see Tebbell and Miles Watts, *The Press and the Presidency,* 215–228. For the language of the congressional resolution on third terms, see ibid., 228. On the Whiskey Ring and Babcock's possible involvement, see Smith, *Grant,* 583–584, 590–593.

42. Smith, *Grant,* 473–474, 586, 607; William B. Hesseltine, *Ulysses S. Grant, Politician* (New York: Simon Publications, 2001), 426.

43. John Russell Young, *Around the World with General Grant: A Narrative of the Visit of General U. S. Grant, Ex-President of the United States to Various Countries in Europe, Asia, and Africa, in 1877, 1878, 1879,* 2 vols. (New York: American News, 1879), 1:4–19.

44. Hesseltine, *Ulysses S. Grant,* 427. See also William S. McFeely, *Grant: A Biography* (New York: Norton, 1981), 452.

45. Young, *Around the World,* 1:i. See also Adam Badeau, *Grant in Peace: From Appomattox to Mount McGregor. A Personal Memoir* (Freeport, N.Y.: Books for Libraries Press, 1971), 265–266.

46. Grant to Childs, 6 June 1877, in John Y. Simon, ed., *The Papers of Ulysses S. Grant,* 32 vols. (Carbondale: Southern Illinois University Press, 1967–2012), 18:210–211; Young, *Around the World,* 1:18 and 1:35.

47. Young, *Around the World,* 1:47 and 1:85. See also Badeau, *Grant in Peace,* 268–269; Hecht, *Beyond the Presidency,* 234–235; McFeely, *Grant,* 460–462.

48. Young, *Around the World,* 1:47, 1:86–95, and 1:120.

49. Because Grant was often seen in MacMahon's presence and frequently had dinner with him, the former president was accused by the French leader's political enemies of harboring militarist sentiments. The fact that the former president had indicated sympathy for Prussia during the Franco-Prussian War did not help matters. The republican poet Victor Hugo had even written a fiery poem attacking Grant just as he arrived in France. Ibid., 1:129–142.

50. Grant to Rear Admiral Daniel Ammen, 25 March 1878, in Simon, ed., *Papers of Ulysses S. Grant,* 18:365–366. Young, *Around the World,* 1:361–375. See also McFeely, *Grant,* 407; Hesseltine, *Ulysses S. Grant,* 429–430; Smith, *Grant,* 609.

51. Grant to Rear Admiral Daniel Ammens, 25 May 1878, in Simon, ed., *Papers of Ulysses S. Grant,* 18:392–393; Young, *Around the World,* 1:378–394.

52. Young, *Around the World,* 1:408–410, 1:426–427.

53. Ibid., 1:411–418 and 2:161.

54. Ibid., 2:432–434.

55. Ibid., 2:458 and 2:483–485. See also Grant to Frederick Dent Grant, 22 August 1878, in Simon, ed., *Papers of Ulysses S. Grant,* 28:459–460.

56. Grant to Frederick Dent Grant, 24 May 1878; Grant to Rear Admiral Daniel Ammen, 25 May 1878; Grant to Major Culver C. Sniffen, 1 July 1878; Grant to Ulysses S. Grant Jr., 4 and 28 August 1878; and Grant to William W. Smith, 1 September 1868, in Simon, ed., *Papers of Ulysses S. Grant,* 28:391–393, 411–412, 445–446, 461–462, 466–467. See also Grant to Elihu B. Washburne, 24 December 1878, in James Grant Wilson, ed., *General Grant's Letters to a Friend, 1861–1880* (New York: T. Y. Crowell, 1897), 86–88.

57. Young, *Around the World,* 2:29.

58. Ibid., 2:159. See also Grant to Elihu B. Washburne, 4 April 1879, quoted in McFeely, *Grant,* 473–474; Grant to Nellie Satoris, 10 August 1879, quoted in Smith, *Grant,* 612.

59. Grant to Nellie Sartoris, 10 August 1879, quoted in Smith, *Grant,* 612.

60. Grant to Adam Badeau, 22 June 1879, in Badeau, *Grant in Peace,* 515. See also Grant to Elihu B. Washburne, 23 July 1879, in Wilson, ed., *General Grant's Letters,* 94–97.

61. Grant to Badeau, 25 August 1879, in Badeau, *Grant in Peace,* 518–519.

62. Mark Twain, *The Innocents Abroad, or The New Pilgrim's Progress* (1869), http://etext.virginia.edu; Grant to William W. Smith, 1 September 1878, in Simon, ed., *Papers of Ulysses S. Grant,* 28:466–467.

63. Charles Neider, ed., *The Autobiography of Mark Twain, Including Chapters Now Published for the First Time* (New York: Harper & Row, 1959), 241–245; Perrett, *Ulysses S. Grant,* 457–460; Smith, *Grant,* 613–614.

64. According to Grant's harshest biographer, William McFeely, his entire world tour had been part of a brilliant campaign strategy by the former president and his supporters to win the presidency. "Cleansed of the odor of corruption by the exhilarating air of travel," McFeely argues, "Grant should once more be put in command of the nation's fortunes. His return to the presidency would seem as irresistible as it was desirable." McFeely, *Grant,* 478–479. The evidence simply does not support such a Machiavellian scheme on Grant's part. Even though considerable speculation had developed even while Grant was traveling abroad that he would seek a third term when he returned to the United States, Young reported that the former president denied categorically that he was interested in winning a third term. McFeely maintains that Young was simply being deceived. If, however, Grant had motives for traveling overseas beyond his desire to see as much of the world as possible, he kept them well hidden, as Young has suggested and other biographers have acknowledged. McFeely, *Grant,* 479; Perrett, *Ulysses S. Grant,* 462–463.

65. Grant to General A. Badeau, 1 August 1879, in Badeau, *Grant in Peace,* 517–518; Josiah Bunting III, *Ulysses S. Grant* (New York: Times Books, 2004), 149.

66. Herbert J. Clancy, *The Presidential Election of 1880* (Chicago: Loyola University Press, 1958), 26–51, 82–121; Hesseltine, *Ulysses S. Grant*, 435–440; Bunting, *Ulysses S. Grant*, 150; McFeely, *Grant*, 482; Smith, *Grant*, 615–617.

67. The quote is from Hecht, *Beyond the Presidency*, 88.

68. Badeau, *Grant in Peace*, 320–323.

69. Grant to Badeau, 7 May 1871, in ibid., 533–534.

70. Young, *Around the World*, 2:156–159.

71. David Pletcher, *Rails, Mines, and Progress* (Ithaca, N.Y.: Cornell University Press, 1958), 149–150 and 160; Hesseltine, *Ulysses S. Grant*, 203; Smith, *Grant*, 78–79.

72. Young, *Around the World*, 2:448; Grant, *Personal Memoirs of U. S. Grant*, 37; Pletcher, *Rails, Mines, and Progress*, 112–114.

73. Pletcher, *Rails, Mines, and Progress*, 159–179; Smith, *Grant*, 618–619; McFeely, *Grant*, 488–489.

74. Badeau, *Grant in Peace*, 353. See also Grant to Elihu B. Washburne, 25 March 1880, in Wilson, ed., *General Grant's Letters*, 106–107; Pletcher, *Rail, Mines, and Progress*, 166–177; McFeely, *Grant*, 488; Hesseltine, *Ulysses S. Grant*, 445. Both McFeely and Hesseltine are incorrect in claiming that the Senate never ratified the treaty.

75. Quoted in Smith, *Grant*, 621.

76. Neider, ed., *Autobiography of Mark Twain*, 236–241.

77. Hesseltine, *Ulysses S. Grant*, 448–454; Smith, *Grant*, 623–624. Twain and Hesseltine state the offer to Grant was 75 percent of the profits; Smith states the offer was 70 percent, citing the *Autobiography* as his source.

78. The quote is from Smith, *Grant*, 625. See also Neider, ed., *Autobiography of Mark Twain*, 250.

79. Simpson, introduction to Grant, *Personal Memoirs of U. S. Grant*, viii–ix.

80. On presidential memoirs, see Geoffrey C. Ward, "When Presidents Tell It Their Way," *American Heritage Magazine* (August/September 1985); Mark Perry, "All the Presidents' Books: Why Do Presidents So Rarely Say Anything Memorable?," *Washington Post*, 13 June 2004; Stanley Renshon, "President Clinton's Memoirs: Caveat Emptor," *Presidential Studies Quarterly* 35 (September 2005): 608–612; Gould et al., "On Presidential Memoirs," *New York Journal News*, 20 June 2004; Kevin Baker, "Getting a Life: What's an Ex-President to Do?" (2000), http://www.kevinbaker.info. Even McFeely, who is more critical of the *Memoirs* than Grant's other biographers, acknowledges "the timeless quality" and "classical force" of the prose. McFeely, *Grant*, 511.

81. Grant, *Personal Memoirs of U. S. Grant*, 664–665.

82. Neider, ed., *Autobiography of Mark Twain*, 252; Howells to Clemens, 11 December 1885, *Selected Mark Twain–Howells Letters, 1872–1910*, ed. Frederick Anderson, William M. Gibson, and Henry Nash Smith (Cambridge, Mass.: Belknap Press of Harvard University Press, 1967), 259; Smith, *Grant*, 627. In addition, see McFeely, *Grant*, 501 and 505; John W. Simon, ed., *General Grant by Matthew Arnold with a Rejoinder by Mark Twain* (Kent, Ohio: Kent State University Press, 1995).

83. Neider, ed., *Autobiography of Mark Twain*, 253; Smith, *Grant*, 627.

84. McFeely, *Grant*, 507–509.

85. "Grant's Tomb: History," http://grantstomb.org.

86. Ibid. Brian Lamb, *Who's Buried in Grant's Tomb? A Tour of Presidential Gravesites* (New York: Public Affairs, 2003), 74–77.

CHAPTER 6: FORMER PRESIDENTS AND THE EMERGENT
MODERN PRESIDENCY

1. Lewis L. Gould, "The President in the Age of the Politco," in *Every Four Years,*
ed. Robert C. Post et al. (Washington, D.C.: Smithsonian Institution, 1980), 123. See also
Ari Hoogenboom, *Rutherford B. Hayes: Warrior and President* (Lawrence: University
Press of Kansas, 1995), 4.

2. Keller, *Affairs of State,* viii.

3. Hans L. Trefousse, *Rutherford B. Hayes* (New York: Times Books, 2002), 36.

4. Hoogenboom, *Rutherford B. Hayes,* 211.

5. Ibid., 211–214, 218–220, 233, 242–244, and 257–263; Trefousse, *Rutherford B.
Hayes,* 40–83.

6. Harry Barnard, *Rutherford B. Hayes and His America* (Indianapolis, Ind.: Bobbs-
Merrill, 1944), 446–447, 456–459, 482–485; Ari Hoogenboom, *The Presidency of Rutherford B. Hayes* (Lawrence: University Press of Kansas, 1988), 52–53.

7. Hoogenboom, *Rutherford B. Hayes,* 5–6. See also Kenneth E. Davison, *The Presidency of Rutherford B. Hayes* (Westport, Conn.: Greenwood Press, 1972), esp. xv–xvii;
Barnard, *Hayes and His America,* 446–447, 456–459, and 482–485.

8. Hoogenboom, *Presidency of Rutherford B. Hayes,* 303–304, 344–345, 347–350,
372–373, 384–387, and 460–461. For an excellent account of Hayes's trip to the Pacific
Northwest, see Davison, *Presidency of Rutherford B. Hayes,* 210–221.

9. John G. Sproat, *"The Best Men": Liberal Reformers in the Gilded Age* (New York:
Oxford University Press, 1968), esp. 4–10. See also Hoogenboom, *Presidency of Rutherford B. Hayes,* 211, 298, 316, 365, 375, 398–399, and 407.

10. Barnes, *Rutherford B. Hayes and His America,* 513.

11. Diary entry for 1 March 1878, in Charles Richard Williams, ed., *Diary and Letters of Rutherford Birchard Hayes: Nineteenth President of the United States* (hereafter
RBH Diary), 5 vols. (Columbus: Ohio State Archaeological and Historical Society, 1924),
3:463. See also Barnard, *Hayes and His America,* 484–486.

12. "The Residence of President Rutherford B. Hayes" and "About Spiegl Grove,"
both at http://www.rbhayes.org; National Park Service, "Survey of Historic Sites and
Buildings: Spiegel Grove, Ohio," http://www.nps.gov.

13. On the Duluth investment, which was suggested to him by the railroad magnate Jay Cooke, and which Hayes came to regret, see Barnard, *Hayes and His America,*
250–251.

14. Hoogenboom, *Rutherford B. Hayes,* 240, 250–252, 256, 268.

15. Hayes to John Sherman, 3 May 1881; Hayes to William Henry Smith, 14 December 1881; Hayes to Guy M. Bryan, 8 October 1882; Hayes to Thomas Donaldson, 10
March 1891, in Williams, ed., *RBH Diary,* 4:14, 4:41, and 4:55.

16. Diary entry for 26 December 1880, in ibid., 3:632.

17. Diary entry for 19 July 1880, in ibid., 3:614.

18. Memorandum for Garfield, 17 January 1881, in ibid., 3:639–640.

19. Hoogenboom, *Presidency of Rutherford B. Hayes,* 214–216; Hoogenboom, *Rutherford B. Hayes,* 455–458.

20. Diary entry for 2 March 1881, in Williams, ed., *RBH Diary,* 3:648; Tebbell and
Miles Watts, *The Press and the Presidency,* 238.

21. Davison, *Presidency of Rutherford B. Hayes,* 227–228; R. B. Hayes to John Sherman, 6 March 1881, in Williams, ed., *RBH Diary,* 3:649; Charles Richard Williams, *The Life of Rutherford Birchard Hayes, Nineteenth President of the United States,* 2 vols. (Boston: Houghton Mifflin, 1914), 2:335–336.

22. Williams, *Life of Hayes,* 2:334–335; Hufbauer, *Presidential Temples,* 26.

23. Hayes to William Henry Smith, 19 December 1881, in Williams, ed., *RBH Diary,* 1:56; Davison, *Presidency of Rutherford B. Hayes,* 229–230; Williams, *Life of Hayes,* 2:332–335.

24. Williams, *Life of Hayes,* 2:352–353.

25. R. B. Hayes to [unidentified], 6 July 1883, in Williams, ed., *RBH Diary,* 4:122; Andrew D. White, *Scientific and Industrial Education in the United States: An Address Delivered before the New York State Agricultural Society* (New York: D. Appleton, 1874), 6. See also Patrick N. Foster, "Lessons from History: Industrial Arts/Technology," *Journal of Vocational and Technical Education* 13 (Spring 1997): 1–11.

26. Barnard, *Hayes and His America,* 506.

27. Hayes to [unaddressed], 6 January 1893, in Williams, ed., *RBH Diary,* 5:133; Barnard, *Hayes and His America,* 506–507.

28. Hayes to Webb C. Hayes, 12 October 1881, in Williams, ed., *RBH Diary,* 4:47–48.

29. Diary entry of 10 December 1881, in ibid., 4:52–53.

30. Hayes to General Eli H. Murray, 29 March 1886, in ibid., 4:278–279.

31. Diary entry of 11 March 1888, in ibid., 4:374.

32. Hayes's views come very close to those whom Nancy Cohen describes as the "ethical economists" of the 1880s. See Cohen, *Reconstruction,* esp. 159–162. On Einstein, see Walter Isaacson, *Einstein: His Life and Universe* (New York: Simon & Schuster, 2007), 240.

33. Diary entries of 4 December 1883 and 24 January 1886, in Williams, ed., *RBH Diary,* 4:261–262, and 4:354–355. In her analysis, Cohen refers only briefly to former President Hayes, who, in most respects, fits her description of a "liberal reformer" as those who sought "to reconcile[e] economic dominance and its attendant symmetries of power with American Democracy." But just as Hayes defies John G. Sproat's characterization of the "best men," so he defies Cohen's characterization of the "liberal reformers" of the late nineteenth century. Cohen, *Reconstruction,* esp. 5–19, 127, and 135.

34. Diary entry of 3 July 1881, in Williams, ed., *RBH Diary,* 4:23–24.

35. Diary entry of 28 August 1881, and Hayes to Emile Kahn, 1 October 1881, in ibid., 4:33, 4:37.

36. Diary entries of 14 and 26 May 1884, in ibid., 4:149 and 4:151. See also Hayes to Mrs. Hayes, 16 January 1885, in ibid., 4:184–185.

37. Diary entries of 23 March 1885 and 13 April 1888, in ibid., 4:198–199 and 4:382–384; Hoogenboom, *Rutherford B. Hayes,* 483, 487, and 501–502.

38. Diary entry of 9 November 1888, in Williams, ed., *RBH Diary,* 4:421–422.

39. Diary entry of 9 November 1892, in ibid., 5:122–123.

40. Diary entry of 19 December 1886, in ibid., 4:299.

41. Hoogenboom, *Rutherford B. Hayes,* 475–476.

42. Diary entries of 7 and 23 February and 3 March 1885, in Williams, ed., *RBH Diary,* 4:188, 4:194–196.

43. Letter from Hayes to Guy M. Bryan, 18 April 1887; diary entries 8 September and 31 December 1891 and 22 June 1892, in ibid., 4:320–321 and 582, 5:22–23, 43, and 68–69.

44. Diary entries of 28 August 1889, in ibid., 4:503–504.

45. Diary entries of 12 December 1890 and 6 February 1891, in ibid., 4:622 and 4:637.

46. Marx, *Health of the Presidents,* 221–230; Bumgarner, *Health,* 115–119.

47. Diary entry of 24 August 1890, in Williams, ed., *RBH Diary,* 4:595; Marx, *Health of the Presidents,* 231–232; Bumgarner, *Health,* 119–120.

48. The quote is from Williams, *Life of Hayes,* 2:397.

49. Marx, *Health of the Presidents,* 232–233; Bumgarner, *Health,* 120.

50. In 1910, when Spiegel Grove was donated by Hayes's son, Webb, to the state of Ohio, the former president and his wife were reinterred on the grounds of the estate.

51. Keller, *Affairs of State,* 122–123; see also Sproat, *Best Men,* 6; Beatty, *Age of Betrayal,* xi; Eric Foner, *Reconstruction,* xxvi, 18–25, footnote 54. Hayes also does not fit the description of liberals of the late nineteenth century who, Nancy Cohen argues, sought to assure civil order and protected emergent corporate capitalism from democratic challenges by transforming liberalism into a form of antidemocratic capitalism. Cohen, *Reconstruction,* 1–19.

52. Cleveland to Wilson S. Bissell, 13 April 1889, and Cleveland to William F. Vilas, 19 April 1889, in Allan Nevins, ed., *Letters of Grover Cleveland, 1850–1908* (Boston: Houghton Mifflin, 1933), 202–204. The standard biography of Arthur is Thomas C. Reeves, *Gentleman Boss: The Life of Chester Alan Arthur* (New York: Knopf, 1975). See esp. 420–424.

53. He had dabbled in Democratic politics, partly because of the party's conservative values and his fear that the merging Republican Party might lead the nation into civil war. In 1865, he ran unsuccessfully for district attorney.

54. Lewis L. Gould, "The Republican Search for a National Majority," in *The Gilded Age,* ed. H. Wayne Morgan (Syracuse, N.Y.: Syracuse University Press, 1970), 171–180; Allan Nevins, *Grover Cleveland: A Study in Courage* (New York: Dodd Mead, 1934), 145–155; Henry F. Graff, *Grover Cleveland* (New York: Times Books, 2002), 40–45.

55. Graff, *Grover Cleveland,* 68, 74, 76, 85, 88–89; Robert E. Welch Jr., *The Presidencies of Grover Cleveland* (Lawrence: University Press of Kansas, 1988), 89–91.

56. Nevins, *Grover Cleveland,* 452–459; Graff, *Grover Cleveland,* 99; Alyn Brodsky, *Grover Cleveland: A Study in Character* (New York: St. Martin's Press, 2000), 255–256.

57. Cleveland to Wilson S. Bissell, 21 October 1891, in Nevins, *Letters of Grover Cleveland,* 269.

58. Cleveland to Williams F. Vilas, 17 August 1890, in ibid., 229–230.

59. Cleveland to Wilson S. Bissell, 8 November 1890, in ibid., 234–236.

60. Cleveland to E. Eller Anderson, 10 February 1891, in ibid., 245–246.

61. Nevins, *Grover Cleveland,* 460–509; 1; Graff, *Grover Cleveland,* 100–110; Brodksy, *Grover Cleveland,* 255–282; Keller, *Affairs of State,* 529–530.

62. According to the historian Ari Hoogenboom, "During the Hayes administration the United States had few problems with foreign governments and little inclination to become an imperialist power." Hoogenboom, *Presidency of Rutherford B. Hayes,* 173–192.

63. Homer E. Socolofsky and Allan B. Spetter, *The Presidency of Benjamin Harrison* (Lawrence: University Press of Kansas, 1987), 47–48.

64. When Harrison entered office in 1889, the United States had been ranked by naval professionals as low as seventeenth among the navies of the world; by the time he left

the White House, it occupied seventh place and was climbing quickly. Walter LaFeber, *The New Empire: An Interpretation of American Expansion, 1860–1898* (Ithaca, N.Y.: Cornell University Press, 1963), 121–127.

65. Charles W. Calhoun, *Benjamin Harrison* (New York: Times Books, 2005), 83.

66. Socolofsky and Spetter, *Presidency of Benjamin Harrison,* 47–48.

67. The quote is from Calhoun, *Benjamin Harrison,* 149.

68. The quotes are from ibid., 150–151.

69. The quotes are from Harry J. Sievers, *Benjamin Harrison, Hoosier President: The White House and After* (Indianapolis, Ind.: Bobbs-Merrill, 1968), 254–255.

70. The quote is from Calhoun, *Benjamin Harrison,* 155.

71. The quote is from ibid., 156.

72. The quote is from Hecht, *Beyond the Presidency,* 214.

73. Allen Sharp, "Benjamin Harrison: High-Priced Counsel," in *America's Lawyer-Presidents: From Law Office to Oval Office,* ed. Norman Gross (Evanston, Ill.: Northwestern University Press, 2004), 195–203.

74. Benjamin Harrison, *Views of an Ex-President: Being His Addresses and Writings on Subjects of Public Interest since the Close of His Administration as President of the United States* (Indianapolis, Ind.: Bobbs-Merrill, 1901); Benjamin Harrison, *This Country of Ours,* 2nd ed. (New York: Charles Scribner's Sons, 1897). The quote is from Sievers, *Benjamin Harrison,* 256.

75. Quoted in Sharp, "Benjamin Harrison," 204.

76. Sievers, *Benjamin Harrison,* 267n80, 268.

77. Harrison to W. H. H. Miller, 28 September 1899, *Papers of Benjamin Harrison* (Washington, D.C.: Library of Congress), microform edition, vol. 175.

78. The quote is from Otto Schoenrich, "The Venezuela–British Guiana Boundary Dispute," *American Journal of International Law* 43 (July 1949): 523–530. See also LaFeber, *New Empire,* 242–283.

79. The article in *Ladies' Home Journal* was republished in Harrison, *This Country of Ours,* 159.

80. "The Great Mass Meeting," Carnegie Hall, New York, 31 October 1894, in Harrison, *Views of an Ex-President,* 410–411.

81. Ibid., 407.

82. "The Obligations of Wealth," address delivered before the Union League Club, Chicago, Illinois, 22 February 1898, in ibid., 331–360.

83. Ibid.

84. The speech in Carnegie Hall can be found as "At the Republican Ratification Meeting," Carnegie Hall, 22 August 1896, in ibid., 426–453.

85. The article on military training was published in the *Century Magazine* and later reprinted in Harrison, *Views of an Ex-President,* 367–370. For his remarks on colonies, see "Statement to Press," *New York Times,* 3 March 1900.

86. Bumgarner, *Health,* 144–145; Marx, *Health of the Presidents,* 271–272.

CHAPTER 7: THE POST-PRESIDENCY AND THE MODERN PRESIDENCY

1. Welch, *Presidencies of Cleveland,* 141–155 and 224; Brodsky, *Grover Cleveland,* 322–332.

2. Cleveland to Don. M. Dickinson, 18 February 1896, in Nevins, *Letters of Grover Cleveland*, 429–430; Welch, *Presidencies of Cleveland*, 201–203.

3. Letter of Cleveland to the Democratic voters, New York *Herald,* 16 June 1896, in Nevins, *Letters of Grover Cleveland,* 440–441; Welch, *Presidencies of Cleveland,* 208–212.

4. Cleveland to Professor Andrew F. West, 8 November 1896, in Nevins, *Letters of Grover Cleveland,* 461; Graff, *Grover Cleveland,* 131–132.

5. The operation had been kept secret to avoid further financial panic. During the operation, the president was strapped to the boat's mast in a sitting position, and his upper jaw was removed using a cheek retractor that avoided external surgery on his face and jaw. His jaw was replaced with a rubber prosthesis that affected neither his appearance nor his speech. Nevins, *Grover Cleveland,* 528–533; Brodsky, *Grover Cleveland,* 304–322.

6. Cleveland to Judson Harmon, 17 April 1899, in Nevins, *Letters of Grover Cleveland,* 515. See also Cleveland to Charles S. Fairchilds, 12 April 1900, in ibid., 529.

7. Cleveland to Don M. Dickinson, 12 October 1900, in ibid., 538–539.

8. Quoted in Brodsky, *Grover Cleveland,* 428.

9. Quoted in George F. Parker, *Recollections of Grover Cleveland* (New York: Century, 1909), 382–385.

10. Bumgarner, *Health,* 140; Welch, *Presidencies of Cleveland,* 210.

11. Cleveland to Alexander E. Orr, 16 November 1896, in Nevins, *Letters of Grover Cleveland,* 461–462.

12. Cleveland to Charles S. Fairchild, 2 April 1897, and Cleveland to the editors of the New York *World,* 14 March 1908, in ibid, 485 and 625–626.

13. Quoted in Brodsky, *Grover Cleveland,* 406–407.

14. Keller, *Affairs of State,* 553–554; Lewis L. Gould, *The Presidency of William McKinley* (Lawrence: University Press of Kansas, 1980), 26–27, 40–44; Kevin Phillips, *William McKinley* (New York: Times Books, 2003), 114.

15. Cleveland's statement to the Associated Press, 24 January 1898, and Cleveland to Richard Olney, 19 June 1897 and 8 July 1898, in Nevins, *Letters of Grover Cleveland,* 478, 491–492, and 501–502.

16. Cleveland to E. C. Benedict, 14 April 1898, in ibid., 499.

17. Cleveland to Charles S. Hamlin, 2 January 1899, in ibid., 502.

18. Cleveland to Judson Harmon, 17 July 1900, and Cleveland to Don Dickinson, 18 December 1900, in ibid., 532–533 and 542–543.

19. Cleveland to Edward M. Shepherd, 12 January 1899, in ibid., 508.

20. Parker, *Recollections of Grover Cleveland,* 250–251. See also Cleveland to President Theodore Roosevelt, 14 October 1900, in Nevins, *Letters of Grover Cleveland,* 560. Brodsky, *Grover Cleveland,* 433–434.

21. From the address at Carnegie Hall, New York City, 21 October 1904, in Albert Ellery Bergh, ed., *Grover Cleveland: Addresses, State Papers and Letters* (New York: Sun Dial Classics, 1909), 440.

22. Cleveland to Richard Watson Gilder, 11 March 1904, in Nevins, *Letters of Grover Cleveland,* 574–576; Nevins, *Grover Cleveland,* 748–751.

23. Nevins, *Grover Cleveland,* 754.

24. Cleveland to Charles S. Hamlin, 14 August 1904, in ibid., 384. See also Brodsky, *Grover Cleveland,* 432.

25. Cleveland to A. B. Farquhar, 12 December 1904, in Nevins, *Letters of Grover Cleveland*, 590–591.

26. Cleveland to E. Prentiss Bailey, 14 March 1908, and Cleveland to the editors of the New York *World*, 14 March 1908, in ibid., 624–625.

27. Cleveland to E. C. Benedict, 7 February 1901, in ibid., 546.

28. Cleveland to Oscar S. Straus, 6 October 1903, and Cleveland to E. C. Benedict, 5 February 1905, in ibid., 571 and 593. See also Graff, *Grover Cleveland*, 134–135.

29. Cleveland to Thomas Fortune Ryan, 10 June 1905, Cleveland to Paul Morton, 6 February 1907, and Cleveland to E. C. Benedict, 3 April 1907, in Nevins, *Letters of Grover Cleveland*, 596–599 and 612–613.

30. Marx, *Health of the Presidents*, 267; Bumgarner, *Health*, 140; Nevins, *Grover Cleveland*, 762–763.

31. Henry F. Pringle, *Theodore Roosevelt: A Biography*, rev. ed. (New York: Harcourt, Brace & World, 1956), vii. The literature on Roosevelt is extensive, but the best of the more recent biographies are H. W. Brands, *T.R.: The Last Romantic* (New York: Basic Books, 1997); Edmund Morris, *Theodore Rex* (New York: Random House, 2001); and Kathleen Dalton, *Theodore Roosevelt: A Strenuous Life* (New York: Knopf, 2002). See also Lewis L. Gould, *The Presidency of Theodore Roosevelt* (Lawrence: University Press of Kansas, 1991), and Louis Auchincloss, *Theodore Roosevelt* (New York: Times Books, 2001).

32. The definitive work on Roosevelt's post-presidency is now Edmund Morris, *Colonel Roosevelt* (New York: Random House, 2010).

33. John Milton Cooper Jr., "Lonesome Lion and Crippled Prophet: Theodore Roosevelt and Woodrow Wilson as Former Presidents," in *Farewell to the Chief: Former Presidents in American Public Life*, ed. Richard Norton Smith and Timothy Walch (Worland, Wyo.: High Plains Publishing, 1990), 3–5.

34. Brands, *T.R.*, ix–x; Auchincloss, *Theodore Roosevelt*, 16.

35. On Roosevelt's coy use of his wartime fame, see Perle Arnold, *Remaking the Presidency: Roosevelt, Taft, and Wilson* (Lawrence: University Press of Kansas, 2009), 21–24.

36. Gould, *Presidency of Theodore Roosevelt*, 147–171 and 197–223.

37. Roosevelt to Cecil Spring Rice, 10 March 1909, in Elting E. Morison, ed., *Letters of Theodore Roosevelt*, 8 vols. (Cambridge, Mass.: Harvard University Press, 1951–1954), 7:2.

38. The quote is from Patricia O'Toole's excellent *When Trumpets Call: Theodore Roosevelt after the White House* (New York: Simon & Schuster, 2005), 41.

39. Ibid., 19–20.

40. Brands, *T.R.*, 204–210, 249–250, 256–257, 267, 404, 432; Dalton, *Theodore Roosevelt*, 123, 139, and 348.

41. The quote is from O'Toole, *When Trumpets Call*, 41.

42. Later *Collier's* and *McClure's* offered him $100,000 for the African articles, but he turned them down. Ibid., 18–21; Brands, *T.R.*, 642–647; Dalton, *Theodore Roosevelt*, 347–348.

43. O'Toole, *When Trumpets Call*, 46–47. The quote is from Brands, *T.R.*, 655.

44. O'Toole, *When Trumpets Call*, 55–67; Brands, *T.R.*, 647–659.

45. Roosevelt to Elihu Root, 17 May 1909, in Morison, ed., *Letters of Theodore Roosevelt*, 7:11; O'Toole, *When Trumpets Call*, 44, 55, and 66–70.

46. He knew that his safari had attracted worldwide attention and that a number of authors were trying to capitalize on this interest by writing books about hunting in Africa. In order not to be preempted by these other writers and to assure large sales of his own book when it was completed, he made sure not to miss any of his deadlines. Roosevelt to Elihu Root, 17 May 1909, in Morison, ed., *Letters of Theodore Roosevelt,* 7:11; O'Toole, *When Trumpets Call,* 44, 55, 66–70.

47. Roosevelt to Gifford Pinchot, 17 January 1910, in Morison, ed., *Letters of Theodore Roosevelt,* 7:45–46. See also Roosevelt to Henry Cabot Lodge, 8 March 1909, and Roosevelt to Henry White, 21 July 1909, ibid., 1–2 and 21.

48. Lodge to Roosevelt, 29 April and 21 June 1909, in Henry Cabot Lodge, ed., *Selections from the Correspondence of Theodore Roosevelt and Henry Cabot Lodge, 1884–1911,* 2 vols. (New York: Charles Scribner's Sons, 1925), 2:333–335 and 2:337–339; Roosevelt to Henry Cabot Lodge, 15 May 1909, in Morison, ed., *Letters of Theodore Roosevelt,* 7:9–10. See also Morris, *Colonel Roosevelt,* 12–13.

49. Lodge to Roosevelt, 21 June 1909, and Roosevelt to Lodge, 26 July 1909, in Lodge, ed., *Selections from the Correspondence,* 2:337–342.

50. Roosevelt to Andrew Carnegie, 18 February 1910, in Morison, ed., *Letters of Theodore Roosevelt,* 7:64 and 7:66–68.

51. Thomas G. Dyer, *Theodore Roosevelt and the Idea of Race* (Baton Rouge: Louisiana State University Press, 1980), esp. 89–122; quote from 118.

52. Roosevelt to Whitelaw Reid, 24 March 1910, in Morison, ed., *Letters of Theodore Roosevelt,* 7:32. See also Roosevelt to Cecil Arthur Spring Rice, 6 October 1909; Roosevelt to Lee, 6 October 1909; and Roosevelt to George Otto Trevelyan, 1 October 1911, all in ibid., 7:33 and 7:350–351.

53. Roosevelt to George Otto Trevelyan, 1 October 1911, in ibid., 7:380–381. See also Sidney M. Milkis, *Theodore Roosevelt, the Progressive Party, and the Transformation of American Democracy* (Lawrence: University Press of Kansas, 2009), 30–37.

54. Roosevelt to Andrew Carnegie, 18 February 1910, in Morison, ed., *Letters of Theodor Roosevelt,* 7:47.

55. The quote is from Morris, *Colonel Roosevelt,* 85.

56. Nathan Miller, *Theodore Roosevelt: A Life* (New York: William Morrow, 1992), 512–513.

57. Roosevelt to Henry Cabot Lodge, 1 August 1910, in Lodge, ed., *Selections from the Correspondence,* 2:386–387, and Roosevelt to Theodore Roosevelt Jr., 22 January 1911, in Morison, ed., *Letters of Theodore Roosevelt,* 7:622.

58. Quoted in Morris, *Colonel Roosevelt,* 96.

59. Dalton, *Theodore Roosevelt,* 363.

60. Roosevelt to Theodore Roosevelt Jr., 11 November 1910, and Roosevelt to Cecil Arthur Spring Rice, 22 August 1911, in Morison, ed., *Letters of Theodore Roosevelt,* 7:159–161 and 7:332–335.

61. The quotes are in Robert S. LaForte, "Theodore Roosevelt's Osawatomie Speech," *Kansas Historical Quarterly* 32 (Summer 1966): 187–200.

62. The quote is in ibid., 196–197. See also Morris, *Colonel Roosevelt,* 109–110.

63. Roosevelt to Henry Cabot Lodge, 12 September 1910, in Lodge, ed., *Selections from the Correspondence,* 2:390–392. See also O'Toole, *When Trumpets Call,* 104–107.

64. Roosevelt to Arthur Hamilton Lee, 16 September 1910, and Roosevelt to Henry Cabot Lodge, 21 September 1910, in Morison, ed., *Letters of Theodore Roosevelt,* 7:129–130 and 7:134–137.

65. His conservative opponents later reported that he won only because he had come to Taft at an earlier meeting in New Haven asking for his support in exchange for endorsing at the Saratoga gathering the president's renomination in 1912. In truth, the New Haven meeting had been arranged in an effort to heal the wounds between the two men; it had been cordial but unproductive. Brands, *T.R.,* 677–680; O'Toole, *When Trumpets Call,* 107–111.

66. Roosevelt to Theodore Roosevelt Jr., 11 November 1910, in Morison, ed., *Letters of Theodore Roosevelt,* 7:159–161; Dalton, *Theodore Roosevelt,* 368.

67. Roosevelt to Benjamin Ide Wheeler, 21 November 1910, in Morison, ed., *Letters of Theodore Roosevelt,* 7:159–161. See also Roosevelt to Theodore Roosevelt Jr., 11 November 1910; Roosevelt to Arthur Hamilton Lee, 11 November 1910; and Roosevelt to Henry Lewis Stimson, 16 November 1910, in ibid., 7:163–165 and 7:169–173.

68. Roosevelt to Arthur Hamilton Lee, 11 November 1910, and Roosevelt to Benjamin Ide White, 21 November 1910, in ibid., 7:163–164 and 7:169–173.

69. *Oultook,* 11 January 1911, in *The Works of Theodore Roosevelt: Memorial Edition,* 24 vols. (New York: Charles Scribner's Sons, 1923–1926), 19:81. See also Roosevelt to Charles Dwight Willard, 28 April 1911, in Morison, ed., *Letters of Theodore Roosevelt,* 7:251; Dalton, *Theodore Roosevelt,* 207.

70. Roosevelt to Jonathan Bourne Jr., 2 January 1911, in Morison, ed., *Letters of Theodore Roosevelt,* 7:196–199.

71. Roosevelt to William Allen White, 12 December 1910, in ibid., 7:181–185.

72. A few months later, however, he offered to raise a division of cavalry should Japan or another major power back rebels in Mexico, then in the throes of a revolution, who might threaten U.S. property in the country or become a danger along the U.S.–Mexican border. Roosevelt to William Howard Taft, 22 December 1910 and 14 March 1911, in ibid., 7:189–192 and 7:243–244.

73. Roosevelt to Charles Dwight Willard, 28 April 1911, in ibid., 7:250–251.

74. O'Toole, *When Trumpets Call,* 126.

75. Roosevelt to James Bryce, 2 June 1911, in Morison, ed., *Letters of Theodore Roosevelt,* 7:275–276. See also Roosevelt to Alfred Thayer Mahan, 3 June 1911; Roosevelt to Hiram Price Collier, 12 June 1911; and Roosevelt to Henry Cabot Lodge, 19 June 1911, in ibid., 7:279–282 and 7:289–290; O'Toole, *When Trumpets Call,* 126–127, 131–133, and 139–141.

76. O'Toole, *When Trumpets Call,* 135–136; Dalton, *Theodore Roosevelt,* 376.

77. Roosevelt to William Allen White, 24 October 1911, in Morison, ed., *Letters of Theodore Roosevelt,* 7:417–418.

78. Roosevelt to John Callan O'Laughlin, 7 February 1911, and Roosevelt to Henry Lewis Stimson, 5 February 1912, in ibid., 7:227 and 7:494–495.

79. Roosevelt to Andrew Carnegie, 5 March 1912, and Roosevelt to Joseph Moore Dixon, 8 March 1912, in ibid., 7:520–524.

80. Roosevelt to William Ellsworth Glassock and Other, 24 February 1912, in ibid., 7:227 and 7:494–495.

81. Roosevelt to Endicott Peabody, 5 May 1911, in ibid., 7:258–259. On Roosevelt's health, see also Morris, *Colonel Roosevelt,* 103–104; Marx, *Health of the Presidents,* 283–297; Bumgarner, *Health,* 154–165.

82. Roosevelt to August Everett Willson, 14 February 1912, in Morison, ed., *Letters of Theodore Roosevelt,* 7:503–504. See also Milkis, *Theodore Roosevelt,* 90–91.

83. Roosevelt to Arthur Hamilton Lee, 14 May 1912, in Morison, ed., *Letters of*

Theodore Roosevelt, 7:544–555; Herbert Eaton, *Presidential Timber: A History of Nominating Conventions, 1868–1960* (New York: Free Press, 1964), 210–214; O'Toole, *When Trumpets Call,* 158–171.

84. Eaton, *Presidential Timber,* 214–217; O'Toole, *When Trumpets Call,* 172–178; Brands, *T.R.,* 713–716.

85. Eaton, *Presidential Timber,* 217–219.

86. Roosevelt to William Dudley Foulke, 1 July 1912, and Roosevelt to Edwin A. Van Valkenburg, 16 July 1912, in Morison, ed., *Letters of Theodore Roosevelt,* 7:568–569 and 7:576–577.

87. Roosevelt to Chase Salmon Osborne, 5 July 1912; Roosevelt to Horace Plunkett, 3 August 1912; and Roosevelt to James Herrick Gipson, 12 October 1912, in ibid., 7:569–570 and 7:591–594.

88. Roosevelt to Arthur Hamilton Lee, 5 November 1912, and Roosevelt to Gifford Pinchot, 13 November 1912, in ibid., 7:633–634 and 7:640–645.

89. Theodore Roosevelt, *Theodore Roosevelt: An Autobiography* (Cambridge, Mass.: Da Capo Press, 1985). See also Morris, *Colonel Roosevelt,* 275–276 and 663, footnote, 276; Miller, *Theodore Roosevelt,* 532–533.

90. See, for example, Roosevelt to Emily Tyler Carol, 4 January 1912, and Roosevelt to Henry Cabot Lodge, 27 February 1913, in Morison, ed., *Letters of Theodore Roosevelt,* 7:688–689 and 7:710; O'Toole, *When Trumpets Call,* 237–238.

91. Roosevelt to Francis Joseph Henry, 13 December 1912, in Morison, ed., *Letters of Theodore Roosevelt,* 7:672–676.

92. The presidential scholar Sidney M. Milkis makes the important point that Roosevelt and his progressive supporters transformed the nature of the political process by subordinating party machinery and local political bosses to direct and mass ("pure") democracy and candidate-centered politics. Progressive issues like the initiative and referendum, recall of elected officials, primaries, and direct election of senators reflected the progessive emphasis on direct democracy. Even Wilson appealed to direct democracy, but within a political structure. One result of this shift away from the power of party machinery largely controlled by political bosses toward mass democracy and candidate-centered politics was increased presidential independence and authority. In terms of the modern presidency, this transformation is what separated Roosevelt as a modern president from his predecessors, including William McKinley. Milkis, *Theodore Roosevelt,* esp. xiii–xiv, 36–62, 147–156.

93. Dalton, *Theodore Roosevelt,* 414–421; O'Toole, *When Trumpets Call,* 242–245.

94. O'Toole, *When Trumpets Call,* 246–247.

95. For the best and most detailed account of Roosevelt's Brazilian expedition, see Morris, *Colonel Roosevelt,* 305–347. But see also O'Toole, *When Trumpets Call,* 254–257; Dalton, *Theodore Roosevelt,* 254–257; and Brands, *T.R.,* 738–743.

96. Quoted in Dalton, *Theodore Roosevelt,* 439.

97. Quoted in ibid., 443. See also Roosevelt to William E. Cadmus, 15 September 1913, in Morison, ed., *Letters of Theodore Roosevelt,* 7:748–750.

98. Roosevelt to Arthur Hamilton Lee, 14 September 1914, and Roosevelt to Hugo Munsterberg, 8 August and 2 November 1914, in Morison, ed., *Letters of Theodore Roosevelt,* 7:794–796, 8:817–818, 8:824–825.

99. Roosevelt to Henry White, 2 May 1913, in ibid., 7:723–724. See also Roosevelt to Hiram Warren Johnson, 20 and 28 April 1913, in ibid., 7:720–722.

100. Roosevelt to Henry Cabot Lodge, 9 September 1913, in ibid., 7:747. On the treaty

with Columbia, see Roosevelt to William Joel Stone, 11 July 1914, in ibid., 7:777–778; Miller, *Theodore Roosevelt*, 538–539; William Henry Harbaugh, *The Life and Times of Theodore Roosevelt* (New York: Collier, 1963), 437. The Senate rejected the agreement, but in 1921, Warren Harding's administration renegotiated a similar treaty without the apology.

101. Roosevelt to Arthur Hamilton Lee, 22 August 1914, in Morison, ed., *Letters of Theodore Roosevelt*, 8:809–812.

102. Roosevelt to Cecil Arthur Spring Rice, 3 October 1914, in ibid., 8:821–822. See also Roosevelt to Hugo Munsterberg, 2 November 1914, in ibid., 825–827.

103. Roosevelt to Albert Apponyi, 17 September 1914, in ibid., 8:819–820. See also Auchincloss, *Theodore Roosevelt*, 126–127; Brands, *T.R.*, 755.

104. *New York Times*, 8 November 1914.

105. Roosevelt to Meyer Lissner, 16 November 1914, in Morison, ed., *Letters of Theodore Roosevelt*, 8:843–845. See also Roosevelt to Rudyard Kipling, 4 November 1914; Roosevelt to Hiram Warren Johnson, 16 November 1914; Roosevelt to William Dudley Foulke, 12 December 1914; Roosevelt to Cecil Arthur Spring Rice, 22 January 1915; Roosevelt to Dwight Emlen, 29 January 1915; Roosevelt to George William Norris, 6 February 1915; Roosevelt to John St. Loe Strachey, 22 February 1915, in ibid., 8:829–831, 8:845–847, 8:865–866, 8:883–886, 8:889, 8:897–903.

106. *New York Times*, 10 March 1918; Roosevelt to Lyman Abbott, 19 June 1914, in Morison, ed., *Letters of Theodore Roosevelt*, 7:768; Morris, *Colonel Roosevelt*, 363, 393, 396; O'Toole, *When Trumpets Call*, 270–271.

107. The quote is from O'Toole, *When Trumpets Call*, 275–276.

108. Roosevelt to Archibald Bulloch Roosevelt, 19 May 1915, and Roosevelt to Arthur Hamilton Lee, 17 June 1915, in Morison, ed., *Letters of Theodore Roosevelt*, 8:922–923 and 8:935–941.

109. The trial was also the second one in two years. The first had involved another libel suit that Roosevelt had brought against a newspaper editor who claimed during the 1912 campaign that Roosevelt was a drunkard. Roosevelt won the case, but he was still angry that his integrity had been impugned. Dalton, *Theodore Roosevelt*, 410, 418, 449, 454–456; Morris, *Colonel Roosevelt*, 404–424.

110. Dalton, *Theodore Roosevelt*, 458–459; Roosevelt to Michael A. Schaap, 22 February 1915, in Morison, ed., *Letters of Theodore Roosevelt*, 8:893.

111. Dalton, *Theodore Roosevelt*, 474. See also Roosevelt to Ethel Eyre Valentine Dreier, 15 October 1915, and Roosevelt to Medeleine Zabriskie Doty, 7 January 1916, in Morison, ed., *Letters of Theodore Roosevelt*, 8:974–975.

112. Roosevelt to Anna Roosevelt Cowles, 27 January 1916, in Morison, ed., *Letters of Theodore Roosevelt*, 8:1007–1008.

113. O'Toole, *When Trumpets Call*, 289–290. Roosevelt had been proposing universal military training since 1914. See Roosevelt to Scott Oliver, 22 July 1915, in Morison, ed., *Letters of Theodore Roosevelt*, 7:949–950. See also Roosevelt to James Edward West, 30 November 1915, in ibid., 8:992–993.

114. The quote is from Miller, *Theodore Roosevelt*, 549. See also Roosevelt to the Progressive National Committee, 22 June 1916, in Morison, ed., *Letters of Theodore Roosevelt*, 8:1067–1074.

115. Brands, *T.R.*, 760–764.

116. Roosevelt to William Franklin Knox, 21 December 1915, in Morison, ed., *Letters of Theodore Roosevelt*, 8:997–998.

117. Roosevelt to Arthur Hamilton Lee, 7 June 1916, in ibid., 8:1052–1056.

118. Roosevelt to George Walbridge Perkins, 3 September 1915, in ibid., 8:971–972.

119. Roosevelt to Henry Cabot Lodge, 7 December 1915 and 6 January 1916, in ibid., 8:995–996 and 8:1000–1002.

120. Roosevelt to Anna Roosevelt Cowles, 3 February 1916, in ibid., 8:1011–1014. See also Roosevelt to Gifford Pinchot, 8 February 1916; Roosevelt to Arthur Hamilton Lee, 18 February 1916, in ibid., 8:1016–1017, 8:1022–1023.

121. Roosevelt to Foster Vincent Brown, 10 May 1916, in ibid., 8:1029–1031 and 8:1038–1039.

122. Roosevelt to William Cameron Forbes, 23 May 1916, in ibid., 8:1044–1045; Brands, *T.R.*, 766–769; Miller, *Theodore Roosevelt*, 549.

123. Roosevelt to Charles Joseph Bonaparte, 29 May 1916, in Morison, ed., *Letters of Theodore Roosevelt*, 8:1049–1050; Eaton, *Presidential Timber*, 251.

124. Eaton, *Presidential Timber*, 255–256.

125. William Allen White, *The Autobiography of William Allen White* (New York: Macmillan, 1946), 526–527; Roosevelt to the conferees of the Progressive Party, 10 June 1916, and Roosevelt to the Progressive National Committee, 22 June 1916, in Morison, ed., *Letters of Theodore Roosevelt*, 8:1060–1061 and 8:1067–1074. See also Eaton, *Presidential Timber*, 256–257.

126. Roosevelt's remarks about "impressions" are in O'Toole, *When Trumpets Call*, 296. See also Miller, *Theodore Roosevelt*, 542; and Auchincloss, *Theodore Roosevelt*, 130.

127. Roosevelt to Julian Street, 3 July 1916, and Roosevelt to Newton Baker, 6 July 1916, in Morison, ed., *Letters of Theodore Roosevelt*, 8:1085–1088.

128. Roosevelt to Corrine Roosevelt Robinson, 21 July 1916, in ibid., 8:1090–1091.

129. Roosevelt to Arthur Hamilton Lee, 28 November 1916; Roosevelt to Benjamin Ide Wheeler, 29 November 1916; and Roosevelt to William Allen White, 1 January 1917, in ibid., 7:1125–1128 and 7:1135–1137.

130. Roosevelt to Newton Diehl Baker, 7 February and 23 March 1917, and Baker to Roosevelt, 9 February 1917, in ibid., 8:1151 and 8:1166.

131. Clemenceau's editorial can be found in ibid., 8:1200–1201n1. See also Roosevelt to Jean Jules Jusserand, 16 February 1917, in ibid., 8:1152.

132. The exchange between House and Roosevelt is from Auchincloss, *Theodore Roosevelt*, 132. For Baker's final rejection of Roosevelt's request and Roosevelt's response, see also Roosevelt to John Callan O'Laughlin, 13 April 1917, and Roosevelt to Newton Diehl Baker, 23 April 1917, in Morison, ed., *Letters of Theodore Roosevelt*, 8:1173–1174 and 8:1176–1183.

133. See, for example, Roosevelt to William Allen White, 3 August 1917, in Morison, ed., *Letters of Theodore Roosevelt*, 8:1216–1217; O'Toole, *When Trumpets Call*, 361–363.

134. Roosevelt to Ernest Lundeen, 7 November 1917, in Morison, ed., *Letters of Theodore Roosevelt*, 8:1250–1251. See also O'Toole, *When Trumpets Call*, 363–364, 397–398.

135. Roosevelt to John Joseph Pershing, 20 May 1917, in Morison, ed., *Letters of Theodore Roosevelt*, 8:1192–1193.

136. Roosevelt to Kermit Roosevelt, 3 July 1917, in ibid., 8:1206–1207.

137. Morris, *Colonel Roosevelt*, 520–534; O'Toole, *When Trumpets Call*, 368–391; Brands, *T.R.*, 794–801.

138. Marx, *Health of the Presidents,* 295; Bumgarner, *Health,* 164.

139. Marx, *Health of the Presidents,* 296–297; Bumgarner, *Health,* 164; O'Toole, *When Trumpets Call,* 402–405.

140. O'Toole, *When Trumpets Call,* 398–399.

141. Both quotes are from ibid., 396. See also Brands, *T.R.,* 804–806.

142. Roosevelt to William Allen White, 3 August 1917. Roosevelt to George William Russell, 6 August 1917, Roosevelt to Kermit Roosevelt, 29 November 1917, and Roosevelt to Charles Harvey Rowell, 17 December 1917, in Morison, ed., *Letters of Theodore Roosevelt,* 8:1216–1220 and 8:1258–1261.

143. Harbaugh, *Life and Times of Theodore Roosevelt,* 469. Barnes's quote is in Miller, *Theodore Roosevelt,* 559.

144. Roosevelt to William Allen White, 4 April 1918, in Morison, ed., *Letters of Theodore Roosevelt,* 8:1305–1306. See also Miller, *Theodore Roosevelt,* 559; O'Toole, *When Trumpets Call,* 399.

145. Roosevelt to Quentin Roosevelt, 1 September 1917, in Morison, ed., *Letters of Theodore Roosevelt,* 8:1232–1234. See also Roosevelt to Theodore Roosevelt Jr., 1 September 1917, in ibid., 8:1230.

146. William Allen White, *Theodore Roosevelt, Masks in a Pageant* (New York: Macmillan, 1928), 283–326.

CHAPTER 8: FORMER PRESIDENTS AS SYMBOLS OF AN ERA

1. Cooper, "Lonesome Lion," 7–8.

2. One of his recent biographers, Judith Icke Anderson, has even suggested that parental pressure and his special emotional bond with his mother provide an explanation for Taft's later inner conflicts, including his willingness to run for president, his sense of dependency and inadequacy, and even his problem with weight. According to her explanation, Taft's wife, Nellie, who was in many ways like his mother, substituted for her as a parental figure driving Taft toward the White House. Judith Icke Anderson, *William Howard Taft: An Intimate History* (New York: Norton, 1981), 42.

3. Ibid., 61.

4. Ibid., 67–84.

5. William Manners, *TR and Will: A Friendship That Split the Republican Party* (New York: Harcourt, Brace & World, 1969), 31–34. David H. Burton, *Taft, Roosevelt, and the Limits of Friendship* (Madison, N.J.: Farleigh Dickinson University Press, 2005), 15, 30, 48, 50–51, 59.

6. The quote is from Manners, *TR and Will,* 47.

7. Lewis L. Gould, *The Modern American Presidency* (Lawrence: University Press of Kansas, 2003), 30–31, 37–41.

8. Taft to Helen Herron Taft, n.d., quoted in Manners, *TR and Will,* 211. In addition to this and other sources cited in the previous chapter, see also Burton, *Taft, Roosevelt,* 101–117; Henry Pringle, *The Life and Times of William Howard Taft,* 2 vols. (Hamden, Conn.: Archon Books, 1964), 2:760–842.

9. William Howard Taft, "The President," 16 November 1912, in *After Dinner Speeches and How to Make Them,* ed. William Allen Wood (Chicago: T. H. Flood, 1914), 32–43.

10. The quote is from Anderson, *William Howard Taft,* 85.

11. Quoted in Pringle, *Life and Times of William Howard Taft,* 2:847–848.

12. Although Taft believed that presidents were "well paid," he expressed doubts that Congress provided enough so that they could save "enough money [while in office] for their retirement." Taft, "President," 39.

13. Taft's remark to the *New York Sun*'s reporter can be found in the *New Haven Journal-Courier,* 5 March 1913. See also Pringle, *Life and Times of William Howard Taft,* 2:849–850.

14. Quoted in Frederick C. Hicks, *William Howard Taft: Yale Professor of Law and New Haven Citizen* (New Haven, Conn.: Yale University Press, 1945), 2–3.

15. William Howard Taft, *Popular Government: Its Essence, Its Permanence, and Its Perils* (New Haven, Conn.: Yale University Press, 1913).

16. David H. Burton, *William Howard Taft: In the Public Service* (Malabar, Fla.: Robert E. Krieger, 1986), 110–111.

17. Hicks, *William Howard Taft,* 29–67.

18. Ibid., 6–8 and 27. See also Taft, "Popular Government," in *The Collected Works of William Howard Taft,* ed. David H. Burton, 8 vols. (Athens: Ohio University Press, 2001–2004), 5:15–159. Alpheus Thomas Mason, *William Howard Taft: Chief Justice* (New York: Simon & Schuster, 1965), 44–51; Burton, *William Howard Taft,* 112–113.

19. William Howard Taft, *The President and His Powers* (New York: Scribner's, 1916), 31–32 and 116–117. See also Burton, *William Howard Taft,* 114–116.

20. For a somewhat different analysis of Taft as a modern president, see Gould, *Modern American Presidency,* 29–41. See also Mason, *William Howard Taft,* 45–47.

21. James F. Vivian, introduction to *William Howard Taft: Collected Editorials, 1917–1921,* ed. James F. Vivian (New York: Praeger, 1990), vii–xv.

22. Quoted in Pringle, *Life and Times of William Howard Taft,* 2:856–857.

23. Quoted in ibid., 2:851.

24. Burton, *Taft, Roosevelt,* 118–119; Pringle, *Life and Times of William Howard Taft,* 2:863–868.

25. Quoted in Pringle, *Life and Times of William Howard Taft,* 2:875; see also 2:869–881.

26. A. L. Todd, *Justice on Trial: The Case of Louis D. Brandeis* (New York: McGraw Hill, 1964), 75–82. See also Mason, *William Howard Taft,* 72–75.

27. William Howard Taft, *The Anti-Trust Act and the Supreme Court* (1914), in Burton, ed., *Collected Works of William Howard Taft,* 5:173–242. See also Burton, *William Howard Taft,* 113–117; Pringle, *Life and Times of William Howard Taft,* 2:881.

28. The quote is from Anderson, *William Howard Taft,* 258.

29. Burton, *William Howard Taft,* 117–118.

30. William Howard Taft, "Address before the World Court Congress," Cleveland, Ohio, 12 May 1915, and Taft, "Address Delivered Before the Convention of the League to Enforce Peace," Philadelphia, 17 June 1915, in Burton, ed., *Collected Works of William Howard* Taft, 7:36–54; Thomas J. Knock, *To End All Wars: Woodrow Wilson and the Quest for a New World Order* (Princeton, N.J.: Princeton University Press, 1992), 55–57. David H. Burton, *Taft, Wilson, and World Order* (Madison, N.J.: Farleigh Dickinson University Press, 2003), 66–69. It is unclear how many people were at Independence Hall; Knock states 120, Burton 300. I have relied on Knock. For an older history of the LEP, see Ruhl J. Bartlett, *The League to Enforce Peace* (Chapel Hill: University of North Carolina Press, 1944).

31. Knock, *To End All Wars*, 57–58.

32. Ibid., 58.

33. Ibid., 76–77; Burton, *Taft, Wilson*, 73–79.

34. Knock, *To End All Wars*, 77–78; Burton, *Taft, Wilson*, 72–73.

35. Knock, *To End All Wars*, 87–88 and 98–104.

36. Burton, *Taft, Wilson*, 94–99.

37. Vivian, introduction, xv–xviii.

38. Ibid., xviii–xx.

39. Ibid., xx–xxiii.

40. The quote is from Knock, *To End All Wars*, 101. See also Burton, *Taft, Wilson*, 101–102 and 104–105.

41. Philadelphia *Public Ledger*, 29 November 1917, reprinted in Vivian, ed., *William Howard Taft*, 9–11.

42. Pringle, *Life and Times of William Howard Taft*, 2:934–940.

43. Philadelphia *Public Ledger*, 5 December 1918, reprinted in Vivian, ed., *William Howard Taft*, 131–133. *New York Times*, 17 November 1918. See also Burton, *Taft, Wilson*, 105–106; Knock, *To End All Wars*, 189–193.

44. Knock, *To End All Wars*, 230–241.

45. "Address delivered at the Metropolitan Opera House," New York City, 4 March 1919, in Burton, ed., *Collected Works of William Howard Taft*, 7:241–254.

46. Knock, *To End All Wars*, 246–257.

47. Philadelphia *Public Ledger*, 2 April 1919, reprinted in Burton, ed., *Collected Works of William Howard Taft*, 7:281–282.

48. Philadelphia *Public Ledger*, 6 March 1920, reprinted in Vivian, ed., *William Howard Taft*, 362–363.

49. Eaton, *Presidential Timber*, 278. See also Pringle, *Life and Times of William Howard Taft*, 2:49–50.

50. Quoted in Pringle, *Life and Times of William Howard Taft*, 2:953–956; Burton, *William Howard Taft*, 122–123.

51. Burton, *William Howard Taft*, 121–123; Pringle, *Life and Times of William Howard Taft*, 2:957–959; Mason, *William Howard Taft*, 76–87.

52. The quote is from Hicks, *William Howard Taft*, 122–142. See also Pringle, *Life and Times of William Howard Taft*, 2:960–961.

53. Taft, *Popular Government*, in Burton, ed., *Collected Works of William Howard Taft*, 5:31. See also Mason, *William Howard Taft*, 44–49 and 60–61.

54. Burton, *William Howard Taft*, 121; Mason, *William Howard Taft*, 50–52, 88–93; Pringle, *Life and Times of William Howard Taft*, 2:973–974.

55. Mason, *William Howard Taft*, 97–98.

56. Taft, *Popular Government*, 5:136.

57. Ibid., 141. See also Mason, *William Howard Taft*, 53–59.

58. Quoted in Taft, *Popular Government*, 5:126.

59. Quoted in ibid., 95. See also Burton, *William Howard Taft*, 126–127.

60. Burton, *William Howard Taft*, 127–130; Mason, *William Howard Taft*, 107–114 and 121–137.

61. Burton, *William Howard Taft*, 127–128; Mason, *William Howard Taft*, 114–120 and 136–137.

62. The quote is from Burton, *William Howard Taft*, 132–133. Pringle, *Life and*

Times of William Howard Taft, 2:965–972. See also Francis Graham Lee, "Commentary," in Burton, ed., *Collected Works of William Howard Taft,* 8:xix–xxii.

63. Quotes are from Lee, "Commentary," xxv.

64. *American Steel Foundries v. Tri-City Central Trades Council* (decided 5 December 1921) In *Bailey v. Drexel Furniture Co.* (1922). However, he held as invalid the Child Labor Tax of 1919, intended to discourage the use of child labor, because it usurped states' rights by interpreting so broadly Congress's taxing powers. He was successful in getting even Brandeis and Holmes to concur in his decision. In *United Mine Workers of America v. Coronado Coal Company* (decided 5 June 1922), his majority opinion reaffirmed unions' liability for damages arising from industrial actions. Francis Graham Lee, ed., *Selected Supreme Court Opinions,* in Burton, ed., *Collected Works of William Howard Taft,* 8:24–29, 73–78, and 8:259–268.

65. *United Mine Workers of America et al. v Coronado Coal Company et al.* (decided 5 June 1922) and *Myers, Administratrix, v. United* States (decided 25 October 1926) in Lee, ed., *Selected Supreme Court Opinions,* 73–78 and 259–268. See also Burton, *William Howard Taft,* 135–138. For a more sympathetic view of Taft's attitude toward unions, see Pringle, *Life and Times of William Howard Taft,* 2:1012–1014, esp. 2:1030–1048. My reading of the *American Steel Foundries Case* is similar to Pringle's. See also Mason, *William Howard Taft,* 236–266.

66. For Taft's comments to Sutherland, see Taft to Sutherland, 2 July 1921, quoted in W. F. Murphy, "In His Own Image: Mr. Chief Justice Taft and Supreme Court Appointments," *Supreme Court Review* (1961): 162. Taft's comments on Cardoza are quoted in Mason, *William Howard Taft,* 170.

67. For Taft's remarks on Hoover, see Mason, *William Howard Taft,* 152. See also ibid., 152–191; Pringle, *Life and Times of William Howard Taft,* 2:1062.

68. Quoted in Burton, *William Howard Taft,* 133. See also ibid., 131–133; Mason, *William Howard Taft,* 218–220 and 225–227; Pringle, *Life and Times of William Howard Taft,* 2:1060.

69. Pringle, *Life and Times of William Howard Taft,* 2:1074–1075; Anderson, *William Howard Taft,* 260.

70. Pringle, *Life and Times of William Howard Taft,* 2:1076.

71. Judith Anderson posits that he needed no longer to rely on food for comfort, as he had before leaving the presidency. Anderson, *William Howard Taft,* 256, 259, and 262. On Taft's health, see also Bumgarner, *Health,* 171; and Marx, *Health of the Presidents,* 304.

72. Bumgarner, *Health,* 172–173; Marx, *Health of the Presidents,* 305–307; Anderson, *William Howard Taft,* 261–263.

73. Mason, *William Howard Taft,* 93.

74. Ibid., 174–175.

75. Ibid., 164.

76. On this point, see Burton, *Taft, Wilson,* 123–129.

77. Edwin Weinstein, a neurologist who has written the most detailed medical and psychological biography of the former president, maintains that Wilson suffered throughout most of his life from serious neurological and other medical problems, including dyslexia, constant headaches and indigestion, and a series of strokes beginning as early as 1896. His neurological problems, Weinstein believes, explain his abrupt changes in personality, including, after his stroke in 1919, his total unwillingness to compromise with the Senate on the League of Nations and a sullenness that led him to a break with some of the

persons closest to him. Edwin A. Weinstein, *Woodrow Wilson: A Medical and Psychological Biography* (Princeton, N.J.: Princeton University Press, 1981). See also Gene Smith, *When the Cheering Stopped: The Last Years of Woodrow Wilson* (Alexandria, Va.: Time-Life Books, 1982), 7–8; August Heckscher, *Woodrow Wilson* (New York: Charles Scribner's Sons, 1991), 612–613. Weinstein's medical diagnosis and his connections between Wilson's psyche and soma remain controversial. Michael Marmor, an ophthalmologist, has even challenged Weinstein's contention that the future president suffered a stroke in 1896 and a syndrome of minor strokes afterward. As for the relationship between Wilson's neurology and his behavior, Marmor concludes, "To call Wilson's behavior quirks at times of crisis a reaction to stroke, or encephalopathy, is to ignore the fact that Wilson—like all of us—reacted to fatigue and distress." However, Marmor concedes that "ample evidence indicates that Wilson had hypertension and arteriosclerosis and had signs of both . . . in 1906. They may indeed have taken a toll from Wilson over the years, and they may be factors to consider in evaluating his overall mental and physical abilities." Michael F. Marmor, "Woodrow Wilson, Strokes, and Zebras," *New England Journal of Medicine* 309 (26 August 1982): 532–533.

78. Quoted in Smith, *When the Cheering Stopped*, x, 5–6, 11, and 24.

79. Weinstein, *Woodrow Wilson*, 335–348; Smith, *When the Cheering Stopped*, 44–50.

80. Arthur Walworth, *Woodrow Wilson*, 2 vols. (New York: Norton, 1978), 374–379; Heckscher, *Woodrow Wilson*, 612–615; Smith, *When the Cheering Stopped*, 90–99, 129.

81. Smith, *When the Cheering Stopped*, 100–109; Heckscher, *Woodrow Wilson*, 614–620; Walworth, *Woodrow Wilson*, 2:374–378.

82. Quoted in Walworth, *Woodrow Wilson*, 2:379.

83. Quoted in Heckscher, *Woodrow Wilson*, 613. See also Smith, *When the Cheering Stopped*, 93–94; Robert M. Saunders, *Beliefs and Behavior* (Westport, Conn.: Greenwood Press, 1998), 233–234.

84. Memorandum by Robert Lansing, 13 February 1920, in Arthur S. Link et al., eds., *The Papers of Woodrow Wilson*, 67 vols. (Princeton, N.J.: Princeton University Press, 1966–present), 64:415–419; Heckscher, *Woodrow Wilson*, 626–627.

85. Joseph P. Tumulty, *Woodrow Wilson as I Know Him* (Garden City, N.Y.: Doubleday, Page, 1921), 415; Memorandum by Robert Lansing, 13 February 1920, and accompanying footnote in Link et al., eds., *Papers of Woodrow Wilson*, 65:415–419.

86. "President Will Never Recover, Is View of Dr. Bevan," 15 February 1920, in Link et al., eds., *Papers of Woodrow Wilson*, 64:432–433.

87. Two letters from Joseph Patrick Tumulty to Wilson, 27 February 1920, in ibid., 64:479–480; Smith, *When the Cheering Stopped*, 134–135, 142–143.

88. Smith, *When the Cheering Stopped*, 18–21, 111–113; H. W. Brands, *Woodrow Wilson* (New York: Times Books, 2003), 111–112.

89. Smith, *When the Cheering Stopped*, 111–112, 116–117, 120–121, 195–197; Robert M. Saunders, *In Search of Woodrow Wilson* (Westport, Conn.: Greenwood Press, 1998), 252–253.

90. Park, "The Aftermath of Wilson's Stroke," 15 March 1920, in Link et al., *Papers of Woodrow Wilson*, 64:525–528.

91. Walworth, *Woodrow Wilson*, 2:398–400.; Saunders, *In Search of Woodrow Wilson*, 258–259; Smith, *When the Cheering Stopped*, 151–152.

92. Heckscher, *Woodrow Wilson*, 636–640; Walworth, *Woodrow Wilson*, 2:402–404;

Smith, *When the Cheering Stopped,* 158–162; Saunders, *In Search of Woodrow Wilson,* 251–252.

93. Smith, *When the Cheering Stopped,* 162–164; Heckscher, *Woodrow Wilson,* 640–641.

94. Donna Evers, "Happy Birthday, Mr. President: Woodrow Wilson and His Post-presidency Kalorama Home," *Washington Life Magazine,* September 2006, http://www.washingtonlife.com.

95. Heckscher, *Woodrow Wilson,* 641.

96. Walworth, *Woodrow Wilson,* 2:411; Heckscher, *Woodrow Wilson,* 641–642 and 646; Smith, *When the Cheering Stopped,* 166. See also Evers, "Happy Birthday, Mr. President."

97. "A News Report," 4 March 1921, in Link et al., eds., *Papers of Woodrow Wilson,* 67:205–212.

98. Ibid.

99. Ibid.

100. Smith, *When the Cheering Stopped,* 166–169 and 207; Walworth, *Woodrow Wilson,* 2:396–397.

101. Quoted in Smith, *When the Cheering Stopped,* 198; see also Walworth, *Woodrow Wilson,* 2:412.

102. Quoted in Smith, *When the Cheering Stopped,* 198.

103. Quoted in ibid., 199.

104. Ibid., 182–183.

105. Weinstein, *Woodrow Wilson,* 360–373.

106. W. H. Murray to Woodrow Wilson, 14 April 1921, and John Randolph Bolling to the Macmillan Company, 15 April 1921, in Link et al., eds., *Papers of Woodrow Wilson,* 67:259.

107. Woodrow Wilson to Ray Stanard Baker, 27 December 1920; Creel to John Randolph Bolling, 29 March and 3 August 1921, in ibid., 67:241–245, 67:249, and 67:363.

108. On Wilson's help to Baker, see, for example, "From the Diary of Ray Stannard Baker," 29 July 1921, in ibid., 67:360–367; Ray Stannard Baker, *Woodrow Wilson and World Settlement,* 3 vols. (Garden City, N.Y.: Doubleday, Page, 1923).

109. On these points, see Stockton Anson to John Grier Hibben, 11 June 1921, in Link et al., eds., *Papers of Woodrow Wilson,* 67:309–311.

110. "From the Diary of Ray Stannard Baker," 13 April 1921, and memorandum by Homer Stiles Cummings, 25 April 1921, in Link et al., eds., *Papers of Woodrow Wilson,* 67:256 and 67:268–270.

111. The two quotes are in Weinstein, *Woodrow Wilson,* 374–375.

112. The first quote is from Walworth, *Woodrow Wilson,* 2:414. The second is from the diary of Ray Stannard Baker, 21 July 1921, in Link et al., eds., *Papers of Woodrow Wilson,* 67:360–361. The third is in Heckscher, *Woodrow Wilson,* 665–666.

113. Quoted in Walworth, *Woodrow Wilson,* 2:414. See also "Will 'Keep His Ideals before Public,' Woodrow Wilson Tells Princeton Students," 12 June 1921, and note 1 attached to Arthur Francis Mullen, 20 June 1921, in Link et al., eds., *Papers of Woodrow Wilson,* 67:366–367; Weinstein, *Woodrow Wilson,* 374.

114. Heckscher, *Woodrow Wilson,* 666; Weinstein, *Woodrow Wilson,* 375.

115. George Creel to Edith Bolling Galt Wilson with enclosure, 19 April 1923, in Link et al., eds., *Papers of Woodrow Wilson,* 68:342–344.

116. Edith Bolling Galt Wilson to George Creel, 24 April 1923, and accompanying note 1 in ibid., 68:347–349; Woodrow Wilson, "The Road Away from Revolution," *Atlantic Monthly* 132 (August 1923): 145–146.

117. Heckscher, *Woodrow Wilson*, 2:651–657.

118. Weinstein, *Woodrow Wilson*, 376; Walworth, *Woodrow Wilson*, 519.

119. "A Radio Address," 10 November 1923, in Link et al., eds., *Papers of Woodrow Wilson*, 68:466–467.

120. *Collier's*, 18 February 1922; Heckscher, *Woodrow Wilson*, 651–657 and 663–665; Walworth, *Woodrow Wilson*, 419.

121. "A News Report," 11 November 1923, in Link et al., eds., *Papers of Woodrow Wilson*, 68:467–471.

122. James Kerney, "Last Talks with Woodrow Wilson" [29 March 1924], in Link et al., eds., *Papers of Woodrow Wilson*, 68:588. See also "News Report: Wilson May Lead Democrats in 1924" [19 September 1923]; Wilson to Ray Stannard Baker, 13 December 1923; "The Final Draft of 'The Document'" [20 January 1924]; "Notes and Passages for an Acceptance Speech" [21 January 1924], in ibid., 425, 499, and 535–544. Historian Robert M. Saunders argues that Wilson had been planning meticulously for another run at the presidency since 1921. According to Saunders, "He fixated on the [Paris peace] as a vehicle for a third term." One reason he gave up his law practice with Colby was his fear that any appearance of improprieties in terms of the clients he represented might be a risk to his presidential ambitions. The evidence simply does not support Saunders's argument. Saunders, *In Search of Woodrow Wilson*, 259–262.

123. James Kerney, "Last Talks with Woodrow Wilson" [29 March 1924]; Wilson to Raymond Blaine Fosdick, 22 October 1923, and footnote 1; Raymond Blaine Fosdick to Wilson, 27 November 1923; Wilson to Raymond Blaine Fosdick, 28 November 1923, in Link et al., eds., *Papers of Woodrow Wilson*, 68:451–452, 68:492–493, and 68:595.

124. *A Tribute to a Great American* (New York: National Committee, 1922), 5.

125. "A Memoradum of an Agreement" [1 October 1923], and Wilson to Cleveland Hoadley, Dodge, 4 October 1923, in Link et al., eds., *Papers of Woodrow Wilson*, 68:438–439 and 68:445. See also Walworth, *Woodrow Wilson*, 416.

126. "News Report: Wilson Is Honored on 67th Birthday: Friends Give Auto," [28 December 1923], in Link et al., eds., *Papers of Woodrow Wilson*, 68:509–510.

127. As the historian John Milton Cooper Jr. has remarked, "Within a generation [after his death], the prophet's visions at home and abroad had become the foundation of national policy for the rest of the century." Cooper, "Lonesome Lion," 8–9.

128. Raymond B. Fosdick, *Chronicle of a Generation: An Autobiography* (New York: Harper and Brothers, 1958), 230–231.

129. Marx, *Health of the Presidents*, 322; Bumgarner, *Health*, 186.

130. Heckscher, *Woodrow Wilson*, 673.

131. Walworth, *Woodrow Wilson*, 2:421–422; Heckscher, *Woodrow Wilson*, 674–675.

132. Donald McCoy, *Calvin Coolidge: The Quiet President* (New York: Macmillan, 1967), 94. See also Robert H. Ferrell, *The Presidency of Calvin Coolidge* (Lawrence: University Press of Kansas, 1998), esp. 1–24, 47, and 51; and David Greenberg, *Calvin Coolidge* (New York: Times Books, 2006), 1–45.

133. On this point, see esp. Greenberg, *Calvin Coolidge*, 6–7, 48, 61–64.

134. Ferrell, *Presidency of Calvin Coolidge*, 39–94; Greenberg, *Calvin Coolidge*, 73–75.

135. Calvin Coolidge, *The Autobiography of Calvin Coolidge* (New York: Cosmopolitan, 1929), 190. At least one historian, Robert Gilbert, has even speculated that the thirtieth president had been "quite ill and quite disabled" during much of his administration and that with his son's death, his presidency "effectively ended." Although Gilbert traces Coolidge's mental and physical state back to the deaths of his mother when he was only twelve years old and of his only sibling five years later, it is a stretch to attribute what Gilbert refers to as Coolidge's "unending depression" and "tendency toward anger and ill humor" to the bereavement he suffered during his formative years. He is on far stronger ground, however, when he argues the lasting impact on Coolidge of his younger son's death. Robert E. Gilbert, *The Tormented President: Calvin Coolidge, Death, and Clinical Depression* (Westport, Conn.: Praeger Press, 2003), 264–265.

136. Gilbert, *Tormented President,* 228–231, 266–268; Greenberg, *Calvin Coolidge,* 17, 100–107.

137. Coolidge, *Autobiography,* 190. On other reasons why Coolidge may have decided not to run in 1928, see Ferrell, *Presidency of Calvin Coolidge,* 192–193; McCoy, *Calvin Coolidge,* 383–392.

138. Quoted in McCoy, *Calvin Coolidge,* 390–391.

139. Richard Norton Smith, "The Price of the Presidency," *Yankee Magazine,* January 1996, http://www.noho.com/calvinc.html.

140. Coolidge, *Autobiography,* 242. Leonard Benardo and Jennifer Weiss, *Citizen-in-Chief: The Second Lives of the American Presidents* (New York: William Morrow, 2009), 51.

141. McCoy, *Calvin Coolidge,* 141, 158, and 395; Greenberg, *Calvin Coolidge,* 151.

142. McCoy, *Calvin Coolidge,* 395–396.

143. Smith, "The Price of the Presidency"; Gilbert, *Tormented President,* 232–233.

144. Coolidge, *Autobiography,* 242–243.

145. Quoted in Gilbert, *Tormented President,* 232.

146. Quoted in Ferrell, *Presidency of Calvin Coolidge,* 201.

147. Ferrell has a more favorable view of the autobiography than the one presented here; ibid. See also McCoy, *Calvin Coolidge,* 399–400; Gilbert, *Tormented President,* 232.

148. Gilbert, *Tormented President,* 234.

149. McCoy, *Calvin Coolidge,* 399–401.

150. Ibid., 412.

CHAPTER 9: THE MODERN POST-PRESIDENCY

1. James Whiteclay Chambers, "President Emeritus," http://www.americanheritage.com.

2. David Burner, *Herbert Hoover: A Public Life* (New York: Knopf, 1979), 3–11; Martin Fausold, *The Presidency of Herbert C. Hoover* (Lawrence: University Press of Kansas, 1985), 1–5.

3. Burner, *Herbert Hoover,* x and 11–14; William Leuchtenburg, *Herbert Hoover* (New York: Times Books, 1985), 4–5; Richard Norton Smith, *Uncommon Man: The Triumph of Herbert Hoover* (New York: Simon & Schuster, 1984), 36–39.

4. Burner, *Herbert Hoover,* 14–16; Leuchtenburg, *Herbert Hoover,* 5–6; Smith, *Uncommon Man,* 65–69.

5. Smith, *Uncommon Man*, 70–71; Burner, *Herbert Hoover*, 16–21.

6. Smith, *Uncommon Man*, 72–73; Burner, *Herbert Hoover*, 21–24.

7. Leuchtenburg, *Herbert Hoover*, 10–11. See also Smith, *Uncommon Man*, 73–77; Burner, *Herbert Hoover*, 28–52.

8. Smith, *Uncommon Man*, 77: Burner, *Herbert Hoover*, 54-; Leuchtenburg, *Herbert Hoover*, 16–18.

9. Burner, *Herbert Hoover*, x-xii, 43, 60, and 63–71; Leuchtenburg, *Herbert Hoover*, 19–20; Smith, *Uncommon Man*, 79–80.

10. Leuchtenburg, *Herbert Hoover*, 24–25; Burner, *Herbert Hoover*, 58–59, 73–74.

11. The quote is from Burner, *Herbert Hoover*, 74.

12. Smith, *Uncommon Man*, 81–87; Burner, *Herbert Hoover*, 72–95; Leuchtenburg, *Herbert Hoover*, 31–32.

13. Joan Hoff Wilson, *Herbert Hoover: Forgotten Progressive* (Boston: Little, Brown, 1975), 28–29.

14. Smith, *Uncommon* Man, 90–91; Leuchtenburg, *Herbert Hoover*, 37–40.

15. When in 1919 money ran out for the ARA, he transformed it into a private organization and raised $30 million to feed millions of displaced children. Under ARA, the European Children's Fund became a forerunner of CARE. Burner, *Herbert Hoover*, 114–137; Smith, *Uncommon Man*, 92; Leuchtenburg, *Herbert Hoover*, 40–42.

16. Herbert Hoover, *American Individualism* (Garden City, N.Y.: Doubleday, Page, 1922), 4, 8–9, and 66; Fausold, *Presidency of Herbert Hoover*, 17–19.

17. Quotes are from Leuchtenburg, *Herbert Hoover*, 40–41.

18. Smith, *Uncommon Man*, 97–98.

19. Ibid., 99–103.

20. Ibid., 104–106.

21. William E. Leuchtenburg, *The Perils of Prosperity, 1914–1932* (Chicago: University of Chicago Press, 1958), 249–251; Smith, *Uncommon Man*, 118–119.

22. Smith, *Uncommon Man*, 115–120.

23. Ibid., 123–140; Leuchtenburg, *Perils of Prosperity*, 251–258.

24. Fausold, *Presidency of Herbert Hoover*, 243–246; Smith, *Uncommon Man*, 140–149.

25. Smith, *Uncommon Man*, 152–164.

26. Fausold, *Presidency of Herbert Hoover*, 218–234; Leuchtenburg, *Herbert Hoover*, 143–145.

27. The quotes are from Fausold, *Presidency of Herbert Hoover*, 234. See also Arthur M. Schlesinger Jr., *The Crisis of the Old Order, 1919–1933* (Boston: Houghton Mifflin, 1957), 444–445, 448, 476–481.

28. Fausold, *Presidency of Herbert Hoover*, 235–236; Smith, *Uncommon Man*, 163–165.

29. The quote is from Schlesinger, *Crisis of the Old Order*, 1; Fausold, *Presidency of Herbert Hoover*, 240.

30. Gary Dean Best, *Herbert Hoover: The Postpresidential Years*, 2 vols. (Stanford, Calif.: Hoover Institution Press, 1983), 1:4–5.

31. Ibid.

32. Quoted in ibid., 1:8.

33. Herbert Hoover, *The Challenge to Liberty* (Rockford, Ill.: Herbert Hoover Presidential Library Association, 1971), 85. See also Best, *Herbert Hoover*, 1:3–4.

34. Hoover, *Challenge to Liberty,* 85. On Hoover's belief that the United States was heading down the road to socialism and totalitarianism, see also Best, *Herbert Hoover,* 1:5–8.

35. Best, *Herbert Hoover,* 1:26–27; Leuchtenburg, *Herbert Hoover,* 150–151.

36. Herbert Hoover, "The Bill of Rights: Address Delivered on Constitution Day," in Herbert Hoover, *American Ideals versus the New Deal* (New York: Scribner Press, 1936), 13–16.

37. Hoover, *American Ideals.*

38. Wilson, *Herbert Hoover,* esp. 27–30; Burner, *Herbert Hoover,* esp. ix–xii.

39. Herbert Hoover, "Spending — Deficits — Debts, and Their Consequences: Address Delivered before the Young Republicans of Eleven Western States," in Hoover, *American Ideals,* 21. See also Burner, *Herbert Hoover,* 330–331; Smith, *Uncommon Man,* 129–130.

40. Best, *Herbert Hoover,* 1:65–73; Smith, *Uncommon Man,* 209–210, 217–221, and 229–231.

41. Best, *Herbert Hoover,* 1:72–73.

42. Smith, *Uncommon Man,* 275–286.

43. Quoted in Leuchtenburg, *Herbert Hoover,* 152; see also 149–152. Smith, *Uncommon Man,* 242.

44. Smith, *Uncommon Man,* 19, 231–233.

45. Presently the Tower houses one of the world's largest collections of documents on communist, Nazi, fascist, and socialist revolutions. Burner, *Herbert Hoover,* 327.

46. Smith, *Uncommon Man,* 177.

47. Ibid., 231.

48. Ibid., 244–245.

49. Quoted in Best, *Herbert Hoover,* 1:80; see also 1:79–87; Smith, *Uncommon Man,* 245.

50. Best, *Herbert Hoover,* 1:87–95; Smith, *Uncommon Man,* 246–249.

51. Quoted in Best, *Herbert Hoover,* 1:110.

52. Ibid., 1:115.

53. Ibid., 1:117.

54. Quoted in Louis Lochner, *Herbert Hoover and Germany* (New York: Macmillan, 1960), 133–135. See also Smith, *Uncommon Man,* 252–253; Best, *Herbert Hoover,* 1:102–103; Burner, *Herbert Hoover,* 332–33; Leuchtenburg, *Herbert Hoover,* 152–153.

55. Leuchtenburg, *Herbert Hoover,* 152–153; Smith, *Uncommon Man,* 253–257.

56. Herbert Hoover, *Addresses upon the American Road, 1933–38* (New York: Charles Scribner's Sons, 1938), 335–342. See also Smith, *Uncommon* Man, 258–259; Best, *Herbert Hoover,* 1:103–104.

57. Interestingly enough, he also criticized the "Jewish influence" on the administration even as he publicly criticized Hitler's persecution of the Jews and worked with leading Jewish leaders and others to rescue Jews from Europe and bring them to the United States. He also looked favorably on Bernard Baruch's plan to establish a home for Jewish refugees in one of the British African colonies, such as Kenya or Rhodesia; Smith, *Uncommon Man,* 266.

58. Herbert Hoover, "We Must Keep Out," *Saturday Evening Post,* 27 October 1939, in Herbert Hoover, *Further Addresses upon the American Road, 1938–1940* (New York: Charles Scribner's Sons, 1940), 139–157.

59. For details of the interaction between the White House and Hoover over the

relief effort, see especially Timothy Walch and Dwight M. Miller, eds., *Herbert Hoover and Franklin D. Roosevelt: A Documentary History* (Westport, Conn.: Greenwood Press, 1998), 168–181.

60. Best, *Herbert Hoover,* 1:116–133, 146–147.

61. Ibid., 1:147–173; Smith, *Uncommon Man,* 273–286.

62. Smith, *Uncommon Man,* 286–291.

63. Ibid., 273.

64. Herbert Hoover, "A Call to American Reason," Chicago (29 June 1941), in Hoover, *Addresses upon the American Road, 1940–1941* (New York: Charles Scribner's Sons, 1941), 87–102.

65. Herbert Hoover, "The Lend Lease Bill: Press Statement," New York City, 10 January 1941, in ibid., 63–65. See also Smith, *Uncommon Man,* 294–295; Best, *Herbert Hoover,* 1:175–180.

66. Herbert Hoover, "Russian Misadventure," *Collier's,* 27 April 1940, reprinted in Hoover, *Further Addresses upon the American Road, 1938–1940,* 158–171; Herbert Hoover, "A Call to American Reason" (29 June 1941), reprinted in Hoover, *Addresses upon the American Road, 1940–41,* 87–102. See also Best, *Herbert Hoover,* 1:187–189.

67. Herbert Hoover, "The Immediate Relation of the United States to This War: A Statement to the American People," New York City, 11 May 1941, reprinted in Hoover, *Addresses upon the American Road, 1940–1941,* 77–86. See also Smith, *Uncommon Man,* 301–307; Best, *Herbert Hoover,* 1:200–205.

68. Quoted in Smith, *Uncommon Man,* 309.

69. Quoted in Best, *Herbert Hoover,* 1:207. On the issue of food rather than troops during World War I, see also the correspondence in Walch and Miller, *Herbert Hoover and Franklin D. Roosevelt,* 193–203.

70. Herbert Hoover and Hugh Gibson, *Problems of Lasting Peace* (New York: Doubleday Doran, 1942), esp. 207–211, 233, and 261. See also Herbert Hoover and Hugh Gibson, *The Basis of Lasting Peace* (New York: D. Van Nostrand, 1945), 1–10 and 42–44.

71. Best, *Herbert Hoover,* 1:211–215. On the issue of whether Hoover was an internationalist, see also Wilson, *Herbert Hoover,* 246–282.

72. Best, *Herbert Hoover,* 1:260–263.

73. Herbert Hoover, "My Personal Relationship with Mr. Roosevelt," 26 September 1958, in Walch and Miller, *Herbert Hoover and Franklin D. Roosevelt.* Even his satisfaction at the reception his books received was diminished by the fact that Undersecretary of State Sumner Welles, Vice President Henry Wallace, Alf Landon, and Wendell Willkie seemed to have preempted his own vision for the postwar world in remarks they made. See also Best, *Herbert Hoover,* 1:220–221.

74. Quoted in Leuchtenburg, *Herbert Hoover,* 155. See also Best, *Herbert Hoover,* 1:258–260.

75. She had also loved the outdoors, had an insatiable curiosity and whimsical mind, and learned to speak eight languages. As the historian Nancy Beck Young has commented, "Although she never advertised her accomplishments, [she] represented a transition between nineteenth century conceptions of demure, receding political wives and the emerging, if incomplete, activism of twentieth century first ladies." Nancy Beck Young, *Lou Henry Young: Activist First Lady* (Lawrence: University Press of Kansas, 2004), 188.

76. The Truman and Hoover presidential libraries have made available online a documentary history of the relationship between Truman and Hoover from the time Truman

took office in 1945 through Hoover's death in 1964. For the chapters of this indispensable resource, all available at the Truman Library Web site (http://www.trumanlibrary.org), see *Hoover and Truman: A Presidential Friendship,* comprising *Part 1—The End of Exile; Part 2—Feeding the World; Part 3—Rebuilding Europe; Part 4—Reorganizing the Executive Branch; Part 5—Not Quite Friends;* and *Part 6—Exclusive Trade Unionists.* On Truman's invitation to Hoover and Hoover's reply, see Truman to Hoover, 24 May 1945; diary of Eben A. Ayers, 24 May 1945; and Hoover to Truman, 26 May 1945, all in *Hoover and Truman, Part 1—The End of Exile.* Truman's recollection of his meeting with Hoover is in Harry S. Truman, *Memoirs: Year of Decisions* (Garden City, N.Y.: Doubleday, 1955), 310–311.

77. For Hoover's detailed account of his meeting with the president and his doubts that anything would come of it, see Hoover, "Notes of Meeting with Truman," 28 May 1945, *Hoover and Truman, Part 1—The End of Exile.* The second quote is from Alonzo L. Hamby, *Man of the People: A Life of Harry S. Truman* (New York: Oxford University Press, 1995), 370. See also Truman, *Memoirs: Year of Decisions,* 472–474. Full documentation of Hoover's role in the relief effort can be found in *Hoover and Truman, Part 2—Feeding the World.* See also Smith, *Uncommon Man,* 346–348, 361–363; Best, *Herbert Hoover,* 2:287–294; Nancy Gibbs and Michael Duffy, *The Presidents Club: Inside the World's Most Exclusive Fraternity* (New York: Simon and Schuster, 2012), 18–37.

78. Donald R. McCoy, *The Presidency of Harry S. Truman* (Lawrence: University Press of Kansas, 1984), 96–97; Smith, *Uncommon Man,* 371–372.

79. "Hoover Commission Memoir," 13 April 1949, in *Hoover and Truman, Part 4—Reorganizing the Executive Branch.* See also "Hoover Statement," *Part 4—Reorganizing the Executive Branch;* "Policy Statement of the Commission on the Organization of the Executive Branch of Government," 20 October 1947, and Hoover, "The Reform of Government" [May 1949], in Herbert Hoover, *Addresses upon the American Road, 1948–1950* (Stanford, Calif.: Stanford University Press, 1951), 112–115 and 146–152. Actually the commission's report was a serious of nineteen reports it issued over a number of months in 1949. However, a commercial publisher published the essence of the reports in a single volume. See *The Hoover Commission Report on Organization of the Executive Branch of the Government* (New York: McGraw-Hill, n.d), esp. v–viii; *Truman in the White House: The Diary of Eben A. Ayers,* ed. Robert E. Ferrell (Columbia: University of Missouri Press, 1991), 20; Burner, *Herbert Hoover,* 337.

80. "Truman Address," 19 October 1948, *Hoover and Truman, Part 5—Not Quite Friends.* See also "Truman Address," 27 October 1948, and "Journal of David Lilienthal," 17 August 1949, ibid., 5–6, and 10.

81. Hoover "Notes of Meeting with Truman," 28 May 1945, and Hoover, "Memorandum on Ending the Japanese War," 30 May 1945, *Hoover and Truman, Part 1—The End of Exile.*

82. Quoted in Wilson, *Herbert Hoover,* 255. See also Smith, *Uncommon Man,* 349–350.

83. For this reason, historians have often lumped Hoover with conservative Republicans of the late 1940s and 1950s, such as senators Robert Taft and John Bricker of Ohio, William Knowland of California, and Colonel Robert McCormick, the publisher of the Chicago *Tribune,* who either emphasized the importance of the Far East over Europe and/ or who wanted the United States to follow an isolationist policy both in Asia and Europe.

84. "On Defense of Europe," in Herbert Hoover, *Addresses upon the American Road, 1950–1955* (Stanford, Calif.: Stanford University Press, 1955), 23–31.

85. Burton I. Kaufman, *The Korean War: Challenges in Crisis, Credibility, and Command* (New York: Knopf, 1986), 122–123.

86. The two quotes can be found in Wilton Eckley, *Herbert Hoover* (Boston: G. K. Hall, 1980), 106. See also Wilson, *Herbert Hoover*, 258–263.

87. The quote is from Hoover, "Where We Are Now," 19 October 1950, in Hoover, *Addresses upon the American Road, 1948–1950*, 91–99. See also Hoover to Arthur Vandenberg, 18 January 1948, and Hoover to Joseph W. Martin, 24 March 1948, *Hoover and Truman, Part 3—Rebuilding Europe;* Herbert Hoover, "On the Committee for the Marshall Plan to Aid European Recovery," 9 February 1948, in Hoover, *Addresses upon the American Road, 1948–1950*, 86–87. See also Wilson, *Herbert Hoover*, 258–261; Smith, *Uncommon Man*, 363–64, 368–370; Best, *Herbert Hoover*, 2:306–310.

88. "Bess W. Truman to Hoover," 22 March 1949," *Hoover and Truman, Part 5— Not Quite Friends.*

89. "Truman to Hoover," 4 October 1955, and "Hoover to Truman," 6 October 1955, *Hoover and Truman, Part 6—Exclusive Trade Unionists.* See also G. W. Sand, *Truman in Retirement: A Former President Views the Nation and the World* (South Bend, Ind.: Justice Books, 1993), 34, 36.

90. Wilson, *Herbert Hoover*, 263–267.

91. Smith, *Uncommon Man*, 396–397.

92. Hoover to Truman, 26 November 1950, *Hoover and Truman, Part 5—Not Quite Friends.*

93. Quoted in Smith, *Uncommon Man*, 389.

94. Ibid.

95. Bumgarner, *Health*, 203–204; Smith, *Uncommon Man*, 404; Burner, *Herbert Hoover*, 337.

CHAPTER 10: THE OFFICE OF EX-PRESIDENT

1. Quoted in Roy Jenkins, *Truman* (New York: Harper & Row, 1986), 1–4. See also Robert H. Ferrell, *Harry S. Truman and the Modern American Presidency* (Boston: Little, Brown, 1983), 40–43.

2. Quoted in Merle Miller, *Plain Speaking: An Oral Biography of Harry S. Truman* (New York: Berkley Books, 1973), 48. See also Alonzo Hamby, *Man of the People: A Life of Harry S. Truman* (New York: Oxford University Press, 1995), 7; David McCullough, *Truman* (New York: Simon & Schuster, 1992), 40.

3. One of Truman's biographers, Alonzo Hamby, even suggests that Truman's later dreams of success, first as an entrepreneur than as a politician, and his efforts at conciliation that often clashed with his male assertiveness were part of his effort to overcome the sense of inferiority and shyness that he had developed as a boy. Another reason may have been his desire to please his demanding father, whom he greatly admired. Throughout his life, he wanted to be "one of the boys." Hamby, *Man of the People*, 8–12, 15. See also McCullough, *Truman*, 41–65; Jenkins, *Truman*, 11–12; Robert Dallek, *Harry S. Truman* (New York: Times Books, 2008), 2.

4. Truman, *Memoirs: Year of Decisions,* 120. Harry S. Truman, *Mr. Citizen* (New York: Popular Library, 1960), 162–179. See also Memorandum, July 1954, in Robert H. Ferrell, ed., *Off the Record: The Private Papers of Harry S. Truman* (New York: Harper & Row, 1980), 306–307. In this memorandum, Truman also provides a brief autobiographical sketch of his political career. For a list of the books he read growing up and the works that most influenced him, see also Truman to Governor Orville Freeman, 7 February 1958, Box 18, Folder "Secretary's Office File," Post-Presidential Papers, Harry S. Truman Library, Independence, Missouri.

5. Hamby, *Man of the People,* 35.

6. Ibid., 57–66.

7. Dallek, *Harry S. Truman,* 3–4.

8. Quoted in Hamby, *Man of the People,* 83; see also 94–199.

9. As the historian Robert Dallek has remarked, Truman "thought of himself as a practical idealist, who was making the best of an imperfect world." Dallek, *Harry S. Truman,* 7.

10. Ibid., 13. See also Ferrell, *Harry S. Truman,* 32–35.

11. Truman took an especial interest in the reconstruction of the White House while he was president. Except for the outer walls, the building, which had been in danger of collapsing, was totally demolished below the third floor and then rebuilt. During the two and a half years that it took to complete the project, Truman frequently walked the construction site and went over every detail of the blueprints. McCullough, *Truman,* 875–887. See also Margaret Truman, *Harry S. Truman* (New York: William Morrow, 1973), 553.

12. The quote is from Dean Acheson, *Present at the Creation: My Years at the State Department* (New York: Norton, 1969), 730. See also McCullough, *Truman,* 895, 899; Hamby, *Man of the People,* 264 and 482–487.

13. Acheson, *Present at the Creation,* 730.

14. The quotes are from Hamby, *Man of the People,* 485. The best known of his outbursts against the press was his response on White House stationery to Paul Hume, the music critic for the *Washington Post,* who had criticized the voice of his daughter, Margaret, after her debut as a singer. Truman exploded when he read the review. "I never met you," he wrote Hume, "but if I do you'll need a new nose and a supporter below." Later the Washington *Star* got hold of the letter and published it. To many Americans, it was final proof that Truman was psychologically unfit to serve as president. Tebbell and Miles Watts, *The Press and the Presidency,* 460–461.

15. The first quote is from McCullough, *Truman,* 875. The second is from Harry S. Truman, *Memoirs: Years of Trial and Hope* (Garden City, N.Y.: Doubleday, 1956), 488–489. See also Truman to Ethel Noland, 2 January 1953, in Ferrell, ed., *Off the Record,* 286–287.

16. Arthur Krock of the *New York Times* reported that Truman told Eisenhower during a conversation they had at the White House in November 1951 that he would support him if he sought the Democratic presidential nomination. Both Truman and Eisenhower later denied the report, and according to Truman's daughter, Margaret, her father never "looked favorably" on his candidacy. More likely he never directly offered to support Eisenhower but suggested strongly that he would like him be the Democratic nominee. Instead, Eisenhower remained silent for two months. Margaret Truman, *Harry S. Truman,* 528–529; Hamby, *Man of the People,* 600–602. See also Jenkins, *Truman,* 191; McCullough, *Truman,*

887–889. See also Gibbs and Duffy, *The Presidents Club,* 57–76. According to Gibbs and Duffy, Truman told Eisenhower at Potsdam as early as 1945 that he would support him for the presidency in 1948. The president later denied making such an offer.

17. Truman to Cabell Phillips, 19 April 1963, Box 15, Folder "Secretary's Office File," Post-Presidential Papers, Truman Papers; Gibbs and Duffy, *The Presidents Club,* 118–123.

18. Even though the president, unlike the senator, did not campaign in the primary (he had failed, in fact, to have his name withdrawn from the primary), his defeat was an embarrassment that contributed to his decision not to seek the Democratic nomination. Truman, *Memoirs: Years of Trial and Hope,* 489–492; Margaret Truman, *Harry S. Truman,* 526–528, 530–531, and 541–542; McCullough, *Truman,* 889–890; Hamby, *Man of the People,* 602–603.

19. Truman, *Memoirs: Years of Trial and Hope,* 492–496; Truman, *Mr. Citizen,* 48–51; Hamby, *Man of the People,* 602–609; Jenkins, *Truman,* 192–198; McCullough, *Truman,* 893–894 and 903–909.

20. Quoted in Jenkins, *Truman,* 198–199. See also Hamby, *Man of the People,* 609–611.

21. Jenkins, *Truman,* 199–200; Hamby, *Man of the People,* 612–613; McCullough, *Truman,* 908–909.

22. Quoted in Margaret Truman, *Harry S. Truman,* 545, See also Steven Neal, *Harry and Ike: The Partnership That Remade the Postwar World* (New York: Simon & Schuster, 2001), 270–271.

23. Craig Allen, *Eisenhower and the Mass Media: Peace, Prosperity, and Prime-Time TV* (Chapel Hill: University of North Carolina Press, 1993), 16–17. See also Neal, *Harry and Ike,* 271–272.

24. Neal, *Harry and Ike,* 274–276.

25. Quoted in Miller, *Plain Speaking,* 341. See also Truman, *Memoirs: Years of Trial and Hope,* 502–503; Margaret Truman, *Harry S. Truman,* 544; McCullough, *Truman,* 910–912.

26. The quote is from Neal, *Harry and Ike,* 275. See also ibid., 275–280 and 286; McCullough, *Truman,* 912.

27. Truman, *Memoirs: Years of Trial and Hope,* 499–500.

28. Ibid., 501. See also Neal, *Harry and Ike,* 284–285.

29. Truman, *Memoirs: Years of Trial and Hope,* 521. See also Truman, *Mr. Citizen,* 13–14; Miller, *Plain Speaking,* 343–345; Neal, *Harry and Ike,* 289–299.

30. Matthew Algeo, *Harry Truman's Excellent Adventure: The True Story of a Great American Road Trip* (Chicago: Chicago Review Press, 2009), 14; Margaret Truman, *Harry S. Truman,* 558–559; Hamby, *Man of the People,* 618.

31. Algeo, *Harry Truman's Excellent Adventure,* 15.

32. Truman to [Marvin] Gates, 7 August 1958, Box 18, Folder "Secretary's Office File," Post-Presidential Papers, Truman Papers. See also Truman, *Mr. Citizen,* 77–80; Margaret Truman, *Harry S. Truman,* 580.

33. Margaret Truman, *Harry S. Truman,* 560–561; Truman, *Mr. Citizen,* 25. For the meeting between Eisenhower and Kennedy at Camp David, see also Gibbs and Duffy, *The Presidents Club,* 136–139.

34. Truman, *Mr. Citizen,* 25–27; Algeo, *Harry Truman's Excellent Adventure,* 22–23.

35. Algeo, *Harry Truman's Excellent Adventure,* 19–21; Truman, *Mr. Citizen,* 31 and 58–59.

36. Algeo, *Harry Truman's Excellent Adventure,* 12; see also 18 and 21–22.

37. The old Truman property has since been turned into a large commercial and real estate enterprise known as Truman Corners.

38. Truman, *Mr. Citizen,* 32–33; McCullough, *Truman,* 928.

39. The quote is from Truman, *Mr. Citizen,* 34. See also Jenkins, *Truman,* 209; Benardo and Weiss, *Citizen-in-Chief,* 61; McCullough, *Truman,* 929.

40. For an excellent account of presidential autobiographies and memoirs, see Hecht, *Beyond the Presidency,* 289–309.

41. Truman, *Mr. Citizen,* 183–184.

42. Truman had sought to be given the same treatment as Eisenhower by the Internal Revenue Service. (Eisenhower had argued successfully that since he was not a professional author, income from his book should not be treated as ordinary income.) When Truman was turned down by the IRS, he held Eisenhower responsible. In fact, the IRS had simply toughened the rules on income from publications and the president had no role in its decision. On the advance, see Hamby, *Man of the People,* 626; McCullough, *Truman,* 932.

43. Truman diary, [April 1953], in Ferrell, ed., *Off the Record,* 289–292. Beginning in 1952, Truman kept an occasional diary, which varied in the number and qualities of entries. The diary was not made available to the public until after Truman's death in 1972. For a more detailed description of the diary and its history, see Ferrell, ed., *Off the Record,* 1–8. See also McCullough, *Truman,* 932.

44. McCullough, *Truman,* 936.

45. Quoted in ibid., 937. See also Sand, *Truman in Retirement,* 18.

46. Hecht, *Beyond the Presidency,* 304; McCullough, *Truman,* 936–937.

47. Truman, *Mr. Citizen,* 36–38.

48. The quote is from ibid., 35. See also Algeo, *Harry Truman's Excellent Adventure,* 26–27.

49. Algeo, *Harry Truman's Excellent Adventure*, 27–29.

50. Ibid. Algeo has written a fascinating account of Truman's road trip. His research for his book involved his re-creation of Truman's trip, including staying at the same motels and eating at the same restaurants as the Trumans whenever possible, and interviewing individuals who might have seen them on their trip. He even tried to locate Truman's New Yorker. When he failed to find it, he tracked down the closest model to it.

51. In 1953, a record 36,190 people were killed in automobile accidents. Ibid., 36–37.

52. Ibid., 172–173.

53. The quote is from Truman, *Mr. Citizen,* 41.

54. Algeo, *Harry Truman's Excellent Adventure*, 111–132.

55. Quoted in ibid., 128.

56. Quoted in ibid., 137.

57. Ibid., 139–140.

58. Ibid., 141–150.

59. Sand, *Truman in Retirement,* 18.

60. The quote is from McCullough, *Truman,* 944. See also Hamby, *Man of the People,* 626.

61. Hamby, *Man of the People,* 626–627; Sand, *Truman in Retirement,* 18–19; McCullough, *Truman,* 945–946.

62. Dean Acheson to Harry S. Truman, 21 June 1955, Old Box 9, Folder "Secretary's Office File," Post-Presidential Papers, Truman Papers; McCullough, *Truman,* 948.

63. On memoirs by presidents since Truman, see Mark Perry, "All the President's Books: Why Do Their Memoirs So Rarely Say Anything Memorable?," *Washington Post,* 13 June 2004; "Gould, Dallek, Shenkman et al. on Presidential Memoirs," New York *Journal News,* 20 June 2004, http://hnn.us/; Geoffrey C. Ward, "When Presidents Tell It Their Way," *American Heritage,* August/September 1985.

64. Quoted in Lawrence O. Burnette Jr., *Beneath the Footnote* (Madison: University of Wisconsin Press, 1969), 156. See also Arnold Hirshon, "The Scope, Accessibility and History of Presidential Papers," *Government Publications Review* 1 (1974): 363–390.

65. The quote is from Hufbauer, *Presidential Temples,* 26.

66. Hirshon, "Scope, Accessibility and History," 377–389.

67. Hufbauer, *Presidential Temples,* 23–33.

68. Raymond Geselbracht and Timothy Walch, "The Presidential Libraries Act after 50 Years," *Prologue Magazine* 28 (Summer 2005), http://www.archives.gov.

69. The quote is in Hufbauer, *Presidential Temples,* 7. But see also Robert F. Worth, "Presidential Libraries: Mines or Shrines?" *New York Times,* 24 April 2002; Jason S. Lantzer, "The Public History of Presidential Libraries: How the Presidency Is Presented to the People," *Journal of the Association for History and Computing* 6 (April 2003), http://quod.lib.umich.edu/j/jahc/3310410.0006.101?rgn=main;view=fulltext; Frank Freidel, "Roosevelt to Reagan: The Birth and Growth of Presidential Libraries," and Don W. Wilson, "Presidential Libraries," both in *Prologue Magazine* 21 (Summer 1989), http://www.archives.gov.

70. The quote is in Hufbauer, *Presidential Temples,* 31.

71. The quote is in Truman, *Mr. Citizen,* 188.

72. The quote is in Sand, *Truman in Retirement,* 32.

73. The quote is in ibid., 33. For an analysis of the meaning of the Benton mural and replication of the Oval Office, see Hufbauer, *Presidential Temples,* 42–67. Hufbauer is highly critical of the mural, which he describes as "a grand history painting of 'American urges westward' that rationalized the dispossession of Native Americans . . . an almost physical need of white Americans to possess and domesticate the body of wild America." Ibid., 48–49. See also Truman, *Mr. Citizen,* 190–191; McCullough, *Truman,* 967–969.

74. Truman, *Mr. Citizen,* 69–70; McCullough, *Truman,* 943.

75. The first quote is in Margaret Truman, *Harry S. Truman,* 562. The second quote is in Sand, *Truman in Retirement,* 34.

76. "History of the Truman Presidential Museum and Library," http://www.trumanlibrary.org. On the activities of the institute, see, for example, "Fifth Annual Report of the Secretary," [1961], Box 6, Folder "Secretary's Office File," Post-Presidential Papers, Truman Papers. See also McCullough, *Truman,* 961–962.

77. Truman, *Mr. Citizen,* 191.

78. The quote is from "Memorandum," [1953], in Ferrell, ed., *Off the Record,* 301–302. On Truman's experiences visiting prestigious universities, see Hamby, *Man of the People,* 631–632; McCullough, *Truman,* 964.

79. Truman to Lyndon Johnson, 23 July and 16 August 1957, Box 10, White House

Famous Names, Lyndon Baines Johnson Papers (hereafter Johnson Papers), Lyndon B. Johnson Library and Museum, Austin, Texas. Truman, *Mr. Citizen*, 190.

80. Sand, *Truman in Retirement*, 13–17.

81. All the quotations are from Hamby, *Man of the People*, 620–621.

82. The first quote is in Neal, *Harry and Ike*, 293. The second is in Conversation Between the President and Mr. Geo. Wallace, 15 January 1954, Old Box 10, Folder "Secretary's Office File," Post-Presidential Papers, Truman Papers.

83. Truman to Paul M. Butler, 8 February 1955, and Truman to Stephen A. Mitchell, 24 February 1955, Box 691, Folder "Political File: Correspondence General, 1955," Post-Presidential Papers, Truman Papers.

84. Truman to Clayton Fritchey, 1 November 1955, Box 691, Folder "Political File: Correspondence General, 1955," Post-Presidential Papers, Truman Papers; Sand, *Truman in Retirement*, 54.

85. Truman, *Mr. Citizen*, 51–52.

86. Truman to W. F. Daniels, 17 May 1956, Old Box 10, Folder "Secretary's Office File," Post-Presidential Papers, Truman Papers. See also Truman, *Mr. Citizen;* Hamby, *Man of the People*, 621–622.

87. Miller, *Plain Speaking*, 186; Hamby, *Man of the People*, 622.

88. The quote is in Neal, *Harry and Ike*, 298. See also Hamby, *Man of the People*, 622.

89. Allen, *Eisenhower and the Mass Media*, 86–149; Hamby, *Man of the People*, 622–623.

90. Truman to Eisenhower, 28 November 1956 [never sent], Box 15, Folder "Secretary's Office File," Post-Presidential Papers, Truman Papers.

91. On Truman as a doting grandfather, see Clifton Daniel, *Growing Up with My Grandfather: Memories of Harry S. Truman* (New York: Carol Publishing, 1995).

92. John Chambers, "Presidents Emeritus," *American Heritage Magazine* 30 (June–July 1979): 18.

93. Wendy Ginsberg, *CRS Report for Congress: Former Presidents: Pensions, Office Allowances, and Other Federal Benefits* (Washington, D.C.: Congressional Research Service, 22 August 2008), 9.

94. Quoted in ibid., 10.

95. On the sale of his Grandview land, see Reece A. Garduer to Rufus Burruss, 10 April 1956, and Rufus Burruss to Commerce Trust Company, 13 September 1956, Box 34, Folder "Harry S. Truman and the Truman File, Legal File," Rufus Burruss Papers, Harry S. Truman Library. On Truman's letter to McCormack, see Truman to John W. McCormack, 10 January 1957, in Ferrell, ed., *Off the Record*, 346–347.

96. Truman to John W. McCormack, 10 January 1957, in Ferrell, ed., *Off the Record*, 346–347.

97. The quotes are in Ginsberg, *CRS Report for Congress*, 10–13.

98. Truman to Lyndon Johnson, 26 August 1959, Box 16, Folder "Secretary's Office File," Post-Presidential Papers, Truman Papers. Although former President Hoover announced his support for the measure, he gave his pension after taxes to charity. Truman remained silent while the measure moved its way through Congress. *New York Times*, 16, 17, 22, 26, and 28 August 1958; Ginsberg, *CRS Report for Congress*, 13. See also Sand, *Truman in Retirement*, 125–126.

99. Truman to John M. Wheeler, 18 December 1959; Fletcher Knebel to Truman, 23

June 1959, and Truman to Knebel, 29 June 1959, attached to Truman to William Hillman, Box 19, Folder "Secretary's Office File," Post-Presidential Papers, Truman Papers.

100. William Hillman to Sam Rosenman, 17 March 1959; memorandum to President Truman from William Hillman and David M. Noyes, 26 May 1959; Bernard Geis to Harry Truman, 11 June 1959; Truman to Bernard Geiss, 5 June 1959 and 1 August 1961; William Hillman to Harry S. Truman, 18 April 1962, and attachment, Box 18, Folder "Secretary's Office File," Post-Presidential Papers, Truman Papers.

101. McCullough, *Truman,* 953–959.

102. Quoted in Miller, *Plain Speaking,* 361.

103. See, for example, Johnson to Truman, 7 December 1956, and Truman to Johnson, 11 December 1956, Box 10, White House Famous Names, Johnson Papers.

104. Truman, *Mr. Citizen,* 53; James Reston, "The Stakes at Chicago," *New York Times,* 16 August 1956.

105. Quoted in McCullough, *Truman,* 970.

106. Truman to Johnson, 11 December 1956, Box 10, White House Famous Names, Johnson Papers.

107. Johnson to Truman, 7 December 1956, Box 691, Folder "Political File, Democratic National Committee," Truman Papers; Johnson to Truman, 17 December 1956, 27 February 1957, and 13 and 14 May 1957, Box 10, White House Famous Names, Johnson Papers.

108. For Truman's fear in 1959 that the chairman of the Democratic National Committee, Paul Butler, was trying to rig the 1960 election in support of Stevenson and his determination not to let that happen, see Truman to Dean Acheson, 22 August 1959, in Ferrell, ed., *Off the Record,* 381–382. See also Truman, *Mr. Citizen,* 54.

109. Quoted in Neal, *Harry and Ike,* 311–312. See also Sand, *Truman in Retirement,* 73; Hamby, *Man of the People,* 624–625.

110. McCullough, *Truman,* 973–974.

111. Both quotes are in Hamby, *Man of the People,* 625. See also Neal, *Harry and Ike,* 313.

112. Truman to India Edwards, 22 November 1960, attached to Edwards to Dr. Philip C. Brooks, 17 December 1960, Box 16, Folder "Tom Edward," Post-Presidential File, Truman Papers; *Kansas City Times,* 15 November 1961.

113. McCullough, *Truman,* 982.

114. Truman to Eisenhower, 24 July 1958, Telephone Conversation between President Truman and Allen Dulles [director of the CIA], 16 July 1958, and Allen Dulles to Truman, 28 August 1958, Boxes 12 and 15, Folder "Secretary's Office File," Post-Presidential File, Truman Papers; *Kansas City Star,* 20 July 1958; Dwight D. Eisenhower, *The White House Years: Waging Peace* (New York: Doubleday and Co., 1965), 276; Transcript of Telephone Conversation between Truman and Dean Acheson, 15 July 1958, Ferrell, ed., *Off the Record,* 365–366; Neal, *Harry and Ike,* 305.

115. Neal, *Harry and Ike,* 317–320.

116. Abraham Feinberg to Truman, 17 November 1961, Box 16, Folder "Secretary's Office File," Post-Presidential Papers, Truman Papers; Neal, *Harry and Ike,* 319.

117. Neal, *Harry and Ike,* 321–324.

118. Quoted in *Washington Post,* 21 March 1968.

119. Hamby, *Man of the People,* 634; McCullough, *Truman,* 987–989.

CHAPTER 11: THE LIMITS OF THE OFFICE OF EX-PRESIDENT

1. Johnson was worn out and certainly less involved publicly and politically than Eisenhower. Even in Johnson's case, it is incorrect, however, to describe him as a "hermit [who] granted only one interview, attended few public meetings, and rarely left the ranch," as his biographer, Doris Kearns, has done, or "as an "exhausted volcano [who spent] his retirement in lonely, bitter semi-exile at his Texas ranch," as the scholar Irina Belinsky has written. Doris Kearns, *Lyndon Johnson and the American Dream* (New York: Harper & Row, 1976), 358; Irina Belensky, "The Making of Ex-Presidents, 1797–1993: Six Recurrent Models," *Presidential Studies Quarterly* 29 (March 1999): 155.

2. Quoted in Kearns, *Lyndon Johnson and the American Dream,* 359.

3. Quoted in Dwight D. Eisenhower, *At Ease: Stories I Told to Friends* (Garden City, N.Y.: Doubleday, 1967), 43.

4. Ibid.; Stephen Ambrose, *Eisenhower: Soldier, General of Army, President-Elect, 1890–1952* (New York: Simon & Schuster, 1983), 9–42.

5. Eisenhower, *At Ease,* 7; William B. Pickett, *Dwight David Eisenhower and American Power* (Wheeling, Ill.: Harlan Davidson, 1995), 7–8.

6. Eisenhower, *At Ease,* 7; Pickett, *Eisenhower and American Power,* 4.

7. Eisenhower, *At Ease,* 24–26.

8. Quoted in Pickett, *Eisenhower and American Power,* 10. See also Piers Brendon, *Ike: His Life and Times* (New York: Harper & Row, 1986), 38–41.

9. Brendon, *Ike,* 43–45.

10. Ibid., 48, 51–53; Ambrose, *Eisenhower: Soldier,* 75–76.

11. Robert Griffith, "Dwight D. Eisenhower and the Corporate Commonwealth," *American Historical Review* 87 (February 1982): 87–122. See also Steven Wagner, *Eisenhower Republicanism: Pursuing the Middle Way* (DeKalb: Northern Illinois University Press, 2006), esp. 4–8 and 145–148.

12. Ambrose, *Eisenhower: Soldier,* 555–561.

13. The quote is from Pickett, *Eisenhower and American Power,* 165. See also Chester J. Pach Jr. and Elmo Richardson, *The Presidency of Dwight D. Eisenhower* (Lawrence: University Press of Kansas, 1991), 226–227.

14. Eisenhower's health problems may also have factored into Nixon's decision.

15. The quote is from Pickett, *Eisenhower and American Power,* 169; Pach and Richardson, *Presidency of Dwight D. Eisenhower,* 227–228.

16. The first quote is from Pickett, *Eisenhower and American Power,* 170; the second and third quotes are from Nancy Gibbs, "When New Presidents Meet Old, It's Not Always Pretty," *Time,* 10 November 2008.

17. Eisenhower Diary, 6 December 1960, in Robert H. Ferrell, ed., *The Eisenhower Diaries* (New York: Norton, 1981), 379–383; Pach and Richardson, *Presidency of Dwight D. Eisenhower,* 229; Stephen E. Ambrose, *Eisenhower: The President* (New York: Simon & Schuster, 1984), 606–607.

18. U.S. National Archives and Records Administration, "President Dwight D. Eisenhower's Farewell Address (1961)," http://www.ourdocuments.gov.

19. "Eisenhower National Historic Site—Eisenhower at Gettysburg," U.S. National Park Service, http://www.nps.gov.

20. William G. Clotworthy, *Home and Libraries of the Presidents* (Blacksburg, Va.: McDonald and Woodward, 1994), 253; Ambrose, *Eisenhower: The President,* 75.

21. Clotworthy, *Home and Libraries of the Presidents,* 253.

22. The quote from Drew Pearson is from *New York Times,* 30 January 1964. On the list of names, see Ann Whitman to Colonel Schultz, Colonel Eisenhower, and Maty Jane McCaffree, 5 January 1961, Box 11, Principal File, Office of Dwight David Eisenhower, Dwight David Eisenhower Papers (hereafter Eisenhower Papers), Dwight David Eisenhower Library, Abilene, Kansas.

23. On the gifts, see Steve Neal, *The Eisenhowers* (Lawrence: University Press of Kansas, 1984), 424.

24. See, for example, Ann C. Whitman to G. Bland Hoke, 30 January 1961, Box 6, Principal File, Office of Dwight D. Eisenhower, Eisenhower Papers. See also Ambrose, *Eisenhower: Soldier,* 436–438, 476–511.

25. Eisenhower to Edgar Eisenhower, 7 January 1961, Box 7, Principal File, Office of Dwight D. Eisenhower, Eisenhower Papers.

26. Ambrose, *Eisenhower: The President,* 631–632.

27. Homer F. Cunningham, *The President's Last Years: George Washington to Lyndon B.* Johnson (Jefferson, N.C.: McFarland, 1989), 270; Brendon, *Ike,* 404.

28. John S. D. Eisenhower, *Strictly Personal: A Memoir* (New York: Doubleday, 1974), 303–304.

29. Ambrose, *Eisenhower: The President,* 635.

30. For other analyses of the two volumes, the first more favorable than the other, see Ambrose, *Eisenhower: The President,* 634–635, and Brendon, *Ike,* 404.

31. Brendon, *Ike,* 405–406; Ambrose, *Eisenhower: The President,* 632–635.

32. Eisenhower Diary, 22 April 1961, in Ferrell, ed., *Eisenhower Diaries,* 386–389.

33. In contrast to later reports that the Bay of Pigs had its origins in Eisenhower's own administration, the former president refused to take any responsibility for the calamity. He even had altered a document suggesting that at one meeting he had approved a plan to invade Cuba. He persuaded Gordon Gray, his national security adviser, who had taken notes of the meeting, that they were inaccurate. Accordingly, Gray deleted the incriminating language. Ambrose, *Eisenhower: The President,* 639–640.

34. Eisenhower to Major General Andrew Goodpaster, 21 August 1961, Box 9, Principal File, Office of Dwight D. Eisenhower, Eisenhower Papers.

35. Ernest R. May and Philip D. Zelikow, eds., *The Kennedy Tapes: Inside the White House during the Cuban Missile Crisis* (New York: Norton, 2002), 405–407; Eisenhower's diary, 29 October and 2 and 5 November 1962, in Ferrell, ed., *Eisenhower Diaries,* 393.

36. Press release from the Council for Economic Growth, 17 July 1961, and Eisenhower to Gabriel Hauge, 6 November 1961, Boxes 6 and 10, Principal File, Office of Dwight D. Eisenhower, Eisenhower Papers.

37. The first quote is Robert F. Kennedy, *Robert Kennedy in His Own Words: The Unpublished Recollections of the Kennedy Years,* ed. Edwin G. Guthman and Jeffrey Shulman (New York: Bantam, 1988), 55. Quoted in Arthur Schlesinger Jr., *A Thousand Days: John F. Kennedy in the White House* (Boston: Houghton Mifflin, 1965), 526; see also 242.

38. Eisenhower to Richard Nixon, 24 August 1961, Box 8, Principal File, Office of Dwight D. Eisenhower, Eisenhower Papers.

39. On Rockefeller, see Tom Wicker, *Dwight D. Eisenhower* (New York: Times Books, 2002), 85–105, 117–118; Ambrose, *Eisenhower: The President,* 559–560, 595.

40. On his complaints about the volume of mail and types of requests he was receiving, see Eisenhower to Gabriel Hauge, 29 April 1961, Box 10, Principal File, Office of Dwight D. Eisenhower, Eisenhower Papers. See also Herbert S. Parmet, *Eisenhower and the American Crusades,* new ed. (New York: Transaction Publishers, 1998), 575.

41. *Northern Virginia Sun,* 27 September 1961, attached to Barry Goldwater to Eisenhower, 3 October 1961, Box 8, Principal File, Office of Dwight D. Eisenhower, Eisenhower Papers.

42. Eisenhower to Barry Goldwater and attachment, 7 October 1961, Box 8, Principal File, Office of Dwight D. Eisenhower, Eisenhower Papers. Parmet, *Eisenhower and the American Crusades,* 575.

43. Quoted in Neal, *Eisenhowers,* 425.

44. The quote is from Ambrose, *Eisenhower: The President,* 645.

45. Eisenhower Diary, 12 October 1968, Box 1, Eisenhower Diaries, Eisenhower Papers.

46. Milton S. Eisenhower, *The President Is Calling* (Garden City, N.Y.: Doubleday, 1975), 389–391.

47. Robert Alan Goldberg, *Barry Goldwater* (New Haven, Conn.: Yale University Press, 1995), 191–193.

48. Ibid., 193.

49. The two quotes are from Neal, *Eisenhowers,* 432.

50. Goldberg, *Barry Goldwater,* 195. See also Neal, *Eisenhowers,* 433; Wagner, *Eisenhower Republicanism,* 140–141.

51. Goldberg, *Barry Goldwater,* 198–199; Neal, *Eisenhowers,* 434; Eisenhower, *The President Is Calling,* 388–389.

52. Goldberg, *Barry Goldwater,* 200–205. Neal, *Eisenhowers,* 435–437; Eisenhower, *The President Is Calling,* 390.

53. Goldberg, *Barry Goldwater,* 207.

54. Neal, *Eisenhowers,* 438–439; Wagner, *Eisenhower Republicanism,* 142–143.

55. The first quote is from Richard Nixon, *RN: The Memoirs of Richard Nixon* (New York: Grosset & Dunlap, 1978), 262. The second is from Goldberg, *Barry Goldwater,* 235.

56. Peter Lyon, *Eisenhower: Portrait of the Hero* (Boston: Little, Brown, 1974), 841; Neal, *Eisenhowers,* 439.

57. Goldberg, *Barry Goldwater,* 189–194; Wagner, *Eisenhower Republicanism,* 144.

58. Mary C. Brennan, *Turning Right in the Sixties: The Conservative Capture of the GOP* (Chapel Hill: University of North Carolina Press, 1995), 1–5 and 11–12; Wagner, *Eisenhower Republicanism,* 145–148.

59. Brendon, *Ike,* 412; Gibbs and Duffy, *The Presidents Club,* 159–160.

60. Brendon, *Ike,* 413. Gibbs and Duffy portray Eisenhower's view of Johnson, at least in the first few years of the Johnson administration, more favorably than the image presented here. *The Presidents Club,* 163–170.

61. Irwin Unger and Debi Unger have Eisenhower playing a more decisive role in Johnson's decision to bomb North Vietnam. See Irwin and Debi Unger, *LBJ: A Life* (New York: Wiley, 1999), 342. So do Gibbs and Duffy, *The Presidents Club,* 171–179. However, the vast literature on the Vietnam War portrays Eisenhower's influence on Johnson's decisions leading to Rolling Thunder as more limited, as does my own reading of the Eisenhower–Johnson relationship at the LBJ Library in Austin, Texas, and the Eisenhower Library in Abilene, Kansas. On the literature on the Vietnam War, see, for example, George C. Herring, *America's Longest War: The United States and Vietnam, 1950–1975* (New York: McGraw-Hill, 2002), 149–155; David Kaiser, *American Tragedy: Kennedy, Johnson, and the Origins of the Vietnam War* (Cambridge, Mass.: Harvard University Press,

2000), 403–409; and Frank Logevall, *Choosing War: The Lost Chance for Peace and Escalation of War in Vietnam* (Berkeley: University of California Press, 1999), 350–351. See also Robert Dallek, *Flawed Giant: Lyndon Johnson and His Times, 1961–1973* (New York: Oxford University Press, 1998), 252–257. Dallek does not even mention Johnson's meeting of 17 February with Eisenhower or any role he might have played in influencing Johnson's decision for a sustained bombing campaign against North Vietnam.

62. The quotes are from Brendon, *Ike,* 413–414.

63. Ibid., 414.

64. Ibid., 413–414.

65. According to the historian Robert H. Ferrell, Eisenhower's problems had to do with his heart. Ferell believes Eisenhower may have suffered a heart attack as early as 1947, and he almost certainly suffered a more serious one in 1949. He also maintains that Snyder, who was not a cardiologist and often made poor medical decisions, purposely hid news of the 1949 attack from the press in order to keep alive any political ambitions Eisenhower may have had. Ferrell bases his claims on a variety of sources, the most important of which was a study made by Dr. Thomas Mattingly, the chief cardiologist at Walter Reed Hospital who later treated Eisenhower after he suffered his heart attack of 1955. Robert H. Ferrell, *Ill-Advised: Presidential Health and Public Trust* (Columbia: University of Missouri Press, 1992), 65–72. In 1997, however, the historian Clarence G. Lasby, who had access to Snyder's extensive collection on Eisenhower's health as well as Mattingly's study, wrote a detailed history of Eisenhower's heart attacks. In it, he rejected Ferrell's assertion that Eisenhower had suffered at least one, and possibly two, heart attacks before the 1955 attack. He acknowledges, however, that Snyder tried to cover up the seriousness of Eisenhower's illnesses and misdiagnosed the cause of his abdominal pains. Lasby's study is more sophisticated and compelling than Farrell's. Clarence G. Lasby, *Eisenhower's Heart Attack: How Ike Beat Heart Disease and Held on to the Presidency* (Lawrence: University Press of Kansas, 1997), esp. 2–5 and 32–50.

66. Lasby, *Eisenhower's Heart Attack,* 72–154; Ferrell, *Ill-Advised,* 80–99.

67. Lasby, *Eisenhower's Heart Attack,* 160–192, Ferrell, *Ill-Advised,* 99–111; Bumgarner, *Health,* 228–230.

68. Lasby, *Eisenhower's Heart Attack,* 206–213 and 240–244; Ferrell, *Ill-Advised,* 128–133.

69. Ambrose, *Eisenhower: The President,* 669.

70. Eisenhower, *Strictly Personal,* 283; Ambrose, *Eisenhower: The President,* 636.

71. Eisenhower, *Strictly Personal,* 328–337; Ambrose, *Eisenhower: The President,* 673–675.

72. Cunningham, *President's Last Years,* 275–276.

73. On Abilene, see Ambrose, *Eisenhower: Soldier,* 26. On life in the hill country, see Merle Miller, *Lyndon: An Oral Biography* (New York: G. P. Putnam's Sons, 1980), 9; Charles Peters, *Lyndon B. Johnson* (New York: Time Books, 2010), 1–2. On the later effects on Johnson of watching his mother have to carry water from the water pump, see Peters, *Lyndon B. Johnson,* 9–10. See also Robert Dallek, *Lone Star Rising: Lyndon Johnson and His Times, 1908–1960* (New York: Oxford University Press, 1991), 28–29.

74. According to Doris Kearns, Johnson may even have internalized a love–hate relationship toward his mother that affected his later need to be accepted, and even loved, by the very people he scorned. Kearns, *Lyndon Johnson and the American Dream,* 24–27, 32–33. See also Dallek, *Lone Star Rising,* 29–33 and 34–38.

75. Kearns, *Lyndon Johnson and the American Dream,* 7–8; Dallek, *Lone Star Rising,* 33–34; Peters, *Lyndon B. Johnson,* 3.

76. Dallek, *Lone Star Rising,* 49–50.

77. The quote is from Kearns, *Lyndon Johnson and the American Dream,* 46. See also Unger and Unger, *LBJ,* 24–25; Dallek, *Lone Star Rising,* 73–75.

78. The quote is from Dallek, *Lone Star Rising,* 77; see also 78–80. Peters, *Lyndon B. Johnson,* 7–8. For the impact of his teaching experience in Cotulla on his later interest in helping poor people, see remarks of Hubert H. Humphrey in Miller, *Lyndon,* xvi–xvii.

79. Kearns, *Lyndon Johnson and the American Dream,* 72–79; Dallek, *Lone Star Rising,* 93–124.

80. Kearns, *Lyndon Johnson and the American Dream,* 80–84; Miller, *Lyndon,* 49–53.

81. Both quotes can be found in Miller, *Lyndon,* xv and xvii.

82. Peters, *Lyndon B. Johnson,* 35–37.

83. Kearns, *Lyndon Johnson and the American Dream,* 102–159; Miller, *Lyndon,* 141–231; Peters, *Lyndon B. Johnson,* 40–41.

84. Kearns, *Lyndon Johnson and the American Dream,* 144–159; Peters, *Lyndon B. Johnson,* 52–59.

85. Kearns, *Lyndon Johnson and the American Dream,* 212–213, 282–285, and 340–341; Dallek, *Flawed Giant,* 592–603; Unger and Unger, *LBJ,* 497–498. For Johnson's distrust of Nixon, even before he became president, and his knowledge of Nixon's effort to undercut his peace initiative with respect to Vietnam, see also Gibbs and Duffy, *The Presidents Club,* 228–231 and 242–249.

86. Randall B. Woods, *LBJ: Architect of American Ambition* (New York: Free Press, 2006), 876–877; Dallek, *Flawed Giant,* 593–594.

87. Dallek, *Flawed Giant,* 595–597. Unger and Unger, *LBJ,* 494–503.

88. Johnson's remarks to Califano are in Joseph Califano, *The Triumph and Tragedy of Lyndon Johnson: The White House Years* (New York: Simon and Shuster, 1991), 253.

89. Mark K. Updegrove, *Second Acts: Presidential Lives and Legacies after the White House* (Guilford, Conn.: Lyons Press, 2006), 71–72.

90. Meeting with President Johnson, 7 February 1969, Walt Rostow to the President, 19 March 1969, and various briefing papers, Box 1, Post-Presidential Intelligence Briefings; Walt Rostow to the President 14 May 1969, Thomas Johnson to Henry Kissinger, 19 May 1969, Tom J. to the President, 4 June 1969, and Lyndon Johnson to Henry A. Kissinger, 28 August 1969, Box 88, Folder "Hon. Henry A. Kissinger," Post-Presidential Name File, Johnson Papers.

91. Kearns, *Lyndon Johnson and the American Dream,* 286. Gibbs and Duffy, in my view, exaggerate the post-presidential friendship Johnson had with Nixon. As even they acknowledge, Johnson regarded Nixon as guilty of treason for undermining his peace initiative. *The President's Club,* 266–269.

92. Robert L. Hardesty, "With Lyndon Johnson in Texas," in Robert L. Hardesty, ed., *The Johnson Years: The Difference He Made* (Austin: University of Texas Press, 1993), 95–96.

93. Miller, *Lyndon,* 529–530; Unger and Unger, *LBJ,* 440–441; Vaughn Davis Bornet, *The Presidency of Lyndon Baines Johnson* (Lawrence: University Press of Kansas, 1983), 296–299.

94. Based on this and other evidence that he has pieced together, the historian of his

presidency, Vaughn Davis Bornet, has even concluded that his health alone led to his decision not to seek reelection in 1968. "So Johnson's withdrawal from candidacy for another term could have been—but clearly was not—due to Tet, the war in general, rival challengers in his party, the protesters, the polls, the 'system' working, any alleged mental quirks or supposed tendencies toward avoiding conflict, or the fear of losing. . . . He and his wife had long been convinced . . . there would be no possibility of living out nine years and two months in power." Bornet, *Presidency of Lyndon Baines Johnson,* 288–305.

95. Dallek, *Flawed Giant,* 548–549 and 563–573; Peters, *Lyndon B. Johnson,* 148–151.

96. Miller, *Lyndon,* 530.

97. Ibid., 544.

98. Kearns, *Lyndon Johnson and the American Dream,* 356–357; Unger and Unger, *LBJ,* 504–505; Peters, *Lyndon B. Johnson,* 155.

99. The quote is from Dallek, *Flawed Giant,* 601.

100. Kearns, *Lyndon Johnson and the American Dream,* 356. See also Robert L. Hardesty, "The LBJ the Nation Seldom Saw," *Office of the President Publications,* Paper 2 (San Marcos: Southwest Texas State University, 1983), http://ecommons.txstate.edu/presopub/2/.

101. U.S. General Services Administration, "Presidential Transition Act of 1963," http://www.gsa.gov. For a list of Johnson's staff, see W. Thomas Johnson to Colonel Robert Schultz, 16 December 1969, Box 85, Folder "Kearns, Dorothy," Post-Presidential Name File, Johnson Papers. On the extension from six to eighteen months, see Tom J. to the President, 25 June 1969, Box 118, Folder "Richard M. Nixon," Post-Presidential Name File, Johnson Papers. On the advance that Johnson and Lady Bird received, see Dallek, *Flawed Giant,* 609.

102. Kearns, *Lyndon Johnson and the American Dream,* 3.

103. Robert Reinhold, "Antiwar Activist Confidante of LBJ," Dallas *Morning News,* 13 June 1971; Kearns, *Lyndon Johnson and the American Dream,* 2–3.

104. Kearns, *Lyndon Johnson and the American Dream,* 4.

105. Ibid., 5–9.

106. Ibid., 10–12.

107. Ibid., 18.

108. Woods, *LBJ,* 880–881; Unger and Unger, *LBJ,* 512–513.

109. Hardesty, "The LBJ the Nation Seldom Saw"; Unger and Unger, *LBJ,* 523.

110. Kearns, *Lyndon Johnson and the American Dream,* 14–15.

111. Ibid.

112. Memorandum for the President from Doris Kearns, 30 July 1970, Box 85, Folder "Doris Kearns," Post-Presidential Name File, Johnson Papers.

113. Memorandum for President Johnson from Tom Johnson, 6 October 1971, Box 6, Folder "Asher, Aaron," Johnson to Wilbur Cohen, 8 February 1972, Box 60, Folder "Wilbur Cohen," Post-Presidential Name File, Johnson Papers.

114. Benardo and Weiss, *Citizen-in-Chief,* 61.

115. Unger and Unger, *LBJ,* 515–516.

116. See, for example, Tom J. to Mr. President, 2 January [1970], Box 27, Folder "Christian, George," Post-Presidential Name File, Johnson Papers. See also Dallek, *Flawed Giant,* 610–611.

117. Tom Johnson to the President, 8 and 27 April 1970, Box 91, Folder "Abe

Fortas," Post-Presidential Name File, Johnson Papers. See also Walter Cronkite, *A Reporter's Life* (New York: Ballantine, 1997), 234; Unger and Unger, *LBJ*.

118. Hufbauer, *Presidential Temples*, 71–73.

119. Miller, *Lyndon*, 550; Hufbauer, *Presidential Temples*, 71–74.

120. Hufbauer, *Presidential Temples*, 74.

121. Ibid., 75–81.

122. The quotes are in Benardo and Weiss, *Citizen-in-Chief*, 93. Hufbauer, who maintains that presidential libraries are the temples of America's civil religion, viewed the library as symbolic of the imperial nature of the American presidency in the last half of the twentieth century and characteristic of "presidential narcissism." Hufbauer, *Presidential Temples*, 68.

123. Miller, *Lyndon*, 550; Hufbauer, *Presidential Temples*, 83–85.

124. Hufbauer has even made the point that a better comparison for the library than the Egyptian pyramids, which were the burying grounds of the deity-like pharaohs, was the ancient Egyptian pylon temples. Not only did they more closely resemble the library architecturally, but they were also living places whose priests were dedicated to serving the deities through rites and ceremonies. Like these priests, Hufbauer argues, "an archivist at the Johnson Library, tending to its millions of documents for years, keeps the deeds of a modern-day leader alive." Hufbauer, *Presidential Temples*, 85.

125. "Memorandum for the Secretary of Defense," from H. R. Haldeman, 7 October 1969, attached to Henry A. Kissinger to Tom Johnson, 7 October 1969, Box 88, Folder "Henry Kissinger," Post-Presidential Name File, Johnson Papers. See also Miller, *Lyndon*, 550.

126. Johnson to Perry R. Bass, 3 February 1970, Box 10, Folder "Bass, Perry and Nancy Lee," Post-Presidential Name File, Johnson Papers.

127. Quoted in Miller, *Lyndon*, 609.

128. The quote is from Dallek, *Flawed Giant*, 609–610. See also Harry J. Middleton, "The President and His Library: My Recollections of Working with Lyndon B. Johnson," in Smith and Walch, *Farewell to the Chief*, 108–111.

129. Middleton, "The President and His Library," 112–113.

130. Quoted in Unger and Unger, *LBJ*, 533.

131. Hardesty, "With Lyndon Johnson in Texas," 106.

132. Ibid., 101–102.

133. Ibid., 101.

134. Dallek, *Flawed Giant*, 612.

135. Unger and Unger, *LBJ*, 512.

136. Updegrove, *Second Acts*, 72–73.

137. Bumgarner, *Health*, 257.

138. Unger and Unger, *LBJ*, 537.

139. The quote is from ibid., *LBJ*, 536–537.

140. The quotes are from Hardesty, "With Lyndon Johnson in Texas," 106.

CHAPTER 12: THE MASS MARKETING OF THE POST-PRESIDENCY

1. All the quotes are from Fawn M. Brodie, *Richard Nixon: The Shaping of His Character* (New York: Norton, 1981), 17. On Goldwater, see Robert Sam Ansom, *Exile: The Unquiet Oblivion of Richard M. Nixon* (New York: Simon & Schuster, 1984), 89–90.

2. Examples of the literature on Nixon's psychology include Brodie, *Richard Nixon;* David Abrahamsen, *Nixon vs. Nixon: An Emotional Tragedy* (New York: Farrar, Straus & Giroux, 1977); and Bruce Mazlish, *In Search of Nixon: A Psychohistorical Inquiry* (New York: Penguin, 1974).

3. Nixon, *RN,* 9 and 12; Richard Nixon, *In the Arena: A Memoir of Victory, Defeat and Renewal* (New York: Pocket Books, 1990), 85–86.

4. Quoted in Monica Crowley, *Nixon Off the Record* (New York: Random House, 1996), 13.

5. Richard Nixon, *Six Crises* (Garden City, N.Y.: Doubleday, 19620, xv.

6. In his memoirs, Nixon wrote that the issue of anticommunism was a legitimate one. More to the point, he argued that it was marginal to the campaign. Voters in 1946 were far more concerned with reigning in government after fifteen years of New Deal programs; with returning to normalcy after having to deal with rationing, food shortages, and inflation; and with hemming in too-powerful labor unions. These were the issues on which, he said, he defeated Voorhis. Nixon's supporters have also made the point that his anticommunism followed from his denunciation of New Deal programs and the power of unions. Nixon, *RN,* 39. David Greenberg, *Nixon's Shadow: The History of an Image* (New York: Norton, 2003), 23–24.

7. Greenberg, *Nixon's Shadow,* 29–30.

8. Kenneth Clawson, "A Loyalist Memoir," *Washington Post,* 9 August 1979.

9. Congress agreed reluctantly to pay the salaries of the federal employees, but later cut his expense grant from $200,000 to $60,000.

10. Quoted in Ansom, *Exile,* 30. See also Jonathan Aitken, *Nixon: A Life* (Washington, D.C.: Regnery Publishing, 1993), 529.

11. Crowley, *Nixon Off the Record,* 9. On Nixon's determination to take charge of his own history, see Elizabeth Drew, *Richard M. Nixon* (New York: Times Books, 2007), 136.

12. Who had ordered him to remove the boxes to San Clemente remains unclear, but almost certainly Nixon was involved because his longtime secretary, Rose Woods, had told Gulley that there were some "personal things [the president] want[ed] done" before leaving the White House. As soon as he returned to California, furthermore, Nixon telephoned Alexander Haig, his former chief of staff, who was still serving in that position under Ford. The former president told Haig that he wanted all of his papers and tapes sent to San Clemente. See Bill Gulley, *Breaking Cover* (New York: Warner Books, 1980), 12–20. See also Ansom, *Exile,* 27–28; Stephen E. Ambrose, *Nixon: Ruin and Recovery, 1973–1990* (New York: Simon & Schuster, 1991), 449–451.

13. Ambrose, *Nixon: Ruin and Recovery,* 449–450.

14. Stanley Kutler, *The Wars of Watergate: The Last Crisis of Richard Nixon* (New York: Knopf, 1990), 556.

15. Ansom, *Exile,* 31.

16. The quotes are in Ambrose, *Nixon: Ruin and Recovery,* 452–453, and Ansom, *Exile,* 31–32.

17. Quoted in Ambrose, *Nixon: Ruin and Recovery,* 452–453; see also 475.

18. Ansom, *Exile,* 34–35.

19. The quote is in Ambrose, *Nixon: Ruin and Recovery,* 456. See also Ansom, *Exile,* 34–35.

20. Ansom, *Exile,* 51–53; Ambrose, *Nixon: Ruin and Recovery,* 457–458.

21. Nixon's comment is in Crowley, *Nixon Off the Record,* 7–8.

22. Ambrose, *Nixon: Ruin and Recovery,* 461.

23. Aitken, *Nixon: A Life,* 532. See also Ambrose, *Nixon: Ruin and Recovery,* 464–465; Ansom, *Exile.*

24. Quoted in Ambrose, *Nixon: Ruin and Recovery,* 459.

25. Quoted in ibid., 465.

26. Ansom, *Exile,* 63–64.

27. Quoted in Ambrose, *Nixon: Ruin and Recovery,* 470.

28. The quote is from *Newsweek,* 11 November 1974. See also Ansom, *Exile,* 73.

29. Ambrose, *Nixon: Ruin and Recovery,* 471–474; Ansom, *Exile,* 78–83.

30. The first quote is in Ansom, *Exile,* 84. The second is in Aitken, *Nixon: A Life,* 534–535.

31. Julie Nixon Eisenhower, *Pat Nixon: The Untold Story* (New York: Simon & Schuster, 1979).

32. Quoted in Ansom, *Exile,* 87.

33. Quoted in ibid., 90.

34. Ibid., 130–134.

35. Gerald R. Ford, *A Time to Heal: The Autobiography of Gerald R. Ford* (New York: Berkley Books, 1980), 348; Ambrose, *Nixon: Ruin and Recovery,* 489–491.

36. Quoted in Ansom, *Exile,* 150.

37. Aitken, *Nixon: A Life,* 536–537; Ansom, *Exile,* 95–96.

38. *Washington Post,* 10 January 1975; *Time,* 10 February 1975. See also Ansom, *Exile,* 92; Ambrose, *Nixon: Ruin and Recovery,* 475.

39. Ansom, *Exile,* 100–101.

40. David Frost, *"I Gave Them a Sword": Behind the Scenes of the Nixon Interviews* (New York: William Morrow, 1978), 13.

41. Ibid., 13–19.

42. Ansom, *Exile,* 112–115.

43. These details can be followed in Frost, *"I Gave Them a Sword,"* 20–85.

44. Ibid., 241–245; Elizabeth Drew, *"Frost/Nixon: A Dishonorable Distortion of History,"* *Huffington Post,* 14 December 2008, http://www.huffingtonpost.com; "The Nation: Nixon Talks," *Time,* 9 May 1977, http://www.time.com; Michael Janusinis, "Is *Frost/Nixon* True? Let's Ask PC Grad Jack Brennan—He Was There," *Providence Journal,* 23 January 2009, http://www.projo.com.

45. Elizabeth Day, "Madly in Love with Absolutely Everyone," *Telegraph,* 11 April 2005, http://www.telegraph.co.uk.

46. Ambrose, *Nixon: Ruin and Recovery.*

47. The quote is in Aitken, *Nixon: A Life,* 538.

48. Ibid., 537–538; Ambrose, *Nixon: Ruin and Recovery,* 512.

49. Ansom, *Exile,* 171–187. Ambrose, *Nixon: Ruin and Recovery,* 513.

50. Ambrose, *Nixon: Ruin and Recovery,* 516–517; James Barber, "Nixon's—Umm—'History,'" *New York Times,* 9 August 1978.

51. Nixon, *RN,* 761.

52. Ibid., 850.

53. Aitken, *Nixon: A Life,* 542.

54. Ansom, *Exile,* 200.

55. Ambrose, *Nixon: Ruin and Recovery,* 527–528.

56. Ralph Blumenthal, "Richard Nixon's Search for a New York Home," *New York Times,* 30 July 2008.

57. Quoted in Crowley, *Nixon Off the Record,* 20.

58. The quotes are in Richard Nixon, *The Real War* (New York: Warner Books, 1981), xiii, 184, and 187.

59. Ronald Steel, "Perfectly Clear," *New York Review of Books,* 26 June 1980.

60. Richard Nixon, *Leaders: Profiles and Reminiscences of Men Who Have Shaped the Modern World* (New York: Warner Books, 1983). On Nixon's remarks, see *New York Times,* 3 September 1982.

61. Ansom, *Exile,* 191–195.

62. Ibid., 195.

63. Ibid., 196–197.

64. Ibid.

65. Roy Reed, "Welcome for Nixon at Oxford Is Warm," *New York Times,* 1 December 1978; Nixon, *In the Arena,* 47–48.

66. Aitken, *Nixon: A Life,* 550.

67. Ibid., 552.

68. Robert Lindsey, "The Ex-President's Men Reunite at San Clemente," *New York Times,* 4 September 1979. See also H. R. Haldeman, *The Ends of Power* (New York: Dell, 1978); John Ehrlichman, *Witness to Power: The Nixon Years* (New York: Simon & Schuster, 1982); Ansom, *Exile,* 205–207.

69. Arnold D. Hirshon, "Recent Developments in the Accessibility of Presidential Papers and Other Presidential Historical Materials," *Government Publications Review* 6, no. 4 (1979): 343–357; Stuart Taylor Jr., "With 50 Suits Pending, Nixon Keeps Lawyers Busy," *New York Times,* 30 October 1980; "Nixon Sues on U.S. Control of Presidential Records," *New York Times,* 19 December 1980.

70. Ambrose, *Nixon: Ruin and Recovery,* 524–525 and 532; Ansom, *Exile,* 207–208.

71. *New York Times,* 8 March 1990.

72. Ansom, *Exile,* 201. John Herbers, "Nixon Views Carter: 'Shrewd' with 'Ruthless' Staff," *New York Times,* 8 September 1980.

73. Quoted in Ambrose, *Nixon: Ruin and Recovery,* 539–540; David Greenberg, "Nixon in American Memory," in *Institutions of Public Memory,* ed. Astrid M. Eckert (Washington, D.C.: German Historical Institute, 2007), 105.

74. Quoted in Ambrose, *Nixon: Ruin and Recovery,* 540.

75. Nixon, *In the Arena,* 79–80; Greenberg, "Nixon in American Memory," 105–106.

76. David M. Alpern, "The Legacy of Watergate," *Newsweek* 14 June 1982; Julie Baumgold, "Nixon's New Life in New York," *New York Magazine* 13 (9 June 1980); "Nixon's Long Road Back," *Newsweek,* 19 May 1986; Greenberg, *Nixon's Shadow,* 290–292. See also Nixon, *In the Arena,* 80–81; Greenberg, "Nixon in American Memory," 98–114.

77. Raymond K. Price, "Nixon's Reassessment Comes Early," in *The Nixon Presidency: Twenty-Two Intimate Perspectives on Richard M. Nixon,* ed. Kenneth W. Thompson (Lanham, Md.: University Press of America, 1982), 389.

78. Alpern, "Legacy of Watergate," 14 June 1982; Drew, *Richard M. Nixon,* 142; Ansom, *Exile,* 242–243. Gibbs and Duffy believe that Nixon exerted considerable influence on Reagan. My own reading suggests that Nixon's influence was more limited. Even they acknowledge that after 1987 it became frayed. Gibbs and Duffy, *The President's Club,* 355–365.

79. Ansom, *Exile,* 241–242.

80. Richard Nixon, *Real Peace: A Strategy for the West* (New York: Touchstone, 1983), esp. 9–10 and 36–37.

81. Richard Nixon, *No More Vietnams* (New York: Arbor House, 1985), esp. 212–237.

82. Richard Nixon, *1999: Victory without War* (New York: Simon & Schuster, 1988), esp. 66–97.

83. Nixon, *In the Arena,* 119–120 and 122–123.

84. Quoted in Ambrose, *Nixon: Ruin and Recovery,* 441. According to Ambrose, a lawsuit in 1990 revealed that Nixon had been indirectly involved with the sale of $180 million in military uniforms to Syria's ally, Iraq, and that John Brennan and John Mitchell, who acted as middlemen in the deal, had made handsome commissions. He suggests that the Syrians may have paid their high price for Nixon's town house because of his involvement in the deal. However, he acknowledges that this connection, or even the possibility that the former president may have received a commission for the deal, cannot be proven. For a description of the Saddlebrook estate, see Ansom, *Exile,* 243.

85. Nixon, *In the Arena,* 139.

86. Ibid., 49–51.

87. The first quote is in Ansom, *Exile,* 245; the second is from *New York Times,* 27 August 1981. See also Ambrose, *Nixon: Ruin and Recovery,* 147, 448–449.

88. *New York Times,* 3 and 5 September 1981, and 26 February 1982.

89. "Nixon Library to Start with Private Financing," *New York Times,* 2 February 1984.

90. "Nixon Library Opens with Pomp, Tributes," *Los Angeles Times,* 20 July 1990, http://www.latimes.com. See also Ambrose, *Nixon: Ruin and Recovery,* 576–809.

91. Crowley, *Nixon Off the Record;* Monica Crowley, *Nixon in Winter* (New York: Random House, 1998).

92. Crowley, *Nixon Off the Record,* 9. Of the presidents who succeeded him into the Oval Office, he was most critical of Jimmy Carter and George H. W. Bush. He viewed Bush as more a crisis manager than a visionary. He also called him the "lesser of the two evils" in the 1992 presidential campaign and criticized him for misjudging developments in the Soviet Union leading to its dissolution following the failed coup against Soviet leader Mikhael Gorbachev in 1991. Finally, he was angry that Bush refused to call on him for advice during the campaign. Ibid., esp. 43 and 96; Gibbs and Duffy, *The President's Club,* 383–394.

93. Crowley, *Nixon off the Record,* 168–169.

94. The quotes are in Richard Nixon, *Seize the Moment: America's Challenge in a One-Superpower World* (New York: Simon & Schuster, 1992), 33; Richard Nixon, *Beyond Peace* (New York: Random House, 1994), 18.

95. *New York Times,* 23 and 27 June 1993.

96. Ibid., 27 June 1993.

97. In a book on Nixon's image, Yale historian David Greenberg concludes, "In the end the polls and the historians and the purveyors of culture all revealed that the dark Nixon—whether seen as crook or conspirator, liar or Machiavellian, or some combination of the above—remained the most enduring identity. . . . The effort to judge Nixon on his entire life and career had to accept that no other president directed a criminal conspiracy

from the White House; that none so grievously traduced the Constitution; that none so eagerly abused his power; that none resigned under duress because of the magnitude and scope of his wrongdoing." Greenberg, *Nixon's Shadow,* 345.

98. The most recent poll of sixty-five of the nation's most prominent American historians, conducted by C-Span in 2009, placed Nixon twenty-seventh among forty-two presidents in the hierarchy of worst to great presidents. Even Nixon's efforts to establish himself as one of the nation's foremost experts on foreign policy were never entirely successful. As Greenberg also points out, "Academic scholars rarely cited his works. Unlike articles by foreign policy thinkers such as Samuel Huntington or Francis Fukuyama, Nixon's ideas provoked no debate." Ibid., 287 and 384.

99. James Cannon, *Time and Chance: Gerald Ford's Appointment with History* (New York: Harper Collins, 1994), 131.

100. Quoted in Cannon, *Time and Chance,* 175.

101. Ronald Brownstein, "The Selling of the Ex-President," *Los Angeles Times,* 15 February 1987. See also Stephanie Smith, *Former Presidents: Federal Pensions and Retirement Benefits* (Washington, D.C.: Library of Congress, updated 2008), 1.

102. Ford, *A Time to Heal,* 44.

103. Cannon, *Time and Chance,* 10.

104. Douglas Brinkley, *Gerald R. Ford* (New York: Times Books, 2007), 151. See also *New York Times,* 23 April 1981. Gibbs and Duffy again argue differently, and, in my opinion, unpersuasively. *The President's Club,* 328–329.

105. Cannon, *Time and Chance,* 237–238.

106. On the sale of Ford's Alexandria residence, see *New York Times,* 27 October 1981.

107. Ford, *A Time to Heal,* xiii–xiv.

108. Brownstein, "The Selling of the Ex-President."

109. Ibid.

110. Ibid.

111. Although this was only half of what Nixon received for his memoirs, the anticipated sales of Ford's memoirs were not nearly as high as those of Nixon, given the latter's notoriety because of Watergate.

112. Brownstein, "The Selling of the Ex-President." On the honoraria that Ford received, see also Laune Johnston and Robert McG. Thomas Jr., "Notes on People; Ford Keeping a Busy Schedule," *New York Times,* 4 May 1981. On the commemorative medals, see Updegrove, *Second Acts,* 121.

113. Jerald terHorst, "President Ford, Inc.," *Washington Post,* 29 May 1977; Brownstein, "The Selling of the Ex-President."

114. Quoted in Brownstein, "The Selling of the Ex-President."

115. *New York Times,* 2 February and 16 July 1981; 15 March and 10 May 1982; and 19 December 1983; Brownstein, "The Selling of the Ex-President."

116. Brownstein, "The Selling of the Ex-President."

117. *New York Times,* 16 and 21 February 1981.

118. Ibid., 19 December 1983.

119. Ibid., 3 March 1982 and 14 August 1983.

120. Ford, *A Time to Heal,* ix.

121. *New York Times,* 18 September 1981; Benardo and Weiss, *Citizen-in-Chief,* 100.

122. *New York Times,* 23 and 28 September 1981.

123. Quoted in *New York Times,* 19 September 1981. See also *New York Times,* 23 April 1981; "History of the Gerald R. Ford Library and Museum (1990)," http://www .fordlibrarymuseum.gov.

124. Ford, *A Time to Heal,* xv–xvi, xxx.

125. Haynes Johnson, "'Oil and Water' Mix on Air Force One: Funeral Flight United the Past Presidents," *Washington Post,* 10 October 1981; Douglas G. Brinkley, *The Unfinished Presidency: Jimmy Carter's Journey to the Nobel Peace Prize* (New York: Penguin, 1998), 67.

126. The quotes can be found in *New York Times,* 12 October 1981.

127. Quoted in Brinkley, *Unfinished Presidency,* 69.

128. Quoted in Mark Bixler, "Friendship Unites Carter and Ford," 21 February 2005, Cox News Service, http://www.oxfordpress.com.

129. The quote is from Cannon, *Time and Chance,* 74–75 and 88–89. See also Brinkley, *Gerald R. Ford,* 74–75.

130. Ford later called himself an enabler for allowing himself to drink with her at the end of a day or at social occasions despite knowing about her condition. The enabler remark is in Bob Greene, *Fraternity: A Journey in Search of Five Presidents* (New York: Crown, 2004), 222–223.

131. Betty Ford, *Betty: A Glad Awakening* (Garden City, N.Y.: Doubleday, 1987), esp. 1–28; Mike Lupica, "Betty Is Ford's Legacy: She Showed No Shame in the Alcohol, Cancer Battles," New York *Daily News,* 2 January 2007; John Robert Greene, *Betty Ford: Candor and Courage in the White House* (Lawrence: University Press of Kansas, 2004), 50–52; Deborah Blumenthal, "A Day in the Life of the Betty Ford Center," *New York Times,* 27 February 1987; "Betty Ford Center: Our History," http://www.bettyfordcenter .org.

132. Brinkley, *Unfinished Presidency,* 68–69; Greene, *Betty Ford,* 113; Scott Kaufman, *Rosalynn Carter: Equal Partner in the White House* (Lawrence: University Press of Kansas, 2007), esp. 150–151.

133. Quoted in Brinkley, *Unfinished Presidency,* 103; see also 118, 138–139.

134. Ibid., 104–105.

135. Jimmy Carter and Gerald Ford, eds., *American Agenda: Report to the Forty-First President of the United States of America* (Campo Hill, Pa.: Book-of-the-Month Club, 1989); R. W. Apple, "2 Ex-Presidents Advise Bush: Forget Vow and Raise Taxes," *New York Times,* 22 November 1988. See also Brinkley, *Unfinished Presidency,* 251–252.

136. Anne McIlree, "Clintons Pal Around with Fords in Colo.," *USA Today,* 16 August 1993; *New York Times,* 1 September 1993; Bill Clinton, *My Life* (New York: Knopf, 2004), 844, 906; Gibbs and Duffy, *The President's Club,* 426–427.

137. *New York Times,* 21 December 1998. For a full discussion of the communications between the White House and former president Ford leading to the joint Ford-Carter statement, see Gibbs and Duffy, *The President's Club,* 450–455.

138. Kenneth R. Bazinet, "Top Medal to Ex-Prez Ford," New York *Daily News,* 12 August 1999.

139. Mary McGrory, "Courage All Around," *Washington Post,* 13 May 2001.

140. Bob Woodward, "Ford Disagreed with Bush About Invading Iraq," *Washington Post,* 28 December 2006.

CHAPTER 13: CITIZEN/POLITICIAN OF THE WORLD

1. Brinkley, *Unfinished Presidency;* Burton I. Kaufman and Scott Kaufman, *The Presidency of James Earl Carter Jr.,* 2nd ed. (Lawrence: University Press of Kansas, 2006), 251–256.

2. Truman, *Mr. Citizen,* 117–126.

3. The first quote is from Marie Hecht, "Today's President," *Chicago Tribune,* 15 January 1977. The second and third are from Benardo and Weiss, *Citizen-in-Chief,* 3. See also "Advisor Role Urged for Ex-Presidents," *New York Times,* 12 January 1954.

4. Gerald R. Ford, "Personal Reflections on My Experience as a Former President," in Smith and Walch, *Farewell to the Chief,* 169.

5. Daniel J. Boorstin, "Saving a National Resource," in Smith and Walch, *Farewell to the Chief,* 139–145.

6. "Former Presidents in American Public Life: A Symposium," in ibid., 150. About the same time, an increasing number of Congress members began to complain of the growing cost of supporting ex-presidents as they lived longer and each new administration meant more funding for staffing and maintaining a new library and museum and for Secret Service protection. A flurry of legislation was introduced to cut back on presidential perks. Leading the charge was Florida senator Lawton Chiles, who ridiculed the new "era of the 'imperial' former presidency with lavish libraries, special staffs and benefits, around-the-clock Secret Service protection for life and other badges of privileges." Besides cuts and limitations on the perks for ex-presidents, he even proposed permitting the federal government a percentage of the royalties received on presidential memoirs. Indiana representative Andrew Jacobs went still further, recommending doing away with all benefits for former presidents because they were making so much money, they no longer needed special treatment. With not a little cynicism, he introduced the "Former Presidents Enough Is Enough and Taxpayers Relief Bill of 1983," which asked, "How many presidents can the American public afford at one time?" Despite the heated rhetoric in Congress, lawmakers made no major changes to the benefits of former presidents. The first quote, by Lawton Chiles, can be found at http://www.quotes.net; the second is in Jonathan Eig, "House Votes to Curb Ex-Presidents Funds," *Los Angeles Times,* 27 July 1985. See also Benardo and Weiss, *Citizen-in-Chief,* 59–61.

7. "President Carter's Farewell Address to the Nation," 14 January 1981, http://www.pbs.org.

8. Jimmy Carter, *Why Not the Best?* (Nashville, Tenn.: Broadman Press, 1975), 8.

9. Ibid., 60.

10. Ibid., 80.

11. Later, Carter wrote in a book about his senatorial campaign, "I was continually reminded by national and world events of these earliest days of my political life and the similar challenges that still confront people everywhere who search for justice, truth, human rights, and governments in which they can have confidence." Jimmy Carter, *Turning Point: A Candidate, a State, and a Nation Come of Age* (New York: Times Books, 1992), 43.

12. *Time,* 31 May 1971.

13. Jimmy Carter, *White House Diaries* (New York: Farrar, Straus and Giroux, 2010), 525–528.

14. Jimmy Carter and Rosalynn Carter, *Everything to Gain: Making the Most of the Rest of Your Life* (New York Random House, 1987), 9.

15. Godfrey Sperling Jr., "A Way Back for Jimmy Carter?" *Christian Science Monitor,* 31 August 1981.

16. The quote is from the British Broadcasting Corporation, "BBC Summary of World Broadcast," 4 September 1981. See also Brinkley, *Unfinished Presidency,* 61–63.

17. Brinkley, *Unfinished Presidency,* 141–142, 203–204, 232–234.

18. Godfrey Sperling Jr., "Jimmy Carter Takes a Look at '84 Race, Arms Race, Mideast," and Richard L. Strout, "Carter Sounds Warning about Declining Global Resources," *Christian Science Monitor,* 12 November 1982 and 3 June 1983; Tom Wicker, "Whatever Became of Jimmy Carter?," *Esquire,* July 1984.

19. Carter and Carter, *Everything to Gain,* 30–31.

20. Quoted in Howard Ousne, "Jimmy Carter Finds His Niche in Work," *Sydney Morning Herald,* 6 September 1986.

21. Ibid. For the mission statement of the Carter Center, see its "Waging Peace, Fighting Disease, Building Hope," and for a detailed chronology and history of the center, see its "Timeline and History of the Carter Center," both at http://www.cartercenter.org.

22. Quoted in Mary McGrory, "Lifeline: Good News in the Swampy Area of Little Black Briefing Book," *Washington Post,* 30 June 1983.

23. Quoted in Kai Bird, "The Very Model of an Ex-President," *Nation,* 12 November 1990. See also Sam Howe Verhovek, "Carter's Decade of Learning about the Poor," *New York Times,* 31 October 1987; Mark A. Uhlig, "Carter Applauds Nicaraguans on Election-Monitoring Plan," *New York Times,* 30 January 1990; Lee Hockstadter, "Carter Played Pivotal Role in Hours after Polls Closed," *Washington Post,* 27 February 1990; Sidney Blumenthal, "The Carter Constituency," *Washington Post,* 21 July 1988; Robert Pittman, "The Rehabilitation of Jimmy Carter," St. Petersburg *Times,* 30 October 1988.

24. Clinton is quoted in *USA Today,* 16 June 1994.

25. Carter's comments can be found in Douglas Jehl, "Carter His Own Emissary, Outpaces White House," *New York Times,* 20 June 1994; Lee Michael Katz, "Carter: 'Nuke Crisis Is Over,'" *USA Today,* 20 June 1994.

26. The quote is in Jehl, "Carter His Own Emissary." See also Brinkley, *Unfinished Presidency,* 409; Judy Keen, "Carter Mission Stirs Confusion/N. Korea Trip Causes Garbled U.S. Message," 20 June 1994; and Robert A. Rankin, "Carter's N. Korean Mission: Unclear. He Returned Home and Pronounced the Nuclear Crisis Over. His Critics Balked and President Clinton Said Not So Fast," *Philadelphia Inquirer,* 26 June 1994.

27. Thomas W. Lippman, "Once Again, Carter Plays Peacemaker; Former President Follows Efforts in North Korea with More Creative Diplomacy," *Washington Post,* 19 September 1994; Juan J. Walte, "11th-Hour Deal Caps a Day of Drama/Carter Rescues Clinton—Again," *USA Today,* 19 September 1994; "Merry Christmas Mr. Karadzic," *New Republic,* 9 and 16 January 1995.

29. Steven Goldstein, "Carter as Diplomat: Blessed Peacemaker or Pawn of Pariahs? The Former President Continues to Get Results on His Diplomatic Missions, This Time in Bosnia. The Criticism Is Continuing as Well," *Philadelphia Inquirer,* 25 December 1994.

30. Updegrove, *Second Acts,* 161.

31. Brinkley, *Unfinished Presidency,* 480.

32. Jimmy Carter, *Palestine: Peace Not Apartheid* (New York: Simon & Schuster, 2006); Jimmy Carter, *White House Diary* (New York: Farrar, Straus and Giroux, 2010);

Jimmy Carter, *The Blood of Abraham: Insights into the Middle East* (New York: Houghton Mifflin, 1986); Jimmy Carter, *We Can Have Peace in the Holy Land: A Plan That Will Work* (New York: Simon & Schuster, 2009); Jimmy Carter, *Keeping Faith: Memoirs of a President* (New York: Bantam Books, 1982); Jimmy Carter, *The Hornet's Nest* (New York: Simon & Schuster, 2003); Jimmy Carter, *The Little Baby Snoogle-Fleejer* (New York: Times Books, 1995); Jimmy Carter, *Always a Reckoning and Other Poems* (New York: Times Books, 1995); Jimmy Carter, *An Hour before Daylight: Memories of a Rural Boyhood* (New York: Simon & Schuster, 2001); Jimmy Carter, *A Remarkable Mother* (New York: Simon & Schuster, 2008); Jimmy Carter, *The Virtues of Aging* (New York: Ballantine, 1998); Jimmy Carter, *Living Faith* (New York: Times Books, 1996); Jimmy Carter, *An Outdoor Journal: Adventures and Reflections* (New York: Bantam Books, 1988).

33. The first quote is in Jonathan Freeland, "I Have Moral Authority," *Guardian*, 7 June 2008, http://www.guardian.co.uk. The second quote is in Goldstein, "Carter as Diplomat."

34. Quoted in Freeland, "I Have Moral Authority."

35. Quoted in Jeffrey Trachtenberg, "I, Jimmy," *Wall Street Journal*, 25–26 February 2006; Curtis Suplee, "The Memoirs Megahype: Carter and Jordan Will Tell You All About It," *Washington Post*, 19 August 1982.

36. Godfrey Sperling Jr., "Is There a Gleam in Jimmy Carter's Eye?," *Christian Science Monitor*, 29 November 1982.

37. Quoted in Trachtenberg, "I, Jimmy." See also Alice Digilio, "The Birth of a Book Salesman; Jimmy Carter Wins With the Sellers, Who Hope His Memoirs Will Be Just What the Readers Want," *Washington Post*, 1 June 1982.

38. For other reviews and comments about the book, see, for example, Robert G. Kaiser, "Wasn't Carter the President Who Said He'd Never Lie To Us?," *Washington Post*, 7 November 1982; Christopher Lehmann-Haupt, "Books of the Times," *New York Times*, 3 November 1982; Suplee, "Memoirs Megahype"; Sperling, "Is There a Gleam?"

39. Quoted in Brinkley, *Unfinished Presidency*, 50; Trachtenberg, "I, Jimmy."

40. The other two finalists were Jean Edward Smith for his 2001 biography, *Grant*, and David McCullough, who was awarded the prize for his 2001 biography of John Adams.

41. Jimmy Carter, *An Hour before Daylight;* Roy Reed, "Miss Lillian's Boy," *New York Times*, 11 February 2001; Gerald F. Kreyche, review of *An Hour before Daylight*, Society for the Advancement of Education, May 2001, http://findarticles.com/p/articles/mi_m1272/is_2672_129/ai_74572256/.

42. Jimmy Carter, *Our Endangered Values: America's Moral Crisis* (New York: Simon & Schuster, 2005).

43. Quoted in Carter, *Palestine*, 189.

44. Ibid., 206. See also Carter, *Blood of Abraham*, 195–208.

45. *New York Times*, 12 January 2007.

46. Carter had earlier rejected an invitation to debate Professor Dershowitz at Brandeis.

47. *New York Times*, 24 January 2007; *Washington Post*, 24 January 2007.

48. *New York Times*, 24 January 2007; *Washington Post*, 24 January 2007.

49. *New York Times*, 24 January 2007.

50. Michael D. Evans, "Jimmy Carter—We Can Have Peace (Without You) in the Holy Land," *Jerusalem Post*, 26 August 2009.

51. Mortimer B. Zuckerman, "The Damage of Jimmy Carter," *U.S. News and World Report,* 28 April and 5 May 2008. See also Carter, *We Can Have Peace,* 117–144.

52. Hilary Leila Krieger, "Jimmy Carter Casts Uneasy Shadow over Jewish Support at Democratic Convention," *Jerusalem Post,* 22 August 2008, and James Gordon Meek, "Carter Talks Up His Hamas Chat," New York *Daily News,* 14 April 2008.

53. Krieger, "Jimmy Carter Casts Uneasy Shadow"; Meek, "Carter Talks Up His Hamas Chat."

54. Jason Koutsoukis, "People of Gaza Treated Like Animals, says Jimmy Carter," Sydney *Morning Herald,* 18 June 2009. For an account of the relationship between Bush 41 and Bush 43 during the latter's presidency, mostly from the perspective of Bush 43, that is largely in accord with what has been stated in these pages, see ibid., 475–488.

55. Carter, *We Can Have Peace,* xix.

56. Ibid., xix, xx, xxiii–iv.

57. St. Petersburg *Times,* 24 December 2009.

58. A number of commentators have taken issue, for example, with his efforts to get the UN Security Council to vote against the efforts of President George H. W. Bush and the U.S. and Arab coalition to eject Saddam Hussein before the first gulf war of 1990–1991. They have also criticized him for being naive in his dealings with foreign leaders, as in North Korea, where, notwithstanding its promises to Carter to give up its nuclear arms program, it has secretly gone ahead with the development of a nuclear weapon. The same naivety applied to the collapse of the cease-fire in the Balkans during the Clinton administration, which he blamed not on the malignity of the Serbs but on Clinton and his European counterparts. Finally, they have also continued to raise questions about how a former leader, who has done more than any other president before him to promote human rights, has been willing to deal with some of the world's worst violators of human rights and international law.

59. Freeland, "I Have Moral Authority"; David Greenberg, "Good Jimmy, Bad Jimmy; The Former President Reminds Us of His Accomplishments since Leaving Office," *Washington Post,* 14 October 2007.

60. "Jimmy Carter's Opinions," Washington *Times,* 23 May 2007; *New York Times,* 11 October 2007.

61. All the comments are from David Saltonstall, "Dem's Fighting Words. Jimmy Carter Gets Flak for Racism Charge—Even from White House," New York *Daily News,* 17 September 2009.

62. Habitat for Humanity, "2010 Jimmy and Rosalynn Carter Work Project" and "August 2011: Community," both at http://www.habitat.org.

63. Jimmy Carter, *Beyond the White House: Waging Peace, Fighting Disease, Building Hope* (New York: Simon & Schuster, 2007), 158–177; "Nigeria: Gowon Hails Cross River on Guinea Worm Eradication," *Africa News,* 10 May 2010.

64. Other organizations that cooperated with the Carter Center have included the River Blindness Foundation and Lions Club International. Carter, *Beyond the White House,* 185–192. See also the Carter Center, "Onchocerciasis Elimination Program of the Americas," http://www.cartercenter.org.

65. Carter, *Beyond the White House,* 185–220.

66. Bloomington *Pantagraph,* 3 October 1999; Lou Cannon, *President Reagan: The Role of a Lifetime* (New York: Simon & Schuster, 1991); William F. Buckley, *The Reagan I Knew* (New York: Basic Books, 2008). For a theme similar to Cannon's, see also Bob

Schieffer and Gary Paul Gates, *The Acting President* (New York: E. P. Dutton, 1989). On the mystery surrounding Reagan, see Alessandra Stanley, "The Reagan We May Never Know," *New York Times,* 5 February 2011.

67. Interestingly, one of his favorite presidents was Calvin Coolidge, who followed a schedule and favored the same small-town values that Reagan did. On Reagan's admiration for Coolidge, see Richard Reeves, *President Reagan, the Triumph of Imagination* (New York: Simon & Schuster, 2005), 79.

68. Reagan's son, Ron Reagan, has even traced his father's worldview to his experience as a lifeguard. "He grew up seeing himself as somebody who saved people's lives," he remarked in 2011. "I think that carried through into his later years as well, the sort of roles he liked to play in movies. He wanted to be the hero." Quoted in Stanley, "The Reagan We May Never Know."

69. Quoted in Garry Wills, *Reagan's America: Innocence at Home* (Garden City, N.Y.: Doubleday, 1987), 55.

70. The quote is from Jules Tygiel, *Ronald Reagan and the Triumph of American Conservatism* (New York: Pearson Education, 2006), 23. See also Ronald Reagan, *An American Life* (New York: Simon & Schuster, 1990), 19.

71. Reagan, *American Life,* 24–25 and 31.

72. Isaiah Berlin, *The Hedgehog and the Fox: Tolstoy's View of History* (Chicago: Ivan R. Dee, 1993).

73. On these points, see Rupert Cornwell, "Ronald Reagan, 1911–2004: A President Whose Optimism Earned Him a Place in History," London *Independent,* 7 June 2004. See also Ron Reagan, *My Father at 100: A Memoir* (New York: Viking Penguin, 2011), 189.

74. In his highly controversial 1999 biography of Reagan, Edmund Morris, who was given unprecedented access to the Oval Office during Reagan's second term, was so baffled by the president that he decided the only way he could write about him was to create a fictional narrator who eyewitnessed different events during Reagan's life. Morris later commented that questioning the president was like "talking into a large, rather cool cave." Edmund Morris, *Dutch: A Memoir of Ronald Reagan* (New York: Random House, 1999), 579. On Ron Reagan's comment, see R. D. Haldenfelds, "Ronald Reagan Puzzle Fits Together on PBS: Documentary Connects Many Pieces in the Life of a Contradictory Man," Akron *Beacon Journal,* 23 February 1998. All the remaining quotes are from Stanley, "The Reagan We May Never Know."

75. Quoted in Harry Levins, "The Great Communicator Ronald Reagan, 1911–2004," St. Louis *Post-Dispatch,* 6 June 2004.

76. Reagan, *American Life,* 31. See also Anastasia Hendrix, "Trouble at Home for Family Values Advocate," San Francisco *Chronicle,* 6 June 2004.

77. Reagan, *American Life,* 20–21 and 29.

78. Ibid., 71–76; Tygiel, *Ronald Reagan,* xi, 28–30.

79. Reagan, *American Life,* 89.

80. Tygiel, *Ronald Reagan,* xii, 35–52.

81. Ibid., 32–33 and 53–54.

82. Reagan was closer to Maureen than Michael, but he and Jane never became close to either of them. Reagan simply did not know how to share affection, even with his children, and Jane was too busy with her budding acting career. The children were raised by nannies and spent most of their young years in boarding schools. Ibid., 70–75. See also Hendrix, "Trouble at Home for Family Values Advocate."

83. Tygiel, *Ronald Reagan.*

84. Cannon, *President Reagan,* 894n144.

85. Quoted in Haynes Johnson, "Reagan's Charm Is Wearing Thin," St. Petersburg *Times,* 29 March 1990.

86. Lou Cannon, "Five Presidents and a Place in History: Past Chiefs and First Ladies Dedicate $57 Million Reagan Library," *Washington Post,* 5 November 1991.

87. "Excerpts from Reagan's Testimony on the Iran-Contra Affair" and "The Nation; Reagan Testifies for Better or Worse," *New York Times,* 23 and 25 February 1990.

88. Johnson, "Reagan's Charm Is Wearing Thin"; See also "Lawyer Says Reagan Told Aide to Give False Data," *New York Times,* 7 September 1989.

89. David Johnston, "North Says Reagan Knew of the Iran Deal," *New York Times,* 20 October 1991. Poindexter's conviction was later thrown out on appeal, and Weinberger was pardoned by President George H. W. Bush in December 1992, a month before he left office.

90. Kitty Kelley, *Nancy Reagan: The Unauthorized Biography* (New York: Simon & Schuster, 1991); Maureen Dowd, "All that Glitters Is Not Real, Book on Nancy Reagan Says," *New York Times,* 7 April 1991.

91. All the quotes are from Desda Moss, "Reagans' Daughter: My Mother Abused Me," *USA Today,* 29 April 1992. See also Patti Davis, *The Way I See It: An Autobiography* (New York: G. P. Putnam's Sons, 1992) esp. 33–42.

92. Kelley, *Nancy Reagan,* 401; Donald Regan, *For the Record: From Wall Street to Washington* (New York: Harcourt Education, 1988), esp. 66–79 and 288–292. Nancy, who was already being referred to as the "dragon lady" for her alleged power as first lady and had been widely criticized for her lavish spending on the redecorating of the White House, had not helped her own cause when she published in 1989 her own memoirs, *My Turn: The Memoirs of Nancy Reagan,* which, as its title suggested, was her effort to strike back at those whom she regarded as her tormenters during her husband's administration. Those persons included virtually every one of Reagan's top aides, including Vice President George Bush, Chief of Staff Donald Regan, Attorney General Edwin Meese, Deputy Chief of Staff Michael Deaver, and the director of the Office of Management, David Stockman. Denying the "frustration of frequently being misunderstood," she also said she was not "as bad or extreme in my power or my weakness, as I was depicted." But she also acknowledged that she sometimes changed her husband's schedule according to the advice of her astrologer and admitted to not being as good a mother as she might have been. See Nancy Reagan with William Novak, *My Turn: The Memoirs of Nancy Reagan* (New York: Random House, 1989). Her book, for which she reportedly received a $2 million advance, was broadly panned by the reviewers as being self-righteous and inappropriate for a first lady. It also made her look hypersensitive, captious, emotionally frail, and, notwithstanding her denials to the contrary, more in control of her husband than considered normal for first ladies. Her admission that she relied on an astrologer and that she could have been a better mother also raised questions about her emotional instability. Finally, as one reviewer pointed out, her book was "one long confirmation of things reporters thought were going on at the Reagan White House but weren't certain about." Fred Barnes, "Partner Shots," *New York Times,* 19 November 1989, and R. W. Apple Jr., "Books of the Times: Nancy Reagan Tells Her Side of the Stories," *New York Times,* 1 November 1989.

93. *New York Times,* 15 April 1990; Gary Sick, *October Surprise: America's Hostages in Iran and the Election of Ronald Reagan* (New York: Random House, 1991).

94. *New York Times,* 4 May 1991.

95. Linda Ellerbee, "Sources Vow Reagan Cut Deal for Timely Release of Hostages," Seattle *Post-Intelligencer,* 22 April 1991; Eric Reguly, "Looking for Truth in a Netherworld," Toronto *Financial Post,* 7 May 1991; Allan Robinson and Martin Mittelstaedt, "Reagan Associate Denies Tie to Hostage Scheme Sources: Dismissed as 'Liars'," *Globe and Mail* (Canada), 13 December 1991.

96. Cannon, *President Reagan.* Michael Gardner, "Starring Ronald Reagan," *Washington Post,* 21 April 1991.

97. Cannon, *President Reagan,* 837.

98. Ibid.

99. Ronald Wilson Reagan, "Farewell Address (January 11, 1989)," http://miller center.org.

100. See, for example, Lou Cannon, "Bittersweet Trip for the Reagans: 'A Time for Tears' Comes before the Return Home," *Washington Post,* 21 January 1989, and Sally Ann Stewart, "Ronald Reagan: 'I'm Still Trying to Get Things Done,'" *USA Today,* 22 June 1989.

101. "Reagan Visits Future Office," *New York Times,* 28 December 1988; Cannon, *President Reagan,* 527–528.

102. Tom Bower, "Spectrum: Welcome to My Fan Club," *London Times,* 5 March 1987. See also Benardo and Weiss, *Citizen-in-Chief,* 102–105.

103. Benardo and Weiss, *Citizen-in-Chief,* 105.

104. Ibid., 105–106.

105. "Reagan Library Is Edging Closer to Reality," *New York Times,* 4 September 1988.

106. Ibid.

107. Cannon, "Five Presidents and a Place in History."

108. Ibid.

109. Many in the industry also thought his purpose in allowing historian Edmund Morris to chronicle his life and in giving him virtually unfettered access to the Oval Office was to have a professional historian and biographer write a volume that would substitute for his own autobiography. Edwin McDowell, "Reagan Agrees to Write Memoirs," *New York Times,* 26 January 1989.

110. Lou Cannon, *Reagan* (New York: G. P. Putnam's Sons, 1982), 353–354.

111. Edwin McDowell, "Reagan Agrees to Write Memoirs," *New York Times,* 26 July 1989; Benardo and Weiss, *Citizen-in-Chief,* 68.

112. The speed with which the 743-page book was written and published at a time when Reagan was engaged in other activities (less than two years from the time of the contract) and Reagan's generous acknowledgment of Lindsey's assistance (he "was with me every step of the way") support this view.

113. Reagan, *American Life,* 92.

114. *Time,* 26 June 1989. See also Updegrove, *Second Acts,* 185–186.

115. "Reagan Lauds Soviet Reforms," Toronto *Star,* 18 September 1990.

116. William Safire, "Recruiting Reagan," *New York Times,* 11 May 1989.

117. What made matters even worse was that the total amount involved in Reagan's deal with Fujisankei was closer to $6 or $8 million than $2 million because the arrangement also involved a private jet, first-class accommodations at some of Japan's finest hotels and resorts, and other perquisites for the former president and twenty others who were

allowed to go with him to Japan. Steven R. Weisman, "Reagan Urges Japan to Look Past Its Success," *New York Times,* 21 October 1989.

118. Safire, "Recruiting Reagan."

119. The Observer, "Colourless Leader with Heart of Gold," Sydney *Morning Herald,* 11 July 1989.

120. Weisman, "Reagan Urges Japan to Look Past Its Success."

121. Both Weisman's and Reagan's remarks are in Steven R. Weisman, "Reagan Warns Japanese on Trade," *New York Times,* 28 October 1989.

122. Terence Smith, "The Reversals of History," *New York Times,* 5 November 1989.

123. Lou Cannon, "The 8 Decades of Ronald Reagan: On His Birthday, He's Hard on Saddam, Soft on Maggie and Still Sweet on Nancy," *Washington Post,* 7 February 1991.

124. *New York Times,* 19 August 1992.

125. Quoted in Ronald Reagan, "Why I'm for the Brady Bill," *New York Times,* 29 March 1991. See also Tom Squitieri, "Reagan Gives Brady Bill Backers a Boost," *USA Today,* 29 March 1991.

126. Buckley, *The Reagan I Knew,* 222–223.

127. Reagan, *My Father at 100,* 205.

128. Ibid., 214–216.

129. Cannon, *President Reagan,* 709–710.

130. Reagan, *My Father at 100,* 217.

131. Reagan's statement, written in longhand, is reproduced in Morris, *Dutch,* 665–666.

132. Reagan, *My Father at 100,* 220. See also Reeves, *President Reagan,* 487.

133. John Hiscock, "Reagan's Decline Severe as Alzheimer's Strengths Grip," *Vancouver Sun,* 6 September 1997.

134. Reagan, *My Father at 100,* 220–221.

135. Dave Saltonstall, "Reagan OK after Surgery," New York *Daily News,* 14 January 2001.

EPILOGUE: BUSH AND CLINTON

1. In 1988, however, he had an autobiography ghostwritten for his presidential campaign. George Bush (with Victor Gold), *Looking Forward: An Autobiography* (New York: Bantam, 1988).

2. Hugh Sidey, "The Presidency: The Grandfather in Chief," *Time,* 28 March 1994.

3. Peter Schweizer and Rochelle Schweizer, *The Bushes: Portrait of a Dynasty* (New York: Doubleday, 2004), 25 and 33–35; Kevin Phillips, *American Dynasty: Aristocracy, Fortune, and the Politics of Deceit in the House of Bush* (New York: Penguin, 2004), 23–24; Herbert Parmet, *George Bush: The Life of a Lone-Star Yankee* (New York: Scribner's, 1997), 23, 34–35.

4. Bush, *Looking Forward,* xvii and 25. See also Parmet, *George Bush,* 23, 30–32.

5. Parmet, *George Bush,* 46–61.

6. Bush, *Looking Forward,* 46.

7. "The George W. Bush Childhood Home: Midland in the 1950s," http://www.bush childhoodhome.org; Parmet, *George Bush,* 69–73.

8. Bush, *Looking Forward,* 66–67; Parmet, *George Bush,* 84–85.

9. Schweizer and Schweizer, *The Bushes,* 143–146.

10. Ibid., 174–179; Tom Wicker, *George Herbert Walker Bush* (New York: Penguin, 2004), 19–20.

11. John Robert Greene, *The Presidency of George Bush* (Lawrence: University Press of Kansas, 2000), 19; Wicker, *George Herbert Walker Bush,* 27.

12. Timothy Naftali, *George H. W. Bush* (New York: Times Books, 2007), 26–27.

13. Hugh Liedtke, for example, was interested in drilling for oil in China, and Bush later helped arrange a meeting between Liedtke and Chinese officials. Shortly thereafter, Liedtke was granted the first drilling rights in China. Schweizer and Schweizer, *The Bushes,* 140.

14. Quoted in Greene, *Presidency of George Bush, 37.*

15. Quoted in Barbara Bush, *Reflections: Life after the White House* (New York: Lisa Drew/Scribner, 2003), 6. See also Roberto Suro, "The Inauguration: Bowing Out: Citizen Bush Goes Home and Says He Is Satisfied," *New York Times,* 21 January 1993.

16. On the honoraria that George and Barbara Bush received, see *Parade,* 7 December 2008, and Updegrove, *Second Acts,* 219.

17. Sidey, "Grandfather in Chief."

18. George Bush, Inaugural Address, 20 January 1989, http://www.barteby.com.

19. Quoted in Parmet, *George Bush,* 348.

20. In his third State of the Union Address before Congress on 29 January 1991, for example, he remarked, "We have within our reach the promise of a renewed America. We can find meaning and reward by serving some purpose higher than ourselves—a shining purpose, the illumination of a thousand points of light." "George H. W. Bush's State of the Union Address, Envisioning One Thousand Points of Light," 29 January 1991, http://www.infoplease.com.

21. Quoted in Sidey, "Grandfather in Chief."

22. Ibid.

23. "Our History," http://www.pointsoflight.org.

24. Barbara Bush, *Reflections,* 59.

25. Ibid., 50 and 65.

26. Ibid., 11–13; Updegrove, *Second Acts,* 219.

27. Barbara Bush, *Barbara Bush: A Memoir* (New York: Charles Scribner's Sons, 1994), 250.

28. Ibid., 250–251, 311–360, and 398–399; Barbara Bush, *Reflections,* 17, 59, and 184–185; "The Barbara Bush Foundation for Family Literacy," http://www.barbarabush foundation.com; Jennifer Harper, "Literacy at Heart of Bush Legacy: President's Mom Raised $30 Million since 1989," Washington *Times,* 19 May 2008; and Allan Peppard, "Benefit Moves to Meyerson," Dallas *Morning News,* 3 August 2003.

29. Michael Duffy, "Bill Clinton and George H. W. Bush," *Time,* 30 April 2006.

30. ABC News, "People of the Year: Bill Clinton and George H. W. Bush," 27 December 2005, http://abcnews.go.com.

31. Quoted in Benardo and Weiss, *Citizen-in-Chief,* 258. See also BBC Monitoring South Asia, "Former U.S. Presidents Arrive in Sri Lanka, 20 February 2005."

32. Quoted in Larry Eichel, "Ex-Presidents to Share Honor; George H. W. Bush and Bill Clinton Were Named Recipients of the Liberty Medal," Philadelphia *Inquirer,* 30 June 2006; Duffy, "Bill Clinton and George H. W. Bush."

33. Quoted in Katy Steinmetz, "Beltway Bash: A Glamorous Night of Tribute to George H. W. Bush," *Time,* 22 March 2011.

34. Sheldon Alberts, "What's with Bill and George? Clinton, Bush Getting Chummy," Montreal *Gazette,* 9 April 2005.

35. "Bill Clinton and George W. Bush Friends," *Right Across the Atlantic,* http://www.theatlanticright.com/.

36. Quoted in Hugh Sidey, "A Former President's Mad Dash to 80," *Time,* 7 June 2004.

37. Robert Kaiser, "Royal Family's Wealth Invested in West," and Michael Abramowitz, "Bush 41 in China: Kinda Like Old Times; Former President Is Back on Familiar, if Changed, Ground," *Washington Post,* 18 February 2002 and 11 August 2008; Phillips, *American Dynasty,* 291–292; Benardo and Weiss, *Citizen-in-Chief,* 68–71. For a good review of Barbara Bush's *Reflections,* see "Books of the Times: A Bush's Keen Eye on Other Bushes," *New York Times,* 20 October 2003.

38. Bush's remarks are in Michael Duffy, "10 Questions for George H. W. Bush," *Time,* 28 April 2011. See also Dr. Zebra, "The Health and Medical History of President George Bush," http://www.doctorzebra.com. On Bush's grin, see Greene, *Fraternity,* 150–151.

39. Quoted in Updegrove, *Second Acts,* 221; see also Barbara Bush, *Reflections,* 166–167.

40. The first quote is in Thomas M. DeFrank, "W to Poppy: You're Bonkers to Sky-drive!," New York *Daily News,* 12 January 2009. The second quote is in Duffy, "10 Questions for George H. W. Bush." See also Barbara Bush, *Reflections,* 285; Matthew Cooper, "Cue Parachute for Bush 41," *Time,* 12 April 2004. See also Sidey, "Former President's Mad Dash."

41. Quoted in Benardo and Weiss, *Citizen-in-Chief,* 108.

42. Douglas Martin, "Michael Halbouty, Oilman of Legend, Dies at 95," *New York Times,* 14 November 2004.

43. By 2004, that cost had increased to $42 million. In 2003, the 1986 legislation was amended to require foundations to raise an endowment equal to 40 percent of the cost of the building. See "Who Should Pay for Presidential Posterity?," *New York Times,* 10 June 2004.

44. "Who Should Pay for Presidential Posterity?," "George Bush Presidential Library Foundation—General Information," and "George Bush Presidential Library Foundation—Mission Statetment," all at http://www.georgebushfoundation.org; Bush School of Government and Public Service at Texas A&M University, http://bush.tamku.edu; Benardo and Weiss, *Citizen-in-Chief,* 108–109; Updegrove, *Second Acts,* 221–222.

45. The first quote is from Schweizer and Schweizer, *The Bushes,* 420. The second is in Naftali, *George H. W. Bush,* 158.

46. Quoted in Schweizer and Schweizer, *The Bushes,* 426.

47. He and Jeb also became the first siblings to govern two states since Nelson and Winthrop Rockefeller were governors of New York and Arkansas from 1967 to 1971. Comparisons even began to be made in the media between the Kennedy and Bush dynasties; ibid., 451–457; "The 1998 Elections: The Nation—Party Leaders; George W. and Jeb Bush are Easily Elected Governors in Texas and Florida," *New York Times,* 4 November 1998; J. Scott Orr and Robert Cohen, "The New American Dynasty: The Bushes Have Eclipsed the Kennedys, Tafts, and Adamses to Become the No. 1 Political Family in U.S. History," Montreal *Gazette,* 14 November 2004.

48. "George Sr. Touts a Third Bush," *Daily Telegraph* (Australia), 6 January 2009.

49. See, for example, Jacob Weisberg, "The Misunderestimated Man," *Slate,* 7 May 2004, http://www.slate.com; Jacob Weisberg, *The Bush Tragedy* (New York: Random House, 2007), esp. xv–xxvii. In addition, see Doug Wead, "Bush Completes Father's Unfinished Business," *USA Today,* 16 June 2003; Alan Brinkley, "In Search of Bush," *New York Times,* 2 March 2008; Charles Truehart, "Oedipus Bush, Slate's Jacob Weisberg Puts President on Couch," *Bloomberg News,* 15 November 2008, http://www.bloomberg.com.

50. George H. W. Bush and Brent Scowcroft, *A World Transformed* (New York: Knopf, 1998), 489.

51. Hugh Sidey, "The Presidency: What Makes Dad Clench His Jaw," *Time,* 16 September 2002.

52. Bob Woodward, *Plan of Attack* (New York: Simon & Schuster, 2004), 421.

53. Ibid.; Sheryl Gay Stalberg, "First Father: Tough Times on Sidelines," *New York Times,* 8 September 2007; Hugh Sidey, "They're Talking About . . . Our Kid," *Time,* 19 December 2004.

54. The first quote is in Stalberg, "First Father." The second can be found in Thomas M. Defrank, "One Proud Poppy, but . . . W. Follies Mar Legacy, Ex-Prez's Aides Gripe," New York *Daily News,* 11 January 2009. The third quote is in Peter Baker, "'I'm Doing Fine,' President Tells Worried Father," *Washington Post,* 13 February 2007.

55. Then there were the numerous honors that Bush 41 received, such as the commissioning in 2009 of the U.S.S. *George H. W. Bush,* the last of the Nimitz-class aircraft carriers. The commissioning ceremony capped off a week of ceremonies that the eighty-four-year-old former president called "the last great event" of his life. Thomas M. Dfrank, "Prez Salutes Dad Aboard Mighty Ship Sailing with H. W. Legacy," New York *Daily News,* 11 January 2009.

56. "Obama Pays Homage to Elder Bush," Dallas *Morning News,* 17 October 2009.

57. Although one can legitimately argue the relative merits of Carter's and Bush's different approaches to their post-presidential years, it is simply wrong to suggest, as at least one historian has done, that Bush's "post-presidential years have not been especially notable except for his having become, along with John Adams, the father of another president." Max J. Skidmore, *After the White House: Former Presidents as Private Citizens* (New York: Palgrave Macmillan, 2004), 154.

58. Because Clinton was born less than nine months after Blythe had returned from military service in Europe and been discharged, and because he was much smarter than either of his parents or other members of his family, at least one historian has speculated that he was really the illegitimate son of someone whom his mother had dated. She has vehemently denied these accusations, maintaining that her son was simply born prematurely. However, according to the nurse, he was "full term, weighing seven and a half pounds when he was born." On this point, see especially Nigel Hamilton, *Bill Clinton: An American Journey, Great Expectations* (New York: Random House, 2003), 33–34.

59. Ibid., 14–33, 35–44. David Maraniss, *First in His Class: A Biography of Bill Clinton* (New York: Simon & Schuster, 1995), 37–38.

60. Maraniss, *First in His Class,* 218.

61. Ibid., 11–15 and 41–47.

62. Ibid., 42, 66, 80, 153.

63. By this time, a lottery system had gone into effect, and Nixon was beginning to withdraw American forces from Vietnam, so fewer men were being drafted. As it happened, Clinton also drew a high lottery number that made it almost certain he would not

be drafted. That said, it is also clear that Clinton had real doubts about the justifiability and morality of the Vietnam War. He was also bothered by the fact that many of his school-mates from Arkansas were serving in Vietnam, and that one of his closest friends from Hot Springs had been killed in the war. As a result, he was conflicted about his decision to avoid the draft and went into a deep depression after he received his draft notice.

64. One of Clinton's biographers, Nigel Hamilton, who has emphasized Clinton's uncontrollable sexual appetite, has even contended that their marriage in 1975 was one of convenience. According to Hamilton, Hillary was aware of Clinton's libido and ongo-ing sexual licentiousness but decided to marry him nevertheless, convinced that he would become president of the United States someday and that she would be an important player in his administration. She insisted from Clinton only that she come first in his life and that he not embarrass her. Hamilton, *Bill Clinton*. See also Carl Bernstein, *A Woman in Charge: The Life of Hillary Rodham Clinton* (New York: Vintage Books, 2008), esp. 8–9 and 88–97. While agreeing with Hamilton that Hillary understood Clinton's sexual compulsions when she married him and believed that he was going to be president of the United States someday, Bernstein presents a much more nuanced account of the relationship between Bill and Hillary than Hamilton, arguing, for example, that they married for love, not sim-ply for convenience. Hillary Clinton maintains that she didn't "remember thinking Bill would be president until years after she married him." On Hillary's account of her relation-ship with Bill before marrying him, see Hillary Rodham Clinton, *Living History* (New York: Simon & Schuster, 2003), 52–75.

65. Hamilton, *Bill Clinton,* 233–243. Bernstein, *A Woman in Charge,* 27, 32, 36, 43–45, 86, 104, 260, and 308–309.

66. Christopher Marquis with Michael Moss, "A Clinton In-Law Received $400,000 in 2 Pardon Cases," and David Johnston and Don Van Natta Jr., "The Clinton Pardons: The Lobbying; Clinton's Brother Pursued Clemency Bids for Friends," *New York Times,* 22 and 23 February 2001.

67. Alison Leigh Cowan, "Plotting a Pardon; Rich Cashed in a World of Chits to Win Pardon," *New York Times,* 11 April 2001; Sally Bedell Smith, *For Love of Politics: Bill and Hillary Clinton—The White House Years* (New York: Random House, 2007), 411, 437–438, and 449.

68. The quotes are from Smith, *For Love of Politics,* 453. See also Clinton, *My Life,* 940–944.

69. Carl Huse with Joyce Walder, "Clintons Agree to Reimburse 27 Gift Givers," and Christopher Marquis, "Clintons Will Return Any Gifts Found to Belong to White House," *New York Times,* 3 and 6 February 2001.

70. Eun Lee Koh, "Neighborhood Report: Harlem; At a Now-Famous Harlem Build-ing, a Little Fish Loses Out to a Big One"; Amy Waldman, "In Harlem, a Hero's Welcome for New Neighbor Clinton"; David W. Dunlap, "Clinton Office Is Furnished Off the Shelf in Nod to Cost," *New York Times,* 4 March 2001 and 21 and 31 July 2001.

71. Although a judge had granted President Clinton's motion that Jones's lawsuit should be dismissed because she was not able to show that she had suffered any damages, Jones appealed her suit to the United States court of appeals. The president agreed to pay her $850,000 (about the cost of her legal fees) in exchange for her dropping her appeal.

72. Carol Felsenthal, *Clinton in Exile: A President Out of the White House* (New York: William Morrow, 2008), 13–14.

73. The most serious was a case by Dolly Kyle Browning, who claimed Clinton had

kept her from getting a publisher for a scarcely fictionalized account of an extramarital relationship she had with Clinton while he was president. Although the case against Clinton was dismissed in June 2002, the cost of defending himself against Browning, who unsuccessfully appealed her case, had also been high. *Dolly Kyle Browning and Direct Outstanding Creations Corporation, Appellants, v. William Jefferson Clinton et al.*, argued 5 April 2002, decided 11 June 2002, http://www.georgetown.edu/.

74. James Fallows, "Post-President for Life," *Atlantic*, March 2003.

75. Richard A. Oppel Jr., "Mrs. Clinton Reports that Her Husband Made $9.2 Million from Speeches Last Year," *New York Times*, 15 June 2002; John Solomon and Matthew Mosk, "Gift of Gab Proves Lucrative for Bill Clinton," *Washington Post*, 23 February 2007; "What Our Ex-Presidents Earn," *Parade*, 7 December 2008.

76. On a controversy over how they met and became good friends, compare John M. Broder and Patrick Healy, "How a Billionaire Friend of Bill Helps Him Do Good, and Well," *New York Times*, 23 April 20; Felsenthal, *Clinton in Exile*, esp. 99–105. For Clinton's one mention of Burkle, see Clinton, *My Life*, 409.

77. The quote is from Laura M. Holson, "Friend Hires Clinton to be an Investment Fund Adviser," *New York Times*, 11 April 2002.

78. Linda Feldmann, "How Voters May React to the Clinton's $109 Million Income," *Christian Science Monitor*, 7 April 2008. See also Don Van Natta Jr. and Joe Becker, "Many Dealings of Bill Clinton Under Review," *New York Times*, 18 November 2008.

79. John M. Broder, "In a Sprawling Memoir, Clinton Cites Storms and Settles Scores," *New York Times*, 19 June 2004.

80. Maureen Dowd, "Noon, High and Low," *New York Times*, 6 June 2004.

81. Clinton, *My Life*, 46–47.

82. Walter Isaacson, "I'm Okay, You're Okay: Bill Clinton's Memoirs Reflect the Tenor of His Times," *Washington Post*, 4 July 2004.

83. Ibid.; Michiko Kakutani, "Books of the Times: A Pastiche of a Presidency, Imitating a Life in 957 Pages," *New York Times*, 20 June 2004; Clinton, *My Life*, 709–710. See also Stanley A. Renshon, "President Clinton's Memoirs: Caveat Emptor," *Presidential Studies Quarterly* 35 (Fall 2005): 608–612.

84. In Britain, the book sold almost 180,000 copies, making it the second best-selling political memoir in British history, behind only Barack Obama's *Dreams from My Father* (1995), which has sold almost 704,000 copies. The figures on sales are derived from a number of sources, but see especially Peter Grier, "George Bush 'Decision Points' — How Many Books Will He Sell?," *Christian Science Monitor*, 9 November 2010, http://www.csmonitor.com; "Rivals: The Best Selling Political Memoirs in Britain," *Economist*, 1 September 2010, http://www.economist.com.

85. Kevin Sack, "Clinton Lays Out Future for Library and Himself," *New York Times*, 3 August 2001; Fallows, "Post-President for Life."

86. The quote is from Clinton, *My Life*, 875. See also Sack, "Clinton Lays Out Future for Library and Himself"; Benardo and Weiss, *Citizen-in-Chief*, 110.

87. David M. Halbfinger, "With Latest Battle Resolved, Clinton Library Work Begins," *New York Times*, 7 June 2002.

88. Benardo and Weiss, *Citizen-in-Chief*, 13, 85, 112–113.

89. The quote is from ibid., 113.

90. The quotes can be found in Todd S. Purdum, "Four Presidents, Past and Present, Exchange Humor and Warm Words," *New York Times*, 19 November 2004. See also

Linton Weeks, "In Little Rock, Bill Clinton Is Still the Life of the Party," *Washington Post,* 19 November 2004.

91. Celia W. Dugger, "Whatever Happened to Bill Clinton? He's Playing India," *New York Times,* 5 April 2001.

92. Amy Waldman, "Clinton, as John Q. Public, Campaigns for Array of Causes," and Lawrence K. Altman, "Clinton Urges Global Planning to Halt HIV," *New York Times,* 11 August 2001 and 12 July 2002; Celia Dugger, "Clinton Makes Up for Lost Time in Battling AIDS," *New York Times,* 29 August 2006.

93. Celia W. Dugger and James Barron, "Forget the U.N.: Clinton Has a League of His Own," *New York Times,* 16 September 2005; Celia Dugger, "Clinton, Impresario of Philanthropy, Gets a Progress Update," *New York Times,* 1 April 2006; "Clinton Foundation History," http://www.clintonfoundation.org; "Clinton Global Initiative," http://www.clintonglobalinitiative.org.

94. All the quotes are in Celia W. Dugger, "Clinton Makes Up for Lost Time."

95. John R. Emshwiller and Jose de Corba, "Bill Clinton's Complex Charities," *Wall Street Journal,* 14 February 2008.

96. The first quote is from ibid. The second is from Bill Clinton, *Giving: How Each of Us Can Change the World* (New York: Knopf, 2007), ix. Because of such criticism at a time when Hillary was running for president, the former president was forced to unwind business interests that could complicate his wife's campaign, including ending his business relationship with the Yucapia companies. Emshwiller and de Cordoba, "Bill Clinton's Complex Charities"; Don Van Natta Jr. and Joe Becker, "Many Dealings of Bill Clinton Under Review," *New York Times,* 18 November 2008; Landon Thomas Jr., "Clinton Foundation's Success Was Buoyed by Donor's Boom Years," *New York Times,* 20 December 2008.

97. Quoted in Julie Bosman, "Bill Clinton Says Critics Distorted Remarks about Obama," *New York Times,* 18 March 2008.

98. Ibid. See also Kate Phillips, "More Finger Wagging from a Miffed Bill Clinton," *New York Times,* 23 March 2008, and John Heilemann and Mark Halperin, *Game Change: Obama and the Clintons, McCain and Palin, and the Race of a Lifetime* (New York: HarperCollins, 2010), 207–215.

99. Heilemann and Halperin, *Game Change,* 344–345, 417–419; "White House Chat for Bill Clinton," *New York Times,* 10 December 2010.

100. Douglas H. Paal, "The Clintons' High-Return Diplomacy," and Mark Landler and Mark Mazetti, "In North Korea, Clinton Helped Unveil a Mystery," *New York Times,* 7 and 19 August 2009.

101. Jim Rutenberg and Kate Zernike, "Bill Clinton, in Demand, Stumps for Obama," *New York Times,* 21 September 2010.

Bibliographic Essay

The literature related to the subject of this book is so vast that it would be impractical to attempt a comprehensive bibliography essay. Instead, I have tailored this essay to nonspecialists, singling out the best and most useful secondary sources, first on the overall topic of the ex-presidency and then for each chapter in the book. For other sources, specialists and general readers are encouraged to consult the footnotes, a number of which amount to short bibliographical essays or my assessment of especially important recent contributions to the historical literature.

GENERAL HISTORIES ON THE EX-PRESIDENCY

The best general history is Marie B. Hecht's *Beyond the Presidency: The Residues of Power* (New York: Macmillan, 1976). Basing her study on primary and secondary sources, Hecht has thoughtful and incisive comments on all the former presidents from Washington to Kennedy. However, the book is arranged topically rather than chronologically and is dated. Also, Hecht offers no overarching theme other than the "residues of power" remaining to ex-presidents.

There are also excellent recent books on twentieth-century former presidents. The best is *Citizen-in-Chief: The Second Lives of the American Presidents* by Leonard Benardo and Jennifer Weiss (New York: HarperCollins, 2009). Except for an excellent introductory chapter on the history of the ex-presidency, however, Bernardo and Weiss also take a topical rather chronological approach to their topic. Another fine study of recent ex-presidents is Mark K. Updegrove's *Second Acts: Presidential Lives and Legacies after the White House* (Guilford, Conn.: Lyons Press, 2006). Updegrove based his book on extensive interviews, including those with Presidents Ford, Carter, and Bush as well as published memoirs, newspapers, and magazines. Also useful are Richard Norton Smith and Timothy Walch, eds., *Farewell to the Chief: Former Presidents in American Public Life* (Worland, Wyo.: High Plains, 1990), and Bob Greene, *Fraternity: A Journey in Search of Five Presidents* (New York: Crown, 2004). The product of a 1989 conference at the Hoover Library,

Farewell to the Chief includes papers on ex-presidents from Roosevelt to Eisenhower by some of the nation's most distinguished scholars and a roundtable discussion on "Former Presidents in American Public Life" with comments by historians, journalists, and President Ford. *Fraternity* consists of interviews Greene held with each of the five presidents from Nixon to Bush. Unfortunately, he provides little context for the interviews, including even when they were held.

CHAPTER 1: WASHINGTON, ADAMS, AND JEFFERSON

Although there is no single study of Washington's retirement years, the final volume, *George Washington: Anguish and Farewell (1793–1799)*, of James Thomas Flexner's multivolume biography, *George Washington*, 4 vols. (Boston: Little, Brown, 1965–1972), is rich in detail about Washington's last eight years. Of the voluminous biographies on Washington, Ron Chernow's recent *Washington: A Life* (New York: Penguin, 2010) is certain to become a classic. Describing the nation's first president as a person of the highest character, Chernow also portrays him as deeply ambitious with a controlled but hypercritical personality. Other shorter, but excellent, Washington biographies include Joseph J. Ellis, *His Excellency: George Washington* (New York: Alfred A. Knopf, 2004); Barry Schwartz, *George Washington: The Making of an American Symbol* (New York: Free Press, 1987); and Richard Norton Smith, *Patriarch: George Washington and the New American Nation* (New York: Mariner Books, 1997).

As in the case of Washington, there is no study of Adams as a former president. But recent excellent biographies include David McCullough's Pulitzer Prize–winning *John Adams* (New York: Simon & Schuster, 2001); John Ferling, *John Adams: A Life* (New York; Henry Holt, 1992); and Joseph J. Ellis, *Passionate Sage: The Character and Legacy of John Adams* (New York: Norton, 1993). A best seller by one of the nation's most popular and well-known historians, *John Adams* is comprehensive and includes a lengthy chapter on Adams's post-presidency. Offering more insight into Adams's character and personality, however, are the volumes by Ferling and Ellis. Ferling is especially strong in discussing Adams's political views and his relationship with his family. Ellis emphasizes the passionate nature of Adams's complex personality. He also offers fine insights into Adams's understanding of American republicanism. Two older but still useful biographies are Page Smith, *John Adams,* 2 vols. (Garden City, N.Y.: Doubleday, 1962), and especially Peter Shaw, *The Character of John Adams* (Chapel Hill: University of North Carolina Press, 1976).

An excellent volume on Jefferson's retirement at Monticello is Allan Pell Crawford, *Twilight at Monticello: The Final Years of Thomas Jefferson* (New York: Random House, 2008). Crawford emphasizes the daily trials that Jefferson, like most Virginia planters, had to endure and his interest in horticulture. He also makes clear Jefferson's profound interest in the development of the economy and the future of republicanism. His descriptions of Monticello are especially useful. The final volume, *The Sage of Monticello* (Boston: Little, Brown, 1981), of Dumas Malone's epic *Jefferson and His Times*, 6 vols. (Boston: Little, Brown, 1948–1981), deals exclusively with Jefferson's years in retirement.

Surprisingly, there are few good biographies of Jefferson. Besides Malone's, the best is Joseph J. Ellis's prizewinning *American Sphinx: The Character of Thomas Jefferson*

(New York: Random House, 1996), and Merrill D. Peterson's older *Thomas Jefferson and the New Nation: A Biography* (New York: Oxford University Press, 1970). Ellis describes Jefferson's character as virtually impenetrable, but he also emphasizes his eternal optimism for the new nation even as he regards him as a disappointed idealist. Clearly biased toward Jefferson, Peterson is meticulous in his description of the many vicissitudes that the nation's third president experienced during his lifetime. Also worth reading for the lasting image of Jefferson is Peterson's landmark *The Jefferson Image in the American Mind* (New York: Oxford University Press, 1960).

CHAPTER 2: MADISON, MONROE, AND QUINCY ADAMS

An excellent volume that deals almost exclusively with Madison's retirement years is Drew R. McCoy, *The Last of the Fathers: James Madison and the Republican Legacy* (New York: Cambridge University Press, 1989). McCoy maintains that the burden of Madison's retirement was preserving the legacy of the Constitution. However, he is highly critical of his role as a member of the 1829 Richmond convention called to draw a new constitution for Virginia.

Of the numerous Madison biographies, the most detailed remains Irving Brant's *James Madison*, 6 vols. (Indianapolis, Ind.: Bobbs-Merrill, 1941–1946), which he has conveniently condensed into a one-volume version, *The Fourth President: The Life of James Madison* (Indianapolis, Ind.: Bobbs-Merrill, 1970). However, a number of more recent studies, including that by McCoy, have questioned several of Brant's conclusions, especially his views on nationalism, as well as a lack of balance in his account of Madison's life. Fortunately, a number of more recent biographies have provided new insight into Madison's political theory. Among these the best are Robert Allen Rutland, *James Madison: The Founding Father* (New York: Macmillan, 1987); Ralph Ketcham, *James Madison: A Biography* (Charlottesville: University Press of Virginia, 1971); Jack N. Rakove, *James Madison and the Creation of the American Republic* (Glenview, Ill.: Scott Foresman, 1990); and Gary Wills, *James Madison* (New York: Times Books, 2002).

Monroe's fight with Congress for additional compensation after he left the presidency is detailed in Lucius Wilmerding Jr., *James Monroe Public Claimant* (New Brunswick, N.J.: Rutgers University Press, 1960). Wilmerding argues that Monroe exaggerated the amount of funds due him. There are few full-length biographies of Monroe. An early but still useful study is W. P. Cresson, *James Monroe* (Chapel Hill: University of North Carolina Press, 1946). However, the standard work remains Harry Ammon, *James Monroe: The Quest for National Identity* (New York: McGraw Hill, 1971). On his presidency, see Noble E. Cunningham Jr., *The Presidency of James Monroe* (Lawrence: University Press of Kansas, 1996).

An excellent study of Quincy Adams's career after he left the presidency is Leonard L. Richards, *The Life and Times of Congressman John Quincy Adams* (New York: Oxford University Press, 1986), which distinguishes between his views on slavery and his fear of the Southern slavocracy. Of the many biographies on his long public career, the standards remain Samuel Flagg Bemis, *John Quincy Adams and the Foundations of American Foreign Policy* (New York: Alfred A. Knopf, 1949), and *John Quincy Adams and the Union* (New York: Alfred A. Knopf, 1956). In these volumes, Bemis continues his famous thesis about the United States' advantages from European distresses. However, Bemis tends to overlook Adams's personal flaws and gives relatively scant treatment to Adams's presidency.

A brilliant one-volume study of Quincy Adams is Paul Nagel, *John Quincy Adams: A Public Life, a Private Life* (Cambridge, Mass.: Harvard University Press, 1997). Nagel is especially good in capturing Adams's complex personality, including his softer side, and makes clear his duty to public service and his desire for public approval balanced by his wish to serve humanity. Also useful is Marie B. Hecht's older *John Quincy Adams: A Personal History of an Independent Man* (New York: Macmillan, 1972), which stresses his ethical side. An excellent short biography is Robert V. Remini, *John Quincy Adams* (New York: Times Books, 2002).

CHAPTER 3: JACKSON, VAN BUREN, AND TYLER

Although there is no single volume on Jackson's post-presidency, the literature on the nation's seventh president is extensive. The most comprehensive biography is Robert Remini's three-volume one, under the titles *Andrew Jackson and the Course of American Empire, 1767–1821* (New York: Harper & Row, 1977), *Andrew Jackson and the Course of American Freedom, 1822–1832* (New York: Harper & Row, 1981), and *Andrew Jackson and the Course of American Democracy, 1833–1845* (New York: Harper & Row, 1984). Regarding Jackson's presidency as vital in transforming the presidency, Remini refers to his veto of the rechartering of the Bank of the United States as the most important veto ever issued by a president. Remini has conveniently abridged his multivolume biography into a single volume, *The Life of Andrew Jackson* (New York: Harper & Row, 1988).

Thee best and most recent Jackson biography is John Meacham's Pulitzer Prize–winning *American Lion: Andrew Jackson in the White House* (New York: Random House, 2008), which stresses his love of country and family and the revolution he brought about in democratizing the nation's politics. But Meacham also makes clear how heartless and ruthless Jackson could be and questions some of his assertions of power. Two other excellent one-volume biographies are Andrew Burstein, *The Passions of Andrew Jackson* (New York: Alfred A. Knopf, 2003), and H. W. Brands, *Andrew Jackson: His Life and Times* (New York: Doubleday, 2005).

Perhaps because of a lack of material on Van Buren, studies of his life are scant. The two best are Donald B. Cole, *Martin Van Buren and the American Political System* (Princeton, N.J.: Princeton University Press, 1984), and Joel H. Silbey, *Martin Van Buren and the Emergence of American Popular Politics* (New York: Rowman & Littlefield, 2002). Both make similar arguments, although Cole emphasizes the way Van Buren adapted to the changing nature of American society while Silbey stresses his political acumen. Silbey is also stronger in his treatment of Van Buren as the candidate of the Free Soil Party. On Van Buren's presidency, consult also Major J. Wilson, *The Presidency of Martin Van Buren* (Lawrence: University Press of Kansas, 1984).

Scholars have also paid relatively scant attention to the life of John Tyler, whose presidential papers were burned during the Civil War. The standard biography remains Oliver Perry Chitwood, *John Tyler: Champion of the Old South* (New York: D. Appleton Century, 1939). More useful to this study has been Robert Seager II, *And Tyler Too: A Biography of John and Julia Gardiner Tyler* (New York: McGraw Hill, 1963), which emphasizes

Tyler's personal and family life as well as his political career. On Tyler's presidency, consult Norma Lois Peterson, *The Presidencies of William Henry Harrison and John Tyler* (Lawrence: University Press of Kansas, 1989).

CHAPTER 4: FILLMORE, PIERCE, AND BUCHANAN

Even though Fillmore left a large quantity of papers, his life remains obscure. Of his few biographies, the best remains Robert Rayback, *Millard Fillmore: Biography of a President* (Buffalo, N.Y.: Buffalo Historical Society, 1959), which is especially useful in tracing his career through the Byzantine maze of New York politics. Also helpful is Robert J. Scarry, *Millard Fillmore* (Jefferson, N.C.: McFarland, 2001). Because of its many inaccuracies, less useful is Benson Lee Grayson, *The Unknown President: The Administration of Millard Fillmore* (Washington, D.C.: University Press of America, 1981). On Fillmore's presidency, see also Elbert B. Smith, *The Presidencies of Zachary Taylor and Millard Fillmore* (Lawrence: University Press of Kansas, 1988).

Although clearly sympathetic to Pierce, two good biographies of New Hampshire's only president are Roy Franklin Nichols, *Franklin Pierce: Young Hickory of the Granite Hills* (Philadelphia: University of Pennsylvania Press, 1931), and especially the two-volume study by Peter Wallner, *Franklin Pierce: New Hampshire's Favorite Son* (Concord, N.H.: Plaidswede, 2004), and *Franklin Pierce: Martyr for the Union* (Concord, N.H.: Plaidswede, 2007). Wallner argues that Pierce was much more in control of his administration than most historians acknowledge. Although much has been written about the coming of the Civil War and some have condemned Buchanan roundly for his handling of the secessionist crisis, historians have otherwise paid scant attention to the nation's fifteenth president. One exception is Philip Klein, *President James Buchanan* (University Park: Pennsylvania State University Press, 1962), a thorough and well-balanced treatment of a president, whom most historians rank among the nation's worst. A more recent but short biography is Jean H. Baker, *James Buchanan* (New York: Times Books, 2004). Ultimately, Baker argues, Buchanan failed to meet his own definition of leadership. On Buchanan's presidency, see also Elbert B. Smith, *The Presidency of James Buchanan* (Lawrence: University Press of Kansas, 1975).

CHAPTER 5: JOHNSON AND GRANT

Most of the coverage on Johnson has been on his struggle with Congress over reconstruction. A notable exception is Hans L. Trefousee, *Andrew Johnson: A Biography* (New York: Norton, 1989). While Trefousee views Johnson with compassion, he is also aware of his character flaws, especially his unbending and narrowly circumscribed personality. A dated and one-sided but still useful biography for its detail and personal interviews is Lloyd Paul Stryker, *Andrew Johnson: A Study in Courage* (New York: Macmillan, 1929). On Johnson's presidency, see also Albert Castel, *The Presidency of Andrew Johnson* (Lawrence: University Press of Kansas, 1979).

In contrast to Johnson, there are excellent biographies of Grant, although none that deal extensively with his post-presidency. Clearly the most comprehensive and best of these is William S. McFeeley's Pulitzer Prize–winning *Grant: A Biography* (New York:

Norton, 1981), and Jean Edward Smith's *Grant* (New York: Simon & Schuster, 2001), which was a finalist for the Pulitzer Prize. Of the two, McFeeley's is the more critical while Smith's is the more nuanced. In the end, Smith concludes, Grant was a flawed but heroic figure. A short but balanced biography is Josiah Bunting III, *Ulysses S. Grant* (New York: Times Books, 2004).

CHAPTER 6: HAYES, CLEVELAND, AND HARRISON

There are a number of biographies on Hayes, but none that provide adequate treatment of his post-presidency. Among the best are Harry Barnard, *Rutherford B. Hayes and His America* (Indianapolis, Ind.: Bobbs-Merrill, 1944); Kenneth E. Davidson, *The Presidency of Rutherford B. Hayes* (Westport, Conn.: Greenwood Press, 1972); Ari Hoogenboom, *Rutherford B. Hayes: Warrior and President* (Lawrence: University Press of Kansas, 1988), and especially Hans L. Trefousse's short but insightful *Rutherford B. Hayes* (New York: Times Books, 2002). Highly favorable in his assessment of Hayes's presidency, Trefousse even concludes that he was an early Progressive.

The literature on Cleveland is extensive, but the classic study remains Allan Nevins, *Grover Cleveland: A Study in Courage* (New York: Dodd Mead, 1934). A more recent biography is Alyn Brodsky's excellent *Grover Cleveland: A Study in Character* (New York: St. Martin's Press, 2000). As the titles of their books suggest, Nevins and Brodsky emphasize Cleveland's positive character. So does Henry Graff in his short but thoughtful *Grover Cleveland* (New York: Times Books, 2002) and an older book by Robert McElroy, *Grover Cleveland: The Man and the Statesman,* 2 vols. (New York: Harper, 1923). For a more critical assessment, see Horace Samuel Merrill, *Bourbon Leader: Grover Cleveland and the Democratic Party* (Boston: Little, Brown, 1957).

There are few full-length biographies of Harrison. By far the most comprehensive is Harry Joseph Sievers's, published in three volumes: *Benjamin Harrison, Hoosier Warrior, 1833–1865* (Washington, D.C.: Henry Regnery, 1952), *Benjamin Harrison, Hoosier Statesman: From the Civil War to the White House, 1865–1888* (New York: University Publishers, 1959), and *Benjamin Harrison, Hoosier President: The White House and the Years After* (Indianapolis, Ind.: Bobbs-Merrill, 1968). A short but useful biography is Charles C. Calhoun, *Benjamin Harrison* (New York: Times Books, 2005), which makes clear how Harrison expanded the bounds of presidential activism. A solid study of Harrison's presidency is Homer E. Socolofsky and Allan B. Spetter, *The Presidency of Benjamin Harrison* (Lawrence: University Press of Kansas, 1987).

CHAPTER 7: ROOSEVELT

As one of the nation's most important presidents, scholars have paid enormous attention to his life. Two recent excellent books on his post-presidency are Patricia O'Toole, *When Trumpets Call: Theodore Roosevelt after the White House* (New York: Simon & Schuster, 2005), and Edmund Morris, *Colonel Roosevelt* (New York: Random House, 2010). O'Toole's title comes from Roosevelt's belief that when trumpets call, only a coward retreats. Even as an ex-president, O'Toole makes clear, Roosevelt remained committed to public duty. *Colonel Roosevelt* is the final volume of Morris's three-volume biography. The first two volumes are *The Rise of Theodore Roosevelt,* rev. ed. (New York: Random

House, 2010), and *Theodore Rex,* rev. ed. (New York: Random House, 2010). Morris's prizewinning trilogy stands as the most comprehensive and complete Roosevelt biography. In *Colonel Roosevelt,* he shows how Roosevelt remained one of the most important political figures even after he left the White House. He also emphasizes Roosevelt's hatred for Wilson.

Three excellent one-volume biographies are Nathan Miller, *Theodore Roosevelt: A Life* (New York: William Morrow, 1992); H. W. Brands, *TR: The Last Romantic* (New York: Basic Books, 1997); and Kathleen Dalton, *Theodore Roosevelt: A Strenuous Life* (New York: Random House, 2002). For a short overview, see also Louis A. Auchincloss, *Theodore Roosevelt* (New York: Times Books, 2001). Auchincloss argues that for Roosevelt, every major decision was a moral one.

CHAPTER 8: TAFT, WILSON, AND COOLIDGE

Two important books on Taft's post-presidency are Frederick Hicks, *William Howard Taft: Yale Professor of Law and New Haven Citizen* (New Haven, Conn.: Yale University Press, 1945), and Alpheus Thomas Mason, *William Howard Taft: Chief Justice* (New York: Simon & Schuster, 1964). Basing his book on extensive interviews with Taft's former colleagues and students at Yale and local newspapers, Hicks emphasizes Taft's career at Yale. As one of the nation's leading legal and constitutional historians, Mason has written a thoroughly documented account of Taft's many activities as chief justice of the Supreme Court, including as a judicial reformer.

A still useful but highly critical biography is Henry F. Pringle, *The Life and Times of William Howard Taft,* 2 vols. (New York: Henry Holt, 1939). Pringle maintains that Taft became increasingly more conservative after he became president. A shorter and more balanced biography is Judith Icke Anderson, *William Howard Taft: An Intimate History* (New York: Norton, 1981). Anderson blames many of Taft's problems, including his decision to run for president and his weight, on his mother and, especially, his wife.

An excellent study of Wilson's post-presidency is Gene Smith, *When the Cheering Stopped: The Last Years of Woodrow Wilson* (Alexandria, Va.: Time-Life Books, 1982). Smith emphasizes Wilson's ongoing medical problems and solitude as an ex-president as well as his thoughts about running for president again in 1920 and 1924. On Wilson's ongoing health problems, see also Edwin A. Weinstein, *Woodrow Wilson: A Medical and Psychological Biography* (Princeton, N.J.: Princeton University Press, 1981).

The classic biography of Wilson remains Arthur S. Link, *Wilson,* 5 vols. (Princeton, N.J.: Princeton University Press, 1947–1965). However, two excellent one-volume studies are Arthur Walworth's Pulitzer Prize–winning *Woodrow Wilson,* rev. ed. (New York: Norton, 1978), and August Hecksher's *Woodrow Wilson* (New York: Charles Scribner's Sons, 1991). Walworth emphasizes Wilson's concern with predatory wealth and refers to his legislative accomplishment as the most momentous economic measures of the twentieth century. For a short overview of Wilson's life, see also H. W. Brands, *Woodrow Wilson* (New York: Times Books, 2003).

The literature on Coolidge is skimpy. The common image of Coolidge as a Scrooge living in a modern version of Babylon can be traced to William Allen White, *A Puritan in Babylon: The Story of Calvin Coolidge* (New York: Macmillan, 1938). More balanced are Charles M. Fuess, *Calvin Coolidge: The Man from Vermont* (Boston: Little, Brown, 1940), and especially Donald R. McCoy, *Calvin Coolidge: The Quiet President* (New York:

Macmillan, 1967). An excellent short biography is David Greenberg, *Calvin Coolidge* (New York: Times Books, 2006). Greenberg makes the important point that Coolidge's views on the prosperity of the 1920s and his failure to do more to regulate the stock market merely reflected the dominant thinking of the time. For Coolidge's presidency, see also Robert H. Ferrell, *The Presidency of Calvin Coolidge* (Lawrence: University Press of Kansas, 1998).

CHAPTER 9: HOOVER

The definitive study of Hoover's post-presidential years is Gary Dean Best, *Herbert Hoover: The Postpresidential Years,* 2 vols. (Stanford, Calif.: Hoover Institution Press, 1985). Best maintains that while Hoover was shunned after leaving the White House, his ideas were not, and contrary to a common image of Hoover, he was always more ahead in his political thinking than most of the Republican Party.

The standard biography of Hoover remains George H. Nash, *The Life of Herbert Hoover,* 3 vols. (New York: Norton, 1983–1986). Excellent one-volume biographies include Richard North Smith, *An Uncommon Man: The Triumph of Herbert Hoover* (Worland, Wyo.: High Plains, 1984), and David Burner, *Herbert Hoover: A Public Life* (New York: Alfred A. Knopf, 1978). Both Smith and Burner note Hoover's shortcomings but acknowledge that he did more than any other previous president to deal with a major economic crisis. Joan Hoff Wilson even makes a strong argument in *Herbert Hoover: Forgotten Progressive* (Boston: Little, Brown, 1975) that Hoover was in fact a Progressive. For an excellent short biography, see also William E. Leuchtenburg, *Herbert Hoover* (New York: Times Books, 2009). While also noting Hoover's many fine qualities, Leuchtenburg concludes that Hoover failed to lead as president and had he been reelected in 1932, it is unlikely that he would have been able to redeem himself.

CHAPTER 10: TRUMAN

Two books on Truman's post-presidency are G. W. Sand, *Truman in Retirement: A Former President Views the Nation and the World* (South Bend, Ind.: Justice Books, 1993), and Matthew Algeo, *Harry Truman's Excellent Adventure: The True Story of a Great American Road Trip* (Chicago: Chicago Review Press, 2009). Although based on the extensive collection of post-presidential papers at the Truman Library, Sand's volume is marred by a lack of balance. The author insists on viewing Truman as a great visionary with few, if any, warts who worked tirelessly to make the world a better place, defined in democratic terms. Algeo confines his book to Truman's road trip after leaving the White House from his home in Independence to the East Coast. Having retraced in detail the former president's exact journey, including eating whenever possible in the same establishments and staying in the same lodging as the former president and his wife, and interviewing those still living who remembered the Trumans' passing through their towns, Algeo offers an entertaining and instructive narrative of how Truman failed in his effort to travel incognito across the country.

There are numerous excellent biographies on Truman that deal extensively with Truman's post-presidency. The two best are David McCullough, *Truman* (New York: Simon & Schuster, 1992), and Alonzo Hamby, *Man of the People: A Life of Harry Truman* (New

York: Oxford University Press, 1995). Without ignoring Truman's many imperfections, both biographers underscore the case for Truman as a champion of the ordinary citizen and as the most uncommon of common people (and presidents). Hamby is especially penetrating in his analysis of the two sides of Truman's personality. These volumes should be supplemented by Merle Miller's extraordinary *Plain Speaking: An Oral Biography of Harry S. Truman* (New York: Berkley, 1973), and Margaret Truman's often insightful *Harry S. Truman* (New York: William Morrow, 1973). For a short overview of Truman's life, see also Robert Dallek, *Harry S. Truman* (New York: Times Books, 2008).

CHAPTER 11: EISENHOWER AND JOHNSON

Despite accusations that Stephen E. Ambrose never held as many personal interviews with Eisenhower as he claimed, his two-volume biography, *Eisenhower: Soldier, General of the Army, President-Elect* (New York: Simon & Schuster, 1983), and *Eisenhower: The President* (New York: Simon & Schuster, 1984), the last three chapters of which are on Ike's post-presidency, remains the most complete on the nation's thirty-fourth president. Also excellent is Jim Newton, *Eisenhower: The White House Years* (New York: Doubleday, 2011). Both biographers regard Eisenhower as among the nation's best presidents. Newton argues that Eisenhower won, rather than merely kept, the peace at times when his advisers were even arguing for the use of nuclear weapons. More critical of Eisenhower is Piers Brendon, *Ike: His Life and Times* (New York: Harper & Row, 1986). On the Eisenhower family, see also Steve Neal, *The Eisenhowers* (Lawrence: University Press of Kansas, 1984), which captures nicely the close and important relationship Eisenhower had with his younger brother, Milton. On Eisenhower's presidency, see Chester J. Pach Jr. and Elmo Richardson, *The Presidency of Dwight D. Eisenhower,* rev. ed. (Lawrence: University Press of Kansas, 1991).

The standard biography of Johnson is Robert Dallek's two volumes, *Lone Star Rising: Lyndon Johnson and His Times, 1908–1960* (New York: Oxford University Press, 1991), and *Flawed Giant: Lyndon Johnson and His Times, 1961–1973* (New York: Oxford University Press, 1998), which captures nicely the political genius but flawed character of this larger-than-life figure. The last chapter of Dallek's biography discusses the mixed character of Johnson's short retirement. A more critical view of Johnson is Robert A. Caro's multivolume biography, still in progress, *The Years of Lyndon Johnson,* 3 vols. (New York: Alfred A. Knopf, 1982–1992), which, at the time of this writing, has only progressed through his years in the Senate. Two important one-volume biographies, which agree with Dallek that Johnson was a flawed giant, are Irwin Unger and Debi Unger, *LBJ: A Life* (New York: Wiley, 1999), and Randall Woods, *LBJ: Architect of American Ambition* (Cambridge, Mass.: Harvard University Press, 2007). For more personal accounts, see Merle Miller, *Lyndon: An Oral Biography* (New York: G. P. Putnam's Sons, 1980), and Doris Kearns, *Lyndon Johnson and the American Dream* (New York: Harper & Row, 1976).

CHAPTER 12: NIXON AND FORD

The most comprehensive biography of Nixon is Stephen E. Ambrose's three-volume *Nixon: The Education of a Politician, 1913–1962* (New York: Simon & Schuster, 1987), *Nixon: The Triumph of a Politician, 1962–1972* (New York: Simon & Schuster, 1989), and

Nixon: Ruin and Recovery (New York: Simon & Schuster, 1991), which contains extensive coverage of Nixon's post-presidency through 1990. Although highly critical of Nixon, Ambrose also treats him with considerable sympathy. A major flaw is the unavailability of most of the Nixon papers when Ambrose was writing his biography. Two excellent one-volume biographies are Herbert S. Parmet, *Richard Nixon and His America* (Boston: Little, Brown, 1990), and especially Jonathan Aitken, *Nixon: A Life* (Washington, D.C.: Regnery Publishing, 1993). Aitken was able to get close to the former president during his trip to England in 1978 and interviewed him on numerous occasions. He finds that Nixon was never comfortable in his own skin. For a revisionist treatment of Nixon, which emphasizes his liberalism, see Joan Hoff, *Nixon Reconsidered* (New York: Basic Books, 1994). A fascinating study of the Nixon image is David Greenberg, *Nixon's Shadow: The History of an Image* (New York: Norton, 2003), which concludes that despite all his efforts to reinvent his image, Nixon has continued to be shadowed by Watergate.

The literature on Ford remains skimpy, especially on his long post-presidential career. Although fewer than 200 pages long, the most complete biography is Douglas Brinkley's highly favorable *Gerald R. Ford* (New York: Times Books, 2007). For a fuller account of Ford's life before becoming president, see James Cannon, *Time and Chance: Gerald Ford's Appointment with History, 1913–1974* (New York: HarperCollins, 1994). Highly critical of Ford's first hundred days as president is Richard Reeves, *A Ford, Not a Lincoln, or Why There Are No Leaders in Washington* (New York: Harcourt Brace Jovanovich, 1975). For a fuller and more balanced account of Ford's presidency, see John Robert Greene, *The Presidency of Gerald R. Ford* (Lawrence: University Press of Kansas, 1995).

CHAPTER 13: CARTER AND REAGAN

A fully researched, well-written, and thoughtful account of Carter's post-presidency through 1998 is Douglas Brinkley, *The Unfinished Presidency: Jimmy Carter's Journey to the Nobel Peace Prize* (New York: Penguin Books, 1998). As his title indicates, Brinkley argues that much of Carter's post-presidency was guided by his efforts to fulfill objectives that he was not able to complete as president, especially in the areas of human rights and peacemaking. He also maintains that his activities as a world citizen made him worthy of the Nobel Peace Prize, which he did not finally receive until 2002.

There are several good biographies of Carter. The best is Peter G. Bourne, *Jimmy Carter: A Comprehensive Biography from Plains to Postpresidency* (New York: Simon & Schuster, 1998). A psychiatrist by training, Bourne was also a White House special assistant to Carter. His biography is balanced and based on extensive research. On Carter's life through the end of his Georgia governorship, see also E. Stanley Godbold Jr., *Jimmy and Rosalynn Carter: The Georgia Years, 1924–1974* (New York: Oxford University Press, 2010). Well written and highly detailed, this is the first volume of a projected two-volume biography. Godbold argues that one cannot understand Carter without understanding his wife because their lives and beliefs were so intertwined. A short overview of Carter is Julian E. Zelizer, *Jimmy Carter* (New York: Times Books, 2010). On Carter's presidency, see Burton I. Kaufman and Scott Kaufman, *The Presidency of James Earl Carter*, rev. ed. (Lawrence: University Press of Kansas, 2006). Both Zelizer and the Kaufmans portray Carter's presidency as a failure despite some significant accomplishment. In concluding epilogues, however, they also regard the thirty-ninth president's ex-presidency as one of the nation's best.

For great personal insight into Reagan, including his post-presidency, see Ron Reagan, *My Father at 100: A Memoir* (New York: Viking Penguin, 2011), a highly sympathetic and beautifully written memoir by Reagan's liberally oriented son. A controversial but highly informative and often incisive biography is Edmund Morris, *Dutch: A Memoir of Ronald Reagan* (New York: Random House, 1999). Allowed to follow Reagan during his second administration, Morris was much criticized for creating the fictitious character of a narrator (himself) and writing his biography as the autobiography of the narrator. Morris has defended his approach, arguing that everything he wrote about Reagan was well documented. His conclusions were highly critical, remarking that Reagan lacked the ability to distinguish between fact and fancy. Other biographies that reach much the same conclusion are Lou Cannon's two volumes, *Reagan* (New York: G. P. Putnam's Sons, 1982), and *President Reagan: The Role of a Lifetime* (New York: Simon & Schuster, 1991), and Bob Schieffer and Gary Paul Gates, *The Acting President* (New York: E. P. Dutton, 1989). For a more sympathetic view, see John Patrick Diggins, *Ronald Reagan: Fate, Freedom, and the Making of History* (New York: Norton, 2007), and Jules Tygell, *Ronald Reagan and the Triumph of American Conservatism,* 2nd ed. (New York: Pearson Education, 2006).

CHAPTER 14: BUSH AND CLINTON

The most thorough biography of Bush is Herbert S. Parmet, *George Bush: The Life of a Lone Star Yankee* (New York: Scribner, 1997). Parmet argues persuasively that despite spending most of his life in Texas, Bush was always guided by his Yankee Republican heritage and his strong sense of noblesse oblige. For a short but still insightful history of Bush's life, see Tom Wicker's sprightly *George Herbert Walker Bush* (New York: Penguin Books, 2004). Wicker, essentially agreeing with Parmet, also emphasizes Bush's natural ability to make friends and his deep sense of loyalty. A critical assessment of the purposely closed but powerfully connected dynastic Bush family is Peter Schweitzer and Rochelle Schweitzer, *The Bushes: Portrait of a Dynasty* (New York: Doubleday, 2004). On Bush's presidency, see also John Robert Greene, *The Presidency of George Bush* (Lawrence: University Press of Kansas, 2000).

On Clinton's post-presidency, see Carol Felsenthal, *Clinton in Exile: A President Out of the White House* (New York: William Morrow, 2008). Felsenthal notes how Clinton made Carter's ex-presidency the model for his own post-presidency. She also makes the point that George Bush's terrible presidency made Clinton's legacy look all that much better.

The best study of Clinton before becoming president is David Maraniss, *First In His Class: A Biography of Bill Clinton* (New York: Simon & Schuster, 1995), which emphasizes Clinton's intelligence, ambitions, and political talents, but also his flawed personality, which Maraniss traces back to his dysfunctional family. The most comprehensive biography is the two volumes by Nigel Hamilton, *Bill Clinton: An American Journey: Great Expectations* (New York: Random House, 2003), and *Bill Clinton: Mastering the Presidency* (New York: Public Affairs, 2007). Although highly informative, the first volume is marred by Hamilton's excessive emphasis on Clinton's sexual exploits. Some of his direct quotes are also dubious. In *The Natural: The Misunderstood Presidency of Bill Clinton* (New

York: Doubleday, 2002), Joe Klein agrees that Clinton suffered from a surplus of libido and a deficit of integrity, but he also concludes that Clinton was the most talented politician of his generation and that his presidency was both substantive and serious. On the often rocky relationship between Hillary and Bill Clinton, even after Clinton became president, see Sally Bedell Smith, *For Love of Politics: Bill and Hillary Clinton: The White House Years* (New York: Random House, 2007). While Smith argues that both Clintons were driven by political ambition, she maintains that Bill was more subtle, circuitous, and creative than Hillary. For the crucial role that Hillary played in Bill's career, consult Carl Bernstein's detailed and informative *A Woman in Charge: The Life of Hillary Rodham Clinton* (New York: Vintage Books, 2007).

Index